GOVERNMENT BY JUDICIARY

LIBERTY FUND

Studies in Jurisprudence and Legal History

*Government by Judiciary: The Transformation of the Fourteenth Amendment*
Raoul Berger

*In Defense of the Constitution*
George W. Carey

*Introduction to the Study of the Law of the Constitution*
A. V. Dicey

*Origins of the Common Law*
Arthur R. Hogue

*Freedom and the Law*
Bruno Leoni

*Lectures on Jurisprudence*
Adam Smith

Raoul Berger

# GOVERNMENT BY JUDICIARY

## The Transformation of the Fourteenth Amendment

Raoul Berger

*with a Foreword by Forrest McDonald*

SECOND EDITION

LIBERTY FUND

*Indianapolis*

1997

This book is published by Liberty Fund, Inc., a foundation established to encourage study of the ideal of a society of free and responsible individuals.

The cuneiform inscription that serves as our logo and as the design motif for our endpapers is the earliest-known written appearance of the word "freedom" (*amagi*), or "liberty." It is taken from a clay document written about 2300 B.C. in the Sumerian city-state of Lagash.

97 98 99 00 01   H   5 4 3 2 1
97 98 99 00 01   P   5 4 3 2 1

Library of Congress Cataloging-in-Publication Data
Berger, Raoul, 1901–
    Government by judiciary : the transformation of the fourteenth
amendment / Raoul Berger with a foreword by Forrest McDonald. —
2nd ed.
        p.      cm.
    Includes bibliographical references and index.
    ISBN 0-86597-143-9 (hardcover). — ISBN 0-86597-144-7 (pbk.)
        1. United States—Constitutional law—Amendments—14th.
    2. Political questions and judicial power—United States.
    3. Civil rights—United States. 4. Judge-made law—United States.
    I. Title.
    KF4558 14th.B47   1997
    342.73'085—DC20
    [347.30285]                                        96-16162

LIBERTY FUND, INC.
8335 Allison Pointe Trail, Suite 300
Indianapolis, Indiana 46250-1687
(317) 842-0880

*For Patty*

All persons born or naturalized in the United States . . . are citizens of the United States and of the State wherein they reside. No State shall make or enforce any law which shall abridge the privileges or immunities of citizens of the United States; nor shall any State deprive any person of life, liberty, or property, without due process of law; nor deny to any person within its jurisdiction the equal protection of the laws.

—FOURTEENTH AMENDMENT, §1

*Nullius in Verbo*
—Motto of the Royal Society, London
Take nobody's word for it; see for yourself

# Contents

Foreword       XV

Preface to the Second Edition       XXI

Acknowledgments       XXIII

Abbreviations       XXIV

## PART I

1. Introduction       3
   *Supplementary Note on the Introduction*       18

2. "Privileges or Immunities"       30
   *Supplementary Note on the Civil Rights Act and the Fourteenth Amendment: Fundamental Rights*       44

3. The "Privileges or Immunities of a Citizen of the United States"       57

4. Negro Suffrage Was Excluded       70
   *Supplementary Note on Suffrage*       85

5. Reapportionment       90

6. The "Open-Ended" Phraseology Theory       116

7. Segregated Schools       132
   *Supplementary Note on Segregated Schools*       146

8. Incorporation of the Bill of Rights in the Fourteenth Amendment       155
   *Supplementary Note on Incorporation*       174

9. Opposition Statements Examined       190

10. "Equal Protection of the Laws"       198

11. "Due Process of Law"                                      221

12. Section Five: "Congress Shall Enforce"                    245

13. Incorporation of Abolitionist Theory in Section One       253
    *Supplementary Note on Abolitionist Influence*            266

                          PART II

14. From Natural Law to Libertarian Due Process              273
    *Supplementary Note on Natural Law and the Constitution* 302

15. "The Rule of Law"                                         307

16. The Judiciary Was Excluded From Policymaking             322
    *Supplementary Note on Exclusion of the Judiciary*        332

17. The Turnabout of the Libertarians                         337

18. Liberals and the Burger Court                             358

19. The Legitimacy of Judicial Review                        369
    *Supplementary Note on the Role of the Court*             378

20. Why the "Original Intention"?                             402
    *Supplementary Note on Original Intention*                410

21. Arguments for Judicial Power of Revision                 428

22. "Trial by Jury": Six or Twelve Jurors?                   448

23. Conclusion                                                457
    *Supplementary Note on the Conclusion*                    466

    Appendix A: Van Alstyne's Critique of Justice Harlan's
    Dissent                                                   471

    Appendix B: Judicial Administration of Local Matters     480

    The Writings of Raoul Berger                              485

    Bibliography                                              493

    Index of Cases                                            517

    General Index                                             525

# *Foreword*

Raoul Berger's original intention, if I may use that phrase in a different way than he does, was not to become a great constitutional historian. Indeed, his work as a scholar is actually the fourth (or fifth, depending on how you count) of the careers he has held during a long and illustrious lifetime.

His first love was and continues to be music. As a youth he studied the violin in New York and Berlin and then went on to make a number of highly praised concert tours, appear as a soloist with the Cleveland Symphony, and serve as second concertmaster with the Cincinnati Symphony Orchestra and first violinist of the Cincinnati String Quartet. But it was difficult in the 1920s, as it is today, to earn a living as a soloist in America, and the drudgery of life in an orchestra began to be numbing to his soul. Accordingly, at the age of twenty-seven, he decided to enroll in college and have a go at making his way in the real world. At thirty-one he entered Northwestern University Law School, and at thirty-four he was ready to hang up his shingle as a practicing attorney.

In 1938, having spent two years in private practice and another taking an advanced degree at Harvard, Berger began his succession of professions in earnest. The first was public service, including stints with the Securities and Exchange Commission and service as general counsel to the Alien Property Custodian and as special assistant to the attorney general. In 1946 he retired from government, and for the next sixteen years he was engaged in private practice in Washington, D.C. Then came yet another calling as a law professor at the University of California, Berkeley, and then at Harvard Law School as Charles Warren Senior Fellow in American Legal History until his retirement in 1976.

In each of these activities Berger achieved considerable distinction, but it was not until he embarked upon his journey as a constitutional scholar that he began rising to greatness. His first book, published in

1969, was *Congress v. The Supreme Court.* In it, he concluded after an exhaustive study of the documentary record that the framers of the Constitution intended that the federal courts have the power to review legislative acts and pass on their constitutionality, though there is no mention of judicial review to be seen in the text of the Constitution—a conclusion that has recently been buttressed by the discovery of some previously unknown documents.[1]

That finding was scarcely revolutionary, for it coincided with the consensus among students of the founding; but the book was marked by several qualities that characterize all of Berger's later works. The quantity of his research is massive but is combined with pinpoint accuracy in dealing with details.[2] His prose is lucid. He brings to his undertakings a zestful enthusiasm, an indication that he is impelled by a sheer love of scholarship—the traditional scholarly ideal that the genuine scholar seeks to know the truth for its own sake—and not by the ideological predilections that distort so much historical research. And, in *Congress v. The Supreme Court* Berger announced his commitment to the ages-old but vitally alive proposition that, when construing a constitution, it is permissible and often necessary to go beyond the text of the document to ascertain, if possible, the intentions of its authors but decidedly not permissible to read into it ideas derived from "natural rights" dogmas or other external values.

Berger's next two books, as Philip Kurland has described them, were "blockbusters," and they won him enthusiastic praise, especially among readers of a liberal persuasion. *Impeachment* coincidentally appeared in 1973, at just the time when President Nixon was headed on a collision course with Congress, though it was a subject on which Berger had been working for several years. The book focuses mainly on the question of the removal of federal judges, but it is a tour de force of English and

1. The documents are the notes of attorneys Edmund Randolph and St. George Tucker in the 1782 case known variously as *Case of the Prisoners* and *Commonwealth v. Caton.* See William Michael Treanor, "The *Case of the Prisoners* and the Origins of Judicial Review," 143 U. Pa. L. Rev. 491–570 (1994).

2. Philip B. Kurland has pointed out that Berger, in the rare instances when he misinterprets his evidence, courageously and candidly acknowledges his error. See Kurland's foreword to Raoul Berger, *Selected Writings on the Constitution* ii (1987).

American constitutional history. *Executive Privilege*, which appeared in 1974, is a devastating rebuttal of the argument that the president can constitutionally withhold from Congress or the courts information relevant to the performance of their duties. (Presidents had been withholding such information for some time, but Berger insists that repeated violations of the Constitution do not make them constitutional but merely compound the evil.)

Berger's niche in the liberal pantheon came tumbling down in 1977 upon the publication of the book you are about to read, *Government by Judiciary*, and suddenly he became a hero to conservatives. His private political beliefs are irrelevant to his work, because he rigorously casts them aside in his research and writing, going wherever the evidence takes him; but it may help the reader if I point out that by and large Berger's predilections have been on the liberal side. He was, after all, a member of the administrations of Franklin Roosevelt and Harry Truman. As he states in the addenda to Chapter 16 of the present edition, his principles are the "standard political principles of the moderate left of the Democratic party," but he makes "no pretense of identifying them with constitutional mandates."

Berger's personal politics had no more influence on the reception of *Government by Judiciary* than they had on his writing of the book. What he learned and reported was that for the better part of a century the Supreme Court had been handing down decisions interpreting the Fourteenth Amendment improperly, willfully ignoring or willfully distorting the history of its enactment. More specifically, he found that the authors of the Amendment, far from contemplating a social and political revolution, as defenders of judicial activism maintained, intended only to protect the freedmen from southern Black Codes that threatened to return them to slavery. More specifically yet, Berger found that the two key passages in the Fourteenth Amendment—privileges or immunities of citizens and due process of law—far from being vague and elastic, as activists maintained, were "terms of art" that had precise, well-understood, and narrow legal meanings. "Equal protection," a new concept, was identified by the framers with the right to contract, to own property, and to have access to the courts.

The implication was that *Brown v. Board* (1954, striking down seg-regation in the public schools), *Baker v. Carr* and *Reynolds v. Sims* (1962 and 1964, respectively, having to do with reapportionment of state leg-islatures), *Roe v. Wade* (1973, making abortion legal), and a vast array of other cases had been decided unconstitutionally, representing not law but the whims and values of the justices of the Supreme Court. No book on the Constitution, with the possible exception of Charles A. Beard's *Economic Interpretation of the Constitution* (1913), has elicited such a storm of controversy.

From the outset, the law reviews teemed with attacks on *Government by Judiciary*, some of them cautious and considered, many slipshod and semihysterical. Berger decided immediately to take each attack seri-ously, to rethink and reexamine his evidence, and to publish a rebuttal. He quotes John Locke as stating that rebuttal is necessary lest victory be "adjudged not to him who had the truth on his side, but by the last word in the dispute." In time, Berger wrote approximately forty article-length rebuttals and one of book length. My own judgment, as I wrote in a review of the book-length rebuttal (Berger's *The Fourteenth Amendment and the Bill of Rights*, 1989), is that Berger defeated his critics "at every turn." This controversy and the now sizable body of rebuttal literature gave rise to the publication of the present edition of *Government by Ju-diciary*, containing the original version liberally sprinkled with fresh addenda.

So thoroughly did Berger rout his critics that, after a decade or so, they virtually stopped trying. Instead, advocates of judicial activism be-gan to assert that neither the words of the Constitution nor the inten-tions of the framers are any longer relevant. Justice William Brennan, for example, declared in 1985 that "the genius of the Constitution rests not in any static meaning it might have had in a world that is dead and gone, but in the adaptability of its great principles to cope with current problems and current needs."[3] (In actuality, as one of Berger's defend-ers, Wallace Mendelson, has pointed out, the only "great principles" to be found in the Constitution are "the consent of the governed, the dif-fusion of power, and the rule of law"—and the Supreme Court has un-

---

3. Brennan speech of October 12, 1985, as reported in most major newspapers.

dermined them all.)[4] Brennan's disciple Justice Thurgood Marshall went even further in this direction. In 1987, amidst the celebrations of the bicentennial of the Constitution, Marshall said, "I do not believe that the meaning of the Constitution was forever 'fixed' at the Philadelphia Convention. Nor do I find the wisdom, foresight, and sense of justice exhibited by the Framers particularly profound. To the contrary, the government they devised was defective from the start." He noted further that "several amendments, a civil war, and momentous social transformation" were necessary before the United States achieved a genuinely "constitutional government."[5]

In the face of such attitudes, one may justifiably question whether the Supreme Court is capable of restoring the constitutional compact to anything resembling its pristine form. But it is true, as the adage has it, that the Supreme Court follows the election returns, and voters have increasingly expressed their frustration with "government by judiciary." It is also true that Congress has the constitutional authority to rein in the Supreme Court through its control over the Court's jurisdiction, its power of the purse, and sundry other means.

I do not know what Raoul Berger thinks of the prospects for a return by any means to constitutional government. I suspect he is hopeful though not optimistic, for he is a man of never-say-die temperament and hard-nosed realism. In any event, if the great desideratum should come to pass, nobody would have done more to bring it about than Raoul Berger, for his writings, in their original form or in the works of disciples and converts, have become common coin of the realm.

Forrest McDonald
University of Alabama

---

4. Wallace Mendelson, "Raoul Berger on the Fourteenth Amendment Cornucopia," 3 Benchmark 211 (1987).

5. Marshall speech of May 6, 1987, as reported in most major newspapers.

# Preface to the Second Edition

The publication in 1977 of *Government by Judiciary* provoked a storm of controversy, leading a critic to exclaim in 1983 that "refuting Raoul Berger has become a cottage industry."[1] Criticism flourishes unabated. A critic more candid than most observed that

> Berger has forced all serious constitutional theorists to deal with questions regarding the proper principles of constitutional interpretation and the proper role of the courts, questions that many theorists, basking in the glow of Warren Court decisions on individual rights, felt content to ignore."[2]

Each critique prompted me to reexamine and retest my conclusions, for scholars are apprehensive whether they have overlooked a fact that will explode their inferences. "The great tragedy of science," Thomas Huxley remarked, is "the slaying of a beautiful hypothesis by an ugly fact."[3] In the eighteen years since publication, I have indited forty-odd responses, in which each respective critique is examined in great—and, I

1. Richard B. Saphire, "Judicial Review in the Name of the Constitution," 8 U. Dayton L. Rev. 745, 753 (1983).

2. Larry A. Alexander, "Modern Equal Protection Theories: A Metatheoretical Taxonomy and Critique," 42 Ohio St. L.J. 3, 4 (1981). C. Vann Woodward wrote, "Raoul Berger's *Government by Judiciary* raises scores of fascinating questions that no one in the field can afford to ignore." Dust jacket of *Government by Judiciary*. Sanford Levinson, himself an activist, wrote of attempts to construct a defense of the modern cases: "it is naive to pretend that the construction will be an easy task or that we can so easily shed the view of the Constitution, and its limits, articulated by Berger." Sanford Levinson, "Book Review," Nation, Feb. 26, 1983, at 248, 250.

"There is no history without polemic . . . without originating in antagonism to something which exists and which it wants to combat and substitute." Umberto Morra, *Conversations With Berenson* 103 (1965).

3. *Oxford Dictionary of Quotations* 269 (3d ed. 1979).

am afraid, tedious—detail. The interested reader will find a bibliography of my responses at the end of the book.[4]

These critiques prompted me to preserve the original text in this second edition so that readers may in the future have before them what excited so much controversy. The materials that have accumulated since 1977 are set forth in greatly abbreviated form as a supplement to a relevant chapter. New material added to the footnotes of the original text is identified by brackets.

A word in extenuation of the profuse quotations. Since my views have been and remain under assault, I prefer not to rely on mere expressions of my opinion but to employ appraisals by others.[5]

This revision was completed in my ninety-fifth year, so the gentle reader should cast upon it a charitable eye, bearing in mind Dr. Johnson's remark about "a dog's walking on his hind legs. It is not done well; but you are surprised to find it done at all."[6] Finally, I am indebted to the Earhart Foundation for a grant that facilitated completion of this second edition.

Raoul Berger<br>
Concord, Massachusetts<br>
1996

---

4. Locke wrote that a rebuttal is required lest victory be "adjudged not to him who had the truth on his side, but by the last word in the dispute." John Locke, *An Essay Concerning Human Understanding* 204–206 (Raymond Wilburn ed. 1942). Jefferson urged Madison to reply to Hamilton's "Pacificus" essays, giving as his reason, "Nobody answers him and his doctrines will therefore be taken for confessed." Stanley Elkins and Eric McKitrick, *The Age of Federalism* 362 (1993).

5. At the conclusion of his *Paradoxes of Legal Science* (1928), Benjamin Cardozo wrote, "I may seem to quote overmuch. My excuse is the desire to make manifest that back of what I write is the sanction of something stronger than my own unaided thought." *Selected Writings of Benjamin N. Cardozo* 313 (Margaret Hall ed. 1947).

6. James Boswell, *The Life of Samuel Johnson* 290 (Everyman ed. 1992).

# *Acknowledgments*

Eminent historians, social scientists, and lawyers have read portions or all of my manuscript and favored me with their suggestions. I do not name them in order to spare them the embarrassment of being associated with my views. Above all I am indebted to them for encouragement.

R. B.

Concord, Massachusetts
August 1977

# Abbreviations

| | |
|---|---|
| *Annals of Congress* | *Annals of Congress* (1st Congress, 1st Session 1789) |
| Bickel | Alexander M. Bickel, "The Original Understanding and the Segregation Decision," 69 Harvard Law Review 1 (1955) |
| Donald, *Sumner I* | David Donald, *Charles Sumner and the Coming of the Civil War* (1960) |
| Donald, *Sumner II* | David Donald, *Charles Sumner and the Rights of Man* (1970) |
| Elliot | Jonathan Elliot, *Debates in the Several State Conventions on the Adoption of the Federal Constitution* (2d ed. 1836) |
| Fairman, *History* | Charles Fairman, *Reconstruction and Reunion 1864–1888*, vol. 6, part 1 of *History of the Supreme Court of the United States* (1971) |
| Fairman, Stanford | Charles Fairman, "Does the Fourteenth Amendment Incorporate the Bill of Rights?," 2 Stanford Law Review 5 (1949) |
| Farrand | Max Farrand, *The Records of the Federal Convention of 1787* (1911) |
| Federalist | *The Federalist* (Modern Library ed. 1937) |
| Flack | Horace Flack, *The Adoption of the Fourteenth Amendment* (1908) |
| *Globe* | *Congressional Globe* (39th Congress, 1st Session 1866) |
| *Globe App.* | Appendix to *Globe* |
| Graham | Howard Jay Graham, *Everyman's Constitution* (1968) |
| James | Joseph B. James, *The Framing of the Fourteenth Amendment* (1965) |
| Kelly, Fourteenth | Alfred H. Kelly, "The Fourteenth Amendment Reconsidered: The Segregation Question," 54 Michigan Law Review 1049 (1956) |
| Kendrick | Benjamin Kendrick, *The Journal of the Joint Committee of Fifteen on Reconstruction* (1914) |
| Levy, *Against the Law* | Leonard W. Levy, *Against the Law: The Nixon Court and Criminal Justice* (1974) |
| Levy, *Warren* | Leonard W. Levy, ed., *The Supreme Court Under Earl Warren* (1972) |
| Lusky | Louis Lusky, *By What Right?* (1975) |
| Poore | Ben P. Poore, *Federal and State Constitutions, Colonial Charters* (1877) |
| TenBroek | Jacobus tenBroek, *Equal Under Law* (1965) |
| Van Alstyne | William W. Van Alstyne, "The Fourteenth Amendment, the 'Right' to Vote, and the Understanding of the Thirty-Ninth Congress," 1965 Supreme Court Review 33 |

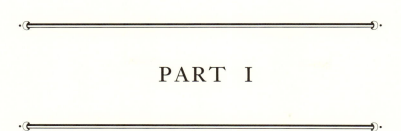

# PART I

# 1

## *Introduction*

My colleagues have learned to respect nothing but evidence, and to believe that their highest duty lies in submitting to it, however it may jar against their inclinations.

—THOMAS H. HUXLEY*

THE Fourteenth Amendment is the case study par excellence of what Justice Harlan described as the Supreme Court's "exercise of the amending power,"[1] its continuing revision of the Constitution under the guise of interpretation. Because the Amendment is probably the largest source of the Court's business[2] and furnishes the chief fulcrum for its control of controversial policies, the question whether such control is authorized by the Constitution is of great practical importance.

Those whose predilections are mirrored in a given decision find such judicial revision an exercise of statemanship.[3] Others consider that a democratic system requires adherence to constitutional limits, by courts no less than presidents.[4] This study seeks to demonstrate that the Court was not designed to act, in James M. Beck's enthusiastic phrase, as a "con-

* T. H. Huxley, *Man's Place in Nature* (1863), quoted in Homer W. Smith, *Man and His Gods* 372 (1953).

1. Reynolds v. Sims, 377 U.S. 533, 591 (1964).

2. Felix Frankfurter, "John Marshall and the Judicial Function," 69 Harv. L. Rev. 217, 229 (1955).

3. For example, Anthony Lewis hailed the Warren Court as the "keeper of the national conscience," in "Historical Change in the Supreme Court," *The New York Times Magazine*, June 17, 1962, at 7, reprinted in *Supreme Court Under Earl Warren* 73, 79, 81 (L. Levy ed. 1972). See also A. S. Miller and R. F. Howell, "The Myth of Neutrality in Constitutional Adjudication," 27 U. Chi. L. Rev. 661, 686, 689 (1960).

4. Chief Justice Marshall stated in M'Culloch v. Maryland, 17 U.S. (4 Wheat.) 316,

tinuing constitutional convention,"[5] that the role assigned to it was far
more modest: to police the boundaries drawn in the Constitution.[6] A
corollary is that the "original intention" of the Framers, here very plainly
evidenced, is binding on the Court for the reason early stated by Madison: if "the sense in which the Constitution was accepted and ratified by
the Nation ... be not the guide in expounding it, there can be no security for a consistent and stable [government], more than for a faithful
exercise of its powers."[7]

The present generation, floating on a cloud of post–Warren Court
euphoria, applauds a Court which read its libertarian convictions into
the Fourteenth Amendment, forgetting that for generations the Court

---

421 (1819), "We admit, as all must admit, that the powers of the government are limited,
and that its limits are not to be transcended." "The theory of our governments," said
Justice Samuel Miller, "is opposed to the deposit of unlimited power anywhere. The executive, the legislative, and the judicial branches of these governments are all of limited
and defined powers." Loan Association v. Topeka, 87 U.S. (20 Wall.) 655, 663 (1874).
"[W]ritten constitutions," and Justice Stanley Matthews, "were limitations upon all the
powers of government, legislative as well as executive and judicial." Hurtado v. California, 110 U.S. 516, 531–532 (1884).

5. In *The Constitution of the United States* (1922), Beck compared "the work of the Supreme Court to that of a 'continuous constitutional convention' which adapts the original
charter by reinterpretation." Quoted in Leonard W. Levy, *Judgments: Essays in American
Constitutional History* 18 (1972). In his recent critique of the "Nixon Court," Levy states
that the "Court is and must be for all practical purposes a 'continuous constitutional convention' in the sense that it must keep updating the original charter by reinterpretation."
L. Levy, *Against the Law* 29, 30 (1974). "Adaptation" and "reinterpretation" are euphe-
misms for "revision" or "rewriting" the Constitution, the function of a constitutional
convention, not the Court. See Louis Lusky, *By What Right?* 21 (1975); Louis Henkin,
"Some Reflections on Current Constitutional Controversies," 109 U. Pa. L. Rev. 637,
658–659 (1961).

Solicitor General Robert H. Jackson, later a Justice of the Court, did not share Beck's
enthusiasm; the pre-1937 Court, he said, "sat almost as a continuous constitutional convention which, without submitting its proposals to any ratification or rejection, could
amend the basic law." R. Jackson, *The Struggle for Judicial Supremacy* x–xi (1941). Ward
Elliott reports that Anthony Lewis (who was a leader in the drive that led to the "reapportionment" decision) asked Solicitor General Archibald Cox (who had filed a brief amicus for reapportionment in Reynolds v. Sims, supra note 1) when the Court announced
its decision, " 'How does it feel like to be present at the second American Constitutional
Convention?' Cox retained enough of his old perspective to answer, 'It feels awful.' "
Ward Elliott, *The Rise of a Guardian Democracy* 370 (1974). See infra Chapter 5 note 1.

6. See infra Chapter 16 at notes 20–28.

7. 9 James Madison, *The Writings of James Madison* 191 (G. Hunt ed. 1900–1910).

was harshly criticized because it had transformed laissez faire into constitutional dogma in order to halt the spread of "socialism."[8] With Brahmin restraint, Justice Holmes commented, in fear of socialism, "new principles had been discovered outside the bodies of those instruments [constitutions] which may be generalized into acceptance of the economic doctrines which prevailed about fifty years ago."[9] In the economic sphere that finally made due process a "dirty phrase."[10] The logic whereby that process becomes sanctified when employed for libertarian ideals has yet to be spelled out.[11] Logic, it is true, must yield to history, but history affords the Court even less support than logic.

Commentary on the Court's decisions frequently turns on whether they harmonize with the commentator's own predilections. My study

8. Joseph H. Choate comprehended that he could rely on the Court to react to the red flag of communism which he waved in Pollock v. Farmers Loan & Trust Co., 157 U.S. 429, 532 (1895). Justice Stephen Field responded in a concurring opinion: "The present assault upon capital is but the beginning. It will be but the stepping stone to others, larger and more sweeping, till our own political contests will become a war of the poor against the rich." Id. 607. On rehearing, Justice Henry B. Brown dissented, saying, "the decision involves nothing less than a surrender of the taxing power to the moneyed class . . . Even the spectre of socialism is conjured up." 158 U.S. 601, 695 (1895). In 1893 Justice David J. Brewer referred to " 'the black flag of anarchism, flaunting destruction to property,' and 'the red flag of socialism, inviting a redistribution of property.' " XVI Proceedings of the N.Y. State Bar Association 37, 47 (1893), quoted in A. T. Mason, "Myth and Reality in Supreme Court Drama," 48 Va. L. Rev. 1385, 1393 (1962). Such citations can be multiplied.

Justice Black reminded the Court of "the extent to which the evanescent standards of the majority's philosophy have been used to nullify state legislative programs passed to suppress evil economic practices." Rochin v. California, 342 U.S. 165, 177 (1952), concurring opinion.

9. Oliver Wendell Holmes, Jr., *Collected Legal Papers* 184 (1920).

10. Herbert Packer, "The Aim of the Criminal Law Revisited: A Plea for a New Look at 'Substantive Due Process,' " 44 S. Cal. L. Rev. 490 (1971). See infra Chapter 14 at notes 64, 77–78.

11. See infra Chapter 14 at notes 80–90; and see Robert G. McCloskey, "Due Process and the Supreme Court: An Exhumation and Reburial," 1962 S. Ct. Rev. 34, 44–45. Although McCloskey was very sympathetic to the Warren Court's goals, he concluded that the distinction does not stand up. Id. at 51. Chief Justice Stone, wrote Learned Hand, "could not understand how . . . when concerned with interests other than property, the courts should have a wider latitude for enforcing their own predilections than when they were concerned with property itself." Learned Hand, "Chief Justice Stone's Conception of the Judicial Function," 46 Colum. L. Rev. 696, 698 (1946).

may be absolved of that imputation: I regard segregation as a blot on our society,[12] and before I began to study the reapportionment issue I was taken with the beguiling slogan "one man, one vote." But almost thirty-five years ago I wrote of a decision that responded to my desires that I liked it no better when the Court read my predilections into the Constitution than when the Four Horsemen read in theirs.[13] Against the fulfillment of cherished ideals that turns on fortuitous appointments must be weighed the cost of warping the Constitution, of undermining "the rule of law." The Court has shown in the past that the Constitution can also be twisted to frustrate the needs of democracy.[14] These statements raise a congeries of questions which have been the subject of interminable controversy to which Part II is addressed.

The task here undertaken is that of an historian, to attempt accurately and faithfully to assemble the facts; that effort constitutes its own justification. For a decade the revisionist historians[15] have been engaged in what has been described as an "extraordinary revolution in the historiography" of Reconstruction,[16] throwing fresh light on the reasons for its limited objectives and its failure. To some extent the legal studies of Charles Fairman in 1949 and Alexander Bickel in 1955[17] had shown that the objectives of the framers of the Fourteenth Amendment were limited. Like the revisionist historians, a lawyer too may take another look after the passage of about a quarter-century. Despite the wilderness of commentary, largely devoted to the due process clause, the historical

12. One reads with horror of the Negro lynchings and torture that found their way into the courts as late as 1938. Paul Murphy, *The Constitution in Crisis Times, 1918–1969* 95, 123 (1972).

13. Raoul Berger, "Constructive Contempt: A Post Mortem," 9 U. Chi. L. Rev. 602, 604–605, 642 (1942).

14. For a withering condemnation of the Court's antidemocritarian course before 1937, see Henry Steele Commager, "Judicial Review and Democracy," 19 Va. Quarterly Rev. 417 (1943).

15. W. R. Brock, Eric L. McKitrick, C. Vann Woodward, David Donald, Harold M. Hyman, Michael L. Benedict. Their works are listed in the bibliography.

16. Alfred H. Kelly, "Comment on Harold M. Hyman's Paper" in *New Frontiers of the American Reconstruction* 40 (Harold M. Hyman ed. 1966).

17. C. Fairman, "Does the Fourteenth Amendment Incorporate the Bill of Rights?" 2 Stan. L. Rev. 5 (1949); Alexander Bickel, "The Original Understanding and the Segregation Decision," 69 Harv. L. Rev. 1 (1955).

warrant for desegregation, reapportionment, and incorporation of the Bill of Rights in the due process clause remains controversial.[18] Little analysis has been devoted to the role of the privileges or immunities clause in the original scheme of things;[19] nor have studies of the equal protection and due process clauses adequately explored what those terms meant to the framers.

In reconstructing the past, historians generally are compelled to rely on accounts written after the event by participants and witnesses, or on the hearsay versions of those who learned at second-hand what had occurred. Such writings are subject to the infirmities of recollection, or of bias arising from allegiance to one side or the other. The historical records here relied on—the legislative history of the Fourteenth Amendment—are of a far more trustworthy character, being a stenographic transcription of what was said in the 39th Congress from day to day by those engaged in framing the Amendment. It is a verbatim account of what occurred, recorded while it was happening, comparable to a news film of an event at the moment it was taking place and free from the possible distortion of accounts drawn from recollection or hearsay. What men say while they are acting are themselves facts, as distinguished from opinions about facts.[20] Such statements constitute a reliable record of what happened as the Amendment was being forged by the framers.

It needs to be emphasized that the records of the 39th Congress are free from the reproach often leveled at legislative history—that it is "enigmatic." A statement such as that of Charles P. Curtis, "It is a hal-

---

18. See Alfred H. Kelly, "Clio and the Court: An Illicit Love Affair," 1965 S. Ct. Rev. 119, 132, 134–135; A. H. Kelly, "The Fourteenth Amendment Reconsidered: The Segregation Question," 54 Mich. L. Rev. 1049, 1081 (1956); Howard J. Graham, *Everyman's Constitution* 314 (1968); William W. Van Alstyne, "The Fourteenth Amendment, The 'Right' to Vote, and the Understanding of the Thirty-Ninth Congress," 1965 S. Ct. Rev. 33; Robert J. Harris, *The Quest for Equality* 55–56 (1960).

19. The leading article, D. O. McGovney, "Privileges and Immunities Clause, Fourteenth Amendment," 4 Iowa L. Bull. 219 (1918) states (at 222 note 2), "this essay . . . might have been entitled the Rule of the Slaughter-House Cases."

20. In Justice Holmes' words, a "party's conduct" may "consist in uttering certain words." Oliver Wendell Holmes, Jr., *The Common Law* 132 (1923).

lucination: this search for intent. The room is always dark"[21] simply cannot stand up against these records. Instead of sparse, cryptic remarks there are, for example, with respect to suffrage, the unequivocal Joint Report of the Committee on Reconstruction which drafted the Amendment; explanations of the Amendment and the antecedent Civil Rights Act of 1866 by the committee chairmen who had them in charge, and by other members of the committees; statements by leaders of the Republican Party which sponsored both, accompanied by a virtually unanimous chorus of fellow Republicans. These are commonly regarded as the best evidence of legislative "intention."[22] Then there are repeated rejections, by heavy pluralities, of extremist efforts to put through legislation or amendments that would confer suffrage. Thus, the records richly confirm Justice Harlan's comment: "The history of the Fourteenth Amendment with respect to suffrage qualifications is remarkably free of the problems which bedevil most attempts to find a reliable guide to present decision in the pages of the past. Instead, there is virtually unanimous agreement, clearly and repeatedly expressed, that § 1 of the Amendment did not reach discriminatory voter disqualifications."[23]

In short, the proof is all but incontrovertible that the framers meant to leave control of suffrage with the States, which had always exercised such control, and to exclude federal intrusion. On traditional canons of interpretation, the intention of the framers being unmistakably expressed, that intention is as good as written into the text.[24] It is, there-

---

21. "A Better Theory of Legal Interpretation," 3 Vand. L. Rev. 407, 409 (1950).

22. H. M. Hart and A. Sacks, *The Legal Process: Basic Problems in the Making and Application of Law* 1266 (1958). Justice Frankfurter stated, "It has never been questioned in this Court that Committee reports, as well as statements by those in charge of a bill or of a report, are authoritative elucidations of the scope of a measure." Schwegmann Bros. v. Calvert Distillers Corp., 341 U.S. 384, 399–400 (1951), dissenting opinion. See also Lusky 45.

23. Oregon v. Mitchell, 400 U.S. 112, 200 (1970), dissenting opinion. Van Alstyne, who is critical of Justice Harlan's view in Reynolds v. Sims (supra note 1), states: "in none of the other kinds of cases where it was brought to bear did it [the historical record] cast the kind of blinding light that Mr. Justice Harlan sees here." Van Alstyne 36.

24. "A thing may be within the letter of a statute and not within its meaning, and within its meaning though not within its letter. The intention of the lawmaker is the law." Hawaii v. Mankichi, 190 U.S. 197, 212 (1903); United States v. Freeman, 44 U.S. (3 How.) 556, 565 (1845); United States v. Babbitt, 66 U.S. 55, 61 (1861); Matthew Bacon, *A New*

fore, as if the Amendment expressly stated that "control of suffrage shall be left with the States." If that intention is demonstrable, the "one man, one vote" cases represent an awesome exercise of power, an 180-degree revision, taking from the States a power that unmistakably was left to them. That poses the stark issue whether such revisory power was conferred on the Court. Because the "intention" of the framers is so crucial to examination of this issue, because a commentator should not pit his mere ipse dixit against the Court's finding, for example, that the historical evidence respecting desegregation is inconclusive, it is not enough to retort that the evidence is overwhelming. It is necessary to pile proof on proof, even at the risk of tedium, so that the reader may determine for himself whether it is overwhelming or inconclusive.

Whether the "original intention" of the framers should be binding on the present generation—a question hereafter discussed—should be distinguished from the issue: what did the framers mean to accomplish, what did the words they used mean to them. That must be the historical focus, not what we should like the words to mean in the light of current exigencies or changed ideals. In the words of the eminent British historians H. G. Richardson and G. O. Sayles, "We must learn, not from modern theorists, but from contemporaries of the events we are studying." We should not impose "upon the past a creature of our own imagining."[25] One hundred and fifty years earlier Justice James Iredell, one of the first Founders to spell out the case for judicial review, stated, "We are too apt, in estimating a law passed at a remote period, to combine in our consideration, all the subsequent events which have had an influence upon it, instead of confining ourselves (which we ought to do) to the existing circumstances at the time of its passing."[26]

---

*Abridgment of the Laws of England*, "Statutes" 1 (5) (7th ed. 1832); infra Chapter 9 note 22.

25. "Parliament and Great Councils in Medieval England," 77 L. Q. Rev. 213, 224 (1961). Miller and Howell label it an "historicist fallacy" to "appraise a former historical era by the criteria of values that have become important since." Supra note 3 at 673.

26. Ware v. Hylton, 3 U.S. (3 Dall.) 199, 267 (1796). In "the construction of the language of the Constitution . . . as indeed in all other instances where construction becomes necessary, we are to place ourselves as nearly as possible in the condition of the men who framed that instrument." Ex parte Bain, 121 U.S. 1, 12 (1887).

In an area of warring interpretations no useful purpose is served by delivering another ex cathedra opinion.[27] A commentator should spread before the reader the evidence on which his opinion is based and comment both on discrepant evidence and on opposing inferences.[28] Consequently, a polemical tone is inescapable; a student of history can no more avoid criticism of views which seem to him erroneous than did the chemists who disputed the tenability of the phlogiston theory of combustion. To avoid that responsibility is to court the charge of ignoring an influential body of contrary opinion, of selecting only the evidence that advances one's own argument, and, even worse, to cast the reader adrift on a sea of conflicting opinions.

Now that the dust has settled, a synthesis of the historical materials that bear on the three controversial areas will furnish some cross-illumination. No synthesis need undertake to trace in complete detail the development of the Amendment and its antecedent bills. Not only is there no need to duplicate the chronological labors that others have already performed, but to do so is to risk swamping the reader in a mass of detail that is bewildering rather than illuminating.[29] Instead my effort will be to focus on the facts that seem to me crucial, to take account of discrepant facts, and to analyze views that are opposed to mine.

Following the lead of Howard Jay Graham and Jacobus tenBroek,[30] academicians have shown a growing tendency to attribute to the framers of the Fourteenth Amendment moral-legal conceptions formulated by some abolitionists during their crusade of the 1830s–1860s, and to read those conceptions of substantive due process and equal protection into the Amendment. Noble enthusiasm is no less prone to distort the vision

27. It is unsatisfying to have the fastidiously detailed study of Fairman dismissed with the phrase that it is "in the opinion of this writer against the weight of the evidence." Kelly, Fourteenth 1081 note 106. As will develop, Kelly was altogether wrong.

28. Sir Herbert Butterfield, *George III and the Historians* 225 (1969).

29. See Bickel; Joseph B. James, *The Framing of the Fourteenth Amendment* (1956); and Horace Flack, *The Adoption of the Fourteenth Amendment* (1908). Walter Bagehot considered that "history should be like a Rembrandt etching, casting a vivid light on important causes and leaving all the rest unseen, in shadow." Quoted in Van Wyck Brooks, *Days of the Phoenix* 135 (1957).

30. Graham; Jacobus tenBroek, *Equal Under Law* (1965). For discussion of the Graham-tenBroek neoabolitionist theory, see infra Chapter 13.

than vulgar prejudice. In evaluating the historical facts we do well to bear in mind Flaubert's view that "personal sympathy, genuine emotion, twitching nerves and tear-filled eyes only impair the sharpness of the artist's vision."[31] Even more, the historian, in the words of C. Vann Woodward, has "a special obligation to sobriety and fidelity to the record."[32]

## Background

The key to an understanding of the Fourteenth Amendment is that the North was shot through with Negrophobia, that the Republicans, except for a minority of extremists, were swayed by the racism that gripped their constituents rather than by abolitionist ideology. At the inception of their crusade the abolitionists peered up at an almost unscalable cliff. Charles Sumner, destined to become a leading spokesman for extreme abolitionist views, wrote in 1834, upon his first sight of slaves, "My worst preconception of their appearance and their ignorance did not fall as low as their actual stupidity . . . They appear to be nothing more than moving masses of flesh unendowed with anything of intelligence above the brutes."[33] Tocqueville's impression in 1831–1832 was equally abysmal.[34] He noticed that in the North, "the prejudice which repels the

---

31. 4 Arnold Hauser, *The Social History of Art* 76 (Vintage Books, undated). Hauser states that Flaubert's view was shared by the Goncourts, Maupassant, Gide, Valéry, and others. "To get at the truth of our system of morality (and equally of the law)," said Holmes, "it is useful to omit the emotion and ask ourselves [how far] those generalizations . . . are confirmed by fact accurately ascertained." Oliver Wendell Holmes, Jr., *Collected Legal Papers* 306 (1920).

32. *The Burden of Southern History* 87 (1960).

33. David Donald, *Charles Sumner and the Coming of the Civil War* 29 (1960).

34. "[W]e can scarcely acknowledge the common features of mankind in this child of debasement whom slavery has brought among us. His physiognomy to our eyes is hideous, his understanding weak, his tastes low; and we are almost inclined to look upon him as a being intermediate between man and the brutes." 1 Alexis de Tocqueville, *Democracy in America* 363 (1900). In the 39th Congress, Robert Hale of New York stated that the District of Columbia "contains a black population which, undoubtedly, approaches to the very extreme of ignorance and degradation . . . a population that has come into this District suddenly, just freed from slavery, with all the marks and burdens upon them that a

negroes seems to increase in proportion as they are emancipated," that prejudice "appears to be stronger in the States which have abolished slavery, than in those where it still exists."[35]

Little wonder that the abolitionist campaign was greeted with loathing! In 1837 Elijah Lovejoy, an abolitionist editor, was murdered by an Illinois mob.[35a] How shallow was the impress of the abolitionist campaign on such feelings is graphically revealed in a Lincoln incident. A delegation of Negro leaders had called on him at the White House, and he told them,

> There is an unwillingness on the part of our people, harsh as it may be, for you free colored people to remain with us . . . [E]ven when you cease to be slaves, you are far removed from being placed on an equality with the white man . . . I cannot alter it if I would. It is a fact.[36]

Fear of Negro invasion—that the emancipated slaves would flock north in droves—alarmed the North.[37] The letters and diaries of Union sol-

---

state of slavery necessarily fixes upon its victims." *Cong. Globe*, 39th Cong. 1st Sess. 280 (1865–1866), hereinafter cited as *Globe*. In citations to the *Globe*, Senators will be identified as such; all others are representatives.

Even one sympathetic to the Negro cause, Senator Henry Wilson of Massachusetts, was constrained to hope in 1864 that "the school house will rise to enlighten the darkened intellect of a race imbruted by long years of enforced ignorance." Quoted in ten-Broek, 164.

35. Tocqueville, supra note 34 at 365, 364.

35a. "[T]he abolitionists were regarded throughout most Northern circles as disagreeable and intemperate radicals and were heckled, harrowed, assaulted and even killed by Northern mobs." Dan Lacy, *The White Use of Blacks in America* 54 (1972).

36. Woodward, supra note 32 at 81. "In virtually every phase of existence Negroes found themselves systematically separated from whites [in the North, 1860] . . . in most places he encountered severe limitations to the protection of his life, liberty, and property." Leon Litwack, *North of Slavery: The Negro in the Free States* 91–97 (1961), quoted in C. Vann Woodward, "Seeds of Failure in Radical Race Policy" in Hyman supra note 16 at 126.

37. Woodward, "Seeds," supra note 36 at 127, 128, 131, 132. Senator Thomas A. Hendricks of Indiana stated, "The policy of the State has been to discourage their immigration . . . to protect white labor. The presence of negroes in large numbers tends to degrade and cheapen labor, and the people have been unwilling that the white laborer shall be compelled to compete for employment with the Negro." *Globe* 2939. The Freedmen's Bureau and Civil Rights Acts "were intended not only to protect the freedmen but also

diers, Woodward notes, reveal an "enormous amount of antipathy towards Negroes"; popular convictions "were not prepared to sustain" a commitment to equality.[38] Racism, David Donald remarks, "ran deep in the North," and the suggestion that "Negroes should be treated as equals to white men woke some of the deepest and ugliest fears in the American mind."[39]

One need not look beyond the confines of the debates in the 39th Congress to find abundant confirmation. Time and again Republicans took account of race prejudice as an inescapable fact. George W. Julian of Indiana referred to the "proverbial hatred" of Negroes, Senator Henry S. Lane of Indiana to the "almost ineradicable prejudice," Shelby M. Cullom of Illinois to the "morbid prejudice," Senator William M. Stewart of Nevada to the "nearly insurmountable" prejudice, James F. Wilson of Iowa to the "iron-cased prejudice" against blacks. These were Republicans, sympathetic to emancipation and the protection of civil rights.[40] Then there were the Democratic racists who unashamedly proclaimed that the Union should remain a "white man's" government.[41] In

to secure a contented black labor force who . . . stayed in the South." Morton Keller, *Affairs of State* 65, 143 (1977).

38. Woodward, supra note 32 at 82, 83. Senator James R. Doolittle of Wisconsin reported that "four out of five" Wisconsin soldiers "voted against Negro suffrage." *Globe* 2165.

39. Donald, *Sumner II* 156–157. An Illinois Radical, John F. Farnsworth, said, " 'Negro equality' is the everlasting skeleton which frightens some people." *Globe* 204. William E. Niblack of Indiana reminded the Congress that in 1851 Indiana ratified a Constitution that excluded Negroes from the State by a vote of 109,976 to 21,084. *Globe* 3212.

"A belief in racial equality," said W. R. Brock, "was an abolitionist invention"; "to the majority of men in the midnineteenth century it seemed to be condemned both by experience and by science." "Even abolitionists," he states, "were anxious to disclaim any intention of forcing social contacts between the races." Brock, *An American Crisis: Congress and Reconstruction* 285, 286 (1963). See infra, Derrick Bell, Chapter 10 at note 6. Racism, Phillip Paludan states, was "as pervasive during Reconstruction as after. Americans clung firmly to a belief in the basic inferiority of the Negro race, a belief supported by the preponderance of nineteenth-century scientific evidence." Phillip S. Paludan, *A Covenant with Death* 54 (1975). See also Keller, supra note 37. Many Republican newspapers in the North opposed "equality with the Negroes." Flack 41. See also Keller, id. 51, 58, 65.

40. *Globe* 257, 739, 911, 2799, 2948.

41. John W. Chanler of New York, *Globe* 48, 218; Senator James W. Nesmith of Oregon, id. 291; Aaron Harding of Kentucky, id. 448; Senator Hendricks of Indiana, id. 880;

the words of Senator Garrett Davis of Kentucky, "The white race . . . will be proprietors of the land, and the blacks its cultivators; such is their destiny."[42] Let it be regarded as political propaganda, and, as the noted British historiographer Sir Herbert Butterfield states, it "does at least presume an audience—perhaps a 'public opinion'—which is judged to be susceptible to the kinds of arguments and considerations set before it."[43] Consider, too, that the Indiana Constitution of 1851 excluded Negroes from the State, as did Oregon,[44] that a substantial number of Northern States recently had rejected Negro suffrage,[45] that others maintained segregated schools.[46] It is against this backdrop that we must measure claims that the framers of the Fourteenth Amendment swallowed abolitionist ideology hook, line, and sinker.[47]

The framers represented a constituency that had just emerged from a protracted, bitterly fought war, a war that had left them physically and emotionally drained. It had begun with a commitment to save the Union and had gone on to emancipate the slaves. Now the war-weary North was far from anxious to embark on fresh crusades for the realization of still other abolitionist goals.[48] While emancipation largely hit slavery in the South, eradication of inequality, as Vann Woodward remarked, required "a revolution for the North as well,"[49] a revolution for which most Republicans were utterly unprepared. Then too, the fact that Republicans and Democrats had been pretty evenly matched over the years, that some districts definitely were swing areas, led Republicans in those areas to be cautious of affronting their constituents.[50] Many moderate and conservative Republicans, as we shall see, were acutely aware of the

---

Senator Garrett Davis of Kentucky, id. 246–250. The sympathetic reformer, Senator William M. Stewart of Nevada, stated, the "white man's government . . . should not be scoffed at; that it was a prejudice in the country that no man has a right to disregard." Id. 1437.

42. Id. 935.

43. Butterfield, supra note 28 at 226; cf. Stewart, supra note 41.

44. For Indiana see supra note 39; for Oregon see Fairman, Stanford 32 note 58.

45. See Van Alstyne's summary, infra Chapter 4 at note 16.

46. See infra Chapter 7 at note 41. As late as 1859 the Ohio Court rejected an attack on segregated schools. Van Camp v. Board of Education, 9 Ohio 407.

47. For additional details see infra Chapter 13.

48. Donald, *Sumner II* 232–233; see also id. 158.

49. Woodward, supra note 32 at 79; see infra Chapter 10 at note 6.

50. David Donald, *The Politics of Reconstruction* 12–13, 61–62 (1965).

impact on elections of sweeping radical claims for political, let alone social, equality for the blacks.[51] While most men were united in a desire to protect the freedmen from outrage and oppression in the South by prohibiting discrimination with respect to "fundamental rights," without which freedom was illusory, to go beyond this with a campaign for political and social equality was, as Senator James R. Doolittle of Wisconsin confessed, "frightening" to the Republicans who "represented States containing the despised and feared free negroes."[52]

A striking reflection of Northern sentiment was furnished by Thaddeus Stevens, the foremost Radical leader. According to his biographer, Fawn M. Brodie, he

> sensed . . . that talk of "social equality" was dangerous politics. When he heard that the ex-slave Frederick Douglass . . . had paraded arm-in-arm with editor Theodore Tilton, he wrote . . . "A good many people here are disturbed by the practical exhibition of social equality in the arm-in-arm performance of Douglass and Tilton. It does not become radicals like us to particularly object. But it was certainly unfortunate at this time. The old prejudice, now revived, will lose us some votes."[53]

As Stevens revealed, most Republicans were politicians first and ideologues afterward.[54] Not civil rights for blacks but the dreaded take-over of the federal government by the South was their obsessive preoccupation. Emancipation brought the startling realization that Southern representation would no longer be limited in the House of Representatives to three-fifths of the blacks, as article I, § 3, provided. Now each voteless freedman counted as a whole person; and in the result Southern States would be entitled to increased representation and, with the help of Northern Democrats, would have, Thaddeus Stevens pointed out at the very outset of the 39th Congress, "a majority in Congress and in the Electoral College." With equal candor he said that the Southern States

---

51. Speaking on June 4, 1866, James Wilson of Iowa said, "I know that many look forward to the fall elections and shiver in the presence of impartial suffrage." *Globe* 2948.

52. Donald, *Sumner II* 158.

53. *Thaddeus Stevens: Scourge of the South* 287 (1959).

54. See James 71.

"ought never to be recognized as valid States, until the Constitution shall be amended . . . as to secure perpetual ascendancy" to the Republican party.[55] The North had not fought and quelled rebellion in order to surrender the fruits of victory to the unrepentant rebels. How to circumvent this possibility was the central concern of the Republicans, and it found expression in § 2 of the Fourteenth Amendment, which reduced representation in proportion as the right to vote was denied or abridged. Unless we seize hold of the fact that, to borrow from Russell R. Nye, "what lies beneath the politics of the Reconstruction period, so far as it touched the Negro, is the prevailing racist policy tacitly accepted by both parties and by the general public,"[56] we shall fail to appreciate the limited objectives of the Fourteenth Amendment. That is the reality underlying the limited purposes of the framers of the Fourteenth Amendment, and which circumscribes the so-called "generality" of "equal protection" and "due process."

Proponents of a broad construction of the Amendment have assumed that advocates of a restricted construction have the burden of proving that the framers' objectives were limited. The shoe is on the other foot; an interpretation that invades what had long been considered the exclusive province of the States, as, for example, criminal procedure, requires some justification. It is not enough in that situation that the words are capable of a broad meaning; the reservation to the States in the Tenth Amendment of powers not delegated to the federal government calls for a clear showing that the successor amendment was designed to curtail those reserved powers.[57] Over the years the Supreme Court, to be sure,

---

55. *Globe* 74; Samuel E. Morison, *The Oxford History of the American People* 714 (1965). Senator John Sherman of Ohio said, "never by my consent shall these rebels gain by this war increased political power, and come back here to wield that political power." *Globe* 745. "I would no more admit the rebels to control these States," said Senator Daniel Clark of New Hampshire, "than I would sail a ship with the mutinous part of a crew, and confine those who were faithful to the captain in the hold or put them in irons." Id. 835.

56. "Comment on C. V. Woodward's Paper," in Hyman, supra note 16 at 148, 151.

57. The governing rule was laid down by Chief Justice Marshall: "an opinion which is . . . to establish a principle never before recognized, should be expressed in plain and explicit terms." United States v. Burr, 25 F. Cas. (No. 14,693) 55, 165 (C.C. Va. 1807). Long before it was stated, "statutes are not presumed to make any alteration in the common law, farther or otherwise than the act expressly declares: therefore in all general

has steadily eroded those reserved powers, but this simply represents another of the usurpations that bestrew the path of the Court. But the historian, looking to the Constitution itself, may not be blind to the fact that, in the words of Willard Hurst, the reservation "represented a political bargain, key terms of which assumed the continuing vitality of the states as prime law makers in most affairs."[58] No trace of an intention by the Fourteenth Amendment to encroach on State control—for example, of suffrage and segregation—is to be found in the records of the 39th Congress. A mass of evidence is to the contrary, and, as will appear, the attachment of the framers to State sovereignty played a major role in restricting the scope of the Amendment. "[W]e ought to remember," Justice Holmes said, "the greater caution shown by the Constitution in limiting the power of the States, and should be slow to construe the [due process] clause in the Fourteenth Amendment as committing to the Court, with no guide but the Court's own discretion the validity of whatever laws the States may pass."[59] The history of the Amendment buttresses the flat statement that no such jurisdiction was conferred.

"What, after all," asked Wallace Mendelson, "are the privileges and immunities of United States citizenship? What process is 'due' in what circumstances? and what is 'equal protection'?"[60] Study of what the terms meant to the framers indicates that there was no mystery. The three clauses of §1 were three facets of one and the same concern: to

---

matters the law presumes the act did not intend to make any alteration; for if the parliament had had that design they would have expressed it in the act." Bacon's *Abridgment*, supra note 24, "Statutes" I (4). An analogous rule was applied to the Constitution in the Slaughter-House Cases, 83 U.S. (16 Wall.) 36, 78 (1872).

Such views were given striking reaffirmation in Pierson v. Ray, 386 U.S. 547, 554–555 (1967). After adverting to the common law immunity of judges from suits for acts performed in their official capacity, the Court stated, "We do not believe that this settled principle was abolished by § 1983, which makes liable 'every person' who under color of law deprives another person of his civil rights . . . The immunity of judges [is] well established and we presume that Congress would have specifically so provided had it wished to abolish the doctrine." Thus the all-inclusive "every person" was curtailed because of an existing common law immunity; the express reservation of power to the States by the Tenth Amendment demands an even more exacting standard.

58. *The Legitimacy of the Business Corporation in the Law of the United States* 140 (1970).
59. Baldwin v. Missouri, 281 U.S. 586, 595 (1930), dissenting opinion.
60. *The Supreme Court: Law and Discretion* 16 (1967).

insure that there would be no discrimination against the freedmen in respect of "fundamental rights," which had clearly understood and narrow compass. Roughly speaking, the substantive rights were identified by the privileges or immunities clause; the equal protection clause was to bar legislative discrimination with respect to those rights; and the judicial machinery to secure them was to be supplied by nondiscriminatory due process of the several States. Charles Sumner summarized these radical goals: let the Negro have "the shield of *impartial laws. Let him be heard in court.*"[61] That shield, it will be shown, was expressed in "equal protection of the *laws*; access to protection by the courts found expression in "due process of law." The framers, it needs to be said at once, had no thought of creating unfamiliar rights of unknown, far-reaching extent by use of the words "equal protection" and "due process." Instead, they meant to secure familiar, "fundamental rights," and only those, and to guard them as of yore against deprivation except by (1) a nondiscriminatory law, and (2) the established judicial procedure of the State.

## Supplementary Note on the Introduction

It is the thesis of this book that the Supreme Court is not empowered to rewrite the Constitution, that in its transformation of the Fourteenth Amendment it has demonstrably done so. Thereby the Justices, who are virtually unaccountable, irremovable, and irreversible, have taken over from the people control of their own destiny, an awesome exercise of power. When Chief Justice Marshall stated that the function of the legislature is to *make* the law, that of the judiciary to *interpret* it,[1] he echoed

---

61. *Globe* 675.

1. This principle lies at the heart of the separation of powers, as Chief Justice Marshall perceived: "The difference between the departments undoubtedly is, that the legislature makes, the executive executes, and the judiciary construes the law." *Wayman v. Southard*, 23 U.S. (10 Wheat.) 1, 46 (1825). Marshall was anticipated by Justice Samuel

Francis Bacon's admonition two hundred years earlier.[2] Much less are judges authorized to revise the Constitution, for as Justice Black, deriding the notion that the Court was meant to keep the Constitution "in tune with the times," stated, "The Constitution makers knew the need for change and provided for it" by the amendment process of Article V,[3] whereby the people reserved unto themselves the right to change the Constitution. Having created a prepotent Congress, being well aware of the greedy expansiveness of power, and knowing that power can be malign as well as benign, the Founders designed the judiciary to keep Congress within its prescribed bounds,[4] what James Bradley Thayer and Learned Hand later called "policing" the constitutional boundaries.[5] *Within* those boundaries, stated Justice James Iredell, one of the ablest of the Founders, the legislature was to be free of judicial interference.[6]

---

Chase in Ware v. Hylton, 3 U.S. (3 Dall.) 199, 223 (1796): "The people delegated power to a *Legislature*, an *Executive*, and a *Judiciary;* the *first* to make; the *second* to execute; and the *last* to declare or expound the laws" (emphasis added). Of the three branches, Hamilton assured the ratifiers, the judiciary is "next to nothing." Federalist No. 78 at 504 (Mod. Lib. ed. 1937).

2. 1 *Selected Writings of Francis Bacon* 138 (Mod. Lib. ed. 1937). Blackstone stated, "Though in many other countries everything is left in the breast of the Judge to determine, yet with us he is only to declare and pronounce, not to make or new-model the law." 3 William Blackstone, *Commentaries on the Laws of England* 335 (1769). James Wilson, second only to Madison as an architect of the Constitution, instructed the judge to "remember, that his duty and his business is, not to make the law but to interpret and apply it." 2 James Wilson, *Works* 502 (Robert McCloskey ed. 1967).

3. Griswold v. Connecticut, 381 U.S. 479, 522 (1965), dissenting opinion. In McPherson v. Blacker, 146 U.S. 1, 36 (1892), the Court rejected the notion that the Constitution may be "amended by judicial decision without action by the designated organs in the mode by which alone amendments can be made." See also Hawke v. Smith, 253 U.S. 221, 239 (1920).

4. In the Virginia Ratification Convention, for instance, John Marshall stated that if Congress were "to go beyond the delegated powers . . . if they were to make a law not warranted by the powers enumerated, it would be considered by the judges as an infringement of the Constitution . . . They would declare it void." 3 Jonathan Elliot, *Debates in the Several State Conventions on the Adoption of the Federal Constitution* 551, 553 (1836).

5. See infra Chapter 16, note 26.

6. Referring to constitutional limitations on legislative power, Justice Iredell declared, "Beyond these limitations . . . their acts are void, because they are not warranted by the authority given. But within them . . . the Legislatures only exercise a discretion expressly confided to them by the constitution . . . It is a discretion no more controllable . . . by a

Unlike the academicians' current infatuation with a revisory judiciary,[7] the Founders had a "profound fear of judicial independence and discretion."[8] They were influenced by the English Puritans' fear that "the laws' meaning could be twisted by means of judicial construction"; they feared the judges' "imposition of their personal views."[9] An important brake on such arrogation was the rule that a document is to be construed in light of the draftsmen's explanation of what they meant to accomplish,[10] the so-called original intention. Jefferson and Madison at-

Court . . . than a judicial determination is by them." Ware v. Hylton, 3 U.S. (3 Dall.) 199, 266 (1726). South Carolina State Highway Department v. Barnwell Bros., 303 U.S. 177, 190–191 (1938), per Stone, J. Champion v. Ames, 188 U.S. 321, 363 (1902): "if what Congress does is within the limits of its power, and is simply unwise or injurious, the remedy is that suggested by Chief Justice Marshall in Gibbons v. Ogden," i.e., look to the people at elections.

7. It was not ever thus. Stanley Kutler, a pervervid activist, noted that "From the early twentieth century throughout the later 1930s, academic and liberal commentators . . . criticized vigorously the abusive powers of the federal judiciary. They accused . . . the Supreme Court of consistently frustrating desirable social policies." He noted that "the judges had arrogated a policy-making function not conferred upon them by the Constitution," which "negated the basic principles of representative government." "After 1937," he observed, "most of the judiciary's long time critics suddenly found a new faith and promoted it with all the zealousness of new converts." Now the courts "matched a new libertarianism . . . with an activist judiciary to protect those values." Stanley I. Kutler, "Raoul Berger's Fourteenth Amendment: A History or Ahistorical," 6 Hastings Const. L.Q. 511, 512, 513 (1978).

Contemporary academicians, Robert Bork noted, "encourage the courts to yet more daring adventures in constitution-making." Robert Bork, Foreword to Gary L. McDowell, *The Constitution and Contemporary Constitutional Theory* viii (1985). However, the new judicial role was extolled only so long as it satisfied activist aspirations. A putative departure from the judicial path of the last forty years (which is no more sacrosanct than the dumped precedents of the prior 150 years) led Dean Guido Calabresi of Yale to declare, "I despise the current Supreme Court and find its aggressive, wilful behavior disgusting." N.Y. Times, July 28, 1991, Op. Ed. Calabresi's complaint is clarified by Anthony Lewis: "we now have a Court dominated by conservative activists, construing laws so as to reach results that they desire." Anthony Lewis, "Winners and Losers," N.Y. Times, Oct. 18, 1989, at A17. But Lewis lauded that very practice when the Warren Court reached results that Lewis desired. See infra note 17.

8. Gordon Wood, *The Creation of the American Republic, 1776–1787* 298 (1969).

9. H. Jefferson Powell, "The Original Understanding of Original Intent," 98 Harv. L. Rev. 885, 891 (1985).

10. Richard Kay, "Book Review," 10 Conn. L. Rev. 800, 805–806 (1978): "To implement real limits on government the judges must have reference to standards which are external to, and prior to the matter to be decided . . . The contents of those standards are

tached great weight to the rule;[11] and Chief Justice Marshall declared that he could cite from the common law "the most complete evidence that the intention is the most sacred rule of interpretation."[12] Here law and common sense coincide. Who better knows what the writer means than the writer himself?[13] John Selden, the preeminent seventeenth-century scholar, stated, "A Man's writing has but one true sense, which is that which the Author meant when he writ it."[14] Such were the views of Hobbes and Locke.[15] To maintain the contrary is to insist that the reader better knows what the writer meant than the writer himself. To recapitulate, antiactivists (originalists) maintain that judges are not authorized to revise the Constitution[16] and that it is to be construed in

---

set at their creation. Recourse to 'the intention of the framers' in judicial review, therefore can be understood as indispensable to realizing the idea of government limited by law." See also W. Lawrence Church, "History and the Constitutional Role of the Courts," 1990 Wis. L. Rev. 1071, 1087–1088.

11. Jefferson pledged in his Inaugural Address to administer the Constitution "according to the safe and honest meaning contemplated by the plain understanding of the people at the time of its adoption—a meaning to be found in the explanations of those who advocated it." 4 Elliot, *supra* note 4 at 466. Madison wrote, "I entirely concur in the propriety of resorting to the sense in which the Constitution was accepted and ratified by the nation. In that sense alone it is the legitimate Constitution. And if that be not the guide in expounding it, there can be no security for a consistent and stable, more than for a faithful exercise of its powers." 3 *Letters and Other Writings of James Madison* 441, 442 (1865).

12. *John Marshall's Defense of McCulloch v. Maryland* 167 (Gerald Gunther ed. 1969).

13. William Cullen Bryant asked, are we "to admit that the Constitution was never before rightly understood, even by those who framed it?" 1 Allan Nevins, *The Emergence of Lincoln* 95 (1950).

14. *Table Talk: Being the Discourses of John Selden, Esq.* 10 (1696). See Supplementary Note on Original Intention.

15. Hobbes wrote that the judge is to be guided by "the final causes, for which the law was made; the knowledge of which final causes is in the legislator." Thomas Hobbes, *Leviathan* pt. 2, chap. 26, §21, p. 191 (1991). Locke stated, "when a man speaks to another, it is . . . [to] make known his ideas to the hearer. That then which words are the marks of are the ideas of the speaker . . . this is certain, their signification, in his use of them, is limited to his ideas, and they can be signs of nothing else." John Locke, *An Essay Concerning Human Understanding* 204–206 (Raymond Wilburn ed. 1947).

16. Louis Lusky, himself an activist, observed that the Court has "a new and grander conception of its own place in the governmental scheme," resting on "two basic shifts in its approach to constitutional adjudication": "assertion of the power to revise the Constitution, bypassing the cumbersome amendment procedure prescribed by Article V," and "repudiation of the limits on judicial review that are implicit in the doctrine of Marbury

light of the Founders' explanations of what they meant to accomplish, no more, no less.

Leading activists Michael Perry and Paul Brest observe that no activist has come up with a satisfactory antioriginalist theory.[17] There are as many theories as activist writers. Indeed, Brest pleads with academe "simply to acknowledge that most of our writings are not political theory but advocacy scholarship—amicus briefs ultimately designed to persuade the Court to adopt our various notions of the public good"— result-oriented propaganda.[18] In their zeal to ameliorate social injustice, academicians undermine the constitutionalism that undergirds our democratic system.[19] Their defense of the Justices' substitution of their own

---

v. Madison." Louis Lusky, "Government by Judiciary: What Price Legitimacy?" 6 Hastings Const. L.Q. 403, 406, 408 (1979). In holding that Congress could not "alter" the Constitution, Marbury made the "implicit" "explicit."

17. By "activists" I mean those who claim that judges are empowered to revise the Constitution and to look for authority outside its text and history. Thus, Paul Brest challenges the assumption that judges are "bound by the text or original understanding of the Constitution." Paul Brest, "The Misconceived Quest for the Original Understanding," 60 B.U. L. Rev. 204, 234 (1980). And the late Robert Cover thrust aside the "self-evident meaning of the Constitution," let alone "the intention of the framers," in favor of an "ideology" framed by judges. Robert Cover, "Book Review," *New Republic*, Jan. 14, 1978, at 26, 27.

Perry urged activists "to get on with the task of elaborating a defensible non-originalist conception of constitutional text, interpretation and judicial role." Michael Perry, "The Authority of Text, Tradition, and Reason: A Theory of Constitutional Interpretation," 58 S. Cal. L. Rev. 551, 602 (1985). For Brest's disappointment with seven activist attempts to frame such a theory, see Paul Brest, "The Fundamental Rights Controversy: The Essential Contradictions of Normative Constitutional Scholarship," 90 Yale L.J. 1063, 1067–1089 (1981). He considers that "no defensible criteria exist" whereby to assess "value-oriented constitutional adjudication." Id. 1065.

18. Brest, supra note 17 at 1109. Anthony Lewis exulted because in the fifteen years since Earl Warren became Chief Justice, the Court "has brought about more social change than most Congresses and most presidents"—"years of legal revolution." Anthony Lewis, "A Man Born to Act, Not to Muse," *New York Times Magazine*, June 30, 1968, reprinted in *The Supreme Court Under Earl Warren* 151 (Leonard Levy ed. 1972); cf. Calabresi, supra note 7.

19. "The two fundamental correlative elements of constitutionalism for which all lovers of liberty must yet fight are the legal limits to arbitrary power and a complete responsibility of government to the governed." Charles H. McIlwain, *Constitutionalism: Ancient and Modern* 146 (rev. ed. 1947). "The fabric of American empire," said Hamilton, "ought to rest on the solid basis of THE CONSENT OF THE PEOPLE," Federalist No. 22 at 141 (Mod. Lib. ed. 1937). James Wilson and others considered that "the binding power

meaning for that of the Founders displaces the choices made by the people in conventions that ratified the Constitution, and it violates the basic principle of government by consent of the governed. The people, said James Iredell, "have chosen to be governed under such and such principles. They have not chosen to be governed or proposed to submit upon any other."[20] Academe has forgotten Cardozo's wise caution: the judges' "individual sense of justice . . . might result in a benevolent despotism if the judges were benevolent men. It would put an end to the reign of law."[21]

When this book appeared in 1977, I anticipated that it would ruffle academic feathers, for it stood athwart the complacent assumption that constitutional limitations[22] must yield to beneficial results, a result-oriented jurisprudence that is a euphemism for the notion that the end justifies the means.[23] The flood of criticism—often ad hominem—surpassed my expectations.[24] Scarcely a month passes without another

---

of the law flowed from the continuous assent of the subjects of law." Bernard Bailyn, *The Ideological Origins of the American Constitution* 174 (1967).

20. 2 G. J. McRee, *Life and Correspondence of James Iredell* 146 (1858).

21. Benjamin N. Cardozo, *The Nature of the Judicial Process* 136 (1921).

22. Chief Justice Marshall asked, "To what purpose are powers limited, and to what purpose is that limitation committed to writing; if those limits may, at any time, be passed by those intended to be restrained?" If, he continued, the Constitution is "alterable when the legislature shall please to alter it . . . then written constitutions are absurd attempts, on the part of the people, to limit a power in its nature illimitable." Marbury v. Madison, 5 U.S. (1 Cranch) 137, 176–177 (1803).

23. Sidney Hook observed that "whoever places greater emphasis upon the product rather than the process, upon an all-sanctifying end rather than upon the means for achieving it, is opening the doors of anarchy." Sidney Hook, *Philosophy and Public Policy* 36 (1980).

24. " 'Criticism,' wrote Johnson in the 60th *Idler*, 'is a study by which men grow important and formidable at a very small expense.' " Augustine Birrell, Obiter Dicta 110 (2d series 1905). Daniel Boorstin observes that most men "hate the necessity of revising their convictions." Daniel J. Boorstin, *The Discoverers* 476 (1983).

Referring to the desegregation and reapportionment decisions, Richard Kay wrote, "These doctrines have now become almost second nature to a generation of lawyers and scholars. Thus it is hardly surprising that the casting of a fundamental doubt on such basic assumptions should produce shock, dismay, and sometimes anger." Kay, supra note 10 at 801.

Aviam Soifer charged me with "the worst type of law-office history," "emphasiz[ing] how badly Berger misuses historical materials." Quoted in Raoul Berger, "Soifer to the

"refutation,"[25] testimony that the corpse simply will not stay buried. Almost all activist critics turn their back on discrepant evidence; they simply will not examine, for example, my detailed demonstration that "privileges or immunities" had become words of art having a limited compass.[26]

Consider the "one man–one vote" doctrine. Section 2 of the Fourteenth Amendment provides that if suffrage is denied on account of race, the State's representation in the House of Representatives shall be proportionally reduced. This constitutes the sole provision for federal intervention. Senator William Fessenden, chairman of the Joint Committee on Reconstruction, explained that the Amendment "leaves the power where it is, but it tells [the States] most distinctly, if you exercise that power wrongfully, such and such consequences will follow."[27] Senator Jacob Howard, to whom fell the task of explaining the amendment because of Fessenden's illness, said, "the theory of this whole amendment is, to leave the power of regulating the suffrage with the people or legislatures of the States, and not to assume to regulate it."[28] It was this "gap" which the Fifteenth Amendment was designed to fill.[29] Plainly

---

Rescue of History," 32 S.Car. L. Rev. 427, 428 (1981). Judge John G. Gibbons (3d Cir.) fired off a papal bull: Berger "is neither talented enough as an advocate nor knowledgeable enough as an historian to be taken seriously in either discipline." Quoted in Raoul Berger, " 'Government by Judiciary': Judge Gibbons' Argument Ad Hominem," 59 B.U. L. Rev. 783 (1979). Hans Baade entitled his critique " 'Original Intention': Raoul Berger's Fake Antique" and declared that his conclusion is summarized by the title of an article, "Misrepresentation in North Carolina," quoted in Raoul Berger, "Original Intent: The Rage of Hans Baade," 71 N.C. L. Rev. 1151, 1152 (1993). William Wiecek dismisses my views as "empty bombast." William H. Wiecek, "The Constitutional Snipe Hunt," 23 Rutgers L.J. 253, 254 (1992).

25. E.g., Baade, supra note 24; Bruce Ackerman, *We the People: Foundations* 91, 334–336 (1991).

26. For an encapsulation of this history, see Supplementary Note on the Civil Rights Act, text accompanying notes 7 through 24.

27. *The Reconstruction Amendments' Debates* 143 (Alfred Avins ed. 1967).

28. Id. 237. See also the *Report of the Joint Committee on Reconstruction*, which drafted the Amendment. Id. 94.

29. For the "gap" materials, see Raoul Berger, "The Fourteenth Amendment: Light From the Fourteenth," 74 Nw. U. L. Rev. 311, 321–323 (1979); United States v. Reese, 92 U.S. 214, 217–218 (1876): the Fifteenth Amendment "has invested the citizen of the United States with a new right." Mark that the "one man–one vote" doctrine rests on the *Fourteenth* Amendment.

the "one man–one vote" doctrine derogates from the exclusive control of suffrage that was left to the States.[30]

Turn to the sacred cow of modern constitutional law, *Brown v. Board of Education*, whereby the Court outlawed segregated schools.[31] Robert Cover of Yale chided me for engaging in a lengthy tour of the historical sources instead of starting from *Brown*, in short, beginning with the end, the *fait accompli*,[32] for *Brown* had no popular mandate. *Brown*, wrote Bruce Ackerman, another advocate of activism, "did not come at [a moment] when a mobilized citizenry was demanding a fundamental change in our fundamental law."[33] The "real significance" of *Brown*, he opines, "lies elsewhere, in the Court's courage in confronting modern Americans with a moral and political agenda that calls upon them to heed the voice of their better selves."[34] Put baldly, the Court had no popular mandate for its revolutionary decision but assumed the role of an Old Testament prophet, enhanced by the sanctions at its disposal.[35]

30. Justice Story declared that "we are not at liberty to add one jot of power to the national government beyond what the people have granted by the constitution." Houston v. Moore, 18 U.S. (5 Wheat.) 1, 48 (1820), dissenting opinion.

31. 347 U.S. 483 (1954). An activist sympathizer asked, "Could it be reasonably claimed that segregation had been outlawed by the Fourteenth when the yet more basic emblem of citizenship—the ballot—had been withheld from the Negro under the amendment?" Richard Kluger, *Simple Justice* 635 (1976).

32. "It is in this recognition of the practical, present and future-looking consequences of constitutional symbols that a proper beginning point for a book on constitutional law must lie." Robert Cover, "Book Review," *New Republic*, Jan. 14, 1978, at 26, 27. The duty of an historian is to ascertain what happened, not to ignore the historical facts for fear of "future consequences."

33. Bruce Ackerman, *We the People: Foundations* 133 (1991). "Only a mobilized mass movement," Ackerman noted, "might encourage progressive Democrats and Republicans to overcome massive Southern resistance to new civil rights legislation." At the time *Brown* was "argued and reargued . . . such a mass movement did not exist." Id. 135. During the oral argument Justice Jackson commented, "realistically the reason the case is here is that action could not be obtained from Congress." Alexander Bickel, *The Supreme Court and the Idea of Progress* 6 (1978). Edmond Cahn stated, "it would have been impossible to secure adoption of a constitutional amendment to abolish 'separate but equal.'" Edmond Cahn, "Jurisprudence," 30 N.Y.U. L. Rev. 150, 156–157 (1955).

34. Ackerman, supra note 33 at 133; Cahn, supra note 33.

35. A similar messianic role is assumed by Justice Brennan with respect to death penalties. Despite the Fifth Amendment's recognition that a person may be deprived of life provided he is accorded due process, despite Brennan's recognition that the majority of

Contrast a few undeniable facts. Congress had "permitted segregated schools in the District of Columbia from 1864 onward";[36] and Senator Charles Sumner vainly fought "to abolish segregated Negro schools in the District of Columbia."[37] How can it be maintained that Congress, after steadfastly refusing to abolish segregated schools in the District, over which it had plenary control, would cram desegregation down the throats of the States? "Negroes were barred from public schools of the North," wrote neoabolitionist Howard Jay Graham, and were "still widely regarded as 'racially inferior' and 'incapable of education.' "[38] Had the framers proposed to bar segregated schools in the North, such interference with state control of internal affairs would have imperiled enactment and adoption of the Fourteenth Amendment.[39] Such a proposal was far from the framers' minds, as is demonstrated by James Wilson's (chairman of the House Judiciary Committee) assurance that the parallel Civil Rights Bill—regarded as "identical" with the Fourteenth

---

his brethren and of his fellow Americans do not share his views, he persists in "striving for human dignity for all," that is, abolition of the death penalty. For extended discussion, see Raoul Berger, "Justice Brennan vs. the Constitution," 29 B.C. L. Rev. 787, 796–798 (1988). See also Supplementary Note on the Role of the Court, notes 19 and 20.

36. Richard Kluger, *Simple Justice* 635 (1976).

37. Kelly, Fourteenth 1049, 1085. When desegregation of the District of Columbia schools was under discussion in April 1860, Senator James Harlan of Iowa said, "I know that there is an objection to the association of colored children with white children in the same schools. This prejudice exists in my own State. It would be impossible to carry a proposition to educate the few colored children that now live in that State in the same school houses with white children. It would be impossible, I think, in every one of the States of the Northwest." Avins, supra note 27 at 22.

38. Howard Jay Graham, *Everyman's Constitution* 290 note 70 (1968).

39. For continued attachment to State sovereignty, see infra pp. 77–80; Berger supra note 29 at 324–326. Lord Acton described the preservation of States' rights as the "redemption of democracy." Robert Speaight, *The Life of Hilaire Belloc* 132 (1957).

Justice Story stated, "it is perfectly clear that the sovereign powers vested in the state governments . . . remain unaltered and unimpaired, except so far as they were granted to the government of the United States." Martin v. Hunter's Lessee, 14 U.S. (1 Wheat.) 304, 325 (1816). Federal invasion of that zone bears the burden of proving that it is authorized by the federal delegation.

Henry Adams wrote, "The doctrine of states' rights was itself a sound and true doctrine; as a starting point of American history and constitutional law there is no other which will bear a moment's examination . . . its prostitution to the base uses of the slave power was one of those unfortunate enlargements which often perturb and mislead history." Henry Adams, *John Randolph* 273 (1882).

Amendment, whose purpose was to safeguard the Bill from repeal—did not require that all "children shall attend the same schools."[40] Prominent academicians, among them leading activists, recognize that segregation was left untouched by the Fourteenth Amendment.[41]

Compare with such incontrovertible facts the imaginary conversation the leading activist theoretician, Ronald Dworkin, held with a framer of the Fourteenth Amendment about segregation: "I don't know what the right answer is to the question of what we've done . . . Nor do I, as it happens, have any particular preferences myself, either way, about segregated schools. I haven't thought much about that either."[42] To change existing practices, particularly in the internal zone left to the States, the

40. Avins, supra note 27 at 163.

41. Paul Brest, "Book Review," N.Y. Times, Dec. 11, 1977, §11 at 10; Sanford Levinson, "The Turn Toward Functionalism in Constitutional Theory," 8 U. Dayton L. Rev. 567, 578 (1983); Nathaniel Nathanson, "Book Review," 56 Tex. L. Rev. 579, 580–581 (1978); Michael Perry, "Interpretivism, Freedom of Expression, and Equal Protection," 42 Ohio St. L.J. 261, 292 (1981); David A. J. Richard, "Abolitionist Political and Constitutional Theory and the Reconstruction Amendments," 25 Loyola L.A. L. Rev. 1143, 1187 (1992); Mark Tushnet, "Following the Rules Laid Down: A Critique of Interpretivism and Neutral Principles," 96 Harv. L. Rev. 781, 800 (1983). Judge Learned Hand said of *Brown v. Board of Education*, "I have never been able to understand on what basis it does or can rest except as a coup de main." Learned Hand, *The Bill of Rights* 55 (1962).

42. Ronald Dworkin, "The Forum of Principle," 56 N.Y.U. L. Rev. 469, 486–487 (1981). Similar fantasizing is exhibited by John Hart Ely: the framers of the Fourteenth Amendment issued on "open-and-across-the-board invitation to import into the constitutional decision process considerations that will not be found in the amendment nor even . . . elsewhere in the Constitution." John Hart Ely, "Constitutional Interpretivism: Its Allure and Impossibility," 53 Ind. L.J. 399, 415 (1978). This at a time when the Dred Scott decision was execrated by the framers. See infra Supplementary Note on the Conclusion, text accompanying notes 21–24. In the introduction to *The Intellectual Adventures of Ancient Man* 3 (Henri Frankfort & H. A. Frankfort eds. 1977), the Frankforts decry the "irresponsible meandering of the mind which ignores reality and seeks to escape from its problems."

John Bingham, draftsman of the Fourteenth Amendment, said that of late the Court had "dared to descend from its high place in the discussion of decisions of purely judicial questions [to "settlement of political questions"] which it has no more right to decide for the American people than the Court of St. Petersburg." 6 Charles Fairman, *History of the Supreme Court of the United States* 462 (1971). Small wonder that section 5 of the Amendment entrusted Congress, not the Court, with power to enforce the Amendment. Ex parte Virginia, 100 U.S. 339, 345 (1879).

federal draftsmen minimally must exhibit a purpose to do so.[43] Ignorance of, or indifference to, such practices does not spell a purpose to
alter them. Dworkin's imaginary framer must have lived in an airtight
cocoon to be oblivious to an issue that reached to the very wellsprings
of the pervasive racism.[44] With William James, we should worry about
"the presumptuous arrogance of theories that ignore, even disdain, the
concreteness of mere fact."[45] Activist criticism of originalism is generally akin to Dworkin's reverie: fantasizing opposed to concrete fact. Of
earlier criticism Lord (Max) Beloff, an Oxford emeritus and longtime
student of American constitutionalism, wrote in a review of my book in
the *Times* of London, "The quite extraordinary contortions that have
gone into proving the contrary make sad reading for those impressed by
the high quality of American legal-historical scholarship."[46]

I came to my study of the Fourteenth Amendment in the service of
no other cause than the integrity of constitutional construction. For that
purpose I sought to ascertain what the framers sought to accomplish,
being without preconceptions as to what the Amendment ought to

43. The governing rule was laid down by Chief Justice Marshall: "an opinion which
is . . . to establish a principle never before recognized, should be expressed in plain and
explicit terms." United States v. Burr, 25 F.Cas. 55, 165 (C.C.D.Va. 1807) (No. 14, 693).
Striking reaffirmation was given to this view in Pierson v. Ray, 386 U.S. 547, 554–555
(1967). After adverting to the common-law immunity of judges from suits for acts performed in their official capacity, the Court stated, "We do not believe that this settled
principle was abolished by § 1983, which makes liable 'every person' who under color of
law deprives another of his civil rights . . . The immunity of judges [is] well established
and we presume that Congress would have specifically so provided had it wished to abolish the doctrine." In a similar context, the Supreme Court declared, "so important a
change . . . if intended, would have been expressly declared." Minor v. Happersett 88
U.S. (21 Wall.) 162, 173 (1874).

44. For citations see supra p. 13; and Index, s.v. "racism." Dworkin might ponder Benjamin Franklin's belief that "patience and accuracy in making observations" are the foundation "on which alone true philosophy can be founded." Carl van Doren, *Benjamin Franklin* 168 (1968). His contemporaries considered Franklin to be one of the foremost
thinkers.

45. William Coles, "A Passionate Commitment to Experience," N.Y. Times, May 29,
1983, § 7.

46. Max Beloff, "Arbiters of America's Destiny," Times (London), Higher Ed. Supp.,
April 7, 1978, at 11.

mean.[47] The Constitution, remarked Paul Brest, "lies at the core" of our "civil religion";[48] until it is changed by amendment, the people are free to govern their own destiny, not to be ruled by "Platonic Guardians" who often are creatures of political accident, virtually irremovable and irreversible. Activist fulminations have not shaken the hope, in the words of Samuel Johnson, that "the most obdurate incredulity may be shamed or silenced by facts."[49] The facts will speak for themselves long after the present controversialists are gone.

47. With Charles McIlwain I can say, "I entered upon this study without preconceptions. During the course of it I came to the conclusion that the weight of contemporary evidence was against some views . . . [T]his has unavoidably given to certain parts of the book a polemical cast, and might lead one to think that it was written from the beginning to bolster a preconceived theory. Such is not the case." Charles McIlwain, *The High Court of Parliament and Its Supremacy* ix (1910).

48. Paul Brest, "The Misconceived Quest for Original Understanding," 60 B.U. L. Rev. 204, 234 (1980).

49. James Boswell, *The Life of Samuel Johnson* 1114 (Everyman ed. 1992).

# 2

## "Privileges or Immunities"

No State shall . . . abridge the privileges or immunities of citizens of the
United States

THE "privileges or immunities" clause was the central provision
of the Amendment's § 1, and the key to its meaning is furnished by the
immediately preceding Civil Rights Act of 1866,[1] which, all are agreed,
it was the purpose of the Amendment to embody and protect. The objectives of the Act were quite limited. The framers intended to confer on
the freedmen the auxiliary rights that would protect their "life, liberty,
and property"—no more. For the framers those words did not have the
sprawling connotations later given them by the Court but, instead, restricted aims that were expressed in the Act. The legislative history of
the Amendment frequently refers to "fundamental rights," "life, liberty,
and property," and a few historical comments will show the ties between
the two.

At Locke's hands, said Edward S. Corwin, natural law dissolves "into
the rights of 'life, liberty, and estate,' " a derivation noted by Francis
Bacon. The trinity was reiterated by Sir Matthew Hale[2] and sharply
etched by Blackstone in his chapter on "The Absolute Rights of Individuals":

> these may be reduced to three principal or primary articles . . . I.
> The right of personal security [consisting] in a person's legal and

1. Act of April 9, 1866, ch. 21, 14 Stat. 27.
2. Edward S. Corwin, "The 'Higher Law' Background of American Constitutional
Law," 42 Harv. L. Rev. 149, 365, 383 (1928).

uninterrupted enjoyment of his life, his limbs ... II. .... the personal liberty of individuals ... [consisting] in the power of locomotion, of changing situations or moving one's person to whatsoever place one's own inclination may direct, without imprisonment, or restraint, unless by due course of law ... III. The third absolute right, inherent in every Englishman ... of property: which consists in the free use, enjoyment and disposal of all his acquisitions, without any control or diminution, save only by the laws of the land.[3]

For Blackstone "due course of law" and the "laws of the land" did not enlarge, they did not add to, the "absolute rights" of an Englishman, but rather marked the sole means whereby those rights might be diminished. These "absolute," "fundamental" rights of "life, liberty, and property" referred, in sum, to (1) personal security; (2) freedom of locomotion; and (3) ownership and disposition of property.

On this side of the water the opening Resolve of the First Continental Congress affirmed that the Colonists "by the immutable laws of nature, the principles of the British Constitution ... 'are entitled to life, liberty, and property.'"[4] Blackstone, whose work was widely circulated in the Colonies, was cited in Federalist No. 84 and paraphrased by Kent.[5] Instead of the "absolute rights" of "life, liberty, and property" the Framers resorted to the terminology of Article IV, §2: "The Citizens of each State shall be entitled to all Privileges and Immunities of Citizens in the several States." These words were construed "confiningly" by Justice Bushrod Washington on circuit, in *Corfield v. Coryell*, as comprising "fundamental" rights such as freedom of movement, freedom from discriminatory taxes and impositions, ownership of property, access to the courts.[6]

3. 1 William Blackstone, *Commentaries on the Laws of England* 129, 134, 138 (1765–1769). These "rights" were read to the House by James F. Wilson, chairman of the House Judiciary Committee, in his exposition of the Civil Rights Bill. *Globe* 1118.

4. *Documents of American History* 83 (Henry Steele Commager ed. 7th ed. 1963).

5. 1 James Kent, *Commentaries on American Law* 607 (9th ed. 1853): "The absolute rights of individuals may be resolved into the right of personal security, the right of personal liberty, and the right to enjoy and acquire property." This too was quoted by Wilson, supra note 3.

6. 6 F. Cas. (No. 3230) 546 (C.C.E.D. Pa. 1823); the full quotation is set forth infra at notes 41–43.

For the "principal spokesmen" and theorists of the abolitionist movement, Lysander Spooner and Joel Tiffany, "privileges and immunities"
meant that a citizen has a right "to full and ample protection in the enjoyment of his personal security, personal liberty, and private property . . .
protection against oppression . . . against lawless violence."[7] This echoes
Blackstone's formulation and in large part anticipates the privileges embodied in the Civil Rights Act of 1866. The sponsors of the Act, Senator
Lyman Trumbull and Representative James F. Wilson, chairmen respectively of the Senate and House Judiciary committees, cited Blackstone,
Kent, and *Coryell*, as did others.[8] And John A. Bingham, draftsman of the
Amendment, stated that he had drawn the "privileges or immunities"
clause of the Fourteenth Amendment from Article IV, §2.[9]

## *The Civil Rights Act of 1866*

The meaning and scope of the Fourteenth Amendment are greatly illuminated by the debates in the 39th Congress on the antecedent Civil
Rights Act of 1866. As Charles Fairman stated, "over and over in this
debate [on the Amendment] the correspondence between Section One
of the Amendment and the Civil Rights Act is noted. The provisions of
the one are treated as though they were essentially identical with those
of the other."[10] George R. Latham of West Virginia, for example, stated
that "the 'civil rights bill' which is now a law . . . covers exactly the same
ground as this amendment."[11] In fact, the Amendment was designed to
"*constitutionalize*" the Act,[12] that is, to "embody" it in the Constitution

7. TenBroek, 108, 110.

8. *Globe* 474–475, 1118, 2765.

9. Id. 1034.

10. Fairman, Stanford 44. It "was in these debates," said Alfred Kelly, that "the Radical [?] ideas as to how far federal guarantees of civil rights as against state action might
properly extend, both by legislation and by constitutional amendment, were first clearly
set down. The debates on the Civil Rights Act are also important . . . because the Civil
Rights Act bore an extremely close relationship to the passage of the Fourteenth Amendment itself." Kelly, Fourteenth 1057.

11. *Globe* 2883.

12. Stevens, id. 2459; Kelly, Fourteenth 1071. Bingham strongly doubted the "power
of Congress to pass" the Civil Rights Bill and insisted upon proceeding by amendment,

so as to remove doubt as to its constitutionality and to place it beyond the power of a later Congress to repeal. An ardent advocate of an abolitionist reading of the Amendment, Howard Jay Graham, stated that "virtually every speaker in the debates on the Fourteenth Amendment—Republican and Democrat alike—said or agreed that the Amendment was designed to embody or incorporate the Civil Rights Act."[13]

Section 1 of the Civil Rights Bill provided in pertinent part,

> That there shall be *no discrimination in civil* rights or immunities . . . on account of race . . . but the inhabitants of every race . . . shall have the *same* right to make and enforce contracts, to sue, be parties, and give evidence, to inherit, purchase, lease, sell, hold and convey real and personal property, and to full and *equal benefit* of all laws and proceedings for the *security* of person and property, and shall be subject to *like* punishment . . . and no other.[14]

---

id. 1291–1292; his doubts were shared by Henry J. Raymond, id. 2502, presumably, as Senator Henderson explained, because the Thirteenth Amendment went no further than to free the slaves, *Appendix to Globe* 122 (hereinafter *Globe App*.). John M. Broomall of Pennsylvania, Thomas D. Eliot of Massachusetts, and Senator James R. Doolittle of Wisconsin also thought it designed to remove constitutional doubts, id. 2498, 2511, 2896. Others like Stevens, James A. Garfield and Rufus P. Spalding of Ohio, and Senator Howard wanted to make the Act secure against repeal by a successor Congress, id. 2459, 2462, 2509, 2896. See also Henry Van Aernam of New York, id. 3069, Thayer, id. 2465. See also infra Chapter 6 at notes 18–19. For additional citations, see tenBroek 244 note 11.

13. Graham 291 note 73; Bickel 47; tenBroek 201, 203, 224; Benjamin Kendrick, *The Journal of the Joint Committee of Fifteen on Reconstruction* 350 (1914). Flack, a devotee of a broad construction of the Fourteenth Amendment, states, "nearly all said that it was butan incorporation of the Civil Rights Bill . . . there was no controversy as to its purpose and meaning." Flack 81, id. 54, 79.

14. Section 1 of the Bill is set out in *Globe* 474 (emphasis added); see also supra note 1. It was anticipated by the Missouri Constitution of 1865: "no person can, on account of color, be disqualified as a witness, or be disabled to contract otherwise than as others are disabled, or be prevented from acquiring . . . property, or be liable to any other punishment for any offense than that imposed upon others for a like offense . . . or be subjected in law, to any other restraints or qualifications in regard to any personal rights other than such as are laid upon others under like circumstances." 2 Ben P. Poore, *Federal and State Constitutions, Colonial Charters* 1136 (1877).

"The master class looked upon any offense as more reprehensible (and therefore subject to more severe penalties) when committed by a slave than when committed by a white man." Kenneth M. Stampp, *The Peculiar Institution* 124 (Vintage Books, 1956).

The specific enumeration was in response to a sentiment expressed at the very outset by Senator John Sherman, who desired to secure such rights to the freedmen, "naming them, defining precisely what they should be."[15] Shortly stated, freedmen were to have the same *enumerated* rights (as white men), be subject to like punishment, suffer no discrimination with respect to civil rights, and have the equal benefit of all laws for the security of person and property. Patently these were limited objectives; the rights enumerated, said William Lawrence of Ohio, were the "*necessary incidents* of these absolute rights," that is, of "life, liberty, and property," lacking which those "fundamental rights" could not be enjoyed.[16] It was these "enumerated rights," "stated in the bill," said Martin Thayer of Pennsylvania, that were "the fundamental rights of citizenship."[17]

Section 1 of the Bill was a studied response to a perceived evil, the Black Codes,[18] which the Republicans averred were designed to set emancipation at naught, to restore the shackles of the prior Slave Codes, and to return the blacks to serfdom. The Bill was necessary, Senator Henry Wilson of Massachusetts said, because the new Black Codes were "nearly as iniquitous as the old slave codes."[19] Citing the prewar Slave

15. *Globe* 42. In a letter to Sumner in 1865, Justin Morrill, soon to be Senator, doubtful whether his suggested words "civil rights, immunities, privileges [have] such a precise and definite meaning as to be practicable," asked "must we specify, rights . . . to hold property, be a party and witness." James 30.

A significant shift from the phraseology of the predecessor Freedmen's Bureau Bill was made in the Civil Rights Bill; the former referred to "civil rights or immunities . . . *including* the right to make and enforce contracts," etc., Bickel 8 (emphasis added); but the Civil Rights Bill phrase "no discrimination in civil rights" was deleted (see infra Chapter 7 at notes 11–15), leaving the provision that blacks should "have the same right to make and enforce contracts," etc., a specific and exclusive enumeration. See infra at notes 15–17.

16. *Globe* 1833 (emphasis added). Senator Sherman said the Bill "defines what are the incidents of freedom." Id. 744. A leading Republican, Samuel Shellabarger of Ohio, explained that "those rights to contract, sue," etc., are "necessary . . . [for] the protection of the rights of person and property of a citizen." Id. 1293.

17. Id. 1151; fully quoted infra note 39.

18. For citations to collections of the Codes, see Bickel 14 note 35.

19. *Globe* 603. The Codes, Wilson said, "Practically made slaves of men we have declared to be free." Id. 39. They "set up elaborate systems of bound apprenticeship, labor restrictions, vagrancy laws, limits on property ownership and craft employment. They

Code of Mississippi, which prohibited the entry of a free Negro into the State, travel from one county to another, serving as a preacher, teaching slaves, and so on, Senator Trumbull stated that "the purpose of the bill ... is to destroy all these discriminations."[20] References to the Black Codes stud the debates:[21] they were described as "atrocious" and "malignant."[22] Samuel W. Moulton of Illinois, William Windom of Minnesota, Thomas D. Eliot of Massachusetts, and Senator Daniel Clark of New Hampshire considered that the Bill was needed to protect the Negro against "damnable violence," "wrong and outrage," "fiendish oppression," "barbarous cruelties."[23] As Senator John B. Henderson, a Republican from Missouri, stated, "though nominally free, so far as discriminating legislation could make him [the black] so he was yet a slave."[24] Republicans did not have to travel beyond the halls of Congress to savor Southern recalcitrance. Toward the close of the debates, Benjamin G. Harris of Maryland, an old-line Democrat, said,

> The States will still retain control and govern in their own way that portion of their population without leave asked of the United States.

---

prescribed white supervision over almost every aspect of black lives ... The bald declaration of Edmund Rhett of South Carolina—'the general interest both of the white man and of the negroes requires that he should be kept as near to the condition of slavery as possible' ... —sums up the purpose of the Black Codes." Morton Keller, *Affairs of State* 203–204 (1977).

20. *Globe* 474.

21. Senator Sumner, id. 95; Senator Timothy Howe of Wisconsin, id. 443; Ignatius Donnelly, id. 588; Senator Daniel Clark, id. 833; Burton C. Cook, id. 1124; William Higby, id. 2882. See the Opelusa Ordinance, id. 516–517. Senator Clark stated, the Master "will allow him no home, that he may become a vagrant. Becoming a vagrant, he will arrest him as a vagabond, and visit him with imprisonment and stripes ... He will shut him off from the courts, seal his mouth as a witness." *Globe* 834. Cook stated, "Vagrant laws have been passed: laws which under the pretense of selling these men as vagrants, are calculated and intended to reduce them to slavery again." *Globe* 1123.

22. Senator Wilson, id. 603; Cook, id. 1123; James Wilson, "barbaric and inhuman," id. 1118.

23. Id. 631, 1159, 2773, 833. Whether the effects of the Black Codes were exaggerated or not is not nearly as important as the aversion to them; it "is incorporated by reference into congressional statements of objectives; it plays a large part in defining those objectives, regardless of the extent to which it was founded on reality and regardless of the motives which underlay its creation." Bickel 14.

24. *Globe* 3034.

> Mr. Speaker, all the efforts made here or elsewhere to educate the
> negro to an equality with the white man in the southern States, ei-
> ther civilly, socially or politically, are perfectly idle. The negro must
> be kept in subordination to the white man.[25]

So it proved.

The explanations of the Civil Rights Bill by the respective committee chairmen made its limited objectives entirely clear. Speaking to "civil rights and immunities," House Chairman Wilson asked,

> What do these terms mean? Do they mean that in all things, civil,
> social, political, all citizens, without distinction of race or color, shall
> be equal? By no means can they be so construed ... Nor do they
> mean that all citizens shall sit on juries, or that their children shall
> attend the same schools. These are not civil rights and immunities.
> Well, what is the meaning? What are civil rights? I understand civil
> rights to be simply the absolute rights of individuals, such as "The
> right of personal security, the right of personal liberty, and the right
> to acquire and enjoy property."

quoting Chancellor Kent.[26] Of "immunities" Wilson said that a black should "not be subjected to obligations, duties, pains and penalties from which other citizens are exempted ... This is the spirit and scope of the bill, and it does not go one step beyond."[27] M. Russell Thayer of Pennsylvania stated that "to avoid any misapprehension" as to what the "fundamental rights of citizenship" are, "they are stated in the bill. The same

25. Id. 3172, 3174.

26. Id. 1117. Wilson quoted *Bouvier's Law Dictionary:* "Civil rights are those which have no relation to the establishment, support, or management of government." Id. Alfred Kelly states that Wilson "declared for a narrow interpretation of the measure in unequivocal terms." Kelly, Fourteenth 1066. But at another point he states that Wilson asserted "*vaguely* that civil rights were only the 'natural rights of man.'" Id. (emphasis added). Such "vagueness" is dispelled by Thayer's explanation infra. See also infra note 55.

Josiah Grinnell of Iowa said, "A recognition of natural rights is one thing, a grant of political franchises quite another." TenBroek 170. Senator Howard stated, the purpose of the Civil Rights Bill "is to secure to these men whom we have made free the ordinary rights of a freeman and nothing else." Id. 504. "Wilson thus presented the Civil Rights Bill to the House as a measure of limited and definite objectives. In this he followed the lead of the majority in the Senate ... And the line he laid down was followed by others who spoke for the bill in the House." Bickel 17.

27. *Globe* 1117.

section goes on to define with great particularity the civil rights and immunities which are to be protected by the bill." And, he added, "when those civil rights which are first referred to in general terms [that is, civil rights and immunities] are subsequently enumerated, that enumeration precludes any possibility that the general words which have been used can be extended beyond the particulars which have been enumerated," that the Bill was for "the protection of the fundamental rights of citizenship and nothing else."[28] Wilson emphasized that the rights enumerated were no "greater than the rights which are included in the general terms 'life, liberty, and property.' "[29] He did not proceed from the dictionary but responded to a sentiment unequivocally articulated by James W. Patterson of New Hampshire in a later discussion of the Fourteenth Amendment, for which he voted. I am opposed, he stated, "to any law discriminating against [blacks] in the security of life, liberty, person, property and the proceeds of their labor. These civil rights all should enjoy. Beyond this I am not prepared to go, and those pretended friends who urge political and social equality . . . are . . . the worst enemies of the colored race."[30]

28. Id. 1151. As Madison said in Federalist No. 41: "For what purpose could the enumeration of particular powers be inserted, if these and all others were meant to be included in the preceding general powers? Nothing is more natural or common than first to use a general phrase, and to explain and qualify it by a recital of particulars. But the idea of particulars which neither explain nor qualify the general meaning . . . is an absurdity." Modern Lib. ed. 269 (1937). Lawrence, an Ohio Radical, said "the privileges referred to in the Constitution are such as are fundamental civil rights, not political rights nor those dependent on local law." *Globe* 1836.

29. *Globe* 1295. While tenBroek, 110, defines privileges and immunities as the right of a citizen to have "protection in the enjoyment of his personal security, personal liberty, and private property . . . protection against the aggression of individuals, communities . . . and domestic states against lawless violence exercised under the form of governmental authority," and while Graham, 236, states the "abolitionist position" was to seek "protection for the fundamental rights of life, liberty, and property," neither is really cognizant of the fact that the Civil Rights Act, and hence the "constitutionalizing" Fourteenth Amendment, had enumerated and defined these rights in restricted terms. I would also, therefore, take exception to Fairman's statement that "vague aspirations" were hung on "privileges or immunities." Fairman, Stanford 139.

30. *Globe* 2699. Patterson voted for the Amendment, id. 2545. Windom said that under the Civil Rights Bill, the Negro "shall have an equal right, nothing more . . . to make and enforce contracts" and so on. "It does not . . . confer the privilege of voting," nor

Such views had been expressed in the Senate by Trumbull, who drafted the Bill: "The bill is applicable exclusively to civil rights. It does not propose to regulate political rights of individuals; it has nothing to do with the right of suffrage, or any other political right."[31] Commenting on *Corfield v. Coryell*, Trumbull stated that such cases had held that under the "privileges and immunities" of Article IV, §2, a citizen had "certain great fundamental rights, such as the right to life, to liberty, and to avail oneself of all the laws passed for the benefit of the citizen to enable him to enforce his rights." These were the rights with which the Civil Rights Bill would clothe the Negro.[32]

*Suffrage*, said Senator Jacob M. Howard in later explaining the Fourteenth Amendment, is not "one of the privileges and immunities thus secured by [Article IV, §2 of] the Constitution"; it is not, said Senator William P. Fessenden of Maine, chairman of the Joint Committee on Reconstruction, a "natural right."[33] Trumbull stated that the Bill "has nothing to do with the right of suffrage, or any other political rights."[34] When Senator Willard Saulsbury, a Democrat of Delaware, sought specifically to except "the right to vote," Trumbull replied: "that is a po-

---

"social privileges. It merely provides safeguards to shield them from wrong and outrage and to protect them in the enjoyment of . . . the right to exist." Id. 1159. [On January 25, 1858, Senator Lyman Trumbull stated, "I have never contended for giving the negro equal privileges with the white man. That is a doctrine I do not advocate." *The Reconstruction Amendments' Debates* 13 (Alfred Avins ed. 1967).]

31. *Globe* 599. As a prelude to the overriding of Johnson's veto, Trumbull stated, "the granting of civil rights does not . . . carry with it . . . political privileges . . . The right to vote . . . depends on the legislation of the various States." Id. 1757. He identified the rights "defined" in §1 as "fundamental rights belonging to every man as a free man." Id. 476. Bickel, 13, states that "Radicals and Moderates alike—who spoke in favor of the bill were content to rest on the points Trumbull had made. The rights to be secured by the bill were those specifically enumerated in section 1."

32. *Globe* 600, 474–475. Senator Henderson said that the Civil Rights Bill was "simply to carry out the provisions of the Constitution which confers upon the citizens of each State the privileges and immunities of citizens in the several States." Id. 3035. As Lawrence stated, "It is idle to say that a citizen shall have the right to life, yet to deny him the right to labor, whereby alone he can live. It is a mockery to say that a citizen may have a right to live, and yet deny him the right to make a contract to secure the privilege and rewards of labor." Id. 1833.

33. Id. 2766, 704.

34. Id. 599.

litical privilege, not a civil right. This bill relates to civil rights only."[35] And he reiterated that the Bill "carefully avoided conferring or interfering with political rights or privileges of any kind."[36] The views of Trumbull and Wilson were shared by fellow Republicans. The "only effect" of the Bill, said Senator Henderson, was to give the blacks the enumerated rights. "These measures did not pretend to confer upon the negro the suffrage. They left each State to determine the question for itself."[37] Senator Sherman said the bill "defines what are the incidents of freedom, and says that these men must be protected in certain rights, and so careful is its language that it goes on and defines those rights, the rights to sue and be sued [etc.] . . . and other universal incidents of freedom."[38] Thayer stressed that the bill did not "extend the right of suffrage," that suffrage was not a "fundamental right."[39] That the purpose of the bill was to *prevent discrimination with respect to enumerated*, fundamental *not political or social rights*, was also stated in one form or another by Cook and Moulton of Illinois, Hubbell, Lawrence, and Shellabarger of Ohio, and Windom of Minnesota.[40]

Since *Corfield v. Coryell*[41] is cited on all hands, it will profit us to consider its bearing on the scope of "privileges or immunities." The actual holding was that the phrase did not confer on an out-of-state citizen the right to dredge for oysters in New Jersey waters. In passing, Justice Washington stated:

35. Id. 606.
36. Id. 1760.
37. Id. 3034–3035.
38. Id. 744.
39. Id. 1151: "the words themselves are 'civil rights and immunities,' not political privileges; and nobody can successfully contend that a bill guarantying simply civil rights and immunities is a bill under which you extend the right of suffrage, which is a political privilege and not a civil right . . . [W]hen those civil rights which are first referred to in general terms are subsequently enumerated, that enumeration precludes any possibility that general words which have been used can be extended beyond the particulars which have been enumerated."
40. Cook, id. 1124; Moulton, id. 632; James R. Hubbell, id. 662; Lawrence, id. 1836; Shellabarger, id. 1293; for Windom, id. 1159, see supra note 30. Further details on the rejection of Negro suffrage are hereinafter set forth in the discussion of suffrage and the Fourteenth Amendment.
41. 6 F. Cas. at 551–552.

> We feel no hesitation in *confining* these expressions to those privi-
> leges and immunities which are, in their nature, *fundamental* . . .
> They may, however, be all comprehended under the following gen-
> eral heads: Protection by the government, the enjoyment of life and
> liberty, with the right to acquire and possess property of every kind
> and to pursue and obtain happiness and safety . . . The right of a
> citizen of one state to pass through, or reside in any other state, for
> purposes of trade, agriculture, professional pursuits,[42] or otherwise;
> to claim the benefit of the writ of habeas corpus; to institute and
> maintain actions of any kind in the courts of the state; to take, hold
> and dispose of property, either real or personal; and an exemption
> from higher taxes or impositions than are paid by the citizens of the
> other state; may be mentioned as some of the particular privileges
> and immunities of citizens, which are clearly embraced by the gen-
> eral description of privileges deemed to be fundamental; to which
> may be added, the elective franchise,[43] as regulated and established
> by the laws or constitution of the state in which it is to be exercised
> . . . But we cannot accede to the proposition . . . that the citizens of
> the several states are permitted to participate *in all* the rights which
> belong exclusively to the citizens of any other particular state.

The last sentence alone militates against an "all-inclusive" reading of
*Corfield*.[44]

In the main, these are the privileges and immunities enumerated in
the Civil Rights Bill. Justice Washington's inclusion of the "elective fran-

42. Emphasis added. Here Justice Washington spoke too loosely. If a State might deny
a nonresident the privilege to dredge for oysters in its waters, all the more might it deny
him the right to practice law in its courts. Bradwell v. State, 38 U.S. (16 Wall.) 130, 139
(1872) held that "the right to admission to practice in the courts of a State" is not a
privilege of a United States citizen.

43. The Supreme Court rejected this notion in Minor v. Happersett, 88 U.S. (21 Wall.)
162, 174 (1874): "This is more than asserting that [citizens] may change their residence
and become citizens of the State and thus be voters. It goes to the extent that while re-
taining their original citizenship they may vote in any State." It must be borne in mind
that Article IV, §2, applies to transient as well as permanent migrants.

44. Emphasis added. That last sentence is at odds with Alfred Kelly's statement that
in the Corfield case "the rights incidental to national citizenship had been described in
*all-inclusive* terms under the comity clause [Article IV, §2]." Kelly, Fourteenth 1059 (emphasis added).

chise," as Charles Fairman remarked, was "plainly wrong."[45] Article IV hardly intended to enable a transient migrant to vote, and this after excluding him from dredging for oysters. From the beginning, admission to suffrage had been the province of the State, as Chief Justice Parker of Massachusetts held at about the same time as *Corfield*, being preceded by Judge Samuel Chase of Maryland.[46] Right or wrong, it was open to Congress to take a narrower view than that of Washington for purposes of the Act which the Fourteenth Amendment was to constitutionalize. Trumbull did just this, saying of Washington, "This judge goes further than the bill" in including the "elective franchise."[47] Graham dwells on the *Corfield* phrase "Protection by the government; the enjoyment of life and liberty . . . and to pursue and obtain happiness."[48] Here, too, the framers could choose to exclude protection for the "pursuit of happiness," but in truth it was to Trumbull's mind a synonym for property: "the great fundamental rights of life, liberty, and the pursuit of happiness."[49] And so it was read by Justice Bradley in the *Slaughter-House Cases:* the rights "to life, liberty and the pursuit of happiness are equivalent to the rights of life, liberty and property."[50] At any rate, the "pursuit of happiness" found no place in the Amendment; in its stead the framers substituted the bare word "property," clinging to the traditional trinity: "life, liberty, and property."

It remains to notice two earlier cases also cited in the debates. In *Campbell v. Morris* (1797), Judge Chase, before long to be a Supreme Court Justice, stated on behalf of the General Court of Maryland that counsel were agreed

> that a particular and limited operation is to be given to these words [privileges and immunities] and not a full and comprehensive one. It is agreed that it does not mean the right of election . . . The court

45. Charles Fairman, *Reconstruction and Reunion, 1864–1888* 1122, vol. 6, pt. 1, of *History of the Supreme Court of the United States* (1971); see supra note 3.

46. Abbott v. Bayley, 6 Pick. 89, 91 (Mass. 1827); Campbell v. Morris, 3 H. & McH. 535, 554 (Md. 1797).

47. *Globe* 475; see Senator Howard, supra at note 33.

48. Graham 332n.

49. *Globe* 475.

50. 83 U.S. (16 Wall.) 36, 116 (1872), dissenting opinion.

are of opinion it means . . . the peculiar advantage of acquiring and holding real as well as personal property, that such property shall be protected and secured by the laws of the state, in the same manner as the property of the citizens of the state is protected. It means, such property shall not be liable to any taxes or burdens which the property of the citizens of the state is not subject to . . . It secures and protects personal rights.[51]

Mark that the emphasis is on freedom from discrimination, on equality with respect to described rights. In 1827, shortly after *Corfield*, Chief Justice Parker declared on behalf of the highest court of Massachusetts, in *Abbott v. Bayley*, that the privileges and immunities phrase confers a "right to sue and be sued," that citizens who remove to a second State "cannot enjoy the right of suffrage," but "may take and hold real estate."[52] Thus, long before 1866 courts had held that "privileges and immunities" were comprised of the rights Blackstone had enumerated; the framers, aware of Blackstone and the decisions, embodied those rights, and those rights only, in the Civil Rights Act of 1866.

That, however, is not the neoabolitionist reading of the history. So Alfred Kelly remarked, "Trumbull made it clear that his notion of the rights incidental to national citizenship were *exceedingly comprehensive* in character . . . Citing the dictum in *Corfield v. Coryell*, he argued that the rights of national citizenship included all 'privileges which are in their nature fundamental' . . . In short, he nationalized the comity clause [Article IV, §2] and turned it into a national bill of rights against the states, as the pre-war antislavery theorists had pretty generally done."[53] Such interpretations are poles removed from Trumbull's carefully restricted explanations. In the debates on the Civil Rights Bill, Trumbull made no mention of the Bill of Rights, but tied the "privileges and immunities" phrase to

51. Supra note 46.
52. Supra note 46. The Abbott and Campbell cases were quoted by Senator Trumbull, *Globe* 474, and at other points in the debates.
53. Kelly, Fourteenth 1062–1063, emphasis added. So too, Kelly reads Bingham's statement that "the protection given by the laws of the States shall be equal *in respect to* life, liberty, and property to all persons" as meaning "a very general requirement of equality on all state legislation of the most inclusive kind" (emphasis added). Id. 1074. There is also the fact that Bingham obtained the deletion of the "no discrimination in civil rights" clause because it was "oppressive." Infra Chapter 7 at notes 13–14.

"certain great fundamental rights such as the right to life, to liberty," and the benefit of laws passed for the enforcement of those rights, explicitly excluding "political" rights. His fellows even more clearly viewed the enumerated rights as restrictive.[54] As the citations to Blackstone and Kent show, "fundamental," "natural" rights had become words of received meaning.[55] TenBroek himself states that "the area of disagreement" about "privileges and immunities was not large, since their natural rights foundation was generally accepted"; they were "the natural rights of all men or such auxiliary rights as were necessary to secure and maintain those natural rights. They were the rights to life, liberty, and property. They were the rights to contract, and to own, use and dispose of property."[56]

Nevertheless, tenBroek remained fuzzy as to the meaning of "fundamental" rights as is shown by his citation to Senator Henderson. After noting Henderson's explanation of the purpose of the Civil Rights Act, to give the rights *therein enumerated* (which he read into the record), and his reference to "those fundamental rights of person and property which cannot be denied to any person," tenBroek concludes: "This was the *sweeping* view of those who sponsored . . . the Fourteenth Amendment.[57] Henderson, however, had emphasized that the "only effect" of the Civil Rights Bill was to give the blacks the rights there listed, that because the "negro is the object of that unaccountable prejudice against race" the "country is not prepared" to give them more.[58]

54. Supra at notes 31–32, 36–38, 26–30.

55. In his 1965 article Kelly himself stated, "Ultimately Revolutionary natural-rights theorists insisted liberty was derived from a state of nature, but it had long before been given a very positive and specific content. It was to be found . . . above all in the common law as expounded by Coke and Blackstone in all their commentaries. The 'rights of Englishmen' were not vacuous; instead they were quite well developed and specific. The notion of pulling new natural rights from the air to allow for an indefinite expansion can hardly be considered to be within the original spirit of the amendment." Kelly, "Clio and the Court: An Illicit Love Affair," 1965 S. Ct. Rev. 119, 154–155. They had been crystallized by Blackstone, supra note 3. Madison, for example, stated in the First Congress that "Trial by jury cannot be considered . . . as a natural right." 1 *Annals of Congress* 437.

56. TenBroek 122–123, 236.

57. Id. 231–232 (emphasis added).

58. *Globe* 3034, 3035. Like tenBroek, Graham, 276, stated that "the evidence in the debates is overwhelming that racial discrimination *very broadly conceived* was the framers' target" (emphasis added). Compare his statement infra Chapter 7 at note 41.

The Graham–tenBroek–Kelly writings have muddied analysis; they are not true to the historical facts. Shortly restated, those facts are that the "fundamental" rights which the framers were anxious to secure were those described by Blackstone—personal security, freedom to move about and to own property; they had been picked up in the "privileges and immunities" of Article IV, §1; the incidental rights necessary for their protection were "enumerated" in the Civil Rights Act of 1866; that enumeration, according to the framers, marked the bounds of the grant; and at length those rights were embodied in the "privileges or immunities" of the Fourteenth Amendment. An argument to the contrary, it may be stated categorically, will find no solid ground in the debates of the 39th Congress.

## Supplementary Note on the Civil Rights Act and the Fourteenth Amendment: Fundamental Rights

The Fourteenth Amendment provides: "No state shall . . . abridge the privileges or immunities of citizens of the United States." Robert Bork considers that the "intended meaning" of the clause "remains largely unknown."[1] I beg to differ. The "intended meaning" of "privileges or immunities" can be explicated by (1) the relation between the Civil Rights Act of 1866 and the Fourteenth Amendment, and (2) by the historical derivation of the terms. We may put to one side *Corfield v. Coryell*,[2] upon which activists beat a tattoo[3] and which, I agree with Bork, is "a singularly confused opinion in 1823 by a single Justice [Bushrod

1. Robert H. Bork, *The Tempting of America: The Political Seduction of the Law* 37 (1990). Ely regards the "Privileges or Immunities Clause as quite inscrutable." John Hart Ely, *Democracy and Distrust* 98 (1980).

2. 6 F. Cas. 546 (C.C.E.D. Pa. 1823) (No. 3230).

3. For recent examples see Raoul Berger, "Constitutional Interpretation and Activist Fantasies," 82 Ky. L.J. 1, 2–6 (1993); Raoul Berger, "Bruce Ackerman on Interpretation: A Critique," 1992 B.Y.U. L. Rev. 1035, 1041–1046.

Washington] of the Supreme Court,"[4] and look rather to the historical derivation of the terms. For as Justice Story stated, if the Framers used terms that had been defined at common law, that definition was "necessarily included as much as if they stood in the text,"[5] as the framers of the Amendment well knew.[6]

## A

The words "privileges and immunities" first appear in Article IV of the Articles of Confederation, which specified "all the privileges of trade and commerce."[7] The words were adopted in Article IV of the Constitution, which, according to Chief Justice White, was intended "to perpetuate [the] *limitations*" of the earlier Article IV.[8] White repeated Justice Miller's statement in the *Slaughter-House Cases* that "There can be but little question that . . . the privileges and immunities intended are the same in each."[9]

Privileges or immunities came into the Fourteenth Amendment by way of the Civil Rights Bill of 1866, which initially referred to "*civil rights or immunities.*"[10] In explaining these terms, Lyman Trumbull, chairman of the Senate Judiciary Committee, read from the Maryland (per Samuel Chase, soon to ascend to the Supreme Court) and Massachusetts cases.[11] Early on these courts had construed Article IV in terms of

4. Bork, supra note 1 at 181; see also supra pp. 39–41.

5. United States v. Smith, 18 U.S. (5 Wheat.) 153, 160 (1820). Chief Justice Marshall stated that if a word was understood in a certain sense "when the Constitution was framed . . . the Convention must have used the word in that sense." Gibbons v. Ogden, 22 U.S. (9 Wheat.) 1, 190 (1824). This was the rule at common law: "If a Statute make use of a Word the meaning of which is well-known at the Common Law, such word shall be taken in the same Sense it was understood at the common Law." 4 Matthew Bacon, A *New Abridgment of the Law* "Statutes" I (4) (3d ed. 1768).

6. Infra text accompanying notes 19 and 20.

7. *Documents of American History* 111 (Henry Steele Commager ed. 7th ed. 1963).

8. United States v. Wheeler, 254 U.S. 281, 294 (1920) (emphasis added). Senator Luke Poland of Maine explained that the privileges or immunities clause "secures nothing beyond what was intended by the original provision of the Constitution," that is, Article IV. *The Reconstruction Amendments' Debates* 230 (Alfred Avins ed. 1967).

9. United States v. Wheeler, id. 296.

10. Avins, supra note 8 at 104 (emphasis added).

11. Id. 121, 122.

trade and commerce.[12] Chase declared, as did Massachusetts Chief Justice Parker, that the words were to be given a "limited operation."[13] Activists ignore those opinions and build entirely on *Corfield*,[14] notwithstanding that Trumbull did not read *Corfield* broadly, stating that it "enumerates the *very rights* set forth in the Bill" and explaining that "the great fundamental rights set forth"[15] in the Bill are "the right to acquire property, the right to come and go at pleasure, the right to enforce rights in the courts, to make contracts,"[16] rights embodied in the Act.

A telling illustration of the "limited" scope of "privileges or immunities" was furnished by John Bingham, an activist mainstay. Despite repeated assurances that the Civil Rights Bill was limited to the specifically enumerated rights, Bingham protested vehemently:

> [C]ivil Rights . . . include and embrace *every* right that pertains to the citizen . . . [it would] strike down . . . every State constitution which makes a discrimination on account of race or color *in any* of the civil rights of the citizen . . . [it would] reform the whole civil and criminal code of every State government.[17]

Consequently the phrase "civil rights and immunities" was deleted, explained James Wilson, chairman of the House Judiciary Committee, in order to remove "the difficulty growing out of any other construction *beyond the specific rights named* in the section . . . [leaving] the bill with the *rights specified*."[18] The House approved the deletion of the "oppressive" words. No activist has attempted to explain why Bingham, after strenu-

---

12. Campbell v. Morris, 3 H. & Mc.H. 535, 554 (Md. 1797); Abbott v. Bayley, 23 Mass. (6 Pick.) 89, 91 (1827).

13. Campbell, id. 554; Abbott, id. 91.

14. Corfield itself stated, "we cannot accede to the proposition . . . that . . . the citizens of the several states are permitted to participate in *all* the rights which belong exclusively to the citizens of any other particular state," 6 F. Cas. at 552 (emphasis added). It is an index of the alleged "breadth" of Corfield that it denied to an out-of-state visitor the right to dredge for oysters in the host State.

15. Avins, supra note 8 at 122.

16. Id. For a narrow view of Corfield, see Phillip S. Paludan, *A Covenant With Death* 268 (1975).

17. Avins, supra note 8 at 186, 188 (emphasis added).

18. Id. 191 (emphasis added).

ously protesting against the oppressive invasion of the States' domain by "civil rights," embraced in the lesser "privileges" of the Amendment the very overbroad scope he had rejected in the Bill.

In truth, the framers regarded "privileges or immunities" as words of art, having a circumscribed meaning. After reading to the Senate from the cases, Trumbull remarked, "this being the construction as settled by judicial decisions."[19] Judge William Lawrence acknowledged in the House "that the courts have by construction *limited* the words 'all privileges' to mean only '*some* privileges.'"[20] Although the Supreme Court noticed the Bingham incident in *Georgia v. Rachel* and concluded that the Bill reached only a "limited category of rights,"[21] it is ignored by activists.

That is likewise the fate of other striking evidence. On January 20, 1871, Bingham submitted a Report of the House Committee on the Judiciary, from which he did not dissent, reciting that the privileges or immunities clause of the Fourteenth Amendment

> does not in the opinion of the committee, refer to privileges and immunities . . . other than those privileges and immunities embraced in the original text of the Constitution, Article IV, Section 2. The Fourteenth Amendment, it is believed, *did not add* to the privileges and immunities before mentioned.[22]

19. Id. 122.

20. Id. 207 (emphasis added). In a similar case the Supreme Court stated, "we should not assume that Congress . . . used the words . . . in their ordinary dictionary meaning when they had already been construed as words of art carrying a special and limited connotation." Yates v. United States, 354 U.S. 298, 319 (1957). Walter Murphy, a critic of my views, concedes that "privileges or immunities" had "become words of art," as Berger "amply demonstrates." Walter Murphy, "Book Review," 87 Yale L.J. 1752, 1758–1759 (1978).

21. 384 U.S. 780, 791 (1966).

22. Avins, supra note 8 at 466 (emphasis added). This was made plain by Samuel Shellabarger in the 39th Congress: "[The Civil Rights Bill] neither confers nor defines nor regulates any right whatever. Its whole effect is not to confer or regulate rights, but to require that whatever of these *enumerated* rights and obligations are imposed by State laws shall be for and upon all citizens alike." Id. 188 (emphasis added). James Wilson said, "We are establishing no new rights . . . It is not the object of this bill to establish new rights." Id. 163.

The Supreme Court likewise declared that the phrase did not add to the privileges or immunities provided by Article IV.[23] What manner of scholarship is it that ignores such weighty evidence? Instead, Erwin Chemerinsky and Bruce Ackerman would attribute to the 1823 *Corfield* case power to expand the 1866 Bill, whose spokesman, after reading from *Corfield*, said it enumerated the "very rights" listed in the Bill.[24]

# B

## THE CIVIL RIGHTS BILL OF 1866

The Civil Rights Bill and the Fourteenth Amendment, activist William Nelson correctly observed, are "inextricably linked."[25] The Amendment was designed to embody the Act in order to prevent its subsequent repeal or, in the alternative, to give it constitutional footing. The evidence that the framers deemed the Act and Amendment "identical" is unequivocal and uncontroverted.[26] That identity is highly important because, as the Supreme Court stated in 1966, "The legislative history of the 1866 Act clearly indicates that Congress intended to protect a limited category of rights."[27] The sponsor of the Act, Senator Lyman Trumbull, chairman of the Senate Judiciary Committee, de-

23. Maxwell v. Dow, 176 U.S. 581, 596 (1900). In Adamson v. California, 332 U.S. 46 (1947), the Court stated, "The Slaughter-House Cases decided . . . that these rights as privileges and immunities of state citizenship, remained under the sole protection of the state governments. This Court, without the expression of a contrary view . . . has approved this determination." Id. 51–52. And it added, "It is the construction placed upon the amendment by Justices whose own experience had given them contemporaneous knowledge of the purposes that led to the adoption of the Fourteenth Amendment." Id. 53.

24. For Chemerinsky see Raoul Berger, "Constitutional Interpretation and Activist Fantasies," 82 Ky. L.J. 1, 2–6 (1993); for Ackerman, see Raoul Berger, "Bruce Ackerman on Interpretation: A Critique," 1992 B.Y.U. L. Rev. 1035, 1041–1046.

25. William Nelson, *The Fourteenth Amendment: From Political Principles to Judicial Doctrine* 104 (1988).

26. See supra pp. 32–33.

27. Georgia v. Rachel, 384 U.S. 780, 791 (1966) (emphasis added). The purpose of the Civil Rights Bill, said Senator William Stewart, "is simply to remove the disabilities existing by laws tending to reduce the negro to a system of peonage [the Southern Black Codes]. It strikes at that; nothing else." Avins, supra note 8 at 204.

scribed its provisions as the "right to acquire property, the right to come and go at pleasure, the right to enforce rights, to make contracts."[28] He is corroborated by the face of the Act.[29] If Act and Amendment are "identical," it follows that the Amendment likewise protects only a "limited category of rights," an unpalatable conclusion that activists simply cannot bring themselves to swallow. But, as Alexander Bickel concluded, "It remains true that an explicit provision going further than the Civil Rights Act would not have carried in the 39th Congress."[30]

So, John Hart Ely rejects the "claim [that] the coverage of the two was meant to be identical."[31] So, too, Paul Dimond dismisses the "claim that the Fourteenth Amendment dealt solely with the rights enumerated

---

Nevertheless Edward J. Erler rejects what he describes as *my* "narrowly limited" view of the Civil Rights Act. Edward J. Erler, "The Ninth Amendment and Contemporary Jurisprudence," in *The Bill of Rights: Original Meaning and Current Understanding* 432, 444 (Eugene W. Hickok ed. 1991). Senator Lyman Trumbull, sponsor of the Civil Rights Bill, referred to "The great fundamental rights set forth in the bill: the right to acquire property . . . to come and go at pleasure, the right to enforce rights in the courts, to make contracts." *Globe* 475.

Erler likewise quotes Thaddeus Stevens' explanation of his advocacy of the Fourteenth Amendment: "Some answer, 'your civil rights bill secures the same things.' That is partly true." From this Erler concludes that "The clear implication of the last statement is that the Fourteenth Amendment was more extensive than the Civil Rights Bill of 1866." Erler, supra at 445. But Erler omits the words that follow "partly true." Stevens explained that the answer was "partly true" because "a law is repealable by a majority," not because the Amendment's coverage was more extensive than the Act. Moreover the framers unanimously regarded Bill and Amendment as "identical," supra pp. 32–33, and Stevens was little likely to repudiate these expressions.

28. Avins, supra note 8 at 122.

29. See supra p. 33.

30. Bickel 1, 61, 62.

31. John Hart Ely, "Constitutional Interpretivism: Its Allure and Impossibility," 53 Ind. L.J. 399, 435 note 129 (1978). Ely grudgingly allows that "there were some actual statements of equivalence, but that they are rare, and generally couched in terms that made clear the speaker's understandable desire to minimize the potentially radical sweep of the constitutional language." Id. Baldly stated, the speakers allegedly sought to conceal from Congress and the people that the words had a "radical sweep." For this there is no evidence, and if there were, concealment of material facts voids ratification. Ely's claim that statements of equivalence were "rare" is belied by the facts. See supra pp. 32–33; see also the additional facts herein recited, infra text accompanying notes 36–45.

in the 1866 Act."[32] Although Michael Zuckert considers my "unrelenting effort" to identify Act and Amendment of "greatest importance," he rejects it on the ground that the language of the Act and that of the Amendment are different, and he asks, if the framers "merely sought to get the Civil Rights Act into the Constitution why did they not simply take the first section and use it for the amendment?"[33] By that logic the argument for incorporation of the Bill of Rights—which Zuckert endorses[34]—collapses. Indeed, the argument for embodiment of the Civil Rights Act is far stronger, because the framers unmistakably and repeatedly stated that Act and Amendment are "identical." Unlike incorporation of the Bill of Rights, there was no confusion on this score. To Zuckert's triumphant query "Why didn't they say so," the answer in Justice Holmes' words is that if "the Legislature has . . . intimated its will, however indirectly, that will should be recognized and obeyed.[35]

To dispose of activist caviling, herewith some additional evidence. Martin Thayer of Pennsylvania explained that "it is but incorporating in the Constitution . . . the principle of the Civil Rights Bill which has lately become a law" in order that it "shall be forever incorporated in the Constitution."[36] On the ratification trail in August 1866, Senator Trumbull "clearly and unhesitatingly declared [Section 1 of the Amendment] to be 'a reiteration of the rights as set forth in the Civil Rights Bill."[37] In Indiana, Senator Henry Lane "affirmed Trumbull's statement concerning the first section";[38] and Senator John Sherman of Ohio endorsed those views in a speech on September 29, 1866.[39] Senator Luke Poland of Maine spoke to the same effect in November 1866.[40] In sum, Joseph

32. Paul Dimond, "Strict Construction and Judicial Review of Racial Discrimination Under the Equal Protection Clause: Meeting Raoul Berger on Interpretivist Grounds," 80 Mich. L. Rev. 462, 495 (1982).

33. Michael Zuckert, "Book Review," 6 Const. Commentary 149, 162 (1991).

34. Id. 161.

35. Johnson v. United States, 163 F. 30, 32 (1st Cir. 1908).

36. *Globe* 2465.

37. Joseph James, *The Framing of the Fourteenth Amendment* 161 (1965).

38. Id. 162.

39. Id. 164.

40. Michael K. Curtis, *No State Shall Abridge: The Fourteenth Amendment and the Bill of Rights* 252 note 46 (1986).

James concluded, "Statements of congressmen before their constituents definitely identify the provisions of the first section of the amendment with those of the Civil Rights Bill."[41]

Horace Flack's canvass of "speeches concerning the popular discussion of the Fourteenth Amendment" led him to conclude that "the general opinion held in the North . . . was that the amendment embodied the Civil Rights Bill."[42] In 1871, James Garfield emphasized that "he not only heard the whole debate [in the 39th Congress] at the time, but I have lately read over, with scrupulous care, every word of it as recorded in the Globe," and stated "this section [1] of the Amendment was considered as equivalent to the first section of the Civil Rights Bill."[43] Earlier Justice Bradley had stated, "the first section of the bill covers the same ground as the fourteenth amendment."[44] Subsequently Justice Field, dissenting in the *Slaughter-House Cases* from emasculation of the "privileges or immunities" clause, stated on behalf of the four dissenters, "In the first section of the Civil Rights Act Congress has given its interpretation to those terms."[45] Activist far-fetched inferences from generalities are no counter to such hard facts.

The modern rights extracted from the Civil Rights Act of 1866 are at a long remove from those envisioned by its framers. Some additional evidence will make that plain. Radical Senator Henry Wilson of Massachusetts urged the framers to ensure that the freeman "can go where he pleases, work when and for whom he pleases, that he can sue and be sued, that he can lease and buy and sell and own property, real and personal"[46]—measures to strike the shackles of the Black Codes. Senator William Windom of Minnesota said that the Civil Rights Bill af-

41. James, supra note 37 at 179.

42. Horace Flack, *The Adoption of the Fourteenth Amendment* 153 (1908). Summarizing Flack, Justice Black stated, "The declarations and statements of newspapers, writers and speakers . . . show very clearly the general opinion held in the North. That opinion, briefly stated, was that the Amendment embodies the Civil Rights Bill." Adamson v. California, 332 U.S. 46, 110 (1947), dissenting opinion.

43. *Cong. Globe* (42d Cong., 1st Sess.) App. 151 (1871).

44. Livestock Dealers' & Butchers' Ass'n v. Crescent City Live-Stock & Slaughter-House Co., 15 F. Cas. 649, 655 (Cir. Ct. D. La. 1870) (No. 8408).

45. 83 U.S. (16 Wall.) 36, 96 (1872).

46. Avins, supra note 8 at 98.

forded the blacks "an equal right, nothing more . . . to make and enforce contracts [etc.] . . . It merely provides safeguards to shield them from wrong and outrage and to protect them in the enjoyment of the right to exist."[47] The framers responded to what Senator Timothy Howe of Wisconsin termed the South's denial to blacks of "the plainest and most necessary rights of citizenship. The right to hold land . . . the right to collect wages by processes of law . . . the right to appear in the courts for any wrong done them."[48] In 1871, Senator Trumbull reminded the Senate that the Act declared that the rights of blacks "should be *the same as* those conceded to whites *in certain respects, which were named in the Act.*"[49] And in 1874, the Supreme Court stated that "the Amendment did not add to the privileges and immunities of a citizen,"[50] which had been construed in terms of trade and commerce.[51]

### FUNDAMENTAL RIGHTS

The current preoccupation with individual rights obscures the Founders' concern in 1787 with the rights of the community rather than the individual. For them "individual rights, even the basic civil liberties that we consider so crucial, possessed little of their modern theoretical relevance when set against the will of the people."[52] "In the Convention and later," wrote Alpheus T. Mason, "states' rights—not individual

47. *Globe* 1159.
48. Id. at Sen. App. 219.
49. Avins, supra note 8 at 548 (emphasis added).
50. Minor v. Happersett, 88 U.S. (21 Wall.) 162, 171 (1874). A Report by the House Committee on the Judiciary submitted by Bingham in 1871 stated that the "Fourteenth Amendment . . . did not add to the privileges or immunities" of Article IV. Avins, supra note 8 at 466. Senator Luke Poland of Maine explained that the privileges or immunities clause "secures nothing beyond what was intended by the original provision of the Constitution," that is, Article IV. Avins, id. 230.
51. See supra pp. 41–42; pp. 45–46.
52. Gordon S. Wood, *The Creation of the American Republic, 1776–1789* 63 (1969). "[T]o the eighteenth-century understanding in general, virtue was 'a positive passion for the public good' . . . Virtue enabled men to put the good of the whole above selfish private advantage . . ." Stanley Elkins and Eric McKittrick, *The Age of Federalism* 535 (1993).
On January 1, 1802, Jefferson wrote to the Danbury Baptist Association he was "convinced that [man] has no natural right in opposition to his social duties." 16 *The Writings of Thomas Jefferson* 281–282 (Andrew A. Lipscomb ed. 1903).

rights—was the real worry,"[53] The Founders were concerned with erecting a structure of government that would diffuse and limit delegated power, not with fortifying individual rights.[54] "It was conceivable," wrote Gordon Wood, "to protect the common law liberties of the people against their rulers, but hardly against the people themselves."[55] As Louis Henkin observed, "the Constitution said remarkably little about rights" because the federal government "was not to be the primary government . . . governance was left principally to the States."[56]

The Colonists claimed "the rights of Englishmen"; what were they? When people in the seventeenth century "talked about rights," Sir William Holdsworth concluded, "they meant the rights which the existing

---

53. Alpheus T. Mason, *The States Rights Debate: Antifederalism and the Constitution* 75 (1964). The "framers of the Constitution and the Bill of Rights believed that state governments were, in some vital respects, safer repositories of power over individual liberties than the federal government." Michael W. McConnell, "Book Review," 54 U. Chi. L. Rev. 1484, 1505–1506 (1987). Benjamin Wright noted that respecting proposals of bills of rights in the ratifying conventions in Massachusetts, South Carolina, and New Hampshire, "members of these conventions were much more perturbed about the rights and powers of the states than about the rights of the people." Benjamin F. Wright, *American Interpretations of Natural Law: A Study in the History of Political Thought* 146 (1931).

John Morley, the eminent English statesman and scholar, considered it a mistake to read into the "constitutional restrictions the protection of individual 'rights' where its founders had merely sought to protect the rights of states." John E. Morgan, *John Viscount Morley* 209 (1924).

54. Justice Brennan, the leading proponent of individual rights, acknowledged that "The original document, before addition of any of the amendments, does not speak primarily of the rights of men, but of the abilities and disabilities of government." William J. Brennan, Address, Georgetown Univ., Oct. 11, 1985, reprinted in *The Great Debate: Interpreting Our Constitution* 18 (1986).

Robert Nagel comments that "The framers' political theory was immediately concerned with organization, not individuals . . . with principles of power allocation." And he notes "a widespread pattern that inverts the priorities of the framers; an obsessive concern for using the Constitution to protect individual rights." Robert Nagel, "Federalism as a Fundamental Value: National League of Cities in Perspective," 1981 Sup. Ct. Rev. 81, 82, 88.

55. Wood, supra note 52 at 63. Forrest McDonald commented that "the liberty of the individual [was] subsumed in the freedom or independence of his political community." Forrest McDonald, *Novus Ordo Seclorum: The Intellectual Origins of the Constitution* 71 (1985).

56. Louis Henkin, "Human Dignity and Constitutional Rights," in *The Constitution of Rights* 210, 213–214 (Michael J. Meyer and William A. Parent eds. 1992); see Pendleton, infra text accompanying note 60.

laws gave them."[57] By 1765 these had crystallized into Blackstone's triad: personal security, personal liberty (i.e., freedom to come and go), and property.[58] The opening resolve of the First Continental Congress affirmed that the Colonies by "the principles of the British Constitution . . . are entitled to life, liberty and property."[59] In the Virginia Ratification Convention, Edmund Pendleton declared, "our dearest rights— life, liberty and property—as Virginians are still in the hands of our state legislatures."[60] Later Justice Story wrote that "the most general rights, which belong to all mankind, may be said to be the right to life, to liberty and to property."[61] And Chancellor Kent paraphrased Blackstone.[62] In 1866, James Wilson, chairman of the House Judiciary Committee, read the Blackstone triad to the 39th Congress and commented, "Thus, sir, we have the English and American doctrine harmonising,"[63] thereby indicating that the rights conferred by the Fourteenth Amendment were confined by the triad, as its due process clause confirmed.

Manifestly the historically limited view of "fundamental rights" cannot sustain the inexhaustible activist claims. Indeed, two leading activist theoreticians admit as much. Paul Brest acknowledges that "Fundamental Rights adjudication is open to criticism that it is *not authorized and not guided* by the text and original history of the Constitution."[64] And

---

57. John W. Gough, *Fundamental Law in English Constitutional History* 39 note 3 (1955).

58. See supra pp. 30–31. By "liberty" Blackstone meant "the power of locomotion . . . moving one's person to whatsoever place one's own inclination may direct." Supra p. 31. That was one of the rights the Civil Rights Act of 1866 provided, as Senator Lyman Trumbull explained—"the right to come and go at pleasure," supra text accompanying note 28, a right that thwarted the Black Codes' attempt to confine blacks to their habitat.

59. *Documents of American History* 80 (Henry Steele Commager ed. 7th ed. 1963). James Otis and Samuel Adams wrote on December 20, 1765, that "The primary, absolute, natural rights of Englishmen . . . are *Personal Security, Personal Liberty and Private Property*." 1 *The Writings of Samuel Adams* 65 (Harry A. Cushing ed. 1904) (emphasis in original).

60. 3 Jonathan Elliot, *Debates in the Several State Conventions on the Adoption of the Federal Constitution* 301 (1836).

61. Unsigned article in Francis Lieber, ed., *Encyclopaedia Americana*, reprinted in James McClellan, *Joseph Story and the American Constitution: A Study in Political and Legal Thought With Selected Writings* 313, 315 (1971).

62. 1 James Kent, *Commentaries on American Law* 607 (9th ed. 1858).

63. Avins, supra note 8 at 164.

64. Paul Brest, "The Fundamental Rights Controversy: The Essential Contradictions of Normative Constitutional Scholarship," 90 Yale L.J. 1063, 1087 (1981) (emphasis in the original).

Michael Perry recognizes that the individual rights which activists champion are judicial constructs of the "modern" Court.[65]

Substantive due process not being as fruitful as of yore, activists have been turning to the Ninth Amendment as a fresh cornucopia of "rights." It provides that "The *enumeration* in the Constitution of certain rights shall not be construed to deny or disparage *others retained* by the people."[66] What is enumerated is embodied in the Constitution; what is retained is not. Reservations are not grants of power to deal with what is retained. Put differently, what is retained is excluded from the federal jurisdiction. This is made clear by Madison's explanation in introducing the Bill of Rights: "the great object in view is to *limit* and qualify the power of Government by *excepting* out of the grant of power those cases in which the Government *ought not to act*."[67] Given that the federal government "ought not to act" in the "excepted" zone, much more was federal action precluded in the "retained" zone.[68] Instead of expanding federal jurisdiction, the Bill of Rights was meant to curtail it. To obviate the implication that the nonmentioned rights "were intended to be *assigned* into the hands of the general Government," Madison stated, this danger would be "guarded against" by the draft precursor of the Ninth Amendment.[69] Justice Black, who read the Bill of Rights into the Fourteenth Amendment, observed that the Ninth Amendment "was intended to protect against the idea that 'by enumerating particular exceptions to the

---

65. Michael Perry, *The Constitution, the Courts, and Human Rights* 91–92 (1982).

It should be noted that "civil rights, such as are guaranteed by the Constitution against State aggression, cannot be impaired by the wrongful acts of individuals, unsupported by State authority in the shape of laws," Civil Rights Cases, 109 U.S. 3, 17 (1883). My study of the 1866 debates persuaded me that such was the framers' design.

66. Emphasis added.

67. 1 *Annals of Congress* 454 (emphasis added).

68. In Federalist No. 82 at 534 (Mod. Lib. ed. 1937), Hamilton stated, "the states will retain all *preexisting* authorities which may not be exclusively delegated to the federal head." In short, what was not delegated (enumerated) is retained.

69. 1 *Annals of Congress* 456 (emphasis added). Justice Story wrote that the Ninth Amendment "was manifestly introduced to prevent any perverse or ingenious misapplication of the well-known maxim, that an affirmation in particular cases implies a negation in all others." Joseph Story, *Commentaries on the Constitution of the United States* § 1007 (5th ed. 1905).

grant of power' to the Federal Government 'those rights which were not singled out, were intended to be assigned into the hands of the General Government.' "[70] The fact that Amendments One through Eight were meant to limit the powers of the federal government militates against a reading of the Ninth that would confer unlimited federal judicial power to create new "rights."[71]

The cheerleader of the cornucopian movement is Randy Barnett.[72] Deploring the Supreme Court's "neglect" of the Ninth Amendment's expansive possibilities, Barnett proffers a "powerful method of protecting unenumerated rights," a "presumption of liberty" that would require a State "to show that the legislation [claimed to be] infringing the liberty of its citizens was a necessary exercise of its police power."[73] But it is for a plaintiff to set forth a cause of action before the State is called upon to prove the negative. To shift the burden of persuasion to the State by Barnett's "presumption of liberty," more is required than bare assertion of an unheard-of claim.[74] Recent Supreme Court pronouncements are unsympathetic to "novel," nontraditional "substantive due process" claims,[75] which are the more compelling when claimants invoke the unidentified rights "retained by the people."

---

70. Griswold v. Connecticut, 381 U.S. 479, 519 (1965). Black relied on the *Annals of Congress*, supra note 67 at 452: "The exceptions here or elsewhere in the constitution, made in favor of particular rights shall not be so construed as to diminish the just importance of other rights retained by the people, or as to enlarge the powers delegated by the constitution; but either as actual limitations of such powers, or as inserted merely for greater caution," that is, as declaratory of existing limitations.

71. Even Lawrence Tribe, whose fertile imagination enables him to toss off novel theories for libertarian goals, "points out the impossibility of viewing the Ninth Amendment as the *source* of rights." Sanford Levinson, "Constitutional Rhetoric and the Ninth Amendment," 64 Chi.-Kent L. Rev. 131 (1988), reprinted in *The Rights Retained by the People* 115, 126 (Randy E. Barnett ed. 1993).

72. Randy E. Barnett, introduction to *The Rights Retained by the People* (Randy E. Barnett ed. 1993). For a critique, see Raoul Berger, "The Ninth Amendment, as Perceived by Randy Barnett," 88 Nw. U. L. Rev. 1508 (1994).

73. Barnett, introduction, id. 10, 11.

74. Barnett believes that the rights retained by the people "are limited only by their imagination," that they are "unenumerable because the human imagination is limitless." Id. 8, 9.

75. See infra Supplementary Note on Incorporation, text accompanying notes 87–91.

# 3

## The "Privileges or Immunities of a Citizen of the United States"

Narrow as was the protection afforded blacks by the "privileges or immunities" clause, it was at least designed to shield them from violence and oppression. Even that limited goal was soon aborted when the Supreme Court divorced the rights of "a citizen of the United States" from the freedom from the discrimination proscribed by the Amendment. Consequently, the provision has become the all-but-forgotten clause of the Constitution.[1] In the *Slaughter-House Cases* the Supreme Court grounded this view in part on the differentiation between the declaration in the first sentence of § 1 that "all persons born or naturalized in the United States . . . are citizens of the United States and of the State wherein they reside" and the second-sentence provision that no State "shall abridge the privileges or immunities of a citizen of the United States." From this Justice Miller deduced that a "citizenship of the United States and a citizenship of a State . . . are distinct from each other," and that § 1 secured only the privileges of a "citizen of the United States."[2] So meager was his catalog of those privileges as to move Justice Field to exclaim that if this was all the privileges or immunities clause

---

1. Colgate v. Harvey, 296 U.S. 404, 443 (1935), Justice Stone dissenting. D. O. McGovney showed that a goodly number of Justice Miller's "national" privileges (infra note 3) can be enforced under some specific, direct constitutional grant. "Privileges and Immunities Clause, Fourteenth Amendment," 4 Iowa L. Bull. 219, 223 (1918). Hence, as Stanley Morrison remarked, "the effect of the decision was to make the privileges and immunities clause practically a dead letter." "Does the Fourteenth Amendment Incorporate the Bill of Rights?" 2 Stan. L. Rev. 140, 144 (1949).

The clause has received little scholarly attention.

2. 83 U.S. (16 Wall.) 36, 74 (1872).

accomplished, "it was a vain and idle enactment."[3] *Slaughter-House* was a five-to-four decision, and Field was joined by Chief Justice Chase and Justices Bradley and Swayne in an opinion that took more accurate account of the framers' intention than did that of Miller.

Preliminarily it will be useful to pull together a few strands that tie the privileges or immunities of § 1 to the specific enumeration of the Civil Rights Act of 1866. There is first the correspondence to the Civil Rights Bill's "civil rights and immunities," "privileges" being narrower than "civil rights," which had been deleted at Bingham's insistence.[4] Second, Chairman Trumbull explained that the Bill had been patterned on the "privileges and immunities" of Article IV, § 2, and its construction by Justice Washington. Third, in introducing the prototype of § 1, Bingham said that the "privileges or immunities" had been drawn from Article IV; fourth, Senator Howard similarly referred back to the Article.[5] Speaking after Howard, Senator Luke P. Poland stated that § 1 "secures nothing beyond what was intended by" the original privileges and immunities provision.[6] More important is the all but universal identification of § 1 with the Civil Rights Act. Why, then, were not the terms of the Act incorporated bodily in § 1? Constitutional drafting calls for the utmost compression, avoidance of the prolixity of a code;[7] "the specific and exclusive enumeration of rights in the Act," as Bickel remarked, presumably was considered "inappropriate in a constitutional provision."[8]

---

3. Id. 96. Among the rights Justice Miller enumerated were the right to come to the seat of government, to assert claims against it, to have access to its seaports, courts, and offices, to have protection abroad, to assemble and petition, to use navigable waters, to become a citizen of another State by residence. Id. 79.

It is anomalous that a "citizen of the United States" is limited to these scanty rights whereas as a "citizen of a State" he may continue to invoke in a sister State the broader rights secured to him by Article IV, § 2. Chambers v. Baltimore & Ohio R.R., 207 U.S. 142, 148 (1907); Blake v. McClung, 172 U.S. 239, 254 (1898).

4. Infra Chapter 7 at notes 11–16.

5. Supra Chapter 2 at notes 6, 9, 32, 33; *Globe* 2765.

6. *Globe* 2961.

7. Cf. M'Culloch v. Maryland, 17 U.S. (4 Wheat.) 316, 407 (1819). In the First Congress, Abraham Baldwin, a Framer, commenting on a proposed amendment that "the President should not turn out a good officer," said that such minute regulation "would have swelled [the Constitution] to the size of a folio volume." 1 *Annals of Congress* 559.

8. Bickel 61.

In sum, the words "privileges or immunities," it is safe to say, were designed to secure "person and property" against violence and oppression by the rights auxiliary to such protection. How was this design separated from the "privileges or immunities of a citizen of the United States"?

Justice Miller correctly stated that Article IV, §2, did not "profess to control the powers of State governments over the rights of its own citizens." Its sole purpose was to require that the rights granted by a State to its "own citizens . . . the same, neither more nor less, shall be the measure of the rights of citizens of other States within your jurisdiction."[9] Without mentioning "citizens of the United States," the courts had construed Article IV to mean that a migrant citizen from one State would enjoy the "fundamental rights" accorded by a sister State to its own citizens.[10] This the framers understood; the cases were quoted, explained, and used as a platform for the Civil Rights Bill.[11] The task, however, was not one of outright adoption but of adaptation. For the Negro did not become a migrant by emancipation; generally speaking, he remained in the same State. But he had experienced a transmigration, from that of a slave, a nonperson,[12] to a freeman, and the framers meant to secure to this transmigrant the rights that Article IV, §2, had guaranteed to a migrant citizen.

Early on, James A. Garfield of Ohio stated, the goal was that "personal liberty and personal rights are placed in the keeping of the nation, that the right to life, liberty, and property shall be guarantied to the citizen in reality . . . We must make American citizenship the shield that protects every citizen, on every foot of our soil."[13] That motive manifestly was at the heart of the Civil Rights Bill: "all persons born in the United States . . . are hereby declared to be citizens of the United States," and it went on to proscribe "discrimination in civil rights or immunities

9. 83 U.S. at 77.

10. Corfield v. Coryell, 6 F. Cas. (No. 3230) 546 (C. C. E. D. Pa. 1823). Abbott v. Bayley, 6 Pick. 89, 91 (Mass. 1827).

11. Trumbull, *Globe* 474, 475, 600; Senator R. Johnson, id. 505; Senator Davis, id. 595–596; Kerr, id. 1269.

12. Roscoe Conkling described a slave as "A man, and yet not a man. In flesh and blood alive; politically dead." Now emancipated, "They are not slaves, but they are not, in a political sense, 'persons.' " *Globe* 356.

13. *Globe App.* 67.

among the inhabitants of any State."[14] A citizen of the United States who was an "inhabitant" of a State was to be free from discrimination. The Bill, Chairman Wilson stated, "refers to those rights which belong to men as citizens of the United States and none other."[15] Raymond of New York said that it provided protection for "citizens of the United States ... against anticipated inequality of legislation in the several States."[16] Cook of Illinois understood the Bill to provide "that as between citizens of the United States there shall be no discrimination in civil rights or immunities. When these rights which are enumerated in this bill are denied to any class of men on account of race or color, when they are subject to a system of vagrant laws which sells them into slavery or involuntary servitude, which operates upon them as upon no other part of the community, they are not secured in the rights of freedom."[17]

In the Senate, Trumbull stated that *Corfield v. Coryell* "enumerates the very rights belonging to a citizen of the United States which are set forth in the first section of the bill."[18] Senator Garrett Davis of Kentucky understood full well what Trumbull was about, and therefore proposed to substitute the Article IV, § 2, formula—"The citizens of each State shall be entitled to all the privileges and immunities of citizens in the several States"—explaining that it would apply "only when a citizen of one State goes into another State," whereas, he stated, Trumbull "proposes now to apply his bill to every citizen of the United States ... where that citizen is domiciled in the State in which he was born." In other words, Trum-

14. *Globe* 474; *Globe App.* 315.

15. Id. 1294. Wilson distinguished these "fundamental" rights from rights under State laws, like the right to attend school, to serve on a jury. Kelly labels this a "restrictive interpretation which actually anticipated the dual citizenship doctrine of the 'privileges and immunities' clause of the Fourteenth Amendment in the *Slaughterhouse Cases*." Kelly, Fourteenth at 1069. Compare Kelly's own "restrictive" view, supra Chapter 2 note 52. Kelly completely misreads Wilson. In tune with the limited Republican goals, he emphasized that "citizens of the United States, as such, are entitled to ... life, liberty, and the right of property." *Globe* 1294. His object was to protect Negroes from violence and oppression whereas Justice Miller rejected even those rights, leaving blacks at the mercy of their former masters.

16. *Globe* 1266.

17. Id. 1124. Shellabarger also referred to "the ordinary rights of national citizenship, such as the right of ... holding land, and of protection." Id. 2104.

18. Id. 475.

bull would legislate "for the resident Negro in Kentucky, born there, who has always lived there, and who intends to remain there," to which, he stated, *Corfield* has no application.[19] Thus, Davis sought to restrict the Bill exactly as Justice Miller later did, but his proposal was stillborn. Instead, Trumbull reasoned from *Corfield* that were a law to declare a "person born in the United States a citizen of the United States, the same rights [listed in *Corfield*] would then appertain to *all* persons who were clothed with American citizenship."[20] After President Johnson's veto of the Bill, Trumbull again stated that "citizens of the United States" have "fundamental rights . . . such as the rights enumerated in this bill," among them, citing Blackstone, that "restraints introduced by law should be *equal to all*" and, quoting Kent, "the right of personal security, the right of personal liberty, and the right to acquire and enjoy property."[21] In short, the Senate rejected the Davis-Miller view in favor of a United

19. Id. 595, 596.

20. Id. 600. The Civil Rights Bill, said Raymond, "is intended to secure these citizens against injustice that may be done them in the courts of those States within which they may reside." Id. 1267. There were, however, some who did not appreciate the difference between Article IV, §2 and §1 of the Amendment; for example, Senator Poland stated that the privileges and immunities clause of §1 "secures nothing beyond what was intended by the original provision" of Article IV, §2. Id. 2961.

21. Id. 1757. Justice Field quoted Senator Trumbull's explanation of the Civil Rights Bill (id. 474): "any statute which is not equal to all, and which deprives any citizen of civil rights, which are secured to other citizens, is an unjust encroachment upon his liberty"; he noted that the Fourteenth Amendment "was adopted to obviate objections which had been raised and pressed with great force to the validity of the Civil Rights Act," and concluded that "A citizen of a State is now only a citizen of the United States residing in that State. The fundamental rights . . . now belong to him as a citizen of the United States." 83 U.S. at 92, 93, 95. Corfield v. Coryell, he stated, "was cited by Senator Trumbull with the observation that it enumerated the very rights belonging to a citizen of the United States set forth in the first section of the act, and with the statement that all persons born in the United States, being declared by the act citizens of the United States, would thenceforth be entitled to the rights of citizens, and that these were the fundamental rights set forth in the act." Id. 98. What Article IV "did for the protection of the citizens of one State against hostile and discriminating legislation of other States," Field summed up, the "Fourteenth Amendment does for the protection of every citizen of the United States against hostile and discriminating legislation against him in favor of others, whether they reside in the same or different States." Id. 100–101. Field was faithful to the legislative history, and it is remarkable that successor judges and scholars did not further explore the path he marked. When, however, he came to substantive due process he forgot about those limited goals.

States citizenship that would clothe *residents* of a State with the "fundamental rights" theretofore conferred on migrants.

Did these views, expressed in connection with the Civil Rights Bill, carry over into the Fourteenth Amendment? Here there is more than the intention to constitutionalize the Civil Rights Act. Frederick E. Woodbridge of Vermont stated that the proposed Bingham prototype was "intended to enable Congress . . . to give all citizens the inalienable rights of life and liberty, and to every citizen in whatever State he may be . . . that protection for his property which is extended to the other citizens of the State."[22] George R. Latham of West Virginia understood the Fourteenth Amendment "privileges and immunities of citizens of the United States" to "provide that no State shall make any discrimination in civil rights of citizens of the United States on account of race . . . the 'civil rights bill' which is now a law . . . covers exactly the same ground."[23] So, too, John M. Broomall of Pennsylvania stated, "We propose, first, to give power to the Government . . . to protect its own citizens within the States," a proposition for which the House had "already voted . . . in the civil rights bill."[24] Ephraim R. Eckley of Ohio also stressed the need to provide "security for life, liberty and property to all citizens of all the States."[25] And Senator Howard referred to the privileges and immunities of Article IV, quoted *Corfield* to explain the terms, and stated that these rights "are secured to the citizens solely as a citizen of the United States."[26] Apart from Garrett Davis' abortive attempt to

22. *Globe* 1088.

23. Id. 2883.

24. Id. 2498.

25. Id. 2535.

26. Id. 2765. So the amended § 1 was understood by Senator Stewart: "It declares that all men are entitled to life, liberty, and property, and imposes upon the Government the duty of discharging these obligations." Id. 2964. After Howard proffered his citizenship definition, Windom summarized the privileges or immunities of § 1 as meaning "Your life shall be spared, your liberty shall be unabridged, your property shall be protected." Id. 3169. See also Bingham: "rights of every person," id. 2542; Farnsworth: § 1 "might as well read . . . 'No State shall deny to any person within its jurisdiction.' " Id. 2539.

[On January 30, 1871, John Bingham submitted a Report of the House Committee on the Judiciary, stating: "The clause of the fourteenth amendment, 'No State shall make or enforce any law which shall abridge the privileges or immunities of citizens of the United States,' *does not*, in the opinion of the committee, refer to the privileges and immunities

limit this objective, no one, so far as I could find, disputed that the purpose of both the Civil Rights Act and the Amendment was to guarantee to "citizens of the United States," whether they were migrants to or residents of a State, the enumerated fundamental rights.

In the process of hammering out the Amendment, the framers had lost sight of the definition of citizenship contained in the Civil Rights Bill, so it was late in the day when Senator Benjamin F. Wade of Ohio remarked anent the word "citizen" in § 1, "that is a term about which there has been a great deal of uncertainty in our government." To "put the question beyond cavil," he proposed to "strike out the word 'citizen' [in what is now the second sentence of § 1], and substitute all persons born in the United States."[27] Howard advanced a counterproposal, the present introductory sentence, "All persons born in the United States . . . are citizens of the United States and of the State wherein they reside." Wade then withdrew his proposal.[28] Presumably the Howard formulation struck Wade as a satisfactory substitute for, not a repudiation of, his own proposal. Although the Negro had been emancipated, the *Dred Scott* decision threw a shadow over his citizenship;[29] the matter had been a source of interminable argument. Trumbull wished "to end that very controversy, whether the Negro is a citizen or not."[30] Howard stated that his definitional amendment of § 1 "settles the great question of citizenship and removes all doubt as to what persons are or are not citizens of the United States." And he further explained, "we desired to put this question of citizenship and the *rights* of citizens and *freedmen* under the civil rights bill beyond the legislative power" of those who would "expose the freedmen again to the oppression

of citizens of the United States *other* than privileges and immunities embraced in the original text of the Constitution, article 4, section 2. The fourteenth amendment, it is believed, *did not* add to the privileges or immunities before mentioned, but was deemed necessary for their enforcement as an express limitation upon the powers of the States." H.R. No. 22, 41st Cong., 3d Sess. 1 (1871) (emphasis added). Reprinted in *The Reconstruction Amendments' Debates* 466 (Alfred Avins ed. 1967).]

27. *Globe* 2768–2769.

28. Id. 2869; cf. with supra at note 26.

29. Referring to the Dred Scott holding that a Negro could be neither a citizen of a State nor of the United States, Justice Miller said, "To remove this difficulty primarily . . . the first clause of the first section was framed . . . That its main purpose was to establish the citizenship of the negro can admit of no doubt." 83 U.S. 72.

30. *Globe* 1285.

of their old masters,"[31] thus confirming that his definition was not a sub rosa abandonment of the paramount goal throughout: protection of the resident Negro against State discrimination. In the House, Thaddeus Stevens of Pennsylvania regarded the Howard interpolation as an "excellent amendment, long needed to settle conflicting decisions."[32] This limited purpose of Howard's definition throws doubt on Miller's view that it was designed to demark the rights of a citizen of the United States from those of a State citizen. Against the manifest purpose of the framers, of which Justice Miller was well aware,[33] his reliance on a rule of construction—to express at one point is to exclude at another—should carry little weight.[34] Rules of construction are useful guides where other light is lacking, but they are not meant to dim or extinguish available light. The cardinal purpose of interpretation, it cannot too often be emphasized, is to ascertain and effectuate, not defeat, the intention of the framers. Once that purpose is ascertained, it may not be thwarted by a rule of construction.[35]

In sum, the purpose of the framers was to protect blacks from discrimination with respect to specified "fundamental rights," enumerated in the Civil Rights Act and epitomized in the §1 "privileges or immunities" clause. To achieve that purpose they made the black *both* a citizen "of the United States and of the State in which he resides." They did not intend by the addition of State citizenship to *diminish* the rights they had

31. Id. 2890, 2896 (emphasis added). Howard stated that his interpolation "is simply declaratory of the law already." Id. 2890. Trumbull had quoted Chief Justice Marshall's statement that "A Citizen of the United States, residing in any state of the Union, is a citizen of that state." Gassies v. Ballon, 31 U.S. (6 Pet.) 761, 762 (1832); *Globe* 1756.

32. *Globe* 3148.

33. Infra at notes 39–40. "It is too clear for argument," said Justice Miller, "that the change in phraseology was adopted understandingly and with a purpose." 83 U.S. 75. That is quite true; but the purpose is that expressed by Trumbull, Stevens, Howard, and Fessenden, not exclusion from the benefits that had been so carefully wrought.

34. Howard, whose purpose Miller sought to ascertain by this rule, stated that it is "a dangerous principle of construction." *Globe* 4001.

35. For example, "The rule of '*ejusdem generis*' is applied as an aid in ascertaining the intention of the legislature, not to subvert it when ascertained." United States v. Gilliland, 312 U.S. 86, 93 (1941). The *expressio unius* rule "serves only as an aid in discovering the legislative intent when that is not otherwise manifest." United States v. Barnes, 222 U.S. 513, 519 (1912).

been at such pains to specify, but the better to *secure* them. The notion that by conferring dual citizenship the framers were separating said rights of a citizen of the United States from those of a State citizen not only is without historical warrant but actually does violence to their intention. Fessenden stated that the definition was framed "*to prevent a State from saying* that although a person is a citizen of the United States he is not a citizen of the State."[36] He did not mean to safeguard State citizenship in order to leave blacks at the mercy of Southern States. It was precisely their abuse of the freedmen that led to the Amendment.

Justice Miller next stressed the serious consequences that would follow adoption of a construction contrary to his own; the effect would be to "degrade the State governments by subjecting them to the control of Congress" in unwonted manner. He read "No State shall make or enforce any law which shall *abridge* the privileges or immunities of citizens of the United States" as transferring "the entire domain of civil right" from the States to the federal government, so that Congress could even "pass laws *in advance*, limiting and restricting the exercise of legislative power by the States."[37] Here Miller imported a term into the clause; "abridge" presupposes preliminary State action; before such abridgment there is nothing upon which to act "in advance." Moreover, Congress was confined to *corrective* measures, as Miller was aware: "If, however, the States did not conform their laws to its [the Amendment's] requirements, *then* by the fifth section . . . Congress was authorized to enforce it by suitable legislation."[38] It was emphatically not authorized to promulgate a general code "in advance."

Miller himself found that "the existence of laws in the States where the newly emancipated negroes reside, which discriminated with gross injustice and hardship against them as a class, was the evil to be remedied"— that is, the Black Codes.[39] The "one pervading purpose," he stated, was "protection of the newly-made freeman and citizen from the oppression

36. *Globe* 2897.

37. 83 U.S. 77–78 (emphasis added).

38. Id. 81 (emphasis added). For the "corrective" purpose of § 1, see infra Chapter 10 at notes 68–92.

39. 83 U.S. 81. Miller referred to the "black codes" and recapitulated some of their harsh provisions; id. 70.

of those who had formerly exercised unlimited dominion over him."[40] Consequently, the Amendment did not encompass "all legislation,"[41] but only discriminatory legislation with respect to specified rights, as Justice Field pointed out: "What, then, are the privileges and immunities which are secured against abridgment by State legislation? In the first section of the Civil Rights Act Congress has given its interpretation of these terms [which] . . . include the right 'to make and enforce contracts . . .' "[42] The correction of discriminatory laws with respect to the enumerated "fundamental rights" would hardly constitute the "court a perpetual censor upon all legislation of the States, on the civil rights of their own citizens."[43] When Miller held that "the citizen of a State" must look to the State for protection,[44] he aborted what he himself had declared to be the "pervading purpose": to protect the Negro from the "evil" of the Black Codes, Codes that handed the Negro back to his oppressors.

Paradoxically, Justice Miller was ready to protect Negroes from "gross injustice and oppression" by resort to the equal protection clause.[45] How,

40. Id. 71, 81. Miller also stated, "We doubt very much whether any action of a State not directed by way of discrimination against the negroes as a class . . . will ever be held to come within the purview of this [equal protection] provision." Id. 81. If this be read as excluding protection for whites, it runs counter to the history of the Civil Rights Bill. Senator Trumbull explained that the Bill "applies to white men as well as to black men. It declares that all persons . . . shall be entitled to the same civil rights." *Globe* 599; see also *Globe* 41, 158, 516. And the Amendment speaks in terms of "persons," in order, Bingham stated, to include "aliens" and "strangers," i.e., whites. Infra Chapter 11 at notes 91–92.

41. Justice Miller's "all legislation" is the more surprising because he noted that "privileges and immunities" was lifted out of Article IV of the Articles of Confederation, where it was particularized—"all the privileges of trade or commerce." Here, he commented, "we have some of these specifically mentioned, enough perhaps to give some general idea of the class of civil rights meant by the phrase." 83 U.S. 75. Self-evidently the privileges subsumed under "trade or commerce" are but a segment of the matters embraced by "all legislation." And his quotation of the Corfield enumeration again suggests that Miller was substituting "statesmanship" for hard-nosed legal interpretation.

42. Id. 96. The Court's statement in Buchanan v. Warley, 245 U.S. 60, 77 (1917), that "The Fourteenth Amendment makes no attempt to enumerate the rights it was designed to protect. It speaks in general terms, and those are as comprehensive as possible," overlooks the framers' limited purposes, plainly expressed in the enumeration of the Civil Rights Act which the Amendment incorporated.

43. 83 U.S. 78.

44. Id. 75.

45. Id. 81.

one wonders, did "equal protection" escape the blight that struck down "privileges or immunities"? It equally "degrad[ed] the State governments by subjecting them to the control of Congress"; it too constituted a "great departure from the structure and spirit of our institutions."[46] And whereas the limits of "privileges or immunities" can be discerned in the rights specified in the Civil Rights Act which § 1 incorporated, there is no clue whatever to the rights comprehended by the Miller formula— equal protection against "gross injustice and hardship." One of the ironies that bestrews the path of the Court is that the censorship abjured by Miller under "privileges or immunities" really became unlimited under the converted due process clause.[47]

No discussion of *Slaughter-House* may fail to take account of Justice Bradley's dissent. Where Field won the concurrence of three associates, Bradley stood alone; where Miller held that protection of the citizen was for the State, Bradley propounded a theory of "absolute" rights that neither State nor nation may invade.[48] That theory, as will hereinafter appear, can draw small comfort from the intention of the framers; and he himself stated with respect to the preexisting Article IV, § 2: "It is true that courts have usually regarded [it] . . . as securing only equality of privileges with the citizens of the State in which the parties are found."[49] In holding that the Amendment was designed to assure similar equality with respect to specified rights among residents of a State, Justice Field staked out a position midway between the extremes of Miller and Bradley, one that honestly reflected the intention of the framers.

There remain some remarks by Senator Trumbull in 1871, which Graham reads as a denial "that the Fourteenth Amendment authorized Congress to protect citizens in their rights of person and property in the States. Such an interpretation [Trumbull] declared, would mean 'anni-

---

46. Id. 78.

47. Consequently I would dissent from Justice Frankfurter's reference to the "mischievous uses to which that [privileges and immunities] clause would lend itself if its scope were not confined to that given to it by all but one of the decisions beginning with the Slaughter-House Cases." Adamson v. California, 332 U.S. 46, 61–62 (1947), concurring opinion.

48. 83 U.S. 114–115.

49. Id. 118.

hilation of the States.' "[50] Little weight has been attached by the Supreme Court to postenactment remarks, even of the Congress itself.[51] When they contradict representations made by the speaker during the enactment process, upon which others have been led to rely, they should be treated with special reserve.[52] Consider, too, the circumstances that gave rise to Trumbull's 1871 remarks. President Grant, Graham recounts, "had just called for a second Force Bill to cope with extralegal suppression of Negro rights. The problem . . . had risen not in the contemplated or familiar form of discrimination by carriers, theaters and inns but in the infinitely more tangled context of Southern whites fighting misrule and military government." Trumbull "flatly declined to go along with the latest proposal"; the tug of new political considerations shaped his version of the past. Now he maintained that the protection afforded by the Fourteenth Amendment was no greater than that accorded by Article IV, § 2, that that section "did not have reference to the protection of those persons in individual rights in their respective States, except so far as being citizens of one State entitled them to the privileges and immunities of citizens in every other"; and that the "fourteenth amendment does not define the privileges and immunities of a citizen of the United States any more than the Constitution originally did."[53]

This was only half the story. Trumbull did not mention his rejection of that very argument by Garrett Davis, that he had read the judicial definitions of the Article IV, § 2, privileges and immunities to the framers and patterned the Civil Rights Bill on *Corfield v. Coryell*, that he adapted the Article IV, § 2, conception—a migrant citizen was entitled to the same fundamental rights as a resident citizen—to the transmigrant black so suddenly released from slavery, named him a citizen of the United States to assure him of the same rights the migrant enjoyed under Article IV. To say in these circumstances that the Fourteenth Amendment "does not define the privileges and immunities" is therefore a half-truth. The terms, in lawyers' jargon, had become "words of

50. Graham 133.

51. Rainwater v. United States, 356 U.S. 590, 593 (1958).

52. Cf. Raoul Berger, *Congress v. The Supreme Court* 48 (1969); Raoul Berger, "Judicial Review: Counter Criticism in Tranquillity," 69 Nw. U. L. Rev. 390, 399–401 (1974).

53. Graham 324, 326, 325.

art"; in borrowing them (with the exclusion of suffrage), Trumbull expressly gave them the meaning which courts had given under Article IV and which he had carefully spelled out in the Civil Rights Bill. It follows that Trumbull's 1871 argument that "the privileges and immunities belonging to a citizen of the United States as such are of a national character," that "National citizenship is one thing and State citizenship another"[54]—the precursor of the *Slaughter-House* dichotomy—was a repudiation of his own explanation to the framers, his enumeration of specific rights in the Bill that were to belong to "citizens of the United States." He could change *his* mind but he could not change that of the 39th Congress which had adopted the Civil Rights Act on the strength of his representations and then went on to incorporate the Act in the Amendment.

54. Id. 528.

# 4

## *Negro Suffrage Was Excluded*

No area of Negro rights considered by the 39th Congress was so extensively discussed as Negro suffrage.[1] The issue was crucial to the maintenance of Republican ascendancy, a goal boldly proclaimed by Stevens at the very outset. Such ascendancy, the mass of Republicans believed, was to be assured through the reduction of Southern representation in the House of Representatives in proportion as a State denied or abridged suffrage, the device embodied in §2 of the Amendment.[2] Some strongly doubted whether the rebel ruling class, outnumbered by blacks, could be induced to "divest itself of the government and hand it over to a subject and despised caste."[3] But it was more important, Senator George H. Williams of Oregon, member of the Joint Committee, candidly avowed, to limit Southern representation than to provide "that negroes anywhere should immediately vote."[4] The fact that Negro suffrage was

1. Van Alstyne 36; James 21.

2. Supra Chapter 1 at notes 55–56. Roscoe Conkling of New York likewise acknowledged that the "representation" proposal "was primarily for party and sectional advantage." Kendrick 204; see also id. 207 and infra note 4.

3. Donnelly remarked, "To pass this law and then hope that South Carolina, moved by the hope of future power, would do justice to the negro is absurd. She has 291,000 whites and 412,000 blacks. To pass such a law would be for the governing power to divest itself of the government and hand it over to a subject and despised caste . . . The same is true, more or less, of all the South." *Globe* 378. Julian of Indiana likewise placed little hope in "representation" as an inducement to the grant of suffrage because southern "scorn of an enslaved and downtrodden race is as intense as ever. They hate the negro." *Globe* 58. Boutwell of Massachusetts admitted "the possibility that ultimately those eleven States may be restored to representative power without the right of franchise being conferred [by them] upon the colored people." *Globe* 2508.

4. *Globe App.* 94. Ward Elliott remarks, "The post–Civil War Radical Republicans, as a group, cared very little for the black vote until they came to believe that it would help

unmistakably excluded from the ambit of the Civil Rights Bill, which proceeded on a parallel track with debate on "representation," lends substance to his avowal. The intention to exclude suffrage from the Amendment as well[5] need not rest entirely on its incorporation of the Civil Rights Act, for there is ample affirmative evidence of that purpose.

Chief Justice Warren held in *Reynolds v. Sims*, a State reapportionment case, that "the right of suffrage can be denied by a debasement or dilution of the weight of a citizen's vote just as effectively as by wholly prohibiting the free exercise of the franchise." The premise, he said, that a State may not deny suffrage was derived from a "conception of political equality . . . [that] can mean only one thing—one person, one vote."[6] Equality, however, did not carry that meaning for the framers;[7] and in a powerful dissent, Justice Harlan reproached the Court "for its failure to address itself at all to the Fourteenth Amendment as a whole or to [its] legislative history."[8] Even one who regards the reapportionment decisions with favor, Carl Auerbach, lamented that "the failure of the Court to mention, let alone deal with, [Harlan's] argument is indeed,

---

to secure their position . . . against a Democratic resurgence. Once convinced that they would profit from the black vote, they passed the Fifteenth Amendment." *The Rise of a Guardian Democracy* 2 (1974); see also id. 204. Section 2 "was not primarily devised for the protection of Negro rights and the provision of Negro equality. Its primary purpose . . . was to put the southern states" under northern control. C. Vann Woodward, "Seeds of Failure in Radical Race Policy," in *New Frontiers of the American Reconstruction* 135 (Harold M. Hyman ed. 1966). Aaron Harding of Kentucky tauntingly asked "if there is a single man among you who would vote for negro suffrage if he believed the negroes would vote the Democratic ticket? Not one, and you know it." *Globe* 449. Although McKee of Kentucky favored the limitation of representation, he opposed Negro suffrage in the District of Columbia because he did not believe "that this race, coming immediately out of bondage, is fit for all rights of citizens." Id. 452. When John Bright expressed "reservations about enfranchising this large unlettered electorate," Sumner wrote, "Without them, the old enemy will reappear . . ." Quoted in Donald, *Sumner II* 201.

5. As Michael Les Benedict justly remarks, the §2 curtailment of representation was "necessary only if Republicans did not intend to force black suffrage on the reluctant South." *A Compromise of Principle: Conservative Republicans and Reconstruction 1863–1869* 136 (1975).

6. 377 U.S. 533, 555, 558 (1964).

7. See W. R. Brock, *An American Crisis: Congress and Reconstruction* (1963). This will be discussed infra Chapter 10.

8. 377 U.S. at 590.

as he charged, remarkable and confounding."[9] Another proponent of those decisions, William Van Alstyne, states that "the majority seems tacitly to have conceded the argument."[10] In 1970 Justice Harlan amplified his dissent in *Oregon v. Mitchell*;[11] both of his dissents are models of scholarly exactitude. Having combed the debates for myself, I can confirm his accuracy and scrupulousness in drawing inferences from the facts; one can only complain that he left so few gleanings for those who came after. Since his discussion in the two opinions covers many pages, and since it is contained in law reports that only scholarly specialists are likely to consult, I have undertaken to compress the materials into smaller compass, particularly because they furnish the springboard for much that is to follow.

## The Grant of Suffrage Was Excluded From § 1

Senator Sumner labeled the right to vote "the Great Guarantee; and *the only sufficient Guarantee*,"[12] without which, said Senator Samuel C. Pomeroy of Kansas, the Negro "has no security."[13] Similar sentiments were expressed by James A. Garfield and James M. Ashley of Ohio, George S. Boutwell of Massachusetts, Ignatius Donnelly of Minnesota, and William A. Newell of New Jersey—Republicans all.[14] Nevertheless, as Senator Trumbull emphasized, it was not included in the Civil Rights Bill. Why not? Because, in the words of David Donald, it was "political dynamite."[15] The reasons have been so admirably compressed by Professor Van Alstyne as to bear quotation in extenso. He notes that the Joint Committee considered a forthright proposal to abolish "any distinctions in political or civil rights . . . on account of race" and states,

9. C. Auerbach, "The Reapportionment Cases: One Person, One Vote—One Vote, One Value," 1964 S. Ct. Rev. 1, 75.

10. Van Alstyne 36.

11. 400 U.S. 112, 152 (1970).

12. *Globe* 685.

13. Id. 1182. Senator Yates of Illinois declared "suffrage . . . the only remedy," id. 3037.

14. Id. 2462, 2882, 310, 589, 867.

15. Donald, *Sumner II* 202. Senator Garrett Davis of Kentucky stated, "Negro suffrage is political arsenic. If it is not, why do not the free States open wide their throats and gulp down the graceful and invigorating draught?" *Globe* 246.

The decision was made, however, not to propose a limited, single purpose amendment; not to advertise the particular issue of Negro suffrage and to dispose of it through a provision instantly invalidating the laws of all states where equal suffrage regardless of race was denied. The reluctance of the Republicans bluntly to dispose of the issue in this fashion is readily explainable; there was not sufficient prospect that the necessary number of votes would ratify such an amendment.

There were, in 1866, but five states in the nation that permitted Negroes to vote on equal terms with whites: Maine, Massachusetts, New Hampshire, Rhode Island, and Vermont. Together, these states contained a mere 6 per cent of the Negro population. New York also permitted Negro suffrage, but only for those possessed of at least a $250 freehold estate, an added "qualification" that whites were not obliged to satisfy. No other state permitted Negroes to vote, regardless of qualification. Moreover, in late 1865, shortly before the Thirty-ninth Congress convened, Connecticut, Minnesota, and Wisconsin voted down impartial suffrage by popular referendum. The Territory of Colorado defeated a referendum for impartial suffrage by a wide margin in September, 1865, and was, nevertheless, admitted to the Union by Congress.

The admission of Colorado, with its ban on Negro voting, followed the admission of Nevada, which had a similar ban, and was in turn followed by the readmission of Tennessee on July 24, 1866. The readmission of Tennessee [*after* submission of the Fourteenth Amendment with its equal protection clause for ratification] was accomplished, moreover, with complete awareness that its general assembly had, on June 5, 1865, restricted the franchise to white males only. Indeed, all these facts were well known to the Congress, and were gleefully recited by some of the Democrats who challenged the Republicans to dare make an issue of Negro suffrage.

All these things and more had a conspicuous and significant influence on the Thirty-Ninth Congress.[16]

---

16. Van Alstyne 69–70. See also infra Chapter 5 at note 74. "The off-year state elections of 1867," during which ratification of the Fourteenth Amendment was debated, "made clear the popular hostility to black suffrage in the North." Morton Keller, *Affairs of State* 81 (1977).

Indeed they had! They explain why the framers rejected Negro suffrage, as may immediately be gathered from two statements among many. Senator Pomeroy stated: "This nation . . . has not yet reached the point of giving all men their rights by a suffrage amendment; three-fourths of the States are not ready."[17] In opening the debate on the Amendment, Senator Jacob Howard stated on behalf of the Joint Committee, "it was our opinion that three-fourths of the States . . . could not be induced to grant the right of suffrage, even in any degree or under any restriction, to the colored race."[18] These views were repeated in the Final Report of the Joint Committee on Reconstruction.[19]

If Negro suffrage was unacceptable to the great mass of Republicans, how can we read into the general terms "equal protection" the very grant they could not swallow? Van Alstyne also notes a number of proposals that would expressly abolish distinctions "in the exercise of the legislative franchise on account of race or color" (including one by Sumner that was rejected by a vote of 38 to 8),[20] and explains that "there was not sufficient prospect that the necessary number of States would ratify such an amendment." Are we to impute to the framers an intention to shroud in ambiguity the Negro suffrage they dared not "advertise" by a "blunt," unequivocal proposal? Something of the sort is suggested by Van Alstyne,[21] but there is no evidence of representations that the Fourteenth would mean one thing in 1866 and the very thing then "feared" in the future. A legislative intention to have words mean one thing in 1866 and the opposite in the future is so remarkable as to call for strict proof, not speculation, particularly when disclosure spelled political disaster.[22] But let me defer comment on this "open-ended" theory, fathered by Alex-

17. *Globe* 1182.
18. Id. 2766.
19. Infra Chapter 5 at note 49.
20. Van Alstyne 69.
21. See infra Chapter 6 at note 53.
22. In an analogous situation Van Alstyne states, "It is even likely, by way of conjecture, that had the subject [reapportionment] been discussed there might have been a disavowal of an intention to apply the Equal Protection clause to malapportionment, at least at that time . . . [But] hypothetical answers to hypothetical questions never actually entertained at the time would be a most dubious basis for expounding the content of 'equal protection' one hundred years later." Van Alstyne 85.

ander Bickel, embraced by Alfred Kelly and Van Alstyne, and then picked up by Justice Brennan, to a later chapter, and for the moment permit the framers to speak for themselves. Because the suffrage issue is so vital for my subsequent discussion of the scope of judicial review, because in the eyes of Justice Brennan the historical record is "vague and imprecise,"[23] it is essential by copious documentation to establish firmly the deliberate exclusion of Negro suffrage.

## NEGRO SUFFRAGE WAS UNACCEPTABLE

With but "6% of the Negro population," New England's advocacy of Negro suffrage, Senator Edgar Cowan of Pennsylvania acidly lectured Sumner, came cheap: "he simply had no understanding of what it is to live in a community surcharged with an idle, dissolute, vicious, ignorant negro population just emerged from slavery."[24] At the other end of the political spectrum, the Radical leader Thaddeus Stevens, also of Pennsylvania, wrote, "In my county are fifteen hundred escaped slaves. If they are specimens of the negroes of the South, they are not qualified to vote."[25] Stevens told Robert Dale Owen, "We haven't a majority, either in our committee or in Congress, for immediate suffrage; and I don't believe the States have yet advanced so far that they would ratify it."[26] William Lloyd Garrison, the indomitable abolitionist, "came out against the forcing of Negro suffrage upon the South."[27]

23. Oregon v. Mitchell, 400 U.S. 112, 278. Justices White and Marshall joined in this opinion.

24. Donald, *Sumner II* 158. Sumner himself had stated that "one must not assume 'that a race, degraded for long generations under the iron heel of bondage, can be taught at once all the political duties of an American citizen' . . . he thought that most of the negroes, free and contented, would remain in the South as 'a dependent and amiable peasantry,' " Donald, *Sumner I* 235. But after 1864 he shifted because, as he wrote, "Without them, the old enemy [slave oligarchy] will reappear . . . and in alliance with the Northern democracy, put us all in peril again." Donald, *Sumner II* 201.

25. Fawn M. Brodie, *Thaddeus Stevens: Scourge of the South* 211 (1959); C. Vann Woodward, *The Burden of Southern History* 92 (1960).

26. James 101.

27. Brodie, supra note 25 at 230–231.

The Republicans were keenly alive to the situation. Very early in the session, Roscoe Conkling explained,

> The northern states, most of them, do not permit negroes to vote. Some of them have repeatedly and lately pronounced against it. Therefore, even if it were defensible as a principle for the Central Government to absorb by amendment the power to control the action of the States in such a matter, would it not be futile to ask three-quarters of the States to do for themselves and others, by ratifying such an amendment, the very thing most of them have already refused to do in their own cases?[28]

Senator Fessenden, chairman of the Joint Committee, said of a suffrage proposal, there is not "the slightest probability that it will be adopted by the States . . . [it] would not commend itself to anybody."[29] Sumner's own Massachusetts colleague, Senator Henry Wilson, a leading Radical, commented on Senator Henderson's proposal of suffrage without distinction of race, "I cannot think . . . there is any hope of adoption after the indications of the last six months."[30] Another Senator who favored Negro suffrage, Doolittle of Wisconsin, said, "out of New England there are not three States in this Union, neither Nevada nor Colorado, nor any of the new States or the old States that will vote for an amendment . . . by which negro suffrage shall be imposed upon the States."[31] Similar remarks were made by still others.[32] On July 21, 1866, shortly after the Amendment passed the Congress, Sumner proposed an amendment to a bill for admission of Tennessee that "there shall be no

28. *Globe* 358. Nathaniel Banks of Massachusetts stated, "The public opinion of the country is such at this precise moment [May 1866] as to make it impossible we should do it." Id. 2532.

29. Id. 704.

30. Id. 1256.

31. Id. 2143. Senator Henderson stated, "the country is not yet prepared" to grant Negro suffrage. Id. 3035. Senator Sherman said, "no man can doubt . . . there was a strong and powerful prejudice in the Army and among all classes of citizens against extending the right of suffrage to negroes." *Globe App.* 127.

32. See: Senator Lane of Kansas, *Globe* 1799; Garfield and Ashley of Ohio, id. 2462, 2882; Senators Howard, Poland, and Sherman, id. 2766, 2963, and *Globe App.* 131.

denial of the electoral franchise, or of any other rights, on account of color or race, but all persons shall be equal before the law." It was voted down without debate, 34 to 4.[33] This background lends meaning to Senator Howard's assurance that "the *first section of the proposed amendment* does not give . . . the right of voting. The right of suffrage is not, in law, one of the privileges or immunities thus secured"[34]—an echo of assurances during debate on the Civil Rights Bill. Bingham likewise stated that "The amendment does not give . . . the power to Congress of regulating suffrage in the several States."[35] In any event, how can we attribute to the ratifiers approval of Negro suffrage when midway in the course of ratification, in the elections of April 1867, Bingham's own State, Ohio, "overwhelmed a negro suffrage amendment by 40,000? In every state where the voters expressed themselves on the Negro suffrage issue they turned it down."[36]

## ATTACHMENT TO STATE SOVEREIGNTY

Notwithstanding that the States' Right doctrine had been badly tarnished by its association with secession, a potent factor in the exclusion of Negro suffrage was a deep-seated attachment to State sovereignty. That this was no mere rationalization for Negrophobia may be gathered from the objection of Senator James W. Grimes of Iowa to a national livestock quarantine measure: "Let us go back to the original condition of things, and allow the States to take care of themselves."[37] On the eve of the Civil War, Lincoln stated in his First Inaugural Address, "The right of each State to order and control its own domestic institutions according to its own judgment exclusively is essential to the balance of powers on which the perfection and endurance of our political fabric

33. *Globe* 4000. His similar motion on July 27 respecting Nebraska was rejected 34 to 5, id. 4222.

34. Id. 2766 (emphasis added).

35. Id. 2542.

36. Woodward, supra note 4 at 137.

37. *Globe* 2446. Senator Henry Anthony of Rhode Island asserted that "he would rather have cholera itself than such a bill." Phillip S. Paludan, *A Covenant With Death* 48 (1975).

depends."[38] So Story had earlier stated,[39] and this view was reiterated by Republicans like Thomas T. Davis, Robert S. Hale, and Giles W. Hotchkiss of New York[40] and Latham of West Virginia. Congress, Latham said, "has no right to interfere with the internal policy of the several states."[41] "The proposition to prohibit States from denying civil or political rights to any class of persons," said Conkling, "encounters a great objection on the threshold. It trenches upon the principle of existing local sovereignty . . . It takes away a right which has been always supposed to inhere in the States."[42] Bingham, a leader in the Negro cause, stated that "the care of the property, the liberty, and the life of the citizen . . . is in the States and not in the federal government. I have sought to effect no change in that respect."[43] It was because of the prevalence of such sentiment that Trumbull, defending the Civil Rights Bill after President Johnson's veto, felt constrained to reassure the Senate that the Bill "in no manner interferes with the municipal regulations of any State which protects all alike in their rights of person and property."[44]

38. Quoted in *Globe* 2096. Governor (soon to be Senator) Yates of Illinois stated in 1865, "I am for unlimited state sovereignty in the true sense, in the sense that the State is to control all its municipal and local legislation and I would be the first to resist all attempts upon the part of the Federal Government to interpose tyrannical usurpation of power in controlling the legislation of States." Paludan, supra note 37 at 34.

39. The State "police power extends over all subjects within the territorial limits of the States and has never been conceded to the United States." Prigg v. Pennsylvania, 41 U.S. (16 Pet.) 539, 625 (1842), quoted in *Globe* 1270. Samuel S. Marshall of Illinois stated, "It is a fundamental principle of American law that the regulation of the local police of all the domestic affairs of a State belong to the State itself, and not to the Federal Government." *Globe* 627.

40. *Globe* 1083, 1085–1086, 1063; infra Chapter 10 at notes 77–78.

41. *Globe* 1295–1296.

42. Id. 358; see also Delano, *Globe App.* 158; Charles A. Eldredge, *Globe* 1154.

43. *Globe* 1292. He repeated, "I have always believed that the protection in time of peace within the State of all the rights of person and citizen was of the powers reserved to the States." Id. 1293. Commenting earlier on Hale's view that "the citizens must rely upon the State for their protection," he said, "I admit that such is the rule under the Constitution as it now stands." Id. 1093. Such reiteration testifies to pervasive uneasiness about the impairment of State sovereignty, uneasiness shared by his fellow Ohioan, Chief Justice Salmon Chase, who regretted that the Joint Committee had gone too far: "Even the loyal people in Northern states, he feared, might oppose the amendment because of its threat to state rights." James 118. This was a man of "radical tendencies." Id.

44. *Globe* 1761.

This sentiment emerges even more sharply when suffrage is in issue, as when Conkling stated that interference therewith "meddles with a right reserved to the States . . . and to which they will long cling before they surrender it."[45] Early in the session, the Radical leader Stevens said of a proposed amendment to reduce State representation in proportion to a denial of Negro suffrage: "I hold that the States have the right . . . to fix the elective franchise within their own States. And I hold that this does not take it from them . . . How many States would allow Congress to come within their jurisdiction to fix the qualification of their voters? . . . You could not get five in this Union."[46] In the Senate, Chairman Fessenden stated, "everybody has admitted from the foundation of the Government down to the present day that the power to fix the qualifications of voters rested with the States," and that the proposed "representation" provision "leaves it just as it was before, and does not change it."[47] After stating his preference for Negro suffrage, Senator Doolittle said that "the Federal Government had no right or constitutional power to impose on a State negro suffrage . . . the right of a State to determine that question was one of the reserved rights of every State." Like Stevens, he averred that "out of New England" no three States would vote for an amendment "by which negro suffrage shall be imposed upon the States."[48] Although Senator Henderson of Missouri was an advocate of Negro enfranchisement, he too stated that he was "not now ready to take away from the States the long-enjoyed right of prescribing the qualifications of electors in their own limits."[49] "The Radical leaders," Flack stated, "were aware as any one of the attachment of a great majority of the people to the doctrine of States rights . . . the right of the States to

45. Id. 358; see also Thomas N. Stillwell of Indiana, id. 670; Senator Cowan, id. 1286; Shellabarger, id. 1293; Senator Poland, id. 2962.

46. Id. 536. Senator Lane of Indiana, who favored strong measures against the rebels, said, "the right to determine the qualifications of electors is left with the several States . . . I do not believe that Congress has a right to interfere between [Indiana] and the people and fix the qualifications of voters." Id. 740.

47. Id. 1279, 1278; see also id. 704. This assurance was meaningless if § 1 conferred suffrage.

48. Id. 2143.

49. *Globe App.* 120.

regulate their own internal affairs."[50] These sentiments were accurately summarized by Justice Miller in 1872, shortly after adoption of the Fourteenth and Fifteenth Amendments:

> we do not see in those amendments any purpose to destroy the main features of the general system. Under the pressure of all the excited feeling growing out of the war, our statesmen have still believed that the existence of the states with power for domestic and local government . . . was essential to the working of our complex form of government.[51]

This "commitment to traditional state-federal relations meant," in the words of Alfred Kelly, that "the radical Negro reform program could be only a very limited one."[52] That it was in fact a program "limited" to a ban on discrimination with respect to "fundamental rights" from which suffrage was excluded is confirmed by §2.

### The Effect of §2

The framers' intention to leave control of suffrage in the States, untouched by §1, is confirmed by §2 of the Amendment. That section provides,

> Representation shall be apportioned among the several States according to their respective numbers, counting the whole number of persons in each State. But when the right to vote at any election . . .

50. Flack 68. "One reason the Reconstruction of the South loomed so high to northerners," Harold Hyman concluded, "was less that blacks were involved than that every one understood the pre-eminence of states . . . in affecting all their citizens' lives." Harold M. Hyman, *A More Perfect Union* 426 (1973). In "early 1865 virtually unhampered state powers were considered fundamental for liberty, federalism and democracy." Id. 301. "A heavy phalanx of Republican politicos, including Sherman and Trumbull . . . were states rights nationalists, suspicious of any new functional path the nation travelled." Id. 304. "No one reading the debates carefully," said Graham at 312, "will question the framers' devotion to federalism, even the extreme Radicals."

51. The Slaughter-House Cases, 83 U.S. (16 Wall.) 36, 82 (1872).

52. Kelly's remark in "Comment on Harold M. Hyman's Paper" in *New Frontiers of the American Reconstruction* 55 (Harold M. Hyman ed.), written in 1966, constitutes to my mind a tacit repudiation of his earlier pieces. Hyman notes Republican unwillingness "to travel any road more rugged than the Civil Rights—Freedmen's Bureau extension—Fourteenth Amendment route that left the states masters of their fates." Hyman, supra note 50 at 470; see also id. 440, 448.

is denied . . . or in any way abridged . . . the basis of representation therein shall be reduced.[53]

The denial is not prohibited, it is not declared void, but as Eckley of Ohio put it, if a State "persists in withholding the ballot" from blacks, she will be "confine[d] . . . to the white basis of representation."[54] It is difficult to dispute Justice Harlan's conclusion that § 2 "expressly recognizes the State's power to deny 'or in any way' abridge the right . . . to vote."[55] Were this doubtful, doubts are dispelled by the "blinding light" of the legislative history.[56] Since that is disputed by Van Alstyne and Justice Brennan, the evidence must be permitted to speak for itself, unfiltered by a commentator's paraphrase.

Bingham, a leading Republican member of the Joint Committee, the pillar of the neoabolitionists, said, "we all agree . . . that the exercise of the elective franchise . . . is exclusively under the control of the States . . . The amendment does not give, as the second section shows, the power of regulating suffrage in the several States."[57] Instead, as he said of a predecessor proviso, it "offers an inducement to those States . . . to make the franchise universal."[58] On the Senate side, Chairman Fessenden said of an earlier provision, H.R. No. 51, couched in terms of racial discrimination respecting suffrage, "It takes the Constitution just as it finds it, with the power in the States to fix the qualifications of suffrage precisely as they see fit . . . If in the exercise of the power you [States] have under the Constitution you make an inequality of rights, then you are to suffer such and such consequences."[59] When illness pre-

53. For earlier variants see James, Index, s.v. "Representation."
54. *Globe* 2535.
55. Reynolds v. Sims, 377 U.S. 533, 594.
56. Van Alstyne, 36, refers to "the kind of blinding light that Mr. Justice Harlan sees here."
57. *Globe* 2542.
58. Id. 432.
59. Id. 1279. Fessenden explained the Committee's espousal of the "representation" provision subsequently embodied in § 2: "we cannot put into the Constitution, owing to existing prejudices and existing institutions, an entire exclusion of all class distinctions." Id. 705. The effect of the proposed amendment, he stated, "is simply to leave the power where it is, and leave it perfectly in the power of the States to regulate suffrage as they please." Id.

vented Fessenden from explaining § 2, Senator Howard stated: "The second section leaves the right to regulate the elective franchise with the States, and does not meddle with that right." Later he added: "We know very well that the States retain the power which they have always possessed of regulating the right of suffrage . . . the theory of this whole amendment is to leave the power of regulating the suffrage with . . . the States."[60] Senator Yates of Illinois recognized that "we do not obtain suffrage now"; Senator Doolittle of Wisconsin stated, the "amendment proposes to allow the States to say who shall vote"; Senator Poland of Vermont would have preferred that "the right of suffrage had been given at once," but realized it was not "practicable"; Senator Howe of Wisconsin likewise preferred to say "no man shall be excluded from the right to vote" to saying "hereafter some men may be excluded from the right of representation."[61]

In the House, Blaine of Maine stated, "The effect contemplated . . . is perfectly well understood, and on all hands frankly avowed. It is to deprive the lately rebellious States of the unfair advantage of a large representation in this House, based on their colored population, so long as that people shall be denied political rights. Give them the vote or lose representation."[62] Conkling stated that the Joint Committee rejected

60. Id. 2766, 3039. Senator Wilson of Massachusetts stated that the "right to vote . . . has been regulated by the State in every State . . . from the beginning of the Government." Id. 1255. Senator Yates of Illinois did "not deny the power of the States to regulate suffrage." Id.

61. *Globe* 3038, 2943, 2963–2964, *Globe App.* 219. Senator Henderson had proposed an amendment to the "representation" proposal, prohibiting discrimination with respect to suffrage (id. 702), but he later supported "representation" because "the country is not yet prepared" for Negro suffrage. Id. 3035. Senator Reverdy Johnson, probably the most open-minded of the Democrats, understood the Amendment to concede "to the States . . . the exclusive right to regulate the franchise" so that the United States would "be impotent to redress" exclusion of blacks. *Globe* 3027. Another Democrat, Senator Davis, stated that the measure "shrinks from . . . openly forcing suffrage upon the States, but attempts by a great penalty to coerce them to accept it." *Globe App.* 240. See also Senator Hendricks, *Globe* 2939.

62. Id. 141. [Joint Committee on Reconstruction, Report No. 112, 39th Cong., 1st Sess. 7 (June 8, 1866), reprinted in Avins, *The Reconstruction Amendments' Debates* 94 (1967), referring to the effect of emancipation upon the three-fifths representation provision, stated: "When all become free, representation for all necessarily follows. As a consequence the inevitable effect of the rebellion would be to increase the political power of

proposals "to deprive the States of the power to disqualify or discriminate politically on account of race or color" and preferred "to leave every State perfectly free to decide for itself . . . who shall vote . . . and thus to say who shall enter into its basis of representation." "[E]very State," he reiterated, "will be left free to extend or withhold the elective franchise on such terms as it pleases, and this without losing anything in representation if the terms are impartial to all." And he summed up, "every State has the sole control, free from all interference, of its own interests and concerns," spelling out that if New York chose to withhold suffrage, "her right cannot be challenged."[63] Stevens, co-chairman of the Joint Committee, stated that the right of a State to disfranchise "has always existed under the Constitution" and the proposed "representation" provision "acknowledges it." He repeated that "the States have the right . . . to fix the elective franchise" and that the proposed representation provision "does not take it from them." In fact, he preferred the reduction of representation to an "immediate declaration" that "would make them [Negroes] all voters"; he did not "want them to have the right of suffrage" until they had been educated in "their duties . . . as citizens."[64] Although Garfield expressed his "profound regret" that the Joint Committee had been unable to "imbed . . . [suffrage] as a part of the fundamental law of the land," he stated, "I am willing . . . when I cannot get all I wish to take what I can get."[65] Similarly, John F. Farnsworth of Illinois stated, "I should prefer to see incorporated into the Constitution a guarantee of universal suffrage; as we cannot get the required two-thirds for that, I cordially support this proposition as the next best."[66]

Nathaniel P. Banks of Massachusetts congratulated the Joint Committee for "waiv[ing] this matter in deference to public opinion," and

---

the insurrectionary States . . . The increase of representation necessarily resulting from the abolition of slavery, was considered the most important element in the questions arising out of the changed condition of affairs, and the necessity for some fundamental action in this regard seemed imperative." The answer was section 2 of the Amendment.]

63. *Globe* 357, 358, 359.
64. Id. 428, 536.
65. Id. 2462.
66. Id. 2540.

George F. Miller of Pennsylvania stated, "This amendment will settle the complication in regard to suffrage and representation, leaving each State to regulate that for itself."[67] Against this mass three Democrats raised the possibility in the House that the amendment might affect suffrage qualifications.[68] On the other hand, leading Democrats—Senators Reverdy Johnson and Garrett Davis—better understood that it left suffrage to the States.[69] These historical materials, which by no means exhaust the quotable statements,[70] seem to me, as to Robert Dixon and Ward Elliott, "overpowering," "overwhelming."[71] In discreetly skirting the issue the Court tacitly acknowledged their unimpeachability. The rebuttal thus eschewed by Chief Justice Warren was undertaken by Professor Van Alstyne, and it emboldened Justice Brennan to pick up the cudgels in a later case, *Oregon v. Mitchell*.

Before examining the Warren and Brennan opinions it is desirable to consider in this setting the argument against reapportionment and its relation to suffrage.

67. Id. 2532, 2510.

68. Niblack, Benjamin M. Boyer of Pennsylvania, and Andrew J. Rogers of New Jersey. Justice Harlan comments on these statements in Oregon v. Mitchell, 400 U.S. at 181–182.

69. Supra note 61.

70. See supra note 55 at 626–632. Samuel McKee of Kentucky, who supported the Amendment, stated, "this House is not prepared to enfranchise all men." *Globe* 2505. William D. Kelley of Pennsylvania said, "Could I have controlled the report of the Committee of Fifteen, it would have proposed to give the right of suffrage to every loyal man." Id. 2469. Boutwell of Massachusetts stated, "The proposition in the matter of suffrage falls short of what I desire . . . I demand . . . the franchise for all loyal citizens." Id. 2508. But like others of the same persuasion, he voted for the Amendment.

Broomall understood § 2 "to limit the representation of the several States as those States themselves shall limit suffrage." Id. 2498. Lawrence said that the "representation" amendment "does not propose to extend the right of suffrage to or to withhold it from any class of people . . . It does not propose to disturb the commonly received construction of the Constitution which leaves to the State the right to determine who shall or shall not be voters." Id. 404. G. F. Miller of Pennsylvania conceded "to each State the right to regulate the right of suffrage . . . they ought not to have a representation for" excluded persons. The Amendment "leav[es] each State to regulate that for itself." *Globe* 2510. See also Thayer, id. 282; Eliot, id. 2511.

71. Robert Dixon, "Reapportionment in the Supreme Court and Congress: Constitutional Struggle for Fair Representation," 63 Mich. L. Rev. 209, 212 (1964); Elliott, supra note 4 at 127.

## Supplementary Note on Suffrage

My view, echoing that of Justice Harlan, is that the framers excluded suffrage from the Fourteenth Amendment. Consideration of the opposing view will be facilitated by encapsulating a few striking evidential items. Section 2 of the Amendment provides that if suffrage is denied on account of race, the State's representation in the House of Representatives shall be proportionately reduced. Senator William Fessenden, chairman of the Joint Committee on Reconstruction, explained that this "leaves the power where it is but tells them [the States] most distinctly, if you exercise the power wrongfully, such and such consequences will follow.[1] Senator Jacob Howard of Michigan, to whom it fell to explain the Amendment because of Fessenden's illness, said,

> We know very well that the States retain the power . . . of regulating the right of suffrage in the States . . . the theory of this whole amendment is, to leave the power of regulating the suffrage with . . . the States, and not to assume to regulate it by any clause of the Constitution.[2]

Howard is confirmed by the Report of the Joint Committee, which drafted the Amendment: "It was doubtful . . . whether the States would surrender a power they had always exercised, and to which they were attached."

---

1. *The Reconstruction Amendments' Debates* 143 (Alfred Avins ed. 1967).

2. Id. 237. A leading Reconstruction historian, C. Vann Woodward, concluded that section 2 of the Fourteenth Amendment "was not primarily devised for the protection of the negro and the provision of negro equality. Its primary purpose . . . was to put the southern states" under Northern control. C. Vann Woodward, "Seeds of Failure in Radical Race Policy," in *New Frontiers of the American Reconstruction* 135 (Harold M. Hyman ed. 1966). For confirmatory historical facts, see Raoul Berger, "Cottrol's Failed Rescue Mission," 37 B.C. L. Rev. 481, 484–485 (1986).

In 1862, John Bingham stated in the 37th Congress that we have "no power whatever over" the right to vote. "The right to vote does not involve the right to citizenship." "The Federal Government has no power to regulate the elective franchise in any state." Avins, supra note 1 at 37.

In consequence the committee recommended Section 2 because it "would leave the whole question with the people of each State."[3] It was this "gap" in the Fourteenth Amendment that led to the adoption of the Fifteenth, which prohibited discrimination with respect to voting on racial grounds.[4] The Fifteenth, the Supreme Court said, testifies that suffrage was not conferred by the Fourteenth Amendment.[5] Justly did Justice Harlan conclude after his own exhaustive survey of the debates that the evidence was "irrefutable and still unanswered."[6] Commentators are widely agreed that suffrage was excluded from the reach of the Fourteenth Amendment.[7]

3. Avins, id. 94. Justice Harlan, who carefully combed the debates, stated, "Not once, during the three days of debate, did any supporter of the Amendment criticize or correct any of the Republicans or Democrats who observed that the Amendment left the ballot exclusively under the control of the States." Oregon v. Mitchell, 400 U.S. 112, 186 (1970), dissenting in part.

For an example of willful disregard of crystal-clear evidence, consider the comments of Justices Brennan, White, and Thurgood Marshall on Justice Harlan's evidence: "We could not accept this thesis even if it were supported by historical evidence far stronger than anything adduced here today. But in our view, our Brother Harlan's historical analysis is flawed by his ascription of 20th-century meanings to the words of 19th-century legislators. In consequence, his analysis imposes an artificial simplicity upon a complex era, and presents, as universal, beliefs that were held by merely one of several groups competing for political power. We can accept neither his judicial conclusion nor his historical premise that the original understanding of the Fourteenth Amendment left it within the power of the States to deny the vote to Negro citizens." Oregon v. Mitchell, 400 U.S. at 251. They brush off the unequivocal explanations of the chairman of the Joint Committee on Reconstruction, of the Senate spokesman who sought to explain the bill, and of the Joint Committee itself. On this issue there *were* no opposing remarks.

4. Raoul Berger, "The Fourteenth Amendment: Light From the Fifteenth," 74 Nw. U. L. Rev. 311, 321–323 (1979). Reprinted in Raoul Berger, *Selected Writings on the Constitution* 148 (1987).

5. United States v. Reese, 92 U.S. 214, 217–218 (1875); Minor v. Happersett, 88 U.S. (21 Wall.) 162, 175 (1874). In March 1869, William Higby, who had been a member of the 39th Congress, stated that the Fifteenth Amendment "insures certain rights . . . not expressed in any part of the Constitution." Avins, supra note 1 at 417.

6. Griswold v. Connecticut, 381 U.S. 479–501 (1965).

7. Henry Abraham, "Book Review," 6 Hastings Const. L.Q. 467–468 (1979); Robert Dixon, "Reapportionment in the Supreme Court and Congress: Constitutional Struggle for Fair Representation," 63 Mich. L. Rev. 209, 212 (1964); Ward E. Y. Elliott, *The Rise of a Guardian Democracy* 127 (1974); Gerald Gunther, "Too Much a Battle With Strawmen," Wall St. J., Nov. 25, 1977, at 4; Morton Keller, *Affairs of State* 66 (1977); Wallace Mendelson, "Book Review," 6 Hastings Const. L.Q. 437, 452–453 (1979); Nathaniel

My reliance on Senator Howard and others indicates to William Nelson that I read "the intention of the authors and ratifiers of the Fourteenth Amendment narrowly," that is, as "not intended . . . to grant blacks voting rights."[8] Yet he notes that "the statement most frequently made in debates on the Fourteenth Amendment is that it did not, in and of itself, confer upon blacks . . . the right to vote."[9] The saving phrase "in and of itself" presumably reflects his fondness for newspaper articles, which prompted him to criticize Alexander Bickel because "Bickel did not spend time examining newspapers systematically,"[10] as if such articles could overcome unequivocal statements in the debates.[11]

More noteworthy are the comments by Chief Justice Warren and Justice Brennan. "The conception of political equality," said Warren, "can mean only one thing—one person–one vote."[12] The framers, however, made unmistakably plain that control of suffrage was to be left to the States notwithstanding their provision for "equal protection." Thus Warren fashioned a principle to override the unmistakable will of the framers. In the eyes of Justice Brennan, the historical record is "vague and imprecise";[13] hence he reasons that "Recognition of the principle 'one man, one vote' as a constitutional one redeems the promise of self-governance by affirming the essential dignity of every citizen to equal participation in the democratic process."[14] In their exercise of *actual* "self-governance," the people adopted the Fifteenth, Sixteenth, and Twenty-sixth Amendments, thereby adjudging that expansion of federal

---

Nathanson, "Book Review," 56 Tex. L. Rev. 579, 581 (1978). For additional citations see Berger, supra note 4 at 311 note 4.

8. William Nelson, *The Fourteenth Amendment: From Political Principle to Judicial Doctrine* 3 (1988).

9. Id. 125. "Most congressional Republicans were aware of (and shared) their constituents' hostility to black suffrage." Keller, supra note 7 at 66–67.

10. Nelson, supra note 8 at 6.

11. Daniel Farber wrote that Nelson "devotes virtually no attention to those debates." Daniel Farber, "Book Review," 6 Const. Commentary 364–365 (1989). For a critique of Nelson's views, see Raoul Berger, "Fantasizing About the Fourteenth Amendment," 1990 Wis. L. Rev. 1043.

12. Reynolds v. Sims, 377 U.S. 533, 558 (1964).

13. Oregon v. Mitchell, 400 U.S. 112, 278 (1970), dissenting in part.

14. Address by Justice Brennan, Georgetown Univ., Oct. 1, 1985, in *The Great Debate: Interpreting the Constitution* 11, 22 (1986).

jurisdiction over suffrage required action by the people themselves, never mind the demands of "dignity." Brennan's attachment to "human dignity" led him to pronounce that it is offended by capital punishment, though he acknowledges that neither the majority of the people nor that of the Court share his view.[15] For him the clear implication of the due process clauses that life may be taken after a fair trial is of no moment. In the face of the ineluctable facts, the conclusions of Warren and Brennan seem to me perverse.

Mention of the Fifteenth Amendment recalls John Hart Ely's assertion that adoption of that Amendment is "extremely damaging . . . to Berger's general claim of the dominance of 'Negrophobia.' "[16] Instead of testifying to abatement of racial prejudice, the Fifteenth Amendment was a response to shifting political exigencies. The primary goal, William Gillette concluded, was enfranchisement of Negroes "outside the deep South" in order to obtain the necessary swing votes of Negroes in the North. A secondary objective, he found, "was to protect the southern Negro against future disfranchisement,"[17] for it had become apparent that military occupation must come to an end and continued control must rest on Negro voters, who would help perpetuate Republican ascendancy.[18] Thaddeus Stevens, leader of the Radicals, therefore began drafting the Amendment "to save the Republican party from defeat."[19] Senator Oliver Morton of Indiana, who had opposed Negro suffrage, now embraced it "as a political necessity."[20] With Negro votes the Republicans could hope to stay in power, the primary aim from the very beginning.[21] Contrast Ely's denial of "the dominance of 'Negropho-

---

15. *The Great Debate*, supra note 14 at 24.

16. John Hart Ely, *Democracy and Distrust* 200 note 70 (1980). Ely was anticipated by Judge John Gibbons, "Book Review," 31 Rutgers L. Rev. 839, 845 (1978). My failure to regard the Fifteenth Amendment as evidence of the abatement of racism is labeled by Gibbons as a "glaring example" of "a narrow, confused, partisan example of special pleading." Id.

17. William Gillette, *The Right to Vote: Politics and the Passage of the Fifteenth Amendment* 46–47, 49–50 (1965).

18. For citations see Berger, supra note 4 at 317 note 34.

19. Gillette, supra note 17 at 34.

20. Id. 57.

21. For citations see Berger, supra note 4 at 317 note 37.

bia'" with the 1869 statement by Senator Henry Wilson, the Massachusetts Radical: "There is not today a square mile in the United States where the advocacy of the equal rights and privileges of those colored men has not been in the past and is not now unpopular."[22] So much, then, for activist denials that suffrage was excluded from the Fourteenth Amendment.

22. *Cong. Globe* (40th Cong., 3d Sess.) 672 (1869).

# 5

# *Reapportionment*

B*AKER v. Carr* (1962), the unprecedented reapportionment decision, said Paul Kauper, opened a "new chapter of judicial adventurism."[1] When the issue was once again presented in *Reynolds v. Sims*, Justice Harlan wrote a dissent that to my mind is irrefutable. The majority of the Court made no pretense of meeting his historical demonstration; it remained for William Van Alstyne to essay a rebuttal. Harlan's reliance on the legislative history to establish the "original understanding," Van Alstyne writes, pertains solely to "exclusive state power over suffrage qualifications" and has no bearing on "the separate issue of malapportionment"; "there was almost no mention of the subject."[2] That fact alone gives one pause: how can a revolution in *Northern* apportionment be based on nonmention?

The dominant purpose of the 39th Congress was to maintain Republican hegemony by reducing Southern representation; and only sec-

1. Paul Kauper, "Some Comments on the Reapportionment Cases," 63 Mich. L. Rev. 243, 244 (1964). In more restrained diction, Archibald Cox instances the reapportionment cases as a "dramatic" example of "reading into the generalities of the Due Process and Equal Protection Clauses notions of wise and fundamental policy which are not even faintly suggested by the words of the Constitution, and which lack substantial support in other conventional sources of law." *The Role of the Supreme Court in American Government* 100 (1976).

Reapportionment may have been "wise," but did it represent the kind of emergency situation that at best arguably excuses judicial revision? Philip Kurland considers that "reapportionment of the state and local legislatures was not among the more pressing problems in post–World War II America." *Politics, the Constitution and the Warren Court* 83 (1970). For an extended and persuasive demonstration that reapportionment was not necessary, see Ward Elliott, *The Rise of a Guardian Democracy* (1974).

2. Van Alstyne 78–79.

ondarily did they think to secure the "person and property" of the Negro from oppression.[3] There were repeated disclaimers of any intention
to interfere with State sovereignty beyond those objectives. Moreover,
while Negro suffrage was predominantly a Southern problem, reapportionment would invade long-established State practices with respect to
*white* voters in the North.[4] But Van Alstyne argues that to read malapportionment in the equal protection clause "is to say *only* that among the
enfranchised [white] elite," qualified by the State to vote, "no invidious
distinction shall be permitted. The States may be as capricious as they
please in withholding the ballot but not in perpetuating elites within the
elite."[5] That is a tremendous "only." Republicans who shrank from interfering with State control of Negro suffrage in the South would
scarcely have dared to impose on the North a radical reconstruction of
white apportionment patterns.[6] Certainly there was no disclosure that

3. Supra Chapter 1 at note 55; Chapter 4 at note 4; Kendrick 207; cf. Van Alstyne 57.

4. Chief Justice Warren, Alfred Kelly states, "carefully neglected the far more important fact that every one of the state legislatures that sent delegates to Philadelphia was
grossly malapportioned by any 'one man, one vote' standard, and the state conventions
that ratified the Constitution were in every instance set up on the same rule of apportionment." "Clio and the Court: An Illicit Love Affair," 1965 S. Ct. Rev. 119 at 136–137.
Justice Story, commenting on the possible introduction of a clause "to regulate the State
elections of members of State legislatures" stated, "It would be deemed a most unwar-
rantable transfer of power, indicating a premeditated design to destroy the State governments. It would be deemed so flagrant a violation of principle as to require no comment." 1 Joseph Story, *Commentaries on the Constitution of the United States* §819 (5th ed.
1905). [In the Convention Nathaniel Gorham said, "[T]he Constitution of [Massachu-
setts] had provided that the [representatives of the] larger districts should not be in an
exact ratio of their numbers. And experience he thought had shewn the provision to be
expedient." 1 *The Records of the Federal Convention of 1787* 405 (Max Farrand ed. 1911).
In the First Congress, Representative Michael Stone of Maryland said, "the representatives of the States were chosen by the States in the manner they pleased." 1 *Annals of
Congress* 765 (1834).]

5. Van Alstyne 80. Stevens stated that "This section [2] allows the States to discriminate *among the same class*, and receive proportionate credit in representation." *Globe* 2460
(emphasis added). So too, the antecedent Civil Rights Bill, Shellabarger stated, "does not
prohibit you from discriminating between citizens of the same race . . . as to what their
rights to testify, to inherit . . . shall be." *Globe* 1293.

6. With reference to a bill introduced by Sumner in March 1867, David Donald states,
"Disturbed by the revolutionary changes Sumner hoped to bring about in the South,
Republican Congressmen were horrified that he proposed to extend them to the North
as well," among them to secure "the elective franchise to colored citizens." Donald, *Sum-*

such intrusion was contemplated;[7] there is in fact striking evidence that malapportionment was an accepted practice. Speaking with respect to reduced representation, Blaine of Maine said,

> if you cut off the blacks from being enumerated in the basis of representation in the southern States the white population of those States will immediately distribute Representatives within their own territory on the basis of white population. Therefore the most densely populated negro districts will not be allowed to offset the most densely populated white districts . . . Do you suppose that the upland districts of Georgia and South Carolina, inhabited largely by whites, will, in the event of adoption of this amendment, allow the distribution of Representatives to be made on the basis of the whole population? By no means. They will at once insist on the white basis within the State.[8]

---

*ner II* 299. Bickel, 16 note 40, states that "Conservative Republicans who considered the Freedmen's Bureau Bill [applicable only in the South] an appropriate concession to offer to the Radicals, evidently felt quite differently about a statute which might be applied in their constituencies." "[N]ational enfranchisement of the Negro—which meant Negro voting in the North—was out of the question." William Gillette, *The Right to Vote: Politics and the Passage of the Fifteenth Amendment* 32 (1965). See also Harold M. Hyman, *A More Perfect Union* 470 (1973).

7. When the Amendment was submitted to the States for ratification, "the northern press," states Flack at 145, "with few exceptions, if any, took the view that the first section of the Amendment re-enacted or gave authority for, the Civil Rights Bill." He quotes a speech of Trumbull in Chicago: § 1 "was a reiteration of the Civil Rights Bill"; and one of Sherman in Cincinnati: "the first section embodied the Civil Rights Bill"; id. 148.

Justice Black, that fervent advocate of reapportionment (Wesberry v. Sanders, 376 U.S. 1 [1964]), stated in his earlier attempt to read corporations out of the Fourteenth Amendment that "the people were not told they [were ratifying] an amendment granting new and revolutionary rights to corporations." Connecticut General Ins. Co. v. Johnson, 303 U.S. 77, 86 (1938), dissenting opinion. Compare supra Chapter 1 note 57. Justice Field, dissenting in Ex parte Virginia, 100 U.S. 339, 362–363 (1879), stated that the provision for Negro jurors was "a change so radical . . . [as] was never contemplated by the recent amendments. The people, in adopting them did not suppose they were altering the fundamental theory of their dual system of government." As we have seen, the framers actually contemplated the continued exclusion of Negro jurors. But the selfsame Field had no difficulty in advocating the tremendous alteration embodied in substantive due process.

8. *Globe* 377. Malapportionment was fastened on the Constitution from the outset by the compromise which permitted three-fifths of the voteless Negro population to be counted for purposes of representation in the House of Representatives. Thereby, as John

Not a hint that this would be unlawful, but, rather, clear recognition that States were free to apportion representation to suit themselves. Although, as Van Alstyne notices, this would leave "areas populated by non-voters without representation (and not merely without a vote in the choice of 'their' representatives),"[9] Bingham replied, "no possible amendment . . . will answer the purpose unless it is followed by further legislation."[10] Bingham thus confirms Blaine's recital of the plenary State power over apportionment and implies that the "representation" (§ 2) proposal was not designed to meet this situation. Van Alstyne's comment that "Blaine's remarks were directed only to the apportionment of congressional rather than state representation" implausibly suggests that the States would be readier to surrender control over their own internal patterns—a suggestion that is incompatible with the pervasive attachment to State sovereignty.

Blaine's remarks did not reflect a fleeting improvisation, but responded to established practice. Earlier he had stated: "As an abstract proposition no one will deny that population is the true basis of representation; for women, children and other nonvoting classes may have as vital an interest in the legislation . . . as those who actually cast the ballot." But, he noted, recognizing existing practice, as had Federalist No. 54 and James Wilson long before,[11] "the ratio of voters to population differs very widely in different sections, from a minimum of *nineteen per cent* to a maximum of *fifty-eight per cent*."[12] Even that uncompromising abolitionist Charles Sumner was reconciled to such practices because they reflected "custom and popu-

---

Quincy Adams remarked, "Every planter South of the Potomac has three votes in effect for every five slaves he keeps in bondage; while a New England farmer who contributes ten-fold as much to the support of the Government has only a single vote" (Nov. 8, 1804). Quoted in Samuel F. Bemis, *John Quincy Adams and the Foundation of American Foreign Policy* 123 note 37 (1949). The result was to give the South twenty-five additional members and to "enable the slave power to keep its grip on the nation." Samuel F. Bemis, *John Quincy Adams and the Union* 417, 446 (1956). Malapportionment was also embedded in the Constitution by the provision for two Senators from each State, although, as Thomas Hartley remarked in the First Congress, "their proportions are as ten to one." 1 *Annals of Congress* 481.

9. Van Alstyne 79 note 142.
10. Id.
11. Infra at notes 26–27, 69–70.
12. *Globe* 141.

lar faith," and could not be changed "unless supported by the permanent feelings and conditions of the people."[13] Then, too, in the congressional debate of June 1868 (that is, prior to ratification of the Fourteenth Amendment), on the readmission of the rebel States, Farnsworth pointed out that the Florida apportionment provision gave "to the sparsely populated portions of the State the control of the Legislature." But Ben Butler responded that the Senate Judiciary Committee "have found the [Florida] constitution republican and proper," as did the Senate, the House Committee on Reconstruction,[14] and the House itself, thus reaffirming that such malapportionment did not violate the guarantee of a "republican form of government," nor the equal protection clause which was the work of Butler and his fellows. The Blaine, Sumner, and Butler statements constitute hard evidence which is not overcome by mere speculation.[15] Since, moreover, most of the States were malapportioned, it is a strained as-

13. "The true basis for representation, Sumner declared in a speech to the [Massachusetts] convention on July 7 [1853], should ideally be founded 'absolutely upon equality' so as to make all men, in the enjoyment of the electoral franchise, whatever their diversity of intelligence, education or wealth, and wheresoever they may be within the Commonwealth, whether in small towns or populous city, 'absolutely equal at the ballot box.' But, he swiftly backtracked, this system of equal representation could not be advantageously instituted 'unless supported by the permanent feelings and conditions of the people.' As the practice of giving Massachusetts small towns disproportionate influence had sprung 'from custom and popular faith, silently operating with internal power, not from the imposed will of a lawgiver' . . . no radical change in the admittedly inequitable system should be tried at present, but instead the rural towns should be given more representation so as to protect the Commonwealth against the 'commercial feudalism' of the big cities." Donald, *Sumner I* 246, quoting 3 Sumner, *Works* 229–258. See supra note 4.

14. Quoted in Reynolds v. Sims, 377 U.S. 533, 605 (1964). Stevens likewise stated that the several constitutions had been pronounced "republican in form." Id. 604 note 42.

15. See Van Alstyne, quoted infra at note 17. "[T]o quarrel with the records without abundant cause is to engage in a desperate cause." H. G. Richardson and G. O. Sayles, "Parliament and Great Councils in Medieval England," 77 L. Q. Rev. 213, 235–236 (1961). Roughly speaking, unless testimony is inherently incredible it must be countered by evidence, not speculation. Phillips v. Gookin, 231 Mass. 250 , 251, 120 N.E. 691 (1918); Messon v. Liberty Fast Freight Co. 124 F.2d 448, 450 (2d Cir. 1942); Eckenrode v. Pennsylvania R. Co., 164 F.2d 996, 999 note 8 (3d Cir. 1947); cf. Miller v. Herzfeld, 4 F.2d 355, 356 (3d Cir. 1925); Magg v. Miller, 296 F. 973, 979 (D.C. Cir. 1924).

sumption that by ratification they surrendered a right they had excercised from the outset, and of which surrender they were totally unapprised.[16]

When Van Alstyne dismissed Harlan's reading of the § 2 phrase "or in any way abridged" because "once the congressional history" of this phrase is "canvassed . . . it becomes clear that the phrase had nothing at all to do with malapportionment," he scuttled his whole case. For, by the same token, the history of the equal protection clause likewise "had nothing at all to do with malapportionment." "There is," he states, "no evidence that § 2 was applicable to abridgment of the right to vote resulting from malapportionment of state legislatures." "It is even likely," he avers, "that had the subject been discussed there might have been a disavowal of an intention to apply the Equal Protection Clause to malapportionment." But "hypothetical answers to hypothetical questions . . . would be a most dubious basis for expounding the content of 'equal protection' one hundred years later."[17] There is no need to speculate because Blaine and others plainly recognized malapportionment as an existing practice that was left untouched. I, too, prefer to eschew speculation, particularly when it is unnecessary. One who would bring an unmentioned depar-

16. After cataloging the "malapportioned" States, Justice Harlan asked, "Can it be seriously contended that the legislatures of the States, almost two-thirds of those concerned, would have ratified an amendment which might render their own State constitutions unconstitutional?" 377 U.S. at 603.

17. Van Alstyne 80, 81, 85. Alfred Kelly also dismisses Harlan's argument; "it neglected one embarrassing fact: both the provision of § 2 and the extensive debate . . . were directed at the possibility of a state's limiting Negro franchise and not to the problem of district legislative apportionment, an entirely different historical question." Kelly, "Clio," supra note 4 at 137. Notwithstanding the difference, Chief Justice Warren built his reapportionment case on "one man, one vote." Because of this "embarrassing fact" Kelly charges that Harlan "indulged in a bit of law office history of his own." Id. That charge, as the above analysis of the same argument by Van Alstyne demonstrates, is without foundation. Nor is Kelly the man to cast stones.

He recorded that when he was retained in the desegregation case to file a historical brief for the NAACP (Kelly, Fourteenth, 1049n), he "manipulated history in the best tradition [?] of American advocacy, carefully marshalling every scrap of evidence in favor of the desired interpretation and just as carefully doctoring all the evidence to the contrary, either by suppressing it when that seemed plausible, or by distorting it when suppression was not possible." Kelly, "Clio," supra note 4 at 144. That is an astonishing admission from a *scholar* who upbraids the Court because it "carefully selected the materials designed to prove the thesis at hand, suppressing all data that might impeach the desired historical conclusion." Kelly, "Clio," supra note 4 at 126.

ture from settled practice within the perimeter of the Amendment has the burden of proof, made heavier here by (1) the fact that Negro suffrage, on which the Court rested its case for reapportionment, was unmistakably excluded; (2) the plainly expressed attachment of the framers to State sovereignty and their intention to intrude no further than the limits of the Civil Rights Act; and (3) the presumption that a diminution of powers reserved to the States by the Tenth Amendment will be clearly stated.[18]

In one form or another, Van Alstyne would put asunder what the Warren Court hath joined; he would jettison the Court's "one man, one vote" postulate. Granting arguendo State power "with respect to outright denials of the right to vote," he asks, "is it equally so with respect to partial disfranchisement through malapportionment?"[19] The simple answer is that the greater includes the less.[20] If a State may altogether *deny* the vote, it may *dilute* it. It was in these terms that Chief Justice Warren rationalized reapportionment: the Constitution, he held, protects the right to "vote," the "right to have one's vote counted." And "the right of

18. See supra Chapter 1 note 57. "An alleged surrender . . . of a power of government . . . must be shown by clear and unequivocal language; it cannot be inferred from . . . any doubtful or uncertain expressions." Belmont Bridge v. Wheeling Bridge, 138 U.S. 287, 292–293 (1891).

Even where States were forbidden to legislate with respect to a particular subject and Congress was empowered to enforce the prohibition, Justice Bradley rejected the assumption that "this gives Congress power to legislate generally upon that subject" as "repugnant to the Tenth amendment." Civil Rights Cases, 109 U.S. 3, 15 (1883). In the Slaughter-House Cases, 83 U.S. (16 Wall.) 36, 78 (1872), Justice Miller rejected a construction which would subject States "to the control of Congress, in the exercise of powers heretofore universally conceded to them" in the absence of "language which expresses such a purpose too clearly to admit of doubt." One may differ with his construction of the Fourteenth Amendment, but the fact remains that he was neither the first nor last to state that rule.

[In United States v. Darby, 312 U.S. 100, 124 (1941), Justice Stone stated, "(the Tenth Amendment) states but a truism that all is retained which has not been surrendered." It was merely "declaratory of the relationship between the national and State governments"; its purpose was "to allay fears that the new federal government might seek to exercise powers not granted, and that the States might not be able to exercise fully their reserved powers."]

19. Van Alstyne 80.

20. "Nothing is more evident than that the greater must include the less." Minor v. Happersett, 88 U.S. (21 Wall.) 162, 175 (1874).

suffrage can be denied by a debasement or dilution of the weight of a citizen's vote just as effectively as by wholly prohibiting the free exercise of the franchise."[21] His premise—that the Constitution, that is, the Fourteenth Amendment, protects the right to vote—is contradicted by historical facts. But his logic is impeccable and may be stated inversely: given a right to deny suffrage, it follows that there is a right to dilute it.

## Republican Form of Government

One of the "other" powers invoked by radical extremists was the guarantee of a "republican form of government."[22] Senator Sumner, its leading advocate, could do no better than to find it "obscure" and to write in 1865 that "the time has come to fix meaning to those words."[23] They were not wrapped in obscurity by the Founders. In the Federal Convention, Edmund Randolph stated that "a republican government must be the basis of a national union; and no state in it ought to have it in their power to *change* its government into a monarchy."[24] This was echoed by Madison in Federalist No. 43: "the superintending government ought clearly to possess authority to defend the system against aristocratic or monarchical innovations . . . [the members of the Union have] the right to insist that the *forms* of government under which the compact was *entered* should be substantially *maintained.*" The guarantee "sup-

21. Reynolds v. Sims, 377 U.S. 533, 554, 555. "The fundamental issue, as [Solicitor General Archibald Cox] puts it, is whether the State law 'arbitrarily and unreasonably apportions its legislature so as to deny the real meaning of the right to vote, i.e., effective participation in democratic government.' " Phil C. Neal, "Baker v. Carr: Politics in Search of Law," 1962 S. Ct. Rev. 252, 285.

My study of the "republican form of government" guarantee, infra at notes 22–47, persuaded me that the Founders had no intention of interfering with State control of suffrage. Justice Stewart's opinion (concurring and dissenting in part) in Oregon v. Mitchell, 400 U.S. 112, 288–290 (1970), pulls together the other textual and historical materials that confirm me in that view.

22. Van Alstyne 49–51.

23. Hyman, supra note 6 at 469. Sumner early invoked the "republican form of government" guarantee to secure blacks against "denial of rights, civil or political," and to make them "equal before the law." *Globe* 92.

24. 1 Max Farrand, *The Records of the Federal Convention of 1787* 206 (1911) (emphasis added).

poses a *preexisting* government of the *form* which is to be guaranteed. As long, therefore, as the *existing* republican forms are *continued* by the States they are guaranteed by the federal Constitution."[25] Although Federalist No. 52 stated that the "definition of the right of suffrage is very justly regarded as a fundamental act of republican government," it concluded that the right must be left to the States because "the different qualifications in the different States [could not be reduced] to one uniform rule."[26] Finally, Federalist No. 54, alluding to the allocation of representation according to the number of inhabitants, added, "the right of choosing their allotted number in each State is to be exercised by such part of the inhabitants as the State itself may designate . . . In every State, a certain proportion of inhabitants are deprived of this right by the Constitution of the State."[27]

Fessenden therefore stood on solid ground when he rebutted Sumner's reliance on the guarantee, saying, "in the very instrument in which the fathers provided that the United States should guaranty to every State a republican form of government they recognized the existence of slavery unmistakably . . . Did they then consider that the obligation to guaranty a republican form of government extended thus far, giving Congress the right to interfere in Virginia to examine her constitution?" When Sumner argued that the guarantee places Congress under a duty to "see that every man votes who ought to vote," said Fessenden, "he goes considerably further than those who made the Constitution ever intended to go." If a State "should choose to have a monarchy, or the controlling portion of the people should choose to have an oligarchy, it then becomes the duty of Congress to interfere."[28] Such was the view of the Fathers, and it was reiterated by other leaders in the 39th Congress. Meeting a query whether a State would "cease to be republican" if it excluded a race from the franchise, Conkling responded that this "has

25. Federalist 282, 283 (emphasis added).
26. Id. 341–342.
27. Id. 356.
28. *Globe* 706. David Donald comments that Sumner's program met with little favor in his own Massachusetts, that it "was not taken seriously," and that his "Republican colleagues greeted his resolutions and bills" with "total silence." Donald, *Sumner II* 234, 235, 240, 243.

always been permitted with universal acquiescence by the courts and the nation."[29] On the admission of Tennessee without provision for Negro enfranchisement, Bingham said in July 1866 that if this was in violation of the guarantee, then Tennessee was in the company of many Northern States. His critics were defeated by a vote of 125 to 12.[30] In the Senate, Trumbull stated, "most of us are here under republican forms of government, just like this in Tennessee."[31]

One of the dissentients, William Higby of California—whom Van Alstyne quotes as saying that no "State which excludes any class of citizens [from voting] on account of race or color is republican in form," and that he was opposed to H.R. No. 51 because "it gives a power to the States to make governments that are not republican in form,"[32]— revealed tellingly that he was merely engaged in wishful thinking. He admitted that by his disenfranchisement test his own State of California is "not republican in form": "I do not believe there is a single State in the Union, except it may be one of the New England States, which is an exception to that general rule ... Now, sir, I am aware that the practice has been very different ... from the establishment of the Government."[33] When Ralph Hill of Indiana stated that, in placing the guarantee in the Constitution, the Framers "spoke with reference to such governments as then existed, and such as these same framers recognized for a long time afterwards as republican governments," Higby replied: "that is a very good answer. It is an answer from a standpoint of seventy-five years ago. I speak from the standpoint of the present time."[34] Like our contemporary apologists for a judicial revisionary power, Higby would

---

29. *Globe* 358–359.

30. Id. 3980. Two of Van Alstyne's dissentients, Higby and Kelley, were among the twelve who voted against the admission.

31. Id. 3988.

32. Van Alstyne 50.

33. *Globe* 427.

34. Id. Shellabarger admitted that although the Southern States disenfranchised blacks, they have "been by common consent regarded as republican and constitutional." Id. 405. See also Thomas A. Jenckes of Rhode Island, id. 387. Replying to Sumner's argument that the limitation of suffrage to whites in the Colorado constitution violated the "republican form of government," Senator Stewart stated, "Nineteen of the free States now exclude blacks from the franchise." Id. 1330–1331.

displace the established, original meaning with his own new one. Given that the Northern States discriminated against voting by blacks, "they were as subject to reconstruction by the federal authority" as was the South. For Radicals, "this whole argument contained political dynamite";[35] and Higby himself admitted, "I do not know that there are half a dozen in this House who will sustain me."[36] Like the 125 to 12 vote on the admission of Tennessee, Higby's concession underscores the framers' indifference to the dissentient views on which Van Alstyne largely pitches his case.

Is it to be wondered that the Court, as Carl Auerbach noted, "agreed in Baker v. Carr that 'any reliance' on the Guarantee clause would be futile?" Auerbach pointed out that the Court "never adequately answered Mr. Justice Frankfurter's argument that the equal protection claim it held to be justiciable was 'in effect a Guarantee Clause claim masquerading under a different label.' In fact the Court was being asked 'to establish an appropriate form of government . . . for all the States in the Union.' "[37] Congress, as Auerbach noticed, had expressed its judgment, in one form or another, "as to the nature of a republican form of government," and it is Congress, not the Court, *Luther v. Borden* held, to whom that function is confided.[38] Where is the evidence that the

35. Donald, *Sumner II* 202.

36. *Globe* 427.

37. Auerbach, "The Reapportionment Cases: One Person, One Vote—One Vote, One Value," 1964 S. Ct. Rev. 1, 85. "Yet to rest the *Reapportionment Cases* on the Guarantee Clause creates difficulties of its own which must be evaluated . . . Historically the system of legislative representation prevailing in a State was intended to be subject to the requirements of the Guarantee Clause while, as we saw, the Equal Protection Clause was not originally intended to deal with this matter." Id. Paul Kauper likewise was critical of the conversion of equal protection to the guarantee of a republican form of government. "This is the central issue in these cases—what form of government is compatible with a representative form of government—and the guarantee of a republican form of government is the explicit constitutional provision relevant to the problem." Kauper, supra note 1 at 244.

38. Auerbach, supra note 37 at 86; 48 U.S. (7 How.) 1 (1849). Auerbach notices the "serious difficulty" posed by the fact that "Congress has admitted states into the Union and declared their forms of government to be 'republican,' even though their constitutions authorized systems of apportionment that the Court would now declare unconstitutional. It would be awkward for the Court to say not only that it has a role in enforcing the Guarantee Clause but that it also may overrule the expressed judgment of

framers who rejected the argument that Congress had power over State suffrage by virtue of the "republican form of government" guarantee meant to confer that power by the "equal protection" clause? It speaks volumes that Sumner, who employed "equality before the law" in a school desegregation case (wherein Chief Justice Shaw held against him),[39] should have turned to the "republican form of government" guarantee in the 39th Congress. After passage of the Amendment he proposed that the admission of Tennessee and Nebraska be conditioned upon no denial of suffrage, a confession that the "equal protection" clause did not preclude such denials.[40]

Van Alstyne attaches considerable weight to Bingham's "unusually rewarding" appeal to "a republican form of government," which Bingham translated as a guarantee of the "right of franchise."[41] His view was not shared by influential Republicans, and in the course of the debates he shifted his position, stating, "we all agree . . . that the exercise of the elective franchise . . . is exclusively under the control of the States."[42] Shortly thereafter he changed course on the very "republican form" guarantee. He had moved for the admission of Tennessee, and Boutwell proposed "a condition precedent" that would require Tennessee to establish "suffrage for all male citizens," without which, he argued, Tennessee would not have a "republican form of government" because of

---

Congress as to the nature of a republican form of government" (in an area which Luther v. Borden held was not for the Court but for Congress). "The Court," Auerbach continues, "thinks it has avoided this contradiction of Congress by resting on the Equal Protection Clause . . . but the Court's explanation is not very satisfactory." Id. 86.

Auerbach finds solace in Justice Frankfurter's statement that "if the 'changing circumstances of a progressive society' for which the Constitution was designed 'yield new and fuller' import to the language of the Equal Protection Clause, they also yield new and fuller import to the language of the Guarantee Clause." Id. 87. Yet Frankfurter could not extend the "new and fuller import" to the reapportionment cases.

39. Cf. Donald, *Sumner I* 180; Kelly, Fourteenth 1056.

40. Senator Sumner proposed as a condition upon the admission of Tennessee that there should be no denial of suffrage; the proposal was rejected by a vote of 34 to 4. Several days later a similar Sumner proposal respecting the admission of Nebraska was defeated by a vote of 34 to 5. *Globe* 4000, 4232.

41. Van Alstyne 51–52; *Globe* 431.

42. *Globe* 2542.

the exclusion of 80,000 blacks.[43] Boutwell was twitted by Bingham: "Why does not the gentleman move for an expulsion of Missouri from representation?" "When [the blacks] shall vote rests with the people of the State. There I leave it." And, he concluded, with respect to the exclusion of Negroes, "So does Ohio, so does Pennsylvania, and so, also, do a majority of the States." Boutwell was voted down 125 to 12.[44]

Bingham is invoked still again by Van Alstyne:

> The second section excludes the conclusion that by the first section suffrage is subjected to congressional law; save indeed, with this *exception*, that as the right in the people of each State to a republican government and to choose their Representatives in Congress is of the guarantees of the Constitution, by this amendment a remedy might be given directly for a case supposed by Madison, where *treason* might change a State government from a republican to a despotic government, and thereby deny suffrage to the people.[45]

Although Van Alstyne finds this statement "puzzling," it suffices to read the words in their ordinary sense: §2 shows that Congress was given no control of suffrage by §1, except in a case of a treasonable shift to a despotic government which does away with all voting. Manifestly, a change from representative government to a dictatorship calls for effectuation of the guarantee. But what light does this shed on the general control of suffrage? No subtle elucidation of this passage can cancel out Bingham's flat-footed statement that "the exercise of the elective franchise is exclusively under the control of the States," at a time when he completely abandoned the "guarantee" as a limitation on State control of suffrage.[46] The Supreme Court confirmed the views of the framers in 1874: "All the States had governments when the Constitution was adopted . . . These governments the Constitution did not change. They were accepted precisely as they were . . . Thus we have unmistakable

---

43. *Globe* 3950, 3975–3976.
44. Id. 3978–3979, 3980.
45. Van Alstyne 62–63; *Globe* 2542; emphasis added; see supra at note 25.
46. *Globe* 2542; and supra at notes 43–44.

evidence of what was republican in form."[47] Unless some special magic was deemed to inhere in the words "equal protection"—a supposition hereinafter examined—the evidence, to my mind, that suffrage was excluded from the Amendment is all but incontrovertible.[48]

The Report of the Joint Committee on Reconstruction, which Stevens, Boutwell, and Bingham signed, furnishes a conclusive summation:

> Doubts were entertained whether Congress had power, even under the amended Constitution, to prescribe the qualifications of voters in a State, or could act directly on the subject. It was *doubtful*, in the opinion of your committee, whether the *States would consent to surrender* a power they had always exercised, and to which they were attached. As the best if not the only method of surmounting the difficulty, and as eminently just and proper in itself, your committee came to the conclusion that political power should be possessed in all the States exactly in proportion as the right of suffrage should be granted, without distinction of color or race. This it was thought *would leave the whole question with the people of each State*, holding out to all the advantage of increased political power as an inducement to allow all to participate in its exercise.[49]

To "leave the whole question with the people of each State" is to say that § 1 left suffrage untouched and that § 2 was merely "an inducement [to the States] to allow all to participate in its exercise."

47. Minor v. Happersett, 88 U.S. (21 Wall.) 162, 175–176.

48. "It is clear," said the Court in Minor v. Happersett, id. 171, "that the Constitution [Fourteenth Amendment] has not added the right of suffrage to the privileges and immunities of citizenship as they existed at the time it was adopted."

49. Report of the Joint Committee on Reconstruction, 39th Cong., 1st Sess. (undated, 1866) xiii (emphasis added). At an early stage Conkling stated that the Committee rejected a proposal "To deprive the States of the power to disqualify or discriminate politically on account of race" and instead approved a proposal. "To leave every State perfectly free to decide for itself, not only who shall vote, but who shall belong to the political community in any way." *Globe* 357. Chairman Fessenden stated that § 2 "leaves the power where it is," i.e., with the States. *Globe* 705. When James M. Ashley of Ohio was asked by his Ohio colleague, Francis LeBlond, "why the gentleman yields the question of suffrage, as he does, in supporting the [representation] proposition of the Committee," he replied, "Because I cannot get it." Id. 2882.

## Chief Justice Warren's Opinion in Reynolds v. Sims

Chief Justice Warren made no allusion to Justice Harlan's historical demonstration of the limited scope of the Fourteenth Amendment, and instead struck off a new version of constitutional principle and history. He premised that "the right to vote freely for the candidate of one's choice is of the essence of a democratic society, and any restrictions on that right strike at the heart of representative government."[50] Were Warren drafting a new Constitution that principle would be unexceptionable. But that was not the established principle at the adoption of the Constitution; nor was it embodied therein. On the contrary, Federalist No. 54 recognized that "in every State, a certain proportion of inhabitants are deprived of this right by the constitution of the State."[51] In the 39th Congress itself, Fessenden said that "everybody has admitted from the foundation of the Government down to the present day that the qualification of voters rested with the States."[52] Such was the clear consensus in the 39th Congress.

Warren postulated that "the conception of political equality from the Declaration of Independence, to Lincoln's Gettysburg Address, to the Fifteenth, Seventeenth and Nineteenth Amendments can mean only one thing—one person, one vote."[53] But Lincoln also bowed to "the right of each State to order and control its own domestic institutions,"[54] and reminded a Negro delegation of the ineradicable prejudice toward blacks, who were "far removed from being placed on an equality with the white man."[55] And if we are to extract a principle from the Fifteenth and Nineteenth Amendments it is that Congress and the people considered that express Amendments were needed to confer suffrage on Negroes and women, that absent these Amendments neither enjoyed "political equal-

---

50. 377 U.S. at 555.

51. Federalist 356; see supra at notes 26–27; infra at notes 69–70.

52. *Globe* 1279.

53. 377 U.S. at 558. This was quoted from the opinion of Justice Douglas in Gray v. Sanders, 372 U.S. 368, 381 (1963).

54. Supra Chapter 4 at note 38.

55. Supra Chapter 1 at note 36.

ity."[56] The point was made by the Court itself in *Minor v. Happersett* (1874), wherein a woman claimed that the Fourteenth Amendment endowed her with suffrage: "after the adoption of the fourteenth amendment, it was deemed necessary to adopt a fifteenth . . . If suffrage was one of the privileges and immunities [of the Fourteenth], why amend the Constitution to prevent its being denied on account of race."[57]

The Seventeenth Amendment likewise speaks against Warren, for it provides, with respect to the popular election of Senators, that "the electors in each State shall have the qualifications requisite for electors of the most numerous branch of the State legislature," qualifications, it will be recalled, that were under exclusive State control from the beginning and were left in place by the Fourteenth Amendment.

Reliance upon the Declaration of Independence, to which the Radical left frequently appealed in the 39th Congress, might be dismissed with the remark of neoabolitionist tenBroek: " 'All men are created equal' proclaimed the Declaration of Independence. All men? Well not quite all— not negro slaves like those owned by Jefferson, among others."[58] To im-

---

56. As Justice Harlan stated, "the very fact that constitutional amendments were deemed necessary to bring about federal abolition of state restrictions on voting by reason of race (Amendment XV), sex (Amendment XIX) . . . is itself forceful evidence of the common understanding in 1869, 1919 . . . that the Fourteenth Amendment did not empower Congress to legislate in these respects." Oregon v. Mitchell, 400 U.S. at 202, dissenting and concurring in part.

57. 88 U.S. (21 Wall.) 162, 175. In United States v. Cruikshank, 92 U.S. 542, 555 (1875), Chief Justice Waite reaffirmed that "the fifteenth amendment has invested the citizens of the United States with a *new constitutional right*, which is exemption from discrimination in the exercise of the elective franchise on account of race. From this it appears that the right of suffrage is not a necessary attribute of national citizenship" (emphasis added).

After indicating that "the 15th and 19th amendments prohibit a State from overweighting or diluting votes on the basis of *race* or *sex*," Chief Justice Warren, quoting a prior opinion, asked, "How then can one person be given twice or ten times the voting power of another person . . . merely because he lives in a rural area." 377 U.S. at 557. Given that discrimination in favor of "rural areas" is historically deep-rooted, orthodox analysis would conclude: because the Fifteenth and Nineteenth govern only "race and sex," not "rural areas." My citation of old cases does not betray a weakness for ancient vintages but responds rather to the weight long given to interpretations contemporary with or close to the event, particularly when they confirm the intention of the framers as disclosed by the legislative history. See infra Chapter 10 note 66.

58. TenBroek 14.

port the Declaration into the Constitution is to overlook their totally
different provenance. The Declaration was a product of rebels and revo-
lutionaries; the Constitution came twelve years later, in no small part as
a recoil from the "excesses" of popularly controlled legislatures.[59] Men of
substance felt threatened and, in the words of John Dickinson, sought to
protect "the worthy against the licentious."[60] TenBroek noted that "Equality was the dominant note in the Declaration," whereas a "stronger position" was accorded in the Constitution to "property,"[61] including property in slaves as the fugitive slave clause testifies. There is no blinking the
fact, as Kent Newmeyer recently reminded us, that the Constitution was
"racist."[62] Jefferson himself, author of the Declaration, predicted emancipation, but wrote: "it is equally certain that the two races will never live
in a state of equal freedom . . . so insurmountable are the barriers which
nature, habit and opinions have established between them."[63] Stevens
powerfully summarized this history at the outset of the 39th Congress:

> Sir, our fathers made the Declaration of Independence; and that is
> what they intended to be the foundation of our Government. If they
> had been able to base their Constitution on the principles of that
> Declaration it would have needed no amendment during all time,
> for every human being would have had his rights; every human be-
> ing would have been equal before the law. But it so happened when
> our fathers came to reduce the principles on which they founded
> this Government into order, in shaping the organic law, an insti-
> tution hot from hell appeared among them . . . It obstructed all their
> movements and all their actions, and precluded them from carrying
> out their own principles into the organic law of this Union.[64]

59. Raoul Berger, *Congress v. The Supreme Court* 10–11 (1969).
60. Quoted in Gordon Wood, *The Creation of the American Republic 1776–1787* 475
(1969).
61. TenBroek 16.
62. "Book Review," 19 Am. J. Legal Hist. 66, 67 (1975). Kelly, however, regards efforts to prove that "the Constitution was exclusively a 'white man's document' " and "to
discount the Declaration of Independence" as a lapse into "a priori, fiat technique." Kelly,
"Clio," supra note 4 at 126 note 26.
63. Quoted in 1 Alexis de Tocqueville, *Democracy in America* 378n (1900).
64. *Globe* 536.

It needs also to be borne in mind that the Declaration was drawn by the Continental Congress, a league of independent States, each of which jealously guarded its independence.[65] One of the reasons advanced by Senator Poland for §1 of the Fourteenth Amendment was doubts as to Congress' power to "destroy all such partial State legislation" as violated the "principles" of the Declaration of Independence.[66] Senator Howard, a favorite of the neoabolitionists, stated that he could not discover the Negro right to vote in the Declaration of Independence and that, "notwithstanding the Declaration of Independence, it is the right of every organized political community to regulate the right of suffrage."[67] Manifestly, Warren's appeal to the Declaration as a guiding principle of constitutional construction is out of tune with the historical facts.

A word about his appeal to James Wilson's 1791 Lectures in Philadelphia: "all elections *ought* to be equal. Elections are equal, when a given number of citizens, in one part of the State, choose as many representatives, as are chosen by the same number of citizens, in any other part of the state."[68] This stated an ideal, not a constitutional requirement. When Wilson turned to the Article I, §2, provision that "the Electors in each state shall have the qualifications requisite for Electors of the most numerous Branch of the State Legislature," he said, "the regulation is generous and wise. It is generous for it *intrusts* to . . . the several *states*, the very important power of ascertaining the qualifications" of the Electors. It was evidence of confidence, "that this foundation should be continued or altered by the States themselves."[69] Wilson was thoroughly aware of the disparate State exclusions from suffrage, having made a survey of the different State constitutions, even noticing that Connecticut provided power to exclude freemen, "according to the sentiments which others entertain concerning their conversations and behavior . . . a power of very extraordinary nature." And he praises "the wisdom . . . which rested one of the principal pillars of the national gov-

---

65. See Raoul Berger, *Executive Privilege: A Constitutional Myth* 103–107 (1974).
66. *Globe* 2961.
67. Id. 2175.
68. Quoted in 377 U.S. at 564 note 41 (emphasis added). The quotation appears at 1 James Wilson, *The Works of James Wilson* 406 (R. G. McCloskey ed. 1967).
69. 1 Wilson, supra note 68 at 407 (emphasis added).

ernment upon the foundations prepared for it by the governments of the several states."[70] Warren's use of Wilson affords striking illustration of the "lawyers history" so justly condemned by Alfred Kelly.

Warren's pervasive error, to my mind, is to substitute twentieth-century logic for the framers' intention, so clearly expressed in the legislative history: "Logically, in a society *ostensibly grounded* on representative government, it would seem reasonable that a majority of the people in a State would elect a majority of that State's legislators."[71] "Ostensibly grounded" refuses to come to terms with the historical fact that suffrage and apportionment were the province of the States. Once again is demonstrated the wisdom of Holmes' aphorism, "a page of history is worth a volume of logic."[72] That history was summarized with crystal clarity in the Report of the Joint Committee on Reconstruction.[73]

## Justice Brennan's Opinion in Oregon v. Mitchell

Justice Brennan recognized that "racial prejudice in the North" was a most "significant" obstacle in the path of equal suffrage:

> Only five New England States and New York permitted any Negroes to vote as of 1866 . . . and extension of the suffrage was re-

70. Id. 409, 411.

71. 377 U.S. at 565 (emphasis added). Ward Elliott justly states that in Reynolds v. Sims the Court fabricated a "fundamental principle of 'one person, one vote' that was exactly the reverse of text and stated intent of the equal protection clause." Elliott, supra note 1 at 129. As a professor, Solicitor General Robert J. Bork wrote, "Chief Justice Warren's opinions in this series of [state legislative apportionment] cases are remarkable for their inability to muster a single respectable supporting argument. The principle of one man, one vote . . . runs counter to the text of the fourteenth amendment, the history surrounding its adoption and ratification and the political practice of Americans from Colonial times up to the day the Court invented the new formula." "Neutral Principles and Some First Amendment Problems," 47 Ind. L.J. 1, 18 (1971).

72. New York Trust Co. v. Eisner, 256 U.S. 345, 349 (1921). Dissenting in a reapportionment case, Justice Stewart stated, "these decisions mark a long step backward into that unhappy era when a majority of the members of this Court . . . convinced themselves and each other that the demands of the Constitution were to be measured not by what it says, but by their own notions of wise policy . . . What the Court has done is to convert a particular political philosophy into a constitutional rule." Lucas v. Colorado General Assembly, 377 U.S. 713, 747–748 (1964).

73. Supra at note 49.

jected by the voters in 17 of 19 popular referenda held on the subject between 1865 and 1868. Moreover, Republicans suffered some severe election setbacks in 1867 on account of their support of Negro suffrage . . .

Meeting in the winter and spring of 1866 and facing elections in the fall of the same year the Republicans thus faced a difficult dilemma: they desperately needed Negro suffrage in order to prevent total Democratic resurgence in the South, yet they feared that by pressing for suffrage they might create a reaction among northern white voters that would lead to massive Democratic electoral gains in the North. Their task was thus to frame a policy that would prevent total Democratic resurgence and simultaneously would serve as a platform upon which Republicans could go before their northern constituents in the fall. What ultimately emerged as the policy and political platform of the Republican Party was the Fourteenth Amendment.[74]

Why could not the Republicans in Congress tell their constituents that unless Negro suffrage was granted Republican hegemony was doomed? Unless Northern voters preferred Democratic resurgence to Negro suffrage, the interests of Republican voters and members of Congress were one and the same. In fact the framers *shared* the prejudices of their Northern constituency, to recall only George W. Julian's statement in the House: "The real trouble is *we hate the Negro*."[75] If the Republicans entertained a secret design to slip suffrage into the Amendment over voter opposition in order to hang on to office, they were betraying their constituency, and for this firm evidence needs to be adduced.

Given the framers' awareness of voter antipathy to suffrage, one would expect Justice Brennan to resolve all doubts in favor of those sentiments. Instead he substitutes twentieth-century speculation for historical fact to effectuate his own predilections and commits the very sin he incorrectly lays at Harlan's door: "historical analysis is flawed by ascription of 20th century meanings to the words of 19th century legislators."[76] For example, Harlan's "view would appear to allow a State to exclude any

---

74. Oregon v. Mitchell, 400 U.S. at 255–256, dissenting in part.
75. *Globe* 257. Similar statements are collected supra Chapter 1 at note 40.
76. 400 U.S. at 251.

unpopular group on the basis of its political opinions."[77] But if State control over suffrage was plenary, if the Amendment left States free to exclude Negroes on account of their color, they were equally free to exclude others for their "political opinions," unpalatable as that appears to twentieth-century thinking. It will be recalled that James Wilson noticed the Connecticut provision for exclusion of freemen, "according to the sentiments which others entertain concerning their conversations and behavior . . . a power of very extraordinary nature." Historical analysis must proceed from the 1866 facts, not reason backward from 1970 predilections. Justice Brennan would substitute his choices for those of the framers; because we dislike a policy today, it does not follow that it is unconstitutional. That standard was rejected both by the Founders and by Chief Justice Marshall.[78]

Justice Brennan's opinion runs to some 38 pages; refutation, as is well known, requires more space than bare assertion; hence only a sampling of the Brennan opinion can here be analyzed. A few examples, however, should suffice to disclose Justice Brennan's preference for speculation over fact. Section 1 began, he notices, as a "provision aimed at securing equality of 'political rights and privileges' "; but the Joint Committee rejected an express reference "to political and elective rights"; it dropped all references to "political rights" and spoke in terms of "privileges and immunities" and equal protection of "life, liberty, and property" by a vote of seven to six. Commenting on these facts, Justice Brennan stated, "the breakdown of the committee vote suggests that . . . no change in meaning was intended," because the "substitute was supported by men of all political views," among them Howard and Boutwell, "who had earlier sought to make the section's coverage of suffrage explicit," and Stevens and Fessenden.[79] But Boutwell, Fessenden, Howard, and Stevens later agreed that the Amendment did not grant suffrage and signed the Joint Committee Report that so stated. To deduce that Bingham merely "sought to do no more than substitute for his earlier specific language more general lan-

---

77. Id. 252 note 4.
78. See infra Chapter 14 at notes 103–104.
79. 400 U.S. 257–260.

guage"[80] ignores the repeated *rejection* of the specific proposals. General language may be construed to comprehend specific language that was earlier approved; but when specific language was rejected, evidence is required to explain why the rejected specific was now embodied in the general, evidence, not speculation. Then, too, Bingham cannot be lifted out of the mainstream of Republican statements that the Amendment *did not* confer suffrage; in fact he himself so stated.[81]

At the instigation of Robert Dale Owen, a reformer, Stevens had submitted a proposal that after July 4, 1876, "no discrimination shall be made . . . as to . . . the right of suffrage because of race." This provision was deleted by the Joint Committee, Justice Brennan notes, but "the reasons for the rewriting are not entirely clear." He notices, however, that in 1875 Owen furnished Stevens' explanation: "several state delegations held caucuses which decided that the explicit references to 'negro suffrage,' in any shape, ought to be excluded from the platform."[82] Is this not a "clear" explanation? By Brennan's own testimony the Republicans feared to endanger the Fall elections by the submission of Negro suffrage. He reasons, however, "Perhaps the changes in § 1 of the Amendment were thought by the Committee to be mere linguistic improvements which did not substantially modify Owen's meaning."[83] The fact is that the 1876 provision was dropped to avoid alienating the electorate. That the "changes" were not "thought by the Committee to be mere linguistic improvements" is once more demonstrated by the unequivocal statement in its Report that suffrage had proven impossible of achievement and was left in the control of the States.

At "the very least," states Justice Brennan, "the Committee must have realized that it was substituting for Owen's rather specific language Bingham's far more elastic language—language that, as one scholar [Alexander Bickel] has noted, is far more 'capable of growth' and 'receptive to "latitudinarian" construction.' "[84] Because, Brennan amplified, "po-

---

80. Id. 260.

81. See infra at notes 91–93.

82. 400 U.S. at 260–262. This incident is more fully discussed infra Chapter 6 at notes 38–41.

83. 400 U.S. at 263.

84. Id.

litical considerations militated against clarification of issues and in favor of compromise," because "much of the North . . . opposed Negro suffrage, and many Republicans in Congress had to seek reelection from constituencies where racial prejudice remained rampant," "what Republicans needed, in the words of Wendell Phillips . . . was 'a party trick to tide over the elections and save time.' "[85] This is the Bickel "open-ended" theory which I shall hereafter examine; and I shall also collate the evidence which repels the conclusion that the framers purposely employed "elastic language" to dupe the voters.

For Justice Brennan "the purpose of §1 in relation to the suffrage emerges out of the debates . . . with an equal obscurity."[86] As exhibit #1 he instances Howard's statement that "the first section of the proposed amendment does not give to either of these classes the right of voting," which is "not as unambiguous as [it] initially appear[s]." This is because after stating that "the right of suffrage was not one of the privileges and immunities protected by the Constitution . . . he read into the record an excerpt from . . . Corfield v. Coryell . . . which listed the elective franchise as among the privileges and immunities."[87] But Senator Trumbull, after calling attention to this *Corfield* listing, had pointed out that suffrage was *not* included in the Civil Rights Bill.[88] One might deduce that Howard felt no need to repeat such a statement after twice stating that the Amendment did not grant suffrage. Moreover, if an ambiguity be assumed, it was cured by his final statement: "the theory of this whole amendment is to leave the power of regulating the suffrage . . . with the States . . . and not to assume to regulate it."[89]

For exhibit #2, Justice Brennan turns to Bingham's "completely incongruous statement": "the exercise of the elective franchise though it be one of the privileges of a citizen of the Republic, is exclusively under the control of the States."[90] Now Bingham was a confused thinker, as I shall show, but on one thing he was clear: the Amendment did not confer suffrage. At

85. Id. 272, 273.
86. Id. 263.
87. Id. 263–264.
88. Supra Chapter 2 at notes 47, 31.
89. *Globe* 3039; and see supra Chapter 4 at note 34.
90. 400 U.S. at 264.

a later point he said: "We all agree . . . that the exercise of the elective franchise . . . is exclusively under the control of the States . . . The amendment does not give, as the second section shows, the power of regulating suffrage in the several States." He further stated, "the second section excludes the conclusion that by the first section suffrage is subjected to congressional law."[91] Thereafter Bingham vigorously defended the exclusion of Negro suffrage from the Tennessee Constitution. When Boutwell objected during the debate on the readmission of Tennessee that in consequence it did not have a "republican form of government," Bingham replied that whether a black "shall vote rests with the people of [Tennessee]. There I leave it . . . I ask the gentlemen to weigh well the question when they come to vote, whether Tennessee shall be rejected only because the majority exercises the same power as to colored suffrage claimed for and exercised by all the other States."[92] This was after Congress submitted the Amendment with its "equal protection" clause to the people, and Bingham was upheld by a vote of 125 to 12,[93] an irreducible fact that speaks more loudly than all of Justice Brennan's speculations. Here were materials that cured the "ambiguity,"[94] that dissipated the "obscurity" conjured up by Justice Brennan, of which he took no notice. And why lean so heavily on the alleged "ambiguities" of two leaders when the vast majority of the leadership and rank and file affirmed or recognized that suffrage was excluded from the Amendment?

Then there is Brennan's citation of Sumner, who was all but ostracized in the Senate, whose proposals were regularly voted down by very large majorities;[95] and his appeal to Stevens' statement that the Amendment "merely allowed 'Congress to correct the unjust legislation of the States, so far that the law which operates upon one man shall operate

91. *Globe* 2542.
92. Id. 3978, 3979.
93. Id. 3980.
94. 400 U.S. at 264.
95. Supra note 40; infra Chapter 7 at note 40. For rejection of another Sumner proposal, see supra Chapter 4 at note 20. A "deep estrangement . . . existed between Sumner and his Republican colleagues . . . More and more Senators came to distrust, when they did not detest, him." Donald, *Sumner II* 248. See also supra notes 6 and 28.

*equally* upon all.' "[96] Stevens sought equality with respect to the rights enumerated in the Civil Rights Act, from which suffrage was excluded. But on the issue of suffrage, he stated, "I hold that the States have the right . . . to fix the elective franchise within their own States. And I hold that this ["representation" proposal] does not take it from them . . . How many States would allow Congress to come within their jurisdiction to fix the qualifications of their voters . . . You could not get five in this Union."[97] It was on Stevens' motion that the Joint Committee adopted a reduction of representation proposal; and it rejected Boutwell's motion to "abolish" any distinction.[98]

Justice Brennan also refers to three Democratic opponents of the Amendment who, more or less clearly, saw in it a grant of suffrage.[99] Opponents of a measure, particularly those who seek to discredit it, are given slight credence, as I shall show; their testimony is not employed to define its scope.[100] What are we to think of Brennan's reference to Senator Stewart, who, "while unhappy that the Amendment did not directly confer suffrage, nevertheless could 'support this plan' because it did 'not preclude Congress from adopting other means by a two-thirds vote' "?[101] Of course Congress could later propose *another* amendment by a "two-thirds vote"; Stewart plainly had no reference to congressional implementation by statute, for that could be done by majority vote, given authorization by the Amendment.

Finally, Justice Brennan takes over Van Alstyne's critique of Harlan's alleged view that "§ 2 is specifically concerned with voting rights, and it provides an exclusive remedy that precludes or preempts application of § 1."[102] Apparently this is based on Harlan's reference to the "Court's utter disregard of the second section which expressly recognized the State's power to deny the right . . . to vote and its express provision of

96. 400 U.S. at 266.

97. *Globe* 536.

98. Kendrick 51, 55.

99. 400 U.S. at 267. Brennan also cites two other Democrats, Boyer of Pennsylvania and Senator Hendricks of Indiana, id. 274.

100. Infra Chapter 9.

101. 400 U.S. at 268.

102. Id. 276–277; Van Alstyne 39.

a remedy for such denial or abridgment."[103] This unduly exalts a loose, passing reference to "remedy." Remedies are given for "wrongs"; it is no "wrong" to exercise the "recognized . . . power to deny the right . . . to vote." Then, too, since § 1 conferred no suffrage, § 2 obviously created no remedy for a nonexistent right. Certainly it gave no "remedy" to the black who was denied a vote. Senator Stewart, a Republican, sardonically commented that § 2 relieves the Negro "from misrepresentation in Congress by denying him any representation whatever."[104] Justice Brennan explains that § 2 "was of critical importance in assuring that, should the Southern States deny the franchise to Negroes, the Congress called upon to remedy that discrimination would not be controlled by the beneficiaries of discrimination themselves."[105] The truth is that § 2 was the core of the Republican program because, as Brennan himself states, the Republicans needed to "prevent total [Democratic] resurgence," "massive electoral gains in the North." Reduction of representation when Negro suffrage was denied was deemed more important than endowing blacks with the vote; perceptive Republicans doubted whether the South would be "induced" to enfranchise Negroes and thus lose control.[106] Section 2, therefore, was not so much a "remedy" to enforce rights which § 1 had not granted as a mechanism to preserve Republican hegemony. Forlorn hopes that the South could thereby be "induced" to confer suffrage were doomed to disappointment.

Enough has been set forth to exhibit Justice Brennan's strange preference for minority Democrats and dissentient radicals like Sumner over the Republican leadership and its followers who enacted the measure and whose utterances are virtually ignored by him, his preference for "ambiguous" utterances rather than the crystal-clear explanations of the self-same speakers, and for speculation over the mass of stubborn evidence to the contrary.[107] Future historians, I confidently predict, will not prefer the "history" of Brennan to that of Harlan.

103. Reynolds v. Sims, 377 U.S. at 594.
104. *Globe* 2801. See also Senator Reverdy Johnson, supra Chapter 4 note 61.
105. 400 U.S. at 277.
106. Supra Chapter 4.
107. Unless evidence is inherently incredible, it must be countered by evidence, not speculation. Supra note 15.

# 6

## The "Open-Ended" Phraseology Theory

We cannot put into the Constitution, owing to existing prejudices and existing institutions, an entire exclusion of all class distinctions.

—SENATOR WILLIAM P. FESSENDEN*

THE "open-ended" theory, shortly stated, is that the framers dared not submit Negro suffrage and the like to the electorate in 1866 and therefore discarded "specific" terms, as Justice Brennan put it, in favor of "far more elastic language—language that, as one scholar [Alexander Bickel] has noted, is far more 'capable of growth' and 'receptive to "latitudinarian" construction.' "[1] This is the classic invocation to extraconstitutional power,[2] power to revise the Constitution under the theory that the framers gave a "blank check to posterity."[3] Bickel had cautiously advanced the theory as a hypothesis; it found favor in scholarly circles,[4] and more positively formulated variants were proffered by Alfred Kelly

---

* *Globe* 705. Fessenden was co-chairman of the Joint Committee on Reconstruction, which drafted the Amendment.

1. Oregon v. Mitchell, 400 U.S. 112, 263 (1970). ["Vague and uncertain laws, and more especially Constitutions, are the very instrument of slavery." 3 Samuel Adams, *The Writings of Samuel Adams* 262 (Harry A. Cushing ed. 1904).]

2. Cf. T. C. Grey, "Do We Have an Unwritten Constitution?" 27 Stan. L. Rev. 703, 712–713, 709 (1975); see infra note 9.

3. "The Constitution is not a blank check to posterity." Ward Elliott, *The Rise of Guardian Democracy* viii (1974). For a similar statement by Justice Black see infra Chapter 11 note 27.

4. Dean Francis Allen stated, "There is evidence that those who drafted Section 1 intended that the meanings of these phrases should evolve and expand with the passage

and William Van Alstyne. It has since been enshrined in an opinion by Justice Brennan; and Justice Black, jumping off from Brennan's paraphrase, announced that it made "the history of the Fourteenth Amendment . . . irrelevant to the present problem."[5] The theory is therefore deserving of close analysis.

### ALEXANDER BICKEL

At the time the "desegregation" case, *Brown v. Board of Education*,[6] was first argued before the Supreme Court, Bickel was a law clerk of Justice Frankfurter, who assigned to him the task of compiling the legislative history of the Fourteenth Amendment, a task he performed brilliantly. When he delivered his memorandum in August 1953, he stated in a covering letter:

> It was preposterous to worry about unsegregated schools, for example, when hardly a beginning had been made at educating Negroes at all and when obviously special efforts, suitable only for the Negroes, would have to be made . . . It is impossible to conclude that the 39th Congress intended that segregation be abolished; *impossible* also to *conclude* that they *foresaw* it might be, *under the language* they were adopting.[7]

In 1962 he again wrote:

> Was it the intention of the framers . . . to forbid the states to enact and enforce segregation statutes? If one goes to the historical materials with this specific question, the only answer is in the negative.

---

of time and changes of circumstance." "The Constitution: The Civil War Amendments: XIII–XV," in *American Primer* 161, 165 (Daniel J. Boorstin ed. 1966). Carl Auerbach likewise noticed general agreement that the original understanding did not comprehend "immediate" suffrage but that Congress wittingly chose "language capable of growth." "The Reapportionment Cases: One Person, One Vote—One Vote, One Value," 1964 S. Ct. Rev. 1, 75–76. Wallace Mendelson said that due process and equal protection "doubtless were designed to have the chameleon's capacity to change their color with changing moods and circumstances." *Justices Black and Frankfurter: Conflict in the Court* viii (1961).

5. 400 U.S. at 139–140.

6. 347 U.S. 483 (1954).

7. Richard Kluger, *Simple Justice* 654 (1976) (emphasis added).

The framers did not intend or expect then and there to outlaw segregation, which, of course, was a practice widely prevalent in the North.[8]

Upon the termination of his clerkship Bickel wrote a farewell letter to Frankfurter in which he adverted to the "living Constitution" dictum of Marshall.[9] But when he revised his memorandum for publication in 1955 he sought more solid footing. Were the amendment a statute, he concluded, a "Court might very well hold" on the basis of the evidence "that it was foreclosed from applying it to segregation in the public schools." Apart from the "immediate effect of the enactment," he asked, "what if any thought was given to the long-range effect" in the future—a possibility he had labeled "impossible" in 1953. Noting the shift from "equal protection in the rights of life, liberty and property" to "equal protection of the laws, a clause which is plainly capable of being applied to all subjects of state legislation,"[10] he asked,

8. Alexander Bickel, *The Least Dangerous Branch* 100 (1962). [In *The Supreme Court and the Idea of Progress* 48 (1978) Bickel stated: "The Framers of the Fourteenth Amendment explicitly rejected the option of an open-ended grant of power to Congress freely to meddle with conditions within the States, so as to render them equal in accordance with Congress's own notions. Rather, federal power, legislative as well as judicial, was to be limited by the terms of the Amendment."

James Wilson, chairman of the House Judiciary Committee, stated, "I fear that comprehensive statesmanship which cares for posterity as well as itself will not leave its impress upon the measure we are now considering." *Globe* 2947. Michael Perry considers that Berger has "devastated the notion that the framers of the Fourteenth Amendment . . . intended it to be open-ended." Michael Perry, "Book Review," 78 Colum. L. Rev. 685, 695 (1978).]

9. Kluger, supra note 7 at 655. Professor Robert McKay "finds the answer in the fact that it is not a statute but in Chief Justice Marshall's words, 'a *constitution* we are expounding.'" Quoted in Louis Pollak, "The Supreme Court Under Fire," 6 J. Pub. L. 428, 440 (1950). That Marshall has been utterly misconstrued down the years is shown infra Chapter 21 at notes 1–28. Here it may be noted that the plea for "growth" is in truth a claim for judicial power to revise the Constitution. In one of the great paradoxes of our time, Justice Black, that supreme "revisionist," dismissed "rhapsodical strains, about the duty of the Court to keep the Constitution in tune with the times. The idea is that the Constitution must be changed from time to time and that this Court is charged with the duty to make those changes . . . The Constitution makers knew the need for change and provided for it" by the amendment process of Article V. Griswold v. Connecticut, 381 U.S. 479, 522 (1965), dissenting opinion.

10. This shift is discussed infra Chapter 11 at note 35.

Could the comparison have failed to leave the implication that the new phrase, while it did not necessarily, and certainly not expressly, carry greater coverage than the old, was nevertheless roomier, more receptive to "latitudinarian" construction? No one made the point with regard to this particular clause. But in the opening debate in the Senate, Jacob Howard was frank to say that only the future could tell what application the privileges and immunities would have.

So, too, Reverdy Johnson, a Democrat, "confessed his puzzlement about the same clause."[11] How does the Howard-Johnson "puzzlement" about "privileges or immunities" advance the argument that "due process" and "equal protection" were understood to be open-ended? Neither Johnson nor Howard expressed uncertainty as to the meaning of *those* terms, and the implication is that there was none, an implication I shall flesh out in subsequent chapters. And given the Republican commitment to a "limited" program of protection for "enumerated" rights,[12] why did Bingham, who had insisted on deletion from the Civil Rights Bill of the words "civil rights" as "oppressive," too "latitudinarian,"[13] now, as author of the Amendment's §1, resort to phraseology that was "roomier, more receptive to 'latitudinarian' construction?" No explanation of his turnabout has been offered, and when we descend from speculation to the facts we shall find that they offer no support for the Bickel hypothesis.

Bickel states that some Republicans referred to "the natural rights of man,"[14] but those rights had been specified in the Civil Rights Act, and the Act was understood to exclude suffrage and desegregation of schools,

---

11. Bickel 60–61.

12. See Kelly infra Chapter 13 at note 53; Thayer supra Chapter 2 at note 28.

13. See infra Chapter 7 at notes 11–17, and 21. [In 1968 Alexander Bickel testified before the Senate Subcommittee on the Separation of Powers in Hearings on the Supreme Court that the "open-ended" Bingham amendment was voted down because "it left Congress too free." The framers thought that section 1 "limited, imposed limits on what Congress could do." An "open-ended power also means that Congress can go there in those States and simply rearrange the social scene, and the legal order in those States, and we don't want that either." *Hearings on the Supreme Court Before the Subcommittee on the Separation of Powers of the Senate Committee on the Judiciary*, 90th Cong., 2d Sess., at 44–45 (June 1968).]

14. Bickel 61.

as Bickel himself noted.[15] The Act, with its restrictive "enumeration" of the rights to be protected, was represented to be embodied in the Amendment. A repudiation of such representations by the framers, in the teeth of their attachment to State sovereignty, their respect for the rights reserved to the States by the Tenth Amendment, needs to be proved, not assumed. And as will appear, the words "equal protection of the laws" evolved side by side with the framers' limited objectives and gave perfect expression to their central goal: to prevent discriminatory legislation with respect to the enumerated rights, and those alone.

Howard knew well enough what "privileges or immunities" comprised. He stated, "we may gather some intimation of what probably will be the opinion of the judiciary by referring to . . . Corfield v. Coryell." He quoted therefrom the reference to those "privileges and immunities which are in their nature fundamental . . . They may be comprehended under the following general heads: protection by the Government, the enjoyment of life and liberty, with the right to acquire property" and so on.[16] The correlation between these rights, the "privileges and immunities" of Article IV, §2, and the Civil Rights Act had been explained by Trumbull. After Howard's speech, Reverdy Johnson moved to strike the "privileges or immunities" clause because he "did not understand what will be the effect of that"; but his motion fell to the ground,[17] testimony that the Senate did not share his doubts. The "puzzlement" of Howard and Johnson cannot cancel out the repeated association of "privileges or immunities" with "security of person and property"; it cannot vitiate the all but universal understanding that the Amendment was to embody the Civil Rights Act, reiterated after Howard spoke. The Act, said Latham, "covers exactly the same ground as this amendment." Senator Doolittle

15. "Natural rights" had acquired a settled common law meaning; supra Chapter 2 note 55. "The obvious conclusion, to which the evidence, thus summarized, easily leads is that section 1 of the fourteenth amendment, like section 1 of the Civil Rights Act of 1866, carried out the relatively narrow objectives of the Moderates, and hence, as originally understood, was meant to apply neither to jury service, nor suffrage, nor miscegenation statutes, nor segregation." Bickel 58.

16. *Globe* 2765.

17. Id. 3041. Just before Johnson spoke, Senator James A. McDougall of California stated that the Civil Rights Act "was simply to carry out the 'privileges and immunities' " provision of Article IV, §2. Id. 3035.

said it "was the forerunner of this constitutional amendment, and to give validity to which this constitutional amendment is brought forward," a view also expressed by Henry Van Aernam of New York.[18] The "privileges or immunities" clause, Senator Poland stated, "secures nothing beyond what was intended by the original provision [Article IV, §2] of the Constitution."[19] In fact, Senator Howard undercuts Bickel, for toward the close of the debates he stated, "the first section of the proposed amendment does not give . . . the right of voting. The right of suffrage is not in law, one of the privileges . . . thus secured."[20] With respect to suffrage, the "Great Guarantee," Howard was quite clear that it was excluded; that concept, at least, could not in future change its skin.

Bickel noticed that the "no discrimination in civil rights" sentence of the Act had been deleted because Republicans "who had expressed fears concerning its reach . . . would have to go forth and stand on the platform of the fourteenth amendment." "It remains true," he said, "that an explicit provision going further than the Civil Rights Act would not have carried in the 39th Congress." And he noted that the Republicans drew back from "a formulation dangerously vulnerable to attacks pandering to the prejudice of the people." But, he asked, "may it not be that the Moderates and Radicals reached a compromise permitting them to go to the country with language which they could, where necessary, defend against damaging alarms raised by the opposition but which at the same time was sufficiently elastic to permit reasonable future advances?"[21] Talk

18. Id. 2883, 2896. Van Aernam stated the Amendment gives "constitutional sanction and protection to the substantial guarantees of the civil rights bill." Id. 3069.

19. Id. 2961.

20. Id. 2766.

21. Bickel 61–62. Earlier Flack had put the matter more bluntly: the "main purpose [of the Radical leaders] in proposing the first section of the Amendment was to increase the power of the Federal Government very much, but to do so in such a way that the people would not understand the great change intended to be wrought in the fundamental law of the land." Flack 69. But, he observed, "had the people been informed of what was intended by the Amendment, they would have rejected it." Flack 237. [In 1830 Madison wrote, "it exceeds the possibility of belief, that the known advocates in the Convention for a jealous grant & cautious definition of federal powers, should have silently permitted the introduction of words or phrases in a sense rendering fruitless the restrictions and definitions elaborated by them." 3 *Records of the Federal Convention of 1787* 483, 488 (Max Farrand ed. 1911).]

of a "compromise" between Moderates and Radicals on "vague" language is without factual basis. Consider the "radical" opposition to readmission of Tennessee because its constitution excluded Negro suffrage, voted down by 125 to 12; or the rejection of Senator Sumner's suffrage proposal by 34 to 4.[22] What need was there to "compromise" with so insignificant a group? Senator Sherman told a Cincinnati audience in September 1866, while the Amendment was up for ratification, "we defeated every radical proposition in it."[23]

Bickel's theory, to speak plainly, is that the compromisers concealed the future objectives that they dared not avow lest the whole enterprise be imperiled; it is an elegant reformulation of conspiratorial purpose. To begin with, this theory posits that the 39th Congress harbored designs not shared by the voters, when, in fact, as Morton Keller remarks, "most congressional Republicans were aware of (and shared) their constituents' hostility to black suffrage."[24] Anticipating that his hypothesis might be "disparaged as putting forth an undisclosed, conspiratorial purpose such as has been imputed to Bingham and others with regard to the protection of corporations,"[25] Bickel invoked statements by Stevens and the Joint Committee Report to the effect that the Amendment's "imperfections" may be cured by "further legislation, enabling acts," by "legislative wisdom"[26]—hardly a warrant for *judicial* changes! What member of the 39th Congress would conclude that by such words was meant that Congress had conferred sub rosa for the future the suffrage it dared not propose in the present? Bickel himself torpedoed that inference.

Observing that Stevens stated the Amendment "falls far short of my wishes . . . but . . . is all that can be obtained in the present state of public opinion . . . I . . . *leave it to be perfected by better men in better times*," Bickel

22. Supra Chapter 5 at note 30; Chapter 4 at note 33.
23. James 167; see also infra Chapter 13 at notes 38–45.
24. Morton Keller, *Affairs of State* 67 (1977); and see infra Chapter 13 at notes 16–17.
25. Bickel 63.
26. Id. "Perhaps the passage of the Civil Rights Act of 1875 ultimately is the most decisive indication of the conviction of a large majority of the Radicals that *Congress* might properly forbid state caste and segregation legislation under the amendment [§5], but again this law implied congressional power and discretion, not necessarily the existence of prior mandatory rights enforceable under the amendment alone." Kelly, Fourteenth 1085 (emphasis added). See infra Chapter 12.

states; "In all probability, the disappointment of Thaddeus Stevens centered on failure to make *any* provision for negro suffrage, immediate *or prospective*."[27] Disappointment over failure to provide for prospective suffrage rules out an open-ended design to authorize such provision in the future. What Stevens meant by "further legislation" does not need construction. As Senator Stewart stated, the Amendment "does not preclude Congress from adopting other means by a two-thirds vote [another amendment] when experience shall have demonstrated . . . the necessity for a change of policy,"[28] as it did before long in recommending the Fifteenth Amendment. Studied ambiguity also collides with Fessenden's suggestion of a change because "there is a little obscurity or, at any rate, the expression in section 4 might be construed to go further than was intended."[29] A "blank check to posterity" is likewise refuted by Chairman Wilson's statement: "I fear that comprehensive statesmanship which cares for posterity as well as for itself will not leave its impress upon the measure we are now considering."[30]

There are also several disclaimers of concealed objectives, of playing a trick upon an unsuspecting people.[31] Charged with "indirection," Fessenden said:

> where a legislator avows his object and his purpose, states what he
> wishes to accomplish and the mode by which he is to accomplish it,
> he is [not] to be charged, although it operates indirectly, with what
> is properly understood by the term "indirection," which conveys the

27. Bickel 45–46 (emphasis added); cf. *Globe* 2459. Stevens stated "prospective" suffrage would be unacceptable; infra at notes 27, 38–41. In explaining §2, Stevens stated, "True it will take two, three, possibly five years before they [Southern States] conquer their prejudices sufficiently to *allow* their late slaves to become their equals at the polls." *Globe* 2459 (emphasis added). This speaks against a §1 power in the future to compel States to grant suffrage; and it is confirmed by Stevens' statement that "The large stride which we in vain proposed is dead." *Globe* 2460.

28. *Globe* 2964.

29. Id. 2941.

30. Id. 2947.

31. In his famous attempt to read corporations out of the Fourteenth Amendment, Justice Black said, "A secret purpose on the part of the members of the Committee, even if such would be the fact, however, would not be sufficient to justify any such construction." Connecticut General Ins. Co. v. Johnson, 303 U.S. 77, 87 (1938), dissenting opinion. Cf. infra Chapter 8 at notes 77 and 95.

idea of a trick, a contrivance, to do something by taking advantage
of others which you cannot do if you make plain to their senses what
is the object.[32]

Shortly after congressional approval of the Amendment, and during the
warm-up for the elections of 1866, a leading Radical, Congressman Robert C. Schenck of Ohio, averred the Democrats "are afraid that it may
have some concealed purpose of elevating negroes . . . [to] make them
voters. It goes to no such length."[33]

   "Equal protection," as will appear, emerged from the framers' intention to outlaw *laws* which discriminated against blacks with respect to
the "coverage of the Civil Rights Act." "Indeed," Bickel himself concluded, "*no specific purpose* going beyond the [limited] coverage of the
Civil Rights Act is suggested; rather an awareness on the part of the
framers that it was *a constitution* they were writing, which led to a choice
of language capable of growth."[34] His appeal to the "awareness" of the
framers assumes what needs to be proved—that there was in fact such a
"choice." Such speculation is rebutted by the very limited objectives of
the Civil Rights Act, embodied in the Amendment, the absence of explanation for a change of direction, and the fact that "due process" and
"privileges or immunities" were deemed to be used in their established
sense. If there was such a "choice,"[35] it cannot harbor a purpose they
confessedly dared not submit. Senator Howard, who has been regarded
as "one of the most reckless of the radicals," one who "served consis-

32. *Globe* 1275.

33. Fairman, Stanford 74–75.

34. Bickel 63 (emphasis added). Yet Bickel noted that "equal protection" had a limited
meaning for the "Moderates, led by Trumbull and Fessenden," the right "of benefitting
equally from the laws for the security of person and property." Id. 56.

35. Bickel also builds on the fact that §1 of the Fourteenth Amendment deals with
discrimination "whether or not based on color" and "this feature of it could not have
been deemed to be included in the standard identification of section 1 with the Civil
Rights Act," an indication of future breadth. Id. 60. But §1 of the Civil Rights Act likewise provided that "the inhabitants of every race and color . . . shall have the same right,"
and the debates show that its coverage extended to whites. As Bickel noticed, Senator
Trumbull stated that "this bill applies to white men as well as black men. It declares that
all persons . . . shall be entitled to the same civil rights." *Globe* 599; Bickel 14 note 36. In
any event, inclusion of whites does not broaden the protection for property and personal
security which the Act provided for both blacks and whites.

tently in the vanguard of the extreme negrophiles,"[36] explained to the
Senate that he would have preferred to

> secure suffrage to the colored race to some extent at least . . . But
> sir, it is not a question what you, or I, or half a dozen other mem-
> bers of the Senate may prefer in respect to colored suffrage . . . the
> question really is, what will the Legislatures of the various States
> . . . do in the premises; what is likely to meet the general approba-
> tion of the people. The Committee were of the opinion that the
> States are not yet prepared to sanction so fundamental a change.[37]

How is Bickel's "undisclosed" purpose to be reconciled with the fact
that an attempt to provide for Negro suffrage *after 1876* was rejected?
Robert Dale Owen, a pro-suffrage reformer, had brought a proposal
which Stevens placed before the Joint Committee. Section 2 of the proposal provided that after July 4, 1876 (a fitting anniversary for enfranchisement), "no discrimination shall be made . . . as to . . . the right of
suffrage."[38] Owen's reason for the "prospective suffrage," he explained
to Stevens, was that "the negro is, for the present, unprepared wisely to
use the right of suffrage."[39] When this provision was noised about,
Stevens told Owen,

> members from New York, from Illinois . . . from Indiana held, each
> separately, a caucus to consider whether equality of suffrage, present
> *or prospective*, ought to form a part of the Republican programme for
> the coming canvass. They were afraid . . . some of them . . . might
> lose their elections . . . [E]ach one of these caucuses decided that
> negro suffrage, *in any shape*, ought to be excluded.[40]

In consequence, the 1876 proposal was dropped and the Committee substituted a "new section simply eliminating from the basis of represen-

---

36. Kendrick 192.

37. *Globe* 2766.

38. Bickel 41–42; Kendrick 83–84.

39. Kendrick 298. This view was shared by Senator Fessenden, *Globe* 704; William A.
Newell of New Jersey, id. 867; and Stevens himself, supra Chapter 4 at note 64. See also
C. Vann Woodward, *The Burden of Southern History* 92 (1960).

40. Kendrick 302 (emphasis added).

tation persons to whom the vote was denied,"[41] the present §2. Add to this Senator Howard's statement of the Joint Committee's opinion that "three-fourths of the States . . . could not be induced to grant the right of suffrage, *even in any degree* or under any restriction, to the colored race,"[42] and we have solid evidence which overcomes speculation that there was an unrevealed purpose to confer broader powers in the future.

### ALFRED KELLY

Kelly does not follow Bickel's theory of a behind-the-scenes "compromise" between Radicals and Moderates, but suggests that the Radicals attempted, baldly stated, to hoodwink the Moderates. He regards it as "highly probable" that the Civil Rights Act "was not intended to bar racial segregation and classification laws." But he finds that

> The intent of certain Radical leaders to go beyond the restrictive enumeration of the Civil Rights Act and to incorporate a series of expansive guarantees in the Constitution is quite clear . . . the *best evidence* of this is the language of the guarantees which Bingham and the other authors of the Fourteenth Amendment incorporated in the first section. The guarantees they finally adopted—privileges and immunities, due process and equal protection—were not at all derived from the Civil Rights Act, which . . . had used the restricted enumerative device. Instead, the authors derived their guarantees deliberately from the prewar Radical antislavery movement.[43]

A Constitution, Chief Justice Marshall stated, cannot have "the prolixity of a code";[44] there the drive is for the most compressed utterance. Moreover, the terms of §1 were far from "vague and amorphous."[45] "Privileges or immunities" was drawn from Article IV, §2, via the Civil Rights

41. Bickel 43.

42. *Globe* 2766 (emphasis added).

43. Kelly, Fourteenth 1069, 1071 (emphasis added).

44. "A constitution, to contain an accurate detail of all the subdivisions of which its great powers will admit . . . would partake of the prolixity of a legal code, and could scarcely be embraced by the human mind." M'Culloch v. Maryland, 17 U.S. (4 Wheat.) 316, 407 (1819); cf. Bickel 61.

45. Kelly, Fourteenth 1071.

Bill, which adopted the established judicial construction.[46] An abolitionist departure needs to be proved, not assumed by reference to "expansive" language. Bingham himself repudiated such notions when he declared that the meaning of "due process" was to be found in the decisions of the courts.[47] That his conception of "equal protection" did not go beyond the ban on discriminatory laws with respect to the enumerated "fundamental rights" is again demonstrated by his defense of Tennessee's disenfranchisement of blacks, regretting that though "We are all for equal and exact justice . . . justice for all is not to be secured in a day."[48]

Next Kelly notices a "curious ambiguity . . . in the Radicals' advocacy of the measure . . . It was as though the Radical leaders were avoiding a precise delineation of legal consequences," this on the basis of their resort to the "technique of lofty, expansive and highly generalized language."[49] Why such avoidance? He explains that

> there was a substantial block of moderate Republicans who had not yet committed themselves entirely to the Radical position . . . if [Bingham et al.] drove home too far the proposition that this amendment would undoubtedly consummate the destruction of all caste and class legislation . . . moderate Republican support might be alienated and the requisite two-thirds majority necessary to the amendment's adoption might not be obtained. Political strategy called for ambiguity not clarity.[50]

Stripped of fig leaves, the Kelly rationale would give the Amendment a meaning which the radicals had concealed even from their Moderate confreres! In truth, there is no evidence of a concealed purpose. How did Bingham's "lofty generalizations" become freighted with a cargo he had severely condemned as "oppressive" and "unjust" when he insisted

46. Andrew J. Rogers charged that §1 "is no more nor less than an attempt to embody in the Constitution . . . that outrageous and miserable civil rights bill"; later he stated that it "simply embodied the gist of the civil rights bill." *Globe* 2538; *Globe App.* 229; quoted in Bickel 48, 54. This was the all but universal view; supra Chapter 2 at notes 10–13.

47. Infra Chapter 11 at notes 36–37.

48. *Globe* 3979.

49. Kelly, Fourteenth 1077.

50. Id. 1084.

upon deletion of the words "civil rights" from the Civil Rights Bill?[50a]
Although Bingham was given to windy oratory,[51] his own words show
that he did not regard "due process," "equal protection," and "privileges
or immunities" as "lofty generalizations," but rather as terms of known
and limited content. For example, he explained that "privileges or immunities" was drawn from Article IV, §2, that "due process" had been
judicially defined. Then, too, Bingham and Stevens are an odd couple to
conspire to pull the wool over the eyes of their colleagues. On the floor
of the House in the 39th Congress, Stevens said of Bingham: "In all this
contest about reconstruction I do not propose either to take his counsel,
recognize his authority, or believe a word he says."[52]

### WILLIAM VAN ALSTYNE

After downgrading some statements in the debates, Van Alstyne nevertheless concludes that "the case can safely be made that there was an
original understanding that §1 of the proposed Fourteenth Amendment
would not itself *immediately* invalidate state suffrage laws severely restricting the right to vote." But, he states, "we cannot safely declare that
there was also a clear, uniform understanding that the *open-ended* phrases
of §1 . . . would foreclose a *different application in the future* [because invalidation of State Negro suffrage laws] was avoided . . . from *fear* that
such an amendment would not be ratified and that its Republican sponsors would be *turned out of office* at the next congressional election."[53]
Van Alstyne reverses the normal order of proof, that a departure from
the norm was intended, that what was unmistakably excluded in 1866

50a. Infra Chapter 7 at notes 11–21.

51. For example, by way of prelude to a quotation from Kent, who had frequently
been cited without florid panegyrics, Bingham must needs gild the lily: "one of those
grand intellects who during life illustrated the jurisprudence of our country, and has left
in his works a perpetual monument of his genius, his learning, and his wisdom." *Globe*
1292. It is instructive to compare the flow of such effusions with the spare, lean style of
Fessenden, Trumbull, and Hale. See also infra Chapter 8 note 54.

52. *Cong. Globe*, 39th Cong., 2d Sess. 816 (Jan. 28, 1867). See also infra Chapter 13
at notes 30–36; Kluger, infra Chapter 7 note 20.

53. Van Alstyne 72 (emphasis added).

was to be embraced in 1966. For such extraordinary drafting *proof*, not speculation, is required.

In an attempt to offer some proof Van Alstyne argues that Congress had based its authority to enact the Civil Rights Act on the fact that it was "appropriate legislation to enforce the mere ban on 'slavery' in §1 of the Thirteenth Amendment." He continues: "fresh from their own experience in developing new applications of the Thirteenth Amendment . . . the Radicals could scarcely have failed to foresee that the still broader contours of the Fourteenth Amendment would offer greater possibilities for the future."[54] Undeniably some appealed to the Thirteenth Amendment for constitutional authority to enact the Civil Rights Act. But there was vigorous opposition. Conkling declared that "Emancipation vitalizes only natural rights, not political rights."[55] And most Republicans held that natural rights did not include the right to vote. Senator Henry Wilson, a Massachusetts Radical, stated that the Thirteenth Amendment "was never understood by any man in the Senate or House to confer upon Congress the right to prescribe or regulate the suffrage in any State . . . If it had been supposed that it gave that power the amendment would never have passed the Congress, never have received the sanction of the States."[56] Considerable impetus to the Fourteenth Amendment was given by Bingham's insistence that there was no constitutional authority for the Civil Rights Bill and that an amendment was required.[57] And the fact that Congress went on to enact the Fourteenth Amendment refutes the view that the Thirteenth was conceived to be "open-ended," to authorize legislation going beyond emancipation.

54. Id. 74–75.
55. *Globe* 356.
56. Id. 1255. "George Ticknor Curtis typified a large stream of conservative constitutionalism in his argument that the Thirteenth Amendment diminished states' powers not one whit beyond abolition." H. M. Hyman, *A More Perfect Union* 428 (1973). Senator Cowan, a Conservative Republican from Pennsylvania, stated that the Thirteenth Amendment was understood merely "to liberate the negro slave from his master." *Globe* 499. On the other hand, Senator Howard, a member of the Judiciary Committee that drafted the Thirteenth Amendment, understood it to authorize the Civil Rights Bill. *Globe* 503. [United States v. Harris, 106 U.S. 629, 643 (1882) rejected the notion that "under a provision of the Constitution which simply abolished slavery and involuntary servitude, we should with few exceptions invest Congress with power of the whole catalog of crimes."]
57. *Globe* 1291.

Even "more significance" is attached by Van Alstyne to what he views as an important parallel between the Civil Rights Act and the Fourteenth Amendment.[58] When Bingham objected that the "no discrimination in civil rights" sentence of the Act was oppressive and invaded States' Rights,[59] the Committee deleted the sentence, and Chairman Wilson explained, "I do not think it materially changes the bill, but some gentlemen were apprehensive that the words we propose to strike out might give warrant for a latitudinarian construction not intended."[60] In contrast, Van Alstyne points out, although "several of the Democrats declared . . . that the Privileges and Immunities Clause would eventually be applied to suffrage . . . the Republicans declined to limit the language of §1 [of the Amendment] to avoid such application." The moral he draws is that the "Civil Rights Act was, of course, a statute; a law not expected to 'endure for ages to come.' The Fourteenth Amendment was something else again."[61] A more prosaic explanation can serve. Bingham was an influential Republican with a following, and the deletion of the "civil rights" sentence, regarded as gratuitous, was a small price to pay for bringing him into camp; whereas the objections of "several Democrats" could safely be ignored because their votes could be written off.[62] The Republicans, who had been assured both during enactment of the Civil Rights Bill and consideration of the Amendment that neither purported to grant suffrage, needed no express exception to make that plain. The established rule is that if a thing is within the intention of the framers, it is as good as written in the text.[63]

---

58. Van Alstyne 75.

59. *Globe* 1291; see Chapter 7 at notes 12–15. Van Alstyne, 76, states that "In spite of the declarations that the bill would not affect voting rights, even Bingham was not satisfied. He moved to strike out the opening general phrase . . . he doubted both the *wisdom* and constitutionality of legislating with respect to the franchise" (emphasis added). Since Bingham was the architect of §1 of the Amendment, how did he become the vehicle of smuggling an undisclosed provision for suffrage into the section?

60. *Globe* 1366; Van Alstyne 77.

61. Van Alstyne 73, 77.

62. Democratic Senator Saulsbury's proposal to add to the Civil Rights Bill "except the right to vote in the State" was rebuffed by Senator Trumbull: "This bill relates to civil rights only, and I do not want to bring up the question of negro suffrage in the bill." *Globe* 606; Van Alstyne 76; cf. supra at note 17.

63. Supra Chapter 1 note 24.

The hypotheses of Bickel, Kelly, and Van Alstyne seem to me a speculative fabric that collapses under the fact, made so clear by the framers, that they did not mean to confer Negro suffrage, present *or prospective*. And the theory runs into another formidable obstacle. During the ratification process, in the summer election campaign of 1866, the Republicans repeatedly assured the people that, in the words of Senator John Sherman of Ohio, the Amendment "was an embodiment of the Civil Rights Bill," itemizing several of its provisions. A similar assurance was given by Senator Lane of Indiana.[64] Congressman Schenck of Ohio repudiated "a concealed purpose" to confer Negro suffrage; his Ohio colleague Columbus Delano stressed that the Amendment was designed to make citizens "safe in the South."[65] Logan of Illinois said it was meant to permit the citizen "to sue and be sued, to own property, to have process of court," a reminder of the limited objectives of the Civil Rights Act, accompanied by a specific disclaimer that §1 "gives the negro the right of suffrage."[66] These and still other representations collected by Charles Fairman militate against a concealed purpose to go beyond the confines of the Act.

Finally, be it assumed that there was an undisclosed purpose, the question arises whether "ratification" extends to objectives that were not disclosed, that were in fact expressly disclaimed. The doctrine of ratification premises that the principal knows what he is ratifying; without full disclosure there can be no ratification.[67] And there is the larger issue of political morality. Ours is a generation insistent on full disclosure, for example, in the marketing of corporate securities. To accept dissimulation as a means of obtaining a constitutional amendment would be to condone lower morals in the halls of Congress than is demanded in the marketplace.[68]

64. Fairman, Stanford 77, 74.

65. Id. 74, 75.

66. Id. 70. James, 179, said, "statements of congressmen before their constituents definitely identify the provisions of the first section of the amendment with those of the Civil Rights Bill."

67. Infra Chapter 8 at note 93. See supra note 21.

68. Justice Douglas wrote, "The principle of full disclosure has as much place in government as it does in the market place," William O. Douglas, "Stare Decisis," 49 Colum. L. Rev. 735, 754 (1949).

# 7

## Segregated Schools

THE "desegregation" decision in *Brown v. Board of Education*[1] was, as Richard Kluger called it, an act of "Simple Justice,"[2] a long over-due attempt to rectify the grievous wrongs done to the blacks. For the legal historian, however, the question is whether the Fourteenth Amendment authorized the Supreme Court to perform that act.[3] For the Court, like every agency of government, may act only within the limits of its constitutional powers. As Lee stated in the Virginia Ratification Convention, "When a question arises with respect to the legality of any power, exercised or assumed," the question will be, "*Is it enumerated in the Constitution?* . . . It is otherwise arbitrary and unconstitutional."[4]

In his illuminating study of the way in which the desegregation case was handled in the Supreme Court, Kluger asks, "Could it be reasonably claimed that segregation had been outlawed by the Fourteenth when the yet more basic emblem of citizenship—the ballot—had been withheld from the Negro under that amendment?"[5] Given the rampant racism in the North of 1866—which still has to loose its grip—it needs to be explained how a North which provided for or mandated segregated schools[6] was brought to vote for desegregation in the Amendment.

When the "desegregation" case came to the Court in 1952, Justice Frankfurter assigned the task of compiling the legislative history of the

1. 347 U.S. 483 (1954).
2. Richard Kluger, *Simple Justice* (1976); hereinafter Kluger.
3. "The result," Archibald Cox stated, "can only be described as a revolution in constitutional law." *The Role of the Supreme Court in American Government* 57 (1976).
4. 3 Jonathan Eliot, *Debates in the Several State Conventions on the Adoption of the Federal Constitution* 186 (1836); Berger, *Congress v. The Supreme Court* 13–16.
5. Kluger 635.
6. Infra at notes 24–25.

Amendment to his brilliant clerk, Alexander Bickel,[7] who was destined to become one of the foremost authorities in the field of constitutional law. Upon completing the assignment, in August 1953, Bickel delivered his memorandum to Frankfurter with a covering letter in which he stated: "it is impossible to conclude that the 39th Congress intended that segregation be abolished; impossible also to conclude that they foresaw it might be, under the language they were adopting."[8] When he later published a revision of that memorandum, he concluded: "there is no evidence whatever showing that for its sponsors the civil rights formula had anything to do with unsegregated schools. Wilson, its sponsor in the House, specifically disclaimed any such notion."[9] Wilson, chairman of the House Judiciary Committee and the House Manager of the Bill, who could therefore speak authoritatively, had advised the House that the words "civil rights . . . do not mean that all citizens shall sit on juries, or that their children shall attend the same schools. These are not civil rights."[10] Wilson's statement is proof positive that segregation was excluded from the scope of the bill.

Another piece of evidence, which Alfred Kelly, one of the historians drawn into the case by the NAACP,[11] considered "very damning," was the "removal of the 'no discrimination' clause from the Civil Rights Bill." The Bill, he stated, "was amended specifically to eliminate any reference to discriminatory practices like school segregation . . . it looked as if a specific exclusion had been made."[12] The deletion was made at the in-

---

7. Kluger 599, 653.

8. Id. 654. Kluger states that the Bickel memorandum held that "the legislative history, while revealing no evidence that the framers of the amendment had intended to prohibit school segregation, did not foreclose future generations from acting on the question, either by congressional statute or by judicial review." Id. 655; see also 634. But this is at odds with Bickel's covering letter, supra Chapter 6 at note 7. In fact, as will shortly appear, the framers deliberately *excluded* school segregation from the ambit of the Civil Rights Bill and therefore of the Amendment.

9. Bickel 56.

10. *Globe* 1117. Wilson's statement is more fully quoted supra Chapter 2 at note 26. He later reiterated that the limited objectives of the bill did not extend to "setting aside the school laws and jury laws." *Globe* 1294.

11. Kluger 626.

12. Id. 635. Among the legal historians drawn into preparation of the briefs by the NAACP was Howard Jay Graham. Id. 625–626. "He was particularly troubled by Rep-

sistence of John A. Bingham, the architect of the Fourteenth Amendment, whom neoabolitionists regard as the conduit through which abolitionist concepts of substantive due process and equal protection were poured into the Amendment.[13] Roughly speaking, he moved for instructions to the Judiciary Committee to strike the "no discrimination" sentence of the Bill,[14] in order to render it "less oppressive and therefore less objectionable." The enactment of laws "for the general government of the people" was reserved to the States; "civil rights," he continued, "include and embrace *every* right that pertains to a citizen as such," including "political rights." On this view the Bill, according to Bingham, proposed "simply to strike down by congressional enactment every state constitution which makes a discrimination on account of race or color *in any* of the civil rights of the citizen." With "some few exceptions every state in the Union does make some discrimination . . . in respect of civil rights on account of color." Hence the "no discrimination" sentence "must be striken out or the constitutions of the States are to be abolished by your act." Deletion of this sentence would remove what he considered the Bill's "oppressive and I might say its unjust provisions," all of which adds up to a States' Rights manifesto. Bingham's censure, how-

---

resentative Wilson's insistence during the phase of the debates dealing with the 'no discrimination' clause that the Civil Rights Bill was not intended to outlaw separate schools. That negative reference, Graham reported, was unfortunate, particularly since he was House Manager of the . . . bill." Id. 634–635.

The "key session" of the NAACP "giant conference running for three days and nights" was "devoted to the papers of [Howard] Jay Graham and Alfred Kelly on the troubling relationship between the Civil Rights Act of 1866, which had been specifically stripped of its broad 'no discrimination' language, and the Fourteenth Amendment, created in its immediate aftermath and conceived, as many historians believed, simply to constitutionalize the rights act." Id. 637. The paper Kelly delivered was on "the damning modification of the Civil Rights Bill in the House and its apparent identity in purpose with the Fourteenth Amendment." He recounted that he "didn't understand the relationship between advocacy and history at that point" and considered the problem "nearly insurmountable." Id. 637.

13. TenBroek 145–148; Graham 280, 283.

14. The Bill is set out in pertinent part supra Chapter 2 at note 14. [Justice Harlan pointed out that Bingham, in the meetings of the Joint Committee on Reconstruction, was "successful in replacing section 1 of Owen's proposal, which read 'No discrimination . . . as to the civil *rights*,' with the 'abridge the *privileges* or immunities of citizens.' " Oregon v. Mitchell, 400 U.S. 112, 172 (1970) (emphasis added).]

ever, does not extend to the *enumerated* rights that follow the "no discrimination" clause; these he quotes with approval, but asserts that the needed reform should be accomplished "not by an arbitrary assumption of power, but by amending the Constitution . . . expressly forbidding the States from any such abuse [that is, denial of said specified rights] in the future."[15] In short, the enumerated rights should be protected by Amendment against State abuse, whereas the "civil rights," which embraced any and every right, should be excised because "oppressive." In this Bingham was in accord with the restricted objectives of almost all of his Republican colleagues who spoke to the measure.[16] Bickel therefore correctly concluded that Bingham, "while committing himself to the need for safeguarding by constitutional amendment the specific rights enumerated in the body of section 1, was anything but willing to make a similar commitment to 'civil rights' in general."[17]

Not without cause was this regarded gloomily in the camp of the NAACP. Kluger relates:

> In calling for the deletion, Bingham, the former abolition theorist, had openly acknowledged that the bill as drafted would have prohibited statutes such as school segregation. Since that broad language was in fact deleted from the final form of the bill and since many of the proponents of the Fourteenth held that the amendment had no purpose beyond constitutionalizing the Civil Rights Act, it had therefore seemed to Kelly, [Thurgood] Marshall, Ming, and others in the NAACP camp that they could not reasonably argue that the framers intended the amendment to prohibit school segregation.[18]

Finally, a "light" broke through, "a really plausible interpretation" dawned on Kelly: "Bingham's objection to the 'no discrimination' was based solely on the apparent lack of constitutional authority for so

15. *Globe* 1291–1293 (emphasis added).
16. E.g., Wilson, supra at note 10.
17. Bickel 24.
18. Kluger 640–641. The noted historian Henry Steele Commager had advised the NAACP that "The framers of the amendment did not, so far as we know, intend that it should be used to end segregation in schools." Id. 620.

sweeping a congressional enactment."[19] This was a "light" that failed. Kelly completely overlooked Bingham's separation between the too-inclusive "civil rights," which were deleted, and the enumerated rights, which, because they also trenched on traditional State governance, required an amendment. Justice Black understood this if Kelly did not.[20]

More important, Chairman Wilson confirms that the deletion was merely designed to repel a "latitudinarian" construction:

> Some members of the House thought, in the general words of the first section in relation to civil rights, it might be held by the courts that the right of suffrage was included in those rights. To obviate that difficulty and the difficulty growing out of any other construction beyond the specific rights named in the section, our amendment strikes out all of those general terms and leaves the bill with the rights specified in the section.

The deletion, Wilson further explained, was made because "some gentlemen were apprehensive that the words we propose to strike out might give warrant for a latitudinarian construction not intended."[21]

To Kelly, who later defended the desegregation decision, Bickel's view "seems a very doubtful reading of Bingham's position. It ignores his extensive extremist antislavery background as well as his position in Congress as one of the strong Radical Republicans."[22] But neither Bingham's

---

19. Id. 641.

20. Justice Black, for whom Bingham is the authoritative expositor, recognized that Bingham objected to the Civil Rights Bill because "it would actually strip the states of power to govern, centralizing all power in the Federal Government. To this he was opposed." Adamson v. California, 332 U.S. 46, 100 (1947), dissenting opinion.

Kluger 641, relates, "One hurdle in the way of [Kelly's] reading of Bingham's intention was a later speech of Thaddeus Stevens, the most powerful man in the House and a strong ally of Bingham. Among other things, Stevens said that a principal purpose of the Fourteenth Amendment had indeed been to re-enact and therefore insure the constitutionality of the Civil Rights Act (even shorn of its broad 'no discrimination' language)—an apparent concession to those who wished to interpret the amendment narrowly. But Kelly concluded that the apparently damaging portion of Stevens' speech had to be considered against the larger political picture and the clear drift of Stevens' generally radical utterances." One thing he was plainly not so radical about was desegregation in the schools. See infra at note 39.

21. *Globe* 1366.

22. Kelly, Fourteenth 1068 note 73. In this very article, however, Kelly concluded, "It

background nor his position had dissuaded him from opposition to Negro suffrage.[23] Moreover, as Bickel informed Justice Frankfurter, "It was doubtful that an explicit 'no discrimination' provision going beyond the enumerated rights in the Civil Rights Bill as finally enacted could have passed in the Thirty-Ninth Congress."[24] At this time "Eight [Northern] states either provided for separate schools or left it up to local communities to adopt that practice if they wished. Five states outside the old Confederacy either directly or by implication excluded colored children entirely from their public schools."[25] Kluger comments, "If Congress and state legislatures had understood that the amendment was to wipe away the practices, surely there would have been more than a few howls."[26] With suffrage unequivocally barred there was no reason to infer that desegregation, a far more touchy matter, was required.

Then there was another thorny fact: "Congress had permitted segregated schools in the District of Columbia from 1864 onward."[27] Sumner's "long fight to abolish segregated Negro schools in the District of Columbia" had been "unavailing."[28] With good reason did Judge E. Barrett Prettyman hold in *Carr v. Corning*[29] that congressional support for

---

seems highly probable, then, that the Civil Rights Act, as finally passed, was not intended to ban state racial segregation and classification laws. The main force of the Conservatives' attack on the 'no discrimination' clause was that it would indeed destroy all race classification laws." Id. 1069–1070.

Bingham's remarks have been subject to varying interpretations, see Bickel 27 note 54; Kelly, Fourteenth 1068. Bickel sums up, "Whatever the ambiguities of his speech, one thing is certain. Unless one concludes that Bingham entertained apprehensions about the breadth of the term 'civil rights' and was unwilling at this stage, as a matter of policy, not constitutional law, to extend a federal guaranty covering all that might be included in that term, there is no rational explanation for his motion to strike it." Bickel 25–26. Certainly Wilson so understood; supra at note 21.

23. E.g., supra Chapter 5 at notes 42–43.

24. Kluger 654–655.

25. Id. 633–634.

26. Id. 635.

27. Id. The problem also troubled Justice Jackson, infra at note 43.

28. Kelly, Fourteenth 1085. For example, when Senator Wilson proposed to allocate funds for the public schools in the District of Columbia, explaining that existing law provided "for the establishment of colored schools" in the District, and the funds would be divided pro rata, Reverdy Johnson asked for and received assurance that "there is no authority to have a mixture of children in any one school." *Globe* 708–709.

29. 182 F.2d 14, 17 (D.C. Cir. 1950).

segregated schools in the District of Columbia contemporaneously with the adoption of the Amendment (and the Civil Rights Act) was conclusive evidence that Congress had not intended §1 of the Amendment to invalidate school segregation laws. Kelly too lightly dismissed this: "technically the parallel is not constitutionally precise or apposite."[30] To the contrary, the parallel is both "precise and apposite." It has long been the rule that laws dealing with the same subject—in pari materia—must be construed with reference to each other, "as if they were one law."[31] The Amendment originated as a congressional Joint Resolution, so it is entirely appropriate to look to the light shed contemporaneously by the District of Columbia bills on the meaning of the Resolution. In truth, it is unrealistic to presume that a Congress which has plenary jurisdiction over the District and yet refused to bar segregation there would turn around to invade State sovereignty, which the framers were zealous to preserve, in order to impose a requirement of desegregation upon the States. The difference was fully appreciated by Senator Henry Wilson, a Radical Republican from Massachusetts, who introduced a bill providing for suffrage in the District of Columbia, but lamented that in "dealing with the States," State "constitutions block up the way and we may not overleap the barriers."[32]

The relation of mixed schools to the limited objectives that were expressed in the Civil Rights Act was lucidly summarized by John L. Thomas of Maryland:

> As a freeman, he is entitled to acquire and dispose of real and other property . . . to have his life, liberty, and person protected by the same laws that protect me . . . so shall he not only have the right to enforce his contract, but to that end shall be received as a witness in a court of justice on the same terms . . . It would be an outrage . . . [if] we were to refuse to throw around them such legal guards as will prove their only protection and secure to them the enforcement of their rights.

30. Kelly, Fourteenth 1085.

31. United States v. Freeman, 44 U.S. (3 How.) 556, 564 (1845). See also infra Appendix A note 46.

32. Phillip S. Paludan, *A Covenant With Death* 50 (1975).

> I will go even further . . . and will vote for all measures to elevate
> their condition and to educate them separate and apart from the
> whites . . . [B]ut when it comes to placing him upon the same social
> and political level as my own race, I must refuse to do it.[33]

There is yet other evidence that the framers had no intention of striking down segregation. The Senate gallery itself was segregated, as Senator Reverdy Johnson mordantly remarked.[34] The Carl Schurz report *Education of the Freedmen* spoke throughout of "'colored schools,' 'school
houses in which colored children were taught.' There were no references
to unsegregated schools, even as an ultimate objective."[35] Instead there
was a pervasive assumption that segregation would remain. Referring to
the burning of black schools in Maryland, Josiah B. Grinnell of Iowa said,
give them schoolhouses and "invite schoolmasters from all over the world
to come and instruct them." Senator Daniel Clark of New Hampshire
stated, "you may establish for him schools." Ignatius Donnelly of Minnesota stated, "Educate him and he will himself see to it that the common
schools shall forever continue among his people."[36] Senator William P.
Fessenden said of the "representation" proposal that was to become §2 of
the Fourteenth Amendment: it "should serve as an inducement to the
southern States to build school houses . . . and educate their colored children until they are fit to vote."[37] In vetoing the antecedent Freedmen's
Bureau Bill, President Johnson noted that it provided for the "erection for

33. *Globe* 263–264. For a similar expression by Patterson of New Hampshire, see supra Chapter 2 at note 30. So, too, Republican Senator Cowan of Pennsylvania was willing
to secure to blacks "their natural rights" but not to desegregate the schools. *Globe* 500.
See also Republican Thomas T. Davis of New York, infra Chapter 10 at note 21.

34. *Globe* 766: "Why is it that [you have] separate places for the respective races even
in your own chamber? Why are they not put together?"

35. Bickel 10 note 29.

36. *Globe* 652, 834, 590; cf. Donnelly, id. 513. Recall Lawrence's exclusion of "political
rights [and] those dependent on local law," as was the privilege of attending public schools,
supra Chapter 2 note 28, and Windom's statement that the Civil Rights Bill does not
confer "the privilege of voting" nor "social privileges." Supra Chapter 2 note 30.

John F. Farnsworth feared that enfranchisement alone might not suffice if it were dependent on reading and writing qualifications, for the States may "exclude him from the
schools." *Globe* 383. See also Frederick Pike of Maine, id. 407. Enfranchisement failed,
as did attempts to open the schools. See infra note 40.

37. Kendrick 206.

their benefit of suitable buildings for asylums and schools," and objected that Congress "has never founded schools for any class of our own people."[38] Thaddeus Stevens "did not publicly object to the separation of the races in the schools although he was against segregation in theory . . . But he never pressed for legal enforcement of this kind of equality, as Charles Sumner did, believing it achievement enough that the South would have free schools at all."[39]

Additional light may be gathered from post–Fourteenth Amendment developments, part of Sumner's continuing campaign for desegregated schools. On March 16, 1867, Sumner moved to amend a Supplementary Bill to require "that State constitutions provide for a system of non-discriminatory public schools." The motion failed; it "went beyond what majority sentiment would sustain."[40] Let an impassioned apostle of the incorporation of abolitionist ideology—Howard Jay Graham—sum up:

> There were many reasons why men's understanding of equal pro-
> tection, as applied to educational matters, was imperfect in 1866 . . .

38. *Globe* 916.

39. Fawn Brodie, *Thaddeus Stevens: Scourge of the South* 320 (1959). Stevens assured the electorate in September 1866 that the Amendment "does not touch social or political rights." James 201. Perhaps the reason, as Rogers noted, was that in "Pennsylvania there is a discrimination between the schools for white children and the schools for blacks. The laws there provide that certain schools shall be set aside for black persons," and inquired whether Congress has a right to "interfere with these statutes." *Globe* 1121. Senator Cowan of Pennsylvania objected to such interference. Id. 500.

40. Fairman, History 329. Sumner "placed little stress upon the Fourteenth Amendment guarantee of equal protection of the laws; too many of his colleagues who had helped draft that ambiguous document would reply that they had never intended to outlaw segregation . . . When Senator Morrill insisted upon learning exactly where in the Constitution the federal government was given control 'over matters of education, worship, amusement . . .' Sumner discovered authorization in the Sermon on the Mount and in the Declaration of Independence." Donald, *Sumner II* 532.

As late as December 1871 Sumner reintroduced a bill which had been adversely reported in 1870–1871: "He maintained that hotels, public conveyances and schools . . . should be opened equally to all." Flack 250. "Without this complementary bill," the Civil Rights Act "was imperfect, he declared," Flack 251. Though there was some contrariety of opinion, id. 253–265, the House, by a vote of 128 to 48, insisted on an amendment "striking out all reference to common schools," id. 275. Senator Morrill opposed the Sumner bill because the "Federal Government had no right to take cognizance of matters of education, amusement . . . it is without warrant in the Constitution," i.e., the Fourteenth Amendment. Id. 252–253.

Negroes were barred from public schools of the North and still widely regarded as "racially inferior" and "incapable of education." Even comparatively enlightened leaders then accepted segregation in the schools.[41]

The "imperfect" "understanding of equal protection" in 1866 means that the framers did not conceive it in the vastly broadened terms given to the phrase by the Warren Court. How did this history fare in the Warren Court?

In his painstaking reconstruction of the progress of *Brown v. Board of Education*, Richard Kluger has furnished some fascinating glimpses behind the portals of the Supreme Court.[42] The case was first argued before the Vinson Court; Chief Justice Vinson "found it 'Hard to get away' from the contemporary view by its framers that the Fourteenth Amendment did not prohibit segregation." Jackson noted, "For 90 years segregated schools [existed] in the city [Washington]."[43] Frankfurter, "a keen observer of his colleagues' voting inclinations," listed Clark—along with Vinson, Reed, and Jackson—as "probable dissenters if the

---

41. Graham 290 note 70. Nevertheless Graham stated that "no one is obliged or disposed to grant—that an outright majority of 1866–1868 did regard race segregation in *their* public schools, as a peculiar form of race discrimination—as one which in *their* judgment, would remain unaffected by the Fourteenth Amendment." Id. 291.

Compare with the foregoing history, in considerable part earlier set forth by Alexander Bickel, Charles Black's recent statement: "I started, virtually [as of NAACP counsel], with Brown v. The Board of Education, a case which seemed to me then and still seems to me to have been as nearly syllogistic as a real law case can be. The Fourteenth Amendment, in *the clear light of its history*, and without any straining or special pleading, forbade *all* discrimination against black people as such, however euphemized and however daubed with cosmetics." C. Black, "The Judicial Power as Guardian of Liberties," statement prepared for delivery at a Symposium on Constitutional Liberties in Modern America, Wayne State University, Detroit, Michigan, October 16, 1976, 2 (emphasis added). Chief Justice Warren's "syllogisms" are examined infra Chapter 13 at notes 56–60. Black's "clear . . . history" seemed "inconclusive" to Chief Justice Warren, who chose rather not to "turn back the clock to 1868." See infra at note 61.

42. Among other things, Kluger consulted the notes of Justices Burton, Frankfurter, and Jackson, and interviewed several of the Justices and the Justices' clerks. Kluger 788–789.

43. Id. 590.

Court voted to overturn *Plessy* in the spring of 1953."[44] If they were to be brought about, time was needed; a decision outlawing segregation by a divided Court would have produced tremendous shock waves.[45] With Bickel's aid Frankfurter framed five questions for reargument, which the Court submitted to counsel and put the case over to the next term.[46] The Frankfurter tactic paid off in an unexpected way: the sudden demise of Chief Justice Vinson just before the *Brown* reargument. How much that mattered may be gathered from Frankfurter's remark: "This is the first indication I have ever had that there is a God."[47] And that remark also reveals that men and votes, not the impalpable "consensus of society" picked up by judicial antennae, are what count.

The most interesting figure was Frankfurter himself. According to William Coleman, who had clerked for him a few years earlier and was the coordinator of research for the NAACP in the various States, Frankfurter "was for ending segregation from the very start."[48] A remarkable fact: Frankfurter, the sworn foe of subjective judgment, who disclaimed enforcement of his own "private view rather than the consensus of society's opinion,"[49] had made up his mind "from the day the cases were

44. Id. 612, 614; Plessy v. Ferguson, 163 U.S. 537 (1896), the "separate but equal" decision.

45. Kluger 600. "Nothing could have been worse, for the Court or the nation itself, than a flurry of conflicting opinions that would confuse and anger the American people." Id. 696. Desegregation could hardly have been imposed upon the nation by a divided Court; the stakes simply were too high. Frankfurter "played a pivotal role in bringing about a unanimous Court" in Brown. Joseph P. Lash, *From the Diaries of Felix Frankfurter* 83 (1975).

46. Kluger 614–616.

47. Id. 656. As Justice Frankfurter was dressing for the Vinson funeral, Bickel overheard him murmuring, "An act of Providence, an act of Providence." Lash, supra note 45 at 83. Compare this with his condemnation of "Law" that turns on "contingencies in the choice of successors." Infra Chapter 17 note 44.

48. Kluger 624, 601. "When President Eisenhower appointed Earl Warren to the Chief Justiceship, Frankfurter took him to school on the issues in the *Brown* case in lengthy talks." Lash, supra note 45 at 83–84. [Alexander Bickel, who was a clerk to Justice Frankfurter at the time *Brown v. Board of Education* was decided, wrote, "(W)hen the inner history of that case is known, we may find that he was a moving force in its decision." Alexander Bickel, *The Supreme Court and the Idea of Progress* 33 (1978).]

49. Infra Chapter 14 at note 50. In a file memorandum, the essence of which Frankfurter communicated to his brethren at a conference, he emphasized, "it is not our duty

taken"[50] that segregation must go! This was before hearing argument or reading briefs in a case of extraordinary national importance.[51] Not that he was unaware of the constitutional obstacles. Kluger recounts that Frankfurter "had studied the history of the Fourteenth Amendment" and concluded that "in all likelihood, the framers of the amendment had not intended to outlaw segregation."[52] His conclusion must have been greatly strengthened by the Bickel memorandum, which he found so impressive that "he had it set up in type in the Court's basement print shop and distributed among the Justices a few days before the Brown reargument."[53] Bickel showed, and his demonstration is yet to be successfully controverted, that the 39th Congress meant to leave segregation "as is"—to the States. After the distribution of the Bickel memorandum, Jackson wrote a file memorandum dated February 15, 1954, in which he stated: "despite my personal satisfaction with the Court's [forthcoming] judgment, I simply cannot find, in surveying all the usual sources of law, anything which warrants me in saying that it is required by the original purpose and intent of the Fourteenth or Fifth Amendment."[54] He told the Conference that he would "file a separate concurring opinion" if the "Court feigned that the Justices were doing anything other than declaring new law for a new day."[55] This, Kluger comments, was asking the

---

to express our personal attitudes towards these issues however deep our individual convictions may be. The opposite is true." Kluger 684. [Justice Frankfurter stated, "Nor should resentment or injustice displace the controlling history in judicial construction of the Constitution." *United States v. Lovett*, 328 U.S. 303, 323 (1946), concurring opinion.]

50. Kluger 601. Bickel justly remarked that were the ultimate "reality" that judicial review spells nothing more than "personal preference," the judicial "authority over us is totally intolerable and totally irreconcilable with the theory and practice of political democracy." *The Least Dangerous Branch* 80 (1962).

51. Justice Jackson "was worried about how a Court decision outlawing segregation could affect the nation's respect for 'a supposedly stable organic law' if the Justices were now, overnight, as it were, to alter an interpretation of the Fourteenth Amendment which had stood for more than three-quarters of a century." Kluger 604.

52. Id. 598. Justice Tom Clark "had been surprised by the legislative history, since he had always thought that one of the avowed purposes of the Fourteenth Amendment had been to abolish segregation." Id. 682.

53. Id. 653.

54. Id. 688–689.

55. Id. 681, 609.

majority to admit that "there was no judicial basis for its decision," that "it was acting in a frankly unjudicial way."[56] Kluger considers it "a scarcely reasonable request to make of the brethren."[57] Why not? What kind of "consensus of society" (which the Court purportedly effectuates) is it that cannot withstand the truth—that effectuation required "new law for a new day"? An adult jurisprudence for an age of "realism" surely called for an end to the pretense that it was the Constitution, not the Justices, who spoke.[58] Concealment suggests there may in fact have been no consensus.[59] Perhaps Jackson's insistence impelled Chief Justice Warren—after labeling the history "inconclusive"[60]—to state that "we cannot turn back the clock to 1868,"[61] a veiled declaration that the intention of the framers was irrelevant and that the Court was revising the Constitution to meet present-day needs.[62]

Justice Frankfurter, the professed devotee of "self-restraint," reached a similar conclusion, but in different rhetoric. He had asked, Justice Burton noted, "What justifies us in saying that what *was* equal in 1868 is not equal now?"[63] and in a file memorandum he formulated his own answer:

56. Id. 690, 683.

57. Id. 683.

58. A deterrent, in Justice Frankfurter's words, was that the decision required "the adjustment of men's minds and actions to the unfamiliar and unpleasant." Id. 615. See infra Chapter 14 notes 140, 143, Chapter 23 at notes 30–34.

59. Edmond Cahn welcomed judicial intervention precisely because no amendment could have been obtained. Infra Chapter 15 at note 14.

60. It had not seemed "inconclusive" to Vinson, supra at note 43; Frankfurter, supra at note 52; Jackson, supra at note 54; Clark, supra note 52; and probably not to Reed, Kluger 595–596, 680–692.

61. 347 U.S. at 489, 492. *Brown* told about Warren's "unabashed and primary commitment to justice and his willingness to shape the law to achieve it." Paul Murphy, *The Constitution in Crisis Times, 1918–1969* 312 (1972). For analysis of Warren's opinion, see infra Chapter 13 at notes 56–61.

62. As Graham, 269, stated, *Brown v. Board of Education* was "decided with scant reference to the historical rebriefings or to framers' intent or original understanding. Rather, political and judicial ethics, social psychology—what the equal protection of the laws means, and must mean in our time, whatever it may have meant to whomsoever in 1866–1868—these were the grounds and the essence of Chief Justice Warren's opinion." "What it must mean in our time" is one way of saying that the Justices may revise the Constitution. Sumner did not rely on equal protection because he knew that many of the draftsmen would affirm "that they had never intended to outlaw segregation." Supra note 40.

63. Kluger 601.

the equality of laws enshrined in a constitution which was "made for an undefined and expanding future ..." ... is not a fixed formula defined with finality at a particular time. It does not reflect, as a congealed summary, the social arrangements and beliefs of a particular epoch ... The effect of changes in men's feelings for what is right and just is equally relevant in determining whether a discrimination denies the equal protection of the laws.[64]

Although the framers were well aware of the nation's "expanding future," they nonetheless, for example, rejected suffrage, "present *or prospective*." They knew that Article V provided the means to avoid "congealment,"[65] as was before long evidenced by adoption of the Fifteenth Amendment. The real issue, therefore, was not whether the Constitution must be "congealed," but rather who was to make the change—the people or the Justices. Buried in Frankfurter's fine phrases is a confession that the people could not be trusted to reflect the "changes in men's feelings" by an amendment, and that in consequence the Justices had to rewrite the Constitution. Even in a memorandum for his own use, Frankfurter could not bring himself to admit that he was "making new law for a new day," but sought to disguise the fact with "majestic generalities."

In Chapter 10 I shall show that the framers employed "equal protection of the laws" to express their limited purpose: to secure the rights enumerated in the Civil Rights Act, and those only, against *discriminatory* State *legislation*. With respect to those rights there could no longer

64. Id. 685. But compare Hamilton, infra Chapter 17 at note 15. Frankfurter's pronouncement that the clearly expressed intention of the framers cannot be regarded as "a fixed formula," cannot be "congealed," is incompatible with his insistence that "very specific provisions" such as the prohibition of "bills of attainder" must be read as "defined by history." Infra Chapter 21 at note 46. Why should an historical definition deserve more respect than the framers' own explanation of their intention? Courts, Frankfurter had stated, "are not designed to be a good reflex of a democratic society." Dennis v. United States, 341 U.S. 494, 525 (1951), concurring opinion.

65. In "recalling that it is a Constitution 'intended to endure for ages to come,' " Justice Black stated, "we also remember that the Founders wisely provided the means for that endurance: changes in the Constitution, when thought necessary, are to be proposed by Congress or conventions and ratified by the States. The Founders gave no such amending power to this Court." Bell v. Maryland, 378 U.S. 226, 342 (1964). See infra Chapter 17 at notes 15–22.

be one *law* for whites and another for blacks. The limitless objectives that Frankfurter read into the phrase were utterly beyond the contemplation of the framers. For the stubborn fact is that racism was, and still remains, an ugly fact of American life;[66] as Jackson's file memorandum stated, "Neither North nor South has been willing to adapt its racial practices to its professions."[67] "It was into this *moral void*," Kluger states, "that the Supreme Court under Earl Warren now stepped,"[68] not to give effect to a national consensus, still less to the Fourteenth Amendment, but to revise it for the people's own good. But "the criterion of constitutionality," said Justice Holmes, "is not whether we believe the law to be for the public good."[69]

## Supplementary Note on Segregated Schools

My demonstration in 1977 that the framers excluded segregated schools from the scope of the Fourteenth Amendment prompted Paul Brest to brand me as a "racist" who "persistently distorted [the historical data] to support his thesis."[1] Aviam Soifer followed suit, emphasizing "how badly Berger misuses historical materials";[2] and William Wiecek charged me

66. For 1866 see supra Chapter 1 at notes 36–46; for the present day, see infra Chapter 17 at note 55, and note 55.

67. Kluger 688.

68. Id. 710, emphasis added.

69. Adkins v. Children's Hospital, 261 U.S. 525, 570 (1923), dissenting opinion.

1. Paul Brest, "Book Review," N.Y. Times, Dec. 11, 1977, §7 at 10. Judge Richard Posner observed, "No constitutional theory that implies that *Brown* . . . was decided incorrectly will receive a fair hearing nowadays, though on a consistent application of originalism it *was* decided incorrectly." Richard A. Posner, "Bork and Beethoven," 42 Stan L. Rev. 1365, 1374 (1990). Lino Graglia comments that "it is politically disqualifying and socially unacceptable to disapprove of *Brown*." Lino A. Graglia, " 'Interpreting' the Constitution: Posner on Bork," 44 Stan. L. Rev. 1019, 1037 (1992).

2. Aviam Soifer, "Protecting Civil Rights: A Critique of Raoul Berger's History," 54 N.Y.U. L. Rev. 651, 654–655 (1979).

with "rap[ing]" rather than respect[ing] Clio."[3] Unmistakably, however, the North was firmly opposed to unsegregated schools.[4] Many commentators, among them leading activists, now agree that the Fourteenth Amendment left segregation untouched.[5] For example, Michael Perry noted that "Berger made it painfully clear that the framers of the Fourteenth Amendment did not mean to prohibit segregated public schooling, (or segregation generally) . . . [a] tragic morally indefensible consensus."[6] Let me add some evidence.

When the District of Columbia schools were under discussion in 1860, Senator James Harlan of Iowa protested,

> I know there is an objection to the association of colored children with white children in the same schools. This prejudice exists in my own State. It would be impossible to carry a proposition in Iowa to

3. William M. Wiecek, "The Constitutional Snipe Hunt," 23 Rutgers L.J. 253–254 (1992).

4. Supra p. 137.

5. Henry J. Abraham, "Essay Review," 6 Hastings Const. L.Q. 467, 467–468 (1979); Bruce Ackerman, *We the People: Foundations* 133, 135 (1991); Larry Alexander, "Modern Equal Protection Theories: A Metatheoretical Taxonomy and Critique," 42 Ohio St. L.J. 3, 6 (1981); Dean Alfange, Jr., "On Judicial Policymaking and Constitutional Change: Another Look at the 'Original Intent' Theory of Constitutional Interpretation," 5 Hastings Const. L.Q. 603, 622, 606–607 (1978); Alexander M. Bickel, *The Least Dangerous Branch* 100 (1962); Paul Brest, supra note 1 at 10; Robert H. Bork, *The Tempting of America: The Political Seduction of the Law* 75–76 (1990); Randall Bridwell, "Book Review," 1978 Duke L.J. 907, 913; John Burleigh, "The Supreme Court vs. the Constitution," 50 Pub. Interest 151, 154 (1978); 6 Charles Fairman, *History of the Supreme Court of the United States* 1179 (1971); Lino A. Graglia, " 'Interpreting the Constitution: Posner on Bork," 44 Stan. L. Rev. 1019, 1037 (1992); Howard Jay Graham, *Everyman's Constitution* 290 note 70 (1968); Justice Robert H. Jackson in Richard Kluger, *Simple Justice* 689 (1976); Michael J. Perry, "Interpretivism, Freedom of Expression, and Equal Protection," 42 Ohio St. L.J. 261, 295 note 144 (1981); Richard Posner, "Bork and Beethoven," 42 Stan. L. Rev. 1365, 1374–1375 (1990); David A. J. Richard, "Abolitionist Political and Constitutional Theory and the Reconstruction Amendments," 25 Loyola L.A. L. Rev. 1187, 1188 (1992); Douglas Martin, "Yale Chief Opens Constitution Talks by Faulting Meese," N.Y. Times, Feb. 22, 1987, at 46; Mark Tushnet, "Following the Rules Laid Down: A Critique of Interpretivism and Neutral Principles," 96 Harv. L. Rev. 781, 800 (1983); G. Edward White, *Earl Warren: A Public Life* 360–361 (1982).

Larry Alexander concluded, "had the framers been asked at the time they were enacting the fourteenth amendment, 'Does your amendment . . . outlaw racial segregation of schools?' they would have answered 'No.' " Alexander, supra at 4.

6. Perry, supra note 5 at 295.

educate the few colored children that now live in the State in the same school houses with white children. It would be impossible, I think, in any one of the States in the Northwest.[7]

That prejudice persisted during the Civil War. Congress had "permitted segregated schools in the District of Columbia";[8] and Senator Charles Sumner vainly sought "to abolish segregated schools in the District."[9] How can it be assumed that the self-same Congress would require the States to adopt the very desegregated schools which it refused to allow in the District?[10] Such an assumption is precluded by James Wilson's assurance that the Civil Rights Bill did not require that all "children should attend the same schools."[11]

The persistent acceptance of segregated schools in the North is further evidenced by the history of the Civil Rights Act of 1875. Although the Act prohibited discrimination with respect to inns, public conveyances, and theaters, Congress, despite Sumner's unflagging efforts, rejected a ban against segregated schools.[12] Senator Aaron Sargent of California urged that the common school proposal would reinforce "what may be perhaps an unreasonable prejudice, but a prejudice nevertheless—a prejudice powerful, permeating every part of the country, and existing more or less in every man's mind."[13] In the House, William Phelps of New Jersey stated, "You are trying to legislate against human prejudice, and you cannot do it. No enactment will root out prejudice, no bayonet will prick it. You can only educate away prejudice."[14]

7. *Globe* 1680.

8. Kluger, supra note 5 at 635. In May 1866, the Senate passed a bill to donate land "for schools for colored children in the District of Columbia." *The Reconstruction Amendments' Debates* 218 (Alfred Avins ed. 1967).

9. Kelly, Fourteenth 1049, 1085 (1956).

10. When Senator Henry Wilson introduced a bill for equal suffrage in the District of Columbia, he lamented that "state constitutions and State laws . . . block up the way, and we may not overleap the barriers." Phillip S. Paludan, *A Covenant With Death* 50 (1975).

11. Avins, supra note 8 at 163.

12. Raoul Berger, "The Fourteenth Amendment: Light From the Fifteenth," 74 Nw. U. L. Rev. 311, 329 (1979).

13. Id.

14. Id. The Act was set aside in the Civil Rights Cases, 109 U.S. 3 (1883). Justice Bradley, who was a contemporary of the Fourteenth Amendment, stated that it "does not

Nor should we congratulate ourselves on greatly improved race re-lations. Arthur Schlesinger, Jr., considers that racism remains "the still crippling disease of American life.[15] A liberal columnist, Tom Wicker, wrote that "the attitudes between the races, the fear and the animosity that exist today, are greater than, let us say, at the time of the *Brown* case, the famous school desegregation decision in 1954."[16] Roger Wilkins, a black commentator, noted that "the attitude of whites to-wards blacks is basic in this country, and that attitude has changed for the worse."[17] Such citations can be multiplied. They caution academe against reading back *its* sentiments into the minds of the 1866 framers. As Peter Gay observed, one who approaches "empirical data . . . by way of a preconceived theoretical bias" is "a poor historian."[18]

That observation and the foregoing history counsel us to reevaluate *Plessy v. Ferguson*.[19] *Plessy* has become a symbol of evil, but that is be-cause we impose "upon the past a creature of our own imagining" in-stead of looking to "contemporaries of the events we are studying.[20] "Separate but equal" was rooted in a harsh reality, noted by Alexander Bickel: "It was preposterous to worry about unsegregated schools . . . when hardly a beginning had been made at educating Negroes at all and when obviously special efforts, suitable only for the Negroes, would have to be made."[21] *Plessy* merely reiterated what an array of courts had been holding for fifty years.

---

authorize Congress to create a code of municipal law for the regulation of private rights." *Id.* 11. James Wilson had assured the framers, "We are not making a general criminal code for the States." *Globe* 1120. John Bingham objected to the words "civil rights" in the Civil Rights Bill of 1866 on the ground that they would "reform the whole civil and criminal code of every State government"; they were deleted. Raoul Berger, *The Four-teenth Amendment and the Bill of Rights* 25–26 (1989).

15. Arthur M. Schlesinger, Jr., *The Disuniting of America* 14 (1992).

16. "Opinions Considered: A Talk With Tom Wicker," N.Y. Times, Jan. 5, 1992, sec. 4 at 4.

17. Roger Wilkins, "Racial Outlook: Lack of Change Disturbs Blacks," N.Y. Times, Mar. 3, 1978, §A at 26.

18. 1 *Historians at Work* 271 (Peter Gay et al. eds. 1975).

19. 163 U.S. 537 (1896).

20. H. G. Richardson & G. O. Sayles, "Parliament and Great Councils in Medieval England," 77 L.Q.R. 213, 224 (1961).

21. Kluger, supra note 5 at 654.

Most post–Civil War decisions cited *Roberts v. City of Boston*,[22] decided in 1849 by the Massachusetts Court per Chief Justice Lemuel Shaw. The school committee had ruled that the common good would be best promoted by maintaining separate primary schools for colored and for white children; the court held that the separation rule was "founded on just grounds of reason and experience."[23] In 1850 the Ohio Supreme Court declared, "As a matter of policy it is unquestionably better that white and colored youth should be placed in separate schools.[24] When the Fourteenth Amendment was invoked in 1871, the Ohio court declared that "Equality of rights does not involve the necessity of educating white and colored persons in the same school."[25] The Nevada court held in 1872 that separate schools do not offend the Fourteenth Amendment,[26] as did the California court in 1874.[27] In 1874 the Indiana court held that the Constitution does not empower Congress "to exercise a general or special supervision over the states on the subject of education."[28]

These earlier cases were cited by Judge William Woods, soon to be elevated to the Supreme Court, in an 1887 Federal circuit court case which held that separate schools for blacks did not constitute a denial of "equal protection."[29] Passing on a New York statute of 1864, the New York court noted in 1883 that separate schools obtain generally in the states of the Union, and do not offend equal protection.[30] Thus *Plessy* was faithful to the framers' design and rested on a long train of cases. We need to recall Huxley's admonition that scientists "respect nothing but evidence" and believe that "their highest duty lies in submitting to it, however it may jar against their inclinations."[31] Are we to demand less of judges?

---

22. 59 Mass. (5 Cush.) 198 (1849).
23. Id. 209–210.
24. State v. Cincinnati, 19 Ohio 178, 198 (1850).
25. State ex rel. Garnes v. McCann, 20 Ohio St. 198, 211 (1871).
26. State ex rel. Stoutmeyer v. Duffy, 7 Nev. 342, 348 (1872).
27. Ward v. Flood, 48 Cal. 36 (1874).
28. Cory v. Carter, 48 Ind. 327, 359 (1874).
29. Bertonneau v. Bd. of Directors, 3 F. Cas. 294 (Cir. Ct. D. La. 1878) (No. 1, 361).
30. People ex rel. King v. Gallagher, 93 N.Y. 438, 449 (1883).
31. Supra p. 3.

## BROWN V. BOARD OF EDUCATION

We should not leave the issue of segregation without taking note of Robert Bork's view that the "result in *Brown* is . . . *compelled* by the original understanding of the fourteenth amendment's equal protection clause."[32] That is a remarkable conclusion. He himself recounts that "no one then imagined that the equal protection clause might affect school segregation."[33] Further, he observes that an "inescapable fact is that those who ratified the amendment did not think it outlawed segregated education or segregation in every aspect of life."[34] And he acknowledges "That the ratifiers probably assumed that segregation was consistent with equality, but they were not addressing segregation."[35] "The text itself," he argues, "demonstrates that equality under law was the primary goal, for it alone was written into the text."[36] Thus his conclusion that "equal protection" overturned an established State institution—segregation—in the North as well as the South rests entirely on the fact that "equal protection" alone "was written into the text."[37] There was no need, however, to write segregation into the text because confessedly "no one then imagined that the equal protection clause might affect school segregation." Why provide against the unimagined?

To overturn the established State control of segregation, the silence of the framers is not enough; minimally there must be an express intent to do so. *Pierson v. Ray* makes the point.[38] It arose under §1983, which provided that "every person who deprives another of his civil rights" shall be liable. At issue was whether a judge was a "person" within the

32. Robert H. Bork, *The Tempting of America: The Political Seduction of the Law* 76 (1990), hereinafter Bork (emphasis added).

33. Id. 75.

34. Id. 75–76.

35. Id. 82.

36. Id.

37. Id. Lino Graglia concluded that "The purpose of the Fourteenth Amendment was not 'equality before the law' between blacks and whites, as the Fifteenth Amendment shows; the Fourteenth was not understood to guarantee blacks the right to vote, and it is fairly clear that 'equal protection' was understood as not prohibiting state antimiscegenation laws, state imposed racial segregation of schools or state laws excluding blacks from jury service." Graglia, supra note 1 at 1038.

38. 386 U.S. 457 (1967).

meaning of the Act. To abolish the common law immunity of judges from suits for acts performed in their official capacity, the Court required a specific provision. Before a State's control over its own residents is curtailed, an equally exacting standard should be demanded.[39]

There is positive evidence that there was no design to impose segregation on the States. Segregated schools were deeply entrenched in the North. The climate of opinion is reflected by the objection of Senator James Harlan in 1860, when the District of Columbia schools were under discussion, to the association of colored children with white in the same schools.[40] Despite Senator Charles Sumner's unflagging efforts to abolish segregated schools in the District,[41] Congress maintained them. It can hardly be assumed that by the word *equal* Congress intended to require the States to adopt the very desegregated schools that it refused to institute in the District of Columbia. Indeed, James Wilson, chairman of the House Judiciary Committee, assured the House that the Civil Rights Bill did not require "that in *all* things . . . all citizens . . . shall be equal," instancing that it did not require that "their children shall attend the same schools."[42]

Nor was "equal protection" conceived in all-encompassing terms. Ely considers the words "inscrutable."[43] Bork himself remarks that to view the words "equal protection" as "general" is "to leave the judges without guidance."[44] That is not his aim; he considers the "general" provision to be limited in terms of the primary purpose of the ratifiers—equality.[45] This is circular reasoning—equal is equal. History discloses a more lim-

---

39. Herbert Wechsler observed that there is "a burden of persuasion on those favoring national intervention" in state matters. Herbert Wechsler, "The Political Safeguards of Federalism: The Role of the States in the Composition and Selection of the National Government," 54 Colum. L. Rev. 543, 545 (1954). The Constitution, stated Justice Brandeis, "preserves the autonomy and independence of the States"; federal supervision of their action "is in no case permissible *except* as to matters specifically delegated to the United States. Any interference . . . *except* as thus permitted is an invasion of the authority of the States." Erie R.R. Co. v. Tompkins, 304, U.S. 64, 78–79 (1938) (emphasis added).

40. Supra text accompanying note 7.

41. Supra text accompanying note 9.

42. *Globe* 1117.

43. John H. Ely, *Democracy and Distrust* 98 (1980).

44. Bork 79.

45. Id. 65.

ited purpose. David Donald, a Reconstruction historian, wrote, "the suggestion that Negroes should be treated as equals to white men woke some of the deepest and ugliest fears in the American mind."[46] George Julian, the Indiana Radical, reflecting widespread opinion, said, "the trouble is we hate the Negro."[47] Although Senator Sumner maintained that suffrage was "the only sufficient guarantee,"[48] it was excluded from the Amendment; and the framers repeatedly rejected proposals to ban *all* discrimination.[49]

The fact is that the framers restricted "equality" to a few *specified* State-created rights. Let me begin with the Civil Rights Bill of 1866, the history of which is highly germane because the framers, without dissent, regarded the Fourteenth Amendment as "identical" with the Bill.[50] It was designed to protect the Bill from repeal by embodying it in the Amendment. Justice Bradley, a contemporary, declared that "the first section of the Bill covers the same ground as the Fourteenth Amendment."[51] Senator William Stewart explained that the Bill was designed "simply to remove the disabilities" imposed by the Black Codes, "tending to reduce the negro to a system of peonage . . . It strikes at that, nothing else."[52] To enable the freedmen to exist, the Bill banned discrimination with respect to the right to own property, to contract, and to have access to the courts,[53] rights that the Supreme Court, after canvassing the legislative history, described in 1966 as "a limited category of rights."[54] Samuel Shellabarger explained that the Bill secures "*equality of protection* in those *enumerated* civil rights which the States may deem proper to confer upon any races."[55] Leonard Myers stated that the Amendment was needed "to provide *equal protection* to life, liberty and

---

46. Donald, *Sumner II* 153.

47. *Globe* 257. For similar remarks see supra pp. 13–14.

48. *Globe* 688. For similar expressions see supra p. 72.

49. Infra pp. 195–196.

50. Infra pp. 32–33.

51. Livestock Dealers' and Butchers' Ass'n v. Crescent City Live-Stock Landing Co., 15 F. Cas. 649, 655 (C. C. D. La. 1870) (No. 8, 408).

52. *Globe* 204.

53. Supra p. 33.

54. Georgia v. Rachel, 384 U.S. 780, 791 (1966).

55. *Globe* 121 (emphasis added).

property, to sue and be sued, to inherit, to make contracts."[56] Thus was "equal protection" wedded to the "limited category of rights" enumerated in the Civil Rights Bill.

Because Bork overlooked the framers' limited conception of "equality," he concluded that "equality and segregation were mutually inconsistent," leaving the courts free to choose between them.[57] The framers, however, as Bork notes, "assumed that equality and state-compelled separation of the races were consistent,"[58] a perfectly rational assumption given their limited conception of "equal protection."

Judge Posner and Lino Graglia agree that Bork's version of originalism is quite flexible, and Graglia notes that Bork defines originalism "in a way that leaves judges with overly broad discretion."[59] For my part, the framers' incontrovertible exclusion of suffrage from the Fourteenth Amendment, for example, leaves no room for judicial "flexibility." So too, Bork finds "majestic generalities" in the Constitution, which Graglia justifiably describes as "the first step toward an expansive view of judicial power."[60] Neither "due process" nor "privileges or immunities" were "majestic generalities"; each had an historically limited content. And equal protection, the legislative history discloses, was also meant to have limited scope.

56. Id. 193 (emphasis added).
57. Bork 82.
58. Id. 81.
59. Lino Graglia, " 'Interpreting' the Constitution: Posner on Bork," 44 Stan. L. Rev. 1019, 1043–1044 (1992). Graglia justly comments that " 'flexible interpretation' [is] a euphemism for short-circuiting the amendment process." Id. 1030.
60. Id. 1044.

# 8

## Incorporation of the Bill of Rights in the Fourteenth Amendment

INVOCATION of the Bill of Rights against the States is of fairly recent origin,[1] whether it be regarded within the older framework of "adoption" or the more recent theory of "incorporation."[2] From the First Amendment's "Congress shall make no law" may be gathered that it was to apply exclusively to Congress, and it was held in *Barron v. Baltimore*[3] that the Bill of Rights had no application to the States, as in fact the First Congress, which drafted the Bill, had earlier made clear.[4] Jus-

---

1. Henkin, "Some Reflections on Current Constitutional Controversies," 109 U. Pa. L. Rev. 637, 644; Lusky 159.

2. For the difference between "incorporation" and "absorption," see Felix Frankfurter, "Memorandum on 'Incorporation' of the Bill of Rights into the Due Process Clause of the Fourteenth Amendment," 78 Harv. L. Rev. 746, 747–748 (1965). For "adoption" see *infra* Chapter 14 at notes 99–122.

3. 32 U.S. (7 Pet.) 243 (1833).

4. It has been little noticed that, as Egbert Benson, speaking with reference to freedom of speech and press, said, all the Committee of Eleven to whom the amendments had been referred "meant to provide against was their being infringed by the [federal] Government." 1 *Annals of Congress* 732. Madison urged that "the State governments are as liable to attack these invaluable privileges as the General Government is, and therefore ought to be as cautiously guarded against." Id. 441. But his attempt failed. Charles Warren, "The New 'Liberty' under the Fourteenth Amendment," 39 Harv. L. Rev. 431, 433–435 (1926). The drive was for protection against the federal government; as Thomas Tucker said, "Five important States have pretty plainly expressed their apprehensions of the danger to which the rights of their citizens are exposed." 1 *Annals of Congress* 757. Elbridge Gerry observed: "This declaration of rights, I take it, is designed to secure the people against the maladministration of the [federal] Government." Id. 749. Earlier James Jackson asked, "Who are Congress, that such apprehensions should be entertained of

tice Harlan spoke truly in stating that "every member of the Court for at least the last 135 years has agreed that our Founders did not consider the requirements of the Bill of Rights so fundamental that they should operate directly against the States."[5] And for a long time the Supreme Court found that the Fourteenth Amendment had made no change in this respect.[6] By means of "selective" incorporation or adoption the Court has worked "a revolutionary change in the criminal process"[7] of the States. Some consider that the Court was "trying to legislate a detailed criminal code for a continental country."[8]

Historically the citizenry have relied upon the States for protection, and such protection was afforded before the Constitutional Convention by a Bill of Rights in virtually every state Constitution. It was not fear of State misgovernment but distrust of the remote federal newcomer that fueled the demand for a federal Bill of Rights which would supply the same protection against the federal government that State Constitutions already provided against the States. This was understood by the framers of the Fourteenth Amendment,[9] and their own attachment to State sovereignty led them to refrain from intruding beyond the ban on discrimination against blacks with respect to certain rights. All else, including suffrage, was left to the States. In particular, Chairman Wilson

---

them?" Id. 442. In presenting the amendments Madison explained that "the abuse of the powers of the General Government may be guarded against in a more secure manner." Id. 432. He added, "If there was reason for restraining the State Governments [by State constitutions] from exercising this power, there is like reason for restraining the Federal Government." Id. 439. The view that prevailed was that of Thomas Tucker: "It will be much better, I apprehend, to leave the State Governments to themselves, and not to interfere with them more than we already do." Id. 755.

5. Duncan v. Louisiana, 391 U.S. 145, 173 (1968), dissenting opinion in which Justice Stewart concurred.

6. The cases are discussed in Stanley Morrison, "Does the Fourteenth Amendment Incorporate the Bill of Rights?" 2 Stan. L. Rev. 140 (1949).

7. Lusky 161.

8. Anthony Lewis, "A Man Born to Act, Not to Muse," in Levy, *Warren* 151, 159.

9. See infra at notes 86–88. It can hardly be gainsaid that "The States have always borne primary responsibility for operating the machinery of criminal justice within their borders, and adapting it to their peculiar circumstances." Justice Harlan, 391 U.S. at 172. Cf. Justice Miller, supra Chapter 4 at note 51. For a century the federal system "permitted States, but forbade Washington, to protect and defend the civil and political rights of citizens." Phillip S. Paludan, *A Covenant With Death* 12 (1975).

emphasized during the debates on the Civil Rights Bill, "We are not making a general criminal code for the States."[10] Since the Amendment indisputably was designed to "incorporate" the guarantees of the Civil Rights Act, evidence is required to show that the framers had moved beyond the limited purposes of the Act.

The architect of the "incorporation" theory, Justice Black, invoked some fragmentary history—utterances in connection with an explanation of "privileges or immunities" by two leading Republican spokesmen, Bingham, author of §1, and Senator Jacob M. Howard, who purported to express the views of the Joint Committee.[11] Such statements are not lightly dismissed, after the manner of Justice Frankfurter, because "Remarks of a particular proponent of the Amendment, no matter how influential, are not to be deemed part of the Amendment."[12] Accepted canons of construction are to the contrary; the paramount consideration is to ascertain the intention of the legislature. That intention may be evidenced by statements of leading proponents,[13] and, if found, is to be regarded as good as written into the enactment: "the intention of the lawmaker is the law."[14] But Black's history falls far short of the "conclusive demonstration" he thought it to be in his famous *Adamson* dissent.[15] The contrary, it may fairly be said, was demonstrated in Charles Fairman's painstaking and scrupulous impeachment of Black's history,[16] buttressed by Stanley Morrison's telling companion article.[17]

10. *Globe* 1120.

11. Fairman states that "The rest of the evidence bore in the opposite direction, or was indifferent." Fairman, Stanford 65. I found no additional confirmation for Black.

12. Adamson v. California, 332 U.S. 46, 64 (1947), concurring opinion. Frankfurter himself later spoke to the contrary, supra Chapter 1 note 22.

13. Wright v. Vinton Branch, 300 U.S. 440, 463 (1937); Wisconsin R.R. Comm. v. C. B. & Q.R.R. Co., 257 U.S. 563, 589 (1922); United States v. Federal Power Commission, 191 F.2d 796, 802 (4th Cir. 1951): "great weight must be accorded . . . to opinions expressed by members of the committees having the legislation in charge."

14. Supra Chapter 1 note 24.

15. Adamson v. California, 332 U.S. at 74.

16. Fairman, Stanford.

17. Supra note 6; Lusky 162. Fairman "conclusively disproved Black's contention, at least, such is the weight of opinion among disinterested observers." Alexander Bickel, *The Least Dangerous Branch* 102 (1962). Levy states, however, that "Fairman's findings were basically negative. He did not disprove that the Fourteenth incorporated the Bill of

Absorption of one or another portion of the Bill of Rights—free speech, for example—antedated *Adamson*,[18] but this was on a selective basis, under cover of due process. To Black this was an abhorrent claim to "boundless power under 'natural law' periodically to expand and contract constitutional standards to conform to the court's conception of what at a particular time constitutes 'civilized decency' and 'fundamental liberty and justice.' " Why, he asked, should the Bill of Rights "be 'absorbed' in part but not in full?"[19] The cure, he maintained, was "incorporation" en bloc. His condemnation was not, however, wholehearted, for he was ready to accept "selective" adoption if he could not obtain wholesale incorporation, suggesting that sacrifice of a desired result was more painful than "boundless power to expand or contract constitutional standards."[20] The words "privileges or immunities" seemed "an eminently reasonable way of expressing the idea that henceforth the

---

Rights; he proved, rather, that there is very little evidence either that its framers intended that result or that the country understood that intention." Levy, *Judgments: Essays in American Constitutional History* 70 (1972). The proposition that "the Fourteenth Amendment incorporated the Bill of Rights" constitutes an invasion of rights reserved to the States by the Tenth Amendment, an invasion of such magnitude as to demand proof that such was the framers' intention. Levy would shift the burden of proof and require Black's critics to prove the negative before he *proved* the intention to incorporate. He himself stated that "Black did not merely misread history . . . he mangled or manipulated it." Levy, *Judgments*, id. 68.

But Justice Black remained unconvinced. Duncan v. Louisiana, 391 U.S. 145, 165, concurring opinion. The Court itself, as Thomas Grey remarked, "clearly has declined" to accept "the flimsy historical evidence" mustered by Black for incorporation. "Do We Have an Unwritten Constitution?" 27 Stan. L. Rev. 703, 711–712 (1975).

18. In Gitlow v. New York, 268 U.S. 652, 666 (1925), the Court "assumed" arguendo that the free speech of the First Amendment is protected by the due process of the Fourteenth. From that assumption grew the absorption of free speech into due process. See infra Chapter 14.

19. 332 U.S. at 69, 86. So too, "When the Court declares that one or the other of the Bill of Rights provisions is 'fundamental' and therefore incorporated, it draws only upon its own sense of what the Fourteenth Amendment *ought* to say." Lusky 163; see also id. 266.

20. 332 U.S. at 89. Black confirmed his compromise in Duncan v. Louisiana, 391 U.S. at 171, concurring opinion. For discussion of the legal consequences presented by the differentiation between "selective" and "full" incorporation, see Louis Henkin, " 'Selective Incorporation' in the Fourteenth Amendment," 73 Yale L.J. 74 (1963).

Bill of Rights shall apply to the States."[21] The two concepts, however, are of entirely different provenance and deal with quite different matters. "Privileges or immunities" has its roots in Article IV, §2, which requires States to accord certain privileges to citizens of a sister State; the Bill of Rights, on the other hand, was designed to protect certain rights against the federal government. The debates in the First Congress contain not the faintest intimation that the "privileges and immunities" of Article IV were being enlarged or, indeed, that the Bill of Rights was in any way related to "privileges and immunities." And, when Justice Bushrod Washington later enumerated those "privileges and immunities," he too made no reference to the Bill of Rights. To read the Bill of Rights into "privileges or immunities" is therefore no more "reasonable" than to read a "bill of attainder" into "habeas corpus."

In *Adamson*, Black appealed to "the original purpose of the Fourteenth Amendment."[22] as disclosed by the Bingham-Howard statements. These statements had reference to the "privileges or immunities" clause, but that clause had been emasculated in the *Slaughter-House Cases*.[23] Hence Black relied on "the provisions of the Amendment's first section, separately, and as a whole" for incorporation of the Bill of Rights.[24] The "privileges or immunities" clause gains no fresh vitality as a component of the "whole" of §1. Reliance on the due process clause runs afoul of Black's statement in the *Adamson* case that in *Chicago, M. & St. P. R. Co. v. Minnesota* (1890)[25] the Court "gave a new and hitherto undisclosed scope for the Court's use of the due process clause to protect property rights under natural law concepts."[26] Substantive due process was fashioned in *Wynehamer v. The People* (1856) to bar abolitionist natural law

21. Duncan v. Louisiana, 391 U.S. at 166, concurring opinion.

22. 332 U.S. at 90.

23. See supra Chapter 3.

24. 332 U.S. at 71.

25. 134 U.S. 418.

26. 332 U.S. at 79. Historically, due process meant service of process (e.g., a writ or summons) in due, i.e., proper, course. Infra Chapter 11 at notes 13–22. Dissenting in Harper v. Virginia Board of Elections, 383 U.S. 663, 675 (1966), Justice Black found "no constitutional support whatever" for the use of the due process clause as "a blank check to alter the meaning of the Constitution as written." For the 39th Congress' narrow view of due process, see infra Chapter 11 at notes 48–52.

claims and confine protection to property; and libertarian due process came long after economic substantive due process. No one in the 39th Congress intimated that the due process clause would incorporate the Bill of Rights; Bingham looked to the judicial decisions for the scope of due process, then purely procedural.[27] Speaking to the Bingham amendment, Chairman Wilson indicated that the due process clause was considered to furnish a "remedy" to secure the "fundamental rights" enumerated in the Civil Rights Act.[28] To transform it into a "source" of other unspecified rights is to set at naught the careful enumeration of rights in the Act, "constitutionalized" by the Amendment, which is incompatible with Black's invocation of the original purpose. In truth, expansion of due process to libertarian claims is largely a product of the post-1937 era; and "substantive equal protection" is a very recent concept indeed. Black's reliance on §1 "as a whole" can therefore be met with the adage "when nothing is added to nothing, the sum is and remains the same—nothing."

Bingham's remarks were addressed to H.R. No. 63, the antecedent Bingham amendment: "The Congress shall have power to make all laws which shall be necessary and proper to secure to citizens of each State all privileges and immunities of citizens in the several States (Art. IV, §2); and to all persons in the several States equal protection in the rights of life, liberty, and property (5th amendment)." This proposal, said Bingham, "stands in the very words of the Constitution . . . Every word . . . is today in the Constitution."[29] It is a mark of Bingham's sloppiness that "every word" was *not* "in the Constitution": "equal protection" was missing altogether. "[T]hese great provisions of the Constitution," he continued, "this immortal bill of rights embodied in the Constitution, rested for its execution and enforcement hitherto upon the fidelity of the

27. 13 N.Y. 378; infra Chapter 11 at notes 23–27, 36–37; Chapter 14 at notes 34–35.
28. Infra at note 36.
29. Kendrick 61; *Globe* 1034. Kendrick comments that when the Bingham amendment was reported to the House, "That body did not receive it with wild enthusiasm, and even denied it the privilege of being considered as a special order. Since to have placed it on the regular calendar would have meant its indefinite postponement, it was recommitted" in the hope of returning on a "more propitious occasion." Bingham "stood almost alone as its champion and defender" when he introduced it. Kendrick 215.

States."[30] As Fairman pointed out, the antecedent of his remark was Article IV, §2, and the Fifth Amendment due process clause which Bingham equated with "equal protection."[31] There is no reason to believe that his subsequent references to the Bill of Rights had broader compass.[32] Certainly his fellow Republicans did not so read his proposed amendment. The radical William Higby of California thought that the Article IV, §2, clause and the Fifth Amendment due process clause constituted "precisely what will be provided" by the Bingham amendment.[33] Another radical, Frederick E. Woodbridge of Vermont, stated: "It is intended to enable Congress by its enactments when necessary to give a citizen of the United States in whatever State he may be, those privileges and immunities which are guarantied to him under the Constitution [Article IV] . . . that protection to his property which is extended to other citizens of the State [due process clause]."[34] Bingham's reference to "the enforcement of the bill of rights, touching the life, liberty, and property . . . within every organized State . . ."[35] would convey to his fellows the technical meaning that had been attached to "life, liberty, and property" in the Civil Rights Bill debate.

Bingham, it will be recalled, had proposed his amendment to avoid doubts as to the constitutionality of the Civil Rights Bill. Wilson, chairman of the Judiciary Committee, joined issue: "in relation to the great fundamental rights embraced in the bill of rights, the citizen . . . is entitled to a remedy. The citizen is entitled to the right of life, liberty and property. Now if a State intervenes, and deprives him, without due process of law, of those rights . . ." And he said, "I find in the bill of rights which the gentleman desires to have enforced by an amendment . . . that 'No person shall be deprived of life, liberty and property without due

30. *Globe* 1034.

31. Fairman, Stanford 26.

32. "No one in debate ever runs down the list of the federal Bill of Rights." Id. 44; see also infra at notes 57–59.

33. *Globe* 1054.

34. Id. 1088. Price of Iowa understood the Bingham amendment "to give the same rights, and privileges, and protection to the citizen of one State going into another that a citizen of that State would have who had lived there for years," i.e., under Article IV, §2; *Globe* 1066.

35. Id. 1291.

process of law.' I understand that these constitute the civil rights . . . to which this bill relates."[36] Implicit in Wilson's formulation is the assumption that no more is needed; and that is likewise the implication of the Higby and Woodbridge remarks about the Bingham amendment.

Far from accepting every word that fell from Bingham as gospel, the framers gave his proposal a chilly reception. According to Kendrick, he "stood almost alone . . . a great many Republicans, including particularly the entire New York delegation, were opposed to the amendment."[37] He tried to soften the opposition by arguing that to oppose his amendment was "to oppose the grant of power to enforce the bill of rights," to perpetuate statutes of confiscation, of banishment, of murder.[38] Bickel considers that Bingham "was suggesting to those members who were alarmed that he had some definite evils in mind, limited and distinct in nature."[39] When we add: (1) the fact that Bingham's amendment was shelved argues against adoption of his views;[40] (2) the fact that the Joint Committee's subsequent rejection of Bingham's motion to add to Owen's proposed amendment the phrase "nor take private property for public use without just compensation"[41] is incompatible with blanket adoption of the first eight Amendments; (3) the fact that Bingham made no reference to inclusion of the Bill of Rights during debate on the final proposal which became §1 of the Amendment; (4) Wilson's emphasis during debate that the Civil Rights Bill embodied the very civil rights embraced by due process protection of life, liberty, and property; and (5) Wilson's assurances during that debate that "we are not making a general criminal code for the States"[42] (suggesting that what was unpalatable in the Bill would be no more acceptable in the Amendment)—it becomes apparent that beyond due process the framers had no intention to adopt the Bill of Rights.

---

36. Id. 1294.
37. Kendrick 214–215; cf. Bickel 42–43; cf. Flack 59.
38. *Globe* 1090–1091.
39. Bickel 39.
40. Id. 40.
41. Id. 42; this was drawn from the Fifth Amendment.
42. *Globe* 1120.

Bingham was in fact utterly at sea as to the role of the Bill of Rights. At first he considered it to be binding upon the States. Thus, after reading the due process clause of the Fifth Amendment as the source of his own proposed amendment, he stated: "this proposed amendment does not impose upon any State . . . an obligation which is not now enjoined upon them by the very letter of the Constitution."[43] For this he appealed to the "supremacy clause" of Article VI, which makes the Constitution binding,[44] hurdling the preliminary question whether the Constitution made the Fifth Amendment binding on the States. Although he noted that *Barron v. Baltimore*[45] held that the Bill of Rights is "not applicable to and do[es] not bind the States,"[46] he stated on February 28: "A State has not the right to deny equal protection . . . in the rights of life, liberty, and property." On March 9 he stated:

> the care of the property, the liberty, and the life of the citizen . . . is *in the States*, and not in the Federal Government. I have sought to effect no change in that respect . . . I have advocated here an amendment which would arm Congress with the power to punish all violations by State officers of the bill of rights . . . I have always believed that *protection* . . . within the States of all the rights of person and citizen, was of the powers *reserved to the States*.[47]

43. Id. 1034. The Bill of Rights, he said, is "to be enforced by State tribunals." Id. 1291.

44. Id. 1034.

45. 32 U.S. (7 Pet.) 243 (1833).

46. *Globe* 1089–1090.

47. *Globe* 1089, 1292–1293 (emphasis added). On February 28 he commented on Hale's statement "that the citizens must rely upon the State for their protection. I admit that such is the rule under the Constitution as it stands." *Globe* 1093. Consider too his statement, "although as ruled the existing amendments . . . *do not bind* the States, they are nevertheless to be enforced and observed in the States." *Globe* 1090 (emphasis added). As Fairman, *History* 334, pointed out, "civil status had been entirely a matter of State concern. Thus when Chancellor Kent discussed the 'Rights of Persons' to 'Personal Liberty and Security' . . . he told of State constitutions and laws." See also Fairman, id. 1368. Speaking of the First Amendment "right . . . to assemble," Chief Justice Waite stated, "For their protection in its enjoyment . . . the people must look to the States. The power for that purpose was originally placed there, and it has never been surrendered to the United States." United States v. Cruikshank, 92 U.S. 542, 552 (1875).

Reservation of "protection" to the States runs counter to rejection of a State's denial of an existing "right to equal protection"; it is incompatible with State "violations" of the Bill of Rights. Apparently unaware that Article IV, §2, protected nonresident migrants, not residents,[48] Bingham said: "No State ever has the right . . . to abridge . . . the privileges and immunities of any citizen of the Republic." Shifting again, he stated: "we all agree . . . that the exercise of the elective franchise, though it be one of the privileges of a citizen of the Republic, is exclusively under the control of the States."[49] "Exclusive control" authorizes a State to "abridge" the privilege. In truth, as Morrison, concurring with Fairman, stated, Bingham's "many statements . . . are so confused and conflicting as to be of little weight."[50] This goes beyond the issue of credibility, which courts test by inconsistent statements. It poses the question: upon which of his conflicting explanations did the framers rely? How can "conclusive" legislative history rest on shifting sands?[51]

In the eyes of Justice Black, "Bingham may, without extravagance be called the Madison of the first section of the Fourteenth Amendment."[52] Shades of Madison! Bingham was a muddled thinker,[53] given to the florid, windy rhetoric of a stump orator, liberally interspersed with invocations to the Deity,[54] not to the careful articulation of a lawyer who addresses himself to great issues. Recall his location of the words "equal

48. See supra Chapter 3 at notes 19–20.

49. *Globe* 2452. But earlier he stated, "I do not admit . . . that any State has a right to disfranchise any portion of the citizens of the United States." *Globe App.* 57.

50. Morrison, supra note 6 at 161; Fairman, Stanford 34–36.

51. Or, as Fairman stated, "When other members were unable to find out what he meant, they can hardly be charged with consenting to his words." Fairman, id. 66.

52. 332 U.S. at 74. The "implied comparison seems a slur upon the sharp-minded Father of the Constitution. For Bingham is one who used ringing rhetoric as a substitute for rational analysis." Wallace Mendelson, "Mr. Justice Black's Fourteenth Amendment," 53 Minn. L. Rev. 711, 716 (1969).

53. Bickel charitably states Bingham was "not normally distinguished for precision of thought and statement." Bickel 25. Fairman considers him "an ardent rhetorician, not a man of exact knowledge or clear conception or accurate language." Fairman, *History* 462; see id. 1289.

54. Three specimens must suffice: late in a debate which had frazzled men's patience, he dwelt on "the departing sun shall have gilded with its last rays the dome of the capitol"; again, "I humbly bow before the majesty of justice, as I bow before the majesty of that God whose attribute it is." *Globe* 2542, 1293.

protection" in the Constitution from which they were notably absent. Hale attributed to Bingham the view that "there had been from first to last, a violation of the provisions of this bill of rights by the very existence of slavery itself,"[55] thereby, as Judge Hale doubtless was aware, converting the Bill into a repealer of several existing provisions that sanctioned slavery—and this in the teeth of the First Congress' express intention to exclude the States from the ambit of the Bill of Rights.[56]

Presumably the framers who listened to Bingham found his frequent shifts of position no less perplexing than they seem to us; consequently, they had an added incentive to cling to the vastly preponderant view that they were merely incorporating the limited provisions of the Civil Rights Act in the Amendment. Whatever be the weight that attaches to Bingham's utterances, it needs to be noted that even his admirers read them restrictively. So, Kelly states that his speech of February 29 "makes it clear that by 'bill of rights' Bingham meant both the guarantees of the comity clause and the guarantee of due process in the Fifth Amendment."[57] And tenBroek asks, "What Bill of Rights? Certainly not the first eight amendments to the Constitution. The answer is not left open

---

When he grasped that Barron v. Baltimore, 32 U.S. (7 Pet.) 243 (1833), held the Bill of Rights inapplicable to the States, he stated, "they are nevertheless to be enforced and observed in the States by the grand utterance of that immortal man, who, while he lived, stood alone in his intellectual power among the living men of his country, and now that he is dead, sleeps alone in his honored tomb by the sounding sea," namely, Daniel Webster. *Globe* 1090.

55. Quoted in Fairman, *History* 1277; *Globe* 1065; compare this with Chapter 5 supra at notes 58–64. For Bingham, enfranchisement of the blacks conformed "exactly to the spirit of the Constitution and according to the declared intent of its framers." *Globe* 430. Yet he stated that "the grant of power" to "secure the enforcement of these provisions of the bill of rights in every State" "would have been [in the Constitution] but for the fact that its insertion . . . would have been utterly incompatible with the existence of slavery in any State." *Globe* 1090. Engulfed by a sea of rhetoric, he never paused to sort out his ideas.

56. The legislative history of the Bill of Rights leaves no doubt that the First Congress designedly excluded States from its operations. Supra note 4.

57. Kelly, Fourteenth 1073 note 88. Graham, 265, states, "no one even pretended that *all* the clauses and guarantees of the Bill of Rights ever could or would be enforced against the States." He concluded that the "odds appear heavily against" imputing to Bingham an intention to include "every clause of each of the eight Amendments," and accepts Fairman's proof that "the entire Bill of Rights was not incorporated," Graham 315 note 80, as does Bickel 5 note 13. What are the criteria for selection?

to conjecture: the Bill of Rights that contain (1) the comity clause . . . which guarantees the privileges and immunities of citizens of the United States; (2) the due process clause of the Fifth Amendment; and (3) the requirement that all shall be protected alike in life, liberty, and property, not explicitly mentioned in either body or amendments . . . this was the 'immortal Bill of Rights' of John A. Bingham."[58] Among the abolitionists themselves there was general agreement only about the due process clause and the First and Fourth Amendments; the "rights in the other amendments," tenBroek says, "received only casual, incidental, and infrequent reference."[59] Justice Black, therefore, would impute to Bingham views which far outran the abolitionist program that allegedly was the source of his inspiration. Before we marshall the evidence which further undermines attribution of Bingham's views to the framers, let us consider the companion remarks of Senator Jacob M. Howard.

By a caprice of fortune—the sudden illness of Chairman Fessenden—it fell to Senator Howard to act as spokesman for the Joint Committee in explaining the Amendment. Up to this point his participation in the debates on the Civil Rights Bill and the several aspects of the Amendment had been negligible. Poles removed from Chairman Fessenden, who "abhorred" extreme radicals, Howard, according to Kendrick, was "one of the most . . . reckless of the radicals," who had "served consistently in the vanguard of the extreme Negrophiles."[60] He had expended "fruitless efforts" to include the right to vote; he and Elihu B. Washburne of Illinois "had been the only Republicans to hold out for black suffrage to the end, all the others proved willing to abandon it."[61] That such a man should speak "for" a Committee in which the "non-radicals clearly outnumbered the radicals," in which, by the testimony of the co-chairmen Fessenden and Stevens, there "was very considerable difference of opinion,"[62] needs to be taken, in the words of the "immortal" Samuel Goldwyn, with "a bushel of salts."

58. TenBroek 214.
59. Id. 127; cf. infra Chapter 11 at notes 48–52.
60. Kendrick 257, 192.
61. James 82; M. L. Benedict, *A Compromise of Principle* 170 (1975).
62. Benedict, id. 34; *Globe* 2332, 3148; James 59.

On May 23 Senator Howard rose in the Senate, alluded to Fessenden's illness, and stated that he would present "the views and the motives which influenced the committee, so far as I understand [them]." After reading the privileges and immunities listed in *Corfield v. Coryell*, he said, "to these privileges and immunities . . . should be added the personal rights guaranteed and secured by the first eight amendments."[63] That is the sum and substance of Howard's contribution to the "incorporation" issue. Justice Black assumed without more ado that Howard "emphatically stated the understanding of the framers."[64] No one, to be sure, rose to challenge Howard's remark, casually tucked away in a long speech.[65] "The argument from silence," as Alfred Kelly observed, "is always more than a little dangerous."[66] But was there really silence? Consider Senator Poland's subsequent statement: "Great differences have existed among ourselves; many opinions have had to yield to enable us to agree upon a plan." A similar statement had been made by Fessenden and repeated by the radical leader Senator Benjamin Wade.[67] Now, after the compromise of such differences about *known* objectives, we are asked to infer that there was unquestioning acceptance of a sweeping, brand-new element, which had received no consideration whatever! Then too, others who spoke after Howard, repeated that the goal was legitimation of the Civil Rights Act. So, Senator Poland observed, "The clause . . . that 'no State shall . . . abridge the privileges and immunities of citizens of the United States' secures *nothing beyond* what was intended by the

63. *Globe* 2764, 2765.

64. 332 U.S. at 73.

65. Flack once more relies on the argument from silence: "Howard's interpretation of the amendment was not questioned by any one . . . this interpretation must be accepted as that of the Committee, since no member of the Committee gave a different interpretation or questioned his statements in any particular." Flack 87. But see Trumbull infra p. 191.

66. Kelly, "Clio and the Court: An Illicit Love Affair," 1965 S. Ct. Rev. 119, 147. Fairman, Stanford 68–69, points out that no newspaper reported Howard's remarkable expansion of the privileges and immunities clause, notwithstanding that application of the Bill of Rights would cut a wide swath through State self-rule. He rightly remarks, "If Senator Howard's statement about Amendments I to VIII had really been accepted at the time, surely one would find it caught up and repeated in contemporary discussion." Id. 137.

67. *Globe* 2964, 2332, 2769–2770.

original [Article IV, §2] provision in the Constitution."[68] If this be not regarded as a delicately phrased repudiation of Howard's addition, at the very least it exhibits a more limited view than that of Howard by a respected Republican.[69] Senator Doolittle stated that the Civil Rights Bill "was the forerunner of this constitutional amendment, and to give validity to which this constitutional amendment is brought forward."[70] Such reminders of known and limited objectives were designed to reassure those whose consent had thus far been won; and they rob Howard's remark of uncontroverted standing.[71]

Account must also be taken of expressions in the House after Howard's speech, for even if his words be taken to express the sentiment

68. Id. 2961 (emphasis added). From Poland's statement, "the last two clauses were . . . in the Declaration of Independence and in the Constitution," Flack distills, "evidently meaning some or all of the first eight Amendments, since one of the clauses [due process] was taken from the Fifth Amendment." Flack 91. Reference to one Amendment does not warrant a deduction that *all* were intended; to the contrary the rule is that to enumerate one is to exclude others.

69. Fairman, Stanford 61, regards Poland's remarks as "quite inconsistent with Howard's speech."

70. *Globe* 2896. On January 30 Howard assured the Senate that the purpose "is to secure" to the blacks "the ordinary rights of a freeman and nothing else . . . There is no invasion of the legitimate rights of the States." Id. 504. Later, after his explanation of the Amendment, he stated that the Committee desired to put the rights conferred by the "civil rights bill beyond the legislative power [to repeal]." Id. 2896. Compare Senator Howe's approval of the Amendment on June 5 because it enumerated the rights of citizenship: to hold land, collect wages, sue, and testify. *Globe App.* 219.

71. To convert the loose statements of Bingham and Howard, as Justice Black did, into the proposition "that one of the chief objects" of §1 "was to make the Bill of Rights applicable to the States," 332 U.S. at 71–72, suggests that Black did not really take time to study the record but relied on the feeble and unsophisticated analysis of Flack. Id. 72 note 5.

Kelly stated that among the "argument[s] for the Black thesis," which Fairman allegedly "ignores," is that Senator Trumbull talked "constantly about 'nationalizing' an already existing 'Bill of Rights' for the states, which he repeatedly asserted to be implicit in the Privileges and Immunities Clause of Article IV of the 'Old Constitution.' " Kelly, "Clio," supra note 66 at 132–133. Kelly's citation to *Globe* 474–475 does not sustain him. Trumbull made no reference to the Bill of Rights, confined his citations to Article IV, §2, and explained that the purpose of the Civil Rights Bill was "to destroy all these [enumerated] discriminations" against the Negroes. The Bill, he stated, "will have *no operation* in any State where the laws are equal, where all persons have the same civil rights without regard to color or race," *Globe* 476 (emphasis added), a statement that spells "hands off" internal State laws that are nondiscriminatory and do not touch "civil rights."

of the Senate, it must not be facilely assumed that it was shared by the House. Nothing was said about the Bill of Rights upon return of the measure to the House[72]—surely a remarkable silence about an extraordinary expansion of jointly accepted goals! Instead, George R. Latham, a West Virginia Republican, remarked, "The 'civil rights bill' which is now a law ... *covers exactly* the same ground as this amendment."[73] Henry Van Aernam of New York said that the Amendment gives "constitutional sanctions and protection to the substantial guarantees of the civil-rights bill."[74] The Latham–Van Aernam remarks, parenthetically, afford additional proof that the earlier Bingham remarks did not represent the thinking of the House. Also significant are Stevens' final remarks lamenting his failure to abolish "all" "inequality" and "distinctions" and explaining that he was constrained to accept so "imperfect a proposition" because he lived "among men and not among angels ... who ... do not choose to yield their opinions to mine."[75] It strains credulity to attribute to "men" who had rejected abolition of "all" distinctions readiness to swallow whole-hog reconstruction of their Northern institutions which had not even been discussed. Instead, the specific incorporation of one portion of the Bill of Rights—the due process clause—and the rejection of another—the just compensation clause—gave the framers ample reason to conclude that "due process" alone was to be "incorporated."[76]

72. Fairman, Stanford 65.
73. *Globe* 2883 (emphasis added).
74. Id. 3069.
75. Id. 3148.
76. In his Adamson concurring opinion, Justice Frankfurter stated that adoption of the due process clause would be "a strange way of saying" that "every State must thereafter initiate prosecutions through indictment by a grand jury, must have a trial by a jury of twelve in criminal cases ... after all, an amendment to the Constitution should be read in a 'sense most obvious to the common understanding *at the time of its adoption*,' " quoting Justice Holmes (emphasis added). Those "conversant with the political and legal history of the concept of due process ... would hardly recognize the Fourteenth Amendment as a cover for the various explicit provisions of the first eight Amendments." 332 U.S. at 63. But no more would such readers guess that the due process clause would authorize judges to select "such provisions of the Bill of Rights as were 'implicit in the concept of ordered liberty.' " Id. 54. Even less would they guess that it would be a "cover" for substantive due process, which was all but unknown to the "common understanding."

Flack's canvass of "speeches concerning the popular discussion of the Fourteenth Amendment" led him to conclude:

> the general opinion held in the North . . . was that the Amendment embodied the Civil Rights Act . . . There does not seem to have been any statement at all as to whether the first eight amendments were to be made applicable to the States or not, whether the privileges guaranteed by those amendments were to be considered as privileges secured by the amendment.[77]

Senator Sherman, for example, told Cincinnati during the campaign for adoption that "the first section was an embodiment of the [Civil Rights] Act."[78] Fairman has collected remarks by five Senators and five Representatives, not one of whom "said that the privileges and immunities clause would impose Articles I to VIII upon the States."[79] We must assume that they knew of no such purpose; men of Sherman's stature may not be charged with a conspiracy to conceal the proposed imposition from the people—certainly not without substantial proof.

---

See infra Chapter 11. "It ought not to require argument," Frankfurter stated, "to reject the notion that due process of law meant one thing in the Fifth Amendment and another in the Fourteenth." Id. 66. Apart from such considerations, the courts were too little trusted by the framers of the Fourteenth Amendment to be entrusted with such vast discretion. Infra Chapter 12.

Although Frankfurter inveighed against a "selective incorporation" without a "calculus for determining which go in and which stay out" as throwing us "back to a merely subjective task," id. 65, he did not really appreciate that his "canons of decency and fairness which express the notions of justice of English-speaking . . . peoples," id. 67, were no less "subjective." Nowhere were those "canons" catalogued with even the specificity of the Bill of Rights, as Frankfurter himself acknowledged: "These standards of justice are not authoritatively formulated anywhere as though they were prescriptions in a pharmacopoeia." Id. 68. For comparison of the Black and Frankfurter approaches, see infra Chapter 14 at notes 44–73.

Writing in 1960, Miller and Howell prophetically stated that Justices Black and Douglas "fail either to realize or be concerned about the fact that if the fourteenth amendment should embrace the procedural rights of the Bill of Rights, the criminal jurisdiction of the fifty states might be entirely disrupted." "The Myth of Neutrality in Constitutional Adjudication," 27 U. Chi. L. Rev. 661, 680 note 76.

77. Flack 153. This was quoted by Justice Black, 332 U.S. at 118, but he appeared oblivious to its implications.

78. Fairman, Stanford 77; see also supra Chapter 6 at notes 64–66.

79. Id. 78.

There is no need to retrace Fairman's examination of the State ratification proceedings;[80] let it suffice that there is no intimation therein that ratification would produce radical changes in the States' judicial machinery, for example, the replacement of an information by a grand jury indictment, of a six-man jury by a jury of twelve.[81] If this was in fact the purpose of the framers, honesty required disclosure.[82] None was made, and the reason, I suggest, is that no such purpose was entertained.

Then there is the remarkable fact that the cases which followed on the heels of the Fourteenth Amendment continued to hold the Bill of Rights inapplicable to State action, without mentioning the Amendment.[83] Oversight will not account for the omission; the Amendment had been widely discussed; bench and bar are alert to every new and relevant enactment; they would not be oblivious to the revolution worked by the alleged incorporation of the Bill of Rights.[84]

80. Id. 81 et seq. See Justice Harlan's dissent in Oregon v. Mitchell, 400 U.S. 112, 196 (1970).

81. Fairman collected examples of State constitutional provisions which "incorporation" would have abrogated and of which, of course, no intimation was given to the State ratifying conventions. Fairman, Stanford 81 et seq. As Justice Frankfurter stated in his concurring Adamson opinion, 332 U.S. at 64, "It could hardly have occurred to these States [which had no rigorous grand jury requirement] that by ratifying the Amendment they uprooted their established methods for prosecuting crime and fastened upon themselves a new prosecutorial system." For a similar expression by Justice Black in a corporate context, see infra at note 95. See also Justice Jackson, dissenting in Beauharnais v. Illinois, 343 U.S. 250, 292–293 (1952), quoted infra note 95.

82. After listening in 1871 to broad claims as to the scope of the Fourteenth Amendment, John B. Storm of Pennsylvania stated, "If the monstrous doctrine now set up as resulting from the provisions of the Fourteenth Amendment had ever been hinted at that Amendment would have received an emphatic rejection at the hands of the People." Quoted in Flack 236–237. Flack, who searched the newspapers of the period quite thoroughly, 332 U.S. at 109, comments, "no doubt [Storm] was right in saying that had the people been informed of what was intended by the Amendment, they would have rejected it." Flack 237, a point unnoticed by Justice Black.

83. Fairman, Stanford 132 et seq.

84. The point was made by Justice Frankfurter with respect to Twichell v. Pennsylvania, 74 U.S. (7 Wall.) 321 (1868), decided only a few months after adoption of the Fourteenth Amendment. Frankfurter, "Memorandum," supra note 2 at 750. See also Mendelson, supra note 52 at 721.

In sum, the framers were motivated by discriminatory denials of "fundamental rights" to the blacks.[85] No trace of a purpose to reconstruct Northern institutions for the protection of white inhabitants against the State will be found in the debates; the frequent expressions of jealous regard for State sovereignty repel such a purpose. When Judge Robert Hale insisted that "the American people have not yet found their State governments are insufficient to protect the rights and liberties of the citizen,"[86] Bingham translated this as "the citizens must rely upon the State for their protection," and added, "I admit that such is the rule under the Constitution as it now stands."[87] It cannot be presumed that the States which, in Stevens' words, would not "allow Congress to come within their jurisdiction to fix the qualifications of their voters,"[88] would tolerate a federal overhaul of their judicial processes that went beyond making them available to Negroes. Such a presumption runs counter to Senator Trumbull's assurance that the "provisions of the [Freedmen's Bureau] bill in regard to holding courts . . . are confined entirely to the rebellious States." "Certainly nobody has ever complained," Senator Cowan said, "that a full and exact measure of justice has not been meted out to him in all our courts . . . I do object to extending it to the loyal States of the North."[89] Subsequently, Trumbull twice stated that the Civil Rights Bill had no ap-

85. The "major inspiration for the 1866 law," says Kelly, "was the resentment and alarm that the enactment of the Black Codes . . . had produced among Radical Republicans." Kelly, "Clio," supra note 66 at 147. "All agree, however, regarding the racial motivation of the Amendment." Graham 274. This view was expressed in the Slaughter-House Cases, supra Chapter 3 at notes 39–40.

86. *Globe* 1064–1065.

87. Id. 1093.

88. Id. 536; to the same effect see Conkling, id. 358. What Howard said, "The Committee were of the opinion that the States are not yet prepared to sanction so fundamental a change as would be the concession of suffrage to the colored race," id. 2766, which would have its greatest impact in the South, is even more applicable to wholesale revision of internal practices affecting whites in the North. Latham, a West Virginia Republican, "denied that Congress had a right to interfere with the internal policy of the States so as to define and regulate the civil rights and immunities of the inhabitants thereof." Id. 1295–1296. The requirement that State laws must not discriminate with respect to certain enumerated rights was an enclave cut out of this general policy. See also the remarks of Hotchkiss, infra Chapter 10 at note 78.

89. *Globe* 334–335.

plication to a State that did not discriminate between its citizens.[90] The constant reiteration that the purpose of the Amendment was to constitutionalize the Civil Rights Act, the frequent tributes to State sovereignty, and recognition of powers reserved to the States by the Tenth Amendment, in which Bingham joined,[91] unite to repel an inference that the framers intended to interfere with State conduct of its own affairs otherwise than is described in that Act. The pervasive attachment to federalism—State control of local institutions—Phillip Paludan repeatedly emphasizes, was "the most potent institutional obstacle to the Negroes' hope for protected liberty"[92]—and even more of an obstacle to federal encroachment on Northern States' control of their own white citizens. If there was a concealed intention to go beyond the Civil Rights Act, it was not ratified because, first, ratification requires disclosure of material facts,[93] whereas there was no disclosure that the Amendment was meant to uproot, for example, traditional State judicial procedures and practices; and, second, a surrender of recognized rights may not be presumed but must be proved. In truth, the Fourteenth Amendment "was presented to the people as leaving control of suffrage in state hands, as representing no change in previous constitutional conditions so far as protection of rights was concerned [beyond banning discrimination], as stripped of radical character."[94]

90. See Trumbull, supra note 71; infra, Chapter 10 at note 49. Bingham insisted on the deletion of no discrimination in "civil rights" because of its "oppressive" invasion of State sovereignty. Supra Chapter 7 at notes 11–17.

91. We need to recall Chief Justice Stone's statement that the Tenth Amendment "states but a truism that all is retained which has not been surrendered." Its purpose was "to allay fears that the new national government might seek to exercise powers not granted, and that the states might not be able to exercise fully their reserved powers." United States v. Darby, 312 U.S. 100, 124 (1941).

92. Paludan, supra note 9 at 15, 13, 51, 54.

93. To bind a principal, ratification must be "with a full knowledge of all the material facts. If the material facts be either suppressed or unknown, the ratification is treated as invalid." Owings v. Hull, 34 U.S. (9 Pet.) 606, 628 (1835), per Justice Story. See also Bennecke v. Insurance Co., 105 U.S. 355, 360 (1881). There must be "an intention . . . to ratify." Flournoy v. Hewgley, 234 F.2d 213, 216 (10th Cir. 1956). To find ratification by implication, "the implication to ratify must be clear." United States v. Pan-American Petroleum Co., 55 F.2d 753, 771 (9th Cir. 1932); "implied ratification is not to be presumed." Id. 772.

94. Paludan, supra note 9 at 52.

Let Justice Black himself, the unremitting champion of "incorporation," sum up, substituting for his word "corporations" the words "judicial processes":

> The states did not adopt the Amendment with knowledge of its sweeping meaning under its present construction. No section of the Amendment gave notice to the people that, if adopted, it would subject every state law . . . affecting [judicial processes] . . . to censorship of the United States courts. No word in all this Amendment gave any hint that its adoption would deprive the states of their long recognized power to regulate [judicial processes].[95]

## Supplementary Note on Incorporation

For William Nelson, "the puzzle of incorporation of the Bill of Rights" has "plagued Fourteenth Amendment historiography for a century."[1] But arguments for "incorporation" are a Johnny-come-lately. For 135 years,

95. Connecticut General Ins. Co. v. Johnson, 303 U.S. 77, 89 (1938), dissenting opinion. It is a profound irony that Black should go on to broaden the Fourteenth Amendment and curtail States' Rights beyond the wildest conceptions of the framers and ratifiers. Or should we rather regard "interpretation" like a meandering river that conforms to a Justice's wandering predilections?

My study of the debates and the history of the period leads me fully to concur with Fairman: "The freedom that states traditionally have exercised to develop their own systems of administering justice, repels any thought that the federal provisions on grand jury, criminal jury, civil jury were fastened upon them in 1868. Congress would not have attempted such a thing, the country would not have stood for it, the legislatures would not have ratified." Fairman, Stanford 137. As Justice Jackson said in a comparable situation, "We are justified in assuming that the men who sponsored the Fourteenth Amendment in Congress, knew of such provisions then in many of their State Constitutions. Certainly they were not consciously cancelling them or calling them into question, or we should have some evidence of it." Beauharnais v. Illinois, 343 U.S. at 292–293, dissenting opinion.

1. William E. Nelson, *The Fourteenth Amendment: From Political Principle to Judicial Doctrine* 117 (1988).

Justices Harlan and Stewart reminded the Court, every member had agreed that the Founders exempted the States from the Bill of Rights.[2] It was Justice Black who, in a dissent, relied on some remarks of John Bingham and Senator Jacob Howard in the 1866 Congress to urge that the Bill of Rights was "incorporated" into the Fourteenth Amendment.[3] For a truly wild flight of fancy, however, Akhil Amar of Yale takes the prize: "both the text of Section One [of the Fourteenth Amendment] and the public gloss Congress placed upon the text *made clear* that what Congress was proposing *was nothing less than a transformation* of the original Bill of Rights."[4] Just what in the "text"—due process, privileges or immunities, equal protection—"made clear" that Congress was importing,[5] let alone "transforming," the Bill of Rights, deponent sayeth not. As the Supreme Court stated in 1874 with respect to Negro suffrage, "So important a change . . . if intended, would have been expressly declared."[6] Unlike "incorporation," which has at least the flimsy basis of Bingham's and Howard's remarks, there is no intimation that the Fourteenth Amendment would "transform" the Bill of Rights. Then there is the fact that those remarks caused hardly a ripple. Horace Flack found no published statement that "the first eight amendments were made applicable to the States."[7] Howard's remark, Charles Fairman recounts, "seems at the time to have sunk without leaving a trace in public dis-

2. Duncan v. Louisiana, 391 U.S. 145, 173 (1968).

3. Adamson v. California, 332 U.S. 46 (1947). Compare Supplementary Note on the Civil Rights Act, text accompanying note 17. The Court, however, as Thomas Grey observed, "clearly has declined" to accept "the flimsy historical evidence" mustered by Black. Thomas C. Grey, "Do We Have an Unwritten Constitution?" 27 Stan. L. Rev. 703, 711–712 (1975); see infra text accompanying note 28.

4. Akhil R. Amar, "The Bill of Rights and the Fourteenth Amendment," 101 Yale L.J. 1193, 1246 (1992) (emphasis added).

5. Amar himself states that "nothing in the text of the [Fourteenth Amendment] would lead an average reader to understand" that the three words "privileges or immunities" encapsulated the first eight amendments. Id. 1244.

6. Minor v. Happersett, 88 U.S. (21 Wall.) 162, 173 (1974). For additional citations see supra Supplementary Note on the Introduction, note 43. In the Civil Rights Cases, 109 U.S. 3, 11 (1883), Justice Bradley, a contemporary of the Amendment, declared that §5 "does not authorize Congress to create a code of municipal law for the regulation of private rights."

7. Horace E. Flack, *The Adoption of the Fourteenth Amendment* 153 (1908).

cussion."[8] This obliviousness is remarkable, for incorporation of the Bill of Rights would drastically reduce the States' self-rule—an unlikely surrender of States' Rights.

The current activist icon, Michael Kent Curtis, who set out to supply an historical footing for "incorporation," admitted that his "thesis is intensely controversial,"[9] and stated that his goal was to find the "probable Republican understanding of a question to which they had paid little direct attention."[10] He reasoned that the key to construction of the 1866 debates is furnished by "certain unorthodox constitutional ideas held by a number of Republicans"[11]—never mind that the greatly preponderant Republican view was to the contrary.[12] Amar noted that "many informed men were simply not thinking carefully about the words of Section One at all."[13] Are we to ground a massive invasion of rights reserved to the States on a fit of absentmindedness? Not if we are to be guided by the Supreme Court.[14] In the *Slaughter-House Cases* Justice Samuel Miller, an informed contemporary of the Fourteenth Amendment, rejected a construction of the Amendment that would subject the States "to the control of Congress, in the exercise of powers heretofore universally conceded to them," in the absence of "language which expresses such a purpose too clearly to admit of doubt."[15] The Federal expansion that activists urge today without a qualm led Justice Brandeis

8. Charles Fairman, "Does the Fourteenth Amendment Incorporate the Bill of Rights?" 2 Stan. L. Rev. 5, 68, 69 (1949).

9. Michael B. Curtis, *No State Shall Abridge: The Fourteenth Amendment and the Bill of Rights* 2 (1986). After citing Curtis, Lino Graglia wrote, "there is very little basis for the implausible proposition that the States that ratified the Fourteenth Amendment understood that it would 'incorporate' the Bill of Rights, making its restrictions applicable to the states, thereby subjecting the states to both expanded federal legislative powers and expanded federal court supervision." Lino A. Graglia, " 'Interpreting' the Constitution: Posner on Bork," 44 Stan. L. Rev. 1019, 1033–1034 (1992).

10. Michael K. Curtis, "The Bill of Rights as a Limitation on State Authority: A Reply to Professor Berger," 16 Wake Forest L. Rev. 45, 57 (1980).

11. Id. 47.

12. See infra Supplementary Note on Abolitionist Influence, text accompanying notes 14–22.

13. Amar, supra note 4 at 1250.

14. Supra text accompanying note 6.

15. 83 U.S. (16 Wall.) 36, 78 (1972).

to say, "in every extension of governmental functions lurks a new danger to civil liberty."[16]

For the moment let me postpone the evidence which led Charles Fairman, and after my own minute scrutiny, myself, to reject the confused and contradictory statements of Bingham, and the remarks of Howard.[17] Our view of Bingham is shared by Alexander Bickel, Leonard Levy, Wallace Mendelson,[18] and even by William Nelson.[19] Michael Zuckert, who regards Curtis favorably, notes that "there was much disagreement among the former abolitionists";[20] there was agreement only about the due process clause and the First and Fourth Amendments.[21] The "rights in the other amendments," wrote Jacobus tenBroek, a neoabolitionist, "received only casual, incidental, and infrequent reference."[22] Alfred Kelly, a dedicated activist, said that Bingham "made it clear that by 'bill of rights' Bingham meant both the guarantees of the comity clause and the guarantees of due process in the Fifth amendment."[23] Leonard Levy concluded that "there is no reason to believe that Bingham and Howard expressed the view of the majority of Congress."[24] Probative legislative history cannot be distilled from such conflicting testimony, characterized by Zuckert as "ambiguity and vacillation."[25]

It bears emphasis that the claim of incorporation "constitutes an invasion of rights reserved to the States by the Tenth Amendment, an invasion of such magnitude as to demand proof that such was the framers' intention."[26] "Incorporation" has not won the Court's assent. Rebuffing

16. Alpheus T. Mason, *Brandeis: A Free Man's Life* 566 (1946). Brandeis believed that the New Dealers' "headlong drive for national power threatened . . . to destroy one of the great bulwarks of liberty—federalism." Id. 558.

17. See Raoul Berger, *The Fourteenth Amendment and the Bill of Rights* 128, 142 (1989).

18. For citations see id. 128.

19. Nelson, supra note 1 at 122. The most recent critic of those views acknowledges that they are "representative of a broadly held scholarly view." Curtis, supra note 9 at 113.

20. Michael Zuckert, "Book Review," 8 Const. Commentary 149, 160 (1991).

21. Jacobus tenBroek, *Equal Under Law* 127 (1965).

22. Id.

23. Kelly, Fourteenth 1049, 1073 note 88.

24. Leonard Levy, *Judgments: Essays on American Constitutional History* 77 (1972).

25. Zuckert, supra note 20 at 156.

26. Michael J. Perry, "Book Review," 78 Colum. L. Rev. 685, 690 (1978). In Federalist

Black's theorizing in *Adamson v. California*, the Court approved the *Slaughter-House Cases* saying, "It accords with the constitutional doctrine of federalism by leaving to the States the responsibility of dealing with the privileges and immunities of their citizens except those inherent in national citizenship,"[27] a meager exception indeed. In 1959 Justice Frankfurter declared on behalf of the Court:

> We have held from the beginning and uniformly that the Due Process Clause of the Fourteenth Amendment does not apply to the States any of the provisions of the first ten amendments as such. The relevant historical materials demonstrate conclusively that Congress and the members of the legislatures of the ratifying States, did not contemplate that the Fourteenth Amendment was a shorthand incorporation of the first eight amendments making them applicable as explicit restrictions upon the States.[28]

The extensive researches of Fairman,[29] which I confirmed, corroborate Frankfurter; our view has won assent even from activists. Michael Perry concluded that Berger's "finding that the fourteenth amendment was not intended to make the Bill of Rights . . . applicable to the States . . . is amply documented and widely accepted."[30] Among those who agree are Dean Alfange, Jr., Alexander Bickel, John Hart Ely, Judge Henry Friendly, Lino Graglia, Thomas Grey, Erwin Griswold, Louis Henkin, Forrest McDonald, Richard A. Posner, and Mark Tushnet.[31]

---

No. 17 at 103 (Mod. Lib. ed. 1937), Hamilton stated that the "one transcendent advantage belonging to the province of the State governments" was "the ordinary administration of criminal and civil justice." Garry Wills observed that to Madison and Hamilton "It seemed inconceivable . . . that a central authority could or would want to descend to enforcement of local laws." Garry Wills, "Introduction" to *The Federalist Papers of Alexander Hamilton, James Madison, and John Jay* xiv (1982).

27. 322 U.S. 46, 51–53 (1947); Slaughter-House Cases, 82 U.S. (16 Wall.) 36, 53 (1972).

28. Bartkus v. Illinois, 359 U.S. 121, 124 (1959).

29. Fairman "conclusively disproved Black's contention, at least, such is the weight of opinion among disinterested observers." Alexander Bickel, *The Least Dangerous Branch* 102 (1962).

30. Michael J. Perry, "Interpretivism, Freedom of Expression, and Equal Protection," 42 Ohio St. L.J. 261, 285–286 (1981).

31. Dean Alfange, Jr., "Book Review," 5 Hastings Const. L.Q. 603, 607 (1978); Bickel, supra note 29 at 102; John Hart Ely, "Constitutional Interpretivism: Its Allure and Im-

Let me set forth some confirmatory considerations. In seeking to read corporations out of the Fourteenth Amendment, Justice Black observed that "the people were not told that they [were ratifying] an amendment granting new and revolutionary rights to corporations."[32] No more were the Northern States told that by the Amendment they were massively curtailing their own rights of self-government. Incorporation was not discussed in the Joint Committee on Reconstruction that drafted the Amendment; it was not debated on the floors of Congress, an extraordinary omission given the vast incursion on State sovereignty by the Bill of Rights. Indeed the North was given to understand that it was unaffected by the companion Civil Rights Bill,[33] the Bill that was considered on all sides to be "identical" with Section One of the Amendment.[34] Plainly the provisions for due process, privileges or immunities, and equal protection did not disclose that the Bill of Rights was incorporated therein. As Justice Frankfurter remarked of the due process clause, it would be "a strange way of saying" that "every State must thereafter initiate prosecutions through indictments by grand jury, must have a trial by a jury of twelve in criminal cases,"[35] for which the Fifth and Sixth Amendments made express provision. Even stranger is the notion that

---

possibility," 53 Ind. L.J. 399, 432 (1978); Henry J. Friendly, "The Bill of Rights as a Code of Criminal Procedure," 53 Calif. L. Rev. 929, 934 (1965); Lino Graglia, " 'Interpreting' the Constitution: Posner on Bork," 44 Stan. L. Rev. 1019, 1033–1034 (1992); Grey, supra note 3 at 711–712 (the Court "clearly has declined" to accept "the flimsy historical evidence" proffered by Black); Erwin N. Griswold, "Due Process Problems Today in the United States," in *The Fourteenth Amendment* 161, 165 (Bernard Schwartz ed. 1970); Louis Henkin, " 'Selective Incorporation' in the Fourteenth Amendment," 73 Yale L.J. 74, 77 (1963); Forrest McDonald, "How the Fourteenth Amendment Repealed the Constitution," Chronicles 29 (October 1989); Richard A. Posner, "Interpreting the Constitution: Bork and Beethoven," 42 Stan. L. Rev. 1365, 1374 (1990) ("thoroughly illegitimate" under original intention); Mark Tushnet, "Following the Rules Laid Down: A Critique of Interpretivism and Neutral Principles," 96 Harv. L. Rev. 781, 789 note 21 (1983).

32. Connecticut General Ins. Co. v. Johnson, 303 U.S. 77, 86 (1938), dissenting opinion.

33. Infra text accompanying notes 102–104.

34. Raoul Berger, "Incorporation of the Bill of Rights: A Response to Michael Zuckert," 26 Ga. L. Rev. 1, 9–12 (1991).

35. Adamson v. California, 322 U.S. 46, 63 (1947).

by those terms the North was surrendering its control over its own internal affairs.

The governing law in 1866 was represented by *Barron v. Baltimore* (1833),[36] which had held that the Bill of Rights did not apply to the States. There Chief Justice Marshall demanded "plain and intelligible language" to demonstrate an intention to curtail the States' control of their internal affairs.[37] Striking reaffirmation of such requirements was furnished in *Pierson v. Ray* (1967),[38] wherein it was held that a statute making "liable 'every person' who under color of law deprived another of his civil rights" did not abolish the common law immunity of judges for acts performed in their official capacity. Congress, the Court stated, "would have specifically so provided had it wished to abolish the doctrine,"[39] this notwithstanding that a judge undeniably is a "person." The "inviolable residuary" sovereignty retained by the States ranks higher than the common law immunity of a judge. Even more does it demand clear expression of a purpose to take over control from the States of their own internal affairs.

The activist "historian" Michael Curtis observed that the framers made "explicit provision" for three distinct changes in existing law. They overruled *Dred Scott* and made a native born black a citizen; they provided for State due process; and they provided that no State could abridge the "privileges or immunities" of a United States citizen.[40] Curtis himself was moved to ask "why 'the Bill of Rights' was not explicitly written into the Fourteenth Amendment, as due process and citizenship were."[41] In the weird and wonderful way that passes for legal reasoning in activist circles, he explained: "the reason, *of course*, is that the rights in the Bill of Rights make up the most important . . . of the rights of a citizen."[42] By this logic, the greater the invasion of the "residuary" sovereignty retained by the States and confirmed by the Tenth Amend-

36. 32 U.S. (7 Pet.) 243 (1833).
37. Id. 250.
38. 386 U.S. 547 (1967).
39. Id. 554–555.
40. Curtis, supra note 9 at 91.
41. Id. 125.
42. Id. (emphasis added).

ment, the less need for disclosure. Put differently, omission of explicit "incorporation" of the Bill of Rights testifies to an intention to comprehend all of its provisions. Why, then, did the framers explicitly include the due process of the Fifth Amendment? Under the *expressio unius* rule all other provisions of the Bill were excluded.[43] And how are we to reconcile with "incorporation" of the Bill of Rights the framers' repeated rejections of proposals to bar *all* discrimination?[44] Curtis himself says of an early draft of the Amendment "which prohibited discrimination in civil rights" that "Its general language failed to take account of and overrule the doctrine of *Barron v. Baltimore* that the Bill of Rights did not limit the States."[45] Total nonmention of "incorporation" weighs more heavily than the ineffectiveness of "general language."

Let me briefly note that the "privileges or immunities" clause was borrowed from Article IV, which had been construed to allow a visitor from one State to engage in trade or commerce in another.[46] A Report of the House Committee on the Judiciary submitted in 1871 by John Bingham recited that the Fourteenth Amendment "*did not add* to the privileges or immunities" of Article IV.[47] The report also quoted Daniel Webster's emphasis that Article IV put it beyond the power of any State to hinder entry "for the purposes of trade, commerce, buying and selling."[48] And in a decision contemporary with the Amendment, the Court said in *Minor v. Happersett*[49] that "The Amendment did not add to the privileges or immunities of a citizen."

A word about Justice Cardozo's statement in *Palko v. Connecticut*[50] that there are principles—among them free speech—"so rooted in the traditions and conscience of our people as to be ranked as fundamental." Unhappily, Madison's proposal that the First Amendment's "free speech"

43. United States v. Arredondo, 31 U.S. (6 Pet.) 691, 725 (1832).
44. Infra pp. 195–196.
45. Curtis, supra note 9 at 84.
46. Campbell v. Morris, 3 H. & McH. 535, 554 (Md. 1797); Abbott v. Bayley, 6 Pick. 89, 91 (Mass. 1827).
47. *The Reconstruction Amendments' Debates* 466 (Alfred Avins ed. 1967).
48. Id.
49. 88 U.S. (21 Wall.) 162, 171 (1874).
50. 302 U.S. 319, 325 (1937).

be extended to the States was rejected.[51] That which the Framers rejected cannot be regarded as part of our tradition. Finally, like Marshall before him, Justice Samuel Miller, a sagacious observer of the political scene, rebuffed in the *Slaughter-House Cases*[52] a construction of the Fourteenth Amendment that would subject the States "to the control of Congress in the exercise of powers heretofore universally conceded to them" in the absence of "language which expressed such a purpose too clearly to admit of doubt."[53] Special force attaches to this statement with respect to "incorporation" of the Bill of Rights, for, apart from the remarks of Bingham and Howard, it is without footing in the debates and the text of the Amendment.

It is time to focus on Bingham and Howard. Justice Black declared that "Bingham may, without extravagance, be called the Madison" of the Fourteenth Amendment.[54] What a comparison! Madison, the informed, precise, painstakingly analytical thinker was worlds removed from Bingham, the careless, inaccurate, stump speaker. This view of Bingham is shared by others.[55] What were his fellows to make of his confused, contradictory utterances? Let me cite chapter and verse.

Bingham's draft of the Fourteenth Amendment provided for "equal protection," and he categorically stated that it "stands in the very words of the Constitution . . . Every word . . . stands in the very words of the Constitution."[56] But the words "equal protection" were *not* in the Constitution until the Fourteenth Amendment put them there. Although he noted that under *Barron v. Baltimore* the Bill of Rights did not apply to the States,[57] he nevertheless considered that the Bill bound State officials to enforce it against the States by virtue of their oath to support the Constitution.[58] Their oath did not bind them to enforce an inapplicable

51. 1 *Annals of Cong.* 435, 755.
52. 83 U.S. (16 Wall.) 36 (1872).
53. Id. 78.
54. Adamson v. California, 322 U.S. 46, 74 (1947).
55. Supra text accompanying notes 17–19.
56. Avins, supra note 47 at 150.
57. *Globe* 1090.
58. Curtis, supra note 9 at 64; *Globe* 1291.

provision. He located "privileges and immunities" in the Bill of Rights,[59] whereas they appear in Article IV of the Constitution, not in the Bill of Rights. He affirmed that the care of life, liberty, and property of a citizen "is in the States, and not in the Federal Government. I have sought to make no change in that respect,"[60]—and then casually stated that the first eight amendments were part of the "privileges or immunities" contained in the Fourteenth Amendment, oblivious to the fact that this entailed a tremendous incursion on the States' right to care for their own citizens. He asserted that "contrary to the *express* letter of your Constitution, 'cruel and unusual punishments' have been inflicted under State laws,"[61] unaware that the Eighth Amendment did not apply to the States. What sense did it make to inveigh against "a reform of the whole civil and criminal Code of every State"[62] and simultaneously maintain that the criminal provisions of the Bill of Rights must be enforced against the States?

Other confused and contradictory utterances could be cited, but I shall close with Bingham's crown jewel. After noting that the first eight amendments did "not bind the States," he declared,

> They are nevertheless to be enforced and observed in the States by the grand utterance of that immortal man [Daniel Webster] who, while he lived, stood alone in his intellectual power among the living men of his country, and now that he is dead, sleeps alone in his honored tomb by the sounding sea.[63]

He was ever intoxicated by his own rhetoric. Webster, of course, would not conceive that his statement would override a Supreme Court decision. And the "grand utterance" cited by Bingham had no more to do with the case than the flowers that bloom in the spring.

There is no need to dwell on the contrariety of opinion among the framers respecting which of the amendments should be embodied in the

59. *Globe* 1089.
60. *Globe* 1292.
61. *Globe* 1290.
62. Avins, supra note 47 at 188.
63. *Globe* 1090.

Fourteenth Amendment.[64] Let it suffice that Thaddeus Stevens, a leader of the Republicans, said of Bingham, "In all this contest about reconstruction, I do not propose to listen to his counsel, recognize his authority, or believe a word he says."[65] No critic of Bingham has been as excoriating. One large question remains; repeatedly I have called upon activists to reconcile Bingham's vehement condemnation of "*civil rights and immunities*"—the original words of the Civil Rights Bill—because the words would reform "the whole criminal and civil Code of every State"[66] with his incorporation of the Bill of Rights, which entailed a massive takeover of State criminal administration.

To comment on Senator Howard in similar detail would be intolerably boring. Because of Senator Fessenden's sudden illness, he was called upon to present the Amendment to the Senate. According to Benjamin Kendrick, the editor of the journal of the Joint Committee on Reconstruction, Howard was "one of the most reckless radicals," who had consistently been "in the vanguard of the extreme Negrophiles,"[67] wherein he was far removed from the pervasive racism of the North. How little his loose utterances are to be trusted is disclosed by his statement that the Amendment "abolishes *all* class legislation,"[68] despite the denial of suffrage to the blacks, and the framers' repeated rejection of proposals to prohibit all manner of discrimination,[69] in which Bingham himself joined.[70]

After Howard spoke, a number of speakers went the other way. Senator Luke Poland said that the Amendment "secures nothing beyond what was intended by the original provision [Article IV] of the Constitution."[71] Senator Timothy Howe spoke of the Amendment in terms of

---

64. For citations see supra pp. 165–166.

65. *Cong. Globe* (39th Cong., 2d Sess.) 816 (1867).

66. Avins, supra note 47 at 186, 188, 191.

67. Benjamin Kendrick, *The Journal of the Joint Committee of Fifteen on Reconstruction* 257, 192 (1914).

68. Avins, supra note 47 at 220 (emphasis added).

69. Infra pp. 195–196.

70. *Globe* 1291.

71. Avins, supra note 47 at 230.

the limited provisions of the Civil Rights Act.[72] In the House, William Windom summarized the meaning of the Amendment as "your life shall be spared, your liberty shall be unabridged, your property shall be protected,"[73] remarks that are incompatible with incorporation of the Bill of Rights. And George Latham stated that the Civil Rights Act "covers exactly the same ground as the Amendment."[74] Leonard Levy concluded, "there is no reason to believe that Bingham and Howard expressed the view of the majority of Congress."[75]

In 1949 Charles Fairman, in what even an activist regards as a "classic" study,[76] thoroughly deflated Bingham and Howard. My independent study of the debates in the 39th Congress confirmed Fairman. At length an activist champion rose to the defense of Bingham and Howard in the person of Michael Curtis, a youthful practitioner in Greensboro, North Carolina, who has made a career of assailing Fairman and myself.[77] That activists should prefer Curtis's evaluation of the evidence to that of Fairman[78] shows the low estate of activist scholarship. For there is a hierarchy of authority; Albert J. Nock adverted to the "great peril" posed by "the inability to appraise and grade one's authorities, the tendency to accept whatever appears on the printed page."[79] Let it suffice

72. Id. 231.

73. Id. 238.

74. Id. 223.

75. Leonard Levy, *Judgments: Essays in American Constitutional History* 77 (1972).

76. William E. Nelson, "History and Neutrality in Constitutional Adjudication," 72 Va. L. Rev. 237, 253 (1986). A fellow activist, Harold Hyman, considers that Fairman's article "shaped much of the constitutional field." Harold Hyman, "Federalism: Legal Fiction or Historical Artifact?" 1987 B.Y.U. L. Rev. 905, 924. Alexander Bickel, who himself had canvassed the legislative history of the Fourteenth Amendment, regarded Fairman's article as "conclusive." Bickel, supra note 31 at 102.

77. Raoul Berger, *The Fourteenth Amendment and the Bill of Rights* 141, 142 (1989). Curtis reminds one of Dr. Samuel Johnson's "When I was beginning in the world and was nothing and nobody, the joy of my life was to fire at all the established wits, and then everybody loved to halloo me on." Louis Biancolli, *The Book of Great Conversations* 144 (1948).

78. Fairman was chosen to cover the Reconstruction era for the history of the Supreme Court of the United States under the Justice Holmes bequest.

79. Albert J. Nock, *Jefferson* 287 (1926). In a letter to Justice Holmes, Harold Laski considered it to be a just criticism that a writer "has no sense of the proportional value of his authorities." 2 *Holmes-Laski Letters: The Correspondence of Mr. Justice Holmes and Harold J. Laski* 1463 (Mark de W. Howe ed. 1953).

that Forrest McDonald stated that I "devastated" Curtis, but engaged in "overkill, roughly comparable to shooting rabbits with a cannon."[80]

## MODERN RIGHTS

In its transformation of the Fourteenth Amendment, the Court has soared beyond the confines of the Bill of Rights to fashion a congeries of individual rights undreamed of by the Founders. Sir William Holdsworth "continually insisted . . . that when people in the seventeenth century [to which the Founders looked] talked about fundamental rights or laws they meant the rights which the existing law gave them."[81] When Samuel Adams claimed "the primary, absolute, natural rights of Englishmen," he listed the Blackstonian trio, "Personal Security, Personal Liberty and Private Property,"[82] liberty being defined by Blackstone as unrestrained freedom to come and go.[83] An activist, Alfred Kelly, concluded that

> The "rights of Englishmen" were not vacuous; instead they were quite well defined and specific. The notion of pulling new natural rights from the air to allow for indefinite expansion can hardly be considered to be within the original spirit of the [Fourteenth] Amendment.[84]

It is still less within the spirit of the Founders. When the Bill of Rights was added, it largely responded to British excesses before and during the Revolutionary War—free speech, quartering of soldiers, unreasonable searches and seizures, the right to bear arms, and sundry procedural provisions to ensure fair trials. How activists can conjure out of these facts provision for illimitable individual rights passes understanding.[85]

Leading activists agree that the modern individual "rights" created by the Court are without foundation in the Constitution. Paul Brest ac-

---

80. McDonald, supra note 31 at 31.

81. John W. Gough, *Fundamental Law in English Constitutional History* 39 note 3 (1955).

82. Samuel Adams, *The Writings of Samuel Adams* 65 (Harry A. Cushing ed. 1904); 1 William Blackstone, *Commentaries on the Laws of England* 125, 129, 138 (1765).

83. Blackstone, supra note 82 at 134.

84. Alfred H. Kelly, "Clio and the Court: An Illicit Love Affair," 1965 Sup. Ct. Rev. 119, 154–155.

85. Supra Supplementary Note on the Civil Rights Act and the Fourteenth Amendment, text accompanying notes 14–18, 23–28, 36–51.

knowledged that "Fundamental rights adjudication is open to the criticism that it is not *authorized* and not *guided* by the text and original history of the Constitution."[86] The individual rights Michael Perry champions, he admits, are constructs of the modern Court.[87] Robert McCloskey, long a student of the Supreme Court, concluded that "during the past 30 years, the Court has built a whole body of constitutional jurisprudence in this field broadly called civil liberties almost out of whole cloth."[88] Activists, Henry Monaghan observed, "outdo one another in urging the imposition of constitutional constraints on the basis of 'rights' whose origins cannot be traced to either the constitutional text or the structure it created."[89]

There are signs on the horizon that a new day is dawning; the talismanic "liberty" is being viewed in more Blackstonian terms. First, the Court recalled that the *core* of "liberty is freedom from bodily restraint."[90] And Justice Scalia stressed that "Without that core textual

86. Paul Brest, "The Fundamental Rights Controversy: The Essential Contradictions of Normative Constitutional Scholarship," 90 Yale L.J. 1063, 1087 (1981) (emphasis added); Paul Brest, "The Misconceived Quest for Original Understanding," 60 B.U. L. Rev. 204, 236 (1980): "Many of what we have come to regard as the irreducible minima of Rights are actually supra-constitutional; almost none of the others are entailed by the text or original understanding."

87. Michael J. Perry, *The Constitution, the Courts, and Human Rights* 91, 92 (1982).

88. *Hearings on the Supreme Court Before the Senate Subcommittee on the Separation of Powers* (90th Cong., 2d Sess.) 98 (June 1968).

89. Henry P. Monaghan, "Our Perfect Constitution," 56 N.Y.U. L. Rev. 353, 354 (1981). Why, asked G. Edward White, should the Court "not openly acknowledge that the source of [newly invented] rights is not the constitutional text but the enhanced seriousness of certain values in American society." G. Edward White, "Reflections on the Role of the Supreme Court: The Contemporary Debate and the 'Lessons' of History," 63 *Judicature* 162, 168 (1979). It is "virtually impossible [to justify providing protection for minorities] on the ground that [the Court] is doing no more than 'finding' the law of the Constitution and fulfilling the intentions of its framers." Jesse H. Choper, *Judicial Review and the National Political Process* 137 (1980). See also Terrance Sandalow, "The Distrust of Politics," 56 N.Y.U. L. Rev. 446, 460 (1981).

90. Foucha v. Louisiana, 112 S.Ct. 1780, 1785 (1992). For the Founders, Gordon Wood concluded, "Liberty was realized when the citizens were . . . willing to sacrifice their private interests for the sake of the community." Gordon S. Wood, *The Radicalism of the American Revolution* 104 (1992), a far cry from the current rampant individualism. See Raoul Berger, "The Ninth Amendment: As Perceived by Randy Barnett," 88 Nw. U. L. Rev. 1508, 1509 (1994).

meaning *as a limitation*, defining the scope of the Due Process Clause 'had at times been a treacherous field for the Court,' giving 'reason for concern lest the only limits to . . . judicial intervention become the predilections of those who happened at the time to be Members of this Court.' "[91] Second, when rights have been claimed as "fundamental," the Court has insisted that they "be an interest traditionally protected by our society."[92] If the claim is novel, its "mere novelty . . . is reason enough to doubt that 'substantive due process' sustains it."[93] Third, "the Court has always been reluctant to expand the concept of substantive due process because guideposts for responsible decision making in this unchartered area are scarce and open ended . . . The doctrine of judicial self-restraint requires us to exercise the utmost care whenever we are asked to break new ground in this field."[94] In sum, the Court is putting the brakes on fresh claims of rights unknown to the law.

Finally, not enough attention has been paid to the impact of "incorporation" on the North, which was led to believe that the draftsmen were aiming at the South alone. "Disturbed by the revolutionary changes Sumner hoped to bring about in the South," his biographer recounted, "Republican Congressmen were horrified when they learned that he proposed to extend them to the North as well."[95] There were few blacks, no Black Codes, no peonage in the North. Almost invariably references in the debates were to oppression in the South, harassment of whites who came South. Congressman William Kelley complained that "Northerners could go South but once there they could not express their thoughts as freemen."[96] Article IV, however, conferred on visitors only the privileges enjoyed by residents, and they criticized slavery at their peril. Richard Yates asked in the Senate, "Do you suppose any of you can go South and express your sentiments freely and in safety?"[97] Columbus Delano pointed out that "the first section

---

91. Michael H. v. Gerald D., 491 U.S. 110, 121 (1989) (emphasis added).
92. Id. 122; see Holdsworth, supra text accompanying note 81.
93. Reno v. Flores, 113 S.Ct. 1439, 1447 (1993).
94. Collins v. City of Harker Heights, 112 S.Ct. 1061, 1068 (1992).
95. Donald, *Sumner II* 299.
96. Zuckert, supra note 20 at 162.
97. Curtis, supra note 9 at 138.

[of the Amendment] was made necessary by the perilous position of Northern men and loyal Southerners in the South."[98] Michael Curtis himself observed that "Republican congressmen typically insisted on protection of individual liberty . . . in the South."[99] A "particularly telling passage," Michael Zuckert exclaims, is James Wilson's statement that blacks "must have the same liberty of speech in any part of the South as they have always had in the North."[100] This statement is indeed "telling"; what it tells us is that the authors of the Fourteenth Amendment believed that the North would not be affected by the Amendment.

There is proof positive that intervention in Northern affairs was not contemplated. Senator Trumbull said, "This bill in no manner interferes with the municipal regulations of any State which protects all alike in their rights of person and property. It would have no operation in Massachusetts, New York, Illinois, or most of the States of the Union."[101] John Bingham, a mainstay of the activist cause, assured the House that "under no possible interpretation can [the Fourteenth Amendment] ever be made to operate in the State of New York while she occupies her present proud position."[102] Referring to the Southern laws that "reduce the negro to a system of peonage," Senator William Stewart said that if all the Southern States would repeal such laws, the Civil Rights Bill would "simply be a nullity," it would have "no operation."[103] After sifting the ratification materials, Joseph James concluded, "wherever the framers discussed the amendment, it was presented as a necessary limitation to be placed on the South."[104] No activist has explained why, in light of this limited purpose, the framers decided to take from the North control in large part of its internal affairs.

98. Joseph B. James, *The Framing of the Fourteenth Amendment* 162 (1965).
99. Curtis, supra note 9 at 56.
100. Zuckert, supra note 20 at 162.
101. Avins, supra note 47 at 200.
102. Id. 155.
103. Id. 204; Bingham to same effect, id. 155.
104. James, supra note 98 at 167. For more extended discussion of the "incorporation" issue, see supra note 17; Raoul Berger, "Incorporation of the Bill of Rights: A Nine-Lived Cat," 42 Ohio St. L.J. 435 (1981); Raoul Berger, "Incorporation of the Bill of Rights: A Reply to Michael Curtis' Response," 44 Ohio St. L.J. 1 (1983).

# 9

## Opposition Statements Examined

THE case for a broad reading of the Fourteenth Amendment has been rested in large part on statements by those who opposed both the Civil Rights Bill and the Amendment. That is a sharp departure from traditional canons of interpretation voiced by Thomas Jefferson; he looked for the "meaning" of the Constitution to the "explanations of those who advocated, not those who opposed it."[1] Like Jefferson, courts look to statements by the advocates of a measure and give short shrift to its opponents.[2] There are sound reasons for that view.

It beclouds analysis merely to identify Senators Willard Saulsbury, Garrett Davis, Thomas A. Hendricks, and Peter G. Van Winkle as "Conservatives,"[3] without adding that they were Democrats adamantly opposed to the Reconstruction measures, who wanted to keep the Negroes in subjection, and of whom Davis and Saulsbury were in the front rank of the assault. Among the opponents was Lovell H. Rousseau of Kentucky, an unabashed racist, who charged that the Freedmen's Bureau Bill "gave negroes the same privileges in railway cars and theaters, and there would be mixed schools."[4] Horace Flack comments that "no one ques-

1. 4 Elliot 446.
2. Statements by "opponents" of a bill "cannot be relied upon as indicative of legislative intent." National Labor Relations Board v. Thompson Products, 141 F.2d 794, 798 (9th Cir. 1944). "If resort to legislative history is had, the statements of those who supported the legislation and secured its passage will be accepted in determining its meaning." Union Starch & Refining Co. v. National Labor Relations Board, 186 F.2d 1008, 1012 (7th Cir. 1951). See also Duplex Co. v. Deering, 254 U.S. 443, 474–475 (1921), and infra at notes 13 and 14.
3. Kelly, Fourteenth 1063, 1070.
4. Cited in Flack at 16. A similar statement was made by John L. Dawson of Pennsylvania, *Globe* 541.

tioned [Rousseau's] statements in regard to these things," and concludes: "Many believed that the negro would be entitled to sit on juries, to attend the same schools . . . It does not appear that *all* of these contentions were specifically contradicted. It would seem reasonable to suppose that . . . these rights could not be legally denied to them."[5] To begin with, there were, for example, a number of specific denials by proponents of the Bill that it provided for Negro service on a jury;[6] it was hardly necessary to pop up like a jack-in-the-box with a retort to each such remark, particularly when the sponsors repeatedly underscored the limited objectives of the Bill. Why should any weight be given to the insistence by Andrew J. Rogers, Democrat of New Jersey, that the Bill would nullify school segregation, coming on the heels of Chairman Wilson's categorical denial, later reiterated, of any such effect?[7]

The length to which the approach of Flack has been carried is illustrated by Alfred Kelly. After noting the various references to constitutionalization of the Civil Rights Act by the Fourteenth Amendment, he states: "All this might well imply that the first section of the proposed amendment was intended to be merely declaratory of the Civil Rights Act, and would not go beyond its rather restrictive guarantees. But a second theme was present in the House debates—the argument that the phraseology of the first section was expansive and 'revolutionary' in character, so that its precise meaning was susceptible to indefinitely broad

5. Flack 16–17, 40 (emphasis added).
6. Infra at notes 25–27.
7. Supra Chapter 7 at note 10. Rogers continued to insist that suffrage was a "civil right" within the meaning of the Civil Rights Bill, *Globe* 1122, although it had been carefully explained by Wilson and Trumbull that it was excluded. Thayer, who followed Rogers, stated, "nobody can successfully contend that a bill guarantying simply civil rights and immunities is a bill under which you could extend the right of suffrage, which is a political and not a civil right." Id. 1151. Rogers illustrates why opposition statements are unreliable. Speaking to §1 of the Amendment, he said, "This section . . . is . . . an attempt to embody in the Constitution . . . that outrageous and miserable civil rights bill," and that the "privileges or immunities" clause embraced the right to vote . . . to marry . . . to be a juror," *Globe* 2538, all of which had been specifically denied by proponents of the bill and, with respect to suffrage, of the Amendment.

Senator Trumbull explained at one point that he did not reply to opposition assertions "because I thought we should soonest get action on the bill by voting silently upon them." Id. 399.

interpretation." And who are the Congressmen avouched for this "revolutionary" reading? A group of Democratic worthies, Benjamin M. Boyer and Samuel J. Randall of Pennsylvania, and Rogers, the " 'bete noire' of the Radicals," says Kelly himself[8]—a man so far out that he was actually embarrassing to his more practiced Democratic colleagues.[9] It is astonishing to derive "revolutionary" principles from the argumentative statements of the very foes who fought even moderate proposals tooth and nail.

Now the Democrats well knew that a broad segment of the Northern electorate was opposed to Negro equality, so their statements, as Charles Fairman noted, were calculated to render the bill "odious."[10] They sought to discredit it, not to make it the instrument of a "revolution" in Negro rights. For the Democrats, color prejudice, Eric McKitrick remarks, "was their greatest asset. All they needed to do was to keep it alive and exploit it in every way."[11] Fairman's admonition against "drawing inferences from a failure to deny such statements in such unreasonable partisan harangues"[12] reflects established interpretive practice most recently restated by the Supreme Court: "[remarks] made in the course of legislative debate or hearings other than by persons responsible for the preparation or the drafting of a bill are entitled to little weight . . . This is especially so with regard to the statements of legislative opponents who '[i]n their zeal to

8. Kelly, Fourteenth 1078–1079. For similar reliance on an array of Democrats, see tenBroek 218–219. In Bell v. Maryland, 378 U.S. 226, 295 (1964), Justice Goldberg stated in a concurring opinion, "opponents . . . frequently complained, without refutation or contradiction, that these measures [Freedmen's Bureau Bill and Civil Rights Bill] would grant negroes the right of equal treatment in places of public accommodation," citing Senator Garrett Davis (Globe 936). On the same page, however, Senator Trumbull stated, "The original act [FBB] and this amendatory bill together were simply designed to protect refugees and freedmen from persecution." Shortly thereafter Chairman Wilson reiterated in the House that the Civil Rights Bill had limited aims, which did not, for example, extend "to setting aside the school laws and jury laws." Globe 1294.

9. Samuel S. Marshall, a fellow Democrat, said, "in many of the extreme views expressed by . . . [Rogers] . . . he does not . . . represent the Democratic portion of this House." Globe 1172. To which Rogers added, "I know that my views are somewhat in advance of those of some members on this side of the House." Id. See also Marshall, id. 1157; William E. Niblack of Indiana, id. 1158.

10. Fairman, Stanford 138.

11. Eric McKitrick, *Andrew Johnson and Reconstruction* 58 (1960).

12. Fairman, *History* 1236.

defeat a bill . . . understandably tend to overstate its reach.'"[13] Or, as it stated on another occasion: "An unsuccessful minority cannot put words into the mouths of the majority."[14]

Several broad constructions cannot, however, quickly be dismissed as calculated partisanship. Senator Edgar Cowan, a conservative Republican of Pennsylvania, read the Bill to mean "that there shall be no discrimination made . . . none in any way," so that Pennsylvania officials could be punished for enforcing its school segregation laws.[15] The Bill, however, was restricted to "civil rights," whose narrow scope was repeatedly emphasized. Then, too, the "no discrimination in civil rights" phrase was later deleted, in order, Chairman Wilson explained, to obviate a "latitudinarian" construction.[16] Another statement, that of Senator Reverdy Johnson, a Democrat of Maryland and respected veteran lawyer, merits notice. He urged that because a Negro would now be authorized to enter into a contract, he could enter into a "contract of marriage" with a white woman and thereby the State miscegenation laws would be invalidated.[17] Tocqueville recorded that "in the North of the Union, marriages may be legally contracted between negroes and whites; but public opinion would stigmatize a man who should connect himself with a negress as infamous."[18] That attitude persisted; Stevens' Negro mistress horrified the abolitionists.[19] Few of the most ardent abolitionists would have dared argue for intermarriage at this time, because it would have wrecked their hope of securing the indispensable "fundamental rights" to blacks.[20] To attribute to the framers an intention by the word "contract" to authorize intermarriage runs counter to all in-

13. Ernst & Ernst v. Hochfelder, 425 U.S. 185, 204 note 24 (1976). See also Justice Frankfurter, quoted in Kluger 668.

14. Mastro Plastics Corp. v. Labor Board, 350 U.S. 270, 288 (1956).

15. *Globe* 500.

16. *Globe* 1366; see Wilson, supra note 8.

17. *Globe* 505–506.

18. 1 Tocqueville, *Democracy in America* 364 (1900).

19. Fawn M. Brodie, *Thaddeus Stevens: Scourge of the South* 20 (1959).

20. Recall Stevens' perturbation upon learning that Theodore Tilton had walked arm-in-arm with ex-slave Frederick Douglass. Supra Chapter 1 at note 53; see also infra Chapter 10 at note 6. Rhode Island enacted a miscegenation statute in 1844. *Globe* 201. Lincoln stated in an address at Columbus, Ohio, September 1859, "I am not . . . in favor of bringing about in any way social and political equality of the white and black races . . . I

tendments. In the House, Samuel W. Moulton of Illinois flatly denied "that it is a civil right for a white man to marry a black woman or for a black man to marry a white woman."[21] Although a contract of marriage, strictly speaking, is a contract, marriage is not in ordinary usage conceived in terms of contract. Given the stated purposes of the Bill, the association of contracts with other property rights, authority to contract could be read as a license for intermarriage only by a strained construction. Senator Johnson himself stated to Fessenden, "you do not mean to do that. I am sure that the Senator is not prepared to go to that extent."[22] Nevertheless, to forestall the possibility that a court might thus broadly construe the Bill, he urged specific exclusion of intermarriage. It would be straining at a gnat to deduce from the omission to make such an exclusion that the Bill contemplated the abolition of miscegenation laws. No court which, like Senator Johnson, would perceive that Congress did "not mean to do that," should so read the Act; for from the bloodletting case in Bologna in the Middle Ages, courts have striven to ascertain and effectuate the intention of the lawmaker.[23] Although President Johnson vetoed the Civil Rights Bill, he referred to "the enumera-

---

am not . . . in favor of making voters or jurors of negroes, nor of qualifying them . . . to intermarry with white people." Id. 3214–3215. He faced up to the realities as President, supra Chapter 1 at note 36. Farnsworth of Illinois, replying to fears of intermarriage expressed by Rogers, said he would "very cheerfully join him in voting the restraining influence of a penal statute." *Globe* 204. Julian of Indiana expressed himself to the same effect. Id. 258. In 1867—while the Fourteenth Amendment was in the course of ratification—the Pennsylvania Supreme Court stated, "The natural law which forbids their intermarriage and that social amalgamation which leads to a corruption of races, is as clearly divine as that which imparted to them different natures." West Chester & Philadelphia Railroad Co. v. Miles, 55 Pa. at 209, 213. See also Morton Keller, *Affairs of State* 150 (1977).

21. *Globe* 632.
22. Id. 506.
23. The question that underlies all "rules for the interpretation of statutes [or Constitutions] . . . is, what was the intention of the legislative body? Without going back to the famous case of the drawing of blood in the streets of Bologna, the books are full of authorities to the effect that the intention of the lawmaking power will prevail even against the letter of the statute . . . The intention of the lawmaker is the law." Hawaii v. Mankichi, 190 U.S. 197, 212 (1903). Blackstone refers to "the Bolognian law . . . 'that whoever drew blood in the streets should be punished with the utmost severity,' " which was held "not to extend to the surgeon, who opened the vein of a person that fell down in the street with a fit." 1 William Blackstone, *Commentaries on the Laws of England* 60.

tion of the rights to be enjoyed" and noted that it did not repeal "State laws on the subject of marriage between the two races."[24]

A similar objection, that of Columbus Delano, an Ohio Republican, was that the "equal benefit of all laws and proceedings for the security of person and property" would extend to the "right of being jurors." Mark that an Ohio Republican said to Chairman Wilson, "I presume that the gentleman himself will shrink from the idea of conferring upon this race now, at this particular moment, the right of being jurors." Wilson countered, "I do not believe it confers that right,"[25] and he reiterated that the limited objectives of the Bill did not extend to "setting aside the school and jury laws."[26] Moulton also denied "that it is a civil right for any one to sit on a jury"; and Ohio Republican William Lawrence stated that the Bill "does not affect any political rights, as that of suffrage, the right to sit on juries . . . That it leaves to the States to be determined each for itself."[27]

The positive explanations that the bill had restricted objectives are fortified by the fact that sweeping proposals to abolish *all* discriminatory classifications[28] repeatedly fell by the wayside, confirming that Congress with open eyes rejected a comprehensive ban against all discriminations. For example, early in the session, on January 12, 1866, Stevens submitted to the Joint Committee on Reconstruction that "*All* laws, state or federal, shall operate impartially and equally on all persons without regard to race or color."[29] On February 19, 1866, Senator Richard Yates of Illinois proposed that "No State shall . . . *in any manner* recognize *any distinction* between citizens of the United States or any State . . . on ac-

24. *Globe* 1679–1680. The veto was overridden in both Houses. Id. 1809, 1861.

25. *Globe App.* 156–157. [Mark Tushnet, "Civil Rights and Social Rights: The Future of the Reconstruction Amendments," 25 Loyola L.A. L. Rev. 1207, 1209 (1992): "during the congressional debates on the adoption of the Fourteenth Amendment, the right to serve on a jury was routinely described as a political right, and the audience was repeatedly assured that the Fourteenth Amendment would not guarantee African Americans that right."]

26. *Globe* 1294.

27. Id. 632, 1832. Madison stated, "Trial by jury cannot be considered as a natural right, but a right resulting from a social compact." 1 *Annals of Congress* 437.

28. TenBroek at 205 collected some proposals.

29. Kendrick 46 (emphasis added).

count of race," and renewed the proposal on March 9, 1866, at which time it was decisively voted down, 38 to 7.[30] Senator Sumner proposed that in the rebel States "there shall be no denial of rights, civil or political, on account of race." This, too, was rejected, 39 to 8;[31] a similar proposal was made by Senator Henderson, and there were others.[32] One and all came to naught.[33] At Bingham's insistence, it will be recalled, the phrase "There shall be no discrimination in civil rights" was deleted from the Civil Rights Bill, leaving the express enumeration of protected privileges and immunities.[34] The plain fact, as Senator Fessenden, the respected chairman of the Joint Committee said, was that "we cannot put into the Constitution, owing to existing prejudices and existing institutions, an entire exclusion of all class distinctions."[35]

In the teeth of this history, to import into the Civil Rights Act views of abolitionists and opponents[36] that so plainly had been rejected, is to thwart, not to effectuate, the intention of its framers. Bickel fairly summarizes the evidence: "The Senate Moderates, led by Trumbull and Fessenden, who sponsored this [civil rights] formula, assigned a limited and well-defined meaning to it," namely, "the right to contract" and so on,

30. *Globe App.* 98; *Globe* 1287 (emphasis added).

31. *Globe* 1287 (emphasis added). Alfred Kelly said of these measures introduced by "the more enthusiastic Radicals" that the "significant" fact is they all "resorted to sweeping and all-inclusive prohibitory language and not mere enumeration alone." Kelly, Fourteenth 1060. Their "significance" resides, rather, in the fact, to use his own words, that "all died early deaths," demonstrating that they were unacceptable to the dominant Republicans.

32. *Globe* 702; supra note 28.

33. As Frederick A. Pike of Maine said of Thomas Eliot's proposal that "the elective franchise shall not be denied or abridged in any State on account of race," "no amendment of that character can pass . . . It is useless to submit such a one to the States when it is sure of rejection." *Globe* 406, 407.

34. Supra Chapter 7 at notes 13–17; supra at note 16.

35. *Globe* 705. A similar statement was made by Stevens, id. 537; see also supra note 32.

36. Kelly tells us that the "mood of the Radicals . . . was 'revolutionary,' " they projected "changes in the southern social order going far beyond the mere destruction of slavery"; "both the Civil Rights Act of 1866 and the Fourteenth Amendment were products of" this "general 'revolutionary' mood." Kelly, Fourteenth 1060–1061. It would also have required "something of a revolution" in the Northern "social order," for which the Republicans were totally unprepared. As we have seen, the "revolutionary" proposals were beaten back time after time. Supra at notes 29–35.

"also a right to equal protection in the literal sense of benefiting equally from the laws *for the security of person and property.*"[37] Even so, James G. Blaine recorded, "it required potent persuasion, reinforced by the severest party discipline, to prevent a serious break in both Houses against the bill"[38]—and this in spite of repeated assurances as to its limited scope. Subsequently, four defectors in the Senate could have defeated the Amendment.[39]

37. Bickel 56 (emphasis added).
38. 2 Blaine, *Twenty Years of Congress* 171, quoted in Flack 19 note 22.
39. James 150.

# 10

# *"Equal Protection of the Laws"*

IT has long been the habit of the Supreme Court to say that the Fourteenth Amendment "speaks in general terms, and those are as comprehensive as possible."[1] Its opinions are replete with references to the "majestic generalities" of the Fourteenth Amendment,[2] to the "vague contours" of the due process clause,[3] and the like. Even Judge Learned Hand, though later dubious whether the Amendment authorized the desegregation decision, had said, "history is only a feeble light, for the rubrics were meant to answer future problems unimagined and unimaginable."[4] And, though Negro suffrage was unmistakably excluded from the Amendment, no less a figure than Justice Holmes held that the equal protection clause self-evidently requires admission of Negroes to a Texas primary: "it seems hard to imagine a more direct and obvious infringement of the Fourteenth. That amendment . . . was passed . . . with a special intent to protect blacks from discrimination against them."[5] Yet, as

1. Strauder v. Virginia, 100 U.S. 303, 310 (1879).
2. Katzenbach v. Morgan, 384 U.S. 641, 649 (1966).
3. Infra Chapter 11 at notes 2–3; Chapter 14 at notes 40–43.
4. *The Spirit of Liberty* 172–173 (Irving Dillard ed. 1952). Yet he could say of the Court's resumption of the "role of a third legislative chamber" in the context of the "desegregation" case, "I have never been able to understand on what basis it does or can rest except as a *coup de main*." Hand, *The Bill of Rights* 55 (1962).
5. Nixon v. Herndon, 273 U.S. 536, 541 (1927). Justice Matthews had earlier cited "the political franchise of voting" as a "self-evident" illustration of "fundamental rights" "because preservative of all rights," Yick Wo v. Hopkins, 118 U.S. 356, 370 (1886), a position that had been pressed by Sumner and others but had been rejected. Supra Chapter 4 at notes 12–14 et seq.

In the same opinion wherein Justice Frankfurter finds it impossible to swallow reapportionment, he states that "the controlling command of Supreme Law is plain and un-

we have seen, the framers meant to outlaw discrimination only with respect to enumerated privileges. Even the abolitionists shrank from complete equality. Derrick Bell points out that "few abolitionists were interested in offering blacks the equality they touted so highly. Indeed, the
anguish most abolitionists experienced as to whether slaves should be
granted social equality as well as political freedom is well documented."[6]

It is the object of this and the succeeding chapter to show that the
framers chose words which aptly expressed, and throughout were wedded to, their limited purposes; that there is virtually no evidence that the
framers meant by resort to those words to open goals beyond those
specified in the Civil Rights Act and constitutionalized in the Amendment.[7] If the terms of the Amendment are "vague," it is because the
Court made them so[8] in order to shield the expanding free enterprise
system from regulation.

Analysis will be facilitated by a breakdown into subsidiary questions:
What privileges were to be protected? Was the protection to be absolute,
that is, to guarantee certain rights to all, or comparative, only to secure
freedom from discrimination if those rights were granted? Do the words
confer upon Congress a general power to legislate for the States or merely
a power to correct State violations? The materials that bear upon these
questions are so intermingled that it is not easy to disentangle them for
separate discussion. Some repetition is therefore unavoidable, but an effort to isolate the several issues is well worth the cost.

---

equivocal" on the issue of Negro disfranchisement: "An end of discrimination against the
Negro was the compelling motive of the Civil War Amendments. The Fifteenth expresses this in terms, and it is no less true of the Equal Protection Clause of the Fourteenth." Baker v. Carr, 369 U.S. 186, 285–286 (1962), citing Nixon v. Herndon, dissenting opinion. The invocation to Holmes cannot overcome the fact that the Fourteenth
Amendment designedly withheld suffrage.

Holmes himself construed a statute "not to include a case that indisputably was within
its literal meaning, but was believed not to be within the aim of Congress." American
Security Co. v. District of Columbia, 224 U.S. 491, 495 (1912). There he *inferred* that
"Congress meant no such result"; here we have proof positive that the framers meant to
exclude suffrage.

6. Derrick A. Bell, Jr., "Book Review," 76 Colum. L. Rev. 350, 358 (1976). See Chapter 1 at notes 38, 39, 53.

7. See supra Chapter 5.

8. See infra Chapter 14 at notes 40–43.

"Equal protection," it has been said, "had virtually no antecedent history."[9] Sumner believed that he may have been "the first to introduce the words 'equality before the law' into American jurisprudence."[10] In truth, the concept that laws should be general, nondiscriminatory in their application, is of long standing. As Locke put it, rulers "are to govern by promulgated established laws, not to be varied in particular cases, but to have one rule for rich and poor."[11] A note to Blackstone stated generality in more limited terms: "*restraints* introduced by the law should be equal to all."[12] Nor was selection of those entitled to equal protection ruled out, as the very exclusion of black slaves from the society attested. The Massachusetts Constitution of 1780 provided that *Christians* "demeaning themselves peaceably shall be equally under the protection of law"; and, like the Civil Rights Act of 1866, that Constitution confined protection to "the enjoyment of his life, liberty and property according to standing laws."[13] As slaves, blacks were chattels, nonpersons singled out for grossly discriminatory treatment and oppression at every step. It would be little exaggerated to say that they were all but unprotected. Declared free by the Thirteenth Amendment, they continued to be treated like slaves,[14] so it was essential to insure that the laws which protected whites would also protect blacks from oppression. In the words of Senator James W. Nye of Nevada, the Negroes "have equal rights to protection—equalized protection under equalized laws."[15] This "equalized protection," it can not be overemphasized, was limited to the rights enumerated in the Civil Rights Act of 1866, as will now appear.

9. Kelly, Fourteenth 1052.

10. Donald, *Sumner II* 149.

11. Quoted in R. J. Harris, *The Quest for Equality* 10 (1960).

12. 1 William Blackstone, *Commentaries on the Laws of England* 127n. The Blackstone note was called to the attention of the 39th Congress by Senator Trumbull. *Globe* 474.

13. Articles III and X; 1 Poore 957–958.

14. Supra Chapter 2 at notes 18–24; Conkling, *Globe* 356; Kenneth M. Stampp, *The Peculiar Institution* 124, 192–236 (1956).

15. *Globe* 1073, 1074.

## What Was Equal Protection to Protect?

The Civil Rights Act, it will be recalled, secured to blacks the *same* right to contract, to hold property, and to sue, as whites enjoyed, and the "*equal* benefit of all laws *for security of person and property.*" "Political rights" were excluded.[16] In describing these aims the framers interchangeably referred to "equality," "equality before the law," and "equal protection" (but always in the circumscribed context of the rights enumerated in the Bill), so that it is reasonable to infer that the framers regarded these terms as synonymous. What is required, said Moulton of Illinois, is "that each State shall provide for equality before the law, equal protection to life, liberty, and property, equal right to sue and be sued."[17] A leading Radical, Samuel Shellabarger of Ohio, said, of the Civil Rights Bill, "whatever rights *as to each of these enumerated* civil (not political) matters the State may confer upon one race . . . shall be held by all races in equality . . . It secures . . . *equality of protection in those enumerated civil rights* which the States may deem proper to confer upon any races."[18] So it was understood by Senator Hendricks, an Indiana Democrat: "To recognize the civil rights of the colored people as equal to the civil rights of the white people, I understand to be as far as Senators desire to go; in the language of the Senator from Massachusetts [Sumner] to place all men upon an equality before the law; and that is proposed in regard to their civil rights." He objected that "in the State of Indiana we do not recognize the civil equality of the races."[19] When Andrew Johnson combed the Bill for objections and vetoed it, he noted that §1 "contains an enumeration of the rights to be enjoyed" and that "perfect equality" was sought with respect to

16. Supra Chapter 2 at note 26 et seq. In 1797 Judge Samuel Chase had decided that the privileges and immunities clause of Article IV required a State to accord an out-of-state citizen the "same" protection for property and "personal rights" and the "same" exemptions from taxes and burdens it afforded to its own citizens. Campbell v. Morris, 3 H. & McH. 535, 554 (Md.).

17. *Globe* 1622.

18. Id. 1293 (emphasis added). Wilson called for a stop to "inhuman" discriminations and for "equality in the exemptions of the law." *Globe* 1118.

19. Id. 601–602.

"these enumerated rights."[20] Thomas T. Davis, a New York Republican, expressed a widely shared feeling in stating, Negroes "must be made equal before the law, and be permitted to enjoy life, liberty, and the pursuit of happiness [property]," but he was against "the establishment of perfect equality between the colored and the white race of the South."[21] While James W. Patterson of New Hampshire was "opposed to any law discriminating against [blacks] in the security and protection of life, liberty, person and property," "beyond this," he stated, "I am not prepared to go," explicitly rejecting "political and social equality."[22] Windom declared that the Civil Rights Bill conferred an "equal right, nothing more . . . to make and enforce contracts," and so on, but no "social privileges."[23] Thus, the concept of "equal protection" had its roots in the Civil Rights Bill and was conceived to be limited to the enumerated rights.

What reason is there to conclude that when the words "equal protection of the laws" were embodied in the Amendment they were freighted with a new cargo of meaning—unlimited equality across the board? The evidence points the other way. In an early version of the Amendment, provision was made for both "the same political rights and privileges and . . . equal protection in the enjoyment of life, liberty and property,[24] an indication that "equal protection" did not include "political rights and privileges," but was confined to "life, liberty, or property." Bingham proposed a substitute, H.R. No. 63, that would empower Congress "to secure . . . all privileges and immunities . . . (Art. IV, Sec. 2); and . . . equal protection in the rights of life, liberty and property (5th Amendment)."[25] "Political rights and privileges" had disappeared; in its place was "privileges and immunities." Neither "privileges and immunities," nor its antecedent, "civil rights," had included "po-

20. Id. 1679–1680. Bickel concluded that the Moderate leadership—Trumbull and Fessenden—had in mind a "limited and well-defined meaning . . . a right to equal protection in the literal sense of benefitting equally from the laws for the security of person and property." Bickel 56.

21. Id. 1085.

22. Id. 2699.

23. Id. 1159. See also John Thomas, supra Chapter 7 at note 33.

24. Bickel 31.

25. Id. 33; Kendrick 61.

litical privileges."[26] Bingham explained that his proposal was aimed at "confiscation statutes . . . statutes of unjust imprisonment" of the "rebel states," the objects of the Civil Rights Bill. It would enable Congress to insure "that the protection given by the laws of the States shall be *equal in respect to* life, liberty and property to all persons."[27] Hale of New York asked him to point to the clause "which contains the doctrine he here announces." Bingham replied, "The words 'equal protection' contain it, and *nothing else*."[28]

Among the statements indicating that §1 was considered to embody the objectives of the Civil Rights Act is that of Latham of West Virginia: "The 'civil rights bill,' which is now a law . . . covers exactly the same ground as this amendment."[29] Stevens explained that the Amendment

> allows Congress to correct the unjust legislation of the States *so far* that the law which operates upon one shall operate *equally* upon all. Whatever law punishes a white man for a crime shall punish the black man precisely in the same way . . . Whatever law protects the white man shall afford *equal protection* to the black man. Whatever means of redress is afforded to one shall be afforded to all. Whatever law allows the white man to testify in court shall allow the man of color to do the same. These are great advantages over their present [Black] codes . . . I need not enumerate these partial and oppressive laws . . . Your civil rights bill secures the same thing.[30]

26. Supra Chapter 2 at notes 26–40.

27. *Globe* 1091, 1094 (emphasis added).

28. Id. 1094 (emphasis added). This interchange with Hale about a provision described by Bingham as "equal *in respect to* life, liberty, and property" (emphasis added), is rendered by Kelly thus: "In other words, the amendment was to impose a very general requirement of equality on *all* state legislation of the most inclusive kind"! Kelly, Fourteenth 1074. "Life, liberty, and property," we have seen, had a limited connotation for the framers.

29. *Globe* 2883; see also supra Chapter 1 at notes 10–13; Chapter 8 at notes 68–70.

30. *Globe* 2459 (emphasis added). Van Alstyne comments on this passage, "Surely the right to vote is one essential protection that white men enjoyed and surely equal protection would require that black men enjoy it to the same extent." Van Alstyne 56. He substitutes twentieth-century logic for the intention of the framers, including Stevens, to exclude suffrage from both the Civil Rights Bill and the Fourteenth Amendment. See infra Appendix A at notes 21–33.

As Bickel noted, the "evils to which the proposal was directed" hark "back to those which had been pointed to in support of the Civil Rights Bill."[31] In attributing to Stevens the view that the Amendment proposed "a congressional guarantee of equality with respect to *all* state legislation,"[32] Alfred Kelly misconceived Stevens' position. Very early in the session he had proposed that "*all* national and State laws shall be equally applicable to every citizen . . . that is the one I love . . . But it would not be wise to entangle the present proposition with that one. The one might drag down the other."[33] And when Stevens summed up his views on the Amendment, he said he had hoped that the people "would have so remodeled all our institutions as to have freed them from *every vestige of . . . inequality* of rights . . . that *no distinction* would be tolerated . . . This bright dream has vanished . . . we shall be obliged to be content with patching up the worst portions of the ancient edifice."[34] Those patches went only to discriminatory punishments, deprivation of judicial redress and the like.

Senator Howard, a far less acute and careful lawyer than Stevens, delivered himself of a looser statement, but even he went on to qualify the general by his enumeration of particulars:

31. Bickel 47. Referring to an earlier Stevens interpellation in a Hale-Bingham colloquy, Kelly states that Stevens "made it clear" he proposed to go "far beyond the scope of the Civil Rights Bill." Kelly, Fourteenth 1073. That concerned a Bingham proposal that "Congress shall have power to make all laws . . . to secure equal protection in the rights of life, liberty, and property." Hale objected, and Stevens asked whether he meant Congress "could interfere in any case where the legislation of a State was equal, impartial to all? Or is it not simply to provide that, where any State makes a distinction in the same law between different classes of individuals Congress shall have power to correct such inequality." *Globe* 1063. The proposal really embodied the former alternative (see infra at notes 76–81 for discussion), and it had to be abandoned. For present purposes, the important thing is that equal protection was limited to "life, liberty, and property," and as the later Stevens statement, quoted supra at note 30, shows, he did not go beyond the rights enumerated in the Civil Rights Act.

32. Kelly, Fourteenth 1073. Apparently Kelly changed his views. In a 1965 article he stated that "so far as I know, there is no instance of any discussion on the floor of either House in terms of anything other than a proposal to guarantee against *certain* forms of *discriminatory* state action." Kelly, "Clio and the Court: An Illicit Love Affair," 1965 S. Ct. Rev. 119, 147 (emphasis added).

33. *Globe* 537.

34. Id. 3148 (emphasis added).

The last two clauses of the first section of the amendment disable a State from depriving . . . any person . . . of life, liberty or property without due process of law, or from denying to him equal protection of the laws. This abolishes *all class* legislation in the States and does away with the injustice of subjecting one caste of person to a code not applicable to another. It prohibits the hanging of a black man for a crime for which the white man is not to be hanged. It protects the black man in his fundamental rights . . . with the same shield which it throws over the white man . . . Ought not the time to be now passed when one measure of justice is to be meted out to a member of one caste while another and different measure is to be meted out to the member of another caste.[35]

By "fundamental rights" Howard was employing the familiar shorthand for the incidents of "life, liberty, or property," repeatedly so identified during the course of the Civil Rights Bill. That by "all legislation" he did not really mean "all" is demonstrated by his statement that §1 "does not . . . give . . . the right of voting"; it is not, he said, "one of the privileges or immunities."[36] One who confessed that suffrage was not granted can hardly have held out in the same breath that "all class legislation" would now be banned, including some for which even greater distaste had been exhibited—desegregation, miscegenation. Reflecting earlier comments on the Civil Rights Bill, Howard stated in the same context that the Amendment "establishes equality before the law," that it will prevent States from "trenching upon these rights and privileges," and will give blacks the "same rights and the same protection before the law" as it gives whites.[37] Patently both Stevens and Howard were addressing themselves to the oppressive discriminations perpetuated by the Black Codes.

Bingham himself contributed a telling bit of evidence against an interpretation of equal protection in unlimited terms. He it was who im-

35. Id. 2766 (emphasis added).
36. Id.
37. Id. To read Howard's "all legislation" literally is also to ignore the proposals to that effect that perished. Supra Chapter 9 at notes 28–35. These facts refute Kelly's statement that Howard "presented in no uncertain terms a powerful and convincing 'broad construction' of the force and scope of the first section," an "extremely latitudinarian interpretation of the due process clause, which he asserted would destroy all class legislation entirely." Kelly, Fourteenth 1081; cf. supra note 32.

ported "equal protection" into the Amendment; speaking toward the close of the session in behalf of the admission of Tennessee despite its whites-only suffrage provision, he said: "One great issue has been finally . . . settled . . . [by the Amendment] the equality of all men before the law."[38] Manifestly an equality that excluded Negro suffrage was not unqualified as he recognized: "We are all for equal and exact justice . . . [but] justice for all is not to be secured in a day." When Joseph H. Defrees of Indiana, like Stevens, said that §1 of the Amendment "places all persons on an equality . . . *so far as* equal protection of the laws is concerned,"[39] he distinguished between full-scale equality and "equal protection of the laws." That distinction was underlined by Samuel Shellabarger, who, speaking to the Civil Rights Bill, confined "equality of protection [to] the enumerated civil rights," if conferred upon whites. Similar remarks were made by Wilson and Moulton.[40] Limited equality was adopted because, as Senator Henderson of Missouri declared early in the session: "A bold declaration of man's equality cannot be carried."[41] His prediction was fulfilled by repeated rejection of proposals to require "all laws" to operate "impartially and equally," to abolish "any distinctions between citizens."[42]

But, it may be asked, does not the differentiation in §1 between "due process" protection of "life, liberty, and property" and "equal protection of the laws" indicate that "equal protection" was now divorced from the earlier limitation to "life, liberty, and property"? Nothing in the debates indicates such a purpose.[42a] "Equal protection of the laws" expressed the central object of the framers: to prevent *statutory* discrimination with respect to the rights enumerated in the Civil Rights Act. That purpose had been loosely expressed in Bingham's earlier formulation: "equal protection in the rights of life, liberty, and property," which he mistakenly

38. *Globe* 3979.

39. *Globe App.* 227 (emphasis added).

40. Supra Chapter 2 at note 26; supra at notes 17–18, 21–23.

41. *Globe App.* 119. See Senator Fessenden, supra Chapter 6, Epigraph. "One is driven by the evidence," Woodward states, to conclude that "popular convictions were not prepared to sustain" a "guarantee of equality." *The Burden of Southern History* 83 (1960); see also Chapter 1 at notes 38–39, 52–53.

42. Supra Chapter 9 at notes 28–35.

42a. Evidence to the contrary is furnished by Farnsworth, infra Chapter 11 at note 98.

identified with the "5th Amendment." Possibly some more perceptive lawyer restored the words "life, liberty, and property" to their Fifth Amendment association with due process, thus insuring access to the courts. At the same time, the established association of due process with judicial procedure made it necessary to block what Stevens denominated "partial and oppressive laws," a purpose succinctly expressed by "equal protection of the laws" to which reference had been made during the debate on the Civil Rights Bill.

## Freedom From Discrimination vs. Absolute Rights

The framers sought only to secure to blacks the same specified rights as were enjoyed by whites; if whites did not have them there was no State duty to supply them to anyone, still less a congressional power to fill the gap. So much appears from Shellabarger's explanation that the Civil Rights Bill secures "equality of protection in these enumerated civil rights which the *States may deem proper to confer* upon any race."[43] Before considering further evidence, let us examine tenBroek's argument to the contrary. His was the most sustained effort to give "equal protection" an "absolute" as distinguished from a nondiscriminatory content. The heart of his argument is:

> the basic notion of this phrase is protection; equality is the condition. The equal protection of the laws cannot be supplied unless the protection of the laws is supplied, and the protection of the laws, at least for men's natural rights, being the sole purpose for which governments are instituted, must be supplied. The clause is thus understood to mean: "Every State shall supply to all persons . . . the protection of the laws and the protection shall be equal to all."[44]

Even on the level of verbal analysis the argument is vulnerable. A "condition" is a "restriction or qualification"; it was therefore not "protection unlimited"—the full protection of which laws are capable—that was mandated, but only that such laws as were enacted should be impartial.

43. Supra at note 18.
44. TenBroek 222.

If the laws supplied no protection, to whites or blacks, there was nothing to which the "equal" condition could attach. To state in this context that " 'equal' protection of the laws and the 'full' protection of the laws are virtually synonyms"[45] departs from a decent respect for words—a half-glass given to all is "equal" though it is not "full."

TenBroek's argument is further flawed by the assumption that the "basic idea" of the equal protection clause is that "protection of the laws . . . *must* be supplied." That may be well enough as a jural postulate,[46] but emphatically it was not the premise of the framers. Translating a remark of Hale as "the citizens must rely upon the State for their protection," Bingham said, "I admit that such is the rule as it now stands."[47] Later he explained that in his proposed amendment, "the care of the property, the liberty, and the life of the citizen . . . is in the States, and not in the Federal Government. I have sought to effect no change in that respect."[48] Because the rule was dear to the framers, Trumbull reassured the Senate that "if the State of Kentucky makes no discrimination in civil rights between its citizens, this bill has no operation whatever in the State of Kentucky."[49] Protection, if given, must be impartial, but the absence of all protection

45. Id. 193.

46. That is likewise Harris' view, supra note 11 at 22, 42.

47. *Globe* 1093. Hale had stated that the "American people have not yet found their State governments are insufficient to protect the rights and liberties of the citizen." Id. 1064–1065. After concurring, Bingham quoted Federalist No. 45: "The power reserved to the Federal States will extend to all the objects, which, in the ordinary course of affairs, concern the lives, liberties and properties of the people." *Globe* 1093.

Shellabarger referred to the "rights which the States may deem proper to confer upon any races," supra at note 18. And Senator Fessenden stated, "The power exists now at the present time in all these States to make just such class or caste distinctions as they please. The Constitution does not limit them." Id. 704.

48. Id. 1292.

49. Id. 600. After the Johnson veto of the Civil Rights Bill, Trumbull reiterated that the Bill "in no manner interferes with the municipal regulations of any State which protects all alike in their rights of person or property." Id. 1761.

Contrast this with tenBroek's deduction from Trumbull's statement, "I take it that any statute which is not equal to all, and which deprives any citizen of civil rights *which are secured to other citizens*, is an unjust encroachment" (emphasis added). TenBroek asks, " 'secured' how? By the only method by which rights can be secured, namely, by supplying protection . . . Hence, deprivation or denial of laws 'not equal to all' will occur just as much by failure to supply the protection . . . as by the Black Codes imposing special burdens on a selected class"! TenBroek 188.

would afford no ground for federal intervention. It does not advance ten-Broek's argument that, in the remarks of the radical extremists Higby-Kelley-Woodbridge, "the qualifying word 'equal' was almost entirely forgotten and 'protection' treated as if it stood alone."[50] Against this unrepresentative fringe there is first the fact that a subcommittee of the Joint Committee had proposed that "Congress shall have power to make all laws . . . to secure all persons . . . *full protection* in the enjoyment of life, liberty and property."[51] Here was a proposal—there were others—that embodied precisely what tenBroek argues for, and its demise demonstrates that the framers had no stomach for "full" protection at the hands of Congress. Their objectives were narrower.

Again and again the framers stated that their purpose was to prevent one law for blacks, another for whites. It was a ban on such discrimination that was expressed in "equality before the law" and "equal protection"—not a mandate that the States must confer rights not theretofore enjoyed by any citizen. In the beginning the Civil Rights Bill had provided:

> There shall be no discrimination in civil rights or immunities . . . but the inhabitants shall have the same right . . . ["as is enjoyed by white citizens"] . . . to full and equal benefit of all laws for the security of person and property, and shall be subject to like punishment . . . and none other.[52]

The word "immunities" carried over into the Amendment, hence Wilson's explanation is germane: "It merely secures to citizens of the United States equality in the exemptions of the law. A colored citizen shall not, because he is colored, be subjected to obligations, duties, pains and penalties from which other citizens are exempted . . . One race shall not be favored in this respect more than another . . . This is the spirit and scope

50. TenBroek 211. But Woodbridge understood the purpose was to strike at discrimination. Infra note 55. Higby is a poor witness for "absolute" protection, for his "extremely anti-Chinese" views led him to maintain that "the Chinese were 'a pagan race' of no virtue and incapable of citizenship," Harris, supra note 11 at 40, and therefore not entitled to equal protection.

51. January 27, 1866, TenBroek 205 (emphasis added).

52. *Globe* 474, 1366.

of the bill, and *it does not go one step beyond*."[53] Although the "no discrimination" clause had been deleted at Bingham's insistence that the words "civil rights" were too broad and "oppressive," the provisions for the "same" rights and immunities remained untouched. It was understood by the framers that discrimination remained the target as Shellabarger illustrates; the Bill would require that whatever of these "enumerated rights and obligations are imposed by State laws shall be for and upon all citizens alike without distinction based upon race"; such rights "shall be held by all races in equality."[54]

That persisted as the ground bass of the Amendment; Stevens explained that it required that a State law "shall operate *equally* upon all. Whatever law punishes a white man for a crime shall punish the black man precisely in the same way and to the same degree."[55] "Equal protection," said Senator Howard, "does away with the injustice of subjecting one caste of persons to a code not applicable to another"; the Amendment "establishes equality before the law."[56] In short, the framers struck at discrimination against the blacks with respect to enumerated privileges and immunities that were accorded to whites; and they chose a word perfectly suited to the purpose. Among the definitions of "equal" are "uniform in effect or operation; neither less nor greater; having the same rights or privileges; impartial." A State provision may be substandard when measured by more enlightened federal or State criteria; but if it is impartial, uniformly applied to all within the State, it satisfies the meaning of "equal."[57]

---

53. Id. 1117 (emphasis added). The word "immunity," said Bingham, means "exemption from unequal burdens." Id. 1089.

54. Id. 1293; see supra at note 18.

55. *Globe* 2459, more fully quoted supra at note 30. Woodbridge read the Bingham prototype amendment to give "to every citizen . . . that protection to his property which is extended to the other citizens of the State." Id. 1088.

56. Id. 2766.

57. In the 1871 debates on the Ku Klux Klan Act, James Garfield, destined before long to become President, "reviewed fully the legislative history of the first section," and stated that "It is not required the laws shall be perfect. They may be unwise, injudicious, even unjust; but they must be equal in their provisions . . . resting upon all with equal weight." *Cong. Globe*, 42d Cong., 1st Sess. App. 153, April 4, 1871.

True it is that Bingham and Lawrence of Ohio maintained that the "fundamental," "natural" rights were "absolute," and could not be withheld.[58] But the Republican majority was content to correct discriminations with respect to those rights. Bingham, on whom tenBroek so often relies, is, we have seen, a confused, imprecise, and vacillating witness.[59] Even so, when pressed by Hale whether his proposal "confers upon Congress a *general power* of legislation" in regard to "protection of life, liberty and property," he replied that it was designed "to see to it that the protection *given* by the laws of the State shall be *equal* in respect to life, liberty and property to all persons."[60] Faced with opposition, Bingham once more retreated—Congress was only to correct discrimination.[61] Nevertheless, tenBroek adopts Bingham's teetering statement that the States were under an absolute duty to protect those privileges. After remarking on Bingham's "immortal Bill of Rights," he loftily dismisses *Barron v. Baltimore*, wherein Chief Justice Marshall held that the Bill of Rights had no application to the States:

> The "immortal Bill of Rights" not binding on the States! How can one refute an axiom? . . . Chief Justices . . . cannot successfully refute an axiom more than any other mortals . . . [Marshall] could not by any pronouncement of his diminish the obligation of the states to protect men in their natural rights of life, liberty, and property.[62]

58. *Globe* 1089–1090, 1832.

59. Supra Chapter 8 at notes 43–56.

60. *Globe* 1094 (emphasis added).

61. "By the Fourteenth Amendment's terms the legal processes (procedures) due equally as protection and remedy to each national citizen were the laws and procedures of a citizen's State. Instead of formulating positively national civil-rights minima, as some Republican Radicals preferred to do, the amendment forbade unequal deprivation of the broad, uncodified mass of civil rights protections which a state professed to afford equally to the generality of its citizens." Harold M. Hyman, *A More Perfect Union* 467–468 (1973).

In 1872 Justice Miller stated, "We doubt very much whether any action of a State not directed by way of discrimination against the negroes as a class . . . will ever be held to come within the purview of this [equal protection] provision." *Slaughter-House Cases*, 83 U.S. (16 Wall.) 36, 81. In 1884, Justice Field stated that the Fourteenth Amendment "only inhibits discriminating and partial enactments, favoring some to the impairment of the rights of others," and does not transfer "to the federal government the protection of all private rights . . ." *Butchers' Union Co. v. Crescent City Co.*, 111 U.S. 746, 759, concurring opinion.

62. TenBroek 214–215; Barron v. Baltimore, 32 U.S. (7 Pet.) 243 (1833).

What tenBroek regards as axiomatic runs counter to statements in the First Congress that the Bill of Rights was to have no application to the States, and in spite of Madison's urging that freedom of speech and press stood in greater need of protection against the States than against the federal government, to the rejection of his proposal that they be made applicable to the States.[63] In 1789 men were more devoted to their States than to the nascent federal government; they feared the centralized, remote power of the newcomer,[64] hence the limitations imposed on the federal government by the Bill of Rights. There is no inkling that in the intervening 75 years the North had become dissatisfied with the protection they were given by the States. On the contrary, they reaffirmed their attachment to State sovereignty in the 39th Congress.[65] They believed that State governments would be more responsive to their needs, more controllable than the federal regime; and they sought to limit federal intrusions to the minimum necessary to protect the personal security of the blacks.

The present generation would read back into the Amendment views that the framers clearly perceived the North would not accept. Much closer to the intention of the framers,[66] the Supreme Court said in 1875, with respect to the First Amendment protection of the right to assemble against "encroachment by Congress": "For their protection in its enjoyment, therefore, the people must look to the States. The power for that purpose was originally placed there, and it has never been surrendered to the United States."[67]

63. Supra Chapter 8 note 4.

64. Raoul Berger, *Congress v. The Supreme Court* 260–263 (1969).

65. E.g., Hale, supra note 47; Chapter 4 at notes 51–52.

66. As long ago as 1454, stated Chief Justice Prisot, "the judges who gave these decisions in ancient times were nearer to the making of the statute than we now are, and had more acquaintance with it." Windham v. Felbridge, Y.B. 33 Hen. 4, f.38, 41, pl. 17, quoted in C. K. Allen, *Law in the Making* 193 (6th ed. 1958). For early American statements to the same effect, see Stuart v. Laird, 5 U.S. (1 Cranch) 299, 309 (1803); Ogden v. Saunders, 25 U.S. (12 Wheat.) 213, 290 (1827). Such cases antedate modern access to legislative history, and I would not suggest that such judges can displace the clearly revealed intention of the framers as disclosed by that history, but would point out that their confirmation of that history lends it added weight.

67. United States v. Cruikshank, 92 U.S. 542, 552 (1875). That plainly appears in the history of the Bill of Rights, supra Chapter 8 note 4. Chief Justice Parker declared in

## Congressional Power: Corrective or General

Does the §1 provision "nor shall any State . . . deny to any person within its jurisdiction the equal protection of the laws" empower Congress to enact laws for direct enforcement thereof? Justice Bradley answered, "How can a prohibition, in the nature of things, be enforced until it is violated?"[68] To convert "No State shall deny" into "Congress shall make" does violence to the text. The distinction between a prohibition of action and a grant of power was well understood by the 39th Congress. Even with respect to the prohibitions directed to Congress by the Bill of Rights, Hale said that the several amendments "do not contain, from beginning to end, a grant of power anywhere. On the contrary, they are all restrictions of power."[69] In addition, there is the fact that "the equality ordained" is, as Dean Phil Neal put it, "a Statewide equality, encompassing the persons 'within its jurisdiction' and not a nationwide or external equality."[70] For it is the "laws" of the State, not of the nation, that are required to afford "equal protection."

Textual analysis is richly confirmed by the legislative history. Shellabarger, an Ohio Radical, argued on behalf of the Civil Rights Bill that "if this section did in fact assume to confer or define or regulate these civil rights which are named . . . then it would . . . be an assumption of the reserved rights of the States . . . Its whole effect is not to confer or regulate rights, but to require that whatever of these enumerated rights and obligations are imposed by State laws shall . . . be without distinc-

---

Abbott v. Bayley, 6 Pick. 89, 93 (Mass. 1827) that "protection of the persons of those who live under this jurisdiction" was left by the Constitution in the States. See also supra Chapter 8 at notes 86–87.

68. United States v. Cruikshank, 25 F. Cas. (No. 14, 897) 707, 714 (C.C.D. La. 1874).

69. *Globe* 1064. Michael C. Kerr of Indiana also rejected the argument that the first ten amendments "are grants of power to Congress . . . Hitherto these amendments have been supposed . . . to contain only limitations on the powers of Congress." Id. 1270.

70. Phil C. Neal, "Baker v. Carr: Politics in Search of Law," 1962 S. Ct. Rev. 252, 293. In Missouri v. Lewis, 101 U.S. 22, 31 (1879), the Court held, "The Fourteenth Amendment does not profess to secure to all persons in the United States the benefit of the same laws and the same remedies. Great diversities in these respects may exist in two States separated only by an imaginary line . . . Each State prescribes its own modes of judicial proceeding."

tion based on race."[71] Shellabarger's assurance to fellow Republicans that State sovereignty was displaced only insofar as corrective measures would require was echoed by his colleagues. Speaking to the final form of the Amendment, Bingham stated: "That great want of the citizen and stranger, protection by national law from unconstitutional State enactments, is supplied by the first section of this Amendment. That is the extent it hath; no more."[72] Stevens said of the same draft that the Amendment "allows Congress to correct the unjust legislation of the States, so far that the law which operates upon one man shall operate *equally* upon all."[73] In the Senate, Howard said that "section one is a restriction upon the States, and does not, of itself, confer any power upon Congress";[74] and that §5 "enables Congress, in case the States shall enact laws in conflict with the principles of the amendment, to correct that legislation by a formal congressional amendment."[75]

Powerful confirmation of such expressions is furnished by the jettisoning of the Bingham amendment (H.R. No. 63), cast in terms of a grant to Congress:

---

71. *Globe* 1293.

72. Id. 2543; see also supra at note 48. Earlier Bingham stated, "The adoption of the proposed amendment will take from the States no rights that belong to the States . . . but in the event they . . . enact laws refusing equal protection to life, liberty or property" Congress can act. *Globe* 1090.

73. *Globe* 2459; see also Trumbull supra at note 49.

74. *Globe* 2766.

75. Id. 2768. Howard also stated, "The great object of the first section of this amendment is, therefore, to *restrain* the power of the States and to *compel them* to respect these great fundamental guarantees." Section 5, he continued, constitutes "a direct affirmative delegation of power to Congress to carry out all the principles of *these* guarantees," i.e., to enforce the "negative" terms of §1. Id. 2766 (emphasis added).

TenBroek would make Howard the exponent of as " 'direct' and 'affirmative' a delegation of power to Congress as could be made" rather than a mere "power to correct state legislation." He argues that if §§1 and 5, in Howard's words " 'establish equality before the law' and 'give to the humblest . . . the same protection before the law as . . . to the most powerful' . . . then certainly the power of Congress may be exercised *whenever* there is *not* equality before the law." TenBroek 230 (emphasis added). Here Howard was speaking of the substantive grant, the "discrimination" that would trigger congressional action, not of the time and corrective nature of that action, about which Howard spoke plainly enough, supra, and which statements tenBroek, 230, overlooked.

The Congress shall have power to make all laws which shall be necessary and proper to secure to the citizens of each State all privileges and immunities . . . and to all persons . . . equal protection in
the rights of life, liberty, and property.[76]

Judge Hale justifiably protested that this "is not a mere provision that
when the States undertake to give protection which is unequal Congress
may equalize it; it is a grant of power in general terms—a grant of the
right to legislate for the protection of life, liberty, and property, simply
qualified with the condition that it shall be equal legislation."[77] Hale's
Republican colleague from New York, Giles W. Hotchkiss, added:

I desire to secure every privilege and every right to every citizen in
the United States that . . . [Bingham] desires to secure. As I understand it, his object . . . is to provide that no State shall discriminate
between its citizens and give one class of citizens greater rights than
it confers upon another. If this amendment secured that, I should
vote for it very cheerfully today . . . I understand the amendment
. . . to authorize Congress to establish uniform laws throughout the
United States upon the subject named, the protection of life, liberty, and property. I am unwilling that Congress shall have any such
power.[78]

Stevens staged a rescue attempt in the form of a rhetorical question addressed to Hale: "is it not simply to provide that where any State makes
a distinction in the same law between different classes of individuals,
Congress shall have power to correct such discrimination and inequal-

76. *Globe* 813, 1034; Bickel 33.

77. *Globe* 1063–1064. When tenBroek, 216, stated that "Bingham and Hale thus completely agree that the equal protection clause was 'a grant of the right to legislate for the
protection of life, liberty, and property simply qualified with the condition that it shall be
equal legislation,' " he was quoting Hale's criticism of the "positive" grant to Congress of
the Bingham amendment, which did not survive. See infra at note 81.

78. *Globe* 1095. Another New York Republican, Davis, who represented "a radical constituency," also opposed the Bingham proposal as an "infringement on the reserved rights
of the States" that would "centralize power in the Federal Government," though he was
pledged to measures "essential to the protection of their [blacks'] just right." Id. 1086,
1083, 1085. But he rejected the proposal as a "grant of original legislation by Congress."
Id. 1087.

ity?"[79] But this put too great a strain on the broader Bingham phraseology, and his approach was abandoned.

That Hale and Hotchkiss voiced the pervasive distrust of a general grant of power to Congress to legislate in the premises may also be gathered from the statement by James F. Wilson of Iowa, chairman of the House Judiciary Committee, that the Bingham proposal was "the embodiment of our greatest danger."[80] Let Henry J. Raymond, an influential New York Republican who voted for the Fourteenth Amendment, sum up: the Bingham amendment "giving to Congress power to secure an absolute equality of civil rights in every State of the Union . . . encountering considerable opposition . . . it was finally postponed"—and never resuscitated.[81] Bingham himself joined ranks when he urged the people, in support of the final draft, to protect "the privileges and immunities of all the citizens of the Republic . . . *whenever* the same shall be abridged or denied by the unconstitutional acts of any State."[82]

Flack comments on this shift from "Congress shall have power" to "no State shall make" that, though the former "was not incorporated into the fundamental law . . . it may properly be asked whether it really did not become a part of it with a mere change in dress but not in meaning."[83] Such flabby analysis that can translate "no" as "yes" has clogged understanding of the Fourteenth Amendment. TenBroek likewise transforms "no State shall make" into the "obligation of the states to 'make or enforce laws' protecting" men in their "natural rights." There "never would have been any historical question about the revolution in federalism worked or confirmed by the Fourteenth Amendment," he maintained, "were it not for the shift from the positive to what at first glance appears

---

79. Id. 1063.

80. TenBroek 217, notes that when the "Congress shall have formula" was reported out by the Joint Committee, "it was recommitted by a vote of 110 to 37, after a debate in which not only Democrats but also conservative Republicans sharply criticized it as effecting a radical redistribution of powers of the states and the national government."

81. *Globe* 2502.

82. Id. 2542 (emphasis added).

83. Flack 64. Yet he notes that "The Radical leaders were as aware as any one of the attachment of a great majority of the people to the doctrine of State Rights . . . the right of the States to regulate their own internal affairs." Id. 68.

to be a negative form of the amendment."[84] That "first glance," as we have seen, is buttressed by the plainly expressed intention of the framers.

TenBroek attempts to torpedo what he considers the three "main-stays" of the "narrow" construction based on a changeover from grant to prohibition, and begins with Stevens' explanation of the final draft, in which he said that it "fell far short of [his] wishes."[85] This, tenBroek argues, referred solely to Negro suffrage, which was not treated in §1 but only in §2 and §3. The argument grasps at straws. Suffrage was a central concern; it had unmistakably been excluded from the Civil Rights Act, the antecedent of §1, so if Stevens was troubled by the failure to provide for suffrage in §2 inferably he considered it also was unprovided for in §1, thus undermining tenBroek's inference that §1 could "hardly [have been] a source of dissatisfaction to him." Such speculation is beside the point. Stevens had disclaimed a grant of original power to Congress, first, by seeking to save the Bingham amendment by reading it merely to confer "power to correct such discrimination,"[86] and later by stating that the final draft "allows Congress to correct the unjust legislation of the States."[87]

The second "mainstay" is that after the shift to the prohibition on States, Andrew J. Rogers, a Democrat and bitter opponent of the several Reconstruction measures, charged that §1 "consolidates everything into one imperial despotism" and "annihilates" States' Rights. TenBroek reinforces this by the testimony of two other Democrats, Aaron Harding and George S. Shanklin of Kentucky, and asks, "Since the amendment was adopted in the teeth of this criticism, might not we as reasonably conclude . . . that the amendment was intended to do the very thing objected to."[88] There is no need to recapitulate the weakness of reliance on opposition obstructiveness designed to inflame the electorate. It is a

---

84. TenBroek 223, 216.

85. Id. 217–218.

86. Supra at note 79. TenBroek, 212 note 8, rightly stated that Stevens' rhetorical question to this effect represented his own view: "The latter half of the sentence shows . . . that Stevens has a mind fixed primarily on the narrower interpretation of equal protection," i.e., the "corrective" role of Congress.

87. Supra at note 73.

88. TenBroek 218–219.

singular approach to legislative history, shared by other proponents of the tenBroek view, to exalt the opposition and all but ignore the statement of objectives by the Republican leadership who carried the day.

Comes now the third "mainstay":

> "No State shall . . ." at first looks like a negative on state action; and section 5, granting enforcement power would accordingly authorize Congress to impose only such restraints as would prevent States from taking the forbidden action. Section 5 would thus authorize nothing more than a corrective removal of prohibited state acts . . . Does not this interpretation render section 5 altogether nugatory? . . . [S]ince the judges would in any event strike down acts transcending the prohibitions of the amendment, a law by Congress would serve no purpose.[89]

TenBroek proves too much; on his reasoning a court equally could proceed without waiting for a general (as distinguished from a corrective) congressional law.[90] The "nugatory" test, therefore, does not clarify whether the congressional power is "corrective" or "general."

James A. Garfield's statement in the 1871 debates, made by a framer in the 39th Congress and faithful to the historical record, is entitled to greater respect than present-day speculation: "soon after the ratification of the Amendment," tenBroek states, Garfield explained that Congress had rejected "a clear grant of power to Congress to legislate directly for the protection of life, liberty, and property within the States" in favor of the present form that "limited but did not oust the jurisdiction of the state over the subjects."[91] Justice Bradley's opinion in the *Civil Rights*

---

89. Id. 220–221.

90. For discussion of the §5 enforcement power, see infra Chapter 12.

91. TenBroek 216–217. See Hyman, supra note 61. Benedict likewise concludes that the Fourteenth Amendment "in no way challenged the tradition that the states had primary jurisdiction over citizens in matters of police regulation . . . Instead, its first and fifth sections gave Congress power to assure that the police regulations would not discriminate against citizens on account of race . . . where the regulation involved some 'fundamental right' of United States citizens . . . it did not transfer to the national government the power to frame all laws touching on these rights. National jurisdiction could arise only through the states prior wrongdoing." M. L. Benedict, *A Compromise of Principle* 170 (1975).

*Cases*, therefore, does not betray, but rather responds to, the intention of the framers. The Amendment, he declared,

> does not authorize Congress to create a code of municipal law for the regulation of private rights; but to provide modes of redress against operation of state laws ... such [congressional] legislation must, necessarily be predicated upon such state laws or state proceedings, and be directed to the correction of their operation and effect ... [U]ntil some state law has been passed ... no [federal] legislation ... can be called into activity.[92]

In sum, the words "equal protection of the laws" were meant to obviate discrimination by laws—that is, statutes—so that with respect to a limited group of privileges the laws would treat a black no differently than a white. If no privilege was accorded to a white, a State was not required to furnish it to anyone. Hence Justice Douglas, in invalidating a State poll tax, was wide of the mark when he based his conclusion, "not on what we think governmental policy should be, but on what the Equal Protection Clause requires." The truth is, as he stated in a preceding sentence, "we have never been confined to historic notions of equality ... Notions of what constitutes equal treatment for purposes of the Equal Protection Clause *do* change."[93] In plain words, Douglas laid claim to power to revise the historic meaning in accord with his own preferences. For Chief Justice Marshall, on the other hand, the words of the Constitution were not to be "extended to objects not ... contemplated by the framers"[94]—let alone unmistakably excluded. As Herbert Packer points

92. Civil Rights Cases, 109 U.S. 3, 11, 13 (1883); see also id. 19. Ten years earlier Justice Bradley had stated on circuit that "there can be no constitutional legislation of congress for directly enforcing the privileges and immunities ... where the State has passed no laws adverse to them ..." United States v. Cruikshank, 25 F. Cas. at 714.

93. Harper v. Virginia Board of Elections, 383 U.S. 663, 670, 669 (1966), but cf. Hamilton, infra Chapter 17 at note 15.

94. Ogden v. Saunders, 25 U.S. (12 Wheat.) 213, 332 (1827), dissenting opinion. In Church of the Holy Trinity v. United States, 143 U.S. 457, 472 (1891), the Court held that though a rector "is within the letter [he] is not within the intention of the legislature, and therefore cannot be within the statute." For a similar holding by Justice Holmes, see supra note 5; see also Robert Bork, infra Chapter 11 at note 80; and see infra Chapter 20.

out, "the new 'substantive equal protection' has under a different label permitted today's justices to impose their prejudices in much the same manner as the Four Horsemen [of the pre-1937 Court] once did."[95]

95. "The Aim of the Criminal Law Revisited: A Plea for a New Look at 'Substantive Due Process,' " 44 S. Cal. L. Rev. 490, 491–492 (1971). Commenting on Brown v. Board of Education, Professor Lusky stated, "Plainly the Court was using the term 'unequal' in a new sense. The 'inequality' prohibited by the Constitution was no longer thought limited to unequal distribution of governmental burdens and benefits, but was held to include measures perpetuating the social isolation of minority groups," Lusky 214, a subject excluded from the Fourteenth Amendment by its framers.

# 11

## *"Due Process of Law"*

nor shall any State deprive any person of life, liberty, or property, without due process of law

To this day," Arthur Sutherland wrote in 1965, "no one knows precisely what the words 'due process of law' meant to the draftsmen of the fifth amendment, and no one knows what these words meant to the draftsmen of the fourteenth amendment."[1] True it is that after the 1880s the phrase was transformed by the Court into one of "convenient vagueness";[2] and such "vagueness" has become the reigning orthodoxy.[3] Whether one can determine "precisely" what due process meant, how-

1. "Privacy in Connecticut," 64 Mich. L. Rev. 283, 286 (1965).

2. Felix Frankfurter, *Mr. Justice Holmes and the Supreme Court* 7 (1938): "phrases like 'due process of law' are, as an able judge [Charles M. Hough] once expressed it, of 'convenient vagueness.' Their ambiguity is such that the Court is compelled to put meaning in the Constitution." Earlier Frankfurter asked, " 'Convenient' for whom or to what end?" Frankfurter, "The Red Terror of Judicial Reform" 40 *New Republic* 110, 113 (1924), reprinted in F. Frankfurter, *Law and Politics* 10, 14 (1938). But as Justice Frankfurter, he declared in 1949 that "Great concepts like . . . 'due process of law' . . . were purposely left to gather meaning from experience. For they relate to the whole domain of social and economic fact." National Ins. Co. v. Tidewater Co., 337 U.S. 582, 646 (1949), dissenting opinion. Compare with Chapter 14 infra at notes 40–43. For the halting, post–Civil War development of substantive due process see Walton H. Hamilton, "The Path of Due Process of Law" in *The Constitution Reconsidered* 167 (C. Read ed. 1938); see also Justice Black, infra note 47.

3. "Due process of law" is among the terms that "doubtless were designed to have the chameleon capacity to change their color with changing moods and circumstances." Wallace Mendelson, *Justices Black and Frankfurter: Conflict in the Court* viii (1961). So too, Leonard Levy stated that due process and equal protection are "purposely protean or undefined words." *Against the Law* 27.

ever, is not nearly so important as the fact that one thing quite plainly *it did not mean*, in either 1789 or 1866; it did not comprehend judicial power to override legislation on substantive or policy grounds. There is first the unmistakable testimony of Alexander Hamilton. Speaking in the New York Assembly in 1787, almost on the eve of the Convention, he stated:

> The words "due process" have a precise technical import, and are only applicable to the process and proceedings of the courts of justice; *they can never be referred to an act of the legislature.*[4]

No statement to the contrary will be found in any of the constitutional conventions, in the First Congress, nor in the 1866 debates.

Hamilton summed up the English and colonial usage, and it is that usage that defines the content of the words "due process of law." It has long been a canon of construction that when the draftsmen employed common law terms, the common law "definitions," as Justice Story stated, "are necessarily included as much as if they stood in the text" of the Constitution.[5] But when so great a master as Judge Learned Hand concludes that the prohibitions of the Fifth and Fourteenth Amendments are cast

---

4. 4 *The Papers of Alexander Hamilton* 35 (H. C. Syrett and J. E. Cooke eds. 1962) (emphasis added); quoted more fully infra note 11.

When Coke asserted in Dr. Bonham's Case that an Act of Parliament could not make a man judge in his own cause, he did not invoke Magna Charta but "common right and reason," Berger, *Congress v. The Supreme Court* 349, which he had identified with the "law of nature," id. 352, 355 note 31, an identification repeated by Justice Hobart, id. 364. By negative implication, the "law of the land" clause of Magna Charta did not, in Coke's eyes, confer authority to set a statute aside as unreasonable. True, Coke also stated in his *Institutes* that if any statute be made contrary to "Magna Charta it shall be holden for none," id. 358 note 43, but this, in my judgment, merely meant, for example, that a statute which authorized the "imprisonment" of a person without the judgment of his peers would be invalid; for he regarded Magna Charta as "fundamental law," id. 358 note 43.

5. United States v. Smith, 18 U.S. (5 Wheat.) 153, 160 (1820). In his Report on the Virginia Resolutions to the Virginia House of Delegates (Sess. 1799–1800), Madison stated, "It is readily admitted that particular parts of the common law may have a sanction from the Constitution, so far as they are necessarily comprehended in the technical phrases which express the powers delegated to the government." 4 Elliot 563. Chief Justice Marshall gave early expression to this view in Ex parte Bollman, 8 U.S. (4 Cranch) 75, 93–94 (1807): "for the meaning of *habeas corpus* resort may unquestionably be had to the common law." So deeply anchored was this presupposition that when the Framers employed the word "treason," they took pains to define it narrowly in order to obviate some of its harsh common law consequences that otherwise might have attached. Article III, § 3(1).

"in such sweeping terms that history does not elucidate their contents,"[6] I may be indulged for piling proof on proof to the contrary.

Our conceptions of due process are traceable to the twenty-ninth chapter of Magna Charta, which, roughly speaking, provided that no man should be deprived of his life, liberty, or property, except by the judgment of his peers or the law of the land.[7] Coke stated that "by the law of the land" was meant "by the due course and process of law."[8] Whether due process and "law of the land" were identical in English law[9] need not detain us; for present purposes it may suffice that both related to *judicial procedures* preliminary to the described forfeitures. Prior to 1789 the several State constitutions employed the "law of the land" terminology, usually in the context of other safeguards for those charged with crimes, suggesting that it was viewed in terms of judicial procedure.[10] That the "law of the land" was understood in Coke's sense is illustrated by Hamilton's 1787 statement.[11] The members of the First

6. *The Bill of Rights* 30 (1962).

7. 4 William Blackstone, *Commentaries on the Laws of England* 424 (1765–1769).

8. 2 Edward Coke's *Institutes* 56, quoted in Hurtado v. California, 110 U.S. 516, 523 (1884).

9. Keith Jurow, "Untimely Thoughts: A Reconsideration of the Origins of Due Process of Law," 19 Am. J. Legal Hist. 265 (1975). ["If we enquire what is meant by the law of the land, the best commentators will tell us that it means due process of law, that is by indictment and presentment . . . and trial and conviction in consequence." 4 Alexander Hamilton, *Works* 232 (H. C. Lodge ed. 1904).]

10. Maryland (1776), 1 Poore 818; Massachusetts (1780), id. 958; New Hampshire (1784), 2 Poore 1282; North Carolina (1776), id. 1410; Pennsylvania (1776), id. 1541–1542; South Carolina (1778), id. 1627; Vermont (1777), id. 1860; Virginia (1776), id. 1909. See infra at notes 24 and 25.

11. Commenting in the New York Assembly on February 6, 1787, on the New York Constitution, Hamilton said, "In one article of it, it is said no man shall be disfranchised or deprived of any right he enjoys under the constitution, but by the *law of the land*, or the judgment of his peers. Some gentlemen hold that the law of the land will include an act of the legislature. But Lord Coke . . . in his comment upon a similar clause in Magna Charta, interprets the law of the land to mean presentment and indictment . . . But if there were any doubt upon the constitution, the bill of rights enacted in this very session removes it. It is there declared that, no man shall be disfranchised or deprived of any right, but by '*due process of law*,' or the judgment of his peers. The words '*due process*' have a precise technical import, and are only applicable to the process and proceedings of the courts of justice; they can never be referred to an act of legislature." The Act was that of January 26, 1787, II Laws of the State of New York 344–345; supra note 4.

Congress, who employed the words "due process" in the Fifth Amendment instead of the "law of the land" contained in the extant State constitutions, presumably intended no departure from prevalent State usage. Given the great respect Coke enjoyed in the colonies, it is reasonable to infer that, like Hamilton, they accepted Coke's identification of the two phrases.[12]

It has been convincingly shown that due process was conceived in utterly procedural terms, specifically, that a defendant must be afforded an opportunity to answer by service of process in proper form, that is, in due course. Starting with an early statute, 28 Edw. III, ch. 3 (1354), which provided that "no man . . . shall be put out of land or Tenement . . . nor put to death, without being brought in to answer by due process of law,"[13] Keith Jurow concluded from a comparison with chapter 10 of the same statute that the due process provision "seems merely to require that the appropriate writ be used to summon the accused before the court

---

Julius Goebel and T. R. Naughton state with respect to seventeenth- and eighteenth-century due process, "The usual and current employment of the phrase in English practice was to designate the judicial order appropriate to a particular procedure and this usage became the rule in eighteenth century New York." *Law Enforcement in Colonial New York (1664–1776)* 385 (1970). In his "Letters of Phocion" Hamilton stated, "due process of law" means "by indictment or presentment." 4 *Works of Alexander Hamilton* 230, 232 (H. C. Lodge ed. 1904).

12. A persuasive explanation of the shift from "law of the land" to "due process of law" was advanced by Justice Curtis in Murray's Lessee v. Hoboken Land & Improvement Co., 59 U.S. (18 How.) 272, 276 (1856). He pointed out that by the Sixth and Seventh Amendments "special provisions were separately made for that [jury] mode of trial in civil and criminal cases. To have followed, as in the state constitutions . . . the words of *Magna Charta*, and declared that no person shall be deprived of his life, liberty, or property but by the judgment of his peers or the law of the land, would in part have been superfluous and inappropriate. To have taken the clause 'law of the land' without its immediate context, might possibly have given rise to doubts, which would be effectually dispelled by using those words which the great commentator on *Magna Charta* had declared to be the true meaning of the phrase, 'law of the land,' in that instrument, and which was undoubtedly then received as their true meaning."

Jefferson recorded that there was never "one of profounder learning in the orthodox doctrines of the British Constitution or what is called British rights" than Coke. Quoted in E. S. Corwin, *The Doctrine of Judicial Review: Its Legal and Historical Basis and Other Essays* 31 (1914).

13. Supra note 9 at 266.

to answer the complaint against him."[14] An earlier statute, 25 Edw. III (1352), had provided that because the "law of the land" required that "none shall be imprisoned, nor put out of his freehold" and so on, henceforth "none shall be taken . . . unless it be by indictment or presentment . . . or by process made by writ original at the common law [and] unless he be duly brought to answer." Jurow concludes that "the word 'process' itself meant writs . . . those writs which summoned parties to appear in court."[15] His reading harmonizes with that of Coke, who, referring to a later statute, 37 Edw. III, ch. 3 cap. 8, explains "without due process of the law" thus: "that is by indictment . . . or by writ originall of the common law. Without being brought in to answer but by due process of the common law. No man may be put to answer without presentment . . . or by writ originall, according to the old law of the land."[16] A Massachusetts measure of 1692, duplicated in the colonies of Connecticut and New York, "ordained . . . no person should suffer . . . without being brought to answer by due course and process of law."[17] Blackstone later recurred to 28 Edw. III for the proposition that "no man shall be put to death without being brought to answer by due process of law."[18] Finally, among the Declarations and Resolves of the First Continental Congress, October 14, 1774, was "the respective colonies are entitled to the common law . . . and . . . to the . . . privilege of *being tried* by their peers . . . according to the due course of that law."[19] "Process," accordingly, was by indictment or writ; it was in "due course," that is, in regular

14. Id. 267.

15. Id. 268, 272; 25 Edw. III st. 5, ch. 4 (1352).

16. Quoted in Hurtado v. California, 110 U.S. at 523. Jurow remarks, "The puzzling thing is that Coke cites 3 Edw. III, ch. 8 rather than 28 Edw. III, ch. 3 to support his interpretation, and when he does cite the latter statute he renders it as 'due process of the common law.' " We may assume with Jurow that "Coke was trying to show that only the common law was the law of the land." Jurow, supra note 9 at 277. For present purposes it suffices that due process, by Jurow's own demonstration, was altogether associated with judicial procedure. In English law, he states, "the term 'due process of law' and the word 'process' were always used in the most precise and consistent way," Jurow, id. 279, as Hamilton clearly perceived.

17. 2 James Kent, *Commentaries on American Law* 608–609 (9th ed. 1853).

18. 4 Blackstone, supra note 7 at 318.

19. *Documents of American History* 83 (Henry Steele Commager ed. 7th ed. 1963) (emphasis added).

course, if the "appropriate" writ was employed.[20] *"Due process" should therefore be regarded as shorthand for Coke's "by the due course and process of law" in judicial proceedings.*[21] These materials demonstrate, parenthetically, that due process was *not* a catchall for all the other safeguards the Bill of Rights provided to a defendant; it had a special and limited function: to insure through service of proper, that is, "due," process that a defendant would be given a chance to answer.[22]

In the interval between 1789 and 1866, the procedural nature of due process received the imprimatur of Kent and Story, who relied on

20. This original meaning of due process as affording a person the opportunity to answer through service of a writ according to established law is incompatible with the "fundamentally fair" procedure structure that the Court has built on the clause. Grey, "Do We Have an Unwritten Constitution?," 27 Stan. L. Rev. 703, 711 (1975). As said by Leonard Levy, "fair trial is a principle of such abstraction, complexity and subjectivity that a judge can play on it as if it were an accordion to be squeezed and stretched to render whatever meaning he seeks to express." *Against the Law* 310.

The foregoing materials cast doubt on Justice Frankfurter's generalization: "Due process of law, as a historic and generative principle, precludes defining, and thereby confining, those standards of conduct more precisely than to say that convictions cannot be brought about by methods that offend 'a sense of justice.' " Rochin v. California, 342 U.S. 165, 173 (1952). His history has very shallow roots.

21. Supra at note 8. [Justice Story noted Coke's explanation that "law of the land" means "due process of law," that is, it requires "presentment and indictment, and being brought to answer thereto, by due process of the common law. So that this clause in effect affirms the right of trial according to the process and proceedings of the common law." 2 Joseph Story, *Commentaries on the Constitution of the United States* 1789 (5th ed. 1905).

Edward S. Corwin, *The Twilight of the Supreme Court* 118–119 (1934): "no one at the time of the framing and adoption of the Constitution had any idea that this clause did more than consecrate a method of procedure against accused persons, and the modern doctrine of due process of law . . . could never have been laid down except in defiance of history." See also id. 95.]

22. I must therefore dissent from Levy's statement that "the history of due process shows that it did mean trial by jury and many of the other traditional rights . . . specified separately in the Bill of Rights," and that the framers "added the due process clause itself, probably as a rhetorical flourish, a reinforced guarantee, and a genuflection towards traditional usage going back to the medieval reenactments of Magna Charta." Levy, *Judgments: Essays in American Constitutional History* 66 (1972). Justice Curtis considered that the Framers carefully avoided surplusage in this respect, supra note 12. And as we have seen, the early statutes identified due process with service of proper process to assure a defendant an opportunity to answer, a guarantee contained in no other provision of the Bill of Rights, and a practice duplicated in early Massachusetts, Connecticut, and New York measures.

Coke.[23] Because lawyers habitually look to judicial decisions for "constitutional law" they have largely overlooked that in virtually all of the State constitutions extant in 1866 the words "due process of law" and "law of the land" were, as Charles E. Shattuck pointed out more than 85 years ago, almost always found "in a section of the Constitution dealing exclusively with the conduct of criminal trials, with the privileges of the accused, with a process in which the whole question is whether the person concerned shall be deprived of one or another of certain rights; that is of life, or *personal* liberty, or property as a penalty for a crime; and it is declared that he shall not without due process of law."[24] The lawyers who framed the Fourteenth Amendment undoubtedly were familiar with this association of due process with judicial procedure,[25] and a departure from this all but universal connotation must be based on more than bare conjecture; the rule is that it must be proved.[26] What Charles P. Curtis, an ardent proponent of judicial "adaptation" of the Constitution, said of the Fifth Amendment could even more truly be said of the Fourteenth. When the framers put due process "into the Fifth Amendment, its meaning was as fixed and definite as the common law could make a phrase. It had been chiseled into the law so incisively that any lawyer, and a few others, could read and understand. It meant a procedural process, which could be easily ascertained from almost any law book."[27]

23. 2 Kent, supra note 17 at 620–621: "by the law of the land [is] understood to mean due process of law, that is, by indictment . . . and this, says Lord Coke, is the true sense of these words." See also 1 Joseph Story, *Commentaries on the Constitution of the United States* § 1789 (5th ed. 1905).

24. "The True Meaning of the Term 'Liberty' in Those Clauses in the Federal and State Constitutions Which Protect 'Life, Liberty and Property,' " 4 Harv. L. Rev. 365, 369 (1891).

In 1866 most State constitutions still adhered to the "law of the land" phraseology. A few had adopted the language of due process or due course of law: Alabama (1865), 1 Poore 49; Connecticut (1818), id. 259; Mississippi (1832), 2 Poore 1068; Nevada (1864), id. 1248; New York (1846), id. 1351–1352; South Carolina (1865), id. 1643; Texas (1866), id. 1785. Constitutions fashioned in the Southern States under Northern military occupation in 1865 and 1866 may be taken to reflect Northern opinion.

25. Before 1866, the due process clause "had been looked upon almost universally as only a procedural guarantee." Benjamin R. Twiss, *Lawyers and the Constitution* 26 (1942); see infra note 48; infra at note 42.

26. Supra Chapter 1 note 57.

27. "Review and Majority Rule," in *Supreme Court and Supreme Law* 170, 177 (Edmond N. Cahn ed. 1954). As Justice Black stated, "there is no constitutional support whatever for

## The 39th Congress

In light of the prominence to which the due process clause has been elevated by the Supreme Court, it is surprising how scanty were the allusions to the clause in the debates of the 39th Congress. It was altogether unmentioned in the Civil Rights Bill; instead the Bill spelled out the concrete rights "to sue, be parties and give evidence"; and it inclusively provided for the "equal benefit of all laws and *proceedings* for the security of person and property." But the debates show plainly enough that by "proceedings" the framers intended to supply judicial protection to Negroes. Senator Daniel Clark of New Hampshire had stated that the Negro "was denied access to the courts, because he had no rights which a white man was bound to respect; he was not permitted to testify because he might tell of the enormities practiced upon him."[28] Samuel McKee of Kentucky asked, "Where is your court of justice in any Southern State where the black man can secure protection?"[29] Senator Henry S. Lane of Indiana stated, "we legislate upon this subject now . . . simply because we fear . . . that the emancipated slaves would not have their rights in the courts of the slave States."[30]

Although due process found no mention in the text of the Bill, its proponents made quite clear that they considered it to be associated with judicial proceedings. John M. Broomall of Pennsylvania explained that blacks were "denied process of law to enforce the right and to avenge

---

this Court to use the Due Process Clause as though it provided a blank check to alter the meaning of the Constitution as written so as to add substantive constitutional changes which a majority of the Court at any given time believes are needed to meet present-day problems." Harper v. Virginia Bd. of Elections, 383 U.S. 663, 675–676 (1966), dissenting opinion. See also infra note 47. But as Alexander Bickel noted, under a "very narrow historical meaning of the Due Process Clause, much else in which Justice Black has joined would be relegated to limbo." *The Least Dangerous Branch* 88 (1962). That does not so much prove his reasoning wrong as a failure to live by it.

28. *Globe* 833. A slave was a chattel and could be neither a party to a suit nor a competent witness against a white. Kenneth M. Stampp, *The Peculiar Institution* 197 (1956).

29. *Globe* 653.

30. Id. 602. Sumner stressed "Equality before the law . . . in court room," id. 674. Raymond stated the Negro "will have access to the courts as a citizen of the United States the same as any other citizen has." Id. 1266.

the wrong," that is, "denied remedy in the courts."[31] The intention to supply a judicial "remedy" by means of "due process" was more sharply articulated by Chairman Wilson: "the citizen . . . is entitled to a remedy . . . The citizen is entitled to the right of life, liberty and property. Now if a State intervenes, and deprives him without due process of law of those rights [which had been enumerated in the Bill] . . . can we not provide a remedy?"[32] Here is the traditional protection afforded by "due process" against the deprivation of life, liberty or property which was later to be expressed in the due process clause of §1. There is no evidence whatsoever that the §1 resort to the due process clause signaled a shift from this intention to furnish a judicial remedy. Evidence to the contrary is furnished by Senator Cowan. Speaking to the Amendment, he said he was opposed to "punishment of any kind upon any body unless by a fair trial where the party himself is summoned and heard in due course of law," the basic conception of due process of law.[33]

The due process clause made its appearance belatedly, almost in a fortuitous manner, deriving from the framers' absorption with equality before the law.[34] At the opening of the session Bingham proposed to "secure to all persons . . . equal protection in the rights [of] life, liberty, and property." Later he explained that the Fifth Amendment contained the very words "equal protection in the rights of life, liberty, and property." "Apparently," Joseph B. James comments, "the words 'due process' did not strike him as outstandingly significant"[35]—and, it may be added, they

31. Id. 1263, 1265; see also Logan, supra Chapter 6 at note 66.
32. Id. 1294.
33. Id. 2899.
34. Infra at notes 56–59. Referring to the due process clause, Bingham said, "Thus, in respect to life, liberty, and property the people by their Constitution declared the equality of all men." *Globe* 1292. When Chief Justice Taft held in Truax v. Corrigan, 257 U.S. 312, 332 (1921) that "Our whole system of law is predicated on the general, fundamental principle of equality of application of the law," he overlooked that (1) Article IV, §2 provided for equality with respect to selected rights; (2) Negroes enjoyed no rights whatsoever; and (3) the Fourteenth Amendment again guaranteed them equality only with respect to selected rights, and pointedly excluded suffrage.
35. *Globe* 14, 1034; James 83. "In comparison with the concept of equal protection of the laws," tenBroek averred, "the due process clause was of secondary importance to the abolitionists"; there was an "interchangeable" usage tied to protection of "natural rights." TenBroek 119–120, 215. "The basic idea," he stated, "is that of 'equal protection' . . .

played no great role in the thinking of his contemporaries. Possibly some more acute lawyer in the Joint Committee, perceiving Bingham's mistaken joinder of "life, liberty, or property" in the Fifth Amendment with "equal protection," restored the original conjunction of "due process" with "life, liberty, or property," thus assuring nondiscriminatory protection by the courts, one of the Civil Rights Act's objectives, and went on to articulate the primary objective of the framers—to prevent discriminatory laws, that is, statutes—by the words "equal protection of the laws." Thus were fashioned the complementary "equal protection" and "due process" clauses, which, as we have seen, were foreshadowed by Blackstone if not by Coke.

Bingham left no room for speculation as to what he meant by "due process." When asked by Rogers, "what do you mean by 'due process of law,' " he curtly replied, "the courts have settled that long ago, and the gentleman can go and read their decisions"—a reply that showed he deemed the question frivolous.[36] As James states, Bingham gave due process the "customary meaning recognized by the courts,"[37] and that meaning was all but universally procedural. Because Bingham "appears to have associated 'equal protection' with 'due process of law,' " Graham concludes that he "probably had a substantive conception of due process."[38] That is like arguing that because "equal protection" outlawed discrimi-

---

other elements were later added—privileges and immunities of citizens, due process of law, political rights. These were all either addenda to the basic notion or an elaboration of it." Id. 207. Hence the "due process clause slipped into a subordinate, almost forgotten position, being commonly read and frequently discussed as if it were a part of the equal protection requirement" (id. 232; see also id. 119–120), as Bingham's statement, supra at note 35, illustrates.

Justice Miller noted in 1878 as a "remarkable" fact that in the century since the Fifth Amendment, due process had "rarely been invoked." Davidson v. New Orleans, 96 U.S. 97, 103 (1877).

36. *Globe* 1089. Dred Scott v. Sandford, 60 U.S. (19 How.) 393, 450 (1857), which employed substantive due process, was scarcely among those "decisions" for it was universally execrated by the abolitionists, and also decried by Lincoln.

37. James 86. That is very old learning: "If a statute make use of a word the meaning of which is well known at the common law, the word shall be understood in the same sense it was understood at common law." Matthew Bacon, *A New Abridgement of the Laws of England* at "Statutes" I (4) (3d ed. 1768). See also supra note 5.

38. Graham 52.

natory statutes, "due process" designed for judicial procedure likewise applied to regulatory statutes. If Bingham entertained that conception, he never expressed it in the debates. According to Graham, "no other member of Congress appears to have used the clause as Bingham [allegedly] did"; and "no other member of the Joint Committee or of Congress . . . manifested his partiality for the due process clause"[39]—a strange inference from his confusion of "equal protection" with the Fifth Amendment! When Stevens explained the Amendment to the House, he made no mention of the clause, but said that the Amendment "allows Congress to correct the unjust legislation of the States, so far that the law which operates upon one shall operate equally upon all," thus exemplifying that freedom from discriminatory laws remained the overriding concern to the end.[40] One of the very few remarks directed to the due process clause, that of Jehu Baker of Illinois, confirms that it was viewed in existing procedural terms: "The Constitution already declares generally that no person shall 'be deprived of life, liberty, or property without due process of law.' This declares particularly that no *State* shall do it."[41]

Before his conversion,[41a] Graham noted that at this time due process was "merely a limitation upon procedure" and stated that the substantive theory "presupposes what was really an extraordinary viewpoint." He himself wrote, "so long as these were the prevailing usages down to 1866 one is hardly warranted in attributing a more subtle or comprehensive purpose without definite, positive evidence."[42] Graham's discovery of abolitionist ideology led him to mute these views but, as we shall see, he failed to offer "definite, positive evidence" that that ideol-

39. Id. 58, 32.

40. *Globe* 2459.

41. *Globe App.* 256. Like Bingham's identification of due process with the judicial decisions, Baker's statement furnishes historical footing for Justice Matthews' "irresistible" conclusion that the due process of the Fourteenth Amendment "was used in the same sense and with no greater extent" than that of the Fifth. Hurtado v. California, 110 U.S. at 535. Later Justice Frankfurter stated, "It ought not to require argument to reject the notion that due process of law meant one thing in the Fifth Amendment and another in the Fourteenth." Adamson v. California, 332 U.S. 46, 66 (1947), concurring opinion. We may safely rely on Hamilton, supra at note 4, for its narrow procedural meaning in the Fifth Amendment, there being no evidence whatever to the contrary.

41a. See infra Chapter 13 at note 4.

42. Graham 35, 36; see also infra at note 48.

ogy was adopted by the framers. The truth is that it was anathema to the centrist-conservative coalition which was in control.[43]

Bingham himself adhered to a procedural view of due process; in mid-August 1866, just two months after passage of the Amendment, he stated in Ohio that §1 "gave 'any citizen' the power to correct wrong by judicial process," thus identifying it with due process.[44] Telling confirmation that "due process" was not conceived in substantive terms is furnished by the fact that Senator Reverdy Johnson, probably the foremost lawyer in the 39th Congress and a member of the Joint Committee, "had not used due process, neither Fifth Amendment due process in *Veazie v. Fenno* nor (apparently) Fourteenth Amendment due process after 1868."[45] "[I]s it conceivable," Graham asked, "that *if* Reverdy Johnson, for example, had clearly understood and intended in 1866 that an added due process limitation against the states would constitute a valuable judicial safeguard for business fighting state regulation, that he himself would fail, as he did in 1869 when arguing the hard-fought case of *Veazie v. Fenno*, to employ the due process clause of the *fifth amendment* in behalf of a corporate client fighting against a drastic federal law?"[46] Since the due process of the Fifth and Fourteenth Amendments were regarded as identical, Graham's rhetorical question suggests that no intimation of substantive content had been voiced in the Joint Committee. And after his review of the railroad battles of the mid-sixties, directed by Reverdy Johnson, which moved from the courts to the Pennsylvania legislature and the halls of Congress, Graham observes: "we find no explicit references in the legislative and congressional debates on the repealers [by the legislature] to violation of *due process as such* . . . [T]hese repealers were regarded only as impairing obligations of contracts, and as having been 'passed without any hearing or judicial determination of the fact of misuse or abuse' . . . What we have to remember is that in 1866 the due process tradition was still on the make."[47]

43. Infra Chapter 13.
44. James 160.
45. Graham 96; Veazie Bank v. Fenno, 75 U.S. (8 Wall.) 533 (1869).
46. Graham 447.
47. Id. 467, 470–471, 487; see also id. 480. If, as is stated by Professor Archibald Cox, "all agree that the [due process] clause calls for some measure of judicial review of leg-

What is the impact of neoabolitionist theorizing on the foregoing facts? The abolitionist theory of racialized substantive due process, Graham tells us, "had gained its original impetus . . . *extra*-judicially, and almost wholly *ante*-judicially . . . *Extra-judicial* due process and *antebellum* equal protection were rankly, frankly heretical."[48] One who maintains that heresy supplanted orthodoxy, and this through the medium of congenitally conservative lawyers in Congress, carries a heavy burden of proof, not at all met by neoabolitionist reliance on Bingham as the instrument of change.[49] The abolitionists themselves by no means saw eye to eye on the subject. Two of their renowned theorists, Lysander Spooner and Joel Tiffany, "refused to rely upon due process" or "thought of it almost entirely as a formal requirement."[50] In Massachusetts, Graham writes, "even abolitionists remained comparatively earthbound . . . Charles Sumner . . . the outstanding black-letter scholar of the movement . . . relied rather on the Republican form of government clause

---

islative enactments," *The Role of the Supreme Court in American Government* 113 (1976), that belief has yet to be rooted in historical fact. The fact is, as Chapter 14 will seek to demonstrate, substantive due process was a judicial construct fashioned in the late nineteenth century to halt the regulation of big business. Justice Black stated that in Chicago, M. & St. P. R. Co. v. Minnesota, 134 U.S. 418 (1890), the Court "gave a new and hitherto undiscovered scope for the Court's use of the due process clause to protect property rights under natural law concepts." Adamson v. California, 332 U.S. at 79, dissenting opinion.

48. Graham 242. "Before there could be clear, general insight into the potentialities of . . . due process," Graham remarked, "there had to be pretty explicit judicial use." Substantive due process, he added, "was not yet an obvious or self-evident proposition." Id. 487, 488. Alfred Kelly observed that in 1860 "these doctrines were outside the pale of constitutional orthodoxy, but the political upheaval incident to the Civil War put a group of old antislavery enthusiasts in a position to control the Thirty-Ninth Congress and to write their radical reformism into the Constitution itself. The debates on the passage of the amendment reveal clearly enough how completely the constitutional ideology of the pre-war antislavery movement shaped the objectives of the Radical Republicans." Kelly, Fourteenth 1054. Chapter 13 infra will demonstrate that "control [of] the Thirty-Ninth Congress" by radical "enthusiasts" is a figment of the neoabolitionist imagination, and that abolitionist ideology fell on stony ground.

49. "The work of Bingham," tenBroek stated, "was the meeting ground, in a sense that the work of no other individual was, of the three concepts and clauses that came to constitute the first section of the amendment." TenBroek 145. Kelly states, "Bingham, principal author of the first section of the amendment, had been a leading congressional antislavery constitutional theorist." Kelly, Fourteenth 1054.

50. TenBroek 121.

and Equality Before the Law."[51] Such divisions indicate that substantive due process was not an idea whose time had come.[52]

Although Graham perceived that evidence of "substantive" intent is lacking when due process is viewed in the frame of corporate protection, he failed to apply the lesson to employment of due process for libertarian purposes. To be sure, the Supreme Court has now dichotomized due process; in the economic sphere the words have become a "dirty phrase,"[53] whereas certain libertarian claims have been given a "preferred position."[54] But support for that distinction will not be found in the history of the Fourteenth Amendment. Rather there was an unmistakable rejection of that most crucial of libertarian rights—the right to vote—and with it the right to attend unsegregated schools.

The extraordinary transformation of due process by the Court[55] has turned the Fourteenth Amendment topsy-turvy. The original design was to make the "privileges or immunities" clause the pivotal provision in order to shield the "fundamental rights" enumerated in the Civil Rights Act from the Black Codes. Intertwined with that enumeration was repeated emphasis on the enjoyment of the "same rights," and "equal benefit of all laws and proceedings for the security of person and property."[56] Trumbull stated, for example, that the Civil Rights Bill "contains but one single principle . . . to establish equality in the civil rights of

51. Graham 539.

52. James Garfield, a participant in the 39th Congress debates, said in discussing a bill for enforcement of the Fourteenth Amendment in 1871, that no State can "deprive any person of those great fundamental rights . . . of life, liberty, and property, except by due process of law; that is, by an impartial trial according to the laws of the land." *Cong. Globe*, 42d Cong., 1st Sess. App. at 152–153, quoted by Justice Black in Adamson v. California, 332 U.S. at 111, dissenting opinion.

53. Supra Chapter 1 at note 10.

54. In a footnote to United States v. Carolene Products Co., 304 U.S. 144, 152–153 note 4 (1938), Justice Stone assigned a preferred position to certain privileges. The genesis and historical footing of that view will hereinafter be discussed.

55. [In 1925 Felix Frankfurter wrote of the due process clauses, "whose contents are derived from the disposition of the Justices." Alexander Bickel, *The Supreme Court and the Idea of Progress* 25 (1978).] Before his discovery of abolitionist ideology, Graham, 112, remarked on the "amazing judicial hybridization of due process of law with the economic tenets of laissez faire [to] which Justice Holmes objected."

56. Supra note 28.

citizens,"[57] among them access to the courts. Throughout the "basic idea," as tenBroek stresses, was that of "equal protection."[58] Farnsworth stated that the Amendment "might as well in my opinion read, 'No State shall deny to any person within its jurisdiction the equal protection of the laws' "; the rest he regarded as "surplusage."[59]

For the framers the three clauses of the Amendment were a trinity, three facets of one and the same purpose. This clearly appears from President Johnson's statement, which accompanied his veto of the Civil Rights Act, that he would *cooperate* "to protect [1] the civil rights of the freedmen [2] by judicial process [3] under equal and impartial laws."[60] *Those* objectives were acceptable to him. In lawyers' parlance, the privileges or immunities clause conferred *substantive* rights which were to be secured through the medium of two *adjective* rights:[61] the equal protection clause outlawed statutory, the due process clause judicial, discrimination with respect to those substantive rights. This adjective duality had been expressed in a Massachusetts measure of 1692 ordaining that "no person should suffer [1] without express law . . . [2] nor without being brought to answer by due course and process of law," a measure duplicated in the colonies of Connecticut and New York.[62] And it found expression in the Fourteenth Amendment, as may be gathered from Senator Howard's explanation that "without this principle of equal *justice* to all men *and* equal protection under the shield of the *law*, there is no republican government." Senator Clark made the point more clearly: "You admit that the *courts* should be open to the black man, and that he should have the protection of the *laws* as fully as the

57. *Globe* 600.

58. TenBroek 207.

59. *Globe* 2539. Windom summarized § 1 in terms of privileges or immunities and equal protection without any mention of due process. Id. 3171.

60. *Globe* 1681.

61. Alone among the Justices, Justice Harlan perceived that the framers expected the "privileges or immunities" clause to be "the most significant portion of § 1," and since it was "expected to be the primary source of substantive protection, the Equal Protection and Due Process Clauses were relegated to a secondary role, as the debates and other contemporary materials make clear." Oregon v. Mitchell, 400 U.S. 112, 163, 164 (1970).

62. 2 Kent, supra note 17 at 608–609.

white man."[63] TenBroek remarks that Bingham "accepted the [aboli-
tionist] amalgamation of natural rights, due process and equal protection."[64] "A common theme of the discussion of the amendment's sup-
porters," Harris comments, "was the mutual interdependence of the
privileges and immunities, due process, and equal protection clauses."[65]
And in answer to the question "equal protection of what?" he replies:
"when the three clauses are read together as they ought to be, it is
equal protection by equal laws pertaining to the rights of life, liberty
and property, and the privileges and immunities of citizenship. Or, as
expressed by Justice Washington, those rights which are in their nature fundamental."[66] But, like tenBroek, Harris does not come to grips
with *the limited meaning* that "natural," "fundamental" rights, that "life,
liberty, or property," had for the framers.[67] Trumbull drew that limited meaning from Justice Washington in drafting the Civil Rights Bill,

63. *Globe* 2766, 833 (emphasis added). So too, Raymond stated that the Civil Rights Bill
"is intended to secure those citizens against injustice that may be done to them in the courts
. . . It is intended to prevent unequal legislation . . . affecting them injuriously." *Globe* 1267.
64. TenBroek 145.
65. R. J. Harris, *The Quest for Equality* 35–36 (1960).
66. Id. 44. The triune analysis undercuts that of Chief Justice Warren in Bolling v.
Sharpe, 347 U.S. 497, 499 (1954): "The Fifth Amendment . . . does not contain an equal
protection clause as does the Fourteenth Amendment . . . But the concepts of equal protection and due process, both stemming from our American ideal of fairness, are not
mutually exclusive. The 'equal protection of the law' is a more explicit safeguard of prohibited unfairness than 'due process of law.' " This is sheer fantasy. Equal protection was
incorporated in the Fourteenth Amendment to bar discrimination by statutes, due process to secure access to the courts; both were antidiscriminatory, but they were designed
to serve quite different purposes. Only eleven years before Warren's statement, the Court
held that because of the absence of "equal protection" from the Fifth Amendment, it
"provides no guaranty against discriminatory legislation by Congress." Detroit Bank v.
United States, 317 U.S. 329, 337 (1943).
67. Thus Harris extracts from the debates the principle "that the equal protection
clause means absolute or perfect equality . . . and condemns *every* discrimination perpetuated by unequal laws." Supra note 65 at 55. Although tenBroek discerned that the
three clauses represented an amalgam for the "protection of natural rights," tenBroek
145, 239, 120, he did not grasp the limited meaning that "natural," "fundamental" rights
had for the framers. Consider only his statement that the "sweeping and comprehensive
meaning of the Fourteenth Amendment . . . turns simply upon the nature of the *statutory*
plan which was sought to be made constitutionally secure by the amendment." TenBroek
203 (emphasis added). This about an Act that painstakingly specified the limited rights
to be protected!

and it was then embodied in the "privileges or immunities" clause. It is striking evidence of the centrality of the privileges or immunities clause for its contemporaries that hard upon the adoption of the Amendment, in the *Slaughter-House Cases*, equal protection and due process, in the words of Justice Miller, had "not been much pressed,"[68] but that the case was almost entirely pitched on the privileges or immunities clause. For it was that clause that contains the substantive rights the Amendment was designed to protect.

As in the case of the "equal protection" clause, the framers were content to bar discrimination, to assure blacks that they would have judicial protection on the same State terms as whites, no more, no less. It should be apparent from the foregoing that the due process clause was not meant to create a new, federal criterion of justice. Like State *laws* at which "equal protection" was aimed, State *justice* had to be nondiscriminatory. It was "equal justice to all men and equal protection under the shield of law" of which Howard spoke.[69] "[E]quality in the protection of these fundamental rights . . . was the common refrain throughout," as is exemplified by Stevens' "Whatever means of redress *is afforded* to one shall be afforded to all,"[70] by Howard's "equal justice to all," and by Trumbull's assurance that the Civil Rights Bill "will have no operation in any State where the laws are equal, where all persons have the same civil rights."[71] Just as the framers disclaimed an intention to displace nondiscriminatory State laws by a general federal code and were content to "correct" discriminatory State laws, so their parallel aim was to secure impartial access to State judicial proceedings,[72] not to write a judicial code for the nation. All this was summed up by Justice Matthews in *Hurtado v. California:* the due process clause of the 14th Amendment "refers

---

68. 83 U.S. (16 Wall.) 36, 80 (1872); Justice Miller, supra note 35.

69. *Globe* 2766.

70. TenBroek 232; *Globe* 2459 (emphasis added). "As Stevens saw it, *discrimination* was the great evil, *equal* protection was the dominant purpose of § 1." Fairman, Stanford 44 (emphasis added). Sumner stated that he wanted "Equality before the law, so that there shall be no ban of color in court room." *Globe* 674.

71. *Globe* 476; see also supra Chapter 10 at note 49.

72. See supra at notes 28–30.

to that law of the land in each State ... 'Each State prescribes its own mode of judicial proceeding.' "[73]

Even less were the framers minded in requiring nondiscriminatory laws and equal judicial process to create a fresh congeries of rights that ranged beyond those enumerated.[74] Having in mind that the Amendment was designed to constitutionalize the Civil Rights Act, it is clear that the "equal protection" and "due process" clauses were merely a compressed version of the original design. All three clauses, tenBroek states, "refer to the protection or abridgment of natural rights,"[75] rights that had been so carefully spelled out in the Civil Rights Act. There is evidence that these clauses simply echoed the Blackstonian formula that the "fundamental rights" could be *diminished* only by "due course of law" or by the "laws of the land," by which was meant general laws that would apply to all alike. Wilson had quoted Blackstone's pairing of "due process of law" and by the "laws of the land" in commenting on the Civil Rights Bill, exhibiting awareness that Blackstone regarded them as the sole means of curtailing the specified rights. He emphasized that the Bill "does not go one step beyond" protection from discrimination with respect to designated "immunities," that "it is not the object of this bill to establish new rights," but to declare "the equality of all citizens in the enjoyment of civil rights and immunities."[76] For the protection of those enumerated rights, "fundamental rights," the framers fashioned impartial access to judicial process and nondiscriminatory legislation. They did not seek to supplant State proceedings and lawmaking, but only to insure, in the words of the Judiciary Committee's interpolation, that an oppressed race should have the "equal benefit of all laws for security of person and property" *"as is enjoyed by white citizens."*[77] This was the purpose constitutionalized by the Fourteenth Amendment.

---

73. 110 U.S. at 535; see also Walker v. Sauvinet, 92 U.S. 90, 93 (1875); cf. supra Chapter 10 at note 70.

74. Recall Bingham's objection to the "oppressive" breadth of the term "civil rights," which was deleted at his insistence. Supra Chapter 7 at notes 11–17; *Globe* 1366.

75. TenBroek 239.

76. *Globe* 1117–1118.

77. Id. 1366; see also supra at note 33.

It is therefore contrary to historical fact to say, as did Justice Black, that "in view of its historical setting and the wrongs which called it into being, the due process provision of the Fourteenth Amendment—just as that in the Fifth . . . was intended to guarantee procedural standards adequate and appropriate, then and thereafter."[78] And it testifies to the potency of unremitting reiteration that even so perspicacious a judge as Justice Harlan could state that "The Due Process Clause of the Fourteenth Amendment requires that those [State] procedures be fundamentally fair in all respects."[79] That is a judicial construct pure and simple; no such mandate can be drawn from the history of the Amendment.

It has been my purpose in this and the preceding chapter to show that the terms "equal protection of the laws" and "due process of law" grew out of the framers' intention to supply, with respect to a selected group of privileges, protection against discrimination either by legislation or by a bar to judicial succor, that these adjective conceptions were intertwined throughout with the framers' solicitude to guarantee those selected substantive rights. Even if I have failed in that purpose, Robert H. Bork's conclusion seems to me controlling:

> The words are general but surely that would not permit us to escape the framers' intent if it were clear. If the legislative history revealed a consensus about segregation in schools and all the other relations in life, I do not see how the Court could escape the choices revealed and substitute its own, even though the words are general and conditions have changed. It is the fact that history does not reveal detailed choices concerning such matters that permits, indeed requires, resort to other modes of interpretation.[80]

The Court, in short, was not empowered to substitute its policy choices for those of the framers.

78. Chambers v. Florida, 309 U.S. 227, 235–236 (1940).

79. Duncan v. Louisiana, 391 U.S. 145, 172 (1968), dissenting opinion. As late as 1894, the Supreme Court declared that the Fourteenth Amendment "conferred no new and additional rights, but only extended the protection of the Federal Constitution over rights of life, liberty, and property that had previously existed under all state constitutions." Mobile & Ohio Railroad v. Tennessee, 153 U.S. 486, 506 (1894).

80. "Neutral Principles and Some First Amendment Problems," 47 Ind. L.J. 1, 13 (1971); see also infra Chapter 21 at note 28.

## Person or Citizen

Few, if any, historical reconstructions can tidily accommodate all the unruly facts. The triune analysis does not fit neatly with the fact that the privileges or immunities clause refers exclusively to "citizens," whereas the equal protection and due process clauses refer to "persons." "In constitutionally defining who is a citizen of the United States," Justice Rehnquist stated, "Congress obviously thought it was doing something, and something important . . . The language of that Amendment carefully distinguishes between 'persons' who, whether by birth or naturalization, had achieved a certain status, and 'persons' in general."[81] That distinction, I suggest, was *not* carefully considered, and it raises a number of perplexing problems. Were the rights of "persons" intended to be broader than those of "citizens"? If so, the unremitting labor to make citizens of blacks was superfluous, especially since suffrage was denied them; for they could have enjoyed as "persons" rights withheld from them as "citizens." Or were "persons," like "citizens," only to receive protection for the "fundamental rights" expressed in the due process words "life, liberty, or property," words Bingham originally had coupled with equal protection. This too would render the privileges or immunities clause supererogatory save as an additional cue to the nature of what was sought to be protected. Nor is it reasonable to conclude that the framers were more solicitous for "persons" than for "citizens." To the contrary, they were almost constantly preoccupied with the plight of the former slaves, who were made citizens for their better protection. All in all, it will not do to read the rights of "persons" more broadly than those that were conferred on "citizens."

Little notice has been taken of the relation in this context between "citizens" and "persons,"[82] and it may be useful to pull the historical

---

81. Sugarman v. Dougall, 413 U.S. 634, 652 (1973), dissenting opinion.

82. Maxwell v. Dow, 176 U.S. 581, 595–596 (1900), presented the question whether a State may provide for criminal trials by a jury of less than twelve. Justice Peckham stated that the rights secured by the Fifth, Sixth, and Seventh Amendments are not "privileges and immunities granted and belonging to the individual as a citizen of the United States, but they are secured to all persons against the Federal Government, entirely irrespective of such citizenship." Hence, he concluded, the privileges or immunities claim

threads together. So far as regards the Civil Rights Bill it is plain, as Wilson stated, that "the entire structure of this bill rests on the discrimination relative to civil rights and immunities . . . on account of race."[83] Originally §1 of the Bill had banned discrimination "in civil rights and immunities among the inhabitants of any State . . . on account of race"; §2 penalized any person who "subjected any inhabitant . . . to the deprivation of any right secured or protected by this act."[84] At the instruction of the Judiciary Committee, Chairman Wilson offered an amendment to §1: "to strike out the words 'but the inhabitants' and insert in lieu the words 'and such citizens,' " so that it would read "no discrimination in civil rights or immunities among the citizens of the United States." He explained that it was "intended to confine the operation of this bill to citizens of the United States, instead of extending it to the inhabitants of the several States, as there seems to be some doubt concerning the power of Congress to extend this protection to such inhabitants as are not citizens."[85] Presumably the doubt was engendered by the fact that the Thirteenth Amendment, the chief reliance for the constitutionality of the Bill, was restricted to enslaved blacks; but the original "discrimination . . . on account of race" adequately responded to that restriction. Later Bingham, apprised by Wilson that the surviving word "inhabitant" in §2 was "in mistake for 'citizen,' " expostulated against the "terrible enormity of distinguishing here in the laws in respect to life, liberty, and property between the citizen and stranger within your gates." That, he said, "is forbidden by the Constitution," citing the association in the Fifth Amendment of "No person" with "life, liberty,

---

"is not protected by a clause which simply prohibits the abridgment of the privileges or immunities of citizens of the United States."

83. *Globe* 1118. Racial discrimination was the acknowledged concern of the Bill: see Trumbull, id. 332, 605; Senator Lane, id. 602; Senator Sumner, id. 674; Senator Sherman, id. 744; Wilson, id. 1117; Senator Howe, *Globe App.* 217. These citations are by no means exhaustive.

But while the "one pervading purpose" as Justice Miller stated was "the freedom of the slave race," supra note 68 at 71, white loyalists who were the victims of discrimination in the South were likewise stated to be "within the intent of the Bingham amendment." See infra at note 91; and see Broomall, *Globe* 1263; Chapter 3 note 40.

84. *Globe* 474–475.
85. Id. 1115.

and property" and asserting that "this bill . . . departs from that great law. The alien is not a citizen. You propose to enact this law, you say, in the interests of the freedmen. But do you propose to allow these discriminations to be made . . . against the alien and stranger?"[86] Although the word "inhabitants" was not replaced by "citizens" in § 2, Wilson continued to refer to the Bill in terms of "citizens," and objected to a proposal to "declare all persons, negroes included, citizens."[87] His understanding that the Bill pertained to "citizens" was shared by William Lawrence and Samuel Shellabarger.[88]

When we turn to the Amendment we find that Bingham pretty consistently sought protection for "persons." In contrast to Stevens, who at the very outset had introduced an amendment requiring all laws to be equally applicable to "citizens," Bingham had proposed to "secure to all persons . . . equal protection in their rights of life, liberty, and property";[89] and this, alongside of a privileges and immunities clause, was later embodied in his prototype amendment.[90] But when challenged, Bingham hedged. Robert S. Hale said, "It is claimed that this constitutional amendment is aimed simply and purely toward the protection of 'American citizens of African descent' . . . I understand that to be the whole intended practical effect of the amendment." Bingham replied, "It is due to the committee that I should say that it is proposed as well to protect the thousands . . . of loyal white citizens . . . whose property . . . has been wrested from them."[91] He recurred, however, to a broader statement: "all persons, whether citizens or strangers . . . shall have equal protection . . . in the rights of life, liberty, and property." Were the word "citizens" used, he stated, "aliens" who were protected by existing constitutional guarantees to "persons" would be excluded.[92] On the other hand, his fellow Republicans—Hiram Price, Thomas T. Davis, Frederick E. Woodbridge,

86. Id. 1292.

87. Id. 1295. There was no need to change "inhabitant" in § 2 because it was limited to deprivations of rights "protected by this act" which extended to "citizens" only.

88. Id. 1832, 1293.

89. Id. 10, 537; id. 14.

90. Id. 813.

91. Id. 1065.

92. Id. 1090, 1292.

and Giles W. Hotchkiss—before and after he spoke, understood his amendment to apply to discrimination between "citizens."[93]

Bingham also described the final version of the Amendment in terms of the "privileges and immunities of all the citizens . . . and the inborn rights of every person."[94] But once again his view apparently did not filter into the minds of his colleagues. The Amendment, as we have seen, was understood to constitutionalize the Civil Rights Bill, which, in the words of M. Russell Thayer, incorporated the Bill's protection of the "fundamental rights of citizenship." Ephraim R. Eckley approved it because it secured "life, liberty, and property to all the citizens."[95] Senator Howard declared, "we desired to put . . . the rights of citizens and freedmen under the civil rights bill beyond the legislative power" of those who would "expose the freedmen again to the oppression of their old masters," and Broomall also referred to the Amendment in terms of "citizens."[96] These references suggest that the minds of most framers were concentrated on the protection of citizens, that they may not have appreciated that the word "persons" was carrying them further. Are so many statements to be viewed as reflecting agreement to use a shorthand version, or do they indicate that Congress did not really grasp that the Amendment applied both to citizens and noncitizens? Bingham never gave thought to the anomalies created by his coupling of the privileges or immunities of "citizens" with the protection of "persons," the fact that he rendered the drive for Negro citizenship and the antecedent specification of the rights epitomized in the privileges or immunities clause superfluous.

Notwithstanding his inept midwifery, the object of the Amendment, whether viewed in the frame of "citizen" or of "person," remains one and the same—the protection of the "fundamental rights" of "life, liberty, or property," which first had been specified in the Civil Rights Bill and then embodied in the privileges or immunities clause.[97] Due pro-

93. Id. 1066, 1087, 1088, 1095.
94. Id. 2452.
95. Id. 2465, 2535.
96. Id. 2896, 2498.
97. Id. 2465; supra Chapter 2. For Wilson, the due process clause served to identify the rights with which the Civil Rights Bill was concerned. Citing the Fifth Amendment,

cess is expressly tied to those rights; the derivation of the equal protection clause shows that it too was designed to shield the same rights against discriminatory laws. As John F. Farnsworth asked, how can a subject "have and enjoy equal rights of 'life, liberty, and the pursuit of happiness' without 'equal protection of the laws'?"[98] Not only is there not the slightest intimation that "persons" were to enjoy broader rights than those that had been so carefully enumerated for "citizens," but those self-same rights of "life, liberty, and property" were repeatedly associated with "persons." One may conclude with tenBroek that "the 'citizen and stranger' are again on the same footing: 'the inborn rights of every person' and 'the privileges and immunities of citizens' are coupled together [by Bingham] and refer to the same rights."[99] Whether the three clauses of § 1 be viewed as a trinity, or whether the equal protection and due process clauses be separated from the privileges or immunities clause by virtue of the differentiation between "citizens" and "persons," the practical effect is the same: protection for the fundamental rights of "life, liberty, and property."

----

"No person shall be deprived of life, liberty, or property without due process of law," he stated, "these constitute the civil rights belonging to the citizens . . . to which this bill relates." *Globe* 1294.

    98. *Globe* 2539.

    99. TenBroek 228.

# 12

## Section Five:
## "Congress Shall Enforce"

Section 5 of the Amendment provides that "The Congress shall have power to enforce by appropriate legislation the provisions of this article." In 1879 the Court declared:

> It is *not said* that the *judicial power* of the general government shall extend to enforcing the prohibitions and protecting the rights and immunities guaranteed. It is *not said* that branch of government shall be authorized to *declare void* any action of a State in violation of the prohibitions. It is the power of Congress which has been enlarged. *Congress is authorized to enforce* the prohibitions by appropriate legislation. Some legislation is contemplated to make the amendment fully effective.[1]

One might read this to mean that the courts are without authority to enforce the Fourteenth Amendment except as Congress empowers them to do so. Nevertheless, Justice Brennan stated in 1970, "we have consistently held that the Amendment grants power to the Court" and brushed the issue aside as "of academic interest only."[2] It is a fact that the Court has exercised the power, but it has never grappled with the questions posed by the text of §5 and by the 1879 opinion. It is never "academic" to inquire into the constitutional authority for action by any

---

1. Ex parte Virginia, 100 U.S. 339, 345 (1879) (emphasis partially added). [During the oral argument on *Brown v. Board of Education*, Justice Jackson asked, "Isn't the one thing that is perfectly clear under the Fourteenth Amendment that Congress is given the power and the duty to enforce the Fourteenth Amendment by legislation?" Alexander Bickel, *The Supreme Court and the Idea of Progress* 6 (1978).]

2. Oregon v. Mitchell, 400 U.S. 112, 264n (1970).

branch of the government. Patently the Court does not derive its power from the text of §5. Whence is it derived? Why did the framers confer the power on Congress rather than the Court?

The preference for Congress over the courts, exhibited by the face of §5, is readily explicable: "Slavery was deeply entrenched in the courts."[3] *Dred Scott* had been so bitterly etched into abolitionist memory that Senator Sumner even sought to bar the customary memorial, placement of Chief Justice Taney's bust in the Supreme Court Chamber, and insisted that his name should be "hooted down in the pages of history."[4] Earlier the fugitive slave decision *Prigg v. Pennsylvania*[5] had incensed the North, and such feelings were exacerbated on the very eve of the Civil War by *Ableman v. Booth*, where an order of the Supreme Court of Wisconsin setting aside a federal commitment of a fugitive slave was reversed.[6] In consequence, Bingham, Stevens, "and others were among the severest critics of the Supreme Court and judicial review . . . [and] viewed it with a profound and ever growing mistrust."[7] James F. Wilson of Iowa rejected "judicial pronouncements" on the "unity of this Republic."[8] Not long after congressional approval of the Amendment, Samuel L. Warner, a Connecticut Republican, said he had "learned to place but little reliance upon the dogmas of [the] Court upon any question touching the rights of humanity."[9]

---

3. TenBroek 149.

4. Donald, *Sumner II* 193. In the House, Stevens referred to "the infamous sentiment that damned the late Chief Justice to everlasting fame; and I fear, to everlasting fire." *Globe* 75. George Bancroft, the historian, stated in a memorial tribute to Lincoln that "The Chief Justice . . . without any necessity or occasion, volunteered to come to the rescue of the theory of slavery." *Globe* 801. Almost twenty years later Justice Harlan delivered himself of more severe strictures in the Civil Rights Cases, 109 U.S. 3, 57 (1883), dissenting opinion.

5. 41 U.S. (16 Pet.) 539 (1842).

6. 62 U.S. (21 How.) 506 (1858). The pot had been kept boiling by a string of fugitive slave decisions, infra Chapter 14 at notes 25–26.

7. Graham 447–448. Courts "had not normally favored abolitionists before the war. There was consequently little inclination to bestow new powers on the judiciary, but rather to lean on an augmented power of Congress." James 184.

8. *Globe* 2947.

9. Fairman, *History* 271. "The Radicals," said R. J. Harris, *The Quest for Equality* 53–54 (1960), "did not trust the judiciary in general and the Supreme Court in particular."

Such statements and sentiments might suggest that the framers intended the § 5 grant of enforcement power to be exclusive, an inference apparently drawn by Judge Learned Hand: "Judicial encroachments upon legislative prerogatives in segregation decisions appeared to Hand to be directly contrary to the intent of the Fourteenth Amendment, which gives Congress power to enforce it through appropriate legislation."[10] Hand could draw on the established canon that the express grant to Congress indicates an intention to withhold the enforcement power from the courts.[11]

It needs to be noticed that in 1866 the lower federal courts had no general jurisdiction of cases alleging a deprivation of rights secured by the Constitution. Although Article III confers jurisdiction of "cases arising under this Constitution," it places creation of the "inferior courts" in the discretion of Congress. Consequently, the Supreme Court held, "Congress may withhold from any court of its creation jurisdiction of any of the enumerated controversies."[12] General jurisdiction of such cases, involving so-called "federal questions," was withheld by Congress from the lower courts until the 1870s.[13] Two related factors also require

---

"Radical Republicans sought to deny the postwar court the power to review congressional Reconstruction." Morton Keller, *Affairs of State* 73 (1977).

10. Kathryn Griffith, *Judge Learned Hand and the Role of the Federal Judiciary* 138 (1973). Hand stated respecting the desegregation decision, "It is curious that no mention was made of section 5, which offered an escape, from intervening, for it empowers Congress to 'enforce' all the preceding sanctions by 'appropriate legislation.' The court must have regarded this as only a cumulative corrective, not being disposed to divest itself of that power of review that it has so often exercised and as often disclaimed." Hand, *The Bill of Rights* 55 (1962).

11. T.I.M.E. v. United States, 359 U.S. 464, 471 (1959); United States v. Arredondo, 31 U.S. (6 Pet.) 691, 725 (1832). The rule was familiar to the Founders. In the First Congress, Egbert Benson said, "it cannot be rationally intended that all offices should be held during good behaviour, because the Constitution has declared one office to be held by this tenure." 1 *Annals of Congress* 505; and see Alexander White, id. 517.

12. Sheldon v. Sill, 49 U.S. (8 How.) 441, 449 (1850).

13. "The Civil Rights Act of 1871 (now 28 U.S.C. § 1343) created original jurisdiction in the district courts over actions [t]o redress the deprivation, under color of any State law . . . of any right . . . secured by the Constitution . . . And the Act of March 3, 1875 (now 28 U.S.C. § 1331), created general federal question jurisdiction in the district courts. The federal courts 'ceased to be restricted tribunals of fair dealing between citizens of different states and became the primary and powerful reliance for vindicating every right

preliminary notice: the existence of the "diversity" jurisdiction of controversies "between citizens of different states," and of appeals to the Supreme Court from State court denials of rights claimed under the Constitution or laws of the United States.[14] But, as the face of the Civil Rights Act discloses, the framers little trusted the State courts to enforce Negro rights;[15] and to have insisted that an impoverished black should pursue his rights in the Supreme Court would have reduced judicial enforcement to an empty promise. The diversity jurisdiction of course was virtually useless to almost all blacks, for their oppressors normally would be residents of the same State.

The framers, however, had made express provision in the Civil Rights Act for federal court jurisdiction to enforce the Act. Section 3 gave (1) the district courts jurisdiction, exclusive of State courts, of all crimes and offenses against the Act; and (2) concurrent jurisdiction with the circuit courts of all causes, civil and criminal, affecting persons who are denied or cannot enforce rights secured by § 1 in State courts; plus (3) rights of removal of criminal or civil actions against persons whose rights were secured by the Act.[16] Nothing in the history of the Amendment suggests an intention to repeal this provision. Instead the question arises: did "incorporation" of the Act in the Amendment carry the enforcement provisions with it? It is unreasonable, however, to attribute to the framers an intention to freeze enforcement provisions—the § 2 fine of $1,000, for example—into the Constitution. Such provisions are generally subject to change in the light of experience, and the need to preserve flexibility with respect to penalties counsels against such an interpretation. On established canons of construction an unreasonable interpretation is to be avoided. Then too, there is no reason to attribute to Congress an intention to surrender any part of its Article III control of the "inferior

---

given by the Constitution, the laws, and treaties of the United States' [citing Felix Frankfurter and James M. Landis, *The Business of the Supreme Court* 65 (1928)]." Paul Brest, *Processes of Constitutional Decisionmaking: Cases and Materials* 1297 (1975).

14. Raoul Berger, *Congress v. The Supreme Court* 274 (1969).

15. Infra at note 16.

16. *Globe App.* 316. McKee of Kentucky asked, "Where is your court of justice in any southern State where the black man can secure protection." *Globe* 653. See also Senator Lane, supra Chapter 11 at note 30.

courts"[17] by a grant of untouchable jurisdiction in the Fourteenth Amendment, particularly at a time when Congress distrusted the courts. Such a surrender calls for more than references to "incorporation"; in an analogous situation the Court has required a specific provision for the change.[18]

In light of the jurisdiction conferred by §3 of the Act, why was there a need for express congressional "power to enforce"? For it is a puzzling fact that the "necessity" of the §5 authorization was stressed. That §5, said George F. Miller of Pennsylvania, "is requisite to enforce the foregoing sections . . . is not contested."[19] Justice Brennan explained that by "including §5 the draftsmen sought to grant to Congress, by a specific provision applicable to the Fourteenth Amendment, the same broad powers expressed in the Necessary and Proper Clause."[20] That leaves the tautology to be accounted for. *Prigg v. Pennsylvania*,[21] a cause célèbre, had decided with respect to the Fugitive Slave Act that Congress has implied power to protect a right derived from the Constitution. Of *Prigg* and the subsequent *Ableman v. Booth*,[22] the abolitionists, we may be sure, were well aware. Practiced lawyers like Senator Reverdy Johnson, Thaddeus Stevens, Judge Robert S. Hale, and Judge William Lawrence would be

17. Supra at note 12.

18. Pierson v. Ray, 386 U.S. 547, 554–555 (1967); see also supra Chapter 1 note 57.

19. *Globe* 2511. Jehu Baker of Illinois declared that §5 "was of course necessary in order to carry the proposed article into practical effect." *Globe App.* 257. See also Senator Poland, *Globe* 2961. Fairman comments, "Poland, like the rest, contemplated action by Congress and ignored direct enforcement by the courts." Fairman, *History* 1296. For a similar comment on Howard, see Fairman, id. 1294.

"Senator Howe, a Radical Republican, went back to Wisconsin and made a major address at Madison on August 10 [1866]; '. . . The only effect of the amendment if adopted is to enable the National Legislature . . . to enforce equal justice, when the several States refuse to enforce it.' " Fairman, Stanford 73–74, quoting the *Chicago Tribune*, August 14, 1866.

20. Katzenbach v. Morgan, 384 U.S. 641, 650 (1966).

21. 41 U.S. (16 Pet.) 539, 618–620 (1842). Justice Bradley stated on circuit, "whenever a right is guaranteed by the constitution . . . Congress has the power to provide for its enforcement, either by implication arising from the correlative duty of the government to protect, wherever a right to the citizen is conferred, or under the general power . . . to make all laws necessary and proper for carrying into execution the foregoing powers." United States v. Cruikshank, 25 F. Cas. (No. 14,897) 707, 709 (C.C.D. La. 1874). He instanced Prigg as an example of the former power.

22. Supra note 6.

familiar with those cases, and one hesitates without more to attribute to the framers an intention merely to confirm such judicial interpretations by express constitutional provision. The "necessity" is perhaps better explained by Laurent B. Frantz: *Prigg* and *Ableman* gave Congress implied power to protect constitutional rights from interference by private individuals, whereas *Kentucky v. Dennison* had denied "implied power to exercise any control over a state's officers and agencies."[23] Since *Dennison* held, and Bingham considered, that *no* branch of the government enjoyed such power over State officers,[24] a grant of power to the judiciary arguably was equally "necessary." No such grant was made in the Amendment. The 1866 congressional grant to the judiciary in the Civil Rights Act was by the *Dennison* test of dubious constitutionality; it could and can be supplemented by delegation from Congress under its §5 "power to enforce." Derived from Congress, the judicial enforcement power can be withdrawn by it from the "inferior courts."

The debates indicate that the framers meant Congress to play the leading role, that they regarded Congress "as the primary organ for the implementation of the guarantees of privileges and immunities, due process, and equal protection."[25] It was "necessary," said Senator Poland, that Congress "enforce the provision . . . and *compel* its observance."[26] Stevens explained that the Amendment "allows Congress to correct the unjust legislation of the States"; and Charles Fairman observed that "Stevens' thought ran to political rather than judicial action."[27] Other framers also

23. "Congressional Power to Enforce the Fourteenth Amendment Against Private Acts," 73 Yale L.J. 1353, 1357 (1964). Chief Justice Taney held in Kentucky v. Dennison, 65 U.S. (24 How.) 66, 107 (1858), with reference to power to compel a Governor to deliver a fugitive from justice to a sister State, "there is no clause or provision in the Constitution which arms the Government of the United States with this power."

24. Bingham stated that "the continued construction of every department of this Government, legislative, executive and judicial . . . has conceded that no such power [to enforce the rights guaranteed to a citizen "from the beginning"] is vested in the Federal Government," and he therefore proposed a grant to Congress. *Globe* 429; see also Howard, infra at note 29.

25. Harris, supra note 9 at 53–54; James 184.

26. *Globe* 2961 (emphasis added). Woodbridge said the Amendment "is intended to enable Congress by its enactments" to give "protection." Supra Chapter 8 at note 34.

27. *Globe* 2459; Fairman, *History* 1284. In "Stevens' mind, it was Congress that was going to correct unjust State legislation." Fairman, Stanford 44.

looked to Congress to undertake "corrective" action.[28] The overtones of such expressions were amplified by Senator Howard: section 5

> constitutes a direct affirmative delegation of power to Congress *to carry out* all the principles of these guarantees, a power *not found in the Constitution* . . . It casts upon Congress the *responsibility* of seeing to it, for the future, that all the sections of the amendment are carried out in good faith, and that no State infringes the rights of person and property . . . I look upon this clause as indispensable for the reason that it thus *imposes upon Congress* this power and *this duty*. It enables *Congress*, in case the States shall enact laws in conflict with the principles of the amendment, *to correct* that legislation by a formal congressional amendment.[29]

Some explanation is required why this "responsibility" to "carry out the principles" of the Amendment did not contemplate congressional rather than judicial initiatives. Why did Hotchkiss protest that § 5 "proposes to leave it to the caprice of Congress" whether or not to enforce antidiscrimination,[30] if it was assumed that the courts could act in the face of congressional inaction? At the outset Conkling stated that all questions "arising upon the construction" of the Amendment would go to the "appropriate forum . . . the forum would be Congress, and also, perhaps the courts."[31] But § 5 made no provision for enforcement by the courts.

Justice Douglas, apparently unaware of the implications of his statement for judicial review, stated that "the manner of enforcement involves discretion; but that discretion is largely entrusted to Congress, not to the courts."[32] The face of § 5 indicates that the "discretion" was *entirely* confided to Congress, and the debates confirm that the "responsibility" for enforcement was imposed upon Congress, thus confirming

28. Supra Chapter 10 at notes 73, 75, 79.

29. *Globe* 2766, 2768 (emphasis added). Justice Brennan cites this passage for "congressional responsibility for implementing the Amendment." Katzenbach v. Morgan, 384 U.S. at 648.

30. *Globe* 1095.

31. Id. 358.

32. Oregon v. Mitchell, 400 U.S. at 143. Professor Willard Hurst stated, "it is pretty plain that the actual framers thought they were delegating the rulemaking power to Congress." "The Role of History," in *Supreme Court and Supreme Law* 60 (Edmond N. Cahn ed. 1954).

the maxim that a direction to act in one mode excludes another.[33] Judge
Learned Hand's inference that the grant to Congress was exclusive is
strengthened by the legislative history. So far as I could find that history
affords no basis for reading into § 5 the judicial power of enforcement it
so plainly withheld. Minimally the legislative history indicates that where
Congress has spoken, that policy ought to be respected.[34]

A reasoned argument for a judicial power of enforcement of the Fourteenth Amendment—apart from that derived from the grant in the Civil
Rights Act of 1866, which Congress is free to withdraw—has yet to be
made. Section 5, I would insist, raises questions which go to the heart of
judicial enforcement of the Amendment, questions which the Court has
never attempted to answer, which have been neglected by scholars, and
to which they might well devote further study.

---

33. Supra note 11.

34. Thus the Equal Educational Opportunities Act of 1974, 20 U.S.C. §§ 1701 et seq.,
undertook to "specify appropriate remedies for the orderly removal of the vestiges of the
dual school system" and to establish priorities for the employment of such remedies. 20
U.S.C. § 1701(b) and § 1713. See also Kelly, supra Chapter 6 note 26.

# 13

## *Incorporation of Abolitionist Theory in Section One*

Enough has been set forth to raise considerable doubt about the Graham-tenBroek theory that §1 of the Fourteenth Amendment embodies the substantive due process–equal protection concepts forged by certain abolitionists in the antislavery crusade of the 1830s–1860s.[1] The abolitionist theorists upon whom Graham and tenBroek relied by no means represented the mainstream of abolitionist theorizing; they were a "handful of relatively unimportant anti-slavery thinkers," overshadowed by the William Lloyd Garrison–Wendell Phillips wing, for whom the natural law of Graham's theologians held no charms.[2] But the fact that a respected historian, Alfred Kelly, considered that Graham and tenBroek "have established quite conclusively that the Fourteenth Amendment both in general ideology and legal phrase was a product of pre-war antislavery theory" and that that view is also taken, albeit less emphatically, by Leonard Levy,[3] calls for further elucidation.

At the outset, it will be recalled, Graham considered that Bingham may have used "due process" in its procedural sense. But on May 4, 1942—he has recorded the date exactly—through a providential "chance

---

1. Graham 155 et seq.; tenBroek 25, 29, 116, 145, 235.

2. Robert Cover, *Justice Accused: Antislavery and the Judicial Process* 155, 150–153 (1975). Cover justly remarks that Graham and tenBroek discovered in the "visions" of this minority "roots for their own constitutional aspirations." Id. 154.

3. Kelly, Fourteenth 1050–1051. Leonard Levy states, "Graham and tenBroek proved that the meaning of Section One must be sought in the pre-1865 period as well as later, and that the evidence of 1866–1868 must be read in the light of a received tradition of abolitionist argument." *Judgments: Essays in American Constitutional History* 70 (1972). See also Thomas Grey, infra Chapter 21 at note 74.

Law Library order" for a work by the abolitionist Theodore Weld, a
shining new world opened up before him.[4] What Graham found is best
summed up in his own words:

> We have been tracing and stressing, not a precise, finished, coher-
> ent, consistent body of constitutional doctrine, still less an authori-
> tative one; rather something still inchoate, derivative, opportunist,
> "sporty and sporting"—hence really a climate of usage, and the so-
> ciology and the geography of professional association, influence and
> knowledge by which due process and equal protection became what
> they did, when and how they did.[5]

This "inchoate" mass allegedly was incorporated in the Fourteenth
Amendment largely through the instrumentality of Bingham, himself an
imprecise thinker who exhibited little more understanding of the Bill of
Rights than Graham credits the abolitionists with.[6]

The Graham-tenBroek theory was spread before the Supreme Court
in *Brown v. Board of Education*, in a brief for which Kelly takes responsibility, and in which Graham collaborated.[7] TenBroek plaintively comments that "it is little short of remarkable that the Chief Justice should
have cut himself off from these historical origins and purposes, casually
announcing, as he did, that 'at best, they are inconclusive.' "[8] It is more
than a little remarkable, it is astounding! Here was a Court that had
invited briefs on the "original understanding";[9] doubtless it would have
rejoiced to base its decision thereon, yet it preferred "political and judicial ethics, social psychology," to their abolitionist history.[10] Such re-

4. Graham 155–156.

5. Id. 543.

6. "That this antislavery constitutional theory was extremely heterodox is clear. It was
not primarily the product of minds trained in vigorous case analysis or statutory construction. It confused moral with civil and constitutional rights. It made the Declaration
of Independence the basic constitutional document . . . the Federal Bill of Rights a *source*
rather than a *limitation* of federal power." Id. 237–238.

7. Kelly, Fourteenth 1049; Graham 268–269.

8. TenBroek 25.

9. Bickel 6.

10. Graham 269. Kelly says of the Court's reaction to his brief, "Equipped with an
impressive mass of historical evidence [which he himself stated "doctor[ed] all the evi-

nunciation by a Court eager to believe suggests a large doubt about the soundness of that history.

Let us begin with Bingham, author of §1 and alleged conduit of abolitionist theology.[11] He inflicted a gaping wound on the conduit theory when he stated, in reply to Rogers, that "the courts have settled [the meaning of due process] long ago."[12] Graham himself wrote that due process "at this time, with a few striking [but uninfluential] exceptions [was] merely a limitation upon procedure."[13] To attribute to Bingham an intention to embody substantive due process in §1, in the face of this statement, it is necessary to charge him with a purpose to conceal his real intention; for if he harbored such an intention, he never revealed it to the 39th Congress. What boots it that Bingham stated in the House, in January 1857, that "absolute equality of all" is a "principle of our Constitution"[14] when he took a firm stand against Negro suffrage in 1866? What matters it that his Ohio district "had been thoroughly abolitionized by the antislavery evangelists in 1835–1837";[15] when Ohio remained a hotbed of Negrophobia; when its Senator Sherman could say in the Senate in 1867, "we do not like Negroes. We do not conceal our dislike";[16] when the Radical George W. Julian of neighboring Indiana could tell the House in 1866, "the real trouble is that *we hate the negro*"?[17] What matters it that "antislavery idealists were backing judicial assault upon segregated

---

dence to the contrary, either by suppressing it . . . or by distorting it . . .] . . . the Court reneged." "As though in embarrassment," the Court "rejected history in favor of sociology." Kelly, "Clio and the Court: An Illicit Love Affair," 1965 S. Ct. Rev. 119, 144. The Court's "embarrassment," I suggest, arose from a hard-headed appraisal of the neoabolitionist theology. It also had before it Bickel's "impressive" compilation to the contrary. Supra Chapter 7 at note 3.

11. Supra Chapter 11 at note 9.

12. *Globe* 1089.

13. Graham 35, 244; see supra Chapter 11 at notes 4–27. For the "exceptions" see infra Chapter 14 at notes 28–35.

14. Kelly, Fourteenth 1052.

15. Graham 280.

16. Woodward, "Seeds of Failure in Radical Race Policy," in *New Frontiers of the American Reconstruction* 128 (Harold M. Hyman ed. 1966).

17. *Globe* 257. "Negrophobia tended to hold even the sparse Reconstruction institutions that the nation created at low throttle, and played a part in Reconstruction incompleteness." Harold M. Hyman, *A More Perfect Union* 447 (1973).

schools" when not long before the Civil War they were rebuffed by the Supreme Courts of Massachusetts and Ohio;[18] when Bingham could acknowledge in the 39th Congress that the Ohio Constitution excluded Negroes from voting;[19] when fellow Republican Columbus Delano shrank from the idea of allowing Negroes to serve as jurors;[20] when "many" Northern newspapers, among them the *Cincinnati Commercial,* were opposed to "equality with the Negroes"?[21]

Bingham's early moral fervor had been diluted by political realities. David Donald states that he "was fully aware that his Ohio district could easily go Democratic, since his own average vote in the elections from 1862 through 1870 was only 50.6 per cent of the total. Bitterly he protested against Radical proposals for 'universal suffrage,' "[22] as is exemplified by his barbed dialogue with Boutwell over the admission of Tennessee sans Negro suffrage.[23] His political instinct did not betray him, for in the April 1867 elections "Ohio overwhelmed a negro suffrage amendment by 40,000."[24] Bingham's change of heart illustrates Russell Nye's pithy summation: after 1865 the "Negro was no longer a problem in morality, but a problem in politics."[25] The "chief trouble no doubt," said Senator Sherman, after the 1867 defeat of the Republican forces in

18. Kelly, Fourteenth 1056.

19. *Globe* 1291.

20. Supra Chapter 9 at note 25.

21. Flack 41; see also Donald, *Sumner II* 158.

22. David Donald, *The Politics of Reconstruction* 46 (1965). Senator Hendricks of Indiana pointed out that "Indiana and Illinois almost continuously were Democratic States," that in Ohio the Democratic party "for half the time had maintained an ascendancy," that for many years it controlled Pennsylvania, and was and is a "mighty power" in New York. *Globe* 368.

23. Supra Chapter 5 at notes 43–44.

24. Supra Chapter 4 at note 36. Michael L. Benedict, who made a "scale" study of voting patterns, concluded that Bingham "led the Republican nonradicals in the House." *A Compromise of Principle* 36 (1975). Bingham's Ohio colleague, Finck, declared on December 21, 1865, that "while I have no ill feeling toward the negro, I shall ever oppose conferring upon him the right of suffrage in Ohio." *Globe* 118.

25. "Comment on C. V. Woodward's Paper" 148, 152, in Hyman ed., supra note 16. Benedict states, "the Republican committee members had eschewed ideology in favor of practicality." Supra note 24 at 182. William Lloyd Garrison "accurately sensed the new mood when he declared that antislavery societies served no useful purpose now that slavery was abolished and closed down the *Liberator*." Donald, *Sumner II* 233.

Ohio, is the Negro "suffrage question . . . it will be a burden in every election."[26] To attribute to this selfsame Ohio an intention to embody in §1 through the medium of Bingham's "vague" phraseology the very suffrage it resoundingly rejected borders on the absurd.

Abolitionist evangelism led Graham and tenBroek to overlook the deep-seated Northern Negrophobia and the fact, noted by C. Vann Woodward, that during the war years "the great majority of citizens in the north still abhorred any association with abolitionists"[27]—hardly fertile soil for the sowing of abolitionist ideology. Senators Fessenden and Grimes, leading Republicans, held "the extreme radicals" in "abhorrence."[28] Senator Cowan, a Pennsylvania conservative Republican, ridiculed the notion that the "antipathy that never sleeps, that never dies, that is inborn, down at the very foundation of our natures," is "to be swept away by half a dozen debates and the reading of half a dozen reports from certain abolitionist societies." He bitterly excoriated the Anti-Slavery Society.[29] To the Moderate leaders the radical leadership was a heavy cross. Many Republicans, reports his biographer, "hated" Stevens. In the Joint Committee, "his own measures were more voted against than

26. Benedict, supra note 24 at 273.

27. *The Burden of Southern History* 73 (1960). Justice Miller, whose "antipathy to slavery" led him to leave Kentucky, wrote in 1854, "An abolitionist has been my abhorrence all my life." Charles Fairman, *Mr. Justice Miller and the Supreme Court* 16–17, 27 (1939). Writing to Harold Laski, October 24, 1930, Justice Holmes stated, "I came to loathe in the abolitionists the conviction that any one who did not agree with them was a knave or a fool." 2 *Holmes-Laski Letters: The Correspondence of Mr. Justice Holmes and Harold J. Laski* 1291 (M. Howe ed. 1953). See also supra Chapter 1 note 36.

28. Kendrick 257. Consider Graham's "the drafters of [§1] . . . Bingham, Stevens . . . Fessenden . . . were men who in their youth and early manhood are known to have been thoroughly exposed to this doctrinal [abolitionist] system," Graham 250, in light of Fessenden's "abhorrence" of "extreme radicals," Bingham's attack upon "oppressive" invasions of States' rights. For Stevens, see infra at notes 30, 35. Of this aspect of Graham's argument, one may borrow his own criticism of "anachronistic thinking" that takes "simple patterns of favorable circumstance as evidence of *much more than that*." Graham 453 (emphasis added). He himself undercuts the neoabolitionist theory when he states with reference to due process and equal protection, "the early antislavery usage and the racial-humanitarian expansion and coverage before the Civil War had got forgotten and eclipsed during Reconstruction." Graham 264.

29. *Globe* 343, 344–345.

voted for."[30] Senator Stewart referred to his "destructive sentiments."[31] Fessenden gleefully reported a tongue-lashing he gave Sumner on the Senate floor, whom he considered "by far the greatest fool of the lot."[32] Consider Senator Trumbull's scathing comment in 1870: "it has been over the idiosyncracies, over the unreasonable propositions, over the impractical measures of . . . [Sumner] that freedom has been proclaimed and established."[33] "More and more Senators came to distrust," David Donald tells us, "when they did not detest him."[34] Stevens excoriated Sumner for halting the Amendment because it did not give Negroes the vote.[35] Between such men there could be no secret protocols that "vague and amorphous" phrases would leave room for what had been rejected.[36]

The Graham-tenBroek theory requires us to believe that a Negrophobic, anti-abolitionist North was ready to embrace the abolitionist program or that the radicals were in a position to dictate the form of the legislation. Indeed, Kelly stated categorically that after the Civil War "a group of old antislavery enthusiasts [were] in a position to control the Thirty-Ninth Congress and to write their radical reformism into the Constitution itself."[37] That is at a long remove from the facts. Among

---

30. Fawn Brodie, *Thaddeus Stevens: Scourge of the South* 259, 268 (1959). Compare this with Kelly's statement, "the Joint Committee was firmly under the control of the Republican Radicals, several of whom, including John A. Bingham and Thaddeus Stevens, had been prominently associated with the radical pre-war antislavery movement." Kelly, Fourteenth 1057. "In fact," Donald states, "the Radical wing of the Republican party had rarely exercised effective control." Donald, *Sumner II* 450. TenBroek, 149, states, "Radical control of Congress hung in a precarious and fluctuating balance." See also Benedict, supra note 24.

31. *Globe* 1106.

32. James 74; Eric L. McKitrick, *Andrew Johnson and Reconstruction* 272 (1960).

33. Benedict, supra note 24 at 39.

34. *Sumner II* 248.

35. Id. Brodie, supra note 30 at 269; *Globe* 2459; cf. id. 1224–1231. Sumner, his biographer remarks, "had gravely objected" to the Fourteenth Amendment, Donald, *Sumner II* 9, presumably because it did not accomplish his abolitionist goals.

36. Kelly, Fourteenth 1071. Kelly states, "the principal Radical leaders concerned with the amendment, notably Bingham, Stevens, Morrill, Fessenden and Howard deliberately sought to go far beyond the guarantees of the Civil Rights Act and to place all civil rights, in the expansive Bingham definition, under federal guarantees of equality against state law." Id.

37. Id. 1054.

the first to discern that underlying political realities called on most Northern Republicans, except for a few Radicals with secure constituencies, to pursue a Moderate course was David Donald: "Moderates had to check extreme Radical proposals or be defeated in the districts they represented"; the "thirty-two Republicans . . . who formed the Moderate faction" were "constantly aware of the need to conciliate the Democrats among their constituents; they were loath to consider imposing . . . Negro suffrage . . . upon the South."[38] Such a one, we have seen, was Bingham. In a recent attempt at more refined "scale" analysis, Michael L. Benedict has classified the Republicans as Conservatives, Moderates (Centrists), and radicals (with a small r). The radicals, he concluded, "did not dominate Congress during the Reconstruction era. More Republican Senators (scaled) consistently conservative than radical"; in the House "consistent nonradicals (Conservatives and Centrists) still outnumbered radicals."[39] One has only to recall that Charles Sumner was not made a member of the Joint Committee and all but excluded from party councils, virtually ostracized,[40] that Stevens regretfully accepted legislation which confessedly fell short of his goals, that Negro suffrage was rejected over Sumner's plea that it was the "Central Guarantee," to realize that Benedict speaks truly. The converse of the fact that the "radicals did not dominate" is that the Conservative-Moderate coalition did.[41] In the Senate a handful of radicals opposed the Fourteenth Amendment,

38. Donald, supra note 22 at 51–52, 61; cf. McKitrick, supra note 32 at 300; see also Benedict, supra note 24 at 56–57.

39. Benedict, supra note 24 at 27, 23; see Donald, quoted supra note 30.

40. Donald, *Sumner II* 149–150, 240, 241, 247–248.

41. "Senate Reconstruction policy after 1865 was framed by a non-radical Joint Committee on Reconstruction and a conservative Judiciary Committee." Benedict, supra note 24 at 37; see id. 29, 146–147; cf. Donald, *Sumner II* 149–150. And see Morton Keller, *Affairs of State* 61 (1977).

Kelly, Fourteenth 1057, states that "the Joint Committee was firmly under the control of Radical Republicans," but Benedict, on the basis of closer analysis, concluded that the "non-radicals clearly outnumbered the radicals." Supra note 24 at 34, 37. Benedict states that "The centrists' work centered on two committees: Fessenden's Joint Committee on Reconstruction and Trumbull's Senate Judiciary Committee. Between them they fashioned the conservative Reconstruction program of the 39th Congress." Benedict, id. 146–147. Kelly's statement, as well as Graham's, that "Ten members of the Joint Committee

evidence that it did not give effect to their wishes.[42] The *New York Herald* remarked that the Amendment "is not the platform of Thaddeus Stevens, Sumner, or any of the noisy radicals in Congress. They can do nothing. It was adopted against all their remonstrances and in spite of their threats."[43] Senator Sherman told a Cincinnati audience in September 1866, while the Amendment was being submitted for ratification, "They talk about radicals; why we defeated every radical proposition in it."[44] Upon the basis of his own studies, Benedict concluded that "the nonradicals had enacted their program with the sullen acquiescence of some radicals and over the opposition of many."[45] What sustenance does this offer for the embodiment of abolitionist ideology in the Fourteenth Amendment?

To Alfred Kelly, "The debates on the passage of the Amendment reveal clearly enough how completely the constitutional ideology of the pre-war antislavery movement shaped the objectives of the Radical Republicans."[46] To my mind, the debates show that—apart from a handful

---

... are known to have grown up in states which were exposed for years to antislavery theory," Graham 313, is vitiated by the fact that the entire committee signed the report, explaining suffrage was unacceptable. Supra chapter 5 at note 49.

42. Cf. Donald, *Sumner II* 247–248.

43. New York Herald, September 28, 1866, quoted in Benedict, supra note 24 at 198. The New York Herald, June 11, 1866, hailed the Amendment as "an ingeniously contrived party platform for the coming fall elections . . . There is nothing here obnoxious to public opinion in the way of negro suffrage." Quoted in Kendrick 352. "The victories Republicans won in 1866," Benedict states, "had demonstrated popular support not for the Radical Republican program but for that of the conservatives and centrists." Benedict, id. at 257; see id. 182, 188. Bingham stated that in the 1866 elections the Amendment was "directly in issue . . . from Maine to California." James 167.

Criticizing the cries of a "white man's government," Stevens said, "I trust the Republican party will not be alarmed at what I am saying. I do not profess to speak their sentiments, nor must they be held responsible for them. I speak for myself." *Globe* 74.

44. James 167. James states it was a "rather consistent practice . . . to disavow all Radical influence in the framing of the congressional proposal." Id. Compare Sherman with Kelly's statement, "The mood of the Radicals was not one of caution and restraint; on the contrary it was 'revolutionary' . . . It is important to understand it, for both the Civil Rights Act of 1866 and the Fourteenth Amendment were products of it." Kelly, Fourteenth 1060–1061.

45. Benedict, supra note 24 at 210. Chairman Fessenden "was unwilling to allow the process of reconstruction to be controlled by the radicals." Kendrick 174.

46. Kelly, Fourteenth 1054.

of extremist radicals and the Democratic opposition, which at every turn sought to besmirch the Republicans with advocacy of all-embracing Negro equality—the Moderate-Conservative coalition steadily adhered to limited objectives: protection of the "person and property" of the Negro against violence and oppression. The means of this protection were carefully specified in the Civil Rights Bill and Congress was repeatedly told that so-called political rights like suffrage, mixed schools, and jury participation were outside the coverage of the Bill. Again and again Congress was told that the Amendment was designed to embody the Civil Rights Act.

A number of questions call for answers by the neoabolitionists. Negro suffrage manifestly was excluded both from the Act and the Amendment. What does this exclusion of Sumner's "Central Guarantee" do to the Graham-tenBroek theory? Why did the Republican majority leave open the door to more abrasive privileges, for example, mixed schools, when they so plainly barred it to suffrage? Why did Chairman Fessenden point out that "existing prejudices" foreclosed "an entire exclusion of all class distinctions"[47] in the Civil Rights Bill, then abruptly embrace that very exclusion in the neoabolitionist version of §1? What caused the Republican majority, who had so firmly pushed through the restricted Civil Rights Bill, suddenly to abandon it in favor of an unrestricted Amendment? Why did "radical control" of the 39th Congress fail in the former and prevail in the latter? Why did Bingham, who objected to "civil rights" as "oppressive" and an encroachment on States' Rights lend himself to abolitionist ideology in drafting §1? It cannot be attributed to a sudden change in the climate of opinion, because Senator Wilson, the Massachusetts Radical, stated in the Senate in January 1869: "There is not today a square mile in the United States where the advocacy of the equal rights and privileges of those colored men has not been in the past and is not now unpopular."[48]

47. *Globe* 705; for a similar remark by Stevens, see id. 537.
48. *Cong. Globe*, 40th Cong., 3d Sess. 672. Russell Nye states, "Neither the antislavery controversy, nor the Civil War, nor the inconclusive maneuvering of Reconstruction made any basic changes in the prevailing attitudes towards race . . . attributes clearly reflected in the congressional politics of Reconstruction." Nye, supra note 25 at 156.

A word about the allegedly "vague and amorphous" nature of the terms used in §1, and Kelly's summation:

> The intent of certain Radical leaders to go beyond the restrictive enu-
> meration of the Civil Rights Act and to incorporate a series of ex-
> pansive guarantees in the Constitution is quite clear. In a general
> sense, the *best evidence* of this is the language of the guarantees which
> Bingham and the other authors of the Fourteenth Amendment in-
> corporated in the first section. The guarantees they finally adopted—
> privileges and immunities, due process and equal protection—were
> not at all derived from the Civil Rights Act, which, with the excep-
> tion of one vague phrase in its final form, had used the restrictive
> enumerative device. Instead the authors derived their guarantees de-
> liberately from the pre-war Radical antislavery movement.[49]

It would be more accurate to say, as Bingham in fact indicated in submitting the Amendment, that two of the clauses—"due process" and
"privileges or immunities"—were drawn from the Constitution,[50] and
under established canons of construction they were to be given their accepted meaning. Bingham himself stated that "due process" was used in
its customary decisional, that is, procedural, sense. The meaning of
"privileges and immunities" had been drawn to the attention of the framers by Chairman Trumbull, who showed that it paralleled—with the
careful exclusion of suffrage—the gloss put upon it by the cases. These
meanings are hardly to be overcome by an "inchoate" meaning favored
by some abolitionists and which was never explained to the framers.
There is also the fact, as Kelly notes, that §1 was presented as "intended
merely to constitutionalize the Civil Rights Act." It does not dispose of
these representations to say that they were made for strategic political
reasons;[51] in the securities field such representations would be branded
as deceptive and misleading.

49. Kelly, Fourteenth 1071 (emphasis added).
50. Id. 1072.
51. Id. 1071. Kelly states that had the Radicals pressed home the proposition that
"their amendment would undoubtedly consummate the destruction of caste and class legislation in the states, an important element of moderate Republican support might be
alienated . . . Political strategy called for ambiguity, not clarity." Id. 1084. For discussion
of this remarkable interpretive approach, see supra Chapter 6.

Remains "equal protection of the laws." The central preoccupation of the framers was the oppression of Negroes under Black Codes and similar discriminatory *laws*. "Equal protection of the laws" perfectly expressed their purpose to halt such discrimination; and the "laws" were such as gave rise to the evils the framers meant to prevent. They did *not* mean to prevent exclusion from suffrage, segregated schools, or miscegenation laws. For this there is evidence in the debates on the Civil Rights Bill. Where is the evidence of a change of purpose? In the case of suffrage, the intention to leave State control of suffrage untouched is plain. It will not do in the face of such facts to infer a "clear intent . . . to go beyond the restrictive enumeration of the Civil Rights Act."

In justice to Kelly, it should be noted that a decade after publication of his article on the Fourteenth Amendment, and under the impact of an "extraordinary revolution in the historiography of Civil War Reconstruction," he tacitly abandoned his earlier analysis.[52] Now he adverted to

> the limitation imposed by the essentially federal character of the American constitutional system, which at last made it *impossible* to set up a comprehensive and *unlimited* program for the integration of the negro into the southern social order. Such a program could have been effected only by a revolutionary destruction of the states and the substitution of a unitary constitutional system . . . [T]he commitment to traditional state-federal relations meant that the radical *Negro reform* program could be *only a very limited one.*[53]

Even less than integration in the South were whites prepared for reconstruction of their institutions to accommodate total Negro integration in the North. It needed no revolution in historiography to learn

52. Kelly, "Comment on Harold M. Hyman's Paper" 40, in Hyman ed., supra note 16. That tacit recantation, published in a sheaf of Reconstruction essays by others, would escape the notice of legal scholars accustomed to search for criticism of the earlier law review article in legal indices.

53. Id. 55 (emphasis added). Benedict comments that "the proposed amendment again demonstrated Republicans' reluctance to expand the national government's jurisdiction over its citizens." Supra note 24 at 170. See also Hyman, supra note 17 at 304, 425, 426, 439, 440, 522–523. The idealistic Graham revealingly states, "The flaws and loopholes . . . were products of a Reconstruction society still willing and able to sacrifice the slave race, to defer protection during the Reconstruction crisis." Graham 297.

that the framers were strongly attached to State sovereignty, that they had "a very limited" program in mind, as was heavily stressed during the debates on the Civil Rights Bill. Fessenden made that plain when he stated that "existing prejudices" barred "an entire exclusion of all class distinctions."[54] A lawyer not committed to the revisionist or any other school, and who holds no brief for "lawyer's history," may be permitted to say that all that was needed was some familiarity with established rules for the interpretation of legislative history, among them to discount heavily oppositionist obstructionism, to read the terms "natural rights" and "fundamental rights" as they had been understood from Blackstone through Kent, as they, so explained Trumbull, were embodied in the Civil Rights Bill, to indulge in something like a presumption that the powers reserved to the States are not diminished by a subsequent amendment in the absence of a clear intention to do so. And above all, to substitute undiluted realism in the appraisal of what happened in 1866 for twentieth-century idealistic fervor, which all too often leads to wishful thinking.[55]

Against this background it is now possible to measure Chief Justice Warren's statement in *Brown v. Board of Education* that the historical evidence is "inconclusive":[56]

> The *most avid* proponents of the post-War amendments undoubtedly intended them to remove all legal distinctions among "all persons born or naturalized in the United States." *Their opponents* just

54. Supra at note 47. Senator Doolittle of Wisconsin, who favored Negro suffrage, recognized that it could not "be imposed upon the [Northern] States." *Globe* 2143; see supra Chapter 4 at notes 28–33. Desegregation of schools was even more unpalatable.

55. In a tacit reference to the neoabolitionist writings, Fairman stated, "some of the studies go to historical origins and through their reinterpretation, report the discovery of high moral purposes which, though lost awhile, are now offered as authentic. In some of these works of great good will it seems as though the fervor to hasten justice now has, however unwittingly, been given ascendancy over devotion to cold truth." *History* 1117.

56. Miller and Howell consider it "rather doubtful that the historical record is so 'inconclusive' as Chief Justice Warren asserted in Brown v. Board of Education . . ., insofar as the framers of the fourteenth amendment had any intent regarding racially segregated schools." "The Myth of Neutrality in Constitutional Adjudication," 27 U. Chi. L. Rev. 661, 674 note 48 (1960). See also Thomas Grey, "Do We Have An Unwritten Constitution?," 27 Stan. L. Rev. 703, 712 (1975).

as certainly were antagonistic to both the letter and spirit of the Amendments and wished them to have the most limited effect. What others in Congress and in the state legislatures had in mind cannot be determined with any degree of certainty.[57]

This sets up an irrelevant antithesis—between the Democrats and "the most avid proponents," the extremist radicals—neither of whom really influenced the outcome. In fact, Democrats often voted with a leading extremist, Sumner, in order "to kill moderate reconstruction proposals."[58] What "others," the decisive Conservative-Moderate coalition, "had in mind" can be determined with considerable "certainty." Chairman Wilson, for example, stated that the terms "civil rights and immunities" in the Civil Rights Bill did not mean that all "children shall attend the same schools," and the evidence demonstrates that he spoke for the framers.[59] On the score of Negro suffrage, the proof that it was deliberately left to the States is indeed "overwhelming." Warren's summation, therefore, hardly does justice to the facts; but it was merely window-dressing for the rationale of his opinion:

> we cannot turn back the clock to 1868 when the Amendment was adopted . . . We must consider public education in the light of its full development and its present place in American life throughout the Nation. Only in this way can it be determined if segregation in public schools deprives plaintiffs of the equal protection of the laws.[60]

Stated baldly, what the framers meant by the words they employed is not binding on the Court; the Court lays claim to power to revise the Constitution to meet present needs. A celebrant of the Warren Court, Paul

57. 347 U.S. 483, 489 (1954) (emphasis added).

58. Donald, *Sumner II* 248. As Senator Yates of Illinois observed, "If we do not meet the views of the Radicals on the one hand, nor the views of the pro-slavery Democracy upon the other, we at all events have the medium, the moderation which has been agreed upon." *Globe* 3038. See supra at note 42.

59. Supra Chapter 2 at note 26; Chapter 6. One of the distinguished lawyers of our generation, Dean Acheson, testified before the Senate in 1971 that "The most complicated thing in the world, race relations, came out of the judges, who took over this problem and found in a phrase, the equal protection of the laws, the way to deal with this complicated question, which didn't deal with it." *Hearings on Executive Privilege before the Senate Subcommittee on the Separation of Powers* 266, 92d Cong., 1st Sess. (July 1971).

60. 347 U.S. at 492–493. See infra Chapter 15 note 11.

Murphy, commented that *Brown* disclosed Chief Justice Warren's "unabashed and primary commitment to justice and his willingness to shape the law to achieve it."[61] He did not merely "shape" the law, he upended it; he revised the Fourteenth Amendment to mean exactly the opposite of what its framers designed it to mean, namely, to leave suffrage and segregation beyond federal control, to leave it with the States, where control over internal, domestic matters resided from the beginning.

## Supplementary Note on Abolitionist Influence

Activists strangely prefer what abolitionists said between 1830 and 1860 outside the halls of Congress to what the framers said in the course of the 1866 debates. The notion that abolitionist theology heavily influenced the framers of the Fourteenth Amendment was floated by Jacobus tenBroek and Howard Jay Graham in the 1960s.[1] Alfred Kelly opined that Graham and tenBroek "have established quite conclusively that the Fourteenth Amendment both in general ideology and legal phrase was a product of radical pre-war anti-slavery theory."[2] That view is shared by Leonard Levy: "Graham and tenBroek proved that the meaning of Section One must be sought in the pre-1865 period as well as later, and that the evidence of 1866–1868 must be read in the light of a received tradition of abolitionist constitutional argument."[3] Recently William Nelson concluded that the Amendment "must be understood as the Republican party's plan for securing the fruits . . . of the three decades of antislavery agitation preceding" the Civil War.[4] It was the Courts, Nel-

---

61. *The Constitution in Crisis Times* 312 (1972).

1. Jacobus tenBroek, *Equal Under Law* (1965); Howard Jay Graham, *Everyman's Constitution* (1968).

2. Kelly, Fourteenth 1049, 1050–1051.

3. Leonard Levy, *Judgments: Essays in American Constitutional History* 70 (1972).

4. William E. Nelson, *The Fourteenth Amendment: From Political Principle to Judicial Doctrine* 61 (1988).

son opines, that transformed "the vague rhetorical principles of the antebellum era . . . into a more precise and consistent body of legal doctrine."[5] "Vague rhetorical principles" that could mean anything to anybody—for example "equality could mean almost anything"[6]—are no principles at all.

Abolitionist speeches during the 1830–1860 drive to abolish slavery did not reflect postwar sentiment in the North. The fact is, wrote Reconstruction historian David Donald, racism "ran deep in the North," and the suggestion that blacks "should be treated as equals to whites woke some of the deepest and ugliest fears in the American mind."[7] Phillip Paludan observed that racism was "as pervasive during Reconstruction as after. Americans clung firmly to a belief in the basic inferiority of the Negro race, a belief supported by the preponderance of nineteenth century scientific evidence."[8] "What lies beneath the politics of the Reconstruction period so far as it touched the Negro," Russell Nye stated,

5. Id. 39. The abolitionists were not only "vague," but they were of divided counsels. David Richards, a devout activist, notes that "abolitionist political and constitutional theory . . . can be divided into at least three antagonistic schools of thought . . . Presumably, however, good historical arguments could discriminate among the various strands of abolitionist thought, and identify the one among them that critically shaped the terms of the Reconstruction amendments." David A. J. Richards, "Abolitionist Political and Constitutional Theory and the Reconstruction Amendments," 25 Loyola L.A. L. Rev. 1181, 1187 (1992). That "discrimination" has yet to be made.

6. Nelson, supra note 4 at 21.

7. Donald, *Sumner II* 202, 252. In an 1831 tour, William Lloyd Garrison found that "a greater revolution in public sentiment was to be effected in the free states—and *particularly in New England*—than at the South. I found contempt more bitter, opposition more active, detraction more relentless, prejudice more stubborn . . . than among slave owners themselves." *Documents of American History* 278 (Henry Steele Commager ed. 7th ed. 1963) (emphasis in original).

8. Phillip S. Paludan, *A Covenant With Death* 54 (1975). See also W. R. Brock, *An American Crisis: Congress and Reconstruction, 1865–1867* 285 (1963). When a generous-hearted English visitor to the United States, W. M. Thackeray, first saw a Negro in 1852, he recorded: "Sambo is not my man & my brother; the very aspect of his face is grotesque & inferior. I can't help seeing & owning this; at the same time of course denying any white man's right to hold this fellow creature in bondage." Gordon N. Ray, *Thackeray: The Age of Wisdom, 1847–1863* 216 (1958). Upon his first sight of slaves in 1834, Charles Sumner wrote, "My worst preconception of their appearance and their ignorance did not fall as low as their actual stupidity . . . They appear to be nothing more than moving masses of flesh unendowed with anything of intelligence above the brutes." Donald, *Sumner I* 29.

"is the prevailing racist policy tacitly accepted by both parties and the general public."[9] Against the racial barrier the waves of prewar abolitionism broke in vain.

Abolitionism was in fact poor soil in which to root protection for emancipated blacks; it had made too many enemies. During the war, C. Vann Woodward recounts, "the great majority of citizens in the North still abhorred any association with abolitionists."[10] Senator Edmund Cowan of Pennsylvania ridiculed the notion that the "antipathy that never sleeps, that never dies . . . [was] to be swept away by . . . the reading of half a dozen reports from certain abolitionist societies."[11] Senator Fessenden, chairman of the Joint Committee on Reconstruction, held "the extreme radicals" in "abhorrence."[12] The fact is that the war-weary North was far from ready to embark on fresh crusades for the realization of abolitionist goals. William Lloyd Garrison, the indomitable abolitionist who had been dragged through the streets of Boston with a rope around his neck, accurately sensed the national mood when he closed down *The Liberator*, declaring that antislavery societies "served no useful purpose now that slavery was abolished."[13]

The abolitionist theorists upon whom Graham and tenBroek relied by no means represented the mainstream of abolitionist thinking; they were a "handful of relatively unimportant anti-slavery thinkers."[14] Robert Cover, himself an activist, observed that Graham and tenBroek discovered in the "vision" of this minority "roots for their own constitu-

---

9. R. B. Nye, "Comment on C. V. Woodward's Paper," in *New Frontiers of the American Reconstruction* 148, 151 (Harold M. Hyman ed. 1966).

10. C. Vann Woodward, *The Burden of Southern History* 73 (1960). Justice Holmes came to dislike the Abolitionists' conviction that "their antagonists must be either knaves or fools." 2 *Holmes-Laski Letters: The Correspondence of Mr. Justice Holmes and Harold J. Laski* 942 (Mark de W. Howe ed. 1953).

11. *Globe* 343–345. In his Second Annual Message, December 1, 1862, President Lincoln "submitted a draft of a constitutional amendment providing for the gradual abolition of slavery (by 1900), for compensation to slaveholders, and for colonization of the freedmen somewhere outside the United States." Forrest McDonald, *The American Presidency: An Intellectual History* 356 (1994).

12. Benjamin Kendrick, *The Journal of the Joint Committee of Fifteen on Reconstruction* 257 (1914).

13. Donald, supra note 7 at 233.

14. Robert M. Cover, *Justice Accused: Antislavery and the Judicial Process* 155 (1975).

tional aspirations."[15] What Graham discovered, in his own words, was "something still inchoate . . . opportunist"; he recognized that the minority theory of due process was "rankly, frankly heretical."[16] Thus Joel Tiffany, a leading minority theorist, held that "slavery was unconstitutional."[17] It takes a great leap of the imagination to assume that such "rankly heretical" theorizing commended itself to the hard-headed lawyers who sat in the 39th Congress, particularly when the minority's own abolitionist brethren rejected "radical anti-slavery thought."[18]

But an activist "scholar," Michael Curtis, triumphantly asks, "If abolitionist ideas were an anathema to most Republican Congressmen, why in the previous session of Congress had they abolished slavery in the states—the main goal of the radical political abolitionists?"[19] It escapes him that a Northerner could oppose slavery and yet remain a racist. The matter was cogently summarized by Henry Monaghan:

> We forget that many mid-nineteenth century Americans, perhaps a clear majority, opposed slavery and racial equality with equal intensity. They could logically believe that emancipation required that the freedman possess certain rights to personal security and property. Simultaneously they could favor rank discrimination against blacks in political and social matters.[20]

15. Id. 154.

16. Graham, supra note 1 at 543, 242. "That the antislavery constitutional theory was extremely heterodox is clear." Id. 237–238.

17. Michael B. Curtis, *No State Shall Abridge: The Fourteenth Amendment and the Bill of Rights* 42 (1986). Curtis, an apologist for abolitionism, recognizes that "the Constitution did not allow interference with slavery in the States." Id. 19.

Lysander Spooner, "the most theoretically profound advocate" of the contrary position, counseled that the constitutional provisions "were to be interpreted not to recognize slavery on the theory that *any interpretation* should be accorded the words, *no matter how textually strained*, that did not recognize slavery." Richards, supra note 5 at 1193 (emphasis added).

18. Curtis, supra note 17 at 42.

19. Id. 118.

20. Henry P. Monaghan, "The Constitution Goes to Harvard," 13 Harv. C.R.–C.L. L. Rev. 117, 126 (1978). For example, Senator James Patterson was "opposed to any law discriminating against [blacks] in the security and protection of life, liberty, property and the proceeds of their labor," but "[b]eyond this," he stated, "I am not prepared to go," explicitly rejecting "political and social equality." *Globe* 2699.

In truth, a Republican conservative coalition, as Michael Les Benedict has shown, "enacted their program with the sullen acquiescence of some radicals and over the opposition of many."[21] Benedict's finding is confirmed by the defeat (125 to 12 in the House, and 34 to 4 in the Senate) of Radical insistence that Tennessee provide for black suffrage.[22] Such action by the Congress, not what some abolitionists had said before the Civil War, illuminates the purposes of the framers.

21. Michael Les Benedict, *A Compromise of Principle* 210 (1974). Benedict found that the centrists' work "centered in two Committees: Fessenden's Joint Committee on Reconstruction and Trumbull's Senate Judiciary Committee. Between them they fashioned the conservative Reconstruction program of the Thirty-ninth Congress." Id. 146–147.

22. *Globe* 3980, 4000.

# PART II

# 14

## From Natural Law to Libertarian Due Process

### Substantive Economic Due Process

THE development of substantive due process was described by Robert G. McCloskey, a friend of the Court, as "the classic example of 'government by judiciary.' "[1] So accustomed are we grown to this development—whereby courts substitute their own views of policy for those of legislative bodies—that one recalls with a start that the doctrine was only launched in the late nineteenth century.[2]

The shift from judicial supervision of procedure *in the courts* to control of *legislative* policymaking constitutes a truly extraordinary transformation. For judicial review was conceived in narrow terms—as a means of policing the constitutional boundaries, the "limits" of a given power. Little did the Framers dream that the judicial power would be construed as a license to supersede the exercise of power by the other branches within those boundaries.[3] In fact, judicial participation in leg-

---

1. *The American Supreme Court* 132 (1960). " 'Government by Judiciary,' is no idle phrase." A. T. Mason and W. M. Beaney, *American Constitutional Law* 21 (1954).

2. See Walton Hamilton, "The Path of Due Process of Law," in *The Constitution Reconsidered* 167 (C. Read ed. 1938); Charles G. Haines, *The Revival of Natural Law Concepts* 104–165 (1930). In Adamson v. California, 332 U.S. 46, 79 (1947), Justice Black said of an 1890 case that it "gave a new and hitherto undiscovered scope for the Court's use of the due process clause to protect property rights under natural law concepts."

3. Judicial review "should be confined to occasions when the statute or order was outside the grant of power to the grantee, and should not include a review of how the power has been exercised." Learned Hand, *The Bill of Rights* 66 (1962); for confirmatory materials, see infra Chapter 16 at notes 20–26. Madison stated that none of the departments

islative policymaking was unmistakably excluded.[4] Under the guise of substantive due process, therefore, the Court has invaded the exclusive jurisdiction of a sister branch; it has violated the injunction of the separation of powers, made explicit in the 1780 Massachusetts Constitution, that "the judiciary shall never exercise the legislative power."[5] And it has encroached on the sovereignty reserved to the States by the Tenth Amendment. It has done this in the name of a self-created doctrine to legitimate the exercise of power once rationalized under the garb of natural law.[6] But neither the Framers of the Constitution nor of the Fourteenth Amendment entertained such notions.

It is axiomatic that all wielders of power, judges included, ever thirst for more.[7] This appetite for extraconstitutional power found classical expression in Justice Samuel Chase's opinion in *Calder v. Bull* (1798). Taking off from an hypothetical horrible—"a law that takes property from *A* and gives it to *B*"—Chase declared that even in the absence of express restraint by the Constitution, "it is against all reason and justice, for a people to entrust a Legislature with such powers . . . the general principles of law

---

"ought to possess, directly or indirectly, an overruling influence over the others in the administration of their respective powers." Federalist No. 48 at 321. See infra note 5. "The judicial cannot prescribe to the legislative department of the government limitations upon the exercise of its acknowledged powers." Veazie Bank v. Fenno, 75 U.S. (8 Wall.) 533, 548 (1869).

4. Infra Chapter 16.

5. Article XXX provided that "the legislative department shall never exercise the executive and judicial powers . . . the executive shall never exercise the legislative and judicial powers . . . the judicial shall never exercise the legislative and executive powers." 1 Poore 960. For the same utterance by Madison, see 1 *Annals of Congress* 435–436.

6. The "modern definition of 'due process' is merely the 'natural justice' . . . under a new name." J. A. C. Grant, "The Natural Law Background of Due Process," 31 Colum. L. Rev. 56, 65 (1931); Haines, supra note 2 at 305, 101, 103; Graham 239. Justice Black referred to the " 'natural law due process notion' by which this Court frees itself from the limits of a written Constitution." In re Winship, 397 U.S. 358, 381 (1970).

7. Madison stated, "It will not be denied, that power is of an encroaching nature, and that it ought to be effectually restrained from passing the limits assigned to it." Federalist No. 48 at 321. One of the ablest of Justices, William Johnson, remarked on "the necessity of watching the advancement of judicial power, in common with all power." Ramsay v. Allegre, 25 U.S. (12 Wheat.) 611, 616 (1827), concurring opinion. Justice Frankfurter commented that "Judicial power is not immune against this human weakness." Trop v. Dulles, 356 U.S. 86, 119 (1958), dissenting opinion. See also infra Chapter 15 at note 37.

and reason" forbid such acts.[8] His appeal to extraconstitutional power was flatly rejected by Justice James Iredell, whose cogent advocacy of judicial review had anticipated that of Hamilton.[9] True, "some speculative jurists," Iredell noted, had stated that "a legislative act against natural justice must, in itself, be void"; but, given a "constitution which imposed no limits on the legislative power . . . whatever the legislative power chose to enact would be lawfully enacted, and the judicial power would never interpose to declare it void."[10] Reflecting David Hume,[11] he said that "the ideas of natural justice are regulated by no fixed standard: the ablest and purest men have differed upon the subject."[12] Natural law therefore differed little from the "mandate from heaven" of a Chinese emperor, which was "so vague that emperors could readily identify their own will with the will of heaven."[13] Dean Pound justly characterized it as "purely personal and arbitrary."[14]

Iredell, not Chase, represented the received opinion. The Founders were deeply committed to positivism, as is attested by their resort to written constitutions—positive law. Adams, Jefferson, Wilson, Madison, and Hamilton, states Robert Cover, "were seldom, if ever, guilty of confusing law with natural right." For them a constitution represented the will of the people "that would determine explicit . . . allocations of power and its corresponding limits." Chase's notion, to borrow from Cover, "that out beyond [a constitution] lay a higher law,"[15] departed from the

8. 3 U.S. (3 Dall.) 386, 388 (1798).

9. Raoul Berger, *Congress v. The Supreme Court* 82–83 (1969).

10. 3 U.S. at 398.

11. "The word natural is commonly taken in so many senses, and is of so loose a signification, that it seems vain to dispute whether justice be natural or not." Quoted in Robert M. Cover, *Justice Accused: Antislavery and the Judicial Process* 23 (1975).

12. 3 U.S. at 398.

13. Herbert Muller, *Uses of the Past* 350 (1952).

14. Roscoe Pound, "Common Law and Legislation," 21 Harv. L. Rev. 383, 393 (1908).

15. Cover, supra note 11 at 29. Cover comments that this "was never a part of the mainstream of American jurisprudence." Id. John Adams and his compeers "used nature to take the measure of law [e.g. "fundamental rights"] . . . but not as a source for rules of decision." Id. 27. But see Haines, supra note 2 at 52–55. Morton Horwitz states that post-Revolution Americans regarded written constitutions as embodying the " 'will' of the people," and "tended to assert the ultimate primacy of the legislature and of statute law," with the result "that the original natural law foundation of common law rules began

Founders' commitment to written limits on all power. That commitment sprang from an omnipresent dread of the greedy expansiveness of power, graphically expressed by Jefferson: "It is jealousy and not confidence which prescribes limited constitutions to bind down those whom we are obliged to trust with power . . . In questions of power, then, let no more be heard of confidence in man, but bind him down from mischief by the chains of the Constitution."[16]

Cover's view may seem to be contradicted by Chief Justice Marshall's reference to natural law in *Fletcher v. Peck*,[17] but Marshall's allegiance to the doctrine is debatable. Justice Frankfurter considered his occasional references to natural law "not much more than mere literary garniture . . . and not a guiding means for adjudication."[18] Let the contrary be assumed,[19] and the Marshall view must yet yield to the Founders' ceaseless emphasis on a federal government of "limited" powers,[20] to the deep distrust of a federal judicial system.[21] Incorporation of natural law as a basic presupposition would set at naught the Framers' efforts to temper

---

to disintegrate." There was a vigorous demand for codification because " 'the very nature of the constitution requires the judge to follow the letter of the law.' " "The Emergence of an Instrumental Conception of American Law, 1780–1820," in 5 *Perspectives in American History* 287, 309–310 (1971). My reasons for concluding that the Founders clung to a "fixed Constitution," to positive, not natural, law, are set forth infra Chapter 21 at note 88 to the end.

16. 4 Elliot 543. In the Virginia Ratification Convention, Francis Corbin stated, "Liberty is secured, sir, by the limitation of its [the government's] powers, which are clearly and unequivocally defined." 3 Elliot 110. In the First Congress, James Jackson said: "we must confine ourselves to the powers described in the constitution, and the moment we pass it, we take an arbitrary stride towards a despotic Government." 1 *Annals of Congress* 489. See also infra Chapter 15 note 19. For additional citations to the Founders, see Berger, supra note 9 at 13–14.

17. 10 U.S. (6 Cranch) 87, 135–136 (1810). This was echoed by Chancellor Kent in Gardner v. Newburgh, 2 Johns. Ch. 162, 166–167 (N.Y. 1816). But as Henry Steele Commager remarked, "the impressive thing is the paucity of such occasions in the first half a century of our history." "Constitutional History and the Higher Law," in *The Constitution Reconsidered* 225 (C. Read ed. 1938).

18. "John Marshall and the Judicial Function," 69 Harv. L. Rev. 217, 225 (1955); see also infra Chapter 21 at notes 12–28.

19. See G. Edward White, *The American Judicial Tradition* 18, 26 (1976).

20. Berger, supra note 9 at 13–16.

21. National Ins. Co. v. Tidewater Co., 337 U.S. 582, 647 (1949), Frankfurter, dissenting opinion; see also Berger, supra note 9 at 260–264.

federal judicial control over the States. And the ongoing debate about the legitimacy of judicial review itself[22] counsels against adoption of the most extreme view of the power—one infinitely expansible by calling on "higher law"; for, as Lord Camden stated, "One should naturally expect that the law to warrant it should be clear in proportion as the power is exorbitant."[23] On this score, finally, when *M'Culloch v. Maryland* came under attack nine years later, Marshall repeatedly and emphatically disclaimed any intimation that constitutional powers could be expanded by construction,[24] assurances that were meaningless if the result could be achieved through the medium of natural law.

The Founders' commitment to written limits on all power received powerful endorsement when a succession of judges, including Shaw, Story, and McLean, put the commands of the Fugitive Slave Act above the agonizing demands of conscience and the higher law. In a typical fugitive slave case, *Miller v. McQuerry*, Justice John McLean stated, "It is for the people . . . in making constitutions and in the enactment of laws, to consider the laws of nature . . . This is a field which judges cannot explore . . . They look to the law, and to the law only."[25] Such were also the views of Justice Story and Chief Justice Lemuel Shaw.[26]

Against this background, judges in whom Chase's yearning for extra-constitutional power survived understandably would be more comfortable with a constitutional catchphrase that "disguised individual opinions and gave them the sanction and prestige of a supreme fundamental

22. See infra Chapter 19 at note 16.

23. Entick v. Carrington, 19 How. St. Tr. 1029, 1065–1066 (1765).

24. *John Marshall's Defense of McCulloch v. Maryland* 185, 182, 184 (G. Gunther ed. 1969), discussed infra Chapter 21 at notes 10–19.

25. 17 F. Cas. (No. 9583) 332, 339 (C.C. D. Ohio, 1853).

26. Shaw stated, "an appeal to natural rights . . . was not pertinent! It was to be decided by the Constitution . . . and by the Law of Congress . . . These were to be obeyed, however disagreeable to our natural sympathies." Account in *The Liberator*, Nov. 4, 1842, at 3, quoted in Cover, supra note 11 at 169. For Story see Cover, id. 171, 193. Still other cases were collected and analyzed by Cover, and he concludes that "The judiciary was superbly consistent in a wide variety of contexts in that positivist approach." Id. 116.

Horwitz considers that "Story's theory in the *Commentaries* is a pure will theory of law, anticipating the most advanced forms of modern, secular, amoral, legal positivism." "The Conservative Tradition in the Writing of American Legal History," 17 Am. J. Legal Hist. 275, 288 (1973).

law."[27] They found it in *Wynehamer v. The People* (1856),[28] the *locus classicus* of substantive due process. But first they too dismissed the doctrine of natural law. Justice Selden declared, "the doctrine that there exists in the judiciary some vague, loose and undefined power to annul a law, because in its judgment it is 'contrary to natural equity and justice,' is in conflict with the first principles of government and can never, I think, be maintained."[29] His associates were equally plainspoken.[30] This, however, did not exemplify a triumph of judicial self-restraint. While barring abolitionist reliance upon natural law, Corwin said, the Court fashioned substantive due process as a means of *confining* protection to vested property rights.[31] But Justice A. S. Johnson cited much the same type of horrible example that had been adduced for resort to natural law, without explaining the leap from procedural due process in a criminal trial to invalidation of a statute, content to appeal to the ostensibly discarded natural law reasoning under a new label.[32]

*Wynehamer*, it needs to be underscored, was a sport; it "found no place in the constitutional law that was generally recognized" in 1856; nor did it thereafter find acceptance.[33] When its argument was pressed on Chief

27. Graham 117.

28. 13 N.Y. 378 (1856).

29. Id. 430.

30. Justice Hubbard stated, "I am opposed to the judiciary . . . declaring a statute invalid upon any fanciful theory of higher law or first principles of natural rights outside the constitution." Id. 453; see also id. 390–391, 476.

31. Edward Corwin, "The Decline of Due Process Before the Civil War," 24 Harv. L. Rev. 460, 471 (1911). He stated that the court was "dismayed by the abolitionists quoting the same [natural rights] scripture to their purposes." Id. Justice Comstock referred to the "great danger in attempting to define the limits" of legislative power, and said that "danger was less apparent" in Marshall's time "than it is now, when theories, alleged to be founded in natural reason or inalienable rights but otherwise subversive of the just and necessary powers of government, attract the belief of considerable classes of men." 13 N.Y. at 391.

32. "For instance, a law that any man who, after the age of fifty years, shall continue to live, shall be punished by imprisonment or fine would be beyond the power of the legislature. It would be so, upon the ground that he cannot be deprived of life, liberty, or property without due process of law." 13 N.Y. at 420.

33. Corwin, supra note 31 at 474–475; Charles Warren, "The New 'Liberty' Under the Fourteenth Amendment," 39 Harv. L. Rev. 431, 442–445 (1926). The Supreme Court dwelled on the procedural aspect of due process in Murray's Lessee v. Hoboken Land &

Justice Ames of the Rhode Island Supreme Court in 1858, he held that the due process clause of the State constitution was not "designed to inhibit the legislature from regulating the vendibility of property" but was the "shield of *one accused of crime*,"[34] as almost all State constitutions made quite plain. Shortly thereafter, in 1866, the New York Court itself repudiated "the inconsiderate dicta of some of the judges" in *Wyne-hamer.*[35] Nevertheless, Justice Miller, recurring to typical natural law examples in 1874, averred, "It must be conceded that there are such rights in every free government beyond the control of the State."[36] Yet Miller himself had categorically rejected such concepts in 1869:

> This whole argument of the *injustice* of the law . . . and of its opposition to the spirit of the Constitution, is too abstract and intangible for application to courts of justice, and is, above all, dangerous as a ground on which to declare the legislation of Congress void by the decisions of a court. It would authorize this court to enforce theoretical views of the genius of government, or vague notions of the spirit of the Constitution and of abstract justice, by declaring void laws which did not square with those views. It substitutes our views

---

Improvement Co., 59 U.S. (18 How.) 272, 276–277 (1856). Although Dred Scott v. Sandford, 60 U.S. (19 How.) 393 (1857), employed substantive due process for protection of property in a slave, over a vigorous dissent by Justice Curtis, that case outraged abolitionist opinion and was roundly condemned in the 39th Congress.

34. State v. Kieran, 5 R.I. 497, 506, 507 (1858) (emphasis added). Chief Justice Ames stated, "Surely, if any clause in the constitution has a definite meaning, which should exclude all vagaries which would render courts the tyrants of the constitution, this clause . . . can claim to have, both from its history and its long received interpretation. It is no vague declaration concerning the rights of property, which can be made to mean anything and everything; but an intensely practical, and somewhat minute provision, guarding the rights of persons *accused of crime*." Id. 505. See also Charles Curtis, supra Chapter 11 at note 27.

35. Metropolitan Board of Excise v. Barrie, 34 N.Y. 657, 668 (1866).

36. Loan Association v. Topeka, 87 U.S. (20 Wall.) 655, 662 (1874). Following in the path of Iredell, Justice Clifford dissented: "Where the constitution of the State contains no prohibition upon the subject . . . neither the State nor Federal courts can declare a statute of the State void as unwise, unjust, or inexpedient . . . unless it be repugnant to the Constitution," quoting Chief Justice Marshall: "The interest, wisdom, and justice of the representative body furnish the only security in a large class of cases not regulated by any constitutional provision [Bank v. Billings, 4 Peters 563]." 87 U.S. at 668–669.

of policy for judicial construction, an undefined code of ethics for the Constitution, and a court of justice for the natural legislature.[37]

That substitution persists now that "due process has come to be the main provision through which natural law theories were made a part of current constitutional law."[38] And it bears emphasis that until deep into the twentieth century the Court did not employ due process to succor the Negro for whose benefit the Fourteenth Amendment was framed, but rather as "a judicial weapon to strike down social legislation."[39]

37. Hepburn v. Griswold, 75 U.S. (8 Wall.) 603, 638 (1869), dissenting opinion. Compare Hamilton, infra Chapter 15 at note 43. "Justice Iredell's scorn of natural law as a limitation on state legislative power might be applied equally well to due process. Since this concept provided no 'fixed standard' all the Court could properly say in raising it as a constitutional bar was that the legislature had passed an act that in the opinions of the judges was inconsistent with abstract principles of justice." Mason and Beaney, supra note 1 at 412.

38. Haines, supra note 2 at 112; see also supra at notes 28–32. Professor Archibald Cox considers "the very persistence of such evocative, rather than sharply definitive, phrases, attests the strength of our natural law inheritance *as authority for legal change.*" *The Role of the Supreme Court in American Government* 113 (1976). He adds, "The Court's persistent resort to notions of substantive due process for almost a century attests the strength of our natural law inheritance in constitutional adjudication." Id. 113. To my mind it merely evidences unquenchable judicial thirst for extraconstitutional power, power that plainly was withheld. For recurrent criticism, see supra notes 6, 36, 37 and infra note 89; see also supra at notes 25–26; infra Chapter 21 at notes 60-63, 87–94. Cox himself has noted that the pre-1937 era "was marked by a vigorous reaction against natural law . . . There was a sense that the Justices made a mess of things when they attempted to enlarge their orbit." Cox, id. 34. That era has been repudiated in the field of economic-substantive due process by the Court itself. Infra at notes 77–78. And proponents of "natural law" must explain why the Founders, who manifestly excluded the judiciary from policymaking, who distrusted judicial discretion, even denied its exercise, could leave the barn door wide to unlimited discretion under natural law.

39. Wallace Mendelson, *Justices Black and Frankfurter: Conflict in the Court* 64 (1961); Wallace Mendelson, *The Supreme Court: Law and Discretion* 21 (1967). In 1917, a Negro leader "insisted on the powerful influence of Supreme Court decisions in snatching liberty from the hands of his race." Phillip S. Paludan, *A Covenant With Death* 5 (1975). See also infra Chapter 17 at notes 67–69.

"For years," Justice Douglas stated, "the Court struck down social legislation when a particular law did not fit the notions of a majority of Justices as to legislation appropriate for a free enterprise system." Poe v. Ullman, 367 U.S. 497, 517 (1961), dissenting opinion. In Ferguson v. Skrupa, 372 U.S. 726, 731 (1963), the Court itself referred to "our

The "convenient vagueness"[40] of due process is of the Court's own making. After noting the "fixed" procedural character of due process, Charles P. Curtis, who rejoiced in judicial "adaptation" of the Constitution, asked: "But who made it a large generality? Not they [the Framers]. We [the Court] did."[41] Justly did Justice Black state that "any broad unlimited power to hold laws unconstitutional because they offend what this Court conceives to be the 'conscience of our people' . . . was not given by the Framers, but rather has been bestowed on the Court by the Court."[42] It is the Court that made due process an obscurantist phrase.[43]

Among the remarkable aspects of this transformation is that Justice Frankfurter, the apostle of "self-restraint," should so warmly have embraced its end-product:[44] "once we go beyond its strictly procedural aspects . . . [it is] precisely defined by neither history nor in terms."[45] How could it be when the Court drew substantive due process out of thin air?

---

abandonment of the use of the 'vague contours' of the Due Process Clause to nullify laws which a majority of the Court believed to be economically unwise . . . We refuse to sit as a 'super-legislature to weigh the wisdom of legislation.' "

40. Supra Chapter 11 at note 2.

41. Curtis, supra Chapter 11 at note 27.

42. Griswold v. Connecticut, 381 U.S. 479, 520 (1965), dissenting opinion. Thereby the Court, as Robert G. McCloskey stated, was enabled "to invalidate any law that struck a majority of the members as 'arbitrary' or 'capricious.' Those wonderfully ambiguous definitions . . . permitted the judiciary to exercise or withhold [their judicial] veto in any given case, subject to no guiding principle except the judges' own sense of discretion." McCloskey, supra note 1 at 152.

43. Charles Fairman refers to "such obscurantist phrases as 'the spirit of our free institutions' [repudiated by Hamilton, infra Chapter 15 at note 46], 'fundamental conceptions lying at the basis of our social compact.' " *Mr. Justice Miller and the Supreme Court 1862–1890* 3 (1939). It is a tribute to the power of ceaseless repetition that even a judge so critical of judicial activism as Justice Harlan should have stated: "the very breadth and generality of the Amendment's provision suggest that its authors did not suppose that the nation would always be limited to mid-19th century conceptions of 'liberty' and 'due process of law' but that the increasing experience and evolving conscience of the American people would add new [meanings]." Duncan v. Louisiana, 391 U.S. 145, 174–175 (1968). I find some difficulty in reconciling this with his condemnation of the "reapportionment" decisions for arguably they responded to an "evolving conscience." Compare infra Chapter 17 at note 62.

44. "The course of history," he remarked, cast responsibilities upon the Court which it would be "stultification" to evade. Rochin v. California, 342 U.S. 165, 173 (1952). See also infra at note 141.

45. Frankfurter, supra note 18 at 228–229.

His revered predecessors, Justices Holmes and Brandeis, understood this full well.[46] His frequent references to the "vagueness" of due process ill fits his deference to the common law meaning of words which have a "deposit of history."[47] Whatever the scope of procedural due process, the "deposit of history" incontrovertibly shows that it did not comprehend a judicial veto of legislation on policy grounds. Frankfurter acknowledged that the "vagueness" of due process "readily lends itself to make of the Court a third chamber with drastic veto power."[48] He wrote in 1926 that, "through its steady expansion of the meaningless meaning of the 'due process' clause of the Fourteenth Amendment, the Supreme Court is putting constitutional compulsion behind the private judgment of its members upon disputed and difficult questions of social policy."[49] Now that he had donned the robe he apparently was satisfied that such power was safe in his hands—a familiar and very human reaction. But he disclaimed enforcement of his own "private view rather than the consensus of society's opinion which, for purposes of due process, is the standard enjoined by the Constitution."[50] "What is this consensus?" George Braden asked, and showed that it bristles with complexities in both definition and ascertainment.[51] "Essentially," Frankfurter explained, what is

46. Arguments contrary to the application of due process to "matters of substantive law" had seemed "persuasive" to Justice Brandeis. Whitney v. California, 274 U.S. 357, 373 (1927), concurring opinion. Shortly thereafter, Justice Holmes stated, "Of course the words 'due process of law,' if taken in their literal meaning have no application to this case; and while it is too late to deny that they have been given a much more extended artificial signification . . ." Baldwin v. Missouri, 281 U.S. 586, 595 (1930). Like Brandeis, Judge Learned Hand "considered the whole concept of [substantive] due process a judicial fabrication." Kathryn Griffith, *Judge Learned Hand and the Role of the Federal Judiciary* 129 (1973).

47. Frankfurter justly stated that "a term gains technical content" by "the deposit of history"; "No changes or chances can alter the content of the verbal symbol of 'jury.' " Rochin v. California, 342 U.S. at 169–170. Indisputably the "technical content" of "due process" was purely procedural, without a trace of "substantive" historical "content," for which we need go no further than Hamilton. See also infra Chapter 21 at note 48.

48. Supra note 18 at 229.

49. *New Republic* (1926), quoted in Philip Kurland, *Politics, the Constitution and the Warren Court* xiv (1970).

50. Louisiana ex rel. Francis v. Resweber, 329 U.S. 459, 471 (1947), concurring opinion. But compare with Hamilton, infra Chapter 17 at note 15.

51. "The Search for Objectivity in Constitutional Law," 57 Yale L.J. 571, 584–585 (1948). Among other things, given that a Justice "knows what he is looking for," how

involved is a "judgment that reflects deep, even if inarticulate, feelings of our society. Judges must divine that feeling as best they can."[52] Does not repudiation of the Court's strictures against the death penalty by legislation in some thirty-odd States demonstrate that the Court is not in possession of a divining rod?[53] The overwhelmingly negative public reaction to Frankfurter's flag-salute opinion indicates that his own powers of divination were unreliable.[54] It furnished proof for his statement that "As history amply proves, the judiciary is prone to misconceive the public good by confounding private notions with constitutional requirements,"[55] and confirmed Learned Hand's belief that the judge "has no right to divination of public opinion which runs counter to its last formal expression."[56]

---

does he "find it? By a Gallup poll? By editorials in leading newspapers . . . By the number of states which follow a given course?" Id. A Frankfurter disciple, Professor Louis Jaffe, stated, "There is no sure way to discover the conscience of the people . . . it is seldom that there is not a great contrariety of representative voices." "Was Brandeis an Activist? The Search for Intermediate Premises," 80 Harv. L. Rev. 986, 998 (1967). In fact, the Court "has demanded a number of social changes which do not command majoritarian support . . . [it] is now often declaring a rule that is unpopular." Lusky 277.

52. Haley v. Ohio, 332 U.S. 596, 603 (1948), concurring opinion. This is squarely opposed to Hamilton's assurance in Federalist No. 78. See infra Chapter 17 at note 15. Frankfurter also stated that a judge should "have antennae registering feeling and judgment beyond logical, let alone quantitative, proof." *Of Law and Men* 39 (Philip Elman ed. 1956), introducing a psychic quality that is itself beyond measurement, and not a little resembles the Chinese emperor's "mandate from heaven" of which he was the sole repository.

53. Furman v. Georgia, 408 U.S. 238 (1972). For a scathing critique of the decision, see Levy, *Against the Law* 389 et seq. In Gregg v. Georgia, 96 S. Ct. 2909, 2928 (1976), Justice Stewart acknowledged that "it is now evident that a large proportion of American society continues to regard [capital punishment] as an appropriate and necessary sanction," pointing to legislative enactments in "at least 35 states" in the wake of Furman "that provide for the death penalty."

54. Minersville School District v. Gobitis, 310 U.S. 586 (1940). Frankfurter utterly misconceived public opinion with respect to a compulsory flag salute in a public school. A. T. Mason, *The Supreme Court: Palladium of Freedom* 165 (1962). Even his close friend Harold Laski thought he was "wrong." J. P. Lash, *From the Diaries of Felix Frankfurter* 69–70 (1975).

55. A. F. of L. v. American Sash Co., 335 U.S. 538, 556 (1949), concurring opinion. Experience has shown, said Professor Lusky, "that the Justices are not endowed with divine insight into the needs of a society." Lusky 107.

56. Learned Hand, *The Spirit of Liberty* 14 (1952). [In the Chinese Exclusion Case, 130 U.S. 581, 600 (1889), the Court cited the Latin maxim leges posteriores priores con-

Frankfurter's "canons of decency and fairness which express the notions of justice of English-speaking people"[57] were scornfully dismissed—paradox of paradoxes—by Justices Black and Douglas, whose record of writing *their* predilections into the Constitution will long be unsurpassed.[58] Justice Black labeled such tests the "catchwords and catchphrases invoked by judges who would strike down under the Fourteenth Amendment laws which offend their notions of natural justice."[59] To him such tests represented a claim of "unlimited power to invalidate laws";[60] for Douglas, judgment would then turn on "the idiosyncracies of the judges."[61] Lest this stamp me as a Black partisan in his running debate with Frankfurter, let me avouch Arthur Sutherland, a Frankfurter friend. He concludes that though Justice Frankfurter was "dissatisfied" with Black's position on incorporation of the Bill of Rights in the Fourteenth Amendment, he "could find no substitute adequate to explain the revisory function of the Supreme Court," that one of his formulas "left us as much at large as we were with mere 'due process of law.'" Is "outraging the Supreme Court's sense of justice," Sutherland asked, "any more definite ... ?"[62]

---

trarias abrogant: "Later laws abrogate prior laws that are contrary to them," i.e., the last expression of the sovereign will control.]

57. Rochin v. California, 342 U.S. at 169. Dissenting from the majority's condemnation of use of a stomach pump to obtain evidence of narcotic traffic, Justice Douglas, seeing that the outlawed practice "would be admissible in the majority of states where the question has been raised," refused to hold that it violates the " 'decencies of civilized conduct' when formulated by responsible courts with judges as sensitive as we are." Id. 177–178.

58. Black was an "overpowering advocate" who believed that he "had a mission to impose his convictions on the nation," Levy, *Against the Law* 36, a conviction shared by Chief Justice Warren and Justice Douglas. Lusky stated that Black "did his full share of judicial constitution-making, stoutly maintaining all the while that he was merely following directions set forth in the text of the Constitution and its Amendments . . . [finding] meanings . . . which none of his colleagues (or any one else) could find there." Lusky 74. See also Kurland, supra note 49 at 4.

59. Griswold v. Connecticut, 381 U.S. at 511 note 4. He rang the changes on this view from Adamson v. California, 332 U.S. 46, 69 (1947), through Sniadach v. Family Finance Corp., 395 U.S. 337, 350, 351 (1969).

60. Rochin v. California, 342 U.S. at 176.

61. Id. 179; see supra note 57.

62. "Privacy in Connecticut," 64 Mich. L. Rev. 283, 285, 287 (1965). Another Frankfurter disciple, Professor Louis Jaffe, wrote, "it must be admitted that the Frankfurterian

Not that Justice Black's insistence on his "impersonal" standard was free of self-delusion. To accomplish control over the States he jumped off from the untenable assumption that the Fourteenth Amendment incorporates the Bill of Rights; upon closer examination it appears that the "specifics" of the Bill of Rights also exhibit "subjective" open spaces.[63] It would take us far afield once more to compare the Black and Frankfurter philosophies.[64] Let it suffice, as George Braden concludes, that both "put into the Fourteenth Amendment what they want to"; [e]ach theory collapses, on analysis, into little more than a front for policymaking."[65] "How can a strict constructionist, so-called, like Black," Philip Kurland rightly asks, "have acquiesced in the reapportionment cases?"[66] Those decisions, in the words of Justice Stewart, "mark a long step backward into that unhappy era when a majority of the members of the Court were thought by many to have convinced themselves and each other that the demands of the Constitution were to be measured not by what it says, but by their own notions of wise political theory."[67] Black it was who declared, "there is no constitutional support whatever for this Court to use the Due Process Clause as though it provided a blank check to alter the meaning of the Constitution as written so as to add substantive constitutional changes which a majority of the Court at any given time believes are *needed to meet present day problems.*"[68] What were the "one man, one vote" decisions in which Black concurred but exactly

---

formulation is somewhat deceptive . . . In a number of cases it is the essence of the problem that the public has been unable to clarify its conscience or formulate a position." "The Court Debated—Another View" (1960), *The New York Times Magazine*, June 5, 1960, in Levy, *Warren* 199, 205. Justice Brennan also charged Frankfurter with subjective standards, unaware, as Leonard Levy stated, that his own "were no less imprecise . . . and subjective." Levy, *Against the Law* 398.

63. See Braden, supra note 51 at 590–591; Mendelson, *Supreme Court*, supra note 39 at 25–26; Mendelson, *Black and Frankfurter*, supra note 39 at 69; Alexander Bickel, *The Least Dangerous Branch* 87–88 (1962).

64. Mendelson, *Black and Frankfurter*, id. 69; Braden, supra note 51 at 582–594.

65. Braden, id. 591, 593–594.

66. Kurland, supra note 49 at 180.

67. Lucas v. Colorado Gen. Assembly, 377 U.S. 713, 747–748 (1964), dissenting opinion.

68. Harper v. Va. Board of Elections, 383 U.S. 663, 675–676 (1966), dissenting opinion (emphasis added).

such instances? For the Fourteenth Amendment, by virtue of its unmistakable history, as good as provides that control of suffrage was left to the States.[69] And what happened, Miller and Howell justly ask, to Frankfurter's "vaunted sense of self-restraint" in the desegregation case,[70] which, to quote his condemnation of a reapportionment decision, was also "a massive repudiation of the experience of our whole past in asserting destructively novel power."[71] That case also interfered with matters that had been a matter of State concern from the beginning, and which the framers of the Fourteenth Amendment plainly intended to leave with the States. Yet Frankfurter "was wary of judicial efforts to impose Justice on the people—to force upon them 'better' government than they were able at the moment to give themselves. It was his deepest conviction that no five men, or nine, are wise enough or good enough to wield such power over an entire nation."[72] The lesson to be drawn from the cross-recriminations of the Justices is that the cry for self-restraint is directed to the other fellow, to decry identification of *his* predilections with constitutional mandates.[73] Each Justice has a blind spot for the identification of his own predilections with constitutional dogma. A beautiful illustration is furnished by Justice Douglas in the contraceptive case *Griswold v. Connecticut*: "We do not sit as a super-legislature to determine the wisdom, need, and propriety of laws that touch economic problems . . . or social conditions. This law, however, operated directly on an intimate relation of husband and wife."[74] The inarticulate premise, as Alpheus Thomas Mason points out, is that "the Court does

69. In Oregon v. Mitchell, 400 U.S. 112, 124–125 (1970), Justice Black stated, "My Brother Harlan has persuasively demonstrated that the Framers . . . intended the States to keep for themselves, as provided in the Tenth Amendment, the power to regulate elections . . . I agree as to the States' power to regulate the elections of their own officials."

70. "The Myth of Neutrality in Constitutional Adjudication," 27 U. Chi. L. Rev. 661, 699 note 108 (1960). Compare supra Chapter 7 at notes 47–53. Justice Frankfurter observed that "The Court is not saved from being oligarchic because it professes to act in the service of humane ends." A. F. of L. v. American Sash Co., 335 U.S. at 555–556.

71. Baker v. Carr, 369 U.S. 186, 267 (1962), dissenting opinion.

72. Mendelson, *Supreme Court*, supra note 39 at 14.

73. Mendelson refers to the "ancient tradition of restraint which all American judges have professed—when their particular 'preferred place' values were not at stake." Id. 13.

74. 381 U.S. at 482; A. T. Mason, "The Burger Court in Historical Perspective," 47 N.Y. State Bar J. 87, 89 (1975); cf. Justice White, infra note 121.

sit as a super-legislature in safeguarding the penumbral rights of privacy."[75] To justify the differentiation Douglas relies on the cobwebby "penumbras formed by emanations,"[76] but in essence he exemplifies the readiness of the Justices to act as a "super-legislature" when their own emotions are engaged.

In the economic realm the Court itself has confessed error. In 1970 it recalled the "era when the Court thought the Fourteenth Amendment gave it power to strike down state laws 'because they may be unwise, improvident, or out of harmony with a particular school of thought' . . . That era has long ago passed into history."[77] "We have returned," it said on another occasion, "to the original constitutional proposition that courts do not substitute their social and economic beliefs for the judgment of legislative bodies who are elected to pass laws,"[78] as had earlier been stated by Justice Holmes.[79] These statements, however, are only accurate in part. At the same time it engaged in this overdue renunciation of usurped power in the economic sphere, the Court expanded the application of substantive due process to libertarian categories to which at length it assigned a "preferred position." To the uninitiated it might seem that if the Fourteenth Amendment, in Justice Holmes' famous phrase, "does not enact Herbert Spencer's Social Statics,"[80] no more does it incorporate Kenneth Clark's social psychology.[81] In this Black and Frankfurter professedly were in accord. Justice Frankfurter stated: "The Constitution does not give us greater veto power when dealing with one phase of liberty than another . . . Our power does not vary according to the particular provision of the Bill of Rights which is invoked."[82] Justice Black affirmed that "The Due Process Clause with an

75. Mason, supra note 74 at 89.

76. 381 U.S. at 484.

77. Dandridge v. Williams, 397 U.S. 471, 485 (1970); see supra note 39.

78. Ferguson v. Skrupa, 372 U.S. at 730.

79. "I cannot believe that the Amendment was intended to give us *carte blanche* to embody our economic or moral beliefs in its prohibitions." Baldwin v. Missouri, 281 U.S. 586, 595 (1930), dissenting opinion.

80. Lochner v. New York, 198 U.S. 45, 75 (1905), dissenting opinion.

81. Clark's psychology was invoked by Chief Justice Warren in Brown v. Board of Education, 347 U.S. 483, 494 note 11 (1954).

82. Board of Education v. Barnette, 319 U.S. 624, 648 (1943), dissenting opinion.

'arbitrary and capricious' or 'shocking to the conscience' formula was liberally used by this Court to strike down economic legislation . . . That formula, based on subjective considerations of 'natural justice,' is no less dangerous when used to enforce this Court's views about personal rights than those about economic rights."[83] The logic that bars the one equally bars the other.

History reveals that property actually was more highly prized by the Founders than "civil liberties." "The great and chief end . . . of men," Locke wrote, in "putting themselves under government, is the preservation of their property."[84] For the Founders property "was the basic liberty, because until a man was secure in his property, until it was protected from arbitrary seizure, life and liberty could mean little."[85] Hence they "warmly endorsed John Adams' deep-seated conviction that 'property is as sacred as the laws of God' ";[86] and such views were expressed in the Convention by Madison: "The primary objects of civil society are in the security of property and the public safety."[87] Neither the Fifth nor the Fourteenth Amendment drew a distinction between "liberty" and "property," and, as Learned Hand remarked, the Framers would have regarded the current reading of the Fifth Amendment as "constituting severer restrictions as to Liberty than Property" as a "strange anomaly." "There is no constitutional basis," he averred, "for asserting

83. Griswold v. Connecticut, 381 U.S. at 522, dissenting opinion.

84. 2 John Locke, *Treatise on Government*, Chapter 2, quoted in J. R. Randall, *The Making of the Modern Mind* 343, 342 (1940).

85. 1 Page Smith, *John Adams* 272 (1962). Anatole France made the point ironically: the poor are as free as the rich to sleep under a bridge. ["For most men, to be deprived of . . . private property would be a far greater and more deeply felt loss of liberty than to be deprived of the right to speak freely." Michael Oakeshott, *Rationalism in Politics* 44 (1962), quoted in James McClellan, *Joseph Story and the American Constitution* 236 (1971). Lynch v. Household Finance Corp., 405 U.S. 538 (1972): ". . . there is no real dichotomy between personal liberties and property rights."]

86. Mason, supra note 74 at 91.

87. 1 Farrand 147. Justice William Paterson, a leading Framer, declared in 1795 that "The preservation of property, then, is the primary object of the social compact." Van Horne's Lessee v. Dorrance, 2 U.S. (2 Dall.) 304, 309 (1795). Quoting Lord Camden in Entick v. Carrington, 19 How. St. Tr. 1029, 1066 (1765), the Supreme Court declared, "The great end for which men entered into society was to secure their property. That right is preserved sacred." Boyd v. United States, 116 U.S. 616, 627 (1886).

a larger measure of judicial supervision over" liberty than property.[88] There is no escape, to my mind, from Stanley Morrison's summation that the difference merely represents "the subjective preferences or convictions of the individual judge."[89]

To this Fred Rodell replies that "regardless of syllogistic consistency about judicial review—this nation puts, or should put, a higher premium on individual dignities and freedoms than on material matters like the getting and keeping of money, and that the Court should honor that preference under the Constitution." Patently what this nation "should put" merely reflects Rodell's own preferences; whether the "nation puts" raises the question: at what point in time? Not from 1788 to the mid-twentieth century of a certainty. If it be the nation today, we have only Rodell's conjecture, a very insecure footing for constitutional doctrine. Leonard Levy correctly points out that such views merely reject the Court's earlier economic predilections because they were "illiberal," not because the Court "made policy," often arbitrarily. And he comments that this view "loses nothing of its monstrous character when the Court is praised sim-

88. Hand, supra note 3 at 50, 51. Commenting on the theory that " 'personal liberties' deserve more stringent protection than 'property rights' because society should assign them greater value," Archibald Cox justly observes that "The rationale merely asserts the conclusion." "The New Dimensions of Constitutional Adjudication," 51 Wash. L. Rev. 791, 797–798 (1976).

89. "What Mr. Justice Black has voted to do [in Adamson] is to abolish substantive due process in the economic field and preserve it in the field of civil liberties. This, however, represents a logical difficulty which is nearly insuperable. If substantive due process is a natural-law gloss in the economic field, it is just as much so in the field of civil liberties. There is no basis for rejecting the doctrine in the one case and adopting it in the other except the subjective preferences of the individual judge. History affords no justification for the choice made. Thus the judge who resorts to natural law to protect civil liberty is using the same techniques as the judges who resorted to natural law to protect economic liberty." Stanley Morrison, "Does the Fourteenth Amendment Include the Bill of Rights?," 2 Stan. L. Rev. 140, 167 (1949). Chief Justice Stone said as much in 1945, see infra at note 137. As late as 1956 the Court held that "as no constitutional guarantee enjoys preference, so none should suffer subordination." Ullmann v. United States, 350 U.S. 422, 428 (1956). Professor Herbert Packer stated, "I find it extraordinarily difficult to draw a distinction between 'economic' legislation and legislation that affects 'fundamental rights.' " "The Aim of the Criminal Law Revisited: A Plea for a New Look at 'Substantive Due Process,' " 44 S. Cal. L. Rev. 490, 493 (1971). See also Levy, *Against the Law* 239; Justices Black and Frankfurter, supra at notes 82 and 83.

ply for reaching the right or just result."[90] Let us now briefly consider the means whereby the distinction was judicially fashioned.

### From Economic Due Process to the "Preferred Position"

The "preferred position" assigned by the Court to "civil liberties" may be traced back to the brief vogue of "liberty of contract." To preserve it, the Court struck down a statute in *Lochner v. New York* (1905)[91] that limited working hours to 10 hours daily and 60 weekly as an interference with a bakery worker's right to work longer hours. Casuistry seldom rose to greater heights. "There is grim irony," Justice Stone later wrote, "in speaking of the freedom of contract of those who, because of their economic necessities, give their services for less than is needful to keep body and soul together."[92] First adopted in *Allgeyer v. Louisiana* (1897),[93] "liberty of contract" flourished so lustily that by 1923 Justice McReynolds could say in *Meyer v. Nebraska*, "without doubt, it denotes not merely freedom from bodily restraint."[94] History disproves the claim. The learning was assembled in two landmark articles by Charles E. Shattuck (1891)[95] and Charles Warren (1926).[96] After collating the earlier history, Shattuck noted Blackstone's summation, defining per-

90. Rodell, "The Crux of the Court Hullabaloo," *The New York Times Magazine*, May 29, 1960, quoted in Levy, *Warren* 192, 195; Levy, id. 186; cf. Cox, supra note 88.

91. 198 U.S. 45 (1905).

92. Morehead v. Tipaldo, 298 U.S. 587, 632 (1936), dissenting opinion. A revealing glimpse of the callousness of the class to which Lochner catered is afforded by the remark of Joseph Choate, the most eminent lawyer of his day, that he saw no reason why "a big husky Irish washerwoman should not work more than ten hours a day in a laundry if she and her employer so desired." Quoted in Ernest Samuels, *Henry Adams: The Major Phase* 412 (1964).

93. 165 U.S. 578 (1897); C. Warren, supra note 33 at 448. But Justice Holmes wrote, "The earlier decisions . . . began within our memory and went no farther than an unpretentious assertion of the liberty to follow the ordinary callings. Later that innocuous generality was expanded into the dogma, Liberty of Contract . . . It is merely an example of doing what you want to do, embodied in the word liberty." Adkins v. Children's Hospital, 261 U.S. 525, 568 (1923), dissenting opinion.

94. 262 U.S. 390, 399 (1923).

95. "The True Meaning of the Term 'Liberty' in Those Clauses in the Federal and State Constitutions Which Protect 'Life, Liberty and Property,'" 4 Harv. L. Rev. 365.

96. Supra note 33.

sonal liberty as the "power of locomotion, of changing situation . . . without imprisonment or restraint of the person."[97] When Warren reviewed the materials some twenty-five years later, he concluded, "there seems to be little question that, under the common law, 'liberty' meant simply 'liberty of the person,' or in other words, 'the right to have one's person free from physical restraint.' "[98] This was the established connotation of "liberty" when the Thirteen State constitutions adopted the "life, liberty, or property" phrase.

Before "liberty of contract" was abandoned, the Justices had timidly extended the concept of "liberty" to freedom of speech. As late as 1922 the Court had held that the Constitution "imposes upon the States no obligation to confer upon those within their jurisdiction . . . the right of free speech."[99] Three years later, in *Gitlow v. New York*, the Court "assume[d] that freedom of speech and of the press are among the fundamental personal rights and 'liberties' protected by the due process clause of the Fourteenth Amendment from impairment by the States."[100] Justice Holmes furnished the clue in his dissenting opinion: free speech "must be taken to be included in the Fourteenth Amendment *in view of the scope that has been given* to the word 'liberty.' "[101] But this was precarious footing; Justice Brandeis averred that free speech and press are protected "from invasion by the States" because they are "fundamental rights comprised within the term 'liberty.' " In one of his finest perorations he attributed it to those "who won our independence," who believed "that this should be a fundamental principle of the American gov-

97. Shattuck, supra note 95 at 377; for Blackstone, see supra Chapter 2 at note 3.

98. Warren, supra note 33 at 440. ["Prior to the Civil War American constitutional law and theory evince a quite surprising unconcern regarding 'liberty' . . . So far as the power of the states was involved, in brief liberty was the liberty which the *ordinary* law allowed and nothing more." Edward S. Corwin, *The Twilight of the Supreme Court* 78 (1934) (emphasis in original).]

99. Prudential Ins. Co. v. Cheek, 259 U.S. 530, 538 (1922).

100. 268 U.S. 652, 666 (1925).

101. Id. 672 (emphasis added). But compare supra note 93. [Justice Brandeis reported that "Holmes was against extending the Fourteenth Amendment. But that meant, Brandeis said, that 'you are going to cut down freedom through striking down regulation of property, but not give protection' (to freedom in other contexts). Alexander Bickel, *The Supreme Court and the Idea of Progress* 27 (1978).]

ernment."[102] Brandeis' attribution to the Founders, as will appear, falls afoul of historical fact. On the eve of *Gitlow*, his foremost disciple, Professor Frankfurter, wrote: "Even the most rampant worshipper of judicial supremacy admits that wisdom and justice are not the tests of constitutionality . . . Particularly in legislation affecting freedom of thought and freedom of speech much that is illiberal would be clearly constitutional."[103] In the post–Warren Court euphoria, when the test of constitutionality is assumed to be that the result is socially desirable, we are apt to overlook Chief Justice Marshall's caution that "The peculiar circumstances of the moment may render a measure more or less wise, but cannot render it more or less constitutional."[104]

Charles Warren tellingly argues that the "free speech" of the First Amendment could not have been comprehended in the due process of the Fifth Amendment because, "having already provided in the First Amendment an *absolute prohibition* on Congress to take away certain rights," it is "hardly conceivable that the framers" would, in the Fifth, provide that "*Congress might take away* the same rights by due process of law."[105]

"The right of free speech," Warren points out, "was not included as one of a person's fundamental . . . rights in any Bill of Rights adopted by any of the States prior to the Federal Constitution."[106] More important, when the First Amendment was proposed, Madison urged the First Congress that "it was equally necessary that [free speech] be secured against

102. Whitney v. California, 274 U.S. 357, 373, 375 (1927), concurring opinion.

103. "Can the Supreme Court Guarantee Toleration?" 43 *New Republic* 85, 87 (1925), quoted in Mendelson, *Black and Frankfurter*, supra note 39 at 54.

104. Supra note 24 at 190–191. "The criterion of constitutionality," said Justice Holmes, "is not whether we believe the law to be for the public good." Adkins v. Children's Hospital, 261 U.S. at 570, dissenting opinion.

105. Warren, supra note 33 at 441.

106. Id. 461. I have checked the constitutions of the original thirteen States and would add a qualification. Article XII of the 1776 Pennsylvania Constitution provided, "the people have a right to freedom of speech, and of writing, and publishing their sentiments; therefore the freedom of the press ought not to be restrained." A similar provision was contained in the 1786 Constitution of Vermont. 2 Poore 1542, 1869. The prohibition, however, is confined to the press. Most of the other States mention only free press.

the State Governments," but his plea was fruitless.[107] Jefferson, the great champion of free speech and free press, wrote in 1804 to Abigail Adams: "While we deny that Congress have a right to controul the freedom of the press, we have ever asserted the rights of the states, and their exclusive right to do so."[108] This was the premise on which the First Congress had acted. One may agree with Justice Cardozo that free speech is "the matrix, the indispensable condition, of nearly every other form of freedom,"[109] but the fact remains that the one time the American people had the opportunity to express themselves on whether free speech was "so rooted in the tradition and conscience of our people as to be ranked as fundamental"[110] was in the First Congress, which drafted the Bill of Rights in response to popular demand. There they voted down interference with State control. Justice Byron White brushed the 1789 history aside as of "little relevance in interpreting the Due Process Clause of the Fourteenth Amendment, adopted specifically to place limitations upon the States."[111] That begs the question. Where is the evidence that in 1866 the framers meant to advance beyond the limited goals of the Civil Rights Act? Where is the evidence that they meant to enlarge the meaning due process had for the Founders in 1789? Instead, the record establishes that the framers had limited objectives; that they carefully avoided encroaching on the States beyond those limits; that they chose technical words apt for their purpose, which, in the case of due process, meant to them access to the courts according to due course of law, not a roving commission to revise State institutions.[112] On the heels of the Fourteenth Amendment Thomas Cooley concluded that "Obstacles

107. Warren, supra note 33 at 434, 435; 1 *Annals of Congress* 435, 755.

108. September 11, 1804, quoted in Frankfurter, supra note 18 at 226; see also Bork, "Neutral Principles and Some First Amendment Problems," 47 Ind. L.J. 1, 22 (1971).

109. Palko v. Connecticut, 302 U.S. 319, 327 (1937).

110. Id. 325.

111. Duncan v. Louisiana, 391 U.S. 145, 153 note 20 (1968).

112. My search of the debates in the 39th Congress turned up two expressions (there may be others) respecting freedom of speech. Price remarked that "for the last thirty years a citizen of a free State dared not express his opinion on the subject of slavery in a slave State," but at the same time he construed "privileges or immunities" to afford to a Northern visitor "the same protection" that a Southern State accorded to its own citizens. *Globe* 1066; see also the remarks of Broomall, id. 1263. Southern citizens, however, enjoyed no greater right to attack the sacred institution—the subject was taboo. Edmund

stood in the way of an unconditional commitment to human freedom. Innovations, he believed, required historical basis, and American history was singularly lacking in precedents for national power used in behalf of individual freedom."[113]

Charles Warren had prophesied in 1926 that by enlarging the Fourteenth Amendment to protect free speech, the Court had opened the door to adoption of the rest of the Bill of Rights.[114] Faced with mounting pressure to do so, Justice Cardozo, in *Palko v. Connecticut* (1937), fashioned a confining doctrine—"ordered liberty": some "immunities that are valid as against the federal government by force of the specific pledges of particular amendments have been found to be implicit in the concept of ordered liberty, and thus, through the Fourteenth Amendment, become valid as against the States."[115] Such portions of the Bill of Rights as had been "absorbed" in the Amendment rested on "the belief that neither liberty nor justice would exist if they were sacrificed." "Absorption" proceeded from those "principle[s] of justice so rooted in the tradition and conscience of our people as to be ranked as fundamental."[116] As in the case of the Chinese "mandate from heaven," we learn a right is "fundamental" only after the Court attaches that label.[117] Cardozo, it needs to be borne in mind, took due process as it was handed to him and therefore could say, "Out of the vague precepts of the Fourteenth Amendment a court frames a rule which is general in form."[118] "Ordered liberty," as Louis Lusky states, "is too vague to describe a national objective. It says that order and liberty are both to be sought, but provides no standard for reconciling the eternal conflict between them."

---

Wilson, *Patriotic Gore* 4, 228, 365 (1962); Kenneth M. Stampp, *The Peculiar Institution* 211–212, 28 (1956). The free speech sought by Price, as in the case of other privileges, was that accorded by the States, provided that it was nondiscriminatory.

113. Paludan, supra note 39 at 263.

114. Warren, supra note 33 at 458-460.

115. 302 U.S. at 324–325.

116. Id. 326, 325, quoted more fully supra at note 110.

117. See infra at note 139. "[W]hether a particular right is denominated as 'fundamental,'" Lusky comments, "depends upon a value judgment so broad" as to be unverifiable "by reference to any known standard." Lusky 264. "[T]here is no authoritative schedule of fundamental rights." Jaffe, supra note 51 at 998.

118. Snyder v. Massachusetts, 291 U.S. 97, 114 (1934).

"It is a vehicle," he justly comments, "for whatever meaning the Court gives it, and thus enables the Court to apply its own conceptions of public policy."[119] Several Justices concur in this view. In a book written by Justice Owen Roberts after his retirement, he stated, in a passage quoted by Justice Douglas, that the cases will fall "on the one side of the line or the other as a majority of nine justices appraise conduct as either implicit in the concept of ordered liberty or as lying without the confines of that vague concept."[120] Justice Byron White likewise regards the concept as no more than a means whereby a majority of the Court can impose "its own philosophical predilections upon State legislatures or Congress."[121] And Justice Black maintained that the concept merely embodied " 'natural law due process' notion[s] by which this Court frees itself from the limits of a written Constitution."[122] Like that of Brandeis, Cardozo's reliance on the "traditions and conscience of our people" is rebutted by the refusal of the First Congress to proscribe *State* interference with free speech and free press. That, to borrow from Learned Hand, was the "last formal expression" of the will of the people. No departure from that will can be found in the history of the Fourteenth Amendment; instead, but for the narrow enclave of the Civil Rights Act, the framers plainly withheld from the Court power to intrude into State regulation of domestic affairs.

119. Lusky 107, 105; see also Jaffe, supra note 51 at 997.

120. *The Court and the Constitution* 80 (1951), quoted in Poe v. Ullman, 367 U.S. at 518–519, dissenting opinion. "Of course," Roberts added, ". . . in this view, the due process clause of the Fifth Amendment . . . may be repetitious of many of the other guaranties of the first eight amendments and may render many of their provisions superfluous," a result that argues against the "absorption" view.

121. Dissenting in Robinson v. California, 370 U.S. 660, 689 (1962), Justice White stated, "I suspect the Court was hard put to find a way to ascribe to the Framers of the Constitution the result reached today rather than to its own notion of ordered liberty. If this case involved economic regulation, the present Court's allergy to substantive due process would surely save the statute and prevent the Court from imposing its own philosophical predilections upon State legislatures or Congress. I fail to see why the Court deems it more appropriate to write into the Constitution its own abstract notions of how best to handle the narcotics problem, for it obviously cannot match either the States or Congress in expert understanding."

122. In re Winship, 397 U.S. 358, 381–382 (1970), dissenting opinion.

About four months after *Palko*, Lusky tells us, Justice Stone, in a foot-note to *United States v. Carolene Products Co.,*[123] "undertook to articulate a more satisfactory justification."[124] At that time Lusky was Justice Stone's law clerk, and he submitted a draft of what eventuated as the second and third paragraphs of the footnote.[125] "It is unnecessary to con-sider," reads paragraph two, "whether legislation which restricts those political processes which can ordinarily be expected to bring about re-peal of undesirable legislation is to be subjected to more exacting scru-tiny . . . than are most other types of legislation." "Nor need we en-quire," paragraph three states, whether statutes that impinge upon religious or racial minorities that were objects of prejudice which might hamper relief through political processes should also be subjected to "more searching judicial scrutiny."[126] Thus, by a disclaimer of the need to decide, in a case that had "curiously not involved liberties in any way,"[127] the Court, as it has so often done, launched a major constitu-tional doctrine. Notwithstanding that it was tucked away in a footnote, it "disturbed" Chief Justice Hughes; consequently, the present first para-graph was added, stating that "there may be a narrower scope" for op-eration of the presumption of constitutionality when legislation "ap-pears on its face to be within a specific prohibition of the Constitution, such as those of the first ten amendments . . when held to be embraced within the Fourteenth."[128] Paragraph one was designed to qualify the second and third paragraphs in order to still Hughes' doubts, as the ex-changes between him and Stone make plain.

Lusky explains that paragraphs two and three "make no reference to the words or intentions of the Constitutors. They speak, rather of the dynamics of government," that is, they assume that "government by the people, and government for the whole people" are "fairly ascribable to

123. 304 U.S. 144 (1938).

124. Lusky 108.

125. A. T. Mason, *Harlan Fiske Stone: Pillar of the Law* 513 (1956); Mason, *The Su-preme Court*, supra note 54 at 151–159.

126. 304 U.S. at 152–153 note 4.

127. Paul Murphy, *The Constitution in Crisis Times, 1918–1969* at 182.

128. Mason, *The Supreme Court*, supra note 54 at 155. In his reply to Hughes, Stone stated that the footnote was a caveat, "without, however, committing the Court to any notion contained in it." Id.

the Constitutors," and that the Court has a "special ability to effectuate them" by acting in the two described situations.[129] And it is the Court itself which is to decide for which purposes it has "special aptitude."[130] Once more the "genius of government" is to override the sovereignty in domestic matters that the Framers reserved to the States; once more their rejection of judicial participation in policymaking[131] and the reservation in 1866 of suffrage and other local matters to the States is ignored. Although the Hughes first paragraph seems narrower, Lusky considers that by it "the Court is left entirely at large. There is virtually no limit to its ability to attribute new meaning to the 'specific prohibitions,' once it is liberated from the need to interpret them as the Constitutors expected." This has "come to be known as the 'preferred position' theory, which affirms that certain rights are . . . so important that the Court should protect them . . . and that the Court's power to select them is limited only by its ability to manipulate words contained in the Constitution. It . . . assumes that any meaning the Court chooses to ascribe to the sacred text will be accepted as authentic revelation."[132] These strictures, it seems to me, are no less applicable to a theory divorced from "the words or intentions of the Constitutors" and founded on "the dynamics of government."

Lusky's pronounced preference for the Stone-Lusky second and third paragraphs of the *Carolene* footnote derives from the belief that it fits in with his newly fashioned theory of the Court's "implied power" to revise the Constitution, his answer to the anguished question, "*By what right* does it revise the Constitution?"[133] His search for a new theory to undergird judicial revision testifies that the footnote is without constitutional roots, that as George Braden says, "it is simply a part of one man's set of values for his society which he holds strongly enough to be willing to enforce when the opportunity arises."[134]

129. Lusky 109.

130. "The Court must take the responsibility for proclaiming its own superior fitness to attain the objective." Lusky 112.

131. Infra Chapter 16.

132. Lusky 111–112.

133. Id. 19.

134. Braden, supra note 51 at 581.

Stone himself, according to Lusky, "seems to have underestimated" the importance of the distinction Lusky draws,[135] illustrating anew the tendency to read into an utterance meaning never contemplated by the author. And before long he was disenchanted with the course pursued by the Court. Long before the Warren Court worked its revolution,[136] Chief Justice Stone wrote (1945): "My more conservative brethren in the old days [read their preferences] into the Constitution . . . [H]istory is repeating itself. The Court is now in as much danger of becoming a legislative and Constitution making body, enacting into law its own pre-dilections, as it was then."[137] His forebodings were overfulfilled; "the Warren Court," Archibald Cox stated, "behaved even more like a Council of Wise Men and less like a Court than the *laissez faire* Justices."[138] Once again Stone exemplifies that the measure of tolerance is effectua-

135. Lusky 312.

136. Infra Chapter 15 note 1. Levy observes that to the eyes of "both the Court's admirers and critics . . . the Justices seemed to consider themselves as movers and shakers of the country's destiny rather than as impersonal spokesmen for the law." Levy, *Warren* 5; cf. infra Chapter 17 note 55.

Professor Abram Chayes remarks that judicial action in the last two decades "adds up to a radical transformation of the role and function of the judiciary in American life . . . Its chief function now is as a catalyst of social change with judges acting as planners of large scale." "The New Judiciary," 28 Harv. L. Sch. Bull. 23, 24 (1976). To accomplish the reform, Archibald Cox states, the courts have been required "to formulate controversial programmes of affirmative action requiring detailed administration for protracted periods under constant judicial supervision." Cox, supra note 38 at 77, a remarkable departure from the nay-saying role of the laissez faire Court. "The decrees thus directly regulate the lives of millions of people without a voice in the decision." Id. 87. See infra Appendix B.

137. A. T. Mason, *Security Through Freedom: American Political Thought and Practice* 145–146 (1955). "Justice Stone was no rabid proponent of expanded judicial power." Lusky 83. Justice Frankfurter was "vehemently opposed to the preferred freedom concept." Mason, *The Supreme Court*, supra note 54 at 173. Judge Learned Hand likewise stated, "I do not think that the interests mentioned in the First Amendment are entitled in point of constitutional interpretation to a measure of protection different from other interests." Hand, supra note 3 at 56. "As several of the Justices have noted in dissent, there is only a verbal difference between the 'fundamental rights' branch of the compelling governmental interest test and the now discredited due process of such cases as Lochner v. New York (1905). Both of them leave the Court entirely at large, with full freedom to enact its own natural law conceptions. The only difference is in the type of interests that are protected." Lusky 266.

138. Cox, supra note 38 at 50.

tion of one's own predilections; when they are exceeded at the hands of other Justices, they are anathematized.

This drastically telescoped survey of divers judicial rationalizations of expanded judicial revision for the benefit of libertarian ideals underlines the wisdom of Judge Learned Hand's conclusion that judges

> wrap up their veto in a protective veil of adjectives such as . . . "reasonable," "inherent," "fundamental" . . . whose office usually, though quite innocently, is to disguise what they are doing and impute to it a derivation far more impressive than their personal preferences, which are all that in fact lie behind the decision.[139]

Because Frankfurter overlooked the fact that "due process" was not a provision "without a fixed technical meaning"—minimally it excluded control over legislation, both in 1789 and 1866—he could allude to "the evolution of social policy by way of judicial application of Delphic provisions of the Constitution."[140] And struggling to arrive at an adequate rationalization of the "desegregation" decision, Frankfurter, we are told, stated in the Conference of the Justices: "It was too bad history had conspired to make the Court the trustee of that incorrigible changeling, the due process clause, and therefore impose upon the Justices a policy-making function unlike that borne by any other court in any other nation."[141] The burden, however, was self-assumed—not unlike the "white man's burden" once employed to justify imperialism. On the most charitable view, Justice Frankfurter had induced a state of self-hypnosis by his frequent incantations to the "convenient vagueness" of due process. Justice Harlan was content, in a case that outraged his sympathies, to state that the historical arguments, among others the limitation of due process to "procedural fairness," "have not been accepted by this Court as

---

139. Hand, supra note 3 at 70; see also Justice Holmes, supra note 93.

140. Frankfurter, supra note 18 at 229, 231. In 1930, however, Professor Frankfurter wrote, "let us face the fact that five Justices of the Supreme Court *are* molders of policy, rather than impersonal vehicles of revealed truth." "The Supreme Court and the Public," 83 Forum 329, 334 (1930), quoted in A. T. Mason, "Myth and Reality in Supreme Court Drama," 48 Va. L. Rev. 1385, 1397 (1962).

141. Richard Kluger, *Simple Justice* 681 (1976). Apparently this is based on a reconstruction of Justice Burton's notes, id. 680. Compare with Frankfurter's views supra at notes 49 and 72.

delineating its scope."[142] Yet he later insisted, with respect to suffrage, that the Court was bound by the framers' intention to exclude it from the scope of the Fourteenth Amendment.

With vision unclouded by claims to power, there is no reason why students of the judicial process should be caught in such toils. It is their duty to discern and proclaim that it is the judges, not the Constitution, that speak, as Frankfurter himself advised President Franklin Roosevelt on the eve of the Court-packing plan,[143] just as in a simpler age the words which fell from the lips of the Delphic Oracle were spoken into a speaking tube by priests secreted below.

Those who consider that judgment is inescapably subjective will chortle that thus far I have merely proved the obvious. But even in their magisterial survey of such inescapability, Arthur S. Miller and Ronald F. Howell state: "It is, of course, only those constitutional provisions of inherent ambiguity that pose problems of interpretation. Where the intention is clear . . . no interpretation is necessary. "[144] Even less is 180-degree *revision* "necessary"; the "ambiguity" of substantive due process was not "inherent" but judicially contrived. Miller and Howell, however, suggest a constrictive criterion, instancing "clear" provisions for the number of Senators, for a President and a Vice-President, and dismissing as a "filo-pietistic notion" something "called the intention of the framers."[145] Nevertheless, they do not suggest that "the judge is wholly free" to sit "kadi-like under a tree dispensing 'justice' by whim or caprice," calling attention to one limitation on such freedom—

142. Poe v. Ullman, 367 U.S. at 540, dissenting opinion: "I believe that a statute, making it a criminal offense for *married* couples to use contraceptives" invades privacy "in the most intimate concerns of an individual's personal life." Id. 539.

143. "People have been taught to believe that when the Supreme Court speaks it is not they who speak but the Constitution, whereas, of course, in so many vital cases, it is *they* who speak and *not* the Constitution. And I verily believe that that is what the country needs most to understand." *Roosevelt and Frankfurter: Their Correspondence, 1928–1945* 383 (M. Freedman ed. 1967). Shortly before Solicitor General Robert H. Jackson became a Justice he wrote, "This political role ["continuous constitutional convention"] of the Court has been obscure to laymen—even to most lawyers." *The Struggle for Judicial Supremacy* xi (1941).

144. Miller and Howell, supra note 70 at 683.

145. Id.

"adherence to precedent."[146] Why should "adherence to precedent" rise above effectuation of the framers' clearly expressed intention, which expresses the value choices of the sovereign people, not merely of judicial predecessors? The Justices themselves are by no means in accord with the now widely shared Miller-Howell view that it is the function of the Court to "update the Constitution."[147] The powerful and repeated dissents across the judicial spectrum, condemning or disclaiming subjective judgment, evidence ongoing soul-searching by members of the Court whether the broad policymaking role academe strenuously defends[148] comports with constitutional limits and the demands of a democratic society.

But this in turn compels us to face the naked question wrung from the lips of Graham. Confronted with the framers' imperfect "understanding of equal protection as applied to educational matters," their acceptance of "segregation in schools," he stated:

> To argue that this means we today are bound by that understanding and practice is to transform the mores and laws of slave code days into constitutional sanctions impossible to be cast off or even moderated ... Does it follow—dare it follow ... [that] we *today* are bound by that imperfect understanding of *equal protection* of the laws?[149]

Graham's inarticulate premise was that change could not be accomplished by amendment as the Constitution provides—desegregation could not win assent of two-thirds of the Congress and three-fourths of the States. Accordingly, it fell to the Court to strike the shackles of the past. Whence does the Court derive the power to free the American people from the "chains of the Constitution," from the "tyranny of the dead," that is, the Founders? Such questions will be considered in subsequent chapters.

146. Id. 676.

147. Id. 684; see also Levy, *Against the Law* 29, 30.

148. Levy id; Miller and Howell, supra note 70 at 689–693. "As dissenting Justices complain ever more often that the Court has revised rather than followed the Constitution, one's readiness to discount their charges as disgruntled polemic becomes gradually less confident." Lusky 75.

149. Graham 290 note 70, 291.

# Supplementary Note on Natural Law and the Constitution[*]

Charles McIlwain observed that natural law appeared "remarkably late" in English law, largely as an attempt to "account for a body of customary law which had long been in existence."[1] Of its surfacing in the United States, cloaked in the garb of substantive due process, Justice Hugo Black justly stated that it was a notion "by which this Court frees itself from the limits of a written Constitution."[2] It is difficult to conclude that the States, whose jealousy of a centralized federal regime moved them grudgingly to dole out enumerated powers while reserving to themselves "residuary, inviolable sovereignty,"[3] nailed down by the Tenth Amendment, left room for resort to natural law that would set their efforts at naught. For natural law little differs from a Chinese emperor's "mandate from heaven," which was "so vague that emperors could readily identify their own will with the will of Heaven."[4]

This was well understood by Justice James Iredell, who declared in *Calder v. Bull* that "the Court cannot pronounce [a statute] to be void, merely because it is in their judgment, contrary to the principles of natural justice. The ideas of natural justice are regulated by no fixed standard: the ablest and purest of men have differed upon the subject."[5] True,

---

[*] For more detailed discussion, see Raoul Berger, "Natural Law and Judicial Review: Reflections of an Earthbound Lawyer," 61 U. Cin. L. Rev. 51 (1992).

1. " '[T]he life and soul of English law has ever been precedent' . . . [O]f a purely speculative basis for the law there is no trace till times that are almost modern. The law of nature, or whatever that speculative basis may be called, appears remarkably late, and when it first appears it comes largely as an attempt . . . to account for a body of customary law which has long been in existence, and whose binding character is unquestioned." Charles H. McIlwain, *The High Court of Parliament and Its Supremacy* 97 (1910). See also Holdsworth, supra Supplementary Note on the Civil Rights Act and the Fourteenth Amendment, text accompanying note 57.

2. In re Winship, 397 U.S. 358, 381–382 (1970), dissenting opinion.

3. Federalist No. 39 at 249 (Mod. Lib. ed. 1937).

4. Herbert Muller, *Uses of the Past* 350 (1952). Dean Pound characterized natural law as "purely personal and arbitrary." Roscoe Pound, "Common Law and Legislation," 21 Harv. L. Rev. 383, 393 (1908).

5. 3 U.S. (3 Dall.) 386, 399 (1798).

Justice Samuel Chase invoked supraconstitutional law,[6] but in what may be regarded as a more solidly rooted decision, he rejected a federal common law of crimes, saying, "the Constitution of the Union, is the source of *all* the jurisdiction of the national government; so that the departments of the government can *never assume any* power that is not expressly granted by that instrument."[7]

A pioneer student of natural law in America, Benjamin Wright, wrote of the Founders, "there were few appeals to the laws of nature . . . with a few exceptions they simply found it unnecessary to their immediate purposes."[8] Consider Edmund Randolph's commonsensical observation in the Convention:

> [a] display of theory, howsoever proper in the first formation of state governments, (seems) *is* unfit here; since we are not working on the natural rights of men not yet gathered into society, but upon those rights modified by society, and (supporting) *interwoven with* what we call (states) the rights of the States.[9]

Tacitly, commented Louis Henkin, "framers of constitutions and bills of rights distinguished between rights that preexisted society and civil rights enjoyed in society."[10] John Adams and his compeers did not "use nature . . . as a source for rules of decision."[11]

The Framers were well aware that laws might offend against natural law and yet not require enforcement. In the federal Convention, James

6. Id. 388, "against all reason."

7. United States v. Worrall, 28 F. Cas. 774, 779 (C.C.D. Pa. 1798) (emphasis added).

8. Benjamin F. Wright, *American Interpretation of Natural Law* 125 (1931). No reference to "natural law" or to the "law of nature" appears in the index to 3 *The Records of the Federal Convention of 1787* (Max Farrand ed. 1911).

9. 2 Farrand, supra note 8 at 137. "The document is in the handwriting of Edmund Randolph with emendations by John Rutledge. In the text here given those portions in parentheses were crossed out in the original, italics represent changes made in Randolph's handwriting." Id. 137 note 6.

10. Louis Henkin, "Human Dignity and Constitutional Rights," in *The Constitution of Rights* 210, 213–214 (Michael J. Meyer and William A. Parent eds. 1992).

11. Robert M. Cover, *Justice Accused: Antislavery and the Judicial Process* 27 (1975). Haines noted that "it is customary to assert that the doctrine of natural rights and natural law has had little acceptance as a basis for judicial decision in the public law of the United States." Charles G. Haines, "The Law of Nature in State and Federal Judicial Decision," 25 Yale L.J. 617, 625 (1916).

Wilson said, "Laws may be unjust . . . may be destructive; and yet not be so unconstitutional as to justify the Judges in refusing to give them effect."[12] George Mason spoke to the same effect.[13] Moreover, the Founders were hostile to the exercise of unlimited power. Justice Story, who was far closer to the Founders than are we, observed that if an English court of equity possessed the "unbounded jurisdiction . . . arising from natural law and justice" ascribed to it, "it would be the most gigantic in its sway, and the most formidable instrument of arbitrary power, that could well be devised."[14]

In what was a cruel test, natural law was rejected in proceedings for enforcement of the Fugitive Slave Act, notwithstanding that the North was aflame with resistance to Southern claimants for return of escaped slaves. When it was argued before the eminent Chief Justice of the Massachusetts court, Lemuel Shaw, that such returns offended natural rights, he declared that "an appeal to natural rights . . . was not pertinent! It was to be decided by the Constitution . . . and by the Law of Congress."[15] In a federal case, Justice John McLean stated, "It is for the people . . . in making constitutions and the enactment of laws, to consider laws of nature . . . This is a field which judges cannot explore."[16] Although Chief Justice Marshall had acknowledged in *The Antelope* that slavery was abhorrent to natural law, he held that long usage had made it legal under the "law of nations."[17]

12. 2 Farrand, supra note 8 at 73.

13. Id. 78.

14. 1 Joseph Story, *Commentaries on the Constitution of the United States* §9 (5th ed. 1905). Earlier Madison opposed incorporation of the common law because it would confer "on the judicial department a discretion little short of a legislative power." The Framers of a Constitution of enumerated powers could not have intended "to introduce in the lump, in an indirect manner . . . the vast and multifarious jurisdiction involved in the common law." Such an "extraordinary doctrine would sap the foundation of the Constitution as a system of limited and specified powers." *The Mind of the Founders: Sources of Political Thought of James Madison* 324, 318, 325 (Marvin Meyers ed. 1973). Parenthetically, mark the rejection of an "open-ended" theory so dear to activists.

15. Cover, supra note 11 at 169.

16. Miller v. McQuerry, 17 F. Cas. 335, 339 (C.C.D. Ohio 1853) (No. 9583).

17. 23 U.S. (10 Wheat.) 66, 89–90 (1825); see also Nevada v. Hall, 440 U.S. 410, 425–426 (1979); Satterlee v. Mathewson, 27 U.S. (2 Pet.) 380, 413 (1829).

All this is of no moment to Suzanna Sherry. Unless we are to view the Framers as "dimwitted," she urges, we must believe that they did not distinguish between "the written judicially enforceable Constitution and the unwritten natural law."[18] They spoke, she reasons, of the Constitution and "unwritten natural law in the same breath . . . without distinguishing between the two, strongly suggest[ing] that they thought of unwritten rights as analogous" to the "legal rights of the Constitution . . . To attribute to them any other conclusion strains credulity."[19] Chief Justice Marshall, however, made this very distinction:

> the powers of the legislature are defined, and limited; and that those limits may not be mistaken or forgotten, the constitution is written. To what purpose are powers limited, and to what purpose is that limitation committed to writing; if these limits may at any time, be passed by those intended to be restrained?[20]

What is resort to natural law but the very attempt to pass the limits "by those intended to be restrained?" Not for nothing did Article VI (2) declare that "This Constitution . . . shall be the supreme law of the land." In place of "higher law" the Constitution itself was to be the "superior, paramount law."[21] That which is paramount—supremely controlling[22]— cannot be superseded by natural law. "[L]aw," Robert Cover observed, "as a sovereign act clearly mandated the subordination of natural law to the constitutions."[23]

Sherry cites Thomas Grey's attribution to the Framers of a "belief in judicially enforceable natural rights."[24] Grey's article deals with pre-1787 "revolutionary thought"[25] and it is studded with preindependence

18. Suzanna Sherry, "The Ninth Amendment: Righting an Unwritten Constitution," 64 Chi.-Kent L. Rev. 1001 (1989), reprinted in 2 *The Rights Retained by the People* 283, 284–285 (Randy E. Barnett ed. 1993).
19. Id. 285.
20. Marbury v. Madison, 5 U.S. (1 Cranch) 137, 176 (1803).
21. Id. 177.
22. Funk and Wagnalls, *Desk Standard Dictionary* (1946).
23. Cover, supra note 11 at 34.
24. Sherry, supra note 18 at 284.
25. Thomas C. Grey, "Origins of the Unwritten Constitution: Fundamental Law in American Revolutionary Thought," 30 Stan. L. Rev. 843 (1978).

utterances, when "higher law" served to justify colonial resistance to Parliament's misrule. Once independence was won, however, the Founders' distrust of judicial hegemony reemerged, as is attested by Hamilton's assurance in Federalist No. 78 that of the three branches the judiciary is "next to nothing." Justice James Wilson, who had been a leading architect of the Constitution, explained in 1791 that judges had been derived from a "foreign source . . . [and] were directed to foreign purposes. Need we be surprised that they were objects of aversion and distrust?" He felt constrained to exhort his fellow citizens that it was time to "chastise our prejudices."[26] Those prejudices militated against a roving commission to judges to transcend a Constitution which set bounds to their powers.

More cautious than Sherry, Grey acknowledges that the effect of a "written Constitution" on the idea that "judicially ascertainable fundamental law could itself have constitutional status remains to be carefully analyzed" and that it "remains to be carefully analyzed" that such judicial review was consistent with "popular sovereignty."[27] Since judges are creatures of the Constitution, and have only such authority as it confers, it must also be shown that the Constitution—the supreme paramount law—empowers a judge to wander outside its confines. Marshall forestalled the need for further demonstration by his declaration that the written limits may not "be passed . . . by those intended to be restrained."

---

26. 1 *The Works of James Wilson* 292, 293 (R. G. McCloskey ed. 1967).
27. Grey, supra note 25 at 893.

# 15

## *"The Rule of Law"*

For a generation the constitutional basis for the "revolutionary" changes wrought by the Warren Court has gone virtually unchallenged.[1] Justice Black, to be sure, unremittingly attacked decisions which to his mind rested on supraconstitutional authority, but his views could be heavily discounted because he himself was guilty of wholesale importation and participated in some of the Court's most debatable constitutional revisions. In a perceptive essay, Thomas C. Grey noticed a turning of the tide, the joinder of distinguished commentators in Black's criticisms; although he dissents, he called for a clear statement and adequate defense of the position.[2] With Grey, I consider the question whether the Court may "enforce principles of liberty and justice" when they are "not to be found within the four corners" of the Constitution as "perhaps the most fundamental question we can ask about our fundamental law," excluding only "the question of the legitimacy of judicial review itself."[3] The issue may for present purposes be stated more concretely: given that the Fourteenth Amendment plainly left suffrage and segregation to the States, may the Court "interpret" it in exact contra-

1. "The 15 years since [Warren] became Chief Justice have been years of legal revolution. In that time the Supreme Court has brought about more social change than most Congresses and most Presidents." Anthony Lewis, "A Man Born to Act, Not to Muse," *The New York Times Magazine*, June 30, 1968, in Levy, *Warren* 151. Justice Douglas complained that one decision entailed a "vast restructuring of American law." Johnson v. Louisiana, 406 U.S 356, 394 (1972), dissenting opinion. Professor Lusky refers to "a revolutionary change in the criminal process." Lusky 161. A. T. Mason, *The Supreme Court: Palladium of Freedom* 170 (1962): "On May 17, 1954, the Court initiated the greatest social revolution of this generation." See also supra Chapter 14 note 136.

2. "Do We Have an Unwritten Constitution?," 27 Stan. L. Rev. 703–705 (1975).

3. Id. 703.

diction of the framers' design—to take control away from the States? Where is the constitutional authority for a power so awesome?

It is important to make clear at this point what Part II of this study is not about. It does not deal with the interpretation of amorphous constitutional provisions such as "commerce,"[4] which, unlike "due process," have no historical content; nor with the weight to be accorded "enigmatic" history. As Part I demonstrated, the framers of the Fourteenth Amendment made their intention abundantly plain: to exclude suffrage and segregation from the ambit of its terms. For me those terms, "equal protection" and "due process," illuminated by clear history, are neither "vague" nor "ambiguous." Nor will I deal with whether or not judicial review is antidemocritarian,[5] for if judicial review of the Warrenite scope was authorized by the Constitution, its antidemocratic nature has constitutional sanction. Nor will the craftsmanship of the Court, about which rivers of ink have been spilled, come into question.[6] If judicial intervention with respect to suffrage, for example, is without constitutional warrant, it cannot be excused by the most elegant craftsmanship. Nor will consideration be given to the extensive debate about

4. Professor Frankfurter commented on Marshall's "use of the commerce clause" to subject state authority "to such limitations as the Court finds it necessary to apply for the protection of the national community" as an "audacious doctrine, which, one may be sure, would hardly have been publicly avowed in support of the Constitution. Indeed The Federalist in effect denied it." *The Commerce Clause Under Marshall, Taney and Waite* 18–19 (1937). Had it been avowed it would have wrecked adoption of the Constitution. For the Founders' jealous attachment to State sovereignty, see Raoul Berger, *Congress v. The Supreme Court* 260–264 (1969). That attachment was made explicit by the Tenth Amendment. That Marshall's views have carried the day is of no moment in a discussion that seeks to build on first principles. See infra at note 15, infra at notes 29–30, 56–57.

5. I consider that Eugene V. Rostow failed to meet Henry Steele Commager's attack on the antidemocratic administration of judicial review up to 1937. Rostow, "The Democratic Character of Judicial Review," 56 Harv. L. Rev. 193 (1952); Commager, "Judicial Review and Democracy," 19 Va. Quarterly Rev. 417 (1943). See infra Chapter 17 at note 69.

Leonard Levy finds the Rostow argument unconvincing and comments, it is "of comparatively recent vintage, raising the suspicion that the arguments have been concocted to rationalize a growing satisfaction with judicial review among liberal intellectuals and scholars." *Judicial Review and the Supreme Court* 24 (Leonard Levy ed. 1967).

6. "Assessment of the Nixon Court's craftsmanship is as subjective as the art of judging, and experts will doubtless disagree, as they have about the Warren Court's craftsmanship." Levy, *Against the Law* 438.

"neutral principles," because I concur with John Ely that if a "neutral principle" "lacks connection with any value the Constitution marks as special," that is, if it is not rooted in the Constitution, "it is not a constitutional principle and the Court has no business imposing it." What is of paramount importance, as Ely stresses, is that the Court "is under obligation to trace its premises to the charter from which it derives its authority."[7] Finally, the "subjectivity" involved in making value choices[8] plays no role in my view of the meaning of the Fourteenth Amendment, for it was not given to the courts to prefer federal judicial control of suffrage to the State control the Amendment deliberately left untouched. The Justices' value choices may not displace those of the Framers,[9] or, as Chief Justice Marshall stated, the words of the Constitution are not to be "extended to objects not . . . contemplated by its framers"[10]—let alone to those which unmistakably were excluded.

Intoxicated by the Warren Court's libertarian breakthrough, academicians have dismissed such restrictions. Fred Rodell exulted that Chief Justice Warren "brush[ed] off pedantic impedimenta to the results he felt were right," that he was not a "look-it-up-in-the-library" intellectual, and that he was "almost unique" in his "off-hand dismissal of legal and historical research from both sides and in [his] pragmatic dependence on the present day results of separate schools."[11] On this view the Constitution itself is a superfluous, even obstructive, "scrap of paper." Leonard Levy labeled this approach as "anti-intellectual,"[12] but Rodell merely expressed in pungent terms what is more decorously phrased by

7. "The Wages of Crying Wolf: A Comment on Roe v. Wade," 82 Yale L.J. 920, 949 (1973). Bruce M. Claggett suggests a "neutral principle," the "intent of the framers which, where knowable, surely should be conclusive." "Book Review," 27 Harv. L. Sch. Bull. 3, 4 (1976).

8. A. S. Miller and R. F. Howell, "The Myth of Neutrality in Constitutional Adjudication," 27 U. Chi. L. Rev. 661 (1960).

9. See infra Chapter 17 at notes 34–35, 62.

10. Ogden v. Saunders, 25 U.S. (12 Wheat.) 213, 332 (1827), dissenting opinion.

11. Fred Rodell, "It Is the Warren Court," *The New York Times Magazine*, March 13, 1966, in Levy, *Warren* 137, 142, 138–139. In both Brown v. Board of Education (desegregation) and Reynolds v. Sims (reapportionment), Rodell takes pleasure in recounting, "Warren was quite unworried that legislative history, dug from a library, might not support his reading." Id. 142.

12. Levy, *Warren* 188.

his fellow "instrumentalists."[13] The underlying reality, as another Warren enthusiast, Edmond Cahn, stated, was that "as a practical matter it
would have been impossible to secure adoption of a constitutional
amendment to abolish 'separate but equal,' only the Court possessed effective power to relieve American education of this incubus," thereby
assuming that it had constitutional warrant.[14]

Inquiry into the source of power to set aside Article V of the Constitution, "which prescribes the Amendment process,"[15] and to impose
a solution on the people that confessedly could not have obtained their
assent is hardly a sheerly antiquarian exercise.[16] Given a Constitution
designed to "limit" the exercise of all delegated power,[17] it is a response
to the admonition contained in the Massachusetts Constitution of 1780,
drafted by John Adams and paralleled in a number of early State constitutions, that "A frequent recurrence to the fundamental principles of
the constitution . . . [is] absolutely necessary to preserve the advantages
of liberty and to maintain a free government . . . The people . . . have a
right to require of their law givers and magistrates an exact and constant

13. E.g., "judicial decisions should be gauged by their results and not by . . . their
coincidence with a set of allegedly consistent doctrinal principles." Miller and Howell,
supra note 8 at 690-691. Warren, said Paul Murphy, "had utilized the judiciary as a constructive policy-making instrument . . . Intent more upon social ends than upon legal
subtleties and refinements, and candidly prepared to say so, he had pushed the nation,
through his Court's legal rulings, to take public actions that Congress was unprepared to
recommend and the executive was incapable, unilaterally, of effectively securing." Murphy, *The Constitution in Crisis Times, 1918-1969* 457 (1972). Apparently this meets with
his approval, id. 466 et seq. He states that McCune (*Nine Young Men* 83 [1947]), praises
the Black-Douglas-Murphy bloc because it " 'would seldom let red tape [!] stand in its
way of arriving at an end it felt desirable.' " Id. 194.

14. Edmond Cahn, "Jurisprudence," 30 N.Y.U.L. Rev. 150, 156-157 (1955). In the
same way, Martin Shapiro assumed the existence of such power when he adverted to
"Learned Hand's eloquent plea for judicial abdication of most of the power of judicial
review," *Law and Politics in the Supreme Court* 24 (1964), when in fact Hand entertained
grave doubts about its legitimacy and therefore would confine it to a narrow compass.

15. Lusky 79; see infra Chapter 17 at notes 15–22.

16. Although poles removed from Rodell's uncritical subjectivity, Leonard Levy lends
credibility to such views by his reference to "an antiquarian historicism that would freeze
[the Constitution's] original meaning . . . and was not intended to." Levy, *Judgments: Essays in American Constitutional History* 17 (1972). The remarks of Jefferson and Madison
plainly look the other way. See infra Chapter 20 at notes 5 and 18.

17. Supra Chapter 1 note 4; Berger, supra note 4 at 13–16.

observance of them."[18] Such provisions evidence what Willard Hurst considers to be "a very basic principle of our constitutionalism . . . a distrust of official power,"[19] as Jefferson's insistence on binding officials "with the chains of the Constitution" attests.[20]

## Constitutionalism and the Rule of Law

When Howard Jay Graham acknowledged that the framers excluded segregation from the compass of "equal protection," but concluded that we dare not be bound by their "imperfect understanding,"[21] he premised that the Court, as it had done in *Brown v. Board of Education* (1954), should strike the "chains of the Constitution." The demands of justice, in short, must rise above the law, or, as libertarians put it, humanitarian goals must override what they regard as arid legalism. To dismiss adherence to "the rule of law," observance of the limitations imposed by a written Constitution, is to strike at the very root of our democratic system.[22] History confirms Justice Black's statement that the struggle for a

18. Article XVIII, 1 Poore 959; New Hampshire (1784), Article 38, 2 Poore 1283; North Carolina (1776), Article XXI, 2 Poore 1410; Pennsylvania (1776), Article XIV, 2 Poore 1542; Vermont (1777), Article XVI, 2 Poore 1860.

19. "Discussion," in *Supreme Court and Supreme Law* 75 (Edmond N. Cahn ed. 1954). James Iredell, who fought against great odds in North Carolina for adoption of the Constitution, stated, "The only real security of liberty . . . is the jealousy and circumspection of the people themselves. Let them be watchful over their rulers." 4 Elliot 130. In Virginia, Randolph said, "I hope that my countrymen will keep guard against every arrogation of power." 3 Elliot 207. Iredell stated that "unlimited power . . . was not to be trusted without the most imminent danger, to any man or body of men on earth." 2 G. J. McRee, *Life and Correspondence of James Iredell* 145–146 (1857–1858). See also Corbin, supra Chapter 14 note 16. The Supreme Court adverted to "Fear of unchecked power, so typical of our State and Federal Governments." Duncan v. Louisiana, 391 U.S. 145, 156 (1968).

20. Supra Chapter 14 at note 16.

21. Supra Chapter 14 at note 9.

22. Supra at note 11. Miller and Howell, supra note 8 at 683, label regard for the "intention of the framers" as a "filiopietistic notion." Cf. Levy, *Judgments* supra note 16. Earlier McDougal and Lans gave vent to a string of spluttering expletives: "absolute artifacts of verbal archeology," "strictly, a matter of concern only to rhetoricians," "the idiosyncratic purposes of the Framers." "Treaties and Congressional-Executive or Presidential Agreements: Interchangeable Instruments of National Policy," 54 Yale L.J. 181, 239 note 104, 291, 212 (1945). If laws were "scorned," John Adams wrote, "in God's name what is ever to be respected? What is there worth living for?" 2 Page Smith, *John Adams* 690 (1962).

written constitution was "to make certain that men in power would be governed by *law*, not the arbitrary fiat of the man or men in power," "according to the 'law of the land,' " not by the "law of judges."[23] The Framers, as will appear, had no stomach for the dispensation of "justice" by a kadi under a tree. Justice, to be sure, is the aim of a democratic state, but there can be no justice without a government of laws, least of all when power is uncurbed. It is for this reason, I suggest, that judges are not required by Article VI, § 3, to take an oath to do justice but rather "to support this Constitution." Our system is committed to "Equal Justice *Under* Law," not to "Justices Above the Law."[24] They were not authorized to revise the Constitution in the interests of "justice."

23. In re Winship, 397 U.S. 358, 384 (1970), dissenting opinion. Chief Justice Waite declared in 1874 that "Our province is to decide what the law is, not to declare what it should be." Minor v. Happersett, 88 U.S. (21 Wall.) 162, 178 (1874). In Houston v. Moore, 18 U.S. (5 Wheat.) 1, 48 (1820), Justice Story declared that the Court was "not at liberty to add one jot of power to the national government, beyond what the people have granted by the constitution," dissenting opinion. For similar expressions by Chief Justice Marshall see infra Chapter 21 at notes 12–19.

24. Cardozo wrote that judges do not have "the right to ignore the mandate of a statute, and render judgment in despite of it." Benjamin N. Cardozo, *The Nature of the Judicial Process* 129 (1921). It is said that when Holmes left the Massachusetts Court for the Supreme Court, "he was admonished to do justice. He responded thoughtfully that his job was merely to enforce the law." Wallace Mendelson, *Justices Black and Frankfurter: Conflict in the Court* 116 (1961). Holmes wrote, "I have said to my brethren many times that I hate justice, which means that I know that if a man begins to talk about that, for one reason or another he is shirking thinking in legal terms." *The Mind and Faith of Justice Holmes* 435 (M. Lerner ed. 1943). See also supra Chapter 14 at notes 37 and 103.

Writing of self-conscious judicial activism, Dean Acheson stated that a judge "may conscientiously be seeking to administer justice, but it is personal justice—the justice of Louis IX or Harun-al-Rashid—not that described on the lintel of the Supreme Court Building, 'Equal Justice Under Law.' " *Morning and Noon* 69 (1965). Lusky suggests that some of the Court's decisions may be inexplicable "except on the premise that the Justices *consider themselves to be above the law*—to be wholly unconstrained by pre-existing principle." Lusky 101. Precisely this won praise from admirers of the Warren Court. Supra at note 11, and notes 11 and 13. See also Levy, supra Chapter 14 at note 136.

In defense of President Ford's pardon of Richard Nixon, Assistant Secretary of Transportation Roger W. Hooker, Jr., stated, "I have never been entirely comfortable with the shibboleth [!] that ours is a nation of laws, not of men. It is true that for the most part it is and should be, but in times of extreme moral crisis throughout history, strong leadership has emerged to supersede the letter of the law and deliver us from the evils of vindictiveness." Hooker, "A 'Quiet, Undramatic' Leader," N. Y. Times, August 19, 1976, at 39. In short, Ford acted above the law to save us from an "extreme moral crisis"!

Mechanical repetition over the years—like a child's unthinking daily pledge of allegiance—has dulled the significance of the rule of law; it has been called a "useful fiction."[25] For the Framers, however, it was the essence of constitutional government. "The government of the United States," said Chief Justice Marshall in one of his earliest decisions, "has been emphatically termed a government of laws and not of men."[26] That the judiciary, too, was meant to stay within bounds was spelled out in the 1780 Massachusetts Constitution, which ordained that the legislature should never exercise judicial power, and never should the judiciary exercise legislative power, so that this may be a "government of laws and not of men."[27] Even more plainly, judges were not left free to exercise the supreme "legislative power" of the people, to revise the Constitution in accordance with their own predilections. As the Massachusetts House wrote to the Earl of Shelburne in 1768, "There are, my Lord, fundamental rules of the Constitution . . . which neither the supreme Legislative nor the supreme executive can alter. In all free states, the *constitution is fixed*; it is from thence, that the legislative derives its authority; therefore it cannot change the constitution without destroying its own foundation."[28] This was addressed to an "omnipotent" Parliament and the Crown under an unwritten Constitution; it was an article of faith among the colonists and Founders.[29] In substituting a written Constitution and expressly providing for change by amendment, they evidenced that they had created a "fixed" Constitution, subject to change

25. Miller and Howell, supra note 8 at 695.

26. Marbury v. Madison, 5 U.S. (1 Cranch) 137, 163 (1803).

27. Massachusetts Constitution of 1780, Article XXX, 1 Poore 960, more fully quoted supra Chapter 14 note 5. The Framers made plain that the judiciary was not to exercise legislative power. Infra Chapter 16 at notes 8–12.

28. *Documents of American History* 65 (Henry Steele Commager ed. 7th ed. 1963).

29. "The colonials shared Bolingbroke's belief in the fixity of the constitution." Julius Goebel, *Antecedents and Beginnings to 1801, History of the Supreme Court of the United States*, vol. 1, p. 89 (1971). "The principle that government must be conducted in conformity with the terms of the constitution became a fundamental political conception." Id. 95.

In 1785 Madison stated that rulers "who overleap the great barrier which defends the rights of the people . . . are tyrants." 2 James Madison, *Writings of James Madison* 185 (G. Hunt ed. 1900–1910). In the Connecticut Convention Oliver Ellsworth stated, Congress may not "overleap their limits." 2 Elliot 196. For other citations see Berger, supra note 4 at 13–14.

by that process alone.[30] That "fixity" was meant to serve as a bulwark for cherished liberties, not a mere parchment. "Our peculiar security," Jefferson declared, "is the possession of a written Constitution. Let us not make it a blank paper by construction."[31] The written Constitution was thus the highest expression of the "rule of law," designed to limit the exercise of power and to make the agents of the people accountable. Once limits are prescribed, Chief Justice Marshall stated, they may not "be passed at pleasure." It was because constitutions were bulwarks against oppression that, in his words, "written constitutions have been regarded with so much reverence."[32]

The Constitution represents fundamental choices that have been made by the people, and the task of the Courts is to effectuate them, "not [to] construct new rights."[33] When the judiciary substitutes its own value choices for those of the people it subverts the Constitution by usurpation of power. No dispensation was given to the Court to step outside its powers; it is no less bound by constitutional limits than are the other branches, as the historical evidence makes plain. First, it was clearly excluded from participation in the making of policy, the function of the legislature.[34] No agent, said Hamilton, "can new-model his commission,"[35] and the most benign purpose does not authorize the judiciary to remodel its powers. Indeed, we need to be rid of "the illusion that personal power can be benevolently exercised."[36] The Founders knew, in

30. Madison stated in the Convention that "it would be a novel and dangerous doctrine that a legislature could change the constitution under which it held its existence." 2 Farrand 92. See infra Chapter 17 at notes 15–22.

31. 8 *Writings of Thomas Jefferson* 247 (P. L. Ford ed. 1892–1899).

32. Marbury v. Madison, 5 U.S. (1 Cranch) 137, 178 (1803).

33. Robert J. Bork, "Neutral Principles and Some First Amendment Problems," 47 Ind. L.J. 1, 8 (1971); see infra Chapter 17 at notes 34–35.

34. See infra Chapter 16 at notes 8–13.

35. "Letters of Camillus," 6 Alexander Hamilton, *Works of Hamilton* 166 (H. C. Lodge ed. 1904). This was said of the President by the foremost advocate of a "strong" presidency. See also supra note 30.

36. Thurman Arnold, "Professor Hart's Theology," 73 Harv. L. Rev. 1298, 1311 (1960). [Speaking of the substitution "of the individual sense of justice," Cardozo said, "That might result in a benevolent despotism if the judges were benevolent men. It would put an end to the reign of law." Benjamin N. Cardozo, *The Nature of the Judicial Process* 136 (1921). See also id. 133, 152, 160.]

Jacob Burckhardt's phrase, that "Power is of its nature evil, whoever wields it."[37] They knew, as Madison stated, that all "power is of an encroaching nature, and that it ought to be effectually restrained from passing the limits assigned to it."[38] "Judicial power," Justice Frankfurter remarked, "is not immune against this human weakness";[39] and the Court's progressive intrusion over the years into the domain of policymaking, from which it was plainly excluded, points the moral. Second, as Chief Justice Warren recognized, "We are oath-bound to defend the Constitution. This obligation requires that congressional enactments be judged by the standards of the Constitution."[40] Substituted judicial made-to-order "standards" are not really the "standards" of the Constitution,[41] as the State "reapportionment" cases plainly evidence. The significance of the judicial oath is illuminated by that of the President, who does not swear to defend the nation, but to "preserve and defend the Constitution,"[42] on the inarticulate premise that the life of the nation hangs on the preservation of the Constitution. Third, conclusive evidence that the judiciary was designed only to police constitutional boundaries, not to exercise supraconstitutional policymaking functions, was furnished by Hamilton. In Federalist No. 78 he stressed that the courts were to serve as "bulwarks of a limited Constitution against legislative encroach-

37. Quoted in Gertrude Himmelfarb, *Victorian Minds* 185 (1968).

38. Federalist No. 48 at 321, quoted more fully supra Chapter 14 note 7.

39. Trop v. Dulles, 356 U.S. 86, 119 (1958), dissenting opinion. Justice Black stated, "The history of governments proves that it is dangerous to freedom to repose such [lawmaking] powers in courts." Katz v. United States, 389 U.S. 347, 374 (1967), dissenting opinion. See also supra Chapter 14 note 7, and John Dickinson, infra Chapter 16 at note 12.

40. Trop v. Dulles, 356 U.S. at 103.

41. "[T]he choice was made by the Framers," Justice Douglas declared, "a choice which sets a standard . . . The Framers made it a standard." Rochin v. California, 342 U.S. 165, 178–179 (1952), concurring opinion. Justice Black stated that "when a 'political theory' embodied in our Constitution becomes outdated . . . a majority of the nine members of this Court are not only without constitutional power but are far less qualified to choose a new constitutional theory than the people of this country proceeding in the manner provided by Article V." Harper v. Virginia Bd. of Elections, 383 U.S. 663, 678 (1966), dissenting opinion. Yet both Black and Douglas joined in the "reapportionment" decisions.

42. Article II, § 1(8). Note John Adams' insistence on "exact" observance of the "fundamental principles of the constitution," supra at note 18, by which he surely included the text and the Framers' explanations.

ments"—a note repeatedly sounded in the subsequent Ratification Conventions.[43] The word "encroachments" posits prior legislative action; it excludes judicial policymaking initiatives on ground of legislative inaction. This is confirmed by Hamilton's statement that the judiciary "can take no active resolution whatever. It may truly be said to have neither FORCE nor WILL, but merely judgment."[44] Chief Justice Marshall rephrased this in unmistakable terms: the Court was only to give "effect to the will of the legislature."[45] Hamilton rejected the argument that the courts were empowered "to construe the laws according to the *spirit* of the Constitution";[46] "penumbras formed by emanations"[47] were not for him. What he meant is made quite clear by his rejection of the notion "that the courts on the pretence of a repugnancy, may substitute their own pleasure to the constitutional intentions of the legislature,"[48] a statement, Louis Lusky notes, that "is hard to square with anticipation of judicial constitution-making power."[49] Finally, well aware that there existed considerable distrust of the proposal for judicial review, Hamilton sought to allay it in Federalist No. 81 by calling attention to the

> important constitutional check which the power of instituting impeachments . . . would give to that body [Congress] upon the members of the judicial department. This is alone a complete security. There can never be danger that the judges, by a series of deliberate

43. Federalist at 508; Berger, supra note 4 at 12–16.
44. Federalist No. 78 at 504.
45. Infra Chapter 16 at note 41.
46. Federalist No. 81 at 524.
47. Griswold v. Connecticut, 381 U.S. 479, 484 (1965). Justice Douglas held that "specific guarantees of the Bill of Rights have penumbras, formed by emanations from those guarantees, that give them life and substance." Webster, as A. T. Mason points out, "defines *penumbra* as a 'marginal region or borderland of partial obscurity.' " "The Burger Court in Historical Perspective," 47 N.Y. State Bar J. 87, 89 (1975). It is an odd conceit that "obscure borderland regions" lend "life and substance" to explicit guarantees. Nor does a region of "partial obscurity" offer the solid footing required for a novel intrusion into the relations of a State with its citizens that the Tenth Amendment protects.
48. Federalist No. 78 at 507. Justice Frankfurter explained that "The reason why from the beginning even the narrow judicial authority to nullify legislation has been viewed with a jealous eye is that it serves to prevent the full play of the democratic process." Board of Education v. Barnette, 319 U.S. 624, 650 (1943), dissenting opinion.
49. Lusky 72.

usurpations on the authority of the legislature, would hazard the united resentment of the body intrusted with it.[50]

These were no idle words, for both the English and the Founders regarded "usurpation" or subversion of the Constitution as the most heinous of impeachable offenses.[51]

Today there is a tendency to reduce the Constitution to the status of a "symbol" of continuity and unity,[52] but for the Founders it was a living reality. They swore the President to "preserve and defend the Constitution" because it represented a "bulwark" of their liberties, not a mere symbol. They indited a charter which delegates power to the "servants and agents of the people,"[53] with "limits," "checks and balances" to guard against its abuse. It bears witness to the creation of a *government by consent* of the sovereign people; "just government," stated the Declaration of Independence, "is founded on the consent of the governed." The terms of

50. Federalist at 526–527. When I first considered this provision in 1969, it was in the context of the congressional power to make "exceptions" to the Supreme Court's appellate jurisdiction, while arguing that that power could not have been designed to curb judicial "excesses," citing Hamilton's statement that the impeachment provision "is the only provision on the point which is consistent with the necessary independence of the judicial character." Federalist No. 79 at 514. When I went on to quote James Wilson's statement that judges were not to be "impeached, because they decide an act null and void, that was made in defiance of the Constitution," Berger, supra note 4 at 290–291, I did not, because the point was not involved, draw the distinction between an exercise by the Court of its jurisdiction to police constitutional boundaries (infra Chapter 16 at notes 5–6, 26–27), which neither the impeachment nor the "exceptions" power can correct, and the usurpation of "legislative power," which is an impeachable offense. The meaning of usurpation was made clear by Iredell: "If Congress, under pretense of executing one power, should in fact usurp another, they will violate the Constitution." 4 Elliot 179. A congressional usurpation can be set aside by the Court; a judicial usurpation, as Hamilton stated, can be met by impeachment.

51. Raoul Berger, *Impeachment: The Constitutional Problems* 33, 39, 86 (1973). [Protesting against a congressional resolution that he had usurped power, President Andrew Jackson declared that the charge that "the President has usurped authority and power not conferred upon him by the Constitution and laws, and that in doing so he violated both . . . (such an act would constitute) a high crime—one of the highest indeed, which the President can commit—a crime which justly exposes him to impeachment by the House." 3 James D. Richardson, comp., *Messages and Papers of the Presidents* 73 (1889–1905).]

52. Bickel, *The Least Dangerous Branch* 31 (1962).

53. "Those in power," said Iredell, are "servants and agents of the people." 4 Elliot 9. Archibald Maclaine stated in the North Carolina Convention that the people can "delegate power to agents." Id. 161. See Hamilton, supra at note 35.

that consent are spelled out in the Constitution. "The people," averred James Iredell, one of the ablest of the Founders, "have chosen to be governed under such and such principles. They have not chosen to be governed or promised to submit upon any other."[54] Substitution by the Court of its own value choices for those embodied in the Constitution violates the basic principle of government by consent of the governed. We must therefore reject, I submit, Charles Evans Hughes' dictum that "the Constitution is what the Supreme Court says it is."[55] No power to revise the Constitution under the guise of "interpretation" was conferred on the Court; it does so only because the people have not grasped the reality—an unsafe foundation for power in a government by consent.

Too much discussion of constitutional law is centered on the Court's decisions, with not enough regard for the text and history of the Constitution itself. We need to recall Justice Gibson's great statement in 1825:

> in questions of this sort, precedents ought to go for absolutely nothing. The Constitution is a collection of fundamental laws, not to be departed from in practice nor altered by judicial decision, and in the construction of it, nothing would be so alarming as the doctrine of *communis error*, which offers a ready justification for every usurpation that has not been resisted *in limine* . . . the judge who asserts [the right of judicial review] ought to be prepared to maintain it on the principles of the Constitution.[56]

54. 2 McRee, supra note 19 at 146. This was powerfully stated in the First Congress by Alexander White of Virginia: "This is a Government constituted for particular purposes only; and the powers granted to carry it into effect are specifically enumerated . . . If these powers are insufficient . . . it is not . . . within our power to remedy. The people who bestowed them must grant further powers . . . This was the ground on which the friends of the Government supported the Constitution . . . [otherwise] the Constitution would never have been ratified" in Virginia. 1 *Annals of Congress* 514–515.

55. Embarrassed by this incautious remark, Hughes explained that he was not picturing interpretation "as a matter of judicial caprice." *The Autobiographical Notes of Charles Evans Hughes* 143 (D. J. Danielski and J. S. Tulchin eds. 1973). One need not charge Justices Field and Pierce Butler with "caprice"; it suffices that they sincerely identified their own predilections with constitutional dogma. Professor Frankfurter wrote to President Franklin Roosevelt that it is the Justices "who speak and not the Constitution." *Roosevelt and Frankfurter: Their Correspondence 1928–1945* 383 (M. Freedman ed. 1967).

56. Eakin v. Raub, 12 S. & R. 330 (Pa. 1825), dissenting opinion. That view was expressed by Justice Holmes and quoted by Justice Brandeis in Erie Ry. Co. v. Tompkins,

Like Chief Justice Burger and Justices Douglas and Frankfurter, I assert the right to look at the Constitution itself stripped of judicial incrustations,[57] as the index of constitutional law and to affirm that the Supreme Court has no authority to substitute an "unwritten Constitution" for the written Constitution the Founders gave us and the people ratified.

Constitutionalism—limited government under the rule of law—was a paramount aim, not to be warped in order to achieve some predilection of any given bench. Solicitor General, later Justice, Robert H. Jackson, perceived, as Chief Justice Warren did not, that "the rule of law is in unsafe hands when courts cease to function as courts and be-

---

304 U.S. 64, 79 (1938), when the doctrine of Swift v. Tyson, 40 U.S. (16 Pet.) 1 (1842), was branded "an unconstitutional assumption of power by courts of the United States which no lapse of time or respectable array of opinion should make us hesitate to correct." [Acquiescence for no length of time can legalize a clear usurpation of power." Thomas Cooley, *A Treatise on the Constitutional Limitations* 106 (8th ed. 1927).

There "can be no doubt that an unconstitutional practice, no matter how inveterate, cannot be condoned by the judiciary." Zweifon v. Mitchell, 516 F.2d 594, 616 (D. C. Cir. 1975). "No one acquires a vested or protected right in violation of the Constitution by long use." Walz v. Tax Comm'n, 379 U.S. 664, 678 (1970). In constitutional questions, "when convinced of former error, this Court has never felt constrained to follow precedent." Smith v. Allwright, 321 U.S. 619, 665 (1944).]

Justice Gibson's opinion is often regarded as impugning judicial review in the federal courts; but Gibson was careful to distinguish between the Pennsylvania Constitution (of 1790, 2 Poore 1548), which contained neither a "supremacy clause" (Article VI, §2), nor an "arising under" clause (Article III, §2), and the federal Constitution, which does. 12 S. & R. at 345, 346, 347, 356, 357. Although Gibson spoke in the context of state powers and duties, federal judges too are "bound" only by "laws" of Congress that are "consistent with the Constitution." Infra Chapter 19 at notes 18–21. Moreover, Gibson made no reference to expressions by the Founders in both the Federal and State Conventions that judicial review was contemplated, infra Chapter 19 at notes 25–28, presumably because they were not germane to the Pennsylvania Constitution under adjudication, and because they had not yet been published.

57. Chief Justice Burger "categorically" rejected the "thesis that what the Court said lately controls over the Constitution . . . By placing a premium on 'recent cases' rather than the language of the Constitution, the Court makes it dangerously simple for future Courts using the technique of interpretation to operate as a 'continuing Constitutional Convention.' " Coleman v. Alabama, 399 U.S. 1, 22–23 (1970). Justice Douglas wrote, a judge "remembers above all else that it is the Constitution which he swore to support and defend, not the gloss which his predecessors may have put upon it." "Stare Decisis," 49 Colum. L. Rev. 735, 736 (1949). Justice Frankfurter stated that "the ultimate touchstone of constitutionality is the Constitution itself and not what we have said about it." Graves v. O'Keefe, 306 U.S. 466, 491–492 (1939), concurring opinion.

come organs for control of policy."[58] Even a celebrant of the Warren era, Thurman Arnold, stated that without a continuing pursuit of "the ideal of the rule of law we would not have a civilized government." But although he labeled it as of "tremendous importance," he viewed it as "unattainable."[59] That is a romantic view which can be invoked to shirk the attainable. Effectuation of the Fourteenth Amendment's decision to leave suffrage to the States, for example, was not "unattainable"; attainment was balked only by the Court's drive to restructure the Constitution. For the Founders "the rule of law" was no "unattainable" ideal, but a basic imperative. And so it must remain. As Charles McIlwain wrote, "The two fundamental correlative elements of constitutionalism for which all lovers of liberty must yet fight are the legal limits to arbitrary power and a complete responsibility of government to the governed."[60]

If this be arid legalism, it was shared by Washington, who stated in his Farewell Address:

> If in the opinion of the People, the distribution or modification of the Constitutional powers be in any particular wrong, let it be corrected by an amendment in the way in which the Constitution designates. But let there be no change by usurpation; for though this, in one instance, may be the instrument of good, it is the customary weapon by which free governments are destroyed. The precedent

---

58. Jackson, *The Struggle for Judicial Supremacy* 322 (1941). And as Justice, one of the most gifted that served on the Court, Jackson "took the notion of a rule of law seriously," G. E. White, *The American Judicial Tradition* 248 (1976); he deemed it inappropriate for judges "to seize the initiative in shaping the policy of the law." And he "attacked the 'cult of libertarian judicial activists' on the Court whose attitude, he felt, 'encourage[d] a belief that judges may be left to correct the results of public indifference to the issues of liberty.' " White, id. 246.

To "engage in result-oriented jurisprudence," Leonard Levy wrote, is to leave "far behind the idea of the rule of law enforced by impersonal and impartial judges." Levy, *Against the Law* 438. Wallace Mendelson stated, "we must begin again the unending struggle for the Rule of Law, for government by something more respectable than the will of those who for the moment hold high office." *The Supreme Court: Law and Discretion* 40 (1967).

59. Arnold, supra note 36 at 1311.

60. *Constitutionalism: Ancient and Modern* 146 (rev. ed. 1947).

must always greatly overbalance in permanent evil any partial or transient benefit which the use can at any time yield.[61]

It is because Americans continue to regard the Constitution as the bulwark of their liberties that they hold it in reverence. "[E]very breach of the fundamental laws, though dictated by necessity," said Hamilton, "impairs the sacred reverence which ought to be maintained in the breasts of the rulers towards the constitution."[62]

61. 35 George Washington, *Writings* 228–229 (J. Fitzpatrick ed. 1940).
62. Federalist No. 25 at 158.

# 16

## The Judiciary Was Excluded From Policymaking

### The Council of Revision

I T is a singular fact that the most significant single piece of evidence that the Framers excluded the judiciary from policymaking—rejection of their participation in a Council of Revision of legislation—went unnoticed by bench and bar until it was called to their attention by a political scientist, Benjamin F. Wright.[1] Not the least remarkable aspect of judicial neglect of this history is that it should finally be invoked by Justices Black (1965)[2] and Douglas (1968),[3] oblivious to the shattering effect that it has on their own sweeping policymaking decisions.

Edmund Randolph proposed in the Convention that the President, "and a convenient number of the National Judiciary, ought to compose a council of revision" to examine every act of Congress and by its dissent to constitute a veto.[4] When his fellow Virginian George Mason argued for judicial participation in the presidential veto, he recognized that judges already

---

1. Benjamin F. Wright, *The Growth of American Constitutional Law* 18–20 (1942); see also A. T. Mason, *The Supreme Court: Palladium of Freedom* 67–70 (1962).

2. Griswold v. Connecticut, 381 U.S. 479, 514 note 6 (1965).

3. Flast v. Cohen, 392 U.S. 83, 107 (1968); Justice Frankfurter had cited it in Board of Education v. Barnette, 319 U.S. 624, 650 (1943): the Framers "denied such legislative powers to the federal judiciary [and] chose instead to insulate the judiciary from the legislative function."

4. 1 Farrand 21.

could declare an unconstitutional law void. But with regard to every law *however unjust oppressive* or pernicious, which did not come plainly under this description, they would be under the necessity as Judges to give it a free course. He wished further use to be made of the Judges, of giving aid in *preventing every improper law.*[5]

A similar differentiation was drawn by James Wilson:

> Laws may be *unjust, may be unwise, may be dangerous,* may be destructive; and yet be *not so unconstitutional* as to justify the Judges in refusing to give them effect. Let them have a share in the Revisionary power [in order to "counteract"] the improper views of the Legislature.[6]

Despite the fact that the proposal had the support of Madison, and, therefore, of perhaps the most influential trio in the Convention, it was rejected for reasons that unmistakably spell out the exclusion of the judiciary from even a share in policymaking. Nathaniel Gorham saw no "advantage of employing the Judges in this way. As Judges they are not to be presumed to possess any peculiar knowledge of the mere policy of public measures."[7] Elbridge Gerry, one of the most vigorous advocates of judicial review, opposed judicial participation in the Council:

> It was *quite foreign* from the nature of ye office to make them *judges of the policy* of public measures . . . It was making Statesmen of the Judges; and setting them up as the guardians of the Rights of the people. He relied for his part on the Representatives of the people as the guardians of their Rights and Interests. It was making the Expositors of the Laws, the Legislators which ought never to be done.[8]

---

5. 2 Farrand 78 (emphasis added).
6. 2 id. 73 (emphasis added).
7. Id.
8. 1 Farrand 97–98; 2 Farrand 75 (emphasis added). Wright stated, "Gerry is not alone in this, for the same point of view is expressed by almost every man who says anything at all on this subject in the Convention and in the ratification controversy." "The judiciary," Wright concluded, "would not be concerned with the policy, the reasonableness or arbitrariness, the wisdom of legislation." Supra note 1 at 18, 244; see also id. 19–20.

Charles Pinckney also "opposed the interference of the Judges in the Legislative business."[9] Rufus King joined in the opposition on the ground that as "the judges must interpret the Laws they ought not to be legislators."[10] Roger Sherman "disapproved of Judges meddling in politics and parties."[11] It is reasonable to infer that John Dickinson expressed a widely shared view in cautioning that "The Justiciary of Aragon . . . became by degrees the law-givers."[12] Plainly the Framers refused to make the judiciary "law-givers," even to the extent of allowing them to share in the legislative making of law, let alone *finally* to decide on policy, an exclusive legislative function.[13] They drew a line between the judicial reviewing function, that is, *policing* grants of power to insure that there were no encroachments beyond the grants, and legislative policymaking *within* those bounds. "Dangerous" and "destructive" as such policies might be, they were yet to be the exclusive province of the legislature. That is the inescapable inference from the facts, and, as will appear, it is fortified by still other historical facts.

Justice Douglas therefore stood on solid ground in stating that "when the Court used substantive due process to determine the wisdom or reasonableness of legislation, it was indeed transforming itself into the Council of Revision which was rejected by the Constitutional Convention."[14] In a remarkable example of compartmentalized thinking he went on to say, "we no longer exercise that kind of power," just as he had

9. 2 Farrand 298.

10. 1 Farrand 108; cf. id. 98.

11. 2 Farrand 300.

12. Id. 299.

13. Mason, *The Supreme Court*, supra note 1 at 70, 94, 117; 1 Julius Goebel, *Antecedents and Beginnings to 1801, History of the Supreme Court of the United States* 238 (1971).

14. Flast v. Cohen, 392 U.S. at 107. Through the due process clauses, A. T. Mason stated, the Court "became the final arbiter of public policy . . . the very authority the framers deliberately refused to confer under the proposed council of revision." Mason, *The Supreme Court*, supra note 1 at 117. Yet Rodell could write that those who complain talk in "abstract phrases"—"judicial usurpation of legislative functions." "The 'Warren Court' Stands Its Ground," *The New York Times Magazine*, September 27, 1964, in Levy, *Warren* 208, 211.

earlier stated in *Griswold v. Connecticut* that the Court no longer acts as a "super legislature"—except in a case touching the "right of privacy."[15]

The history of the Council of Revision also serves to refute the view that judicial review is an expression of "distrust in popular government,"[16] or, in Corwin's oft-quoted phrase, having bet on democracy, the Framers then "covered their bet."[17] The "cover," however, went no further than to prevent the legislature from "overleaping its bounds." In fact the judiciary was *excluded* from halting "dangerous . . . destructive" legislation that was within those bounds. If the Framers "covered their bet," they gave the last trump to Congress: judges who usurped power, for example, exercised a power withheld, said Hamilton, could be impeached. The Founders unequivocally rejected the judiciary as "guardians of the people"; they preferred, in Gerry's words, to put their trust in "the Representatives of the people." For judicial review was an innovation by no means universally admired; it was a departure from Blackstone's "omnipotent parliament."[18] Having "smarted" under the "omnipotent power of the British parliament," said James Iredell, we should "have been guilty of . . . the grossest folly" had we "established a *despotic* power among ourselves."[19] If this could be said of a legislature that could be turned out of office periodically, constitution-makers were even less ready to entrust unlimited power to an untried, unelected judiciary appointed for life.

The judicial role, it cannot be unduly emphasized, was limited to policing constitutional boundaries. James Wilson said it is necessary that Congress be "kept within prescribed bounds, by the interposition of the judicial department."[20] The courts, said Oliver Ellsworth, were a "check" if Congress should "overleap their limits," "make a law which the Constitution does not authorize."[21] Judges, John Marshall stated in the Vir-

15. Supra Chapter 14 at note 74.

16. Wallace Mendelson, *Justices Black and Frankfurter: Conflict in the Court* 126 (1961).

17. Quoted in Mason, *The Supreme Court*, supra note 1 at 63: "Judicial review represents an attempt by American Democracy to cover its bet."

18. Raoul Berger, *Congress v. The Supreme Court* 38–42, 29 (1969).

19. 2 G. J. McRee, *Life and Correspondence of James Iredell* 145–146 (1857–1858).

20. 2 Elliot 445.

21. Id. 196.

ginia Convention, could declare void "a law not warranted by any of the powers enumerated."[22] Hamilton stressed that the courts were to serve as "bulwarks of a limited Constitution against legislative encroachments."[23] But "within those limits," Madison said, there were "discretionary powers."[24] The exercise of that discretion, as we have seen, is for the branch to whom it has been confided. No one, so far as my search of the several convention records uncovered, looked to the Court for "leadership" in resolving problems that Congress, the President, or the States failed to solve. That view is a product of post-Warren euphoria. The courts were expected to "negative" or set aside unauthorized action, to "check" legislative excesses, to "restrain" Congress within its prescribed "limits," to prevent the "usurpation" of power. The Court, in other words, was to act as *nay-sayer*, not as initiator of policy. Justice Stephen Field, supreme activist of his time, stated upon his retirement in 1897 that "This negative power, the power of resistance, is the only safety of a popular government."[25]

When, therefore, James Bradley Thayer and Learned Hand insisted that the role of the Court was to police the boundaries of constitutional grants, not to interfere with the exercise of legislative or executive dis-

22. 3 Elliot 553. For additional citations, see Berger, supra note 18 at 13–16.

23. Federalist No. 78 at 508. At another point he stated that the courts were an "excellent barrier to encroachments and oppressions of the representative body." Id. 503.

24. 1 *Annals of Congress* 438 (1789). "The Legislative powers," Madison stated, "are vested in Congress, and are to be exercised by them uncontrolled by any of the Departments, except the Constitution has qualified it otherwise." Id. 463.

[Story extolled the common law because it "controls the arbitrary discretion of judges, and puts the case beyond the reach of temporary feelings and prejudices." James McClellan, *Joseph Story and the American Constitution* 98 (1971).

Madison stated in the Convention that "the collective interest and security were much more in the power belonging to the Executive than to the Judiciary department . . . in the adminstration of the former much greater latitude is left to opinion and discretion than in the administration of the latter." 2 *The Records of the Federal Convention of 1787* 34 (Max Farrand ed. 1911).]

25. Letter to the Court, October 12, 1897, 168 U.S. 713, 717 (1897). Gouverneur Morris stated that it was the judicial function to reject a "direct violation of the Constitution." 2 Farrand 299. The Court "gained its power as an agency trusted to establish and enforce constitutional limitations on the excessive use of governmental authority," i.e., in excess of granted authority. Paul Murphy, *The Constitution in Crisis Times, 1918–1969* 154 (1972).

cretion *within* those boundaries,[26] they rested firmly on the authority of Hamilton and the preponderant view of the Founders. For 150 years the Court was content with this policing function;[27] even the headstrong laissez-faire Court merely acted as a nay-sayer. It fell to the Warren Court to *initiate* policy when the legislative and executive failed to act, to take the lead in deciding what national policy ought to be.[28] But the failure of Congress to exercise legislative power does not vest it in the Court.

## Judicial "Discretion" in 1787

A common historicist fallacy is to import our twentieth-century conceptions into the minds of the Founders. At the adoption of the Constitution the notion that judges, for example, could *make law* as an instrument of social change was altogether alien to colonial thinking. "Instrumentalism" was yet to come. In a valuable essay Morton J. Horwitz observed that "fear of judicial discretion had long been part of colonial political rhetoric" and described the prevalent jural conceptions

26. J. B. Thayer, "The Origin and Scope of the American Doctrine of Constitutional Law," 7 Harv. L. Rev. 129, 135 (1893); Learned Hand, *The Bill of Rights* 66, 31 (1962). That control of executive discretion lies beyond the judicial function was held in Marbury v. Madison, 5 U.S. (1 Cranch) 137, 169–170 (1803), and in Decatur v. Paulding, 39 U.S. (14 Pet.) 497, 515 (1840).

27. Cf. Murphy, supra note 25 at 154. Professor Kurland stated, "the Court would remain true to its function of preserving the original meaning of the Constitution if it were to act more aggressively to prevent the executive from overreaching his constitutionally limited function." *Politics, the Constitution and the Warren Court* 17 (1970). "Throughout most of our history the form of the Supreme Court's contributions to public policy was negative." Archibald Cox, "The New Dimensions of Constitutional Adjudication," 51 Wash. L. Rev. 791, 813 (1976).

28. "[T]here *were* outrages in American life . . . no other arm of government was doing anything about them." Anthony Lewis, "A Man Born to Act, Not to Muse," *The New York Times Magazine*, June 30, 1968, in Levy, *Warren* 151, 159 (1968). See also Martin Shapiro, *Law and Politics in the Supreme Court* 247–248 (1964). In the words of Professor Lusky, the Court is "acting as a prime mover rather than a modulator of efforts at change initiated elsewhere . . . As a prime mover . . . it has demanded a number of changes which do not command majoritarian support." Lusky 227. See also supra Chapter 14 note 136. For the transformation of the judicial function this has entailed, see Appendix B. See also infra Chapter 20 note 8.

that combined to circumscribe the judicial function in the eighteenth century.[29] There was first the fact that the common law rules—that is, judicially enunciated rules in the field of contracts and the like—"were conceived of as '*founded in principles, that are permanent*, uniform and universal.' " Consequently, judges "conceived their role as merely that of discovering and applying preexisting legal rules" and derived "the rule of strict precedent" from such "preexisting standards discoverable by judges." It followed that "judicial innovation itself was regarded as an impermissible exercise of will."[30] Horwitz cites the statement of Chief Justice Hutchinson of Massachusetts in 1767: "the *Judge* should never be the *Legislator*: Because then the Will of the Judge would be the Law: and this tends to a State of Slavery."[31] Not long afterward Edward Gibbon wrote, "the discretion of the judge is the first engine of tyranny."[32] Horwitz concluded that "In eighteenth century America, common law rules were not regarded as instruments of social change; whatever legal change took place generally was brought about through legislation . . . American judges . . . almost never self-consciously employed the common law as a creative instrument for directing men's energies towards

29. "The Emergence of an Instrumental Conception of American Law, 1780–1820," in 5 *Perspectives in American History* 287, 303 (1971).

30. Id. 296, 297, 298. Zephaniah Smith, Chief Justice of Connecticut, stated, "Judges have no power to frame laws—they can only expound them." 1 Z. Smith, *A System of Laws of the State of Connecticut* 93–94 (1795–1796). Lord Mansfield's reforming work "convinced Thomas Jefferson that a check need be established on the common law powers of judges." Horwitz, supra note 29 at 310. This in the field of commercial, not constitutional, law.

31. Horwitz, id. 292. For additional materials illustrating the Founders' aversion to judicial discretion, see Gordon Wood, *The Creation of the American Republic 1776–1789* 301–302 (1969). As one writer put it, if the judges "put such a construction on matters as they think most agreeable to the spirit and reason of the law . . . they assume what is in fact the prerogative of the legislature." Wood, id. 302.

32. 4 Edward Gibbon, *The History of the Decline and Fall of the Roman Empire* 518 (Nottingham Soc. undated). Blackstone had written, "law, without equity, though hard and disagreeable, is much more desirable for the public good than equity without law; which would make every judge a legislator, and introduce most infinite confusion." 1 Blackstone, *Commentaries on the Laws of England* 62 (1765–1769). Wendell Phillips quoted Lord Camden: "The discretion of a Judge is the law of tyrants . . . In the best of times it is often times caprice—in the worst, it is every vice, folly and passion, to which human nature is liable." Quoted in Robert Cover, *Justice Accused: Antislavery and the Judicial Process* 152 (1975).

social change."[33] Those who would rest an implied power of judges to act as such instruments of social change in the field of constitutional law have the burden of producing evidence that the Framers intended to depart from these norms. The exclusion of judges from the Council of Revision alone points to the contrary.

"Instrumentalism," Horwitz shows, largely began to develop in the early nineteenth century—after the adoption of the Constitution; the examples he cites are all drawn from application of common law; not once is a judicial claim of power to alter a statute, let alone a constitution, asserted. To such negative implications may be added Hamilton's statement in the very context of judicial review (Federalist No. 78), that the judicial role is one of "judgment" not "will," that "to avoid arbitrary discretion in the courts, it is indispensable that they should be bound down by strict rules and precedents, which serve to define and point out their duty in every particular case that comes before them."[34] What could be further from the current freewheeling conception of judicial review than these words by the foremost apologist for judicial review, designed to reassure opponents of ratification? Courts were not merely to be "bound down" by the "chains of the Constitution," but by "strict rules and precedents" as well. Even when the tide began to turn toward instrumentalism, Judge William Cranch of the Circuit Court for the District of Columbia stated in his preface to 1 Cranch of the Supreme Court's decisions (1803): "In a government which is emphatically stiled a government of laws, the least possible range ought to be left for the discretion of the judge."[35]

33. Supra note 29 at 287.

34. Horwitz, supra note 29 at 309–326; Federalist No. 78 at 504, 510. Kent stated that without the common law, i.e., the precedents, "the courts would be left to a dangerous discretion to roam at large in the trackless field of their own imaginations." 1 James Kent, *Commentaries on American Law* 373 (9th ed. 1858).

35. 5 U.S. (1 Cranch) iii (1803). Cranch was a nephew of, and appointed by, President John Adams, and a classmate and esteemed friend of his cousin John Quincy Adams. *Life in a New England Town: 1787, 1788. Diary of John Quincy Adams* 21 note 2 (1903). Horwitz quotes an unpublished opinion on circuit by Justice William Johnson (1813) that to invite "judicial discretion" would "increase the oddity of the state of things" in that the judiciary "would be left at large to be governed by their own views on the Fitness of things." Supra note 29 at 306–307.

There are also contemporary judicial statements that display the circumspection with which the judges approached the novel task of judicial review. In one of the earliest State cases, *Commonwealth v. Caton* (1782), Edmund Pendleton, president of the highest Virginia court, stated: "how far this court . . . can go in declaring an act of the Legislature void, because it is repugnant to the Constitution, without exercising the Power of Legislation, from which they are restrained by the same Constitution? is a deep, important, and I will add, an awful question"[36]—which, he rejoiced, he had no occasion to decide. Subsequently, Pendleton served as the presiding officer of the Virginia Ratification Convention, and it is unlikely that he translated the examples furnished by his colleagues, all addressed to checking encroachments on reserved powers, into unlimited power of review. No one remotely intimated that there would be judicial power to rewrite the Constitution.[37] Nothing could have been better calculated to defeat ratification than a claim of judicial power that would leave the States altogether at the mercy of the federal courts;[38] and such State jealousy was met by the Judiciary Act of 1789 which withheld from the inferior federal courts jurisdiction of cases "arising under" the Constitution.

Even with respect to the policing function, Justice James Iredell, who had been one of the most cogent advocates of judicial review, stated in 1798 that the power to declare a legislative act "void is of a delicate and awful nature, [hence] the Court will never resort to that authority but in a clear and urgent case."[39] In *M'Culloch v. Maryland* Chief Justice Marshall indicated that something like a "bold and plain usurpation to which the constitution gave no countenance" was required "to invoke the ju-

36. Commonwealth v. Caton, published in 2 *Letters and Papers of Edmund Pendleton* 416, 422 (D. J. Mays ed. 1967).

37. For citations to Madison, Marshall, and Nicholas, see Berger, supra note 18 at 77, 140, 15.

38. Cf. id. 263.

39. Calder v. Bull, 3 U.S. (3 Dall.) 386, 399 (1798); Justice Chase said, "a very clear case." Id. 395. Earlier, Iredell, rebutting criticism of judicial review by Richard Spaight (then a delegate to the Convention), had stressed that an Act "should be unconstitutional beyond dispute before it is pronounced such." 2 McRee, supra note 19 at 175.

dicial power of annulment."[40] And in 1824 he averred that "judicial power is never exercised for the purpose of giving effect to the will of the judge; always for the purpose of giving effect to the will of the legislature."[41] For Chief Judge Cardozo, Marshall's statement was the expression "of an ideal," which "Marshall's own career" illustrates "is beyond the reach of human faculties to attain."[42] It would be more accurate to say, as Charles L. Black pointed out, that it reflected the colonists' conception that "*Law is a body of existing and determinate rules,*" which "*is to be ascertained*" by the judge by consulting "statutes, precedents and the rest," and that "the function of the judge was thus placed in sharpest antithesis to that of the legislator," who alone was concerned "with what the law ought to be."[43] So Marshall understood the judicial role: "Courts are mere instruments of the law and can will nothing. When they are said to exercise a discretion, it is a mere legal discretion, a discretion to be exercised in discerning the course *prescribed by law*"[44]—that is, by the legislators or the people gathered in Convention.

Marshall, it needs always to be remembered, had fought on behalf of judicial review in the Virginia Ratification Convention and was well aware of the views entertained by the Founders. His 1824 statement confirms that among the presuppositions the Founders brought to the several conventions was a bias against judicial discretion and policymaking. There is no evidence whatsoever that these presuppositions were thrown overboard in the creation of the judiciary. To the contrary, the established presumption is that the Founders created a judiciary in familiar terms, except insofar as they envisaged its "policing" function. Judicial alteration of the fundamental law ran counter to their belief in a "fixed Constitution"; it

40. 17 U.S. (4 Wheat.) 316, 402 (1819).

41. Osborn v. Bank of the United States, 22 U.S. (9 Wheat.) 738, 866 (1824).

42. Benjamin N. Cardozo, *The Nature of the Judicial Process* 169–170 (1921). It is not merely an "ideal" but a requirement of the separation of powers, supra Chapter 15 at notes 27, 43–49. Marshall recognized judicial limits in his pseudonymous defense of M'Culloch v. Maryland, to meet stormy charges of judicial usurpation. See infra Chapter 21 at notes 12–19. Least of all can the judiciary say one thing and do another; it cannot afford conflicts between word and deed. Nor does Marshall's disregard of constitutional bounds legitimate his displacement of the Framers' "will" by his own.

43. Black, *The People and the Court* 160 (1960).

44. Osborn v. Bank, 22 U.S. at 866 (emphasis added).

was altogether outside their contemplation, as Hamilton made plain.[45] Justice Frankfurter, therefore, was close to the mark in stating that the Framers were on guard "against the self-will of the courts."[46]

## Supplementary Note on Exclusion of the Judiciary

Activists forget, or overlook, the framers' exclusion of the judiciary from policymaking. A proposal for judicial participation in the president's veto was rejected on the ground, among others, that the Justices had no special competence in the field of policy.[1] Benjamin Wright stated that "the same point of view was expressed by almost every man who says anything at all on this subject at the Convention and in the ratification controversy." The judiciary, he concluded, "would not be concerned with the policy, the reasonableness or arbitrariness, the wisdom of legislation."[2]

These views were reflected by the judiciary. In one of the earliest and strongest decisions to lay claim to the power of judicial review, *Kamper v. Hawkins*, Judge Henry explained:

> The judiciary from the nature of the office . . . could never be designed to determine upon the equity, necessity or usefulness of a law: that would amount to an express interfering with the legislative branch . . . [N]ot being chosen immediately by the people, nor being accountable to them . . . they do not, and ought not, to represent the people in framing or repealing any law.[3]

45. The foregoing materials, to my mind, refute Bickel's view that the Framers "certainly had no specific intent relating to the nature and range of the power" of judicial review. *The Least Dangerous Branch* 104 (1962).

46. National Ins Co. v. Tidewater Co., 337 U.S. 582, 647 (1949), dissenting opinion.

1. Supra pp. 322–324.

2. Benjamin F. Wright, *The Growth of American Constitutional Law* 244 (1942). This was likewise the view of Madison; see *The Mind of the Founders: Sources of Political Thought of James Madison* 360 (Marvin Meyers ed. 1981).

3. 3 Va. (1 Va. Cas.) 20, 47 (1793).

This was the contemporaneous view. In *Ware v. Hylton*, Justice James Iredell, who anticipated Hamilton's defense of judicial review in Federalist No. 78, declared, "These are considerations of policy, considerations of extreme magnitude, and certainly entirely incompetent to the examination and decision of a Court of Justice."[4] For long that remained the view of the Supreme Court.[5]

Despite the Court's exclusion from policymaking, activists hail it as "*conscience to the country*."[6] For Bruce Ackerman, the "real significance" of *Brown v. Board of Education*[7] lies in "the Court's courage in confronting modern Americans with a moral and political agenda that calls upon them to heed the voices of their better selves."[8] This was not a mere "call" but a binding decision, notwithstanding that the citizenry did not demand "a fundamental change in our fundamental law."[9] Ackerman reminds us of Robespierre: "If Frenchmen would not be free and virtuous voluntarily, then he would force them to be free and cram virtue down their throats."[10]

4. 3 U.S. (3 Dall.) 199, 260 (1796).

5. Nebbia v. New York, 291 U.S. 502, 537 (1934): "The courts are without authority to declare such [State economic] policy. With the wisdom of the policy adopted . . . the courts are both incompetent and unauthorized to deal."

6. Anthony Lewis, "Historical Change in the Supreme Court," in *The Supreme Court Under Earl Warren* 81 (Leonard Levy ed. 1972) (emphasis added); Arthur S. Miller & Ronald F. Howell, "The Myth of Neutrality in Constitutional Adjudication," 27 U. Chi. L. Rev. 661, 689 (1960).

With the changing of the guard on the Court, it appears that it was the activists' own conscience that they cherished, not that of the nation. The point is exemplified by the heated invective of Dean Calabresi; see supra Supplementary Note on the Introduction note 7, a shift from activist rejoicing in the "revolutionary" changes made by the Warren Court.

7. 347 U.S. 483 (1954).

8. Bruce Ackerman, *We the People: Foundations* 133 (1991). The claim that "our 'insulated' judiciary has done a better job of speaking for our better selves turns out to be historically shaky." Alexander M. Bickel, *The Least Dangerous Branch* 57 (1962).

9. Ackerman, supra note 8 at 133.

10. 2 Crane Brinton, John B. Christopher, and Robert L. Wolff, *A History of Civilization* 115 (1960). From "their experiences under the Protectorate, Englishmen learned that . . . the claims of self-appointed saints to know by divine inspiration what the good life should be and to have the right to impose their notions on the ungodly could be as great a threat as the divine right of kings." W. H. Auden, "Introduction" to Sydney Smith, *Selected Writings of Sydney Smith* xvi (W. H. Auden ed. 1956).

Activist Mortimer Adler gives the game away; he upbraids Robert Bork because he "find[s] no grounds for doing what must be done in the crucial cases in which the majority legislation is unjust without being unconstitutional."[11] A philosopher may long for the freedom of a kadi to decide as he will, but as Chief Justice Marshall said, "Whatever might be the answer of a moralist . . . a jurist must search for its legal solution in those principles of action which are sanctioned by usage,"[12] and even more, by the Constitution. To determine what is "unjust" we should first ask what is "just." Cardozo struggled to define "justice" and concluded that "when all is said and done," it "remains to some extent . . . the synonym of an aspiration, a mood of exaltation, a yearning for what is fine and high."[13] This offers scant support for encroachment on the "residuary and inviolable" jurisdiction of the States over personal affairs of their citizens.[14] For the Founders the "unjust" was not equivalent to the "unconstitutional." James Wilson, second only to Madison as an architect of the Constitution, flatly declared that "laws may be unjust," even "dangerous," and yet not be "unconstitutional," a view likewise expressed by George Mason.[15]

But Suzanna Sherry maintains that we are free to make our own "moral choices."[16] Of course; but it does not follow that they must be made for us by unelected, unaccountable judges. Nevertheless she urges that they "have some obligation to oversee the community's moral

11. Mortimer Adler, "Robert Bork: The Lessons to Be Learned," 84 Nw. U. L. Rev. 1121, 1125 (1990). Justice Frankfurter cautioned, "Nor should resentment against an injustice displace controlling history in judicial construction of the Constitution." United States v. Lovett, 328 U.S. 303, 323 (1946), concurring opinion.

12. The Antelope, 23 U.S. (10 Wheat.) 66, 121 (1825).

13. Benjamin N. Cardozo, *The Growth of the Law* 87 (1924).

14. Federalist No. 41 at 249 (Mod. Lib. ed. 1937). In Tyson v. Banton, 273 U.S. 418, 446 (1927), Justice Holmes stated "that a state legislature can do whatever it sees fit to do unless it is restrained by some express prohibition in the Constitution . . . and that the Courts should be careful not to extend such prohibitions beyond their obvious meaning by reading into them conceptions of public policy that the particular Court may happen to entertain," dissenting opinion.

15. 2 *The Records of the Federal Convention of 1787* 73, 78 (Max Farrand ed. 1911).

16. Suzanna Sherry, "The Ninth Amendment: Righting an Unwritten Constitution," 64 Chi.-Kent L. Rev. 1001 (1989), reprinted in 2 *The Rights Retained in the People* 283, 293 (Randy Barnett ed. 1993).

choices."[17] Not a shred of evidence remotely suggests that the Founders contemplated that judges would serve as arbiters of morals. Their function, Marshall pointed out, was merely to "construe," to "interpret" laws,[18] not to infuse them with moral content. Having rejected judicial participation in policymaking, the Framers were little likely to embrace judicial supervision of morals. What ground was there for attributing special competence to judges in the field of morals? Jefferson spoke powerfully to the contrary: "I cannot give up my guidance to the magistrate, because he knows no more the way to heaven than I do, and is less concerned to direct me than I am to go right."[19] Activist John Ely remarked that perhaps judges are not "best equipped to make moral judgments, in particular that they are [not] better suited to the task than legislators."[20] If morals are to be the guide, it is questionable "whether the Court is as competent as Congress to divine the character of . . . tradition and consensus."[21] Rapaczynski observes the judges' "absence of special competence . . . in matters of general morality."[22] Then too, Perry considers that "Political-moral philosophy, after all, is in a state of serious disarray,"[23] a view shared by Larry Simon.[24] But Stephen Macedo protests

17. Id.

18. Chief Justice Marshall stated, "The difference between the departments undoubtedly is that the legislature makes, the executive executes, and the judiciary construes the law." Wayman v. Southard, 23 U.S. (10 Wheat.) 1, 46 (1825). The separation of powers guards this difference.

19. Saul K. Padover, *Jefferson* 44 (abridged ed. 1970).

20. John Hart Ely, "Foreword: On Discovering Fundamental Values," 92 Harv. L. Rev. 5, 35 (1978) (bracket in original).

21. Michael J. Perry, *The Constitution, the Courts, and Human Rights* 108 (1982).

22. Andrzej Rapaczynski, "The Ninth Amendment and the Unwritten Constitution: The Problems of Constitutional Interpretation," 64 Chi.-Kent L. Rev. 177, 208 (1988). Stephen Macedo notes the "complexity of moral issues and the tendency of moral judgments to be colored by personal feelings." Stephen Macedo, "Reason, Rhetoric, and the Ninth Amendment: A Comment on Sanford Levinson," 64 Chi.-Kent L. Rev. 163, 173 (1988).

23. Michael J. Perry, "The Authority of Text, Tradition, and Reason: A Theory of Constitutional Interpretation," 54 S. Cal. L. Rev. 551, 592–593 (1985).

24. "[M]oral theory today is in a conceptual melange." Larry Simon, "The Authority of the Constitution and Its Meaning: A Preface to a Theory of Constitutional Interpretation," 58 S. Cal. L. Rev. 603, 619 (1985). The "controversy that surrounds many of the Court's human rights cases—the death penalty and abortion cases are good examples—

that preclusion of a judicial moral test will leave unreasonable legislation untouched.[25] That is precisely what the Founders intended.[26]

Activists' solicitude for judicial "supervision" of morals is but another aspect of their attempts to maintain the revisionary gains of the Warren Court. As Mark Tushnet notes, academe applauds Supreme Court "embodiments of principles of justice, defined as the standard political principles of the moderate left of the Democratic party."[27] Those principles likewise are mine; but I make no pretense of identifying them with constitutional mandates.

---

shows that neither the public nor the courts share a consensus on what Perry views as moral issues." John B. McArthur, "Abandoning the Constitution: The New Wave in Constitutional Theory," 59 Tul. L. Rev. 280, 291 (1984).

25. Stephen Macedo, "Originalism and the Inescapability of Politics," 84 Nw. U. L. Rev. 1203, 1212 (1990).

26. Supra, text accompanying notes 2–4.

27. Mark Tushnet, "Truth, Justice, and the American Way: An Interpretation of the Public Law Scholarship in the Seventies," 57 Tex. L. Rev. 1307, 1322 (1979).

# 17

## The Turnabout of the Libertarians

Wᴴʏ did the libertarians, after decades of berating the Court for reading its laissez-faire predilections into the Constitution and imposing its own economic policy on the nation,[1] turn around and defend it for pursuing the same course with respect to libertarian values? One may view the turnabout merely as another illustration of "whose ox is gored";[2] but perhaps the explanation lies deeper. Arthur Sutherland explained that between 1920 and 1940 academe "viewed the federal judiciary with dismay" and was "deeply imbued with faith in majorities." A "change of political theory developed" between 1938 and 1948, deriving from "Hitler's popularity among the German people, public support of the Un-American Activities Committee and McCarthy Hearings" and so on, for "votaries of unreviewed majoritarianism" suddenly realized that "unrestricted majorities could be as tyrannical as wicked oligarchs . . . We could not say in plain terms that occasionally we have to select wise and able people and give them the constitutional function of coun-

1. In the pre-1937 era, Archibald Cox states, "Historians and politicians were 'proving' that judicial review was a usurpation of power defeating the original intent. There was a sense that the justices made a mess of things when they attempted to enlarge their orbit, as they did in resisting government regulation of the economy." *The Role of the Supreme Court in American Government* 34 (1976).

2. An unconscious example is Rodell's statement in 1964: "Not since the Nine Old Men of unhallowed memory struck down the first New Deal almost 30 years ago . . . has any Supreme Court used its politico-legal power so broadly and boldly as did Earl Warren's," a performance that gave him joy, whereas the predecessors were "unhallowed." Fred Rodell, "The Warren Court Stands Its Ground," *The New York Times Magazine*, September 27, 1964, in Levy, *Warren* 208, 209.

tering the democratic process."[3] Looking back in 1976 and writing with equally praiseworthy candor, Archibald Cox, who had played a major role as Solicitor General in persuading the Supreme Court to adopt some of the epochal decisions of the 1960s,[4] stated:

> By the 1950s the political atmosphere had changed. The legislative process, even at its best, became resistant to libertarian, humanitarian, and egalitarian impulses. At worst, the legislatures became repressive, in the libertarian view, because of the Cold War, increased crime, the fear of social disorder, and perhaps, the strength of established economic and political power . . . [I]n the new era these impulses were not shared so strongly and widely as to realize themselves through legislation. They came to be felt after the early 1950s by a majority of the Supreme Court Justices, perhaps by the fate which puts one man upon the Court rather than another, perhaps because the impulses were felt more strongly in the world of the highly educated.[5]

Mark that these "impulses" were "not shared so strongly and widely as to realize themselves through legislation," that they "were felt more strongly in the world of the highly educated," and were realized through the "fate which puts one man upon the Court rather than another." Because for the nonce the majority of the Court shared the predilections of the "highly educated," the latter looked kindly upon the Court's imposition of its will upon the people.[6] But, as Myres McDougal wrote some years ago, "Government by a self-designated elite—like that of benevolent despotism or Plato's philosopher kings—may be a good form of government for some, but it is not the American way."[7] No intellec-

3. "Privacy in Connecticut," 64 Mich. L. Rev. 283–284 (1965).
4. See Ward Elliot, *The Rise of a Guardian Democracy* (1974).
5. Cox, supra note 1 at 35.
6. Writing in September 1976, Professor Joseph W. Bishop, Jr., stated, "Those who favor abortion, busing . . . and oppose capital punishment, call themselves and are generally regarded as liberals. But they obviously have no faith whatever in the wisdom or the will of the great majority of the people, who are opposed to them. They are doing everything possible to have these problems resolved by a small minority in the courts or the bureaucracy." Bishop, "What is a Liberal—Who is a Conservative?," 62 *Commentary* 47.
7. McDougal and Lans, "Treaties and Congressional–Executive or Presidential Agreements: Interchangeable Instruments of National Policy," 54 Yale L.J. 181, 577–578 (1945).

tual but can from time to time be disappointed by the vox populi, whether it be by the choices it makes—Richard Nixon, for example—or its imperviousness to the cultural values intellectuals cherish. In some it leads to a sense of alienation from the commonality; but, as Winston Churchill observed, the alternatives to democracy are even worse. With Lincoln, I cling to faith in the ultimate good sense of the people;[8] I cannot subscribe to the theory that America needs a savior, whether in the shape of a President or of nine—oftimes only five—Platonic Guardians.

It does not dispose of the uncomfortable historical facts to be told that "the dead hand of the past need not and should not be binding," that the Founders "should not rule us from their graves."[9] To thrust aside the dead hand of the Framers is to thrust aside the Constitution. The argument that new meanings may be given to words employed by the Framers[10] aborts their design; it reduces the Constitution to an empty shell into which each shifting judicial majority pours its own preferences. It is no answer to argue, as did Charles Curtis, "we cannot have our government run as if it were stuck in the end of the eighteenth century when we are in the middle of the twentieth,"[11] because, as Willard Hurst replied, "the real issue is *who is to make the policy choices* in the twentieth century: judges or the combination of legislature and electorate that makes constitutional amendments."[12] Since, for example, it would have been impossible to secure a desegregation amendment,[13] the libertarians premise that submission of such an issue to the people by amendment is at all costs to be avoided. McDougal and Lans genteelly

8. President Charles W. Eliot of Harvard University wrote, "I should like to be saved from loss of faith in democracy as I grow old and foolish." Ernest A. Samuels, *Henry Adams: The Major Phase* 359 (1964).

9. *Judicial Review and the Supreme Court* 143 (Leonard Levy ed. 1967); Arthur S. Miller, "An Inquiry Into the Relevance of the Intentions of the Founding Fathers, With Special Emphasis Upon the Doctrine of Separation of Powers," 27 Ark. L. Rev. 584, 601 (1973).

10. Infra Chapter 20 at notes 28–39.

11. "The Role of the Constitutional Text," in *Supreme Court and Supreme Law* 64, 68 (Edmond N. Cahn ed. 1954).

12. Willard Hurst, "Discussion," in *Supreme Court and Supreme Law*, id. 75 (emphasis added). Hurst also disposed thereby of the citation to Holmes' "The present has a right to govern itself." Leonard Levy, *Judgments: Essays in American Constitutional History* 17 (1972). For Holmes' views see infra Chapter 21 at notes 33–42.

13. Supra Chapter 15 at note 14.

explained that because "the process of amendment is politically difficult, other modes of change have emerged."[14] In less opaque terms, the cumbersomeness of the process authorizes the servants of the people informally to amend the Constitution without consulting them! That, however, collides head-on with Hamilton's assurance in the midst of his defense of judicial review in Federalist No. 78:

> Until the people have, by some solemn and authoritative act, annulled or changed the established form, it is binding upon themselves collectively, as well as individually; and no presumption, or even knowledge of their sentiments, can warrant their representatives in a departure from it, prior to such an act.[15]

Neither Frankfurter's finely tuned antennae for ascertaining the inarticulate sentiments of the people, nor "even knowledge of their sentiments, can warrant" a "departure from" the Constitution by the Justices. Change, thus laid down the leading expositor of judicial review,

14. McDougal and Lans, supra note 7 at 293. Chief Justice Burger stated, "however cumbersome or glacial, this is the procedure the Constitution contemplated." Wheeler v. Montgomery, 397 U.S. 280, 284 (1970), dissenting opinion.

It is ironical that libertarians who argue for judicial "adaptation" of the Constitution because amendment is cumbersome should, like Eugene V. Rostow, state, "Given the possibility of constitutional amendment, there is nothing undemocratic in having responsible and independent judges act as important constitutional mediators." "The Democratic Character of Judicial Review," 66 Harv. L. Rev. 193, 197 (1952). Judges, in short, may alter the Constitution because resort to the people is onerous, but that very cumbersome process is recommended to the people to curb judicial infractions; cf. infra note 31.

15. Federalist No. 78 at 509. For a similar comment by Jefferson see infra at note 90. Compare this with Alexander Bickel's view that "The Framers knew . . . that nothing but disaster could result for government under a written constitution if it were generally accepted that the specific intent of the framers of a constitutional provision is ascertainable and is forever and specifically binding, subject only to the cumbersome process of amendment." *The Least Dangerous Branch* 106 (1962). See also Madison, 1 *Annals of Congress* 739. Elias Boudinot, erstwhile President of the Continental Congress, referred in the First Congress to "the great danger" in "modifying the principles of the Constitution." We "may begin with the alpha and go to the omega, changing, reversing, and subverting every principle contained in it . . . [T]his never was the intention of our constituents; they never sent us here for the purpose of altering the system of Government; they reserved that power to themselves." 1 *Annals of Congress* 530. See also Alexander White, supra Chapter 15 note 54.

must come via amendment. The reason was put in a nutshell by Bruce Claggett. The Constitution requires that:

> changes in our fundamental law be made only when and if they have been subjected to the degree of deliberation and commanded the preponderance of assent, involved in adoption and ratification of a constitutional amendment . . . [T]he requirement was agreed upon (what legitimacy has our scheme of government had except as a compact?) and unilateral change involves usurpation, at least as much when effected by a court as by a majority in Congress. If one thinks the more-than-simple majorities required for constitutional change are too onerous, one disagrees with the Constitution itself.[16]

It is not as if the difficulties of amendment were unperceived by the Founders. Patrick Henry argued in the Virginia Ratification Convention that "four of the smallest states, that do not collectively contain one tenth part of the population . . . may obstruct the most salutary . . . amendments."[17] But James Iredell expressed the prevailing view: the Constitution "can be altered with as much regularity, and as little confusion, as any Act of Assembly; not, indeed, quite so easily, which would be extremely impolitic . . . so that alterations can without difficulty be made, agreeable to the general sense of the people."[18] In Massachusetts, Charles Jarvis said, "we shall have in this article an adequate provision for all purposes of political reformation."[19] In the First Congress, Elbridge Gerry, one of the important Framers and erstwhile President of the Continental Congress, stated: "The people have" directed a "particular mode of making amendments, which we are not at liberty to depart from . . . Such a power [to alter] would render the most important

16. "Book Review," 27 Harv. L. Sch. Bull. 3, 4–5 (1976). See also supra Chapter 15 at note 61. For what consent meant to the Founders, see supra Chapter 15 at note 54.

17. 3 Elliot 49.

18. 4 Elliot 177.

19. 2 Elliot 116. In the Virginia Convention, Judge Edmund Pendleton stated, "remote possible errors may be eradicated by the amendatory clause in the Constitution . . . the system itself points out an easy mode of removing errors which shall have been experienced." 3 Elliot 303. This was a judge who had faced up to the issue of judicial review, supra Chapter 16 at note 36, and it speaks volumes that it never occurred to him that there might be an even easier judicial way of revision than the "easy mode" provided by Article V.

clause of the Constitution nugatory."[20] In other words, Article V constitutes the *exclusive* medium of change, under the long-standing maxim that to name a particular mode is to exclude all others.[21] And, as Gerry stated, "an attempt to amend" the Constitution in "any other way" but by Article V "may be a high crime and misdemeanor," that is, an impeachable offense for subversion of the Constitution.[22] Because arguments to the contrary are couched obliquely—for example, "each generation of citizens must in a very real sense interpret the words of the Framers to create its own Constitution"[23]—one is apt to overlook that these are arguments for "change" outside Article V, by the judicial "interpreters" rather than the people. Libertarians, in short, would read the exclusivity of Article V out of the Constitution and cede to the Court a power that is to be exercised only by the people, and then only in accordance with its terms. The "shackles" from which libertarians would free us had the sanction of the people expressed through their State conventions, whereas judicial revision represents only the will of judges who would circumvent submission of a change to the people.

The Court itself, however, has not been overeager to acknowledge the crown academe would press upon its brow; it has never in terms asserted a right to strike the shackles of the past. Though it has often repudiated the design of the Framers, it has done so by indirection, by resort to "lawyer's history,"[24] to far-fetched theorizing in search of an

20. 1 *Annals of Congress* 503 (1789).

21. See supra Chapter 12 note 11.

22. 1 *Annals of Congress* 503 (1789); see Hamilton, supra Chapter 15 at note 50.

23. McDougal and Lans, supra note 7 at 215.

24. "The present use of history by the Court is a Marxist-type perversion of the relation between truth and utility. It assumes that history can be written to serve the interests of libertarian idealism. The whole process calls to mind the manipulation of scientific truth by the Soviet Government in the Lysenko controversy. The Court's purposes may be more laudable . . . but the assumptions about the nature of reality are the same." Alfred H. Kelly, "Clio and the Court: An Illicit Love Affair," 1965 S. Ct. Rev. 119, 157. Nevertheless Kelly applauded the decision in the desegregation case. Thomas Grey comments on the Court's "resort to bad legislative history and strained reading of constitutional language to support results that would be better justified by explication of contemporary moral and political ideals not drawn from the constitutional text." "Do We Have an Unwritten Constitution?," 27 Stan. L. Rev. 703, 706 (1975). See also Charles A. Miller, *The Supreme Court and the Uses of History* (1969).

anchor in the Constitution. Robert Bork justly comments that "The Supreme Court regularly insists that its results . . . do not spring from the mere will of the Justices in the majority but are supported, indeed compelled, by a proper understanding of the Constitution . . . Value choices are attributed to the Founding Fathers, not to the Court."[25] Let Chief Justice Warren himself furnish an example: "The provisions of the Constitution are not time-worn adages or hollow shibboleths. They are vital living principles that authorize and limit governmental power in our Nation. They are the rules of government."[26] As Bork observes, "The way an institution advertises tells you what it thinks its customers demand."[27] Were the issue put squarely to the American people whether they would elect to have the Court strike the "shackles" of the past or to live under the constraints of the Constitution, I doubt not that they would resoundingly prefer the "idiosyncratic purposes of the Framers"[28] to those of the Justices.[29]

25. "Neutral Principles and Some First Amendment Problems," 47 Ind. L.J. 1, 3–4 (1971); see Grey, supra note 24.

26. Trop v. Dulles, 356 U.S. 86, 103 (1958).

27. Bork, supra note 25 at 4.

28. McDougal and Lans, supra note 7 at 291. Professor Lusky also prefers "misgovernment by law" to "enlightened government by decree." Lusky 271. Hans Linde remarks that the "whole enterprise of constitutional law rests, after all, on the premise that the nation cares about its Constitution, not about its courts." "Judges, Critics and the Realist Tradition," 82 Yale L.J. 227, 256 (1972).

"In Professor [David] Truman's terms, large numbers of, and perhaps most, Americans entertain certain expectations or values about the Court's neutrality—values that have been called the 'judicial myth' [D. Truman, *The Governmental Process* 498 (1948)]." Martin Shapiro, *Law and Politics in the Supreme Court* 29 (1964). From childhood on the American expectation that the umpire will not espouse the cause of the opposing side is no "myth." If judicial umpires alone are not impartial arbiters let that fact be made known. See infra Chapter 23 at notes 30–35.

29. Judicial idiosyncrasy finds ready illustration in Justice Douglas. For example, he joined in the decision in Williams v. Florida, 399 U.S. 78 (1970), holding that the phrase "trial by jury" did not require a jury of twelve. But he dissented when the Court held in Johnson v. Louisiana, 406 U.S. 356 (1972), that these words did not require a unanimous verdict, condemning "this radical departure from American traditions"—"two centuries of American history are shunted aside." Id. 381, 383. For centuries both a 12-man jury *and* a unanimous verdict had been indissoluble components of trial by jury. See infra Chapter 22. Douglas weakly sought to distinguish the 12-man jury decisions because "neither evidence nor theory suggested the 12-man jury decision was more favorable to the

Some have sought a rationale in common law affirmations. Alexander Bickel referred to Holmes' statement that it is "revolting" to adhere to a rule of law, the grounds of which "have vanished long since."[30] Holmes wrote in the frame of the common law, where the courts have long been entrusted with the task of shaping the law of contracts and the like. If the results were at times displeasing to Parliament, they could be over-ruled in easy fashion by an act of Parliament. Decisions of constitutional question cannot, however, be overruled by the legislature; resort must be had to the "cumbersome" amendment process—it took eighteen years to overrule the income tax decision![31] Then, too, if the common law is to serve as a model, it needs to be remembered that at the adoption of the Constitution judicial discretion was feared and confined by strict ad-herence to precedent as a curb on the "impermissible exercise of will,"[32] a course far removed from the present Court's habit of leaving "prece-dents in a shambles."[33] Nevertheless, a free and easy judicial approach to constitutional "adaptation" derived in no small part from the freedom American courts assumed in the early nineteenth century to reshape the common law for the benefit of an emerging entreprenurial system. Wit-ting or unwitting, it was a carryover from a practice so plainly described by Chancellor Kent in extolling his own role in the shaping of American

accused than six." Id. 382 note 1. On that analysis his appeal to history was superfluous. See also supra Chapter 14 at note 74.

30. Bickel, supra note 15 at 16. For a similar view, see Levy, *Judgments*, supra note 12 at 17. But compare Justice Holmes, infra note 32.

31. P. B. Kurland, *Politics, the Constitution and the Warren Court* 176–177 (1970); Raoul Berger, *Congress v. The Supreme Court* 207 (1969); Pollock v. Farmers Loan & Trust Co., 157 U.S. 429 (1895). Justice Brandeis stated, "In only two instances—the Eleventh and the Sixteenth Amendments—has the process of constitutional amendment been success-fully resorted to, to nullify decisions of this Court." Burnet v. Coronada Oil & Gas Co., 285 U.S. 393, 409 note 5 (1932), dissenting opinion.

32. Supra Chapter 16 at notes 30–35, 44. Even in the adjudication of common law cases, the norm was to leave "novel and unique" changes to the legislature, not "to re-place a durable impersonal body of common law principles with intuitive individual no-tions of justice in a given case." G. E. White, *The American Judicial Tradition* 277 (1976). Or, as Justice Holmes stated, "judges do and must legislate, but they can do so intersti-tially; they are confined from molar to molecular motions. A common law judge could not say I think the doctrine of consideration a bit of historical nonsense and shall not enforce it." Southern Pacific Co. v. Jensen, 244 U.S. 205, 221 (1917), dissenting opinion.

33. Levy, *Against the Law* 260.

equity jurisdiction: "I might once & a while be embarrassed by a technical rule, *but I most always found principles suited to my views of the case.*"[33a] This remarkable confession that law was to be manipulated to achieve a desired result—"my views of the case"—might perhaps be extenuated in an area where courts had been left to make the initial choices. But no such authority was conferred in the policing of constitutional boundaries. For, as Judge J. Skelly Wright observed (in an article devoted to castigating the "self-appointed scholastic mandarans" who criticized the Warren Court): "Constitutional choices are in fact different from ordinary decisions . . . the most important value choices have already been made by the framers of the Constitution." Judicial "value choices," he continued, "are to be made only within the parameters" of those choices.[34] If, as Judge Wright declared, even "imprecise" constitutional guarantees "provide a direction, a goal," and "rule out many alternative directions, goals,"[35] all the more does the exclusion of suffrage from the Fourteenth Amendment, for example, leave no room for judicial choices such as "one man, one vote."

"Instrumentalism" describes the approach derived from early-nineteenth-century common law practice, a view, Hans Linde points out, later expressed in the "realist canon" that new decisions are to "be measured by instrumental success in effecting a socially desirable outcome."[36] But at the adoption of the Constitution judges were considered to be without discretion to alter the law. And "desired" by whom? Oft-times the "sense of the community" has turned on the opinion of a swing man, for example, Justice Owen Roberts, whose change of position in 1937

33a. Quoted in Morton J. Horwitz, *The Transformation of American Law* 125 (1977). This "transformation," Horwitz justly concludes, "enabled emergent entreprenurial and commercial groups to win a disproportionate share of wealth and power in American society." More crudely stated, the courts loaded the costs of an expanding industrial society on those least able to bear it—"forced subsidies to growth coerced from victims of the process." Id. xvi.

34. "Professor Bickel, The Scholarly Tradition, and the Supreme Court," 84 Harv. L. Rev. 769, 777, 784, 785 (1971). See also Hamilton, infra Chapter 21 at note 93; Linde, supra note 28 at 254; Justices Black and Douglas, supra Chapter 15 note 41; Cardozo, supra Chapter 15 note 24.

35. Wright, supra note 34 at 785; see supra at note 15.

36. Supra note 28 at 228–229.

on minimum wages was perhaps not entirely coincidental.[37] When the
Court splits 5 to 4 it evidences a deep cleavage as to the "desired" result.
Frequently an "outcome" that is stubbornly resisted by a dominant majority of the Court is quickly adopted upon the retirement of one or
more Justices when their replacements transform the dissenting minority into a new majority. On the heels of a decision that declared the
greenback law unconstitutional, President Grant "carefully chose men
who he had reason to believe would uphold the Legal Tender Acts." His
hopes were gratified by a 5-to-4 reversal.[38] Such swings of the pendulum are a commonplace of Supreme Court history: constitutional law is
given a "new look" when a Warren succeeds a Vinson, a Goldberg succeeds a Frankfurter. The changes can be fateful. Vinson "held fast to the

37. White, supra note 32 at 193. Of the overruled decision, Adkins v. Children's Hospital, 261 U.S. 525 (1923), T. R. Powell said that 5 Justices invalidated the minimum
wage law that 35 judges (including 4 Justices) held valid. Powell, *Vagaries and Varieties in
Constitutional Interpretation* 40 (1956). Roberts, as Fred Rodell remarked, was "the perfect
personification of the chanciness of government by judges. It was he who . . . changed his
mind and his major votes three separate times . . . on the bed-rock issue of governmental
power to regulate business; it was he who, by holding the decisive Court vote . . . was for
years the most powerful person in the United States." And he owed his appointment to
the accident that Judge John Parker was turned down by the Senate. Rodell, *Nine Men*
221–222 (1955). Alexander Bickel observed that 5 to 4 opinions highlight "the fact that
one man had the decision . . . It just makes unavoidable for everybody the awareness of
the authoritarian nature of the institution, and of how narrowly that authority resides in
one individual perhaps." *Hearings on the Supreme Court Before the Senate Subcomittee on the
Separation of Powers* 108, 90th Cong., 2d Sess. (June 1968).

38. R. H. Jackson, *The Struggle for Judicial Supremacy* 42 (1941). The overruled decision had been procured by Lincoln in the same fashion. He "confided that he chose
Salmon Chase as Chief Justice . . . chiefly because '. . . we wish for a Chief Justice who
will sustain what has been done in regard to . . . legal tenders.' Chase had been Lincoln's
Secretary of the Treasury . . . and had supported the Legal Tender Acts." Jackson, id.
32–33. Chase performed as expected and then came Grant's turn.

In the same way, Richard Nixon selected men who would give effect to his desires.
"That the Nixon Court favored law-enforcement values is no surprise. Burger, Blackmun, Powell and Rehnquist got their seats on the bench because of their supposed or
known lack of sympathy for the rights of the criminally accused." Levy, *Against the Law*
422. Dissenting in Boys Market v. Clerks' Union, 398 U.S. 235, 256 (1970), from the
discard of a 1962 precedent, Justice Black stated, "Nothing at all has changed, in fact,
except the membership of the Court and the personal opinion of one Justice." It has been
said that American constitutional history may be viewed as a "series of minor courtpack-
ing plans." White, supra note 32 at 197.

position that the judiciary should not be an aggressive instrument for invalidating school segregation."[39] He was succeeded in the midst of the desegregation case by Warren,[40] and Rodell tells us he learned from law clerks that "in conference at least three Justices came close to dissenting until their new Chief put on all the pressure he could wield."[41] A similar "major turning point" marked the succession of Frankfurter by Goldberg.[42] Citations can be multiplied. Should what is "socially desirable" for a nation of 200 million people turn on such accidents?[43] Should grave national policy be the sport of circumstance? Justices themselves have inveighed against the creation of novel constitutional doctrine on so fortuitous a base.[44] These shifts in opinion underscore Justice Jackson's aphorism: "we are not final because we are infallible, but we are infallible only because we are final."[45] Just as "perception of community stan-

---

39. Paul Murphy, *The Constitution in Crisis Times, 1918–1969* 309 (1972). "The Chief Justice [Vinson] found it 'Hard to get away' from the contemporary view by its framers that the Fourteenth Amendment did not prohibit segregation." Richard Kluger, *Simple Justice* 590, 589 (1976).

40. Cf. Cox, supra at note 5.

41. Fred Rodell, "It Is the Warren Court," *The New York Times Magazine*, March 13, 1966, in Levy, *Warren* 136, 139. Rodell adds, "I tell this tale—and let him who can prove it wrong deny it—to illustrate the result-minded pragmatism and power of Earl Warren." Id. After the first argument before Chief Justice Vinson, "Frankfurter . . . listed Clark—along with Vinson, Reed and Jackson—as probable dissenters if the Court had voted to overturn Plessy in the spring of 1953." Kluger, supra note 39 at 612. Bickel, who had served as a law clerk to Justice Frankfurter when the desegregation case first was argued before the Vinson Court, stated, "there is reason to believe that had Chief Justice Vinson lived, something very different from the opinion read by Earl Warren . . . would have come down." Alexander M. Bickel, "Is the Warren Court Too 'Political?,' " *The New York Times Magazine*, September 25, 1966, in Levy, *Warren* 216, 217.

42. "Today [1964] the close civil liberties cases (as opposed, in legal parlance, to those involving Negroes' civil *rights*), which used to come down predictably while Frankfurter sat, five to four against the liberty claimed, have for the past two terms come down just as predictably five to four the other way." Fred Rodell, supra note 2 at 208, 211.

43. Murphy, supra note 39 at 428.

44. Such shifts, Justice Frankfurter stated, afford "fair ground for the belief that Law is the expression of chance . . . of unexpected changes in the Court's composition and the contingencies in the choice of successors." United States v. Rabinowitz, 339 U.S. 56, 86 (1950), dissenting opinion. Yet he regarded Vinson's demise as providential. Supra Chapter 7 at note 47. To the same effect, Justice Black, supra note 38; Justice Stewart, Mitchell v. W. T. Grant Co., 416 U.S. 600, 636 (1974).

45. Brown v. Allen, 344 U.S. 443, 540 (1953), concurring opinion.

dards varies" from Justice to Justice, so no agreement on such matters is to be found in academe, for law professors also are not agreed upon what results are "good."[46] Were there such agreement, the judgment of cloistered scholars is no substitute for the will of the people.

Even when the Court is unanimous, it is not peculiarly fitted to be a thermometer of community feeling, as the Framers emphasized during their discussion of judicial participation in the Council of Revision. The Sixteenth Amendment attests that the Court did not represent the sense of the community when it declared the income tax unconstitutional.[47] Its recent decision that the age-old death penalty for murder constitutes "cruel and unusual punishment" quite plainly is opposed to popular sentiment.[48] So, too, the procedural safeguards required of States for criminals run counter to public opinion.[49] Some consider that the Court's rul-

---

46. Levy, supra note 9 at 199–200; J. H. Ely, "The Wages of Crying Wolf: A Comment on Roe v. Wade," 82 Yale L.J. 920, 944 (1973).

47. So too, Justice Holmes pointed out in Lochner v. New York, 198 U.S. 45, 75 (1905), that the majority was deciding the case "upon an economic theory which a large part of the country does not entertain," dissenting opinion.

48. Furman v. Georgia, 408 U.S. 238 (1972); see supra Chapter 14 note 53.

Justice Black's invocation to history in 1971 deserves notice: "These words cannot be read to outlaw capital punishment because that penalty was in common use and authorized by law . . . at the time the Constitution was adopted. It is inconceivable to me that the framers intended to end capital punishment by the [Eighth] Amendment." McGautha v. California, 402 U.S. 183, 226 (1971), concurring opinion. See infra Chapter 21 note 39. The case for rejection of judicial policymaking and for a restricted judicial function is even stronger. Supra Chapter 16.

Like politics, adjudication makes strange bedfellows. Chief Justice Burger, dissenting in Furman v. Georgia, stated, "a punishment clearly permissible under the Constitution at the time of its adoption and accepted as such by every member of the Court until today, is suddenly so cruel as to be incompatible with the Eighth Amendment." 408 U.S. at 381–382. And in Trop v. Dulles, 356 U.S. at 99, Chief Justice Warren stated that "the death penalty has been employed throughout our history, and, in a day when it is still widely accepted, it cannot be said to violate the constitutional concept of cruelty."

49. In 1968, "a Gallup poll revealed that the majority believed that the Court was 'too soft' on criminals, protected their rights at the expense of society." Levy, *Against the Law* 3. Richard Nixon rode into office in no small part because of his appeal to "law and order." The "people think that the Court has contributed to the crime wave." Kurland, supra note 31 at 95. Levy states that Congress regarded one such decision as " 'a harmful blow at the nationwide effort to control crime' " and enacted a countermeasure. Levy, *Against the Law* 252.

ings on obscenity do not reflect popular opinion;[50] and in the result the nation is deluged by a flood of blatant pornography and filth that the people are powerless to deal with.[51] Even desegregation, an undeniably noble goal, did not have[52] and does not have the consent of the nation. The Report of the National Advisory Commission on Civil Disorders found "pervasive racism" across the country,[53] as is evidenced by continued resistance in the North to busing. An admirer of *Brown v. Board of Education*, Anthony Lewis, ruefully wrote in May 1974 that the issues of race and poverty are "much more complicated, more intractable than we imagined."[54] Soberly appraising the situation in the Fall of 1975 Derrick Bell, a black scholar, stated that "Today, opposition to desegregation is, if anything, greater than it was in 1954." He referred to "nationwide opposition to meaningful implementation of school desegregation," saying, "it should now be clear that Brown can [not] integrate our schools."

50. Professor Louis Jaffe stated it is overwhelmingly the case that "the 'public conscience' does not support the claim" of constitutional protection for "obscenity," commenting that "the Legislatures, Federal and State, had openly and universally for upwards of 100 years seen fit to condemn obscenity." "The Court Debated—Another View," *The New York Times Magazine*, June 5, 1960, in Levy, *Warren* 199, 205; cf. Kurland, supra note 31 at 31, and J. W. Bishop, "The Warren Court Is Not Likely to be Overruled," *The New York Times Magazine*, September 7, 1969, in Levy, *Warren* 93, 103.

51. Archibald Cox adds, "One wonders, too, whether the Supreme Court, in extending the protection of the First Amendment to sheer vulgarity, useful only in its ability to shock, does not give the vulgarities an imprimatur which contributes to the lowering of public discourse." Cox, supra note 1 at 47–48.

52. Supra Chapter 15 at note 14.

53. Lewis M. Steel, "Nine Men in Black Who Think White," *The New York Times Magazine*, October 13, 1968, in Levy, *Warren* 83, 91.

54. "A Time to Celebrate," N.Y. Times, May 13, 1974, at 29. He added, "we seem unlikely to solve [the problems] soon, to the general satisfaction, in terms of either law or politics." On October 16, 1976, Professor Charles Black stated, "To the *victims* of inequality, inequality is often perceived as a denial of liberty . . . The poor are indeed unfree . . . [But] reliance on the judiciary to correct this kind of unfreedom is tragically misplaced . . . [W]hat will be wanted, and indispensably needed, is that major shift of resources, and that systematic reorganization, which cannot succeed without very weighty action by the political branches. The most serious single mistake possible at this time would in my judgment be to write Congress off, and to try to tackle poverty by invoking the judicial power." Address, "The Judicial Power as Guardian of Liberties," before a symposium on "The Supreme Court and Constitutional Liberties in Modern America," Wayne State University, Detroit, Mich.

The "real sickness is that our society in all its manifestations is geared to the manifestations of white superiority."[55] Bell's careful bill of particulars raises large doubts whether the disease is curable by judicial fiat. This is not to deny that the side-effects of *Brown* in other areas of desegregation have been beneficial in the extreme. Here our focus is on the absence of a national consensus, the fact that the desegregation decree did not and still does not represent the "sense of the community," but is rather a prime example of how the Justices imposed their will upon the people. Justice Black, who was ready enough to impose his own will, rightly declared that there is no "gadget which the Court can use to determine what traditions are rooted in the conscience of the people."[56]

If the argument of necessity can be made for desegregation because segregation is a reproach to our society, what need was there for the Court's decision that the centuries-old requirement of trial by a jury of 12 was not binding on the present? No social urgency called for judicial tampering with what had been a central concern of the Founders.[57]

55. Derrick Bell, "The Burden of Brown on Blacks: History Based on Observations on a Landmark Decision," 7 N.C. Cent. L.J. 25, 26, 36 (1975). See also Thomas Sowell, "A Black 'Conservative' Dissents," *The New York Times Magazine*, August 8, 1976, at 14. The issue of racial discrimination "has been fanned into the most protracted, rancorous, and divisive domestic blaze of the post-war era." Chester E. Finn, Jr., "Book Review," *Commentary* 78 (April 1976). Philip Kurland had written in 1970 that the segregation "cases demonstrate, I think, that rapid movement toward equality of the races is not attainable through the judicial process. The Court has moved faster than society is prepared to go." Kurland, supra note 31 at 113.

56. Griswold v. Connecticut, 381 U.S. 479, 519 (1965). Levy numbers Black, Douglas, and Warren among the Justices who believed that "they have a mission to impose their convictions upon the nation," to "mold its public policy," Levy, *Warren* 110. "Earl Warren is the closest thing the United States has had to a Platonic Guardian, dispensing law from a throne without any sensed limits of power except what is seen [by him] as the good of society." Anthony Lewis, "A Man Born to Act, Not to Muse," *The New York Times Magazine*, June 30, 1968, in Levy, *Warren* 151, 161. Professor Louis Henkin stated, there is "a preference by some Justices for results which fit an image of the nation not projected by the Constitution and which the Justices cannot prove to be justified by history, need, the philosophy of the people, or anything better than the Justices' faith or inclination." Henkin, "Some Reflections on Current Constitutional Controversies," 109 U. Pa. L. Rev. 637, 660 (1961).

57. For a powerful critique of the 6-man jury decision see Levy, *Against the Law* 259 et seq. My own studies have convinced me that the Founders unfailingly identified trial by jury with a jury of 12. See infra Chapter 22.

What urgent necessity dictated overthrow of the death penalty to which more than half of the States are attached? Such decisions confirm Hamilton's prescient caution in Federalist No. 25: "every breach of the fundamental laws, though dictated by necessity, . . . forms a precedent for other breaches where the same plea of necessity does not exist at all."[58]

For a realistic and unusually candid disclosure of the uses of instrumentalism we are indebted to a member of the Nixon administration, Donald E. Santarelli, an Associate Deputy Attorney General, who described himself in April 1973 as in charge of "an idea shop," which "work[s] on concepts" and "plans" for the President. He considered that the "separation of powers is obsolete," that the

> Constitution is flexible . . . Your point of view depends on whether you're winning. The constitution isn't the real issue in this; it is how you want to *run the country*, and achieve national goals. The language of the Constitution is not at issue. It is what you can interpret it to mean in the light of modern needs. In talking about a "Constitutional crisis" we are not grappling with the real needs of running the country but are using the issues for the self-serving purpose of striking a new balance of power . . . Today, the whole Constitution is up for grabs.[59]

To my knowledge, the Nixon administration did not repudiate this interview, and it was tacitly confirmed by Richard Nixon himself. As said by Leonard Levy, "Nixon's search for conservative strict constructionists has been more than a candid attempt to alter the trend of decisions, it is an acknowledgment that at the very apex of our government of laws and not of men, the men who interpret the laws, rather than the laws themselves, are the decisive factors.[60] It is difficult to deny that "a result-oriented adjudication . . . is a corruption of the judicial process, that leaves too far behind the rule of law enforced by impersonal and objective judges."[61]

58. Federalist No. 25 at 158.
59. *The New Yorker*, April 28, 1973, at 32–34.
60. Levy, *Warren* 9.
61. Levy, *Against the Law* 438; cf. Kathryn Griffith, *Judge Learned Hand and the Role of the Federal Judiciary* 192 (1973). An admirer of judicial policymaking averred that the

Instrumentalism, in short, substitutes the will of the Justices for that of the people. That requires more than jurisprudential justification, more than a response to the needs of a changing world; it calls for the informed "consent of the governed." Although Justice Harlan, in measuring the impact of the Fourteenth Amendment on voting, stated that "the amending process is not the only way in which constitutional understanding alters with time . . . as conditions change the Constitution changes as well," he went on to say:

> when the Court gives the language of the Constitution an unforeseen application, it does so, whether explicitly or implicitly, in the name of some underlying purpose of the Framers . . . [T]he federal judiciary . . . has no inherent general authority to establish norms for the rest of society . . . When the Court *disregards the express intent* and understanding of the Framers, it has invaded the realm of the political process to which the amending power was committed, and it has violated the constitutional structure which it is its highest duty to protect.[62]

In terms of this discussion, the limited goals of the Fourteenth Amendment were explained to the people; they gave their consent in conformity with Article V, and if their decision needs to be changed, let it be, as President Washington counseled, by action in the same constitutional manner: let the people decide.

Instead of searching for the "sense of community," some would have the Court serve as a "national conscience," as "an educational body . . . teachers in a vital national seminar."[63] That notion, Wallace Mendelson stated, "sounds strange in the mouths of its liberal sponsors. By their standards, most of the Court's teaching in this area has been erroneous"[64]— let alone that the Court has not been content merely to teach but has

---

Court "has ceased to be a student of law . . . It has become the crusading political philosopher of populism." Shapiro, supra note 23 at 252.

62. Oregon v. Mitchell, 400 U.S. 112, 202–203 (1970) (emphasis added).

63. A. S. Miller and R. F. Howell, "The Myth of Neutrality in Constitutional Adjudication," 27 U. Chi. L. Rev. 661, 689 (1960). Rostow, supra note 14 at 208. See also infra at note 81.

64. Wallace Mendelson, "Mr. Justice Frankfurter: Law and Choice," 10 Vand. L. Rev. 333, 341 (1957).

imposed its teachings on the nation. There is no need to dwell on the fact that judges of high stature—Black, Frankfurter, Learned Hand, and Robert Patterson—have rejected the roles of preacher, teacher, crusader;[65] instead, let us examine how this "conscience" has served the nation. Careful scholars confirm Robert H. Jackson's stricture: "time has proved that [the Court's] judgment was wrong on most of the outstanding issues upon which it has chosen to challenge the popular branches."[66] Consider first the Japanese relocation case, which stands as a dreadful precedent for racial concentration camps; the Court failed 70,000 Japanese at the very moment they stood most in need of protection against West Coast hysteria.[67] From the very outset the Court gutted the minimal protection afforded the Negro by the Fourteenth Amendment. By a series of decisions, Leonard Levy said, "the Court crippled and voided most of the comprehensive program for protecting the civil rights of Negroes after the Civil War. These decisions paralyzed or supplanted legislative and community action and played a crucial role in destroying public opinion that favored meeting the challenge of the Negro problem."[68] The record, said Henry Steele Commager, with respect to the pre-1937 Court,

> discloses not a single case, in a century and a half, where the Supreme Court has protected freedom of speech, press . . . against Congressional attack. It reveals no instance . . . where the Court has intervened on behalf of the underprivileged—the Negro, the alien,

65. Black: Jaffe, supra note 50 at 204–205; Frankfurter: "From the Wisdom of Felix Frankfurter," 3 *Wisdom* 25 (1959), quoted in Griffith, supra note 61 at 209; Hand: *The Bill of Rights* 71 (1962); Patterson: Griffith, id. 88.

Miller and Howell, supra note 63 at 678, noted a "lack of consensus on the Court as to the appropriate role of the judiciary."

66. Jackson, supra note 38 at x, 37; Robert Dahl, "Decision-Making in a Democracy: The Supreme Court as a National Policy-Maker," 6 J. Pub. Law 279, 292–293 (1957). The "Supreme Court, mainly during history, though not in recent decades, work[ed] as a buttress against the expansion of individual liberty and civil rights." James McGregor Burns, "Dictatorship—Could It Happen Here?," in *Has the Court Too Much Power?* 234, 236 (C. Roberts ed. 1974).

67. E. V. Rostow, "The Japanese-American Cases—A Disaster," 54 Yale L.J. 489 (1945); Levy, supra note 9 at 20.

68. Levy, supra note 9 at 33–34. "Meanwhile," Levy states, "millions of Negroes suffered lives of humiliation for five or more decades . . . because the Court betrayed the intent of the Reconstruction Amendments." Id. 35.

women, children, workers, tenant farmers. It reveals, on the contrary, that the Court has effectively intervened, again and again, to defeat Congressional attempts to free the slave, to guarantee civil rights to Negroes, to protect workingmen, to outlaw child labor, to assist hard-pressed farmers, and to democratize the tax system.[69]

So wretched a performance, I suggest, inspires little confidence in the Court as the "national conscience." In their rapture over the Warren Court's adoption of *their* predilections, the libertarians tend to overlook that "A single generation's experience with judicial review . . . does not wipe out the experience of a century and a half."[70] Already there are anguished outcries that the Burger Court is acting "against the law."[71] But the name of the game is "Two Can Play";[72] once the legitimacy of judicial policymaking is recognized, new appointees may properly carry out the policies which they were appointed to effectuate.[73]

What the "national conscience" is at any given moment depends on shifting personnel and the nature of the appointees. The replacement of one or two Justices may result in a complete reversal of the prevailing conscience, as when Chief Justice Warren succeeded Chief Justice Vinson. How can we put our trust in a conscience that changes color with every judicial succession, itself subject to shifting political winds?

The conscience of the nation is a tender thing, and one may well shrink from entrusting it to some of the incumbents who have served over the years. Shall we prefer the Four Horsemen to Brandeis and Stone as keepers of the conscience? Learned Hand believed that judges "must be expected to express the points of view of the class to which they be-

69. Henry Steele Commager, "Judicial Review and Democracy," 19 Va. Quarterly Rev. 417, 428 (1943). See also John Frank, "Review and Basic Liberties," in *Supreme Court and Supreme Law* 109, 114 (Edmond N. Cahn ed. 1954).

70. Levy, supra note 9 at 23.

71. Levy, *Against the Law*, some aspects of which are discussed infra Chapter 18.

72. In 1942 I pointed out that the "reconstructed" Court was sanctifying the deplorable example of the "Four Horsemen" and that that stamp of approval might yet come back to haunt the libertarians. Raoul Berger, "Constructive Contempt: A Post-Mortem," 9 U. Chi. L. Rev. 602, 604–605 (1942). For a similar expression, see Richard Goodwin, "The Shape of American Politics," *Commentary* 25, 26–27 (June 1967), quoted in Kurland, supra note 31 at 18.

73. See supra at note 60.

long rather than that of the whole community."[74] Justice Field's close ties with the railroad barons of the West Coast furnishes one example,[75] Chief Justice Taft another. Although Taft confessed to feeling "less acute and more confused" as he grew older, he felt duty-bound "to stay on the Court in order to prevent the Bolsheviki from getting control."[76] Presumably Brandeis was one of the "Bolsheviki";[77] and Taft opposed the appointments of Cardozo and Learned Hand because they might "herd" with Brandeis.[78] Justice Brewer's overheated warnings against the "black flag of anarchism . . . and the red flag of socialism"[79] long furnished the rallying cry of the embattled Court, which felt duty-bound to save "society from itself."[80]

Now it was the turn of the libertarians to look to the Court as the savior of democracy. Edmond Cahn considered that it was incumbent upon a judge to shoulder his moral responsibility rather than to defer to community standards, preferring the "wisdom" of such a judge as Learned Hand.[81] But Learned Hand in his wisdom wanted Platonic Guardians no more than did Elbridge Gerry 173 years earlier.[82] It is

74. Griffith, supra note 61 at 90; Hand, *The Spirit of Liberty* 203 (I. Dillard ed. 1952).

75. Graham 14, 102–103. For other justices with similar ties, see Fred Rodell, *Nine Men* 30–31(1955). Justice Samuel Miller wrote, "It is vain to contend with judges who have been at the bar the advocates for forty years of railroad companies . . . when they are called upon to decide cases where such interests are in contest." Quoted in Charles Fairman, *Mr. Justice Miller and the Supreme Court* 374 (1939).

76. Levy, *Judgments*, supra note 12 at 98.

77. In 1920 W. H. Taft referred to "the new school of constitutional construction" led by Brandeis and Clarke, which tended to encourage "Socialist raids on property." Taft, "Mr. Wilson and the Campaign," 10 Yale Rev. (N.S.) 1 (October 1920), quoted in 1 *Holmes-Laski Letters: The Correspondence of Mr. Justice Holmes and Harold J. Laski* 347 note 1 (M. Howe ed. 1953).

78. A. T. Mason, *The Supreme Court: Palladium of Freedom* 122 (1962). Taft considered "Hand had proved his poor judgment in 1912, when he 'turned out to be a wild Roosevelt man, a progressive.' " Id. See also White, supra note 32 at 179–180.

79. See supra Chapter 1 note 8.

80. Robert McCloskey, *The American Supreme Court* 165 (1960). Justice Field was convinced "that the salvation of democracy lay in a judicial trusteeship." Graham 149.

81. Edmond Cahn, *The Moral Decision: Right and Wrong in the Light of American Law* 310, quoted in Griffith, supra note 61 at 158.

82. Hand, supra note 65 at 73; Gerry, supra Chapter 16 at note 8. Hand considered that the law "must be content to lag behind the best inspiration of its time until it feels behind it the weight of such general acceptance." Supra note 74 at 15–16. See also supra

disheartening to go over the roster of "wise and able men" to whom
Arthur Sutherland would confide "the constitutional function of coun-
tering the democratic process." Rodell justly refers to Truman's "inept
cronies";[83] the revulsion not long since against some proposed Nixon
appointments, including an ineffable trio who shall here be nameless,[84]
illustrates that the nation's salvation is dependent upon the "luck of the
draw." Anthony Lewis observed that "the run of Supreme Court appointments in our history has not been particularly distinguished."[85]
Levy more bluntly stated that they have run from "mediocre to
competent"[86]—with a few distinguished exceptions such as Holmes and
Brandeis, who often were relegated to dissent.[87] Learned Hand, one of

at note 65. And always there is the question whether even "general acceptance" can dis-
pense with amendment under Article V. See Hamilton, supra at note 15.

83. "It Is the Warren Court," supra note 41 at 145.

84. Levy, *Against the Law* 44, 48.

85. "What Qualities for the Court?," *The New York Times Magazine*, October 6, 1957,
in Levy, *Warren* 114, 119. Writing of the Associate Justices, many of whom he knew
personally, John Quincy Adams said, "Not one of them, except Story, has been a man of
great ability. Several of them have been men of strong prejudices, warm passions, and
contracted minds." Quoted in Samuel F. Bemis, *John Quincy Adams and the Union* 406
note 79 (1956).

86. *Judgments*, supra note 12 at 105. He adds, "the politics of appointment . . . are
surely not calculated to bring the ablest men to our supreme tribunal." For a scathing
critique of the run of appointments over the years, see Rodell, *Nine Men*. Robert G. Mc-
Closkey, a searching student of the Court, said that at any given time "You are not likely
to find more than a handful who are capable of performing the rather awesome intellectual task that these ventures of [the Justices] involve. We have had on the Court in
modern times, I would say offhand maybe three . . . Frankfurter, Jackson, and probably
Harlan, but they in general, were swimming against the tide." *Hearings*, supra note 37 at
109. Philip Kurland likewise testified that "the personnel of the Court is not up to the
task that has been assigned to it." Id. 149. Paul Freund, who as chief aide to the Solicitor
General was in a position to observe the Court at close quarters, is quoted as saying that
Justice George Sutherland "did not have a very 'searching mind.' McReynolds was a very
'idiosyncratic' man and was often 'childish and peevish.' " Tim Cooper, "Freund: 40 Years
of Supreme Court History Recalled." 64 Harv. L.S. Rec. 1, 9 (1977).

87. Morris R. Cohen wrote to Frankfurter in January 1936, "you think in terms of
Holmes, Brandeis and Cardozo, and you think more men of that type would make the
Supreme Court a good institution. In this you ignore the fact that it is only by accident
that men of that type can get on the Supreme Court and that when they do they are more
likely to be on the minority side." L. C. Rosenfield, *Portrait of a Philosopher: Morris Raphael
Cohen in Life and Letters* 270 (1962), quoted in Joseph P. Lash, *From the Diaries of Felix
Frankfurter* 55 (1975).

the wisest and most profound jurists, disclaimed any knowledge of how to choose Platonic Guardians.[88] A succession of presidents have demonstrated that they know still less.

One who studies the course of events since the advent of the Warren era is struck by how short is the memory of man. One hundred years of judicial misrule have been wiped out by a fifteen-year interlude during which libertarian aspirations at length were gratified. Now the intellectuals eagerly embraced the Court as a "law-giver," forgetful of Tocqueville's comment on the then prevailing respect for the judiciary that imprudent appointments might bring forth evil fruit.[89] Do we need Hitler or Indira Gandhi to remind us that the lesson of history is: put not your trust in saviors? The enduring strength of our institutions is not a little due to our veneration of the Constitution as the bulwark of our liberties. We need to take to heart a statement made by Jefferson when he was President and had been urged to take a dubiously broad view of his own powers:

> I had rather ask for an enlargement of power from the nation, where it is found necessary, than to assume it by a construction which would make our powers boundless. Our peculiar security is in possession of a written Constitution. Let us not make it a blank paper by construction. If [power is boundless] then we have no Constitution. If it has bounds, they can be no other than the definition of the powers which that instrument gives.[90]

For him those definitions were to be read in light of the explanations made to those who ratified the Constitution.[91]

---

88. Hand, supra note 65 at 73.

89. "[I]f the Supreme Court is ever composed of imprudent men or bad citizens, the Union may be plunged into anarchy or civil war." 1 Alexis de Tocqueville, *Democracy in America* 150 (1900).

90. Letter to Wilson Cary Nicholas, September 7, 1803, 8 *The Writings of Thomas Jefferson* 247 (P. L. Ford ed. 1897).

91. See infra Chapter 19 at note 42.

# 18

## *Liberals and the Burger Court*

LAMENTATIONS over the "regressive" course of the Burger Court in the field of civil liberties fill the air. *The New York Times*, for example, stated: "There was a time not so far distant when the United States Supreme Court was the staunch and ultimate defender of civil rights and liberties . . . [T]he Court seems clearly to be beating a path of retreat from its once proud forward position in this delicate and difficult area of the relationship between citizen and state."[1] Undoubtedly the Court is tilting the scales from what many regarded as excessive tenderness toward criminals;[2] it is haltingly attempting to return some criminal administration to the States.[3] But, as Leonard Levy points out,

1. N.Y. Times, March 31, 1976, at 36; see also Nathan Lewin, "Avoiding the Supreme Court," *The New York Times Magazine*, October 17, 1976, at 31.

2. Edward R. Korman, "Book Review," 4 Hofstra L. Rev. 549, 556 (1976), refers to "the near hysterical response in certain quarters that accompanies every opinion of the 'Nixon Court' affirming the conviction of a murderer, rapist or robber." Professor Louis Jaffe stated that judges "have been insensitive to the public's need for a sense of security." "Was Brandeis an Activist? The Search for Intermediate Premises," 80 Harv. L. Rev. 986, 1002 (1967).

3. Cf. Stone v. Powell, 96 S. Ct. 3037 (1976), limiting the use of habeas corpus for review of state court convictions on the basis of illegally obtained evidence.

"Between 1937 and 1961 the Court's constitutional rulings in criminal cases had rarely touched law enforcement and trial practices that were generally permitted by state law and were in widespread use." Lusky 159. Justice Harlan, dissenting in Chapman v. Alabama, 386 U.S. 18, 46–47 (1967), stated, "I regard the Court's assumption of what amounts to a general supervisory power over the trial of federal constitutional issues in state courts as a startling constitutional development that is wholly out of keeping with our federal system and completely unsupported by the Fourteenth Amendment where the source of such power must be found." A swing of the pendulum was acknowledged by Justice Lewis F. Powell in an address on August 11, 1976, before the American Bar Association convention. The changes were due to a " 'leveling off' in activism by the

"That the Nixon Court favored law-enforcement values" should come as "no surprise. Burger, Blackmun, Powell and Rehnquist got their seats on the bench because of their supposed or known lack of sympathy for the rights of the criminally accused."[4] This, however, is only the latest of what G. E. White felicitously described as a "series of minor court-packing plans."[5] Now that a new set of predilections is displacing their own, libertarians who rejoiced in the "creative" role of the "wise and able men" are despondent. But the "revolutionary" changes in the criminal process[6] by the Warren Court had not won the assent of the people.[7] And it cannot be gainsaid that the Burger Court rulings in this area are closer to the original design than were those of the Warren Court. For, as we have seen, the Bill of Rights was not made applicable to the States, either by its framers or in the 39th Congress.

Not that the Burger Court is abjuring lawmaking; its "six-man jury" decision furnished evidence to the contrary.[8] It has not held that the Court has no business regulating State death penalties because the "cruel and unusual punishment" phrase of the Bill of Rights has no application to the States, or because, as Chief Justices Warren and Burger and Justice Black stated, it did not encompass a death penalty for murder.[9] Instead, in *Gregg v. Georgia* and companion cases it has weighed whether a death penalty is or is not a "cruel and unusual punishment" on an apothecary's scale.[10] It would be inopportune to show in detail that the "strict constructionist" Burger Court clings as firmly to judicial gover-

---

Court"; "a more traditional, and in my view, a sounder balance is evolving between the rights of accused persons and the right of a civilized society to have a criminal justice system that is effective as well as fair." N.Y. Times, August 12, 1976, at 18.

4. Levy, *Against the Law* 422 (1974).

5. G. E. White, *The American Judicial Tradition* 197 (1976).

6. Lusky 161.

7. See supra Chapter 17 note 49. "The Court's 'coddling' of criminals became a major issue in the 1968 elections; [after the election] new appointees were selected in part on their commitment to law enforcement and their hostility to 'criminal forces.' " White, supra note 5 at 364–365.

8. Infra Chapter 22.

9. Supra Chapter 17 note 48.

10. Gregg v. Georgia, 96 S. Ct. 2909 (1976).

nance as its predecessor.[11] Archibald Cox observed that "the new Justices seem not to shrink from using constitutional law as an instrument of reform when an existing rule offends their preferences."[12]

It is more to the purpose to examine how the Burger Court has thrown "liberal" analysis into disarray, as Leonard Levy's recent book *Against the Law: The Nixon Court* illustrates. Levy's earlier studies give evidence of incisive analysis and a richly stocked mind; but *Against the Law* leaves one with a baffling sense of ambivalence, of seeming unawareness that his views are often incongruent. In what follows I am not to be taken as a partisan of the Burger Court, but rather as seeking to test Levy's theories by his criticism of that Court. By way of background let us begin with his sympathetic introduction to a group of articles on the Warren Court. The phrases of the Constitution are "Delphic"; the Court

> is indeed, and cannot help but be [a superlegislature]. The reason is simply that the Constitution, as Jefferson said in exasperation, is "merely a thing of wax" which the Court "may twist and shape into any form they please . . ." Judge Learned Hand observed that . . . "The words [a judge] must construe are empty vessels into which he can pour nearly anything he will." Legal erudition, legal rules, legal logic, legal precedents do not decide cases involving the ambiguous clauses of the Constitution . . . Inevitably, then, our constitutional law is subjective in character and to a great degree result oriented.[13]

11. See infra Chapter 22.

12. "The New Dimensions of Constitutional Adjudication," 51 Wash. L. Rev. 791, 803 (1976). Cf. Justice White, Roberts v. Louisiana, 96 S. Ct. 3001, 3020 (1976); see also Cox, *The Role of the Supreme Court in American Government* 34 (1976).

13. Levy, *Warren* 7, 9, 10. Why then criticize Justice Rehnquist's approach as "that of an ideologue advocating the embodiment of his political choices in constitutional law"? Levy, *Against the Law* 58. And if "legal rules, legal precedents" and the like "do not decide cases" then Rodell was not "anti-intellectual" in dismissing the "look-it-up-in-the-library" intellectual. Supra Chapter 15 at notes 11–12.

Jefferson was lamenting that the Court had *made* of the Constitution "a thing of wax," letter to Spencer Roane, September 6, 1819, 12 *Works of Thomas Jefferson* 135, 137 (Fed. ed. 1905). He had hoped that officials would be bound "from mischief by the chains of the Constitution." See also infra Chapter 20 at note 6. So too, Learned Hand's reference to words as "empty vessels" must be balanced against his confession of failure to understand the Court's function as a "third legislative chamber" except as a *coup de main*. *The Bill of Rights* 55 (1962).

Levy continues in this strain in his commentary on the Burger Court: "From the beginning . . . the Court . . . read the Constitution to mean whatever it wanted. Despite pretenses to the contrary, the Court could do no other, for . . . American constitutional law exists in the collective eye of those who happen at any moment in time to dominate the Court."[14] If this be so, how can the decisions of the "Nixon Court" be "Against the Law"? And "why," to borrow Levy's adoption of Justice Black's rhetorical question, "have a written Constitution at all if its interpreters are left only to the admonitions of their own consciences?"[15] Is this reconcilable with Levy's view that the Court "is and must be for all practical purposes a 'continuous constitutional convention' in the sense that it must keep updating the original charter . . . it simply cannot decide cases on the basis of what the Constitution says"?[16]

Given that constitutional law is "inevitably . . . result-oriented," one can understand Levy's view that any decision other than *Brown v. Board of Education* "would have been unthinkable, unbearable, unspeakable"[17] (though not to Chief Justice Vinson and Justices Reed and Jackson),[18] that "strict constructionism means reversing the decision of Appomatox . . . a return to . . . Jim Crow."[19] That is not a return that I should recommend, but is this not the very "reasoning backwards" so vigorously condemned by Levy: "In constitutional cases . . . the judge who first chooses what the outcome should be and then reasons backwards to apply a rationalization replete with rules and precedents has betrayed his calling; he has decided on the basis of prejudice and prejudgment, and has made constitutional law little more than the embodiment of his policy preferences, reflecting his subjective predilections."[20] That, however, is "inevitable" once it is postulated that "our constitutional law is

14. Levy, *Against the Law* 25.

15. Levy, *Warren* 186.

16. Levy, *Against the Law* 29–30. "Burger was quite accurate when he accused the Court of operating as a 'continuing constitutional convention.' It cannot operate in any other way." Id. 230.

17. Levy, *Warren* 10, 20.

18. Supra Chapter 7 at notes 43–44, 54–55.

19. Levy, *Against the Law* 30–31.

20. Levy, *Warren* 186.

subjective in character and to a great degree result-oriented."[21] Nevertheless Levy states that "result-oriented constitutional adjudication . . . is a corruption of the judicial process that leaves too far behind the rule of law enforced by impersonal or objective judges."[22] He himself avers, however, "We may not want judges who start with the answer rather than the problem . . . but as long as mere mortals sit on the Court and must construe that majestic but muddy Constitution, we will rarely get any other kind."[23] Yet he emphasizes in *Against the Law* that "result-oriented jurisprudence . . . [is a] judicial monstrosity that gains nothing when the Court reaches a just result merely because of its identification with underdog litigants."[24]

Now unless I am sadly at sea, it seems to me that Levy is riding off in opposite directions. He cannot at one and the same time maintain that the words of the Constitution "are empty vessels into which [a judge] can pour nearly anything he will" and then insist that the "*purpose* of the Sixth Amendment was to *bind* the federal government to the system of trial by jury that was traditional and familiar."[25] On that analysis the words "trial by jury" are not "empty vessels" but have a fixed content. So, too, he has been unable to decide whether a result-oriented jurisprudence is "inevitable" or a "monstrosity." It may be one or the other, but it cannot be both.[26] The core of Levy's complaint, unless I grossly misconceive his concluding remarks, seems to be against the Burger Court's craftsmanship, its failure "to weigh criticism," "to develop carefully reasoned judgments," "to make bad law in the sense of being badly crafted."[27] But, as he recognizes, "experts will doubtless disagree" about "the Nixon Court's

21. Levy, *Against the Law* 35.

22. Id. 438.

23. Id. 35.

24. Id. xiii.

25. Id. 289 (emphasis added).

26. So, too, affirmation that "inevitably . . . constitutional law is subjective," supra at note 13, is incompatible with Levy's statement that the Brennan-Marshall explanations "were like Band-Aids covering their very personal and humanitarian reading of present-day values," Levy, *Against the Law* 398, as well they might do in "updating" the Constitution. For similar criticism see Robert H. Horn, "Book Review," 88 Harv. L. Rev. 1924, 1925 (1975).

27. Levy, *Against the Law* 438–439. "His alarm arises more from the style, manners and rationale with which the decisions have been rendered than from the decisions them-

craftsmanship" as "they have about the Warren Court's craftsmanship."[28] Whether it be good or bad, however, is of no moment in a jurisprudence that is "inevitably . . . result-oriented." The result, not the reasoning, is what counts.[29]

Some of Levy's severest strictures are reserved for the Burger Court's treatment of precedents: one new reading "left its precedents in shambles"; the Court "obliterates them."[30] Yet, he considers that "precedents do not decide cases."[31] And in disregard of precedents the Burger Court yields the palm to its predecessor. "The list of opinions destroyed by the Warren Court," Philip Kurland observed, "reads like a table of contents from an old constitutional law casebook."[32] It is difficult to agree that Chief Justice Burger "displayed an egregious contempt for precedents" when he rejected the "thesis that what the Court said lately controls over the Constitution."[33] He may be indulged in re-

---

selves . . . he concentrates his detailed analytical criticism on the *how* instead of the *what*." D. G. Stephenson, "Book Review," 61 Va. L. Rev. 1338, 1341 (1975).

28. Levy, *Against the Law* 438.

29. Stephenson, supra note 27 at 1344, justly remarks, "*what* the Court does has a greater and more lasting effect on its place in the political system than *how* it reaches its judgment." One has only to compare the impact of the "desegregation case" with its inadequate reasoning. Levy, finding a decline in Justice Douglas' analytical powers, remarks that "Douglas's opinions provoked some of his liberal admirers to take the cynical position that if constitutional adjudication is basically result-oriented, Douglas voting for the 'right' side was better than any Nixon appointee voting the other way." Levy, *Against the Law* 38. See Rodell, supra Chapter 15 at note 11, Chapter 17 note 41.

30. Levy, *Against the Law* 260, 423.

31. Id. 34.

32. *Politics, the Constitution and the Warren Court* 90 (1970). An ardent admirer of the Warren Court stated that "in a whole series of precedent-shattering decisions, the Court extended the protection of parts of the Bill of Rights well beyond old-established limits and set aside several past Court rulings to do so . . . [a] well-nigh unprecedented display of judicial power." Fred Rodell, "The 'Warren Court' Stands Its Ground," *The New York Times Magazine*, September 27, 1964, in Levy, *Warren* 209, 210.

33. Levy, *Against the Law* 28–29. Like Chief Justice Burger, Justices Douglas and Frankfurter claimed the right to look at the Constitution rather than what the Court had said about it. Supra Chapter 15 note 57.

Burger spoke in a "right to counsel" case, Coleman v. Alabama, 399 U.S. 1, 22 (1970), dissenting opinion. Levy notes that at the adoption of the Constitution, "the counsel clause . . . meant no more than the right to retain counsel of one's choice at one's own expense," that it was only in 1938 that the Court held counsel must be supplied, and "that rule was not extended to state crime proceedings until 1963." Levy, *Against the Law* 197.

turning to older precedents that the Warren Court had only recently discarded,[34] particularly since, as Justice Henry Baldwin early observed, "There is no more certainty that a last opinion is more correct than the first."[35] Let Levy sum up:

> In all these cases ... the Burger Court no less than the Warren Court displayed an audacious disregard for and circumvention of precedents, clearly revealing its own values and policy choices. Despite pretenses to the contrary, it could do no other for as beauty exists in the eye of the beholder, so American constitutional law exists in the collective eye of those who happen at any moment to dominate the Supreme Court.[36]

Such are the fruits of a value-oriented system which makes of "constitutional [case] law" a veritable whirligig. No rhetoric can disguise that this is but the kadi administering justice under a tree.

Where Levy entertained misgivings about judicial review but swallowed them,[37] Charles Black was an uncurbed partisan of the Warren Court, a panegyrist of Justice Black who sought to justify the policy-

---

Similarly Levy complains that Kirby v. Illinois, 406 U.S. 682 (1972), "emasculated" United States v. Wade, 388 U.S. 218 (1967) (right to counsel at police lineup). Why should the Burger Court feel bound by a "precedent" first created only five years earlier? Levy notices that "Congress viewed Wade as a 'harmful blow at the nation-wide effort to control crime.' " Levy, id. 252.

34. Consider Justice Brennan's dissent in United States v. Ash, 413 U.S. 300, 326 (1973): "today's decision marks simply another step towards the complete evisceration of the fundamental constitutional principles *established* by this Court *only six years* ago" (emphasis added).

Horn, supra note 26 at 1926–1927 comments, "In large part these decisions were less than a decade old when the Burger era opened. Professor Levy is entitled to regard them as 'settled meanings of the Constitution' (422) regardless of how greatly these Warren Court decisions unsettled what in some instances had been an apparently settled meaning since the Bill of Rights itself had been adopted," i.e., for 150 years.

35. Livingston's Executor v. Story, 36 U.S. (11 Pet.) 351, 400 (1837), dissenting opinion. See also Justice Jackson's comment on judicial infallibility, supra Chapter 17 at note 45.

36. Levy, *Warren* 251.

37. "If there must be an answer, the most satisfying is the most equivocal or gingerly balanced, that of the mugwump caught in the classic stance with his mug on one side of the fence and his wump on the other." *Judicial Review and the Supreme Court* 42 (Leonard Levy ed. 1967).

making ways of the Court to man.[38] Now Black has come forth with a semi-recantation, taking on himself some of the blame for encouraging a result-focused jurisprudence.[39] The "fresh raw wound" caused by the Burger Court's death penalty cases of July 2, 1976, set him to "wondering whether we liberals . . . may not be in part to blame for a . . . quite evident trend toward the point of view that reason doesn't matter much, and can be brushed aside, if only the result is thought desirable."[40] One should not be captious with a repentant sinner, but Black's semi-recantation contains the seeds of further error; and, as one who wrote in 1942 that the test of constitutionality cannot be the embodiment of predilections which I share,[41] I may be forgiven for seeking to lay those errors bare.

There is first Black's repeated appeal to "reason."[42] The recent death-penalty cases moved him to ask "whether we do well to entrust this Court with the job of a rational defense of ordered liberty—and even whether we did well to refrain from talking too loud about it when the same [Burger] Court without adequate reason given, decided the abortion case as it did."[43] Like Professor Black, I too am a devotee of reason and well recall the richly deserved criticisms of the Warren Court, couched in

38. C. L. Black, *The People and the Court* (1960); *Hugo Black and the Supreme Court: A Symposium*, "Foreword" by C. L. Black (S. P. Strickland ed. 1967). As Levy observed, "the defense of judicial review has come mainly from those who have welcomed the trend of judicial decision in recent years and have rushed to the Court's protection." Supra note 37 at 24.

39. Address, "The Judicial Power as Guardian of Liberties," before a symposium on "The Supreme Court and Constitutional Liberties in Modern America," Wayne State University, Detroit, Mich., Oct. 16, 1976 hereinafter cited as Black, Wayne.

40. Id. 2.

41. Supra Chapter 1 at note 13.

42. The death-penalty "cases represented as definite an abandonment of the responsibility to justify a result by coherent reason as has ever occurred in the history of the Court." Black, Wayne 4. He urges that the bar "never cease to call the Court to account, and to urge reason upon it," id. 9, lest a "miasma of illegitimacy . . . hang about all judicial work." Id. 10. Even more vital is it that the Court must act within the bounds of its authority for, as he states, it is "a prime political postulate that the government is not to travel outside its allocated sphere," supra note 38 at 41, and that also goes for the judiciary.

43. Black, Wayne 7.

terms of deplorable "craftsmanship"[44]—without a peep from Black.[45] He himself recognizes that "painstaking reason often leads to different results in different minds" and that "no important result is dictated wholly by reason; there must lie at its heart a normative judgment not reachable by reason alone."[46] In other words, "reason" starts from premises that another may reject. Chief Justice Warren proceeded in *Reynolds v. Sims* (reapportionment) from the Declaration of Independence and the Gettysburg Address, notwithstanding that the framers of the Fourteenth Amendment found that the Declaration had not deprived the States of control over suffrage, and that Lincoln saw no prospect of Negro "equality." And he totally ignored the incontestable evidence that Justice Harlan spread before the Court that the framers excluded suffrage from the scope of the Amendment. Even now Black does not ask whether the Justices may displace the framers' value-choices with their own "normative judgments."

The frailty of "reason" is further illustrated by Black himself; he regards *Brown v. Board of Education* "as nearly syllogistic as a real law case can be. The Fourteenth Amendment, in *the clear light of its history* . . . forbade *all* discrimination against black people."[47] He may be indulged for his inability to abandon a view to which he was committed as a member of the NAACP legal counsel in that case; he "threw all his passionate brilliance into the NAACP effort."[48] But, to the astonishment of Kelly,

44. Black's Yale colleagues, Alexander Bickel and Harry Wellington, wrote in 1957, "The Court's product has shown an increasing incidence of the . . . formulation of results accompanied by little or no effort to support them in reason." "Legislative Purpose and the Judicial Process: The Lincoln Mills Case," 71 Harv. L. Rev. 1, 3 (1957). Dissenting Justices complained that the Warren majority failed to "confront complicated constitutional issues with professional expertise and consistency." Levy, *Warren* 17. Kurland observed that "the defenders of the [Warren] Court do not tend to argue that the opinions are well reasoned." Supra note 32 at 183. See also supra at note 28.

45. He considered protests against the "reasoning" in the Brown case as "wrong." Black, Wayne 3. In other contexts he now bemoans his own silence, infra at note 51.

46. Black, Wayne 11.

47. Id. 2 (emphasis added). In 1959 he wrote that the case "was a debatable one." Supra note 38 at 137. His Yale colleague, Bickel, wrote what Justice Frankfurter considered an "impressive" memorandum, and advised that "it is impossible to conclude that the 39th Congress intended that segregation be abolished." Supra Chapter 7 at note 8.

48. Kluger 645.

Graham, and others, the "clear" neoabolitionist history they pressed on the court was branded by Chief Justice Warren—anxious though he was to rule in favor of desegregation—as "inconclusive." How can we rely on "reason" that converts the very limited and "clear" purposes of the framers into a ban on "all" discrimination?

Black recalls that he "expressed some doubt about the application of the equal protection clause to legislative apportionment, in *Baker v. Carr*, but, looking back, I know that I muted that doubt." Came *Oregon v. Mitchell*, and Professor Black perceived "that the plurality opinion of four was plainly wrong, and the deciding concurrence of Mr. Justice Black so egregiously wrong as to be . . . all but incredible."[49] In justice to Justice Black, it deserves to be repeated that he recanted (though without so stating) with respect to apportionment for State offices, saying that he "agreed" with Justice Harlan's demonstration that control over suffrage was deliberately left by the framers with the States.[50] Of this Professor Black says not a word. One of the remarkable aspects of his address in fact is that not once does he advert to the historical limitations on judicial policymaking with respect to the Bill of Rights, segregation, and reapportionment set forth by Fairman, Bickel, and Harlan; he puts his trust in "reason." Because reason can lead in different directions, however, the all-but-incontestable proof that suffrage was left by the framers to the States, offers a safer, surer mooring.

But to resume Professor Black's threnody; looking back to the Warren Court's extension of the school desegregation case "to other forms of segregation, involving neither schools nor children" in cases "decided *per curiam* and without opinion," Black now wishes that he "had fullthroatedly joined Herbert Wechsler in his protest against this procedure, which was so self-evidently wrong that one is ashamed to have glossed it over just because the result was what one wanted and thought right."[51] This was more than a departure from a lawyer's "commitment . . . to rea-

49. Black, Wayne 3–4.
50. "My Brother HARLAN has persuasively demonstrated that the Framers . . . intended to keep for themselves . . . the power to regulate elections . . . I agree as to the State's power to regulate the elections of their own officials." Oregon v. Mitchell, 400 U.S. 112, 124–125 (1970), concurring and dissenting in part.
51. Black, Wayne 8–9.

son";[52] it represents a departure from standards that led the people to place their trust in scholars. Like scientists, constitutional scholars, as Thomas Huxley said upwards of a century ago, should "respect nothing but evidence, and . . . believe that their highest duty lies in submitting to it, however it may jar against their inclinations."[53] That duty carries with it, I submit, publication, not suppression, of scholarly findings.

*Oregon v. Mitchell* induced some soul-searching in Black: "What if all this *is turned on us?* If real reason goes out of fashion, can we be sure it will not happen? . . . Have we not, after all, asked for it?"[54] It is not unfair to conclude, I trust, that Black's jeremiad illustrates once more the "whose ox is gored" adage. He held his peace when "the result was what one wanted and thought right," but now protests against a departure from "reason" when he is "heartbroken that the legal killing of people is to be resumed."[55] Not a word about the manifest preference of the people to the contrary, about the formidable evidence that the Fourteenth Amendment did not make the Bill of Rights applicable to the States, that the death penalty was not deemed a "cruel and unusual punishment" by the Framers—a view to which the Supreme Court adhered until 1972.[56] Instead Black apparently remains faithful to a judicial power to revise the Constitution—if only it be clothed in "reason."

---

52. Id. 9.
53. Supra Chapter 1 epigraph.
54. Black, Wayne 4 (emphasis added).
55. Id. 2.
56. Supra Chapter 17 note 48.

# 19

## The Legitimacy
## of Judicial Review

THE most fundamental question of all, as Thomas Grey rightly stated, is "the legitimacy of judicial review itself,"[1] a question that goes beyond the scope of the power to its very existence, however limited. After remarking, "Whether this enormous power can fairly be deduced from the language of the Constitution, and whether the framers of that instrument intended to confer it on the Justices, has been the subject of vast learned controversy . . . unlikely ever to be resolved," Joseph Bishop reassuringly stated, "No matter; the power exists."[2] It is true that the power has long been exercised, but whether it "exists"—has constitutional warrant—is something else again. Edmond Cahn, however, opined that "it is too late to reopen the question of whether the Court ought to determine constitutional issues."[3] On the contrary, it is never too late to challenge the usurpation of power; one gains no title by prescription against the government,[4] still less against the sovereign people. Power reserved to the people by the Tenth Amendment cannot be taken over

1. "Do We Have an Unwritten Constitution?," 27 Stan. L. Rev. 703 (1975).
2. "The Warren Court Is Not Likely to Be Overruled," *The New York Times Magazine*, September 7, 1969, in Levy, *Warren* 93–94. See also E. V. Rostow, "The Democratic Character of Judicial Review," 66 Harv. L. Rev. 193, 196 (1952). But see infra Chapter 21 at note 44.
3. Edmond Cahn, "Brief for the Supreme Court," *The New York Times Magazine*, October 7, 1956, in Levy, *Warren* 28, 29; cf. Robert G. McCloskey, *The American Supreme Court* 17–18 (1960). But see infra Chapter 23 at note 2.
4. United States v. 1,629.6 Acres of Land, County of Sussex, Del., 503 F.2d 764, 767 (3d Cir. 1974); United States v. Oglesby, 163 F. Supp. 203, 204 (W.D. Ark. 1958); Blask v. Sowl, 309 F. Supp. 909, 914 (W.D. Wis. 1967).

by "squatter sovereignty." "It will not be denied," Chief Justice Marshall stated, "that a bold and daring usurpation might be resisted, after an acquiescence still longer and more complete than this."[5] In *Erie Ry. Co. v. Tompkins* the Court, per Justice Brandeis, branded its own course of conduct stretching over one hundred years as "unconstitutional,"[6] in a situation not nearly as important as the "enormous power" to impose the judicial will upon the nation. Usurpation—the exercise of power not granted—is not legitimated by repetition.[7] The people, as John Adams inscribed in the Massachusetts Constitution of 1780, are ever entitled to demand of their magistrates an "exact and constant observance" of the principles of the Constitution,[8] above all, to exercise no powers not granted. We may not, therefore, shut our eyes to the issue of legitimacy.

In the course of a penetrating summary of the issues posed by judicial review, Leonard Levy states: "The charges of usurpation most certainly cannot be proved; it is without merit. The difficulty is that the legitimacy of judicial review in terms of the original intent cannot be proved either."[9] This attempt at even-handed analysis overlooks the fact that under a Constitution which delegates and limits power, the burden is on a claimant to point to the source of his power—failing which, it is a usurpation.[9a] After dwelling on the materials which led him to conclude that the framers left a "very incomplete and extraordinarily ambiguous record,"[10] Levy comments on Charles Black's argument that judicial re-

5. M'Culloch v. Maryland, 17 U.S. (4 Wheat.) 316, 401 (1819). Hamilton stated that judicial "usurpations on the authority of the legislature" would be impeachable. Supra Chapter 15 at note 50.

6. 304 U.S. 64, 77–78 (1938): referring to Swift v. Tyson, 40 U.S. (16 Pet.) 1 (1842), the Court held, "the unconstitutionality of the course pursued [by the courts] has now been made clear, and compels us" to "abandon" the "doctrine so widely applied throughout nearly a century." For Justice Brandeis' quotation from Justice Holmes, see supra Chapter 15 note 56.

7. Powell v. McCormack, 395 U.S. 486, 546–547 (1969): "That an unconstitutional action has been taken before surely does not render the same action any less unconstitutional at a later date." See also Ogden v. Saunders, 25 U.S. (12 Wheat.) 213, 290 (1827).

8. Massachusetts Constitution, 1780, Part the First, Article XVIII, 1 Poore 959, quoted more fully supra Chapter 15 at note 18. See also supra Chapter 15 note 19.

9. *Judicial Review and the Supreme Court* 2 (1967); cf. McCloskey, supra note 3 at 8–9.

9a. See infra Chapter 23 at note 2.

10. Levy, supra note 9 at 3.

view has been "legitimized by popular acquiescence, and therefore popular approval, over the course of American history." In Black's own words, "the people have, precisely through the political process, given the stamp of approval in the only way they could give approval to an institution in being—by leaving it alone." To this Levy retorts: "The simple fact is that at no time in our history have the American people passed judgment, pro or con, on the merits of judicial review over Congress. Consent freely given, by referendum, by legislation, or by amendment is simply not the same as failure to abolish or impair."[11] If in fact no provision for judicial review was made by the Constitution, Black's argument would substitute for the constitutional machinery for change by amendment revision by tacit acquiescence. Neglect or inaction would excuse noncompliance with the amendment provision; usurpation would be legitimized by inertia. But, as Hamilton stated in Federalist No. 78, the Constitution is "binding"—"until the people have, by some *solemn and authoritative act*, annulled or changed the established form."[12] The Black argument, which takes little or no account of historical roadblocks, is, as Willard Hurst said in an analogous context, "a way of practically reading Article V out of the Constitution."[13]

To read popular acquiescence in judicial vetoes as ratification of a judicial power to change the Constitution offends against still another requirement: complete disclosure. The people could rely on Hamilton's rejection in Federalist No. 78 of the possibility that "the courts on the

11. Id. 30–31. In the same essay, however, Levy earlier stated, "Long acquiescence by the people and their representatives has legitimated judicial review ... Judicial review, in fact exists by the tacit consent of the governed." Id. 12.

12. Quoted in full, supra Chapter 17 at note 15 (emphasis added).

13. Willard Hurst, "Discussion" in *Supreme Court and Supreme Law* 74 (E. Cahn ed. 1954). Learned Hand also adhered to amendment as the proper means of change. Kathryn Griffith, *Judge Learned Hand and the Role of the Federal Judiciary* 83 (1973). Justice Black rang the changes on this theme, e.g., in Griswold v. Connecticut, 381 U.S. 479, 522 (1965).

The issue has generally been ignored by the instrumentalists. Yet it is central, for as Lusky asks, "does establishment of new constitutional rules by the Court offend Article V ... which prescribes the amendment process? Does it outrage the principle of separation of powers? ... In short, is the Court guilty of plain usurpation?" Lusky 79. Elbridge Gerry, as we have seen, regarded change outside Article V as a subversion of the Constitution and impeachable. Supra Chapter 17 at notes 20–22.

pretense of repugnancy, may substitute their own pleasure to the constitutional intention of the legislature," on his representation that the judges had no warrant to depart from the Constitution. As Lusky put it, the people expect the Justices to view the Constitution as expressing "the will of those who made" it and "to ascertain their will."[14] Until the Court candidly discloses—as Justice Jackson vainly urged—that it is "making new law for a new day," the people can hardly be held to acquiesce in what they have not been told. They have been told that the Court speaks with the voice of the Constitution;[15] they are constantly told that "the *Constitution* (not the Justices) requires." And that cannot be converted into ratification of progressive judicial violation of its limits.

On Levy's view that judicial review has no sure constitutional basis[16] and that it has not been "approved" by the American people, it is, like Mahomet's coffin, suspended in midair. Thus, the awesome power of judicial review is left altogether without footing. My own studies, set forth in *Congress v. The Supreme Court* (1969), convinced me that judicial review *was* contemplated and provided by the Framers, albeit limited to policing constitutional boundaries and divorced from participation in policymaking. The fundamental importance of legitimacy impels me to comment briefly on Levy's objections to the evidence avouched for it.

Levy begins by asking, if the Framers "intended the Court to have the power, why did they not provide for it?"[17] In my view they did. Article III, § 2, extends the judicial power to cases "arising under this Con-

14. Federalist 507; Lusky 31–32.

15. Professor Felix Frankfurter wrote President Franklin Roosevelt, "People have been taught to believe that when the Supreme Court speaks it is not they who speak but the Constitution, whereas, of course . . . it is *they* who speak and *not* the Constitution. And I verily believe that that is what the country needs most to understand." *Roosevelt and Frankfurter: Their Correspondence 1928–1945* 383 (M. Freedman ed. 1967). But as a Justice, sitting on the desegregation case, he could not bring himself to tell the people, as Justice Jackson urged, that the Justices were "declaring new law for a new day." Supra Chapter 7 at notes 52, 55. See also supra Chapter 17 at notes 25–26.

16. Levy, supra note 9 at 2. After examining the arguments pro and con, Archibald Cox likewise concludes that the argument for judicial review "hardly adds up to conclusive proof that the basic charter, as originally adopted, conferred supremacy upon constitutional questions to the Judicial Branch." *The Role of the Supreme Court in American Government* 16 (1976).

17. Levy, supra note 9 at 2.

stitution"; one who claims that a constitutional right was invaded presents such a case. Article VI, §2, provides that "This Constitution and the Laws . . . which shall be made in Pursuance thereof . . . shall be the supreme Law of the Land; and the Judges in every State shall be bound thereby." Federal judges and all federal and State officials were no less "bound" than State judges by the "supreme Law."[18] If a judge is "bound" *only* by a law "in pursuance" of the Constitution, that is, consistent therewith, by necessary implication he is *not bound* by an inconsistent law.[19] Obviously a judge would be required to make a preliminary decision whether or not he was "bound" by the law, exercising the judicial power to decide lodged in a federal judge by Article III.[20] As said by Herbert Wechsler, federal judges "enforce the Constitution" because "they must decide a litigated issue that is otherwise within their [Article III] jurisdiction and in doing so must give effect to the supreme law of the land."[21] In other words, a judicial issue is presented by the question whether a statute is the "supreme Law of the Land" and the Article III "judicial power" embraces such questions. Read together, Articles III and VI therefore confer the power of judicial review. Those who find it difficult to draw these deductions should bear in mind that *the Framers so understood* the two provisions, the evidence for which I have supplied in 86 heavily documented pages.[22]

18. Raoul Berger, *Congress v. The Supreme Court* 236–344 (1969).

19. To the Founders "in pursuance thereof" meant "consistent with." Id. 228–236.

20. Id.

21. Quoted in id. 245 note 101.

22. Id. 198–284. Levy asserts that "Articles III and VI . . . established . . . judicial review . . . over the acts of the states, the subordinate agencies within the federal system, but not over the President and Congress." Levy, supra note 9 at 7. But Article VI refers to "laws of the United States which shall be made in pursuance" of the Constitution; only congressional laws consistent with the Constitution are made the "supreme law of the land." The companion argument—that only state judges are "bound" by the Constitution—would free every other official, state or federal, from constitutional bonds, an absurd result, and one incompatible with the Founders' design. Berger, supra note 18 at 236–242. Levy's inarticulate premise, that the Framers were more solicitous to protect Congress than the States from review, runs counter to historical fact. The Founders cherished the States as the bastion of their rights and *feared* the remote and new federal government; they sought to protect the States against federal incursions, and to do so initially confided judicial review to the State courts. Id. 258–278. They repeatedly referred

Next Levy turns to "Corwin's vacillations" which allegedly testify "to the confusing and inconclusive nature of the evidence."[23] Undeniably Corwin swung like a pendulum, but the important question is not what he thought but what are the facts. Now the facts, set forth by Charles Beard, criticized by Corwin in 1913, but richly confirmed by Corwin in 1914,[24] are in the words of his 1914 summary:

> That the members of the Convention of 1787 thought the Constitution secured to the courts . . . the right to pass on the validity of acts of Congress under it cannot reasonably be doubted. Confining ourselves simply to the available evidence that is strictly contemporaneous with the framing and ratifying of the Constitution, as I think it only proper to do, we find the following members of the Convention that framed the Constitution definitely asserting that this would be the case . . . True these were only seventeen names out of a possible fifty-five, but let it be considered whose names they are. They designate fully three-fourths of the leaders of the Convention.[25]

Only two men, Gunning Bedford and John Mercer, who carried little weight, expressed a contrary view.[26] As Corwin stated, "on no other feature of the Constitution with reference to which there has been any considerable debate is the view of the Convention itself better attested."[27] To these seventeen are added a number of prominent Founders, such as Oliver Ellsworth of Connecticut and John Marshall of Virginia, who spoke in the Ratification Conventions. After painstakingly sifting all the evidence I concluded that Beard and the 1914 Corwin evaluation were fully supported.[28]

---

to judicial review as a curb on *congressional* encroachments. Id. 13–14; Hamilton, supra Chapter 15 at note 50. See Hamilton, infra note 33.

23. Levy, supra note 9 at 3.

24. For a critique of Corwin's 1913 review, see Berger, supra note 18 at 106–114. His reversion in 1937 to his 1913 view was colored by his espousal of the Court-packing plan as a means of halting the Court's assault on the New Deal. For comment on some of his 1937 views, see Berger, id. at 114 note 312.

25. More fully quoted in Berger, id. 104–105.

26. Id. 69 note 109, 63.

27. Id. 105.

28. Id. 47–141.

A few comments seriatim on the selected items Levy would discredit will suffice. When the Convention discussed the "arising under" clause, Madison "expressed doubt about 'going too far' and advocated that jurisdiction over such cases be 'limited to cases of a Judiciary Nature.' "[29] This merely sought to obviate a roving commission to declare legislation unconstitutional and to confine that function to properly litigated cases. Levy himself explains that the Court "cannot strike down an act at will, however unconstitutional, it must wait passively for a zealous litigant to raise a real case or controversy over which it has jurisdiction."[30] The Convention did not see need to act on Madison's suggestion because of the general belief that "the jurisdiction given was constructively limited to cases of a Judiciary Nature"[31]—to "cases or controversies." Levy also stresses Madison's inconsistent positions.[32] Undoubtedly Madison was inconsistent over the years. Who is not? But if we look to what he said in the Federal and State Conventions—the proper frame, as Corwin noted, because those utterances were meant to influence fellow delegates—there is actually little or no inconsistency. On July 23, 1787, Madison declared that "A Law violating a constitution established by the people themselves, would be considered by the judges as null and void,"[33] a view often expressed by other Founders, including Marshall in the Virginia Convention.[34] On August 27 Madison stated: "The right of expounding the Constitution in cases not of this [Judiciary] nature ought

29. Levy, supra note 9 at 5.
30. Id. 27–28.
31. 2 Farrand 430.
32. Levy, supra note 9 at 4–6.
33. Berger, supra note 18 at 73. Following William Crosskey, Levy states this was "wrenched out of context to give the misleading impression that Madison supported judicial review over Congress," whereas Madison referred "to the possibility that state judges would declare unconstitutional a state act in violation of the federal constitution." Levy, supra note 9 at 4. But Levy himself calls attention to Hamilton's explanation "that the Court's power was intended to hold Congress in check, thereby safeguarding the States against national aggrandizement." Levy, id. 6. The Founders were far more concerned about checking Congress than the States. Supra note 22. See also Madison's statement that the Bill of Rights, aimed at Congress, would enable the courts to act as a bulwark. Infra Chapter 21 at note 65.
34. Berger, supra note 18 at 15–16.

not to be given to that Department."[35] By plain implication, if the right *was* of a Judiciary Nature, "the right of expounding" was given, and "expounding" had been employed by the Members to include decisions on constitutionality, which embraced "laws of the United States [congressional acts] . . . in pursuance" of the Constitution.[36]

Then Levy turns to Hamilton: "it is not irrelevant" that Hamilton's own plan made no provision "for any sort of judicial review."[37] I suggest that it is utterly irrelevant. Hamilton did not propose to submit a complete scheme of government, but merely "to suggest the amendments which he should probably propose to the plan of Mr. R[andolph] in the proper stages of its future discussion." The Randolph plan provided for a judiciary as a "check" on the legislature.[38] Levy also depreciates Hamilton's exposition of judicial review in Federalist No. 78 because it adopted Robert Yates' demonstration (in opposition to adoption of the Constitution) that it provided for judicial review.[39] Adoption of an opponent's argument generally is a tacit tribute to its force. Levy explains that

> Hamilton tried to convince his readers that the Court's power was intended to hold Congress in check, thereby safeguarding the states against national aggrandizement. A few [?] advocates of the Constitution, like Oliver Ellsworth and John Marshall, sought in the same manner to allay popular apprehensions that Congress might exceed its power . . . Their remarks, like Hamilton's in #78, are evidence of shrewd political tactics, not of the framers' intention to vest judicial review in the Supreme Court over acts of Congress.[40]

35. Id. 74.

36. Id.; see also Index s.v. "Expounding."

37. Levy, supra note 9 at 6; but see Hamilton, supra note 33.

38. 1 Farrand 291, 28; Berger, supra note 18 at 19 note 53.

39. Levy, supra note 9 at 6. For Yates see Berger, supra note 18 at 201–202. Yates had been anticipated by James Iredell, an advocate of the Constitution and judicial review, in a reply to Richard Spaight, who had written him from the Convention. Berger, id. 82–83.

Levy also argues, supra note 9 at 7, that Hamilton argued in Federalist No. 78 "from general principles" rather than from the words of the Framers. Since he was defending their handiwork, he had to appeal to outside authority—the argument from principle.

40. Levy, supra note 9 at 6.

If they did not mean what they were saying (as to which there is no evidence whatever),[41] they were guilty of false representations to "allay" fears on which votes depended. Those who voted for adoption of the Constitution were entitled to rely on such representations; consequently, the Constitution is to be construed, in Jefferson's words, in accordance with the "meaning contemplated by the plain understanding of the people at the time of its adoption—a meaning to be found in the explanation of those who advocated it."[42] Let it be assumed that the remarks of Madison and Hamilton are open to Levy's doubts, they cannot tip the scales against the clear recognition of judicial review by 15 members who spoke to the issue in the Convention, plus 6 or 7 delegates who spoke thereafter.[43]

Finally, Levy finds it "striking . . . that there were so few State precedents prior to the Convention."[44] That is not surprising in view of the short span between 1776 and 1787, during most of which the States were fighting for survival. If some "precedents" are "spurious" in light of present-day research, the important fact is that they were thought to exemplify judicial review.[45] What men think the facts are is more influential than the actual facts.[46] Levy himself says, "The idea of judicial review was, nevertheless, rapidly emerging, a fact which adds retrospective significance to the few precedents."[47] The decade preceding adoption of the Constitution was one of great intellectual ferment in which, Gordon Wood has shown, a revolution in political thinking was taking place.[48] The postulate, for example, that sovereignty was in the people,

41. Laurent Frantz observed of a similar argument, "the issue is not what Madison really thought but how the First Amendment was presented to those who voted for its enactment." "Is the First Amendment Law?—A Reply to Professor Mendelson," 51 Calif. L. Rev. 729, 739 (1963).

42. Berger, supra note 18 at 120.

43. Id. 112–113.

44. Levy, supra note 9 at 8.

45. Berger, supra note 18 at 38–39.

46. Charles Evans Hughes said of the colonists' reliance on Magna Charta, "It matters not whether they were accurate in their understanding of the Great Charter, for the point is . . . what the colonists thought it meant" in framing their own constitutional provisions. C. E. Hughes, *The Supreme Court of the United States* 186 (1928).

47. Levy, supra note 9 at 11.

48. *The Creation of the American Republic 1776–1787* 389, 524, 555, 564, 589 (1969); the changes proceeded at a rapidly accelerating pace, id. 92, 259, 300, 318.

that rights need not flow from the Crown, was far more revolutionary than judicial review.[49] The Founders, as Corwin emphasized, took "Federalism, checks and balances, judicial review . . . not in the form of institutions tested and hammered into shape by practice, but as raw ideas."[50] What has since become obscure to this generation was clear enough to a great contemporary, James Wilson, second only to Madison as an architect of the Constitution and chief advocate in Pennsylvania of its adoption. In 1790–1791 he was a Justice of the Supreme Court as well as a professor of law in Philadelphia. In the course of a series of Lectures on Law he declared that under the Constitution the effect of legislative "extravagancies may be prevented . . . by the judicial authority." "Every transgression" of the constitutional "bounds of legislative power" shall thus be "adjudged and rendered vain and fruitless."[51]

Were the evidence that judicial review was contemplated and provided for by the Framers far less weighty, it should yet be preferred to a theory which rests judicial review on no evidence at all, for that represents a naked usurpation of power nowhere granted. If, however, judicial review is in fact derived from the text and history of the Constitution, it must be within the compass envisaged by the Framers— policing of boundaries and exclusion of policymaking reserved to the legislature. History cannot be invoked to establish the power, then discarded when seen to limit its scope.

## Supplementary Note on the Role of the Court

Whether the Court may "enforce principles of liberty and justice" when they are not "found within the four corners" of the Constitution is regarded by Thomas Grey as "perhaps the most fundamental question we

49. Id. 344–389.
50. Berger, supra note 18 at 46.
51. Id. 150–151.

can ask about our fundamental law."[1] Philip Kurland considers "the usurpation by the judiciary of general governmental powers on the pretext that its authority derives from the fourteenth amendment" as "the most immediate constitutional crisis of our present time."[2] It is not as if the issue is wrapped in mystery. When Chief Justice Marshall stated that "The difference between the departments undoubtedly is, that the legislature makes, the executive executes, and the judiciary construes the law,"[3] he echoed Francis Bacon's admonition two hundred years earlier that *making* law is not for judges,[4] reiterated by Justice James Wilson in the early days of the Republic and restated down the years.[5] The point was pungently made in 1767 by Chief Justice Hutchinson of the Massachusetts Court: "the *Judge* should never be the *Legislator* because then the Will of the Judge would be the Law: and this tends to a State of Slavery."[6]

1. Thomas C. Grey, "Do We Have an Unwritten Constitution?" 27 Stan. L. Rev. 703 (1975).

2. Letter to Harvard University Press, Aug. 15, 1977. Michael Perry considers the legitimacy of judicial "constitutional policymaking" the "central problem of contemporary constitutional theory." Michael Perry, *The Constitution, the Courts, and Human Rights* 6 (1982).

3. Wayman v. Southard, 23 U.S. (10 Wheat.) 1, 46 (1825).

4. 1 *Selected Writings of Francis Bacon* 138 (Mod. Lib. ed. 1937). This is a view of long standing. Bracton wrote his treatise in 1250 because there were "judges who decided cases according to their own will rather than by the authority of the laws." Bracton, *Treatise on the Laws and Customs of England* 19 (Samuel Thorne ed. 1968). In a Year Book, one judge rebuked another who had stated that "law is what the judges choose." Frederick Pollock, "Judicial Caution and Valour," in *Jurisprudence in Action* 371 (1953).

5. 2 *The Works of James Wilson* 502 (R. G. McCloskey ed. 1967); Minor v. Happersett, 88 U.S. (21 Wall.) 162, 178 (1874). "When once it is established that Congress possess the power to pass an act, our province ends with its construction . . . [T]he province of the courts is to pass upon the validity of laws, not to make them, and when their validity is established, to declare their meaning and apply their provisions. All else lies beyond their domain." The Chinese Exclusion Case, 130 U.S. 581, 603 (1889), per Justice Field for a unanimous Court. The "Judicial process is too remote from conditions . . . It is not accessible to all the varied interests that are in play in any decision of great consequence . . . [I]t is in a vast, complex, changeable society, a most unsuitable instrument for the formulation of policy." Alexander M. Bickel, *The Supreme Court and the Idea of Progress* 175 (1978).

6. Morton J. Horwitz, "The Emergence of an Instrumental Conception of American Law, 1780–1820," in 5 *Perspectives in American Legal History* 287, 292 (1971). A leading activist, Charles Black, confirms that for the colonists, "The function of the judge was

In departing from the demands of the separation of powers,[7] the Court, Louis Lusky has observed, engaged "in a dazzling display of seemingly free-hand constitution-making without apparent concern for the intention of the Constitutors."[8] The result, to borrow from Abram Chayes, an admirer of the Court's expanded role, has been "a radical transformation of the role and function of the judiciary in American life . . . Its chief function now is as a catalyst of social change with judges acting as planners and even managers of large scale intervention in social and economic life."[9] In a familiar image, James Iredell, a pioneer advocate of judicial review, compared the constitutional delegations of

---

thus placed in sharpest antithesis to that of the Legislator," who alone was concerned "with what the law ought to be." Charles L. Black, Jr., *The People and the Court: Judicial Review in a Democracy* 160 (1960).

7. In his Farewell Address, Washington stated, "It is important" that our delegates "confine themselves within their respective Constitutional spheres, avoiding in the exercise of the powers of one department to encroach upon another. The spirit of encroachment tends to consolidate the powers of all the departments in one, and thus to create . . . a real despotism." George Washington, *Writings* 228 (John C. Fitzpatrick ed. 1940).

The Court declared that the Framers divided the government "into three defined categories . . . to assure . . . that each Branch of government would confine itself to its assigned responsibility . . . [T]o maintain the separation of powers, the carefully defined limits on the power of each Branch must not be eroded." Immigration & Naturalization Serv. v. Chadha, 462 U.S. 919, 951, 957 (1983). Justice Brandeis stated, "The doctrine of separation of powers was adopted . . . to preclude the exercise of arbitrary power." Myers v. United States, 272 U.S. 52, 292 (1926), dissenting opinion.

8. Louis Lusky, *By What Right?* 263–264 (1975). Not all activists were "dazzled"; they variously assailed the decisions as "gibberish," "wanton"; others pointed to "lunatic," "inconsistent" decisions, a veritable "shambles," upon which they vainly strove "to superimpose a facade of rationality." For the citations see Raoul Berger, "Paul Brest's Brief for an Imperial Judiciary," 40 Md. L. Rev. 1, 15–16 (1981).

9. Abram Chayes, "The New Judiciary," 28 Harv. L. Sch. Bull. 23, 24 (Feb. 1976). Though sympathetic to judicial revisionism, Lawrence Church finds it hard to swallow cases such as Missouri v. Jenkins, 495 U.S. 33, where the lower federal courts "intervened to reform the public school system in Kansas City," "force[d] very large tax increases," "dictated the planning process for expenditure of the proceeds," and in short "essentially took over the whole public policy process." W. Lawrence Church, "History and the Constitutional Role of the Courts," 1990 Wis. L. Rev. 1071, 1100. The "amount required to be spent grew to about $400 million in one school district"; and Church questioned "whether an expenditure of the magnitude ordered by the lower courts is constitutionally acceptable." Id. 1100 note 97. Given that resources are finite, the State was deprived of the right to decide where expenditures are most needed.

power to "a great power of attorney, under which no power can be exercised but what is expressly given."[10] Hamilton, and before him Blackstone, stated that "an agent cannot new model the terms of his commission."[11] Plainly a power to sell a mule does not authorize sale of the barn.

Ours, as Chief Justice Marshall stated, is a government of limited powers:

> That those powers may not be mistaken or forgotten, the Constitution is written. To what purpose are powers limited, and to what purpose is that limitation committed to writing, if those limits may, at any time, be passed by those intended to be restrained?[12]

From this it follows, as Justice Story declared, the Constitution is "to have a fixed, uniform, permanent construction." It should be "not dependent upon the passions or parties of particular times, but the same yesterday, today, and forever."[13] In our own time, Justice Holmes declared that it is not the function of judges to "renovate the law. That is not their province."[14] And defending *McCulloch v. Maryland*, Chief Jus-

10. 4 *Debates in the Several State Conventions on the Adoption of the Federal Constitution* 148 (Jonathan Elliot ed. 1836).

11. 6 *The Works of Alexander Hamilton* 166 (H. C. Lodge ed. 1904) (the phrase was omitted in 20 *The Papers of Alexander Hamilton* 6 [H. C. Syrett and J. E. Cooke eds. 1962]); 3 William Blackstone, *Commentaries on the Laws of England* 327 (1765–1769). The Justices were pointedly excluded from any share in legislative policy making; when it was proposed by Madison and James Wilson that the Justices assist the President in exercising the veto power, the proposal was rejected because "It was quite foreign from the nature of the office to make them judges of the policy of public measures." For citations see supra pp. 323–324.

12. Marbury v. Madison, 5 U.S. (1 Cranch) 137, 176 (1803).

13. 1 Joseph Story, *Commentaries on the Constitution of the United States* §426 (1905). Chief Justice Thomas Cooley, a contemporary of the Fourteenth Amendment, wrote, "a constitution is not to be made to mean one thing at one time and another some subsequent time when the circumstances may have [changed]." 1 Thomas Cooley, *A Treatise on the Constitutional Limitations* 123–124 (1927). He added, "the meaning of the Constitution is fixed when it is adopted." Id. at 124. Presumably, he reflected accepted learning of the day, thereby barring the activist argument that the Fourteenth Amendment was intended to be "open-ended," to mean one thing in 1866, and another today. See supra pp. 116–121.

14. Oliver Wendell Holmes, Jr., *Collected Legal Papers* 239 (1920).

tice Marshall wrote that the exercise of the judicial power "cannot be the assertion of a right to change that instrument."[15]

Activists like to regard the Court as "conscience to the country," and the guardian of the people[16]—until it happens to go counter to a particular activist desire.[17] Justice Brennan maintains that death penalties are "fatally offensive to human dignity"—never mind that they are authorized by the Fifth Amendment after a fair trial. Although he acknowledges that his view is not shared by a "majority [70 percent] of [his] fellow countrymen," he hopes "to embody a community striving for all."[18] This is to assume that a Justice knows better what is for the people's good than they themselves. Sidney Hook, a hardheaded philosopher, decries those "who know better what basic needs of men and women *should* be, who know . . . what they require *better* than those who have them or should have them."[19] The theory that government "can identify what people would *really* want were they enlightened" was rejected by Lord Noel Annan, then Vice-Chancellor of the University of London, for that would justify the state "in ignoring what ordinary people say they desire or detest."[20]

The Founders, it bears repetition, did not share present-day activist enthusiasm for judges. Judges, Justice James Wilson reminded his fellow

15. *John Marshall's Defense of McCulloch v. Maryland* 209 (Gerald Gunther ed. 1969).

16. Anthony Lewis, "Historical Change in the Supreme Court," in *The Supreme Court Under Earl Warren* 151 (L. Levy ed. 1972). Arthur J. Miller & Ronald F. Howell, "The Myth of Neutrality in Constitutional Adjudication," 27 U. Chi. L. Rev. 661, 689 (1960).

17. Dean Calabresi of the Yale Law School wrote, "I despise the current Supreme Court and find its aggressive, willful statist behavior disgusting." Guido Calabresi, "What Clarence Thomas Knows," N.Y. Times, July 28, 1991, Sec. 4 at 15.

18. Raoul Berger, "Justice Brennan's 'Human Dignity' and Constitutional Interpretation," in *The Constitution of Rights, Human Dignity, and American Values* 129, 130 (Michael J. Meyer and William A. Parent eds. 1992). Opposed to Brennan's "human dignity" is the fact that "in every [colonial] punishment the authorities were determined to expose the offender to scorn . . . persons with a brand on their forehead or a piece of ear missing were forever exposed to the contempt" of their fellows. Gordon S. Wood, *The Radicalism of the American Revolution* 73 (1992). See also Raoul Berger, *Death Penalties: The Supreme Court's Obstacle Course* 117–118 (1982).

19. Sidney Hook, *Philosophy and Public Policy* 28–29 (1980) (emphasis in original).

20. Noel Annan, "Introduction" to Isaiah Berlin, *Personal Impressions* xvii (1981) (emphasis in original). See also supra Supplementary Note on Exclusion of the Judiciary at note 10.

Americans, had been objects of "aversion and distrust."[21] It defies common sense to urge that the judiciary, which Hamilton was constrained to assure the Ratifiers was "next to nothing,"[22] was authorized to revise the Constitution. Such an authorization, Michael Perry commented, would "have been a remarkable delegation for politicians to grant to an institution like the Supreme Court, given the electorate's long-standing commitment to policy making . . . by those accountable, unlike the Court, to the electorate."[23] That no such delegation was made is attested by the historical evidence that I have set out elsewhere in voluminous detail. Here the barest summary must suffice. (1) The founders believed in a fixed Constitution of unchanging meaning.[24] (2) They accorded an inferior place in the federal scheme to the judiciary, deriving from suspicion of innovations by judges theretofore regarded with "aversion and distrust."[25] (3) They had a "profound distrust" of judicial discretion.[26] (4) They were attached to the separation of powers and insisted that courts should not engage in policymaking but act only as interpreters.[27] (5) Above all, judges were not to act as revisers of the Constitution, for

21. 1 Wilson, supra note 5 at 292. Trevelyan wrote that England "was represented by Governors, Colonels and Captains of the British upper class, often as little suited to mix with a democratic society as oil with vinegar." G. M. Trevelyan, *Illustrated History of England* 550 (1956).

22. Federalist No. 78 at 504 (Mod. Lib. ed. 1937). Gouverneur Morris, that deep-dyed Federalist, stated that federal judges "will never be so wild, so absurd, so mad as to pretend that they are superior to the legislative power of America." Howard Swiggett, *The Extraordinary Mr. Morris* 362 (1952).

23. Perry, supra note 2 at 201. For the exclusion of the Justices from policymaking, see supra note 11. Perry found "no plausible textual or historical justification for constitutional policymaking by the judiciary." Id. 24. Justice Holmes stated that "this Court always had disavowed the right to intrude its judgment upon questions of policy or morals." Hammer v. Dagenhart, 247 U.S. 251, 280 (1918), dissenting. He was anticipated by Madison: "questions of policy and expediency are unsusceptible of judicial cognizance and decision." James Madison, "Veto Messages," in *The Messages and Papers of the Presidents* 570 (James D. Richardson comp. 1897).

24. Supra text accompanying note 13.

25. Supplementary Note on the Introduction, supra text accompanying notes 7 and 8.

26. Supplementary Note on the Introduction, supra text accompanying note 7.

27. Supra text accompanying notes 3–6. Article XXX of the 1780 Massachusetts Constitution provides that the "judicial shall never exercise the legislative or executive powers." 1 *Federal and State Constitutions, Colonial Charters* 960 (Benjamin Perley Poore ed. 1877). Similar provisions are contained in a number of other State Constitutions.

that function had been reserved to the people themselves by Article V, the provision for amendment of the Constitution.[28]

In the Convention Elbridge Gerry refused to set up the judges "as the guardians of the Rights of the people," preferring to rely "on the Representatives of the people as the guardians of their rights and interests."[29] That belief was later echoed by Justice Brandeis, who referred to the deep-seated conviction of the American people that they "must look to representative assemblies for the protection of their liberties."[30] Platonic Guardians have enjoyed small favor in our polity. Judge Learned Hand, one of the wisest judges, disclaimed any knowledge of how to choose Platonic Guardians and had no desire to live under their guardianship.[31] And wonder of wonders, Justice Brennan declared "Justices are not platonic guardians appointed to wield authority according to their personal moral predilections."[32] To be sure, this was said during his confirmation hearings; during his incumbency he became a veritable paragon of Platonic Guardians.

Judges are not oracles who, indifferent to the passions of the time, divine the true meaning of the Constitution. What a judge is "really discovering" on his interpretive voyage, correctly observes John Hart Ely,

28. Madison considered that the Constitution "can be altered by the same authority *only* which established it . . . a regular mode of making proper alteration has been inserted in the Constitution itself." 3 *Letters and Other Writings of James Madison* 143, 145 (1865). In McPherson v. Blacker, 146 U.S. 1, 36 (1892), the Court rejected the notion that the Constitution may be "amended by judicial decision without action by the designated organs in the mode by which alone amendments can be made." See also Ullmann v. United States, 350 U.S. 422, 428 (1956). Even Justice Brennan assured the Senate—during his confirmation hearings—that "The only way to amend the Constitution . . . is by the method provided in the Constitution." Sanford Levinson, "The Turn Toward Functionalism in Constitutional Theory," 8 U. Dayton L. Rev. 567, 572 (1983), though he turned 180 degrees on the Bench.

29. 2 *Records of the Federal Convention of 1787* 75 (Max Farrand ed. 1911). Chief Justice Marshall stated that "The wisdom and discretion of Congress . . . are the restraints on which the people must often rely solely, in all representative governments," Gibbons v. Ogden, 22 U.S. (9 Wheat.), 1, 197 (1824).

30. Myers v. United States, 272 U.S. 52, 294–295 (1926), dissenting opinion.

31. Learned Hand, *The Spirit of Liberty* 147 (Irving Dillard ed. 1952).

32. Quoted by Robert Bork, "Address," in *The Great Debate: Interpreting Our Written Constitution* 43, 45 (1986).

"are his own values."[33] Judging in terms of personal preferences has long been condemned; Blackstone disapproved of judges whose decisions would be regulated "only by their own opinions."[34] Marshall declared that "the judicial power is never exercised for the purpose of giving effect to the will of the judge."[35] "Under the guise of interpreting the Constitution," said Justice Moody, "we must take care that we do not import into the discussion our personal views of what would be wise, just, and fitting rules . . . and confound them with constitutional limitations."[36] Recently Judge Richard Posner commented that "a judge ought not to substitute personal values for those that are part of the text, structure and history of the Constitution."[37] Even activists acknowledge the rule,[38] perhaps perceiving that the substitution "of the individual sense of justice . . . would put an end to the rule of law."[39] Then too, as James Wil-

---

33. John Hart Ely, "Foreword: On Discovering Fundamental Values," 92 Harv. L. Rev. 5, 16 (1978). The judge, wrote Learned Hand, "has no right to divinations of public opinion which run counter to its last formal expressions." Learned Hand, supra note 31 at 14. Nonoriginalists, Leonard Levy observed, "tend to stress current values, usually their own, which they find in some philosophy or alleged consensus of which they approve, and they insist that judges ought to decide accordingly." Leonard Levy, *Original Intent and the Framers' Constitution* xv (1988).

Speaking of good and evil, Hobbes said there is "nothing simply and absolutely so; nor any common Rule of Good and Evill, to be taken from the nature of the objects themselves." Thomas Hobbes, *Leviathan* pt. I, chap. 5, §7, p. 39 (1991).

34. 1 William Blackstone, *Commentaries on the Laws of England* 269 (1765).

35. Osborn v. Bank of United States, 22 U.S. (9 Wheat.) 738, 866 (1824).

36. Twining v. New Jersey, 211, U.S. 78, 106–107 (1908). Justice Douglas declared, "Our personal preferences, however, are not the constitutional standard." Zorach v. Clausen, 343 U.S. 306, 314 (1952).

37. Address by Judge Posner, 35 Harv. L. Bull. 34 (1987).

38. Owen Fiss remarks that the judge may "not . . . express his . . . personal beliefs . . . as to what is right or just." Owen M. Fiss, "The Supreme Court, 1978 Term—Foreword: The Form of Justice," 93 Harv. L. Rev. 1, 12–13 (1979). See also Mark V. Tushnet, "A Note on the Revival of Textualism in Constitutional Theory," 58 S. Cal. L. Rev. 683, 690 (1985).

39. Benjamin N. Cardozo, *The Nature of the Judicial Process* 136 (1921). " 'There is not,' says a distinguished writer 'in the whole compass of human affairs, so noble a spectacle as that which is displayed in the progress of jurisprudence; where we may contemplate the cautious and unwearied exertion of a succession of wise men, through a long course of ages, withdrawing every case, as it arises, from the dangerous power of discretion, and subjecting it to inflexible rules.' " Fortunatus Dwarris, *A General Treatise on Statutes* 713 (1848), citing Sir James Mackintosh, *Of a General Discourse on the Study of the Law of Nature and Nations.*

son emphasized in the Convention, laws "may be unjust" and yet be "constitutional."[40]

Activists seek to reshape the Constitution on behalf of "human rights" and of greater protection of "minorities." We have seen that the Founders were more concerned with the rights of the community than with those of the individual,[41] that they regarded the rights expressed in Blackstone's triad as "fundamental,"[42] that this triad, the 39th Congress was told, also represented the American view.[43] A leading activist theoretician, Paul Brest, acknowledges that "Many of what we have come to regard as the irreducible minima of rights are actually supraconstitutional; almost none of the others are entailed by the text or original understanding."[44] Activists would have the courts decide, Michael Perry observes, "what rights, beyond those specified by the framers, individuals should . . . have against government."[45]

Activist efforts to enlarge judicial protection of minorities would jettison a central tenet of our democratic system—majority rule. Of course, if specific provision is made in the Constitution for such protection, it must be given effect. But, as Hamilton stated in Federalist No. 22, "To give a minority a negative upon the majority . . . [is] to subject the sense of the greater number to that of the lesser."[46] Madison was of the same

40. 2 Farrand, supra note 29 at 73. George Mason was of the same opinion. Id. at 78. Chief Justice Marshall said, "the peculiar circumstances of the moment may render a measure more or less wise, but cannot render it more or less constitutional." *John Marshall's Defense of McCulloch v. Maryland* 190–191 (Gerald Gunther ed. 1969). Helvering v. Davis, 301 U.S. 619, 644 (1937): "Our concern here, as often, is with power, not with wisdom."

41. Supra Supplementary Note on the Civil Rights Act and the Fourteenth Amendment, text accompanying notes 52–55. Forrest McDonald observed that "the liberty of the individual [was] subsumed in the freedom of independence of his political community." Forrest McDonald, *Novus Ordo Seclorum: The Intellectual Origins of the Constitution* 71 (1985).

42. Supra Supplementary Note on the Civil Rights Act and the Fourteenth Amendment, text accompanying notes 58–63.

43. Id. text accompanying note 63.

44. Paul Brest, "The Misconceived Quest for the Original Understanding," 60 B.U. L. Rev. 204, 236 (1980).

45. Perry, supra note 2 at 93 (emphasis added).

46. Federalist No. 22 at 135–136 (Mod. Lib. ed. 1937). In the Convention, James Wilson said, "The majority of people wherever found ought in all questions to govern the minority." 1 Farrand, supra note 29 at 605.

mind; criticizing a proposal that more than a majority ought to be required for a quorum, he said that it would reverse a "fundamental principle of free government," because "It would be no longer the majority that would rule; the power would be transferred to the minority."[47] And Jefferson concurred that the "will of the Majority should always prevail."[48] Activists would substitute the "tyranny" of the minority for the "bugaboo" of majority "tyranny";[49] they would have the tail wag the dog. Randall Bridwell properly asks, "what makes the tyranny of the minority . . . better than the tyranny of the majority?"[50] Activists' insistence on enlarged judicial protection illustrates once more their preference for judicial governance, as is exemplified by Robert Cover. He unabashedly thrust aside "the self-evident meaning of the Constitution" because "we" have decided to "entrust" judges with framing an "ideology" whereby to test legislation[51] and, it may be added, discard the Framers' choices.

---

47. Federalist, No. 58 at 382–383. The great historian of Rome Theodor Mommsen praised "every Constitution however defective, which gives free play to the free self-determination of a majority of citizens." 3 *Historians at Work* 288 (Peter Gay et al. eds. 1975).

48. Alpheus T. Mason, *The States Rights Debate: Antifederalism and the Constitution* 169 (1964). Theophilus Parsons, later Chief Justice of Massachusetts, said of the extent to which men part with their natural rights upon entering society, that "the only judge is the majority." Benjamin F. Wright, *American Interpretations of Natural Law* 109–111 (1931).

Mason concluded that the "experience of the past one hundred and fifty years has revealed the danger that, through judicial interpretation, the constitutional device for the protection of minorities from oppressive majority action, may be made the means by which the majority is subject to the tyranny of the minority." Alpheus T. Mason, *Harlan Fiske Stone: Pillar of the Law* 331 (1956).

49. Sidney Hook, who united philosophy with practical wisdom, wrote, "the dictatorship of the majority [is a] bugaboo which haunts the books of political theorists but has never been found in the flesh in modern history." Terrance Sandalow, "Judicial Protection of Minorities," 75 Mich. L. Rev. 1162, 1191 (1977). Dean Jesse Choper considered it "virtually impossible to justify the Court's actions [in providing vigorous protection for rights of minorities] on the ground that it is doing no more than 'finding' the law of the Constitution and fulfilling the intention of its framers." Jesse H. Choper, *Judicial Review and the National Political Process* 137 (1980).

50. Randall Bridwell, "The Scope of Judicial Review: A Dirge for the Theorists of Majority Rule?" 31 S. Car. L. Rev. 617, 654 (1980).

51. Robert Cover, "Book Review," *New Republic*, Jan. 14, 1978, at 26, 27. Mortimer Adler also dismisses "an appeal to the letter of the law or to the original intention of its framers" in order to meet cases in which "majority legislation is unjust without being

A fellow activist, Arthur S. Miller, concluded, however, that the Justices have not been prepared "for the task of constitutional interpretation."[52] With the exception of a few, such as Felix Frankfurter, who was a long-time student of the Court's way with the Constitution, most appointees have been plucked from busy law practices which afforded little occasion for plumbing the depths of constitutional law. Many appointments—some astonishing—have been the fruit of political expediency. When the Court splits 5 to 4 on important issues, a swing Justice is clothed with awesome power to control our destiny.[53] It needs to be borne in mind that the Constitution contains no specific provision for judicial review. What legitimacy it has largely rests on the legislative history, which contemplates no more than policing constitutional boundaries,[54] limits which Chief Justice Marshall declared were not to be "transcended."[55] Incensed by my challenge to cherished Warren dogma,[56] activists launched a campaign to refute and discredit "Gov-

---

unconstitutional." Mortimer Adler, "Robert Bork: The Lessons to Be Learned," 84 Nw. U. L. Rev. 1121, 1125, 1139 (1990).

52. Arthur S. Miller, "The Elusive Search for Values in Constitutional Interpretation," 6 Hastings Const. L.Q. 487, 500 (1979): "Few have the broad gauged approach and knowledge," Miller adds, essential to "search for and identify the values that should be sought in constitutional adjudication." Id. 507.

53. Alexander Bickel observed that 5 to 4 opinions highlight "the fact that one man had the decision . . . It just makes unavoidable for everybody the awareness of the authoritarian nature of the institution, and of how narrowly that authority rests in one individual perhaps." *Hearings on the Supreme Court Before the Senate Subcommittee on the Separation of Powers* 108 (90th Cong., 2d Sess., June 1968).

54. For instance, Marshall stated in the Virginia Ratification Convention, "If they [Congress] were to make a law not warranted by any of the powers enumerated, it would be considered by the judges as an infringement of the Constitution." 3 Elliot, supra note 10 at 553–554. So Justice Story concluded: "If there be an excess by overleaping the just boundary of the power, the judiciary may generally afford the proper relief." Story, supra note 13 at §432. There was never a hint that the courts might rewrite the Constitution. A branch that was "next to nothing" was too frail to support such a burden.

55. Marbury v. Madison, 5 U.S. (1 Cranch) 137, 176 (1803).

56. The doctrines which *Government by Judiciary* challenged, observed Richard Kay, "have now become almost second nature to a generation of lawyers and scholars. Thus it is hardly surprising that the casting of a fundamental doubt on such basic assumptions should produce shock, dismay, and sometimes anger." Richard Kay, "Book Review," 10 Conn. L. Rev. 801 (1978). Daniel Kommers commented, "The tendency of many reviewers of Berger's book is to dismiss his theory out of hand, in part because the modern

ernment by Judiciary." Let us examine how they have dealt with the questions it raises.

### ACTIVIST THEORIZING

A dispassionate Canadian observer commented that while "American scholars struggle to offer some theoretically valid account of the jurisprudential enterprise," they are "energized by a growing sense of desperation."[57] It is impossible in the limited compass of a supplement to

---

liberal mind just cannot imagine turning the clock back to the days prior to *Brown v. Board of Education* and in part because of the fundamental fairness or simple justice for which *Brown* stands. But, as Berger suggests, if the Supreme Court's purpose is to establish justice without reference to the original intent of the framers, then what remains to circumscribe Judicial power? Berger's critics have given singularly unsatisfactory answers to this question." Donald Kommers, "Role of the Supreme Court," 40 *Review of Politics*, 409, 413 (1978).

" 'There is little doubt that the debate over the Constitution has reached a new intensity, and that the discussion has vast implications,' said Morton Horwitz, a leftist legal historian at Harvard Law School." Ethan Bronner, "S-t-r-e-t-c-h-i-n-g the Constitution," Boston Sunday Globe, May 8, 1988, at A27.

57. Allan C. Hutchinson, "Alien Thoughts: A Comment on Constitutional Scholarship," 58 S. Cal. L. Rev. 701 (1985). Paul Brest examined "seven representative scholars who favor one or another form of fundamental rights adjudication" and found that they espouse different theories revolving around different concepts and sources of "morals." Paul Brest, "The Fundamental Rights Controversy: The Essential Contradictions of Normative Constitutional Scholarship," 90 Yale L.J. 1063, 1067 (1981). He wrote that "no defensible criteria exist" whereby to assess "value-oriented constitutional adjudication." Id. 1065. According to Michael Perry, activists have not come up with "a defensible nonoriginalist conception of constitutional text, interpretation and judicial role." Michael J. Perry, "The Authority of Text, Tradition and Reason: A Theory of Constitutional Interpretation," 58 S. Cal. L. Rev. 551, 602 (1985). John McArthur correctly concluded that in general "noninterpretivism [nonoriginalism] is merely a political argument for values non-interpretivists prefer to those in the Constitution." John B. McArthur, "Abandoning the Constitution: The New Wave in Constitutional Theory," 59 Tul. L. Rev. 280, 281 (1984).

Earl Maltz observes that "the premises from which the various commentators proceed vary so widely that the achievement of consensus is likely to be impossible." Earl M. Maltz, "Murder in the Cathedral: The Supreme Court as Moral Prophet," 8 U. Dayton L. Rev. 623 (1983). The eminent British historian A. L. Rowse considers that "the true historian . . . reveres the fact rather than any theory." A. L. Rowse, *A Cornishman at Oxford* 269 (1965). Compare the activist jungle of theory with the observation of Thomas Grey, himself an activist, that the "originalist" view is "of great power and compelling simplicity . . . deeply rooted in our history and in our shared principles of political legitimacy. It has equally deep roots in our formal constitutional law." Thomas Grey, "Do We Have an Unwritten Constitution?" 27 Stan. L. Rev. 703, 705 (1975).

deal with activist criticism in the comprehensive fashion of the nearly forty responses I published. There the reader will find a detailed dissection of such criticism;[58] here I shall limit myself to a few activist arguments which, to my mind, reveal the untenable nature of activist analysis.

Let me begin with Stanley Kutler's argument that "judicial policy-making fills a vacuum created when politically accountable legislatures . . . abdicate their proper policy role."[59] But legislative power can not light on the shoulders of the Court because of congressional inaction. "[I]t is a breach of the National fundamental law," the Court declared, "if Congress gives up its legislative power and transfers it to . . . the Judicial branch."[60] Rightly did Gerald Gunther reject "the view that courts are authorized to step in when injustices exist and other institutions fail to act. That is a dangerous—and I think illegitimate—prescription for judicial action."[61] Justice Story emphasized that "the power of redressing the evil lies with the people by an exercise of the power of amendment. If they do not choose to apply the remedy, it may fairly be presumed that the mischief is less than what arises from a further extension of the power."[62] The vacuum theory is itself vacuous.

58. See bibliography of the writings of Raoul Berger at end of the book. "[F]ree controversy is the only road by which we poor mortals can arrive at historical truth." George M. Trevelyan, *An Autobiography and Other Essays* 72 (1949).

59. Stanley I. Kutler, "Raoul Berger's Fourteenth Amendment: A History or Ahistorical," 6 Hastings Const. L.Q. 511, 523 (1979). Anthony Lewis exclaimed, "there *were* outrages in American life . . . no other arm of government was doing anything about them." Anthony Lewis, "A Man Born to Act, Not to Muse," in *The Supreme Court Under Earl Warren* 159 (L. Levy ed. 1972).

60. Buckley v. Valeo, 424 U.S. 1, 121–122 (1976). "A constitutional power may not be delegated"; United States v. Morton Salt Co. 338 U.S. 632, 647 (1950). It is a maxim of the common law: *delegatus non potest delegare,* i.e., a delegate cannot delegate the power delegated to him. It was restated by Locke: "The legislature cannot transfer the power of making laws to any other hands, for it being but a delegated power from the people, they who have it cannot pass it over to others." John Locke, *Two Treatises of Government* §141 at 380 (Peter Laslett ed. 1960).

61. Gerald Gunther, "Some Reflections on the Judicial Role: Distinctions, Roots and Prospects," 1979 Wash. U. L.Q. 817, 825. In Terminiello v. Chicago, 337 U.S. 1, 11 (1948), dissenting opinion, Justice Frankfurter stated, "We do not sit like a kadi under a tree dispensing justice according to considerations of individual expediency." For additional citations see Raoul Berger, "Paul Brest's Brief for an Imperial Judiciary," 40 Md. L. Rev. 1, 23 note 137 (1981).

62. Story, supra note 13 a §426.

Paul Brest adopts Owen Fiss' suggestion that the "legitimacy" of the courts "depends not on the consent . . . of the people, but rather on [the courts'] *competence*, on the special contribution they make to the quality of our social life."[63] Such a tenet was disclaimed by the Court; speaking by Justice Jackson, it declared,

> Nor does our duty to apply the Bill of Rights to assertions of official authority depend upon our possession of marked competence in the field where the invasion of rights occurs . . . But we act in these matters not by authority of our competence but by force of our commissions.[64]

Expertise does not confer power; it merely invites employment. "An argument for letting the expert decide," said Judge J. Skelly Wright, "is an argument for paternalism and against democracy."[65] Fiss' strange reliance on judicial "competence" is highlighted by his observation that judges

> are lawyers, but in terms of personal characteristics they are no different from successful businessmen or politicians. Their capacity to make a special contribution to our social life derives not from personal traits or knowledge, but . . . from the definition of the office in which they find themselves and through which they exercise power.[66]

63. Brest, supra note 44 at 226 (emphasis added). G. Edward White asserts that "craft techniques justif[y] the judiciary's substitution of its judgment for those of electorally accountable institutions." G. Edward White, "Judicial Activism and the Identity of the Legal Profession," 67 *Judicature* 246, 252 (1983). For a striking example of such "craft techniques," see Bolling v. Sharpe, infra text accompanying notes 90–96.

64. West Virginia State Bd. of Ed. v. Barnette, 319 U.S. 624, 639–640 (1943). Brest overlooks that the basic issue "is not a question of judicial institutional *capacity*; it is rather one of constitutional *legitimacy*." Henry J. Abraham, "Book Review," 6 Hastings Const. L.Q. 467, 470 (1979) (emphasis in original).

65. John Hart Ely, *Democracy and Distrust: A Theory of Judicial Review* 134 (1980). Woodrow Wilson wrote, "What I fear is a government of experts. God forbid that in a democratic country we should resign the task and give the government to experts." Richard Hofstadter, *Anti-Intellectualism in American Life* 209 (1963).

66. Perry, supra note 2 at 99. Alan Dershowitz comments that the Court consists of nine men "who are generally mediocre lawyers, often former politicians . . . almost al-

Entry into office confers expertise! A seasoned judge J. Clifford Wallace observed, "I do not believe that one gains wisdom or a keener perception of social value merely by becoming a judge."[67]

Some apologists for a revisionist Court parade the horribles; thus Gerald Lynch urges that the "consequences of insisting that the 'original intention' be honored across the board" would be that "the States need not enforce the Bill of Rights, protect First Amendment freedoms, or abandon 'de jure schools segregation,' entailing, in short, the rejection of 'virtually all of the Supreme Court's fourteenth amendment jurisprudence.' "[68] He is horrified that "Berger's theory would deny us *Brown*,"

---

ways selected on the basis of political considerations." Alan Dershowitz, "Book Review," N.Y. Times, Nov. 2, 1980, sec. 7 at 9. Justice Story told Chancellor Kent, "We began with first rate men for judicial trusts, and we have now got down to third rate." James McClellan, *Joseph Story and the American Constitution* 80 (1971). Judge Richard Posner notes that "Judgeships normally are rewards for political service" and comments, "politics does play a large role in federal judicial selection." "Few judges," he considers, "in our history are thought to have performed with great distinction." Richard Posner, *The Federal Courts: Crisis and Reform* 31, 42 (1985).

Alexander Bickel observed, "The vagaries of the subjective individual judgments that the Justices were pressing into service as the law of the Constitution [re obscenity] merely caused intellectual anguish to professional observers of the Court." He referred to "the erratic and apparently inarticulable subjectivity of the Court's obscenity decisions" and concluded that "the Court is not the place for the heedless break with the past . . . or for the action supported by nothing but rhetoric, sentiment, anger, or prejudice." Alexander Bickel, *The Supreme Court and the Idea of Progress* 51, 77, 87 (1978).

67. J. Clifford Wallace, "The Jurisprudence of Judicial Restraint: A Return to the Moorings," 50 Geo. Wash. L. Rev. 1, 6 (1981). Shortly before his appointment to the Court, Solicitor General Robert H. Jackson wrote, "time has proved that [the Court's] judgment was wrong on the most outstanding issues upon which it chose to challenge the popular branches." Robert H. Jackson, *The Struggle for Judicial Supremacy* x (1941). Terrance Sandalow considers that the legislature is a better instrument of change than the courts because the lawmakers "are amenable to popular control through ordinary political processes," a vital need if law is to respond "to the interests and values of the citizenry." Terrance Sandalow, "Judicial Protection of Minorities," 75 Mich. L. Rev. 1162, 1166 (1977).

68. Gerald Lynch, 63 Cornell L. Rev. 1091, 1094 (1978). Commenting on the argument that rejection of the notion that the Fourteenth Amendment incorporated the Bill of Rights would be followed by dire consequences, Lino Graglia sapiently observed, "we have very little reason to fear that the horribles will actually occur or that they would prove to be horrible . . . [T]he nation did manage to survive and prosper for most of its history with the states unrestricted by the national Bill of Rights." Lino A. Graglia, " 'Interpreting' the Constitution: Posner v. Bork," 44 Stan. L. Rev. 1019, 1034 (1992).

the "touchstone of constitutional theory."[69] Baldly stated, if a result is benign, ergo it is constitutional; the end justifies the means. Against the "consequences" of repudiating unconstitutional decisions, however, should be weighed the cost of countenancing undeniable judicial arrogations of power, the Court's operation as a continuing constitutional convention.[70]

The view that it is too late to effectuate the unmistakable intention of the Framers is tantamount to claiming that long-standing usurpation confers title. But squatter sovereignty does not run against the people. No one, the Court declared, "acquires a vested interest or protected right in violation of the Constitution by long use";[71] and Chief Justice Thomas Cooley wrote, "Acquiescence for no length of time can legalize a clear usurpation of power."[72] A striking illustration is furnished by *Erie R.R. Co. v. Tompkins*, where the Court by Justice Brandeis, quoting Justice Holmes, branded the century-old *Swift v. Tyson* as "an unconstitutional assump[tion] of power by courts of the United States which no lapse of time or respectable array of opinion should make us hesitate to correct."[73] Long before, Dante wrote that "usurpation of a right does not create a right."[74] If prior decisions represent usurpation, let our guide be Washington's admonition in the Farewell Address: "let there be no change by usurpation; for though this, in one instance, may be the instrument of good, it is the customary weapon by which free governments are destroyed."[75] To repudiate past infractions is to pledge anew to abide by the Constitution, which the Justices are sworn to support.

Brest challenges the assumption that judges are "bound by the text or original understanding of the Constitution."[76] But Chief Justice Mar-

69. Gerald Lynch, "Book Review," 63 Cornell L. Rev. 1091, 1099 (1978).

70. "To the originalist the most relevant, usually dispositive consequence of a failure to follow the law is the usurpation of the right of his fellow citizens to self government." Graglia, supra note 68 at 1047.

71. Walz v. Tax Comm'n, 397 U.S. 664, 678 (1970); Powell v. McCormack, 395 U.S. 486, 546, 547 (1969).

72. 1 Cooley, *Constitutional Limitations* 150 (1927).

73. Erie R.R. Co. v. Tompkins, 304 U.S. 64, 79 (1938).

74. Will Durant, *The Age of Faith* 1063 (1950).

75. 35 *The Writings of George Washington* 229 (John C. Fitzpatrick ed. 1940).

76. Brest, supra note 44 at 224.

shall asked, "Why does a judge swear to discharge his duties agreeably to the Constitution . . . if that Constitution forms no rule for his government?"[77] Brest reasons that "the authority of the Constitution derives from the consent of its adopters," but they are "dead and gone" and "their consent cannot bind succeeding generations."[78] The Court, whom Brest would free from the shackles of the Constitution, has spoken to the contrary: "Our Constitution is a covenant running from the first generation of Americans to us and then to future generations. It is a coherent succession."[79]

Consent or no, the Justices remain bound by their oath to support the Constitution. If, moreover, the Constitution, lacking renewed consent, is not binding, what becomes of judicial authority? For judges are creatures of the Constitution and have only such authority as it confers. What, too, of the hundreds of decisions handed down by judges while the Constitution lacked fresh consent that were therefore unsanctioned? The American people, of course, do not share Brest's opinion; indeed, he notes that "the citizenry at large habitually invoke the Constitution," that it "lies at the core of the American 'civil religion.' "[80] Every amendment the people have adopted testifies that, except for the respective changes, the Constitution was entirely satisfactory—an inferential renewed "consent." Brest's demand for recurrent consent is met by the rule that an enactment remains in force until superseded or repealed.

Indifference to the facts permeates the highest activist quarters. Benno Schmidt, former Dean of Columbia Law School and former President of Yale University, contended that "the Fourteenth Amendment guar-

77. Marbury v. Madison, 5 U.S. (1 Cranch) 137, 180 (1803).

78. Brest, supra note 44 at 225.

79. Planned Parenthood of Southeastern Pennsylvania v. Casey, 112 S. Ct. 2791, 2833 (1992). In Ogden v. Saunders, 25 U.S. (12 Wheat.) 213, 355 (1827), Chief Justice Marshall dissenting, joined by Justice Story, stated, "In framing an instrument, which was intended to be perpetual, the presumption is strong, that every important principle introduced into it is intended to be perpetual also." Edmund Burke saw society as a "partnership not only by those who are living, but between those who are living, those who are dead, and those who are to be born." Herbert Sloan, "The Earth Belongs in Usufruct to the Living," in *Jeffersonian Legacies* 281, 299 (Peter Onuf ed. 1993).

80. Brest, supra note 44 at 234.

anteeing of due process was deliberately cast in 'indeterminate terms.' "[81] Now the due process clause of the Fourteenth Amendment, said the Supreme Court, was identical with that of the Fifth.[82] Charles Curtis wrote that when the framers put due process "into the Fifth Amendment, its meaning was as fixed and definite as the common law could make a phrase . . . It meant a procedural process, which could be easily ascertained from almost any law book."[83] On the eve of the Convention Hamilton stated:

> The words "due process" have a precise technical import, and are only applicable to the process and proceedings of the courts of justice; they can never be referred to an act of legislature.[84]

Judge William Lawrence, one of the framers of the Fourteenth Amendment, quoted the Hamilton definition to the House in 1871,[85] shortly after adoption of the Amendment; and in the same year, another framer, James Garfield, destined to be a martyred president, said that due process of law meant an impartial trial according to the law of the land.[86] Dean John Hart Ely found no references in the legislative history that gave the due process clause of the Fourteenth Amendment "more than a procedural connotation,"[87] as my own extended delving in the records likewise found. To describe "due process" as "indeterminate," therefore, is to fly in the face of the historical evidence. Of the same order is

81. Douglas Martin, "Yale Chief Opens Constitutional Talk by Faulting Meese," N.Y. Times, Feb. 22, 1987, sec. 1 at 46.

82. Hurtado v. California, 110 U.S. 516, 535 (1884): "the [phrase] was used in the same sense and with no greater extent."

83. Charles Curtis, "Judicial Review and Majority Rule," in *Supreme Court and Supreme Rule* 170, 177 (Edmond N. Cahn ed. 1954).

84. 4 *The Papers of Alexander Hamilton* 35 (H. C. Syrett and J. E. Cooke eds. 1962). Edward Corwin concluded that "no one at the time of the framing and adoption of the Constitution had any idea that this clause did more than consecrate a method of procedure against accused persons." Edward S. Corwin, *The Twilight of the Supreme Court* 118–119 (1934).

85. *The Reconstruction Amendments' Debates* 479 (Alfred Avins ed. 1967).

86. Id. 529.

87. John Hart Ely, "Constitutional Interpretivism: Its Allure and Impossibility," 53 Ind. L.J. 399, 416 (1978). John Bingham gave due process the "customary meaning recognized by the courts." Joseph B. James, *The Framing of the Fourteenth Amendment* 86–87 (1965).

Schmidt's statement that "Despite the clear probability that its authors did not intend it as such, the Amendment's general language allowed it to be used to spur 'a revolution in race relations.' "[88] "General language" cannot overcome a specific intention. A considerable body of opinion, including that of leading activists, agrees that the Fourteenth Amendment left segregation untouched.[89]

We must not omit an example from the hand of the Master himself. In *Bolling v. Sharpe* Chief Justice Warren erroneously found that the Fourteenth Amendment prohibited racial segregation in State schools,[90] a prohibition rested in *Brown v. Board of Education*[91] on the equal protection clause. Having located the State prohibition, Warren stated, "it would be *unthinkable* that the same Constitution would impose a lesser duty on the Federal government."[92] But it was not the "same" Constitution; the Fifth Amendment, adopted in 1789, contained no equal protection clause. The very addition of "equal protection" in the Fourteenth Amendment argues against its inclusion in the due process of the Fifth. The interests of symmetry could not overcome the fact that Congress had rejected Senator Charles Sumner's unremitting efforts to banish segregation from the federal enclave, the District of Columbia schools.[93] John Hart Ely, to whom Warren is a "carefully" chosen "hero," says *Bolling* is "gibberish both syntactically and historically."[94] And Brest considers that it "is not supported by even a generous reading of the fifth amendment."[95] In his adulatory biography of Warren, G. Edward White concluded that "when one divorces Warren's opinions from their ethical premises, they evaporate." Warren's "justifications for a result were often conclusory statements of what he perceived to be ethical imperatives."[96] Such was the Warren legacy; and as Mark Tush-

88. Martin, supra note 81.

89. Supra Supplementary Note on the Introduction at note 41.

90. 347 U.S. 497, 500 (1954).

91. 347 U.S. 483 (1954).

92. Bolling v. Sharpe, 347 U.S. at 500 (emphasis added).

93. Supra Supplementary Note on the Introduction, text accompanying note 37.

94. Ely, supra note 65 at Dedication and 32.

95. Brest, supra note 44 at 233.

96. G. Edward White, *Earl Warren: A Public Life* 367 (1982). Warren made no bones about his revisory function: "We will pass on a document [Bill of Rights that] will not

net notes, activist theorizing is "plainly designed to protect the legacy of the Warren Court."[97]

In 1976 Abram Chayes wrote that judicial action in the two prior decades "adds up to a radical transformation of the role and function of the judiciary . . . its chief function now is as a catalyst of social change with judges sitting as planners on a large scale."[98] Unless the Fourteenth Amendment authorizes this "transformation," it was a naked arrogation in the teeth of the Founders' exclusion of the Justices from policymaking,[99] and of Hamilton's assurance that of the three branches the judiciary was "next to nothing."[100] Let us then consider whether the Amendment was intended to enlarge the Court's jurisdiction.

To begin with, the Court was then at the very nadir of public confidence. The disastrous *Dred Scott* decision was so deeply etched into Northern memory that Senator Charles Sumner even sought to bar the customary placement of Chief Justice Taney's bust in the Supreme Court chamber, stating that his name should be "hooted down in the pages of history."[101] In fact, the framers bitterly resented the Court's intrusion

---

have exactly the same meaning it had when we received it from our fathers." Id. 223. On the other hand, Marshall declared, if a word was "understood in a [certain] sense . . . when the Constitution was framed . . . the convention must have used it in that sense," and it is that sense which is to be given effect. Gibbons v. Ogden, 22 U.S. (9 Wheat.) 1, 190 (1824).

Judge Richard Posner observed, "as the courts move deeper into subjects on which there is no ethical consensus, judicial activism in the form attributed by Professor [G. E.] White to Chief Justice Warren becomes ever more partisan and parochial, lawless, and finally reckless." Richard Posner, *The Federal Courts: Crisis and Reform* 215 (1985).

97. Mark Tushnet, "Legal Realism, Structural Review, and Prophecy," 8 U. Dayton L. Rev. 809, 811 (1983).

98. Abram Chayes, "The New Judiciary," 28 Harv. L. Sch. Bull. 23, 24 (February 1976). See also Lusky, supra Supplementary Note on the Introduction at note 16 and Lewis, id. at note 18.

99. Supra Supplementary Note on Exclusion of the Judiciary, text accompanying notes 1–5.

100. Federalist No. 78 at 504 (Mod. Lib. ed. 1937).

101. David Donald, *Charles Sumner and the Rights of Man* 193 (1970). See also supra Chapter 12 at note 4. In 1871 Senator James Nye of Nevada said that the Dred Scott "decision was an outrage upon the Constitution," and the American people. Avins, supra note 85 at 428. And Senator Jacob Howard added, "It was a partisan political decision, the purpose of which was to establish . . . for all time to come the legality, the rightfulness and even the piety of slavery . . . The comment made upon that great wrongful judicial

into "settlement of political questions" which, said John Bingham, "it has no more right to decide for the American people than has the Court of St. Petersburg."[102] It was such sentiments that led Congress to withdraw jurisdiction in *Ex parte McCardle*,[103] a case then under advisement by the Supreme Court. And this hostility found expression in §5 of the Amendment: "The *Congress shall have power* to enforce by appropriate legislation the provisions of this article." The Court was under no illusions as to the meaning of §5, saying in 1879:

> It is not said that the judicial power . . . shall extend to enforcing the prohibitions . . . It is the power of Congress which has been enlarged.[104]

Thus the framers of the Fourteenth Amendment were altogether unlikely to enlarge the jurisdiction of the federal courts.

The fundamental error in activist thinking is laid bare by Eric Foner. He regards Reconstruction as effecting a "revolution,"[105] and believes that the Fourteenth Amendment was not "a minor adjustment to the Constitution" but "a change in its basic structure."[106] Phillip Paludan, whose "major concern . . . is that of the national protection for Negro rights,"[107] comes to the contrary conclusion, for reasons which are incontestable. Apart from the pervasive racism[108] which clogged the way, the vast majority cherished the federal system and clung to States' rights.[109] Respect for federalism, Paludan concluded, was "the most po-

---

decision is to be seen in the dreadful war through which we have just passed." Avins, id. at 429.

102. Charles Fairman, *Reconstruction and Reunion*, 6 *History of the Supreme Court of the United States* 462 (1971).

103. 74 U.S. (7 Wall.) 506 (1868); see Raoul Berger, *Selected Writings* 239 (1987).

104. Ex parte Virginia, 100 U.S. 339, 345 (1879).

105. Eric Foner, "The Supreme Court's Legal History," 23 Rutgers L.J. 243, 245 (1992).

106. Id.

107. Phillip S. Paludan, *A Covenant With Death* 24 (1975).

108. Supra pp. 10–13, 255–256; Paludan, supra note 107 at 54, 102, 216. Paludan's mentor, Harold Hyman, stated that "Negrophobia tended to hold even sparse Reconstruction institutions . . . at low throttle, and played a part in Reconstruction's incompleteness." Harold M. Hyman, *A More Perfect Union* 447 (1973).

109. Paludan, supra note 107 at 11, 49, 55.

tent obstacle to the Negroes' hope for protected liberty."[110] "To secure his equality," he wrote, "the freedman would require a major constitutional upheaval," but the populace "loved" federalism more than equal protection for blacks.[111] "Federalism remained a barrier to equal rights."[112] Thus John Bingham, draftsman of the Fourteenth Amendment, felt constrained to assure the House, "God forbid that by [the Amendment] we should strike down the rights of States."[113] Chief Justice Thomas Cooley, the chief constitutional authority of the period, considered that the Amendment had "not been agreed upon for the purpose of enlarging the sphere of powers of the general government, or of taking from the States any of those just powers of government which . . . were 'reserved to the States respectively.' The existing division of sovereignty is not disturbed by it."[114] And his compeer, John Norton Pomeroy, found that the "state police power, the power to legislate to secure the health and safety of its citizens had [not] been rescinded by the fourteenth amendment."[115] There was "general acceptance of the constitutional views of Pomeroy and Cooley."[116]

Let me brush in some confirmatory facts. The immediately antecedent Civil Rights Act, which the Amendment was designed to embody to prevent its repeal,[117] was triggered by the Black Codes, whereby the South sought to return the freedmen to serfdom.[118] Both were designed to save them from oppression and to enable them to exist. Discussing the Amendment, for which he voted, Senator James Patterson of New Hampshire said, "I am opposed to any law discriminating against [blacks]

110. Id. 15, 49. "No one reading the debates carefully will question the framers' devotion to federalism, even the extreme Radicals." Howard Jay Graham, *Everyman's Constitution* 312 (1968).

111. Paludan, supra note 107 at 12–13.

112. Id. 52.

113. Id. 59.

114. Id. 272. Senator Lyman Trumbull, author of the Civil Rights Bill of 1866, declared in 1871, "The States were, and are now, the depositaries of the rights of the individual against encroachment. The fourteenth amendment has not changed an iota of the Constitution as it was originally framed." Id. 59.

115. Id. 241.

116. Id. 282.

117. Supra pp. 32–33.

118. Raoul Berger, *The Fourteenth Amendment and the Bill of Rights* 23–25 (1989).

in the security of life, liberty, person and property . . . Beyond this I am not prepared to go."[119] One of the "authorities," Harold Hyman, whom Foner believes "have greatly expanded the horizon of legal scholarship,"[120] observed that Patterson did not "want to undermine state power in any *drastic* fashion."[121] Another Foner "authority," William Nelson, describes as a "key fact" the Northern goal of imposing restraints on the South "*without altering radically* the structure of the federal system or *increasing markedly* the power of the federal government."[122] The North, moreover, was given good reason to believe that the "alterations" in the South did not extend to the North.[123] Then too, a war-weary North was little minded to embark on fresh crusades for abolitionist goals. As Henry Monaghan emphasized, midcentury Americans "opposed slavery and racial equality with equal intensity."[124]

Since Foner invokes the Civil Rights Act of 1866 in aid of his vision,[125] we may begin with the Supreme Court's conclusion in *Georgia v. Rachel* (1966) that "The legislative history of the 1866 Act clearly indicates that Congress intended to protect *a limited category* of rights."[126] In 1866, Senator Lyman Trumbull, draftsman of the Bill, explained that "The great fundamental rights set forth" in the Bill are "the right to acquire property, the right to come and go at pleasure, the rights to en-

119. *Globe* 2699.

120. Foner, supra note 105 at 244.

121. William E. Nelson, *The Fourteenth Amendment: From Political Principle to Judicial Doctrine* 7 (1988) (emphasis added). Hyman observed that "A heavy phalanx of Republican politicos, including Sherman and Trumbull . . . were states rights nationalists, suspicious of any new functional path the nation travelled." Hyman, supra note 108 at 304. He noted Republican unwillingness "to travel any road" that did not leave "the states masters of their fates." Hyman, id. 470.

122. Nelson, supra note 121 at 197 (emphasis added).

123. Supra, Supplement to Chapter 8, text accompanying notes 95–104.

124. Henry P. Monaghan, "The Constitution Goes to Harvard," 13 Harv. C.R.–C.L. L. Rev. 117, 126 (1978). "A belief in racial equality," wrote the English scholar W. R. Brock, "was an abolitionist invention; . . . to the majority of men in the mid-nineteenth century it seemed to be condemned both by experience and by science." W. R. Brock, *An American Crisis: Congress and Reconstruction* 285 (1963). Americans "clung firmly to a belief in the basic inferiority of the Negro race, a belief supported by the preponderance of nineteenth century scientific evidence." Paludan, supra note 107 at 54.

125. Foner, supra note 105 at 246.

126. 384 U.S. 780, 791 (1966).

force rights in the courts, to make contracts and to inherit and dispose of property."[127] These were carried into the Act, and Act and Amendment were viewed as "identical."[128] Pomeroy stated that the Amendment secured to all an equal right to enter or leave the State, to acquire and transfer property, to sue and be sued, to make contracts and to hold a lawful occupation."[129] Justice Bradley, a contemporary, declared that the "first section of the bill covers the same ground as the fourteenth amendment,"[130] as leading senators confirmed during the ratification campaign.[131] Against this background Foner's assertion that the Amendment changed the "basic structure" has not a leg to stand on.

127. Avins, supra note 85 at 122. Sidney George Fisher, a contemporary commentator on Reconstruction, defined "civil rights" as "the right to acquire property, to make contracts, to sue and be sued, to give testimony in court, to work for whomever he pleased"— the rights embodied in the Civil Rights Act. Paludan, supra note 107 at 217.

128. Supra pp. 32–33. See supra Supplementary Note on the Civil Rights Act and the Fourteenth Amendment, text accompanying notes 25–26.

129. Paludan, supra note 107 at 241. Pomeroy believed that the Fourteenth Amendment "mirrored the view of the rights protected under the Civil Rights Bill." Id. 235.

130. Live-Stock Dealers' and Butchers' Ass'n v. Crescent City Live-Stock Landing & Slaughter-House Co., 15 F. Cas. 649, 655 (C. C. D. La. 1870) (No. 8408).

131. Raoul Berger, "Incorporation of the Bill of Rights: A Response to Michael Zuckert," 26 Ga. L. Rev. 1, 10–11 (1991).

# 20

## *Why the "Original Intention"?*

URRENT indifference to the "original intention"—shorthand for the meaning attached by the Framers to the words they employed in the Constitution and its Amendments—is a relatively recent phenomenon. Those who would adhere to it are scornfully charged with "filiopietism," "verbal archeology,"[1] "antiquarian historicism that would freeze [the] original meaning" of the Constitution.[2] We are told that the Framers intended to leave it "to succeeding generations [meaning judges] . . . to rewrite the 'living' constitution anew,"[3] an argument opposed to historical fact. The sole and exclusive vehicle of change the Framers provided was the amendment process; judicial discretion and policymaking were in high disfavor; all "agents and servants of the people" were to be "bound by the chains" of a "fixed Constitution." Certainly Justice Story did not regard himself as holding a commission "to rewrite the 'living' constitution anew":

> Nor should it ever be lost sight of that the government of the United
> States is one of limited and enumerated powers; and that a depar-

1. Myres McDougal and Asher Lans, "Treaties and Congressional-Executive or Presidential Agreements: Interchangeable Instruments of National Policy," 54 Yale L.J. 181, 212, 214, 291 (1945).

2. Leonard Levy, *Judgments: Essays in American Constitutional History* 17 (1972).

3. A. S. Miller, "An Inquiry Into the Relevance of the Intentions of the Founding Fathers, With Special Emphasis Upon the Doctrine of the Separation of Powers," 27 Ark. L. Rev. 584, 595 (1973). The Constitution was "not intended to" "freeze its original meaning." Levy, supra note 2. Professor Miller might have cited Edward Corwin, who, in 1925, dismissed "speculative ideas about what the framers of the constitution . . . intended it should mean" because "the main business of constitutional interpretation . . . is to keep the constitution adjusted to the advancing needs of time." *American Constitutional History* 108 (Mason and Garvey eds. 1964).

ture from the true import and sense of its powers is pro tanto, the establishment of a new Constitution. It is doing for the people, what they have not chosen to do for themselves. It is usurping the functions of a legislator.[4]

Why is the "original intention" so important? The answer was long since given by Madison: if "the sense in which the Constitution was accepted and ratified by the Nation . . . be not the guide in expounding it, there can be no security for a consistent and stable government, more than for a faithful exercise of its powers."[5] A judicial power to revise the Constitution transforms the bulwark of our liberties into a parchment barrier. This it was that caused Jefferson to say, "Our peculiar security is in the possession of a written constitution. Let us not make it a blank paper by construction."[6] Given a system founded on a dread of power, with "limits" to fence it about, those who demand compliance with those limits (pursuant to the counsel of four or five early State constitutions) are not to be charged with invoking the shades of the Framers in order to satisfy "the need for certainty . . . If we pretend that the framers had a special sort of wisdom, then perhaps we do not have to think too hard about how to solve pressing social problems."[7] The issue rather is whether solution of those "pressing social problems" was confided to the judiciary.[8]

Effectuation of the draftsman's intention is a long-standing rule of interpretation in the construction of all documents—wills, contracts, statutes—and although today such rules are downgraded as "mechanical" aids, they played a vastly more important role for the Founders. Hamil-

---

4. 1 Story, *Commentaries on the Constitution of the United States* §426 at 325–326 (5th ed. 1905). "It is not the function of the courts or legislative bodies . . . to alter the method [for change] which the Constitution has fixed." Hawke v. Smith, 253 U.S. 221, 227 (1920). See also supra Chapter 17 at notes 15–22.

5. Supra Chapter 1 note 7; see infra note 38.

6. See supra Chapter 17 at note 90.

7. Miller, supra note 3 at 595–596.

8. "[S]ince the mid-1950's the Supreme Court also has become the principal agent of change within our political order. Tackling political issues that the 'political' branches could not, would not, or dared not touch, the Court assumed the responsibility for political innovation, forcing changes long blocked by a Congress or by state legislatures dominated by minority elements." Rondel G. Downing, "Judicial Ethics and the Political Role of the Courts," 35 L. & Contemp. Prob. 94, 102 (1970). See also supra Chapter 16 note 28.

ton, it will be recalled, averred: "To avoid arbitrary discretion in the courts, it is indispensable that they should be bound down by *strict rules* and precedents, which serve to define and point out their duty in every particular case that comes before them."[9] That Hamilton was constrained thus to reassure the ratifiers testifies to prevailing distrust of unbounded judicial interpretive discretion.[10] Some fifty years later, Justice Joseph Story, perhaps the greatest scholar who sat on the Supreme Court, emphasized that such rules provided a "fixed standard" for interpretation,[11] without which a "fixed Constitution" would be forever unfixed. The Constitution, in short, was written against a background of interpretive presuppositions that assured the Framers their design would be effectuated.

The rules governing "intention" reach far back in legal history; but for our purposes it suffices that English case-law emphasis on effectuation of the "original intention" was summarized in Bacon's *Abridgment* (1736)[12] and restated in 1756 by Thomas Rutherforth,[13] in a "work well known to the colonists."[14] Rutherforth assimilated the interpretation of statutes to that of contracts and wills and stated that "The end, which interpretation aims at, is to find out what was the intention of the writer,

9. Supra Chapter 16 at note 34 (emphasis added). This conception was deeply rooted in the common law. Chief Justice Fortescue, Corwin tells us, was guided by maxims which "constituted the very substance of the peculiar science of the judges"; and Coke paid reverence to such "fundamental points of the common law," among them, borrowed from Coke by "early American judges and lawyers," are "the numerous rules for the construction of written instruments which were originally adapted from the same sources to the business of constitutional construction." E. S. Corwin, "The 'Higher Law' Background of American Constitutional Law," 42 Harv. L. Rev. 149, 365, 370, 371 (1928).

10. Jefferson expressed confidence in the judiciary if "kept strictly to their own department." 5 *The Writings of Thomas Jefferson* 81 (P. L. Ford ed. 1892–1899).

11. 1 Story, supra note 4, §400 at 305. The object of such standards is to avoid "the passions and prejudices of the day." Id.

12. Matthew Bacon, *A New Abridgment of the Laws of England*, "Statute" I (5) (1736). Citations herein are to the 3d ed. 1768. Justice Story stated that "Bacon's Abridg. title Statute I contains an excellent summary of the rules for construing statutes." 1 Story §400 at 305 note 2.

13. *Institutes of Natural Law* (1754–1756).

14. Robert M. Cover, *Justice Accused: Antislavery and the Judicial Process* 12 (1975). Some of Rutherforth's criteria are quoted in 1 Story §402.

to clear up the meaning of his words."[15] And he concluded that "the intention of the legislator is the natural measure of the extent of the law."[16] The influence of these presuppositions on the Founders is no matter of conjecture. On the heels of the Convention, Justice James Wilson, a leading participant, said: "The first and governing maxim in the interpretation of a statute is to discover the meaning of those who made it."[17] Not long thereafter Jefferson pledged as President to administer the Constitution "according to the safe and honest meaning contemplated by the plain understanding of the people at the time of its adoption—a meaning to be found in the explanations of those who advocated . . . it."[18] That view was echoed by Chief Justice Marshall, himself a participant in the Virginia Ratification Convention: if a word "was so understood . . . when the Constitution was framed . . . [t]he convention must have used it in that sense."[19] It was reaffirmed by Justice Holmes: an amendment should be read in a "sense most obvious to the common understanding at the time of its adoption."[20]

Enchanted by judicial fulfillment of libertarian hopes, academe, on one ground or another, has endeavored to discredit "original intention," to rid us of the "dead hand of the past."[21] But neither has openly been repudiated by the Court. To the contrary, it has been the Court's practice over the years to consult the intention of the Framers; the Court's concern, as Louis Pollak remarked, "for the original intent of the framers of the Constitution remains high."[22] An arresting example is fur-

15. 2 Rutherforth, supra note 13 at 307, 309. Story likewise stated, "The first and fundamental rule in the interpretation of all instruments is, to construe them according to the sense of the terms and the intention of the parties." 1 Story §400.

16. 2 Rutherforth, supra note 13 at 364.

17. 1 *The Works of James Wilson* 75 (McCloskey ed. 1967).

18. 4 Elliot 446.

19. Gibbons v. Ogden, 22 U.S. (9 Wheat.) 1, 190 (1824). See also infra note 39.

20. Eisner v. Macomber, 252 U.S. 189, 220 (1920), dissenting opinion.

21. Supra Chapter 17 at note 9. McDougal and Lans, supra note 1 at 545: the "dead cannot bind the living."

22. Louis Pollak, "The Supreme Court Under Fire," 6 J. Pub. L. 428, 441 (1957). "[A]ll questions of constitutional construction," Justice Horace Gray stated, are "largely a historical question." Sparf v. United States, 156 U.S. 51, 169 (1895), dissenting opinion. Bickel brushed aside "the proposition that the original understanding is simply not relevant. For arguments based on that understanding . . . have been relied on by judges well

nished by the exchange between two "activists," Justices Black and Goldberg, aligned on opposing sides. To Black's condemnation of judicial "amendment," Goldberg responded: "Of course our constitutional duty is to construe, not to rewrite or amend the Constitution! . . . Our sworn duty to construe the Constitution requires, however, that we read it to effectuate the intent and the purposes of the Framers."[23] So, too, both Justices Black and Frankfurter, on opposite sides of the fence in *Adamson v. California*, invoked the original intention.[24]

To impeach the "original intention," academicians sought to discredit resort to "legislative history" in general on the ground that the records are incomplete,[25] that they are inconclusive because strewn with conflicting claims. Such charges are irrelevant to the records of the 39th Congress, a "complete" verbatim record of the entire debates. Insofar as there were conflicting opinions, the views of racist Democrats who sought to kill both the Civil Rights Bill and the Fourteenth Amendment carry no weight; those of a handful of radical dissentients for whom neither Bill nor Amendment went far enough are overborne by the will of the great Republican majority—for example, to leave control of suffrage to the States. That will is implicitly stated in the §2 curtailment of representation when a State denies or abridges suffrage—recognition of power to do so; it is unequivocally confirmed by the Report of the Joint Committee on Reconstruction, by those in charge of the Bill and the Amendment, and by many others in the course of the debates. On a

---

aware that it is a *constitution* they were expounding." Alexander M. Bickel, "The Original Understanding and the Segregation Decision," 69 Harv. L Rev. 1, 3–4 (1955).

23. Bell v. Maryland, 378 U.S. 226 (1964). Black: "changes in the Constitution . . . are to be proposed by Congress or conventions and ratified by the States. The Founders gave no such amending power to this Court." Id. 342, dissenting opinion; Goldberg, id. 288, concurring opinion.

24. 332 U.S. 46, 63–64, 72–73 (1947). For Frankfurter, see also supra Chapter 14 note 44.

25. John Wofford, "The Blinding Light: The Uses of History in Constitutional Interpretation," 31 U. Chi. L. Rev. 502, 504–506 (1964). The intentions of the Framers "are clothed in mystery." Miller, supra note 3 at 596. Miller goes further: "even if that history is clear, it is really not relevant." Id. 598. Compare with Bickel, supra note 22, and with Miller and Howell supra Chapter 1 note 25.

centuries-old canon of interpretation, that intention is as good written into the text.[26] When a legislature "has intimated its will, however indirectly," Justice Holmes held, "that will should be recognized and obeyed . . . it is not an adequate discharge of duty for courts to say: 'We see what you are driving at, but you have not said it.' "[27] The intention of the sovereign people, whether expressed in convention or through the amendment process, demands even greater obedience.

Another attempt to dissolve traditional bonds was by way of semantics. To demonstrate that "only present current meanings are pertinent,"[28] Charles Curtis delivered himself of a "profound discourse on the meaning of meaning,"[29] liberally sprinkled with Aristotelian essences and linguistics.[30] But four years earlier, in an article giving some sage counsel to draftsmen, Curtis advised, "What the author of a legal document is trying to control is the future . . . to control this person's conduct in the future"[31]—more graphically expressed in Jefferson's "bind him down . . . by the chains of the Constitution." If that be the purpose of drafting, as seems indisputable, it is aborted by a theory that leaves another person free to read his own meaning into the draftsman's words. Commenting on Curtis' "meaning of meaning," Willard Hurst matter-of-factly pierced to the heart of the matter: "When you are talking about constitutional law, you are talking about the balance of power in the community and the question of how you find meaning boils down concretely here to who finds the meaning."[32] May the Justices supplant the value-

26. Bacon's *Abridgment*, "Statute" I (5): "A thing which is within the intention of the makers of a statute, is as much within the statute as if it were within the letter." The principle has often been applied by the Supreme Court. See supra Chapter 1 note 24.

27. Johnson v. United States, 163 F. 30, 32 (1st Cir. 1908); quoted in Keifer & Keifer v. R.F.C., 306 U.S. 381, 391 note 4 (1939).

28. "The Role of the Constitutional Text" in *Supreme Court and Supreme Law* 64, 68 (Edmond N. Cahn ed. 1954).

29. Paul A. Freund, "Discussion," in id. 71.

30. Curtis, id. 68–70.

31. C. P. Curtis, "A Better Theory of Legal Interpretation," 3 Vand. L. Rev. 407, 423 (1950).

32. Willard Hurst, "Discussion," in *Supreme Court and Supreme Law* 74 (Edmond N. Cahn ed. 1954).

choices of the Framers with their own? An officeholder like Santarelli appreciated such realistic implications.[33]

If the Court may substitute its own meaning for that of the Framers it may, as Story cautioned, rewrite the Constitution without limit. But, Leonard Levy maintains: "Whatever the framers of the Fourteenth intended, there is no reason to believe that they possessed the best insights or ultimate wisdom *as to the meaning of their words* for subsequent generations . . . Words do not have fixed meanings. As Justice Holmes once remarked, a word is 'the skin of living thought and may vary greatly in color and content according to the circumstances and time in which it is used.' "[34] Of course, were Holmes *drafting* he would use words in their present meaning, but that is a far cry from the view that he would feel free to substitute his own meaning in a subsisting document for that of bygone draftsmen. As we have seen, he felt bound to give effect to the intention of the legislators, and it will hereafter appear that he held that words must be given the meaning they had at the time they were set down.[35] There is, moreover, a serious flaw in the Levy analysis, which appears more plainly in John Wofford's statement that if "the meaning of a word is its use, and if its use can never be found apart from its context, then we need only add that an inseparable constituent of context is the time at which the use occurs to show that a past meaning can not bind the present."[36] Now one who reads what another has written or seeks to interpret it does not in common usage really "use" the word. It is the writer who "used" it, and the traditional function of interpretation, as Rutherforth stated above 200 years ago, is to ascertain "what was the intention of the *writer*?"[37] On the Levy-Wofford analysis we are free to read Hamlet's statement that he "can tell a hawk from a handsaw," then meaning a heron, as if he referred to our pointed-tooth cutting tool because the meaning of "handsaw" has changed, reducing Shakespeare to nonsense.[38] Even

33. Supra Chapter 17 at note 59.
34. Levy, supra note 2 at 71 (emphasis added).
35. Infra Chapter 21 at notes 38–42.
36. Wofford, supra note 25 at 523.
37. Supra at note 15 (emphasis added).
38. Paul Brest states, "suppose that the Constitution provided that some acts were to be performed 'bi-weekly.' At the time of the framing of the Constitution, this meant only

Humpty-Dumpty did not carry it so far as to insist that when Alice "used" a word *he* could dictate what *she* meant. With Willard Hurst, I would underscore that "if the idea of a document of superior authority"—the "fixed Constitution" to which the Founders were attached—"is to have meaning, terms which have a precise history filled content to those who draft and adopt the document [such as "due process"] or to which they attach a clear meaning [such as "equal protection"] must be held to that precise meaning."[39] To hold otherwise is to convert the "chains of the Constitution" to ropes of sand.

Like the Constitution, the Fourteenth Amendment was written against the Bacon-Rutherforth background, clearly restated in 1860.[40] Even Charles Sumner, archradical of the 39th Congress, was well aware that

---

'once every two weeks'; but modern dictionaries, bowing to pervasive misuse, now report 'twice a week' (i.e., semi-weekly) as an acceptable definition. To construe the definition now to mean 'semi-weekly' would certainly be a change of meaning (and an improper one at that)." Paul Brest, *Processes of Constitutional Decisionmaking: Cases and Materials* 146 note 38 (1975).

That has been the accepted view: "The Constitution is a written instrument. As such its meaning does not alter. That which it meant when adopted it means now . . . 'Any other rule of construction would abrogate the judicial character of this court, and make it the mere reflex of the popular opinion or passion of the day.' " South Carolina v. United States, 199 U.S. 437, 448, 449 (1905). See also Hawke v. Smith, 253 U.S. at 227. On the opposite view constitutional limitations are writ on water.

39. W. Hurst, "The Process of Constitutional Construction," in *Supreme Court and Supreme Law* 55, 57 (Edmond N. Cahn ed. 1954). From the beginning the courts looked to the common law for the meaning of constitutional terms. Chief Justice Marshall declared with respect to the word "treason," "It is scarcely conceivable that the term was not employed by the framers of our constitution in the sense which had been affixed to it by those from whom we borrowed it. So far as the meaning of any terms, particularly terms of art, is completely ascertained, those by whom they are employed must be considered as employing them in that ascertained meaning." United States v. Burr, 25 F. Cas. (No. 14,693) 55, 159 (C.C. Va. 1807). See also Ex parte Grossman, 267 U.S. 87, 108–109 (1925); United States v. Wong Kim Ark, 169 U.S. 649, 654 (1898). In the Convention, John Dickinson cited Blackstone to show that ex post facto means retroactivity in criminal cases. 2 Farrand 448. See also supra Chapter 11 note 5; infra Chapter 22 notes 6 and 42.

40. Vaughan Hawkins, "On the Principles of Legal Interpretation, With Reference Especially to the Interpretation of Wills," 2 Jur. Socy. Papers 298 (1860):

in the interpretation of written language . . . the object is a single one—to ascertain the meaning or intention of the writer—to discover what were the ideas existing in his mind, which he desired and endeavored to convey to us . . . we desire . . . to know what the writer meant by the language he used.

Quoted in Curtis, supra note 31 at 407.

> Every Constitution embodies the principles of its framers. It is a tran-
> script of their minds. If its meaning in any place is open to doubt, or
> if words are used which seem to have no fixed signification, we can-
> not err if we turn to the framers; and their authority increases in pro-
> portion to the evidence which they left on the question.[41]

A "transcript of their minds" was left by the framers in the debates of the
39th Congress, and they left abundant evidence that, for example, in
employing "equal protection of the laws" they had in mind only a ban
on discrimination with respect to a limited category of "enumerated"
rights. Disregard of that intention starkly poses the issue whether the
Court may "interpret" black to mean white, to convert the framers' intention to leave suffrage to the States into a transfer of such control to
the Supreme Court.

## Supplementary Note on Original Intention

Notwithstanding Thomas Grey's view that interpretivism (resort to the
original intention) is a tradition "of great power and compelling simplicity . . . deeply rooted in our history and in our shared principles of
political legitimacy [with] equally deep roots in our formal constitutional law,"[1] and Robert Bork's conclusion that until quite recently "there
was never any doubt" that the "Constitution was to be construed so as
to give effect, as nearly as possible, to the intention of those who made
it,"[2] "it is currently fashionable," Frederick Schauer observes, "to make

41. *Globe* 677.
1. Thomas C. Grey, "Do We Have an Unwritten Constitution?" 27 Stan. L. Rev. 703,
705 (1975).
2. Robert Bork, "Foreword" to Gary L. McDowell, *The Constitution and Contemporary
Constitutional Theory* v (1985). Jacobus tenBroek, an early neoabolitionist, wrote in 1939
that the Court "has insisted, with almost uninterrupted regularity, that the end and object
of constitutional construction is the discovery of the intention of those persons who formulated the instrument." Jacobus tenBroek, "Use by the United States Supreme Court
of Extrinsic Aids in Constitutional Construction," 27 Calif. L. Rev. 399 (1939).

sport of the ability to determine original intent with any degree of certainty."[3] Leading activists categorically reject resort to original intention: the Grand Panjandrum of activist theorists, Ronald Dworkin, asserts "there is no such thing as the intention of the Framers waiting to be discovered."[4] His coadjutor, Paul Brest, flatly declares, "It is simply not possible . . . to determine the adopter's specific intentions."[5] Herein I shall collate some historical evidence that refutes such rash assertions.

## THE AMERICAN SCENE

Early American distrust of the judiciary[6] suggests that a doctrine which confined judicial discretion would be welcome. H. Jefferson Powell, the activist "discoverer" of what original intention *really* meant,[7] recounts that the English Puritans' suspicion of judges traveled to America.[8] They feared that judges would "undermine the legislative prerogatives of the people's representatives by engaging in the corruptive process of interpreting legislative texts"; they feared that the "advantages of a known and written law would be lost if the laws' meaning could be twisted by judicial construction";[9] and they opposed the "judges imposition of their personal views."[10] Came the Jeffersonian "revolution of 1800" and the Republican victors, Powell notes, viewed it as "the people's endorsement" of original intention.[11] In 1838 the Supreme Court declared that construction

3. Frederick Schauer, "Easy Cases," 58 S. Cal. L. Rev. 399, 437 note 99 (1985).

4. Ronald Dworkin, "The Forum of Principle," 56 N.Y.U. L. Rev. 469, 477 (1981).

5. Paul Brest, "Who Decides?" 58 S. Cal. L. Rev. 661, 662 (1985).

6. Justice Wilson noted in 1791 that judges "were objects of aversion and distrust." 1 James Wilson, *The Works of James Wilson* 292 (R. G. McCloskey ed. 1967).

7. H. Jefferson Powell, "The Original Understanding of Original Intent," 98 Harv. L. Rev. 885 (1985).

8. Id. 891.

9. Id. 892.

10. Id. 891.

11. Id. 934. In his Inaugural Address, President Jefferson pledged to administer the Constitution "according to the safe and honest meaning contemplated by the *plain understanding of the people at the time of its adoption*—a meaning to be found in the explanations of those who advocated . . . it." 4 *Debates in the Several State Conventions on the Adoption of the Federal Constitution* 446 (Jonathan Elliot ed. 1836) (emphasis in original). During the debate on ratification of the Constitution, the Federal Farmer referred to "the spirit and true meaning of the Constitution, as collected from what must appear to have been the intention of the people when they made it." 2 *The Complete AntiFederalist* 322 (Herbert J. Storing ed. 1981).

must necessarily depend on the words of the Constitution; the meaning and intention of the conventions which framed and proposed it for adoption and ratification to the conventions . . . in the several States . . . to which the Court has always resorted in construing the Constitution.[12]

"By the outbreak of the Civil War," Powell observes, "intentionalism in the modern sense reigned supreme."[13]

The framers of the Fourteenth Amendment were cognizant of this practice. Senator Charles Sumner, leading proponent of broad rights for the freedmen, said that if the meaning of the Constitution "in any place is open to doubt, or if words are used which seem to have no fixed signification [e.g., equal protection], we cannot err if we turn to the framers; and their authority increases in proportion to the evidence they have left on the question."[14] This was also the approach of confreres who sat with him in the 39th Congress. In 1871, John Farnsworth of Illinois said of the Amendment, "Let us see what was understood to be its meaning at the time of its adoption by Congress."[15] James Garfield rejected an interpretation that went "far beyond the intent and meaning of those who amended the Constitution."[16] Such sentiments found unequivocal expression in 1872 in a unanimous Senate Judiciary Committee Report, signed by senators who had voted for the Thirteenth, Fourteenth, and Fifteenth Amendments:

> In construing the Constitution we are compelled to give it such interpretation as will secure the result which was intended to be accomplished by those who framed it and the people who adopted it
> . . .
> A construction which should give the phrase . . . a meaning differing from the sense in which it was understood and employed by the people when they adopted the Constitution, would be as unconstitutional as a departure from the plain and express language of the

12. Rhode Island v. Massachusetts, 37 U.S. (12 Pet.) 657, 721 (1838); see also Carpenter v. Pennsylvania, 58 U.S. (17 How.) 456, 463 (1854).
13. Powell, supra note 7 at 947.
14. *Globe* 677.
15. *The Reconstruction Amendments' Debates* 506 (Alfred Avins ed. 1967).
16. Id. 528.

Constitution in any other particular. This is the rule of interpretation adopted by all commentators on the Constitution, and in all judicial expositions of that instrument.[17]

Contrast this with G. Edward White's comment that the "singularly eccentric feature of Berger's theory of constitutional interpretation ["judges are absolutely bound by the text and [its] history"] is that there is *no evidence* of such as requirement."[18]

Two items of evidence should suffice to confute the assertions of Dworkin & Co. that there is "no evidence" of original intention: the exclusion of suffrage and of segregation from the ambit of the Fourteenth Amendment. Senator Jacob Howard, to whom it fell to explain the Amendment, stated:

> We know very well that the States retain the power . . . of regulating the right of suffrage in the States . . . the theory of this whole amendment is, to leave the power of regulating the suffrage with . . . the States, and not to assume to regulate it.[19]

Respecting segregation, Congress "had permitted segregated schools in the District of Columbia,"[20] over which it has plenary control; and Senator Sumner vainly "fought to abolish Negro Schools in the District."[21] A Congress which refused to abolish segregation in the District was altogether unlikely to compel States to outlaw it. That is confirmed by the assurance of James Wilson, chairman of the House Judiciary Committee, that the Civil Rights Bill did not require that all children "shall attend the same school."[22] The claims that there is no evidence of original intention run counter to the facts.

17. Id. 571–572.

18. G. Edward White, "Judicial Activism and the Identity of the Legal Profession," 67 *Judicature* 246, 248 (1983) (emphasis added).

19. Avins, supra note 15 at 237; see supra Supplementary Note on the Introduction, text accompanying notes 27–29, and Supplementary Note on Suffrage.

20. Richard Kluger, *Simple Justice* 635 (1976).

21. Kelly, Fourteenth 1049, 1085.

22. Avins, supra note 15 at 163; see supra Supplementary Note on Segregated Schools, Supplementary Note on the Introduction, text accompanying note 37. Even critics of originalism agree that segregation was left untouched by the Fourteenth Amendment; see supra Supplementary Note on the Introduction at note 41.

Inasmuch as the Fourteenth Amendment has become a mini-Constitution—according to Justice Frankfurter, "the largest source of the Court's business"[23] and because its framers undeniably contemplated that their "intention" would be binding, it may seem as a practical matter gratuitous to probe further into the roots of original intention. But as Justice Frankfurter remarked, "legal history still has its claims,"[24] particularly since Chief Justice Marshall declared that he could cite "from the [common law] the most complete evidence that the intention is the most sacred rule of interpretation."[25] Let us then look at the common law.

### ENGLISH SOURCES

We need to remember Hamilton's "The rules of legal interpretation are rules of *common sense*,"[26] as was illustrated in 1305 in *Aumeye's Case* when Chief Justice Bereford cut off comment of counsel on the Statute of Westminster II with the words "Don't bother interpreting the statute for us: we know it better than you do, for we made it."[27] Who knows better what the writer meant by his words than he himself? "Of course," Justice Holmes stated, "the purpose of written instruments is to express some intention . . . of those who write them, and it is desirable to make that purpose effectual."[28] To exalt the reader above the writer is to go beyond Humpty Dumpty, who was content to claim, "When *I* use a word

---

23. Felix Frankfurter, "John Marshall and the Judicial Function," 69 Harv. L. Rev. 217, 229 (1955).

24. Federal Power Comm'n v. Natural Gas Pipeline Co., 315 U.S. 575, 609 (1942), concurring. Frankfurter stated, "Legal doctrines . . . derive meaning and content from the circumstances that gave rise to them and from the purposes they were designed to serve. To these they are bound as is a live tree to its roots." Reid v. Covert, 354 U.S. 1, 50 (1957), concurring.

25. *John Marshall's Defense of McCullough v. Maryland* 167 (Gerald Gunther ed. 1969). "The development of our values over the course of nearly two centuries has been in the direction of strengthening belief in the wisdom of the framers' intentions." Terrance Sandalow, "Constitutional Interpretation," 79 Mich. L. Rev. 1033, 1062 (1981).

26. Federalist No. 83 at 539 (Mod. Lib. ed. 1937).

27. Hans W. Baade, " 'Original Intention': Raoul Berger's Fake Antique," 70 N.C. L. Rev. 1523, 1530 n. 63 (1992).

28. Oliver Wendell Holmes, Jr., *Collected Legal Papers* 206 (1920).

. . . it means just what I choose it to mean."[29] John Selden, the preeminent seventeenth-century legal scholar, said that "a Man's writing has but one true sense; which is that which the Author meant when he writ it."[30] Earlier Thomas Hobbes and John Locke had written to the same effect.[31] They were anticipated by the courts; herewith a few examples.

(1) Chief Justice Frowycke, a fifteenth-century sage, recounted that in 1285 the judges asked the "statute makers whether a warrantie with assettz shulde be a barre" in the Statute of Westminster and "they answered that it shulde. And so in our dayes, have those that were the penners & devisors of statutes bene the grettest lighte for expocision of statutes."[32]

(2) Lord Chancellor Hatton, writing circa 1587–1591, said, "when the intent is proved, that must be followed . . . but whensoever there is a departure from the words to the intent, that must be well proved that there is such a meaning."[33]

(3) In the *Magdalen College Case* Coke stated that "in acts of Parliament which are to be construed according to the intent and meaning of the makers of them, the original intent is to be observed."[34]

(4) Samuel Thorne, an eminent scholar in the field, concluded that "Actual intent . . . is controlling from Hengham's day to that of Lord Nottingham (1678)."[35]

---

29. Lewis Carroll, "Through the Looking Glass," *Oxford Dictionary of Quotations* 135 (3d. ed. 1979) (emphasis in original).

30. *Table Talk: Being the Discourses of John Selden, Esq.* 10 (1696).

31. Hobbes and Locke are quoted supra Supplementary Note on the Introduction at note 15.

32. *A Discourse Upon the Exposicion & Understanding of Statutes* 151–152 (Samuel Thorne ed. 1942). An English historian, S. B. Chrimes, concluded that "the rule of reference to the intention of the legislators . . . was certainly established by the second half of the fifteenth century." S. B. Chrimes, *English Constitutional Ideas in the Fifteenth Century* 293 (1936).

33. Christopher Hatton, *A Treatise Concerning Statutes and Acts of Parliament and the Exposition Thereof* 14–15 (1677).

34. 11 Co. Rep. 66b, 73b, 77 Eng. Rep. 1235, 1245 (1615).

35. *A Discourse*, supra note 32 at 60 note 126. For extended discussion of the English and American sources, see Raoul Berger, " 'Original Intention' in Historical Perspective," 54 Geo. Wash. L. Rev. 296 (1986); Raoul Berger, "The Founders' Views—According to Jefferson Powell," 67 Tex. L. Rev. 1033 (1989); Raoul Berger, "Original Intent: The Rage of Hans Baade," 71 N.C. L. Rev. 1151 (1993).

Jefferson Powell attempts to explain away these and still other utterances. He acknowledges that "The central concept—the goal—of common law interpretation was indeed what the common lawyers called 'intention,' " and that they "often sounded remarkably like contemporary intentionalists."[36] "There is no disagreement," he writes, "over the proposition that the common lawyers, and most of the founders, thought that interpretation ought to subserve a document's [i.e., the draftsman's] 'intent' . . . The debate instead is over what 'intent' *meant*."[37] His answer is a confessedly "curious" theory that " 'intention' was an attribute or concept attached primarily *to the document itself*, and not elsewhere,"[38] that the "basic notion of 'intent' [is] a product of the interpretive process rather than something locked into the text by its author."[39] Thus, despite their constant differentiation between "words" and "intention," between the "maker's intention" and his words, the common-law lawyers, according to Powell, excluded the actual intention and looked for it only in the words. One who would substitute a recondite explanation for a simple differentiation labors under a heavy burden. It would have been far simpler merely to inquire what the *words* "meant."[40] If we are to look only at the words, then, said Justice Holmes, "we inquire, not what this man meant, but what those words would mean in the mouth of a normal speaker."[41] Then too, Lord Chancellor Hatton's demand for proof "when

36. H. Jefferson Powell, "The Modern Misunderstanding of Original Intent," 54 U. Chi. L. Rev. 1513, 1533 (1987).

37. Id. 1538 (emphasis added).

38. Id. 1534 (emphasis added).

39. Powell, supra note 7 at 899.

40. Contrast with Powell's web spinning Justice Story's admonition: "Constitutions are not designed for metaphysical or logical subtleties . . . for elaborate shades of meaning, or for the exercise of philosophical acuteness . . . the people make them, the people adopt them . . . [and] must be supposed to read them, with the help of common sense, and cannot be presumed to admit in any of them any recondite meaning or extraordinary gloss." 1 Joseph Story, *Commentaries on the Constitution of the United States*, §451 (5th ed. 1905).

41. Oliver Wendell Holmes, Jr., *Collected Legal Papers* 204 (1920). Apparently reflecting Francis Lieber's views on hermeneutics, Bouvier's *Law Dictionary* speaks of "interpretation" as seeking the "meaning which those who used [the words] were desirous of expressing."

there is *a departure from the words* to the intent" posits resort to extrinsic evidence, for to return to the words would undo the "departure."

Powell's stellar exhibit of what he himself terms "this [to us *curious*] *usage* of 'intent' "[42] is Hamilton's 1791 statement during the controversy over the constitutionality of a national bank. Since the Framers' intention plainly barred his path,[43] he was constrained to argue that "whatever may have been the intention of the framers of a constitution or of a law, that intention is to be sought in the instrument itself."[44] This was bare assertion, unsupported by a single citation, in the teeth of the common law.

Powell's unpracticed hand is betrayed by two other citations: the first, an eighteenth-century contract treatise that stated, "The law of contracts is not concerned with any one's 'internal sentiments' but only with their 'external expression.' "[45] That is to say, the case presented a subjective, unexpressed intent. There one party claimed that he had understood a term in a special, *undisclosed* sense to the detriment of the other party. There being no evidence that he had attached that special meaning to the term, he was held to have used the words "according to their common acceptation."[46] In other words, no intent was expressed.

Of the same nature is Powell's second citation; Chief Justice Fleming said in 1611, the "intention and construction of words shall be taken according to the vulgar and usual sense";[47] Powell adds, without any

42. Powell, supra note 36 at 1534 (emphasis added).

43. The Convention records plainly show that the Framers rejected a proposal empowering Congress to grant charters of incorporation. Incorporation of a bank had been the subject of controversy in Pennsylvania and New York, and the Framers feared that such a proposal would excite prejudice and impede ratification of the Constitution. 2 *Records of the Federal Convention of 1787* 616 (Max Farrand ed. 1911). Even when limited to corporations for canals the proposal was defeated by a vote of 8 to 3 a few days before the close of the Convention, at which Hamilton was present. But in 1791 he pretended to find the facts "confused." 8 *Papers of Alexander Hamilton* 111 (H. C. Syrett and J. E. Cooke eds. 1965).

44. *Papers of Hamilton*, supra note 43.

45. Powell, supra note 7 at 895, quoting 1 J. Powell, *Essay Upon the Law of Contracts and Agreements* 372–373 (1790).

46. J. Powell, *Essay*, id. 372–373.

47. Powell, supra note 7 at 895 note 48, quoting Hewitt v. Painter, 1 Bulstrode 174, 175–176, 80 Eng. Rep. 864, 865 (1611).

factual basis, "not according to any particular meaning the parties may have intended."[48] Fleming referred to the sale of eighteen barrels of ale which, according to "common usage," did not include the barrels. In the absence of proof that the parties intended otherwise, "common usage" would prevail, leading Fleming to say, the *intent of the parties never was* that the vendee should have the barrels, but only the ale."[49] Had there been evidence of "intent," it would have carried the day.

That Powell was driven to invoke such inapposite citations testifies to the hollowness of the activist case against originalism. As Justice Harlan remarked, "the transparent failure of attempts to cast doubt on the original understanding is simply further evidence of the force of the historical record."[50] Indeed, Powell cannot altogether stifle his common-law heritage: he acknowledges that "it is natural, inevitable, and appropriate that we should look to the founders for enlightenment."[51] Most enlightening is their own explanation of what they intended by their words.[52]

Powell's "curious" usage was repudiated by the House of Lords in 1992. Turning to the very Parliamentary explanations that Powell rejects, the Law Lords in *Pepper v. Hart*[53] reversed an exclusionary practice that first appeared in 1769,[54] and underscored the fact that contemporary legislative explanations are the best evidence of legislative

48. Powell, supra note 7 at 895.

49. 80 Eng. Rep. at 865 (emphasis added).

50. Oregon v. Mitchell, 400 U.S. 112, 200 (1970), dissenting in part.

51. H. Jefferson Powell, "How Does the Constitution Structure Government? The Founders' Views," in *A Workable Government? The Constitution After 200 Years* 15 (Burke Marshall ed. 1987).

52. Powell cites "modern students of hermeneutics" who "attack non-author based interpretation as an abstract and ultimately hopeless search for a text's meaning." Powell, supra note 7 at 896 note 54.

53. [1993] A. C. 593, H.L. (E.). I am indebted for the citation to Professor Gary McDowell of the University of London.

54. The exclusionary practice took off from a two-sentence statement by Justice Willes in Millar v. Taylor, 4 Burr 2303, 2332 (1769) [1993] A.C. 630E. His was one of four seriatim opinions, and his remark went unnoticed by his Associate Justices; it made no mention of the prior common law to the contrary, and the point was not argued by counsel. See Raoul Berger, " 'Original Intent,' A Response to Hans Baade," 70 Tex. L. Rev. 1535, 1537 (1992).

purpose. The financial secretary to the Treasury had assured the House of Commons that the Act "was not intended to impose" a particular tax,[55] and the issue posed was whether to depart from previous authority which forbade reference to proceedings in Parliament. Lord Griffiths said, "the object of the court in interpreting legislation" is "to give effect to the true purpose of legislation."[56] Noting that the courts consulted other "extraneous material,"[57] he asked, "Why then cut ourselves off from the one source in which may be found an authoritative statement of the intention with which the legislation is placed before Parliament?"[58] Lord Browne-Wilkinson, in whose opinion all but one Law Lord concurred, also asked, why "should the courts blind themselves to a clear indication of what Parliament intended in using these words?"[59] And he answered, "we are much more likely to find the intention of Parliament [in the debates] than anywhere else," adding, there is a "basic need for the courts to give effect to the words enacted by Parliament, in the sense that they were intended by Parliament to bear."[60]

Finally, original intention acts as a brake on unlimited judicial discretion, a discretion the Founders profoundly feared.[61] If, writes Earl Maltz, "intent is irrelevant and the text ambiguous, courts are left with no constitutional source that defines the limits of their authority."[62] Richard Kay explains:

55. Pepper v. Hart, supra note 53 at 616G.

56. Id. 617E–F.

57. Id. 617F. For example, "information as to the mischief aimed at," id. 635C, which goes back to Heydon's Case, 3 Co. Rep. 7a, 76 Eng. Rep. 637 (1584).

58. Pepper v. Hart, supra note 53 at 617F. The point was made in Raoul Berger, " 'Original Intent': The Rage of Hans Baade," 71 N.C. L. Rev. 1151, 1168 (1993).

59. Pepper v. Hart, supra note 53 at 635A.

60. Id. 635G (quoting Reg. v. Warner [1969] 2 A.C. 256, 279); id. 637H. I came to the same conclusion; see Raoul Berger, "Original Intention in Historical Perspective," 54 Geo. Wash. L. Rev. 296 (1986); Raoul Berger, "The Founders' Views—According to Jefferson Powell," 67 Tex. L. Rev. 1033, 1055–1076 (1989).

61. Gordon S. Wood, *The Creation of the American Republic, 1776–1789* 298 (1969).

62. Earl M. Maltz, "Federalism and the Fourteenth Amendment: A Comment on *Democracy and Distrust*," 42 Ohio St. L.J. 209, 210 (1981). Lawrence Church, who is unsympathetic to originalism, recognizes that if judges "are not bound by the intent of the Founders . . . then there may be no limits at all to their power." W. Lawrence Church, "History and the Constitutional Role of the Courts," 1990 Wis. L. Rev. 1071, 1087–1088.

To implement real limits on government the judges must have reference to standards which are external to, and prior to, the matter
to be decided. This is necessarily historical investigation. The content of those standards are set at their creation. Recourse to the intention of the framers in judicial review, therefore, can be understood as indispensable to realizing the idea of government limited
by law.[63]

More broadly speaking, Judge Frank Easterbrook points out that "Constitutional interpretation . . . is a process of holding an actual government within certain bounds."[64]

Activists' writings do not proffer a viable alternative; they are, Mark
Tushnet observed, "plainly designed to protect the legacy of the Warren
Court."[65] Another activist, Paul Brest, adjures his fellows "simply to ac-
knowledge that most of our writings are not political theory but advo-
cacy scholarship—amicus briefs ultimately designed to persuade the
Court to adopt our various notions of the public good."[66] The evidence

63. Richard S. Kay, "Book Review," 10 Conn. L. Rev. 801, 805–806 (1978). The rule
of law requires that we "be governed by the same pre-established rules and not by the
whim of those charged with executing those rules." Philip Kurland, "Curia Regis: Some
Comments on the Divine Right of Kings and Courts 'To Say What the Law Is,' " 23 Ariz.
L. Rev. 581, 582 (1981). Justice Story praised the rules "for the construction of statutes
. . . to limit the discretion of judges." James McClellan, *Joseph Story and the American
Constitution* 362–363 (1971). As a practical matter, resort to original intention "avoids
uncertainty and arbitrariness and promotes predictability and consistent application."
J. M. Balkin, "Constitutional Interpretation and the Problem of History," 63 N.Y.U. L.
Rev. 911, 928–929 (1988).

64. Frank H. Easterbrook, "The Influence of Judicial Review on Constitutional
Theory," in *A Workable Government? The Constitution After 200 Years* 172 (Burke Marshall
ed. 1987).

65. Mark Tushnet, "Legal Realism, Structural Review, and Prophecy," 8 U. Dayton L.
Rev. 809, 811 (1983). See also supra Supplementary Note on the Introduction at note 16.

66. Paul Brest, "The Fundamental Rights Controversy: The Essential Contradictions
of Normative Constitutional Scholarship," 90 Yale L.J. 1063, 1109 (1981). See Brest's
rejection of the rationalizations of "seven representative [activist] scholars." Id. 1067–
1089. Justice Scalia considers it a grave defect of the nonoriginalists that they have been
unable to agree on an alternative theory. Antonin Scalia, "Originalism: The Lesser Evil,"
57 U. Cin. L. Rev. 849, 862–863 (1989). He observes, "surely there must be general agreement not only that judges reject one exegetical approach (originalism), but that they adopt
another," adding that "it is hard to discern any emerging consensus among the nonoriginalists as to what this might be." Id. 855. See supra note 52.

above set forth, which is but a small part of the facts collected else-where,[67] demonstrates, in my judgment, that original intention is deeply rooted in Anglo-American law[68] and that it serves as a brake on judges' imposition of their personal preferences under the guise of interpreta-tion.[69] The argument to the contrary, we have seen, cannot withstand scrutiny, so that to borrow from the French savant, Raymond Aron, our case once more "justifies itself by the falseness of the beliefs that oppose it."[70]

### JAMES HUTSON'S CRITIQUE OF THE SOURCES

It remains to examine the doubts shed by James Hutson on the reli-ability of the sources.[71] Hutson was solely concerned with the 1787 pe-riod. Since, however, the great bulk of contemporary constitutional liti-gation arises under the Fourteenth Amendment, it is to be noted that the records of the 1866 Amendment have not been impeached and, in my judgment, are unimpeachable. They are a day-to-day stenographic record of the debates, and their veracity is attested by a striking incident. In 1871 John Bingham challenged James Garfield's account of a remark in 1866 by Thaddeus Stevens. Garfield responded,

67. See the Berger citations, supra note 35.

68. Chief Justice Marshall stated that he could cite from the common law "the most complete evidence that the intention is the most sacred rule of interpretation." *John Marshall's Defense of McCulloch v. Maryland* 167 (Gerald Gunther ed. 1969).

69. Henry Monaghan observes that "any theory of constitutional interpretation which renders unimportant or irrelevant questions as to original intent, *so far as that intent can be fairly discerned*, is not, given our tradition, politically or intellectually defensible." Henry P. Monaghan, "The Constitution Goes to Harvard," 13 Harv. C. R.–C.L. L. Rev. 117, 124 (1978) (emphasis in original). For an assessment of the opposing views, see Randall Bridwell, "The Scope of Judicial Review: A Dirge for the Theorists of Majority Rule?" 31 S.C. L. Rev. 617 (1980); William Gangi, "Judicial Expansionism: An Evaluation of the Ongoing Debate," 8 Oh. N.U. L. Rev. 1 (1981); Gary L. McDowell *The Constitution and Contemporary Constitutional History* (1985).

70. Raymond Aron, "Pensées," N.Y. Times, Oct. 23, 1981, at E19. Chief Justice Tho-mas McKean told the Pennsylvania Ratification Convention, "refutation of an argument begets a proof." 2 Elliot, supra note 11 at 54.

71. James Hutson, "The Creation of the Constitution: The Integrity of the Docu-mentary Records," 65 Tex. L. Rev. 1 (1986).

my colleague can make but he cannot unmake history. I not only heard the whole debate at the time, but I lately read over with scrupulous care, every word of it as recorded in the Globe. I will show my colleagues that Mr. Stevens did speak.[72]

This is an attestation that the records confirmed his recollection. Because few constitutional cases nowadays arise under the 1787 Constitution, Hutson's critique has little practical consequence. Nevertheless a historian may take exception to Hutson's criticism of the 1787 records.

Hutson properly exonerates Madison from charges that he falsified the records, considering Madison's Notes as "a faithful account of what he recorded at the Convention in 1787."[73] Since, as Hutson recounts, Madison obtained copies of set speeches from the speakers,[74] what he recorded in such cases presumably corresponded to what was said. Indeed, Hutson observes, "if his notes . . . are compared with the fragmentary records of the debates left by other delegates . . . a rough approximation between the different accounts is evident—demonstrating that Madison was not inventing dialogue, but was trying to capture what was said."[75] My own research confirmed, for example, that on the issue of judicial participation in the Council of Revision to assist in the presidential veto, the Notes of Madison, Yates, King, and Pierce are in substantial accord.[76] So too, Madison's account of the Convention's rejection of federal charters of incorporation, which he himself had proposed,[77] was corroborated by McHenry's notes[78] and by Abraham Baldwin, who was present and later reminded Justice Wilson, a participant in the debate, that the Convention had rejected the power to create corporations.[79]

---

72. *The Reconstruction Amendments' Debates* 527 (Alfred Avins ed. 1967).

73. Hutson, supra note 71 at 22.

74. Id. 31.

75. Id. 33.

76. 1 Farrand, supra note 43 at 97–98 (Madison); id. 105 (Yates); id. 108 (King); id. 109 (Pierce); see also the confirmatory note recorded in the Journal respecting participation in the veto. 2 id. 72.

77. 2 id. 615–616.

78. Id. 620.

79. 3 id. 375, 376.

But Hutson concluded on the basis of hypothetical calculations that Madison "may have recorded only a small part of each day's proceedings."[80] As much can be said of every recording secretary of a corporate or association meeting, whose recitals are often much more truncated than those of Madison. If the recording was incomplete, that does not impeach the veracity of what was recorded.[81] Madison was unlikely to omit fresh material. Leonard Levy, although he was taken with Hutson's critique, recognizes that "the very real possibility exists that Madison consistently and accurately caught the gist of the debates."[82]

Hutson finds another feature of Madison's notes "troublesome."[83] Inasmuch as Madison did not prepare his remarks in advance and could hardly speak and record at the same time, his later reduction of his remarks to writing leads Hutson to conclude that "speeches written and 'improved' after the event and large scale deletions [omissions] are reminiscent of Genet [a disruptive French agent], Lloyd and the shorthand reporters, however different Madison's motives may have been."[84] This is a sorry analogy. Driven by his desire to influence the political scene, Genet was not overly scrupulous,[85] and Lloyd, Hutson shows, was probably bought and paid for by the Federalists.[86] It is therefore a mistake to bracket the high-minded Madison—who was endeavoring to set forth *his own views*—with Genet who engaged in misrepresenting those of another, and with the venal Lloyd. Whether or not Madison's recorded remarks represent a complete reflection of his speeches in the Convention, they yet constitute an undeniable statement of his own views. As President, Jefferson relied on *"the plain understanding of the people at the time of [the Constitution's] adoption*—a meaning to be found in the expla-

80. Hutson, supra note 71 at 34.

81. As John Marshall asked in the Virginia Ratification Convention: "Because it does not contain all, does it contain nothing?" 3 Elliot, supra note 11 at 560.

82. Leonard Levy, *Original Intent and the Framers' Constitution* 288 (1988). Long since Thucydides observed that "at such a distance of time [the historian] must make up his mind to be satisfied with conclusions resting upon the clearest evidence which can be had." Daniel J. Boorstin, *The Discoverers* 565 (1983).

83. Hutson, supra note 71 at 35.

84. Id.

85. Id. 9–12.

86. Id. 22–23.

nation of those who advocated it."[87] Would Jefferson have rejected Madison's "explanation" because he set it down after he had spoken it?

Hutson is more critical of the reports of the State Ratification Conventions. Jonathan Elliot, who published those debates, confessed that "in some instances" the expressions "have been inaccurately taken down."[88] Shorthand reporting was in its infancy;[89] the reporters were inexpert;[90] some were paid by the Federalists or were biased in their favor;[91] and in Pennsylvania and Connecticut the reporter deleted virtually all of the Antifederalist remarks.[92] Despite this, suppression of the Antifederalist remarks was compensated in part by the fact that James Wilson laced his speeches in the Pennsylvania Convention with restatements of Antifederalist arguments and refutations thereof. His assurances that the proposed Constitution did not go to the alarming lengths portrayed by the Antifederalists are more important than their claims. For they were the defeated opponents whose remarks, on settled rules of construction, would not count as legislative history.[93]

Nor does suppression of opposition remarks undermine the reliability of *Federalist* statements. Wilson's statements, constituting the lion's share of the published Pennsylvania debates, were "corrected" by him or his agent.[94] Hutson tells us that in Massachusetts "ghostwritten" speeches were inserted in the report,[95] no doubt with the principal's approval. The fact that a speech is "ghostwritten" does not render it less the speech of one who adopts it. In New York, Hutson recites, speakers "revised" their remarks.[96] More than once it has befallen me to marvel at garbled stenographic versions of my oral remarks, and I have welcomed the opportu-

87. 4 Elliot, supra note 11 at 446 (emphasis in the original).

88. Hutson, supra note 71 at 20.

89. Id. 19.

90. Id. 23–24.

91. Id. 23.

92. Id. 21–22.

93. Jefferson sought for the meaning of the Constitution "in the explanations of those who advocated it." Supra text accompanying note 88. See also Ernst & Ernst v. Hochfelder, 425 U.S. 185, 204 (1976); Mastro Plastics Corp. v. NLRB, 350 U.S. 270, 288 (1956).

94. Hutson, supra note 71 at 23.

95. Id. 21.

96. Id. 22.

nity to "revise" them, more truly to reflect the sentiments I had uttered. "Revised their remarks" is not presumptively a sinister act. By revising their remarks, the Federalists testified that *their* views were faithfully presented. They assumed that their remarks would be publicized and took pains to make them accurate. "Federalist stalwarts," Hutson states, "sent pre-publication excerpts from Lloyd's [Pennsylvania] debates to partisans in other states to furnish Federalist orators arguments for ratification,"[97] thereby evidencing their satisfaction with Lloyd's reporting. Their statements were in fact designed to serve as "Federalist campaign literature,"[98] to allay the fears aroused by Antifederalists. Now to discard those representations on the plea that the Antifederalist statements were unrecorded is, as Justice Story wrote in another context, to commit a "fraud upon the whole American people."[99]

On several occasions it has fallen to me to trace a particular issue through the several Conventions, and I have found remarkable unanimity. That *all* reports were unreliable in such particulars is highly improbable. Widely scattered "inexpert" transcribers do not commit one and the same error unless they are engaged in a widespread conspiracy. Thus:

(1) There was remarkable unanimity in the Federal Convention, *The Federalist*, and the Ratification Conventions that the Senate was to participate in *making* treaties, not merely to rubber-stamp them after they had been made by the President. The unanimity on so important an issue deserves a detailed account.

As late as August 6 the Convention's Committee on Detail draft provided that "the Senate . . . shall have power to make treaties."[100] During the debate Madison "observed that the Senate represented the States alone," and consequently "the president should be an agent in Treaties."[101] As the Convention drew to a close, the Committee of Eleven

97. Id. 23.
98. Id.
99. "If the Constitution was ratified under the belief, sedulously propagated on all sides, that such protection was afforded, would it not be a fraud upon the whole American people to give a different construction of its powers." Story, supra note 40 at §1084.
100. 2 Farrand, supra note 43 at 183.
101. Id. 392.

proposed on September 4 that "The President by and with the advice and consent of the Senate shall have power to make treaties."[102] Rufus King observed that "as the Executive was here joined in the business, there was a check [on the Senate] which did not exist in [the prior] Congress."[103] In Federalist No. 38 Madison wrote that the Constitution "empowers the Senate with the concurrence of the Executive to make treaties."[104]

Clear-cut confirmation is furnished by Hamilton in Federalist No. 75:

> [T]he vast importance of the trust, and the operations of treaties as laws, plead strongly for the participation . . . of the legislative body in the office of making them . . . It must indeed be clear to a demonstration that the joint possession of the power in question, by the President and Senate, would afford a greater prospect of security, than the separate possession of it by either of them.[105]

Such expressions likewise were voiced in the Ratification Conventions. Hamilton explained in New York that "They, together with the President, are to manage all our concerns with foreign nations."[106] And Chancellor Livingston said that the Senate is "to form treaties with foreign nations."[107] In Pennsylvania James Wilson stated, "nor is there any doubt [that] the Senate and President possess the power of making [treaties]."[108] In North Carolina, Samuel Spencer said that the Senate is "in effect, to form treaties."[109]

(2) There was likewise virtual unanimity on the issue of judicial review. The evidence is so voluminous as to counsel against repetition of the details contained in my *Congress v. The Supreme Court*.[110] Hutson states that Marshall complained that his speeches were inaccurately re-

102. Id. 495.
103. Id. 540.
104. Federalist No. 38 at 240 (Mod. Lib. ed. 1937).
105. Id. No. 75 at 486, 488.
106. 2 Elliot, supra note 11 at 291, 305.
107. Id.
108. Id. 506.
109. 4 id. 116.
110. Raoul Berger, *Congress v. The Supreme Court* at 120–143 (1969).

corded.[111] On the issue of judicial review, however, his remarks are in accord with those of George Nicholas, George Mason, Edmund Randolph, Edmund Pendleton, Madison, and even that bitter opponent of the Constitution Patrick Henry.[112] In addition to these records from Virginia, there are substantial confirmations that judicial review was contemplated by Oliver Ellsworth and James Wilson in the Connecticut and Pennsylvania Ratification conventions, by Robert Yates in his "Letters of Brutus," and by Luther Martin of Maryland.[113] All were Framers.

Now, the Constitution makes no express provision for judicial review. Are we better off with *no* evidence that the Framers contemplated judicial review, with a glaring arrogation of power? I do not pretend that these examples exhaust the subject, but they suffice to caution against hastily discarding the several Convention records as altogether lacking in credibility. Such caution is the more requisite because in many particulars Madison's Notes are corroborated by *The Federalist* wherein *Publius*, according to Thomas Jefferson and Edward Corwin, purported to express the sentiments of the Convention.[114] Then too, Madison's Notes and *The Federalist* were often echoed in the state Ratification Conventions, as appears from the foregoing discussion of the treaty power and judicial review. Such parallelism demands explanation other than across-the-board venality and inexpert transcription. Despite Madison's "dissatisfaction" with the reporting of the Virginia Convention, he repeatedly counseled resort to the Ratification records for light as to the meaning of the Constitution. It is doubtful whether we are better situated to evaluate them than one who participated in the debates.

111. Hutson, supra note 71 at 23–24.

112. Berger, supra note 110, id. 140 (Marshall); id. 15 (Nicholas); id. 139 (Mason); id. 138 (Randolph); id. 202 (Pendleton); id. 139 (Madison); id. 137 (Henry).

113. Berger, supra note 110 at 124 (Ellsworth); id. 201–202 (Yates); 3 Farrand, supra note 43 at 220 (Martin).

114. Jefferson regarded The Federalist as "evidence of the general opinion of those who framed" the Constitution. Clinton Rossiter, *Alexander Hamilton and the Constitution* 52 (1964). Corwin wrote, "It cannot be reasonably doubted that Hamilton was here, as at other points, endeavoring to reproduce the matured conclusions of the Convention." Edward Corwin, *The Doctrine of Judicial Review* 44 (1914).

# 21

## Arguments for Judicial Power of Revision

### Chief Justice Marshall

WHERE early claims to extraconstitutional power were made in the name of "natural law," the present fashion is to invoke the "living Constitution" when it is sought to engraft or amputate a limb.[1] Commentators at a loss to justify judicial arrogations fall back on Marshall's sonorous reference to a "constitution intended to endure for ages to come."[2] In an oft-quoted apostrophe, Justice Frankfurter declared that it "expressed the core of [Marshall's] constitutional philosophy . . . the single most important utterance in the literature of constitutional law."[3] It has become a mythic incantation.[4] Chief Justice Hughes, when con-

---

1. The "doctrine of the living Constitution amounts to little more than willful disregard of the express or implied intent of the framers." James McClellan, *Joseph Story and the American Constitution* 116–117 (1971). Thomas Grey more diplomatically states that "Our characteristic contemporary metaphor is 'the living Constitution' . . . sufficiently unspecific to permit the judiciary to elucidate the development and change in the content of those rights over time." "Do We Have an Unwritten Constitution?," 27 Stan. L. Rev. 703, 711 (1975).

2. Auerbach, "The Reapportionment Cases: One Person, One Vote—One Vote, One Value," 1964 S. C. Rev. 1, 75; cf. Louis Pollak, "The Supreme Court Under Fire," 6 J. Pub. L. 428, 441 (1957).

3. Frankfurter, "John Marshall, and the Judicial Function," 69 Harv. L. Rev. 217, 218–219 (1955). That utterance, Frankfurter said, requires "a spacious view in applying an instrument of government 'made for an undefined and expanding future.'" Youngstown Sheet & Tube Co. v. Sawyer, 343 U.S. 579, 596 (1952). Compare the severely restricted gloss Marshall put upon his words, infra at notes 12–18. And compare the Founders' views as to change by amendment. Supra Chapter 17 at notes 15–22.

4. "It is important," said Justice Frankfurter, "not to make untouchable dogmas of the fallible reasoning of even our greatest judge." Frankfurter, supra note 3 at 219.

fronted by the "mortgage moratorium"–"impairment of contract" problem, declared:

> If by the statement that what the Constitution meant at the time of its adoption it means today, it is intended to say that the great clauses of the Constitution must be confined to the interpretation which the framers, with the conditions and outlook of their time would have placed upon them,[5] the statement carries its own refutation. It was to guard against such a narrow conception that Chief Justice Marshall uttered a memorable warning—"We must never forget that it is a *Constitution* we are expounding . . . a constitution intended to endure for ages to come, and consequently to be adapted to the various *crises* of human affairs."[6]

At best Marshall's dictum represents a self-serving claim of power to amend the Constitution. In Justice Black's words, "in recalling that it is a Constitution 'intended to endure for ages to come,' we also remember that the Founders wisely provided for the means of that endurance: changes in the Constitution are to be proposed by Congress or conventions and ratified by the States."[7] Claims to the contrary need to be measured by Lord Chief Justice Denman's observation that "The practice of a ruling power in the State is but a feeble proof of its legality."[8] Such judicial claims stand no better than the bootstrap "precedents" created by a number of presidents for reallocation to themselves of the warmaking power confided to Congress, in justification of single-handed

5. Many are the instances in which the Framers *did* place an interpretation upon their words, or used words of known common law meaning. To phrase the issue in terms of what meaning they "*would* have placed upon them" beclouds it.

6. Home Building & Loan Assn. v. Blaisdell, 290 U.S. 398, 442, 443 (1934). Small as is my esteem of Justice Sutherland, I consider nevertheless that his dissent has a firmer historical base. My friends inquire whether I am not troubled to find myself in such company. Edmund Wilson called this "the 'bed-fellow' line of argument, which relies on producing the illusion of having put you irremediably in the wrong by associating you with some odious person who holds a similar opinion." Edmund Wilson, *Europe Without a Baedeker* 154 (1966). To which I would add, "I would rather be right with my enemy than wrong with my friend."

7. Bell v. Maryland, 378 U.S. 226, 342 (1964); cf. supra Chapter 15 at note 61; Chapter 17 at notes 15–22.

8. Stockdale v. Hansard, 112 E. R. 1112, 1171 (Q. B. 1839).

commitments of the nation to war, as in Vietnam.[9] But the fact is, as I shall show, that Marshall's words have been removed from context, that he flatly repudiated the revisory power Hughes attributed to him, and that other Marshall utterances also show that the conventional view of *M'Culloch* does not represent the "core of his constitutional philosophy."

Marshall's dictum was uttered in *M'Culloch v. Maryland;* the issue was whether the Constitution empowered Congress to establish the Bank of the United States, and that turned on whether a bank was a proper *means* for execution of other expressly granted powers. Marshall reasoned that a government "intrusted with such ample powers" as "the great powers, to lay and collect taxes; to borrow money; to regulate commerce,"

> must also be intrusted with *ample means* for their execution. The power being given, it is in the interest of the nation to facilitate its execution . . . This could not be done, by confining the *choice of means* to such narrow limits as not to leave it in the power of congress to adopt any which might be appropriate . . . To have prescribed the means by which government should, in all future time execute its powers, would have been . . . [to give the Constitution] the properties of a legal code.[10]

Manifestly, this was merely a plea for some freedom in the "choice of means" to execute an existing power, not for license to create a fresh power at each new crisis. Marshall himself flatly denied such license-claims in a pseudonymous debate with Judges Spencer Roane and William Brockenbrough of Virginia.

*M'Culloch* immediately had come under attack. To Madison the Court's ruling seemed

> to break down the landmarks intended by a specification of the powers of Congress, and to substitute, for a definite connection between means and ends, a legislative discretion as to the former, to which no practical limits can be assigned . . . [A] regular mode of making proper alteration has been providently provided in the Constitution itself. It is anxiously to be wished . . . that no innovation

9. See Raoul Berger, *Executive Privilege: A Constitutional Myth* 75–88 (1974), for citations.

10. 17 U.S. (4 Wheat.) 316, 407, 408, 415 (1819) (emphasis added).

may take place in other modes, one of which would be a constructive assumption of powers never meant to be granted.[11]

Thus, the chief architect of the Constitution rejected the replacement of the amendment process by judicial revision as an "assumption of powers never meant to be granted." Even more severe strictures were published by Roane and Brockenbrough. Marshall leapt to the defense under a pseudonym; speaking to the "intended to endure for ages" phrase, he said:

> it does not contain the most distant allusion to *any extension by construction of the powers* of congress. Its sole object is to remind us that a constitution cannot possibly enumerate *the means* by which the powers of government are to be carried into execution.[12]

Again and again he repudiated any intention to lay the predicate for such "extension by construction." There is "not a syllable uttered by the court" that "applies to an enlargement of the powers of congress."[13] He rejected any imputation that "those powers ought to be enlarged by construction or otherwise."[14] He emphasized that "in all the reasoning on the word 'necessary' the court does not, in a single instance, claim the aid of a 'latitudinous' or 'liberal' construction."[15] He branded as a "palpable misrepresentation" attribution to the Court of the view of the "necessary and proper clause" "as augmenting those powers, and as one which is to be construed 'latitudinously' or even 'liberally.' "[16] "It is not pretended," he said of the "choice of means," "that this right of selection may be fraudulently used to the destruction of the fair landmarks [Madison's term] of the constitution."[17] Finally, the exercise of the judicial power to decide all questions "arising under the constitution and laws" of the United States *"cannot be the assertion of a right to change that in-*

11. H. C. Hockett, *The Constitutional History of the United States 1826–1876* 4 (1939); see supra Chapter 15 at note 61; Chapter 17 at notes 15–22; for the explanation of Madison's anxiety see infra at note 20 and note 22.

12. *John Marshall's Defense of McCulloch v. Maryland* 185 (G. Gunther ed. 1969) (emphasis added).

13. Id. 182.

14. Id. 184.

15. Id. 92.

16. Id. 97.

17. Id. 173.

*strument.*"[18] Slender as was the justification for invocation of Marshall's dictum prior to Gerald Gunther's discovery of Marshall's Defense, it has been shattered altogether by Marshall's categorical disclaimer of judicial "right to change that instrument."[19]

Before leaving *M'Culloch*, account should be taken of a proposal in the Federal Convention to authorize Congress "to grant charters of incorporation." Rufus King pointed out that it "will be referred to the establishment of a Bank, which has been a subject of contention" in Philadelphia and New York. Modified to apply only to canals, it was voted down 8 to 3.[20] Louis Pollak points out that "This legislative history was known at the time *M'Culloch v. Maryland* was decided, for Jefferson had utilized it in his 1791 memorandum to Washington opposing the Bank Bill."[21] As a successor to Jefferson as Secretary of State, Marshall had more reason than most to know. His omission to notice it is the more puzzling in light of his allusion to the heated debate on the subject in 1789.[22] For the moment discussion of a possible clash between word and deed may be deferred to examination of other Marshall opinions—strangely never mentioned in the "living Constitution" incantations—which adhere to the "constitutional philosophy" he proclaimed in the Roane-Brockenbrough debates.

In *Ogden v. Saunders*, Marshall stated that the words of the Constitution are not to be "extended to objects not . . . contemplated by its framers."[23] In *Gibbons v. Ogden* he stated that if a word was understood in a certain sense "when the Constitution was framed . . . [T]he convention must have used it in that sense," and it is that sense that is to be

18. Id. 209 (emphasis added).

19. Commenting on the impact of that Defense, Professor Gunther observes that "If virtually unlimited congressional [or judicial] discretion is required to meet twentieth century needs, candid argument to that effect, rather than ritual invoking of Marshall's authority, would seem to me more clearly in accord with the Chief Justice's stance." Supra note 12 at 20–21.

20. 2 Farrand 321, 325, 615–616.

21. Pollak, supra note 2 at 441 note 87.

22. Supra note 10 at 401. In the February 1791 debate Madison "well recollected that a power to grant charters of incorporation had been proposed in the General Convention and rejected." 2 *Annals of Congress* 1896 (1791).

23. 25 U.S. (12 Wheat.) 213, 332 (1827), dissenting opinion.

given judicial effect.[24] In *Osborn v. Bank of the United States*, he stated: "Judicial power is never exercised for the purpose of giving effect to the will of the judge; always for the purpose of giving effect to the will of the legislature"[25]—that is, of the "original intention." In *Providence Bank v. Billings*, he stated: "The constitution . . . was not intended to furnish the corrective for every abuse of power which may be committed by the State governments. The interest, wisdom, and justice of the representative body and its relation with its constituents furnish the only security . . . against unwise legislation generally," echoing Gerry's rejection of judicial "guardians."[26] These statements are irreconcilable with the interpretation Hughes put on the *M'Culloch* dictum. Their significance was summed up by Marshall's associate, Justice Henry Baldwin, who, after noting Marshall's "a constitution we are expounding," went on to say, "no commentator ever followed the text more faithfully, or ever made a commentary more accordant with its strict intention and language."[27]

The evidence, I submit, calls for an end to the incantatory reliance on Marshall's "a Constitution . . . to be adapted to the various crises of human affairs." If the Constitution is to be altered by judicial fiat, let it not be under seal of a reading Marshall himself repudiated.[28]

## Mr. Justice Holmes

Another lofty dictum canonized by proponents of judicial lawmaking is that of Justice Holmes in *Missouri v. Holland*:

> when we are dealing with words that also are a constituent act, like the Constitution . . . we must realize that they have called into life a being the development of which could not have been foreseen completely by the most gifted of its begetters. It was enough for them to realize or to hope that they had created an organism; it has

24. 22 U.S. (9 Wheat.) 1, 190 (1824); see supra Chapter 20 note 38; infra Chapter 22 note 6.

25. 22 U.S. (9 Wheat.) 738, 866 (1824).

26. 29 U.S. (4 Pet.) 514, 563 (1830).

27. H. Baldwin, *A General View of the Origin and Nature of the Constitution and Government of the United States* 100 (1837).

28. See supra note 19.

taken a century and cost their successors much sweat and blood to prove that they created a nation. The case before us must be considered in the light of our whole experience and not merely in what was said a hundred years ago.[29]

The magic spell of the superb literary artist must not blind us to the narrow issue actually decided; for it is a fundamental tenet of case law that all statements in a case are to be confined to that decision.[30] At issue was whether the treatymaking power extended to an agreement with Great Britain for the protection of migratory birds which annually traversed parts of the United States and of Canada. Addressing the argument that the treaty infringed powers reserved to the States by the Tenth Amendment, Holmes held, "Wild birds are not in the possession of any one; and possession is the beginning of ownership. The whole foundation of the State's rights is the presence within their jurisdiction of birds that yesterday had not arrived, tomorrow may be in another State, and in a week a thousand miles away." He therefore found that the "States are individually incompetent to act," that the national interest in such migratory birds was of the "first magnitude" and "can be protected only by national action in concert with that of another power,"[31] and concluded that "it is not lightly to be assumed that in matters requiring national action, 'a power which must belong to and somewhere reside in every civilized government' is not to be found."[32] Holmes might have cited Hamilton's explanation that the treaty power was to have "the most ample latitude—to render it competent to all the stipulations which the exigencies of national affairs might require."[33] Instead he rose to one of his great rhetorical flights:

29. 252 U.S. 416, 433 (1920).

30. Marshall dismissed his own dicta in Marbury v. Madison when they were pressed upon him in Cohens v. Virginia, 19 U.S. (6 Wheat.) 264, 399 (1821), saying that dicta do not receive the careful consideration accorded to the "question actually before the court."

31. 252 U.S. at 434, 433.

32. Id. 433. But Madison stated, "Had the power of making treaties, for example, been omitted, however necessary it might have been, the defect could only have been lamented, or supplied by an amendment of the Constitution." 2 *Annals of Congress* 1900–1901 (February 2, 1791).

33. "Letters of Camillus," 6 Hamilton, *Works* 183 (Lodge ed. 1904).

The case before us must be considered in the light of our whole experience and not merely in that of what was said a hundred years ago. The treaty . . . does not contravene any prohibitory words to be found in the Constitution [nor in its history]. The whole question is whether it is forbidden by some invisible radiation from the general terms of the Tenth Amendment. We must consider what this country has become in deciding what the Amendment has reserved.[34]

The reader will indulge an attempt at more pedestrian analysis. The Tenth Amendment, on which *Missouri* relied, provides that "The powers not delegated to the United States by the Constitution, nor prohibited by it to the States, are reserved to the States respectively, or to the people." Given that in this area a State is "incompetent" to act, it could hardly lay claim to a "reserved" power to do so. According to Hamilton, a power to enter into "*all* the stipulations which the exigencies of national affairs might require" *had* been delegated to the United States. It follows that a plenary treaty power did not invade a nonexistent State power.[35] Consequently *Missouri v. Holland* furnishes no warrant for encroachment upon actual, reserved State powers, nor for revision of express or implicit constitutional provisions because a new day has dawned.

The cases which confirm that Holmes respected and adhered to the intention of the draftsmen may for the moment be deferred while we consider Holmes' dicta in *Gompers v. United States:* "[the] provisions of the Constitution . . . are organic living institutions transplanted from English soil. Their significance is to be gathered not simply by taking the words and a dictionary but by considering their origin and the line of their growth."[36] Like "living constitution" the words "the line of their

34. 252 U.S. at 433–434.

35. Willard Hurst, who served as law clerk to Justice Holmes and wrote a valuable monograph on Holmes' view of constitutional history, states that in Missouri v. Holland Holmes "in effect . . . says that *when all other evidence* of the Constitution-makers' intent *fails*, we must yet be guided by what we know to be their most general objective . . . to provide a structure within which the future may settle its own problems." "The Process of Constitutional Construction," in *Supreme Court and Supreme Law* 55, 57–58 (Edmond N. Cahn ed. 1954) (emphasis added). This is no license to ignore "evidence of the Constitution-makers' intent."

36. 233 U.S. 604, 610 (1914).

growth" have become a shibboleth of judicial lawmaking, for a Constitution, be it remembered, "grows" only by judicial accretions. *Gompers*
merely involved the meaning of a common law term, "contempts" of
court, and the legal meaning of that term could no more be ascertained
by resort to a dictionary than could that of "trial by jury" or "habeas
corpus." For that purpose resort to the common law was essential, and
in traditional fashion Holmes looked to the common law for the "origin" and "line of growth" of contempts. The issue was whether a criminal contempt lies for violation of an injunction. Justice Holmes held:
"So truly are they crimes that . . . in the early law they were punishable
only by the usual criminal procedure" and in England still "are tried that
way."[37] By this "origin" and "line of growth" he was not remotely claiming judicial power to "change" the Constitution, but was giving a common law term its traditional meaning.

Other Holmes opinions confirm that such a claim was far removed
from his thinking. In *Johnson v. United States* he held that when a legislature "has intimated its will . . . that will should be recognized and
obeyed."[38] Although this referred to a statute, Holmes scarcely attached
more importance to the will of a legislature than to that of the people
met in convention. Indeed, he applied the parallel rule to an Amendment in the subsequent case of *Eisner v. Macomber*: "I think that the word
'incomes' in the Sixteenth Amendment should be read in 'a sense most
obvious to the common understanding at the time of its adoption.' "[39]
Earlier, in *Lochner v. New York*, he had protested against the majority's
identification of its economic predilections with the Fourteenth Amendment,[40] and a few years after *Gompers*, in *Baldwin v. Missouri*, he stated:

> I have not yet adequately expressed the more than anxiety that I feel
> at the ever increasing scope given to the Fourteenth Amendment in
> cutting down what I believe to be the constitutional rights of the

37. Id. 610–611.
38. 163 F. 30, 32 (1st Cir. 1908).
39. 252 U.S. 189, 219–220 (1920). In Weems v. United States, 217 U.S. 349, 389, 397
(1910), Justice Holmes joined in a dissent by Justice Edward White stating that the meaning of "cruel and unusual punishment" was to be derived from English and pre-1787
State practices.
40. 198 U.S. 45, 75 (1905).

States. As the decisions now stand, I see hardly any limit but the sky to the invalidating of those rights if they happen to strike a majority of this Court as for any reason undesirable. I cannot believe that the Amendment was intended to give us *carte blanche* to embody our economic or *moral beliefs* in its prohibitions . . . Of course the words "due process of law," if taken in their literal meaning, have no application to this case; and while it is too late to deny that they have been given a much more extended and artificial signification, still we ought to remember the great caution shown by the Constitution in limiting the power of the States, and should be slow to construe the clause in the Fourteenth Amendment as committing to the Court, with no guide but the Court's own discretion, the validity of whatever laws the States may pass.[41]

In short, Holmes deplored judicial invasion of rights reserved to the States, condemned uncurbed judicial discretion to identify personal predilections with constitutional mandates, and recognized the perversion of due process that made such practices possible—all of which is diametrically opposed to the current reading of the *Gompers* and *Holland* dicta. Those who march under the pennons of those dicta have overlooked Holmes' statement that "I do not expect or think it desirable that the judges should undertake to renovate the law. That is not their province."[42]

## Mr. Justice Frankfurter

Proponents of a power to "adapt" the Constitution to current needs also quote a dictum of Justice Frankfurter in *Youngstown Sheet & Tube Co. v. Sawyer*: "It is an inadmissibly narrow conception of American constitutional law to confine it to the words of the Constitution and to disregard the gloss that life has written about them."[43] Once again this is a statement lifted from its context. Frankfurter had in mind the rule that a long-standing executive interpretation illuminates an ambiguous provision: "In short, a systematic, unbroken executive practice, long pursued

41. 281 U.S. 586, 695 (1930) (emphasis partially added).
42. Oliver Wendell Holmes, Jr., *Collected Legal Papers* 239 (1920); see also supra Chapter 17 note 32.
43. 343 U.S. at 610–611, concurring opinion.

to the knowledge of Congress and never before questioned . . . may be treated as a gloss on 'Executive Power' vested in the President." To avert a too-sweeping implication he explained that "Deeply embedded traditional ways of conducting a government *cannot supplant the Constitution* or legislation; but they give meaning to the words of the text or supply them,"[44] that is, if the meaning is otherwise obscure.

That Frankfurter did not refer by such a "gloss" to judicial encrustations is inferable from his assertion on another occasion of a right to look to the Constitution itself rather than to what his predecessors had said about it.[45] Then, too, in *United States v. Lovett* he had distinguished "broad standards," which "allow a relatively wide play for individual legal judgments," from "very specific provisions" such as the prohibition of "bills of attainder," which must be read as "defined by history. Their meaning was so settled by history that definition was superfluous."[46] To be sure, he placed "due process of law" among the "broad standards"; in this, however, he was mistaken, for history leaves no doubt that there was no "substantive" due process, that due process did not apply to legislative action but was confined to procedure in the courts, as was unmistakably expressed by Hamilton in 1787. The purely "procedural" content of due process was, in the words of Charles Curtis, "as fixed and definite as the common law could make a phrase."[47] Frankfurter himself adverted to the "fundamental principles that inhere in 'due process of law' as understood at the time of the adoption of the Constitution."[48] Under his own criterion respecting common law terms—they must be read as "defined by history"—we cannot, to borrow from one of his opinions, "extend the definitions . . . Precisely because 'it is *a constitution* we are expounding' . . . we ought not to take liberties with it."[49] And precisely because, in Frankfurter's own words, "there was a deep distrust of

44. Id. 610 (emphasis added).
45. Supra Chapter 15 note 57.
46. 328 U.S. 303, 321 (1946), concurring opinion.
47. Supra Chapter 11 at note 27.
48. Anti-Fascist Refugee Committee v. McGrath, 341 U.S. 123, 161–162 (1951), concurring opinion.
49. National Ins. Co. v. Tidewater Co., 337 U.S. 582, 646 (1949), dissenting opinion.

a federal judicial system"[50] in 1787, and of the courts in 1866 as well, we should not read "due process" to confer untrammeled lawmaking power on the judiciary. Although the "deepest conviction" he cherished was that "no five men, or nine, are wise enough or good enough to wield such power over an entire nation,"[51] it was not deep enough to overcome his confidence in his own wisdom when he ascended to the bench.[52]

To convert the Marshall-Holmes-Frankfurter statements into constitutional dogma is both to disregard how narrow were their actual decisions and their reaffirmations that judges are under a duty to effectuate the original understanding and to respect the historical meaning of common law terms. Reliance on those statements for a doctrine of judicial power to "change" the Constitution only exposes the hollowness of the case for judicial revisionism.

Proponents of a "living Constitution" often twit me with the discrepancy between Marshall's deeds and his words. It is true that some of his decisions may be regarded as judicial lawmaking. Willard Hurst observed that "To rule that a corporation charter enjoyed the protection of a 'contract' under the constitutional provision [impairment of contracts clause] was a clear-cut act of judicial law-making."[53] And if knowledge can be brought home to Marshall that the Convention had specifically rejected a proposal for incorporation of banks, his disclaimers respecting *M'Culloch* might be regarded as "fraudulent."[54] But such examples afford a sad triumph for revisionists. To do what one disclaims as he acts is a reproach to any man, all the more when it is done by the oracles of the law whom we are urged to regard as the "national conscience." Of no one should more fastidious morality be required than of the Supreme Court.

50. Id. 647.
51. Supra Chapter 14 at note 72.
52. See supra Chapter 7 at notes 48–53, 63–65, and Chapter 14 at notes 140–141.
53. *The Legitimacy of the Business Corporation in the Law of the United States* 63 (1970).
54. See supra at note 17.

## Professors Thomas C. Grey and Louis Lusky

Sensible of the deficiences of conventional arguments for judicial law-making, Thomas Grey and Louis Lusky have proffered new theories on which the function should be based. Grey would invoke a continuing "natural law" tradition, while Lusky finds that the Founders conferred an "implied right" of judicial revision.

Grey espouses the Court's "role as the expounder of basic national ideals of individual liberty and fair treatment, even when the content of these ideals is not expressed as a matter of positive law in the written Constitution."[55] He concedes, however, that "such a role . . . is more difficult to justify than is the role assigned by the pure interpretive model," his label for Justice Black's restrictive view of judicial review.[56] That view, he states, "is one of great power and compelling simplicity . . . deeply rooted in our history and in our shared principles of political legitimacy. It has equally deep roots in our formal constitutional law."[57] The "grave difficulties" that attend the lawmaking model explain the judicial tendency, he continues, "to resort to bad legislative history" to support desired results. If "judges resort to bad interpretations in preference to honest exposition of deeply held but unwritten ideals, it must be because they perceive the latter mode of decision-making to be of suspect legitimacy."[58]

To answer the "question whether in our Constitution we have actually granted this large power to our judges" he briefly sketches an argument that he hopes to expand and document later.[59] His posits that the generation that framed the Constitution was attached to "the concept of a 'higher law' protecting 'natural rights,' and taking precedence over ordinary positive law . . . Thus in the framing of the original American constitutions it was widely accepted that there remained unwritten but still binding principles of higher law. The Ninth amendment is the textual expression of this idea in the Federal Constitution." It was

55. Grey, supra note 1 at 706.
56. Id. 706, 705.
57. Id. 705.
58. Id. 706; cf. supra Chapter 7 at notes 54–59.
59. Grey, supra note 1 at 715 note 49.

"widely assumed," he states, "that judges would enforce as constitutional restraints the unwritten natural rights."[60] Since Grey postponed documentation for these propositions, detailed commentary is not possible. Robert Cover concluded, however, that the Founders were attached to positive rather than to natural law.[61] Judicial review was an innovation that had excited the animosity of several State legislatures;[62] its proponents advocated it in restricted terms: the policing of constitutional "limits."[63] My own study of the records of the Federal Convention uncovered no intimations that natural law would empower judges to rise above the positive limitations of the Constitutions; evidence to the contrary may be postponed to examination of the Lusky thesis, for that evidence, I consider, refutes both the Grey and Lusky theories.

Here it may suffice to inquire in what way the "Ninth amendment is the textual expression" of the "idea" that "there remained unwritten but still binding principles of higher law." Were they binding on the courts? The Amendment provides: "The enumeration in the Constitution, of certain rights, shall not be construed to deny or disparage others retained by the people." Because certain nonenumerated rights are "retained by the people," it does not follow that federal judges are empowered to enforce them. Apart from "diversity" suits between citizens of different States, fashioned to "insure fair dealing between citizens of different States,"[64] federal jurisdiction is limited to cases "arising under this Constitution," for example, one invoking Fourth Amendment guarantees. It needs at least to be asked whether federal courts are authorized to enforce extraconstitutional "rights" that have neither State nor federal sanction. An implication to the contrary may be drawn from Madison's explanation in the First Congress immediately following his reference to the Ninth Amendment. If the guarantees of the Bill of

60. Id. 715–716. For the settled scope of "natural rights," see Kelly, supra Chapter 2 note 55.

61. Chapter 14 at note 15. Professor Cox alludes to "a deep and continuing American belief in natural law." *The Role of the Supreme Court in American Government* 16 (1976). For additional quotations from Cox, see supra Chapter 14 note 38.

62. Raoul Berger, *Congress v. The Supreme Court* 38, 40, 42 (1969).

63. Id. 13–14.

64. See supra Chapter 12 note 13.

Rights, he said, would be incorporated in the Constitution, the "independent tribunals of justice . . . will be naturally led to resist every encroachment upon rights *expressly stipulated* for in the Constitution by the Declaration of Rights."[65] The appeal to the Ninth Amendment was made by Justice Goldberg in *Griswold v. Connecticut*,[66] but the cases he cited lend no support for invocation of the Ninth Amendment; they involve either Bill of Rights guarantees that the Court has embodied in the Fourteenth Amendment, or rights like those of the right to travel or to associate which the Court found protected by the "liberty" of the Fifth and Fourteenth Amendment due process clauses.[67] In short, when the Court deemed a right worthy of protection it grounded intervention on the Bill of Rights or the Fourteenth Amendment, rendering resort to the Ninth Amendment superfluous. For me, as for Justice Black, the Amendment "was passed not to broaden the powers of this Court . . . but . . . to limit the Federal Government to the powers granted."[68]

Grey considers that the Fourteenth Amendment likewise was influenced by "natural rights":

> Natural rights reasoning in constitutional adjudication persisted up to the Civil War, particularly with respect to property and contract rights, and increasingly involving "due process" and "law of the

65. 1 *Annals of Congress* 439 (emphasis added).

66. 381 U.S. 479, 492 (1965), concurring opinion. Compare with Chief Justice Marshall, supra at note 26. Dissenting, Justice Black replied, "the Ninth Amendment was intended to protect against the idea that 'by enumerating particular exceptions to the grant of power to the Federal Government,' those rights which were not singled out were intended to be assigned" to it. 381 U.S. at 519, quoting 1 *Annals of Congress* 439.

67. Cantwell v. Connecticut, 310 U.S. 296 (1940): First Amendment—freedom of religion; New York Times Co. v. Sullivan, 376 U.S. 254 (1964): First Amendment—freedom of speech; Kent v. Dulles, 357 U.S. 116 (1958) and Aptheker v. Secretary of State, 378 U.S. 500 (1964): Fifth Amendment "liberty"—right to travel; Gideon v. Wainright, 372 U.S. 335 (1963): Sixth Amendment—right to counsel; N.A.A.C.P. v. Alabama, 357 U.S. 449 (1958): Fourteenth Amendment "liberty"—freedom of association; Bolling v. Sharpe, 347 U.S. 497 (1954): Fifth Amendment "liberty"—desegregated schools in District of Columbia.

Instead of employing the language of "natural rights" the Court has enjoyed equal freedom by resort to "fundamental rights"; we learn that some right is "fundamental" only after the Court attaches the label. Supra Chapter 14 note 117. But that judicial practice cannot draw on the embodiment of "natural law" in the Constitution.

68. Griswold v. Connecticut, 381 U.S. at 520.

land" clauses in constitutional texts. At the same time, an important wing of the anti-slavery movement developed a natural-rights constitutional theory, built around the concepts of due process, of national citizenship and its rights, and of the human equality proclaimed in the Declaration of Independence.

Though this latter movement had little direct effect on pre–Civil War decisions, it was the formative theory underlying the due process, equal protection and privileges and immunities clauses of the 14th amendment. Section 1 of the 14th amendment is thus properly seen as a reaffirmation and reenactment in positive law of the principle that fundamental human rights have constitutional status.[69]

Prior to the Civil War the courts were most inhospitable to "natural rights" as Robert Cover convincingly shows in his review of the fugitive slave cases.[70] Even in a "property" case, *Wynehamer v. The People*, the court dismissed claims based on "natural law" and fabricated a novel theory of "substantive due process." But that theory found no favor with other courts[71] until the Supreme Court, under ceaseless prodding by Justice Field, embraced it in the 1890s. It is true that the framers embodied "fundamental human rights" in the Civil Rights Act and thence in the Fourteenth Amendment, but those were regarded as restricted in scope and enumerated, for example, the right to own property, to contract; "political and social" rights were unmistakably excluded.[72] The equality (only partially) envisaged in the Declaration of Independence plainly found no place in the thinking of the framers of the Fourteenth Amendment.[73] Grey's reference to the "constitutional theory" of a "wing of the anti-slavery party" that allegedly "was the formative theory" underlying §1 invokes the Graham-tenBroek-Kelly theory, which simply cannot stand up against the historical facts.[74] In the history of the Fourteenth Amendment, it may confidently be stated, there is not a glimmering of intention to authorize judges to enforce rights beyond those

69. Supra note 1 at 716.
70. Supra Chapter 14 at notes 25–26.
71. Id. at notes 28–35.
72. Supra Chapter 2 at notes 26–30, 35–36, 39.
73. Supra Chapter 4 at notes 57–66; Chapter 2 at notes 26, 30; Chapter 10 at note 6.
74. Supra Chapter 13.

enumerated in the Civil Rights Act. Far from endowing the judiciary with a broad power to enforce "natural rights" going beyond those so enumerated, the courts were pointedly omitted from the §5 power to enforce even the rights granted by §1.[75]

Lusky, who sought an improved rationale for judicial intervention in behalf of libertarian ideals as long ago as 1938, when he aided Justice Stone in fashioning the *Carolene Products* footnote,[76] was at last driven to ask: "*By what right* does [the Court] revise the Constitution?"[77] His attempt to supply an answer by way of a theory of "implied power" to do so is set forth in his book *By What Right?* Many of his comments on the cases are rewarding, but strange is his line of demarcation. Down to 1961 or 1962 "the Court maintained its traditional passive posture,"[78] but after 1962 it engaged in "a dazzling display of seemingly freehand constitution-making without apparent concern for the intention of the Constitutors."[79] Few would regard *Brown v. Board of Education* (1954) as exemplifying the Court's "passive posture"; the evidence set forth in Chapter 6 hereof demonstrates that it was "making new law for a new day. " In fact, Lusky praises "the tremendously valuable work it has done in the past third of a century." It "has performed splendidly" as the "citadel of the republic—the main instrument for societal self-perfection,"[80] a performance far removed from a "passive posture."

Lusky's anxiety was aroused by the "neoprivacy" (contraceptive and abortion) cases, where the discredited "substantive due process began to reappear . . . under a different banner bearing the watchword privacy."[81] These are the cases he regards as "usurpation of power."[82] Yet neither the constitutional text nor its history forbid judicial interference with State regulation of the right of privacy, whereas the history of the Fourteenth Amendment plainly does preclude such interference with State control of

75. Supra Chapter 12.
76. Supra Chapter 14 at notes 123–125.
77. Lusky 19.
78. Id. 274.
79. Id. 263–264.
80. Id. 6.
81. Id. 337; see also id. 336, 339–341.
82. Id. 6.

suffrage and segregation. We may therefore with Justice Harlan view the State reapportionment cases "as a much more audacious and far-reaching judicial interference with the state legislative process . . . than the comparatively innocuous use of judicial power in the contraceptive case."[83] Presumably Lusky considers that the desegregation and reapportionment cases meet the criteria he suggests for employment of the "implied power" to revise the Constitution, but he himself recognizes that whether those tests are "so vague as to be illusory" poses a question "on which the validity of the [implied power] must stand or fall."[84] Examination of that question may be dispensed with because, as will appear, his *argument* for existence of the "implied power" is fundamentally defective, and because the materials I shall set out to demonstrate that defect equally dispose of Grey's resort to "natural law."

Lusky bases his "implied power" to "revise the Constitution . . . exercising the prerogatives of a continuing constitutional convention," upon a sweeping assumption:

> One perpetrates no violence upon logic or known historical facts by assuming that the Founding Fathers *intended* . . . (c) to empower the Court to serve as the Founders' surrogate for the indefinite future—interpreting the Constitution not as they themselves would have directed if they had been consulted in 1787, but as is thought right *by men who accepted the Founders' political philosophy—their commitment to self-government and the open society—and consider themselves obligated to effectuate that philosophy in the America of their own day.*[85]

This assumes the answer to the very question in issue: did the Framers empower the judges to revise the Constitution. It assumes that the Framers handed the constitution-changing function to a "surrogate," whose crystal-gazing as to effectuation of their "political philosophy" is made a substitute for the express terms of the Constitution. Such divination

---

83. The quotation is in the paraphrase of Professor Paul Kauper, "Penumbras, Peripheries, Emanations, Things Fundamental and Things Forgotten: The Griswold Case," 64 Mich. L. Rev. 235, 256 (1965).

84. Lusky 270, 318.

85. Id. 21.

recalls the Chinese emperor's "mandate from heaven." Lusky's assumption does in fact do "violence . . . to known historical facts."

He considers that Marshall "unfolded the doctrine of implied powers" in *M'Culloch v. Maryland*, drawing on Marshall's statement that, given ample powers, the government "must also be entrusted with ample means for their execution."[86] But ample means to execute *existing* powers cannot stretch to their expansion or to creation of *new* powers. Marshall himself disclaimed "any extension by construction of the powers of Congress"; he held that the judicial power "cannot be an assertion of a right to change" the Constitution.[87] The generation that framed the Constitution was devoted to a "fixed constitution"; courts "were not regarded as instruments of social change."[88] Judicial participation in legislative policymaking was forthrightly rejected; despite arguments by George Mason and James Wilson that judicial review confined to violation of some constitutional provision would not allow judges to set aside oppressive though constitutional laws, the Framers would not, as Elbridge Gerry stated, make judges the "guardians of the people."[89] Now Lusky would have it that the Framers turned policymaking over to the judges in toto, constituting them a super legislature, notwithstanding Hamilton's reassuring quotation of Montesquieu: "of the three powers— the judiciary is next to nothing."[90]

Hamilton alone presents an insuperable obstacle to the Grey-Lusky theories. Presumably inspired by States' Rights distrust of a federal judiciary,[91] he averred that the Constitution is "binding" on all, including the peoples' representatives, who have no "warrant" to make "a departure" from it "until the people" have changed it by a "solemn and au-

---

86. Id. 81.

87. Supra at notes 10–18.

88. Supra Chapter 16 at note 33. In the North Carolina Convention Timothy Bloodworth stated, "I wish to leave no dangerous latitude of construction." 4 Elliot 50. Elbridge Gerry stated in the First Congress, "The people of America can never be safe, if Congress have a right to exercise the power of giving constructions to the Constitution different from the original instrument." 1 *Annals of Congress* 523. Chief Justice Marshall was well aware of the continuing vitality of such fears. Supra at notes 14–16.

89. Supra Chapter 16 at note 8.

90. Federalist No. 78 at 504n.

91. Supra at note 50; see also Berger, supra note 62 at 263, 267–269.

thoritative act,"[92] that is, by amendment. He stated that "the intention of the people ["ought to be preferred"] to the intention of their agents." That he meant to leave no room for displacement of that "intention" by the Justices is underscored by his scornful dismissal of the notion that "the courts on the pretense of a repugnancy may substitute their own pleasure [for] the constitutional intentions of the legislature."[93] As Lusky himself comments, this "is hard to square with anticipation of judicial constitution-making power."[94] It is not "hard to square," it is impossible—as Hamilton's further statement that judges would be impeachable for "deliberate usurpations on the authority of the legislature" confirms. What "usurpations" could there be if judges were empowered to act as "surrogates" of the Founders or to enforce the wide-open spaces of "natural law"? Both the Grey and Lusky theories set at naught the "limits" so carefully framed by the Founders; both would circumvent the Article V method of change by amendment.

92. Supra Chapter 17 at note 15.

93. Federalist No. 78 at 506, 507.

94. Lusky 72. Lusky's reliance on the practice of "successive generations of Justices," id. 95, does not advance his argument because: (1) no chain of argument is stronger than its weakest link—the original source of the power; (2) what a wielder of power claims is but "feeble proof of its legality," supra at note 8; and (3) usurpation is not legitimated by repetition. Powell v. McCormack, 395 U.S. 486, 546–547 (1969). His reliance on United States v. Curtiss-Wright Corp., 299 U.S. 304 (1936), for a theory of "implied power," Lusky 90, leans on a case that has been widely criticized, and as Justice Jackson pointed out, proceeded under a delegation from Congress. Youngstown Sheet & Tube Co. v. Sawyer, 343 U.S. 579, 635–636 note 2 (1952), concurring opinion; David Levitan, "The Foreign Relations Power: An Analysis of Mr. Justice Sutherland's Theory," 55 Yale L.J. 467 (1946); Raoul Berger, "War-Making by the President," 121 U. Pa. L. Rev. 29, 69–75 (1972); C. A. Lofgren, "United States v. Curtiss-Wright Export Corporation: An Historical Reassessment," 83 Yale L.J. 51 (1973).

Lusky handsomely discloses that some of his "most perceptive Columbia colleagues" view his "implied power" theory skeptically because "(1) it affirms the legitimacy of constitutional rules not rooted in the constitutional text. (2) . . . it suggests . . . that the Court . . . can itself initiate changes in the law." Lusky 25. He advances his theory "not because it is more nearly 'correct' but because it is more *useful*." Id. 26 (emphasis added).

# 22

## *"Trial by Jury":*
## *Six or Twelve Jurors?*

THE increasingly free and easy judicial revision of constitutional norms is strikingly exemplified by *Williams v. Florida*,[1] wherein
the Supreme Court, for the first time in our history, held that a 6-man
jury satisfies the requirement of trial by jury. By Justice White's own
testimony a 12-man jury has been the invariable common law practice
since "sometime in the 14th century"—600 years. The Court held in
1930 that "it is not open to question . . . that the jury should consist of
twelve men, neither more nor less."[2] But because history furnishes no
explanation why the number 12 was chosen, Justice White dismisses it
as "an historical accident, unrelated to the great purposes which gave
rise to the jury in the first place."[3] Adherence to a practice for 600 years
renders its "accidental" origin irrelevant, for as Coke stated, "usage and
ancient course maketh law"[4]—all the more when that usage is embodied
with full awareness in a written Constitution. The case for the practical

1. 399 U.S. 78 (1970).
2. Patton v. United States, 281 U.S. 276, 288 (1930). Among the remarkable aspects
of Florida v. Williams is that Chief Justice Burger, appointed by President Nixon as a
"strict constructionist," "join[ed] fully in Mr. Justice White's opinion for the Court." 399
U.S. at 105. Yet on the very same decision day, he stated in Coleman v. Alabama, 399 U.S.
1, 22 (1970), dissenting opinion, "While I do not rely solely on 183 years of contrary
constitutional interpretation, it is indeed an odd business that it has taken this Court
nearly two centuries to 'discover' a constitutional mandate to have counsel at a preliminary hearing," a statement even more applicable to the "discovery" that the 12-man jury
was not an essential component of trial by jury.
3. 399 U.S. at 89–90.
4. 1 Coke, *Institutes of the Laws of England* 155a (London, 1628–1641).

448

wisdom of 12 jurors has been made by Hans Zeisel, Leonard Levy and others,[5] so I shall focus on Justice White's extraordinary approach to constitutional interpretation.

From Chief Justice Marshall onward the meaning of common law terms or institutions, which had a fixed content at the time they were incorporated into the Constitution, is to be ascertained by resort to that content.[6] With little short of disdain Justice White rejects that meaning as representing "mystical or superstitious insights into the significance of '12.' "[7] "Typical" of such "superstition" is a dithyramb by that great "mystic" Lord Coke, in his crabbed explication of Littleton on Tenures: "it seemeth to me, that the law in this case delighteth herselfe in the number of 12; for there must not onely be 12 *jurors* for the tryall of all matters of fact but 12 judges of ancient time for tryall of matters of law *in the Exchequer* Chamber ... And that *number of twelve* is much respected in *holy writ*, as in 12 *apostles*."[8] When men are moved to make exalted, mystical-religious explanations, it is because they deeply venerate the established practice.

Trial by jury was a central pillar of the society the colonists sought to erect; for centuries it had served as cherished buffer against oppressive prosecutors and judges.[9] Blackstone, whose *Commentaries* were widely circulated in the colonies, and whose influence on this issue can be traced into the very terms of a number of State constitutions and utterances of the Founders, stated, "the liberties of England cannot but subsist so long as this *palladium* remains sacred and inviolate."[10] The North Carolina Constitution of 1776 provided that "the ancient mode of trial by jury ...

5. For citations and discussion, see Levy, *Against the Law* 270–276.

6. See Chapter 20 notes 38, 39; Chapter 21 at note 24. In Townsend v. Sain, 372 U.S. 293, 311 (1963), the Court stated that the "historic conception of the writ [of habeas corpus] anchored in the ancient common law and in our Constitution ... has remained constant to the present day." See infra note 42, and supra Chapter 11 note 5; Chapter 20 note 39.

7. 399 U.S. at 88; cf. Justice Holmes, supra Chapter 17 note 32.

8. Supra note 4. Justice White notes that "The singular unanimity in the selection of the number twelve to compose certain judicial bodies, is a remarkable fact in the history of many nations." 399 U.S. at 89 note 23.

9. 399 U.S. at 87.

10. 4 Blackstone, *Commentaries on the Laws of England* 350 (London 1765–1769).

ought to remain sacred and inviolable."[11] Massachusetts, New Hampshire, Pennsylvania, and Vermont provided that it "shall be held sacred";[12] Georgia, South Carolina, and New York, that it was "inviolate forever."[13] In the Virginia Ratification Convention the Wythe Committee recommended an amendment: that "the ancient trial by jury is one of the greatest securities to the rights of the people, and is to remain sacred and inviolable."[14] George Mason in Virginia termed it "This great palladium of national safety," and James Iredell in North Carolina referred to it as "that noble palladium of liberty."[15] No element of judicial proceedings or power aroused such anxious inquiry as did trial by jury. Every facet of an institution held "sacred" by the Founders, therefore, needs to be approached with respectful regard.

Except for partial rejection of a jury of the "vicinage," of which more hereafter, there is no indication that any incident of trial by jury was to be more "sacred and inviolate" than another. To the contrary, the First Continental Congress laid claim to the "inestimable privilege of being tried by their peers of the vicinage, according to the due course of the common law";[16] this was repeated in the Maryland Constitution of 1776.[17] South Carolina provided that "the trial by jury, as heretofore used . . . shall be forever inviolably preserved."[18] That usage had been described by Coke as already "very ancient"[19] and was reformu-

11. Article XIV, 2 Poore 1410. For complete discussion of colonial and State sources, and Founders' utterances, see F. H. Heller, *The Sixth Amendment to the Constitution of the United States* 16–34 (1951).

12. Massachusetts (1780), Article XV, Declaration of Rights, 1 Poore 959; New Hampshire (1784), Article 20, 2 Poore 1282; Pennsylvania (1776), Article XI, 2 Poore 1542; Vermont (1777), Chapter I, Sec. XIII, 2 Poore 1860.

13. Georgia (1777), Article LXI, 1 Poore 383; South Carolina (1790), Article XI, Sec. 6, 2 Poore 1633; New York (1777), Article XLI, 2 Poore 1339.

14. 3 Elliot 658.

15. Mason, id. 528; Iredell, 4 Elliot 148.

16. Resolve of October 14, 1774, quoted in Duncan v. Louisiana, 391 U.S. 145, 152 (1968).

17. Declaration of Rights, Article III, 1 Poore 817; "according to the course of that [common] law."

18. Supra note 13. For similar provisions see North Carolina (1776), Article IX, 2 Poore 1409; Pennsylvania, Article IX, Sec. 6, 2 Poore 1554.

19. Supra note 4 at 155b.

lated in Bacon's Abridgment as calling for a "petit jury . . . precisely of twelve, and is never to be either more or less," as Chief Justice Matthew Hale had earlier stated.[20] This "most transcendent privilege," Blackstone stated, required a jury of 12.[21] In the Virginia Ratification Convention, Governor Edmund Randolph said: "There is no suspicion that less than twelve jurors will be thought sufficient."[22] Julius Goebel adverted to "popular sensitivity regarding any tampering with the 'inestimable right of jury trial,' " and concluded that "any suggestion that the jury system as then entrenched might be amended in any detail was beyond tolerance."[23] In the Virginia Ratification Convention, Grayson, for example, stated that "it is generally thought by Englishmen, that [trial by jury] is so sacred that no act of the [omnipotent] Parliament can affect it."[24] How can this be reconciled with Justice White's refusal to "ascribe a blind formalism to the Framers"? Far from being "wholly without significance 'except to mystics,' "[25] the Framers would have regarded tampering with the number "12" as shaking the very pillars of the temple.

## A Jury of the Vicinage

Justice White attached great weight to the Framers' refusal to embody in the Constitution a traditional component of trial by jury—that the jury be drawn from the "vicinage," the "neighborhood, or in medieval England, jury of the county."[26] Article III of the Constitution provides that the jury trial "shall be *held* in the State where the said Crimes shall have been committed"; it does not purport to direct how the jury shall be drawn, and no illumination is furnished by the "very scanty history"

20. Bacon's *Abridgment*, "Juries" (A) at 234; 2 Hale, *History of the Pleas of the Crown* 161 (1736).

21. 3 Blackstone 379; see also id. 358, 365.

22. 3 Elliot 467.

23. 1 Julius Goebel, *Antecedents and Beginnings to 1801, History of the Supreme Court of the United States* 141, 493 (1971).

24. 3 Elliot 569.

25. 399 U.S. at 103, 102.

26. Id. 93 note 35.

of the provision.[27] It received opposing interpretations in the Virginia Ratification Convention: Madison met an objection "that there was no provision for a jury from the vicinage" with the reply "if it could have been done with safety, it would not have been opposed,"[28] implying that Article III did not require that jurors be drawn from the vicinage. On the other hand, Randolph, who also had been a delegate to the Federal Convention, stated in Virginia, "nor is a jury from the vicinage in criminal cases excluded. This house has repeatedly resounded with this observation—that where a term is used, all its concomitants follow."[29] In the upshot, the Virginia Convention attached to its approval an amendment proposing trial by a jury of the vicinage.[30] And Justice White remarked that "concern" over failure to "preserve the common law right to be tried by a 'jury of the vicinage' . . . furnished part of the impetus for introducing" the Sixth and Seventh Amendments.[31]

In the First Congress, Madison proposed a jury "of the vicinage, with the requisite unanimity for conviction, of the right of challenge, and other accustomed requisites."[32] It passed the House but was rejected by the Senate; went to Conference and emerged in what ultimately became the final version of the Sixth Amendment: a "jury of the State and district wherein the crime shall have been committed." This Justice White properly views as "a compromise between broad and narrow definition" of the term "vicinage."[33] The compromise sprang from the fact noted by Madison that "In many of the States, juries . . . are taken from the State at large; in others, from districts of considerable extent; in very few from the County alone. Hence a dislike to the restraint with respect to *vicinage*."[34] What this history proves, is that the "vicinage" States did

27. Id. 93.

28. 3 Farrand 332; cf. infra note 34. Grayson, a Virginia opponent of adoption, charged that Article III abandoned "vicinage," 3 Elliot 568–569, a view shared by Holmes in the Massachusetts Convention, 2 Elliot 109–110.

29. 3 Elliot 573.

30. Id. 658.

31. 399 U.S. at 93–94.

32. Quoted, id. 94.

33. Id. 94–96.

34. Quoted, id. 95 note 39. In the Pennsylvania Ratification Convention James Wilson had stated, "there is no particular regulation made, to have the jury come from the

not have the votes to overcome a constitutional modification of the common law *in this respect*. Does it follow that the Founders meant also to curtail the right to challenge jurors, for example, which the Virginia Ratifiers were assured had been left intact by Article III,[35] or to abolish the "mystic" number "12"?

Justice White draws three negative implications, which cast "considerable doubt on the easy assumption in our past decisions that if a given feature existed in a jury at common law in 1789, then it was necessarily preserved in the Constitution."[36] First, "the mere reference to 'trial by jury' in Article III was not interpreted to include" vicinage.[37] But there was more than a "mere reference": trial by jury was qualified by "shall be held in the State," which raised differences of opinion whether or not vicinage was affected. At most, Article III modified the common law in that respect alone. Second, "provisions which would have explicitly tied the 'jury' concept to the 'accustomed requisites' of the time were eliminated." Justice White recognizes that this elimination is "concededly open to the explanation that the 'accustomed requisites' were thought to be already included in the concept of a 'jury.' But that explanation is no more plausible than the contrary one: that the deletion had some substantive effect."[38] The assumption that the "accustomed requisites" already were thought to be included in the concept of a "jury" was not left to speculation. The Ratifiers had been assured again and again in Virginia by John Marshall, by Edmund Pendleton, the Mentor of its highest court, and by Randolph, that the words "trial by jury" embraced all its attributes, such as the right to challenge jurors.[39] Curtailment of the

---

body of the county in which the offense was committed; but there are some States in which this mode of collecting juries is contrary to their established custom . . . In some states, the juries are not taken from a single county." 2 Elliot 450.

35. See infra note 39.

36. 399 U.S. at 92–93.

37. Id. 96.

38. Id. 96–97.

39. Pendleton: "It is strongly insisted that the privilege of challenging, or excepting to the jury, is not secured. When the Constitution says that the trial shall be by jury, does it not say that every incident will go along with it?" 3 Elliot 546; see also id. 547. Marshall re right of challenging: "If we are secure in Virginia without mentioning it in our Constitution, why should not this security be found in the federal court?" Id. 559. Randolph:

vicinage requirement responded to the preponderant State practice; but the nonvicinage States were no less attached to a jury of "12" than the "vicinage" adherents,[40] so that curtailment of vicinage does not argue for abandonment of "12." In *Pierson v. Ray* the Supreme Court refused to read *comprehensive* language to abolish a much less treasured common law practice in the absence of a specific expression of intent to do so.[41] Here, where ratification by the people is involved, it is even more important to demand a specific expression of intention to discard the treasured unanimous verdict by a jury of 12. Nothing in the Sixth Amendment phrase "a jury of the State and district" warned the people that by ratification they would surrender those attributes of a jury trial. Then, too, although the Founders, in framing the treason clause, had drastically narrowed the definition of "treason," Chief Justice Marshall looked to the common law for other aspects of "treason."[42] Like Marshall, we may conclude that a partial departure from the common law with respect to vicinage does not spell wholesale repudiation of other concomitants of trial by jury, that to embrace the contrary view is to do violence to the Framers' reverence for the institution.

Third, Justice White reasoned, "where Congress wanted to leave no doubt that it was incorporating existing common law features of the jury system, it knew how to use express language to that effect. Thus, the Judiciary Bill . . . provided in certain cases for the narrower 'vicinage' requirement which the House had wanted to include in the Amendment."[43] Now, as Justice White noticed, "the Senate remained opposed to the vicinage requirement, partly because in their view the then-

"That the incident is inseparable from the principal, is a maxim in the construction of laws." Id. 463; and see supra at note 29.

40. "The States which had adopted constitutions by the time of the Philadelphia Convention in 1787 appear for the most part to have either explicitly provided that the jury would consist of 12 . . . or to have subsequently interpreted their jury trial provisions to include that requirement." 399 U.S. at 98 note 45. Cf. Parker v. Munday (N.J. 1791), 1 Coxe's L. Rep. 70, 71 (1816).

41. See supra Chapter 1 note 57.

42. United States v. Burr, 25 F. Cas. (No. 14,693) 55, 159 (C.C. Va. 1807): Treason "is a technical term . . . It is scarcely conceivable that the term was not employed by the framers of our constitution in the sense which had been affixed to it by those from whom we borrowed it." See also supra note 6.

43. 399 U.S. at 97.

pending judiciary bill—which was debated at the same time as the Amendments—adequately preserved the common law vicinage feature—making it unnecessary to freeze that requirement into the Constitution."[44] "Vicinage" was specifically named because compromise of a disputed point so required. So, too, Justice White reads the Seventh Amendment provision that in civil cases "no fact tried by a jury, shall be otherwise reexamined in any Court . . . than according to the common law" against adoption of the 12-man jury.[45] Again this arose out of the need to resolve a particular controversy. Strenuous objections had been made in the Ratification Conventions to the provision for the Supreme Court's appellate jurisdiction of "questions both of law and fact" on the ground that facts found by a jury should be unreviewable. No aspect of judicial review excited greater opposition;[46] as Patrick Henry stated in Virginia: "The unanimous verdict of twelve impartial men cannot be reversed."[47] From settlement of a particular controversial issue it cannot be deduced that the Framers thereby intended to discard rights that had not once been challenged. Justice White, in my judgment, did not succeed in justifying a departure from the rule that common law terms must be given the meaning they had at the time of adoption.[48]

When Madison sought to explain the relation of Article III to vicinage, he said: "It is a misfortune in any case that this trial should be departed from, yet in some cases it is necessary."[49] There the real "necessity" was that Virginia stood in a decided minority in its attachment to "vicinage"; it could not muster votes to overcome resistance to *this* aspect of jury trial. Since trial by jury was a fabric woven of many strands—a "seamless web"—we should be slow to countenance a rent, particularly one not dictated by the most urgent need. What necessity impelled the Court to jettison the "very ancient" 12-man jury?

The Court had painted itself into a corner when it held that the Fourteenth Amendment made the "trial by jury" provision of the Bill of

---

44. Id. 95.
45. Id. 97.
46. For citations see Raoul Berger, *Congress v. The Supreme Court* 286–287 (1969).
47. 3 Elliot 544.
48. Supra note 42.
49. Quoted in 399 U.S. at 93 note 35.

Rights mandatory on the States,[50] a position, as we have seen, that is without historical warrant. Since some States employed less than 12 men, the Court, as Justice Harlan observed, recognized that the 'incorporationist' view . . . must be tempered to allow the States more elbow room in ordering their own criminal systems."[51] The Burger Court is presently retreating from the Warren Court's imposition of federal requirements on State practice,[52] and it might well have concluded that the quite recent extension of the Sixth Amendment's trial by jury to the States was ill-considered and, therefore, as Justice Harlan stated, the Burger Court's decision in *Duncan v. Louisiana* should be overruled.[53] Instead, it chose to rupture a 600-year practice in order to adhere to a dubious decision, illustrating what Washington and Hamilton had warned against: a usurpation to meet a great emergency breeds usurpations where no emergency exists.

50. "In Duncan v. Louisiana, 391 U.S. 145 (1968), we held that the Fourteenth Amendment guarantees a right to trial by jury in all criminal cases that, were they to be tried in a federal court—would come within the Sixth Amendment's guarantee." 399 U.S. at 86.

51. 399 U.S. at 118, dissenting opinion.

52. Supra Chapter 18 note 3.

53. 399 U.S. at 118.

# 23

## Conclusion

THE historical records all but incontrovertibly establish that the framers of the Fourteenth Amendment excluded both suffrage and segregation from its reach: they confined it to protection of carefully enumerated rights against State discrimination, deliberately withholding federal power to supply those rights where they were not granted by the State to anybody, white or black. This was a limited—tragically limited—response to the needs of blacks newly released from slavery; it reflected the hagridden racism that held both North and South in thrall; nonetheless, it was all the sovereign people were prepared to do in 1868.

Given the clarity of the framers' intention, it is on settled principles as good as written into the text. To "interpret" the Amendment in diametrical opposition to that intention is to rewrite the Constitution. Whence does the Court derive authority to revise the Constitution? In a government of limited powers it needs always be asked: what is the source of the power claimed? "When a question arises with respect to the legality of any power," said Lee in the Virginia Ratification Convention, the question will be, "*Is it enumerated in the Constitution? . . .* It is otherwise arbitrary and unconstitutional."[1] Or, as James Iredell put it, a law "not warranted by the Constitution . . . is bare-faced usurpation."[2] Hamilton made clear that action not warranted by the Constitution is no less a usurpation at the hands of the Court[3] than of a President. The suffrage-segregation decisions go beyond the assumption of powers "not warranted" by the Constitution; they represent the arrogation of powers

1. 3 Elliot 186.
2. 4 Elliot 194.
3. Supra Chapter 17 at note 15.

457

that the framers plainly *excluded*. The Court, it is safe to say, has flouted the will of the framers and substituted an interpretation in flat contradiction of the original design: to leave suffrage, segregation, and other matters to State governance. It has done this under cover of the so-called "majestic generalities" of the Amendment—"due process" and "equal protection"—which it found "conveniently vague," without taking into account the limited aims those terms were meant to express. When Chief Justice Warren asserted that "we cannot turn back the clock to 1868,"[4] he in fact rejected the framers' intention as irrelevant. On that premise the entire Constitution merely has such relevance as the Court chooses to give it, and the Court is truly a "continuing constitutional convention," constantly engaged in revising the Constitution, a role clearly withheld from the Court. Such conduct impels one to conclude that the Justices are become a law unto themselves.[5]

Can it be, then, that in a civilized society there exists no means of ridding ourselves of such a blight as segregation? No cost, it can be argued, is too high to be rid of the incubus. Archibald Cox observes: "To have adhered to the doctrine of 'separate but equal' would have ignored not only the revolution sweeping the world but the moral sense of civilization. Law must be binding even upon the highest court, but it must also meet the needs of men and match their sensibilities," and it is for judges to "make law to meet the occasion."[6] But, as Cox recognized, these "libertarian, humanitarian, and egalitarian" impulses "were not shared so strongly as to realize themselves through legislation," still less through an amendment. They were only realized through the "fate which puts one man on the Court rather than another."[7] I cannot bring myself to believe that the Court may assume a power not granted in order to correct an evil that the people were, and remain, unready to

4. Supra Chapter 7 at note 61.

5. "[T]he Justices have given serious cause for suspicion that they have come to consider the Court to be above the law." Lusky vii; and see id. 101. See Levy, supra Chapter 14 note 136; Murphy, supra Chapter 15 note 13; and Lewis, supra Chapter 17 note 56.

6. *The Role of the Supreme Court in American Government* 110 (1976). Cox does not regard the segregation decisions as "wrong even in the most technical sense," id. 109, although he states, "Plainly, the Court was not applying customary constitutional principles." Id. 60.

7. Id. 35.

cure. Justification of judicial usurpation—the label Hamilton attached to encroachments on the legislative function—on the ground that there is no other way to be rid of an acknowledged evil smacks of the discredited doctrine that "the end justifies the means."[8] John Stuart Mill cautioned against man's disposition "to impose [his] own opinions . . . as a rule of conduct on others."[9] The Inquisition burned heretics at the stake to save their souls.

Then there are the costs to constitutional government[10] of countenancing such usurpation. As the Court itself has demonstrated, unconstitutional action to cure a manifest evil establishes a precedent, as Washington and Hamilton warned, that encourages transgressions when such urgency is lacking. Time and again the Justices themselves have accused their brethren of acting without constitutional warrant. So to act is to act unconstitutionally; in another field the Court itself branded its own course of conduct over a hundred-year span as "unconstitutional."[11] "In a government of laws," Justice Brandeis cautioned, "existence of the government will be imperilled if it fails to observe the law scrupulously."[12] Justice Frankfurter added that "Self-willed judges are the least defensible offenders against government under law."[13] How long can public respect for the Court, on which its power ultimately depends, survive if

8. Lord Chancellor Sankey stated, "It is not admissible to do a great right by doing a little wrong . . . It is not sufficient to do justice by obtaining a proper result by irregular or improper means." Quoted by Chief Justice Warren in Miranda v. Arizona, 384 U.S. 436, 447 (1966). Levy observes that scholars "cannot be ignored and cannot be gainsaid when they insist that any means to a justifiable end is, in a democratic society, a noxious doctrine." Levy, *Warren* 190.

9. More fully quoted, infra note 20.

10. Cox states, "Nearly all the rules of constitutional law written by the Warren Court relative to individual and political liberty, equality, criminal justice, impress me as wiser and fairer than the rules they replace. I would support nearly all as important reforms if proposed in a legislative chamber or a constitutional convention. In appraising them as judicial rulings, however, I find it necessary to ask whether an excessive price was paid for enlarging the sphere and changing the nature of constitutional adjudication." Cox, supra note 6 at 102.

11. Erie Ry. Co. v. Tompkins, 304 U.S. 64, 77–78 (1938).

12. Olmstead v. United States, 277 U.S. 438, 485 (1928).

13. "From the Wisdom of Felix Frankfurter," 3 *Wisdom*, No. 28, p. 25 (1959), quoted by Kathryn Griffith, *Judge Learned Hand and the Role of the Federal Judiciary* 209 (1973).

the people become aware that the tribunal which condemns the acts of others as unconstitutional is itself acting unconstitutionally? Respect for the limits on power are the essence of a democratic society; without it the entire democratic structure is undermined and the way is paved from Weimar to Hitler.[14]

Proponents of the "original understanding," Sanford Levinson justly charges, are rarely prepared to press it all the way: "Thus opponents of the [Vietnam] war eager to return to the original understanding of the War Power are not likely to be eager to return to what was probably the rather conservative initial understanding of freedom of speech."[15] Rigorous constitutional analysis halts at the door of particular predilections. Setting practical considerations aside for the moment, intellectual honesty demands that the "original understanding" be honored across the board—unless we are prepared to accept judicial revision where it satisfies *our* predilections, as is the current fashion. But that is to reduce "law" to the will of a kadi. The list of cases that would fall were the "original understanding" honestly applied is indeed formidable. As Grey summarizes, "virtually the entire body of doctrine developed under the due process clauses of the 5th and 14th amendments," the core "requirement of 'fundamentally fair' procedures in criminal and civil proceedings," and "everything that has been labeled 'substantive due pro-

---

14. As Professor Charles Black stated, when urging noninterference with the Warren Court, "constitutional legality is indivisible . . . the right to wound one part of the body as you may desire is the right to destroy the life." *The People and the Court* 190 (1960). Madison said, "It is our duty . . . to take care that the powers of the Constitution be preserved entire to every department of Government; the breach of the Constitution in one point, will facilitate the breach in another." 1 *Annals of Congress* 500.

In a review of Alexander Bickel's last work, *The Morality of Consent*, Professor Alan M. Dershowitz states that Bickel saw "the Nixon Presidency and Watergate as the 'utterly inevitable' consequence of the undisciplined liberalism and 'result-orientation' of the Warren Court." Dershowitz comments, "A strange relationship, probably wrong and surely overstated." "Book Reviews," *The New York Times Book Review*, September 21, 1975, at 1. But Nixon's "idea" man, Donald Santarelli, quite plainly had learned from the Warren Court. Supra Chapter 17 at note 59.

Jefferson "foresaw that if the Constitution were ever destroyed, it would be destroyed by construction or interpretation, in final analysis, by the federal judiciary." Caleb P. Patterson, *The Constitutional Principles of Thomas Jefferson* 70 (1953).

15. S. Levinson, "Fidelity to Law and the Assessment of Political Activity," 27 Stan. L. Rev. 1185, 1200 note 68 (1975).

cess' would be eliminated," even though it "must constitutionally free the federal government to engage in explicit racial discrimination," for "there is no textual warrant for reading into the due process clause of the fifth amendment any of the prohibitions directed against the states by the equal protection clause." He adds, "there is serious question how much of the law prohibiting state racial discrimination can survive honest application of the interpretive ["original understanding"] model. It is clear that the equal protection clause . . . was *not* intended to guarantee equal political rights, such as the right to vote or to run for office, and perhaps including the right to serve on juries."[16] But because repudiation of the cases would have undesirable consequences, it does not follow that the prior determinations were authorized by the Constitution.[17] Whatever may be the merit of Judge Joseph Hutcheson's method of decision in common law cases—first a "hunch," then a hunt for legal rationalization[18]—such reasoning backward in constitutional cases displaces choices already made by the Framers. It perilously resembles the subordination of "law" to the attainment of ends desired by a ruling power which was the hallmark of Hitlerism and Stalinism.

Had it fallen to me, therefore, to decide some of the "substantive due process" and "equal protection" cases *ab initio*, I should have felt constrained to hold that the relief sought lay outside the confines of the judicial power.[19] It would, however, be utterly unrealistic and probably im-

16. Grey, "Do We Have an Unwritten Constitution?," 27 Stan. L. Rev. 703, 710–712 (1975). An earlier illustrative list had been furnished by Bork, "Neutral Principles and Some First Amendment Problems," 47 Ind. L.J. 1, 11–12 (1971). If effect be given to the framers' intention, the decision in Strauder v. Virginia, 100 U.S. 303 (1879), that Negroes must be permitted to serve as jurors, was wrongly decided. See Chairman Wilson, supra Chapter 2 at note 26, the colloquy between Wilson and Delano, and remarks by Moulton and Lawrence, supra Chapter 9 at notes 25–27.

17. Supra Chapter 14 at notes 103–104.

18. J. C. Hutcheson, "The Judgment Intuitive: The Function of the 'Hunch' in Judicial Decision," 14 Cornell L.Q. 274, 287 (1929). See also Martin Shapiro, *Law and Politics in the Supreme Court* 15 (1964).

19. Justice Stevens recently expressed a similar view. Runyon v. McCrary, 96 S. Ct. 2586 (1976), presented the issue whether the federal Act of 1866 prohibits private schools from excluding qualified children on racial grounds:

There is no doubt in my mind that that construction of the statute would have amazed the legislators who voted for it . . . [S]ince the legislative his-

possible to undo the past in the face of the expectations that the segregation decisions, for example, have aroused in our black citizenry— expectations confirmed by every decent instinct. That is more than the courts should undertake and more, I believe, than the American people would desire. But to accept thus far accomplished ends is not to condone the continued employment of the unlawful means. If the cases listed by Grey are in fact in contravention of the Constitution, the difficulty of a rollback cannot excuse the *continuation* of such unconstitutional practices.

This is not the place to essay the massive task of furnishing a blueprint for a rollback. But the judges might begin by curbing their reach for still more policymaking power, by withdrawing from extreme measures such as administration of school systems—government by decree— which have disquieted even sympathizers with the ultimate objectives. Such decrees cannot rest on the assertion that the *Constitution demands* busing, when in truth it is the Justices who require it[20] in contravention of the framers' intention to leave such matters to the States. The doctrinaire extension of false doctrine compounds the arrogation. So too, greater restraint in reapportionment matters, the return of the administration of local criminal, libel, and obscenity law to the States would not only respond to constitutional limitations but to preponderant public sentiment. Judges should take to heart Justice Holmes' admonition in *Baldwin v. Missouri*:

> we ought to remember the great caution shown by the Constitution in limiting the power of the States, and should be slow to construe the clause in the Fourteenth Amendment as committing to the

---

tory discloses an intent not to outlaw segregated schools at that time, it is quite unrealistic to assume that Congress intended the broader result of prohibiting segregated private schools. Were we writing on a clean slate, I would therefore vote to reverse.
Concurring opinion.

20. Cf. Lino A. Graglia, *Disaster by Decree* (1976). Justice Rehnquist reminded us of John Stuart Mill's statement, "The disposition of mankind, whether as rulers or as fellow citizens, to impose their own opinions and inclinations as a rule of conduct on others, is so energetically supported by some of the best and some of the worst feelings incident to human nature, that it is hardly ever kept under restraint by anything but of power." Mill, *On Liberty* 28 (1885), quoted in Furman v. Georgia, 408 U.S. 238, 467 (1972), dissenting opinion.

Court, with no guide but the Court's own discretion, the validity of whatever laws the States may pass.[20a]

His counsel is heavily underscored by the manifest intention of the framers to limit federal intrusion into State internal affairs to a plainly described minimum.

All this may seem like idle theorizing in light of Justice Stone's famous dictum that "the only check upon our own exercise of power is our own sense of self-restraint."[21] Were this true, it would offend against one of the most fundamental premises of our constitutional system. "Implicit in the system of government [the Framers] designed," Alpheus Thomas Mason stated, "is the basic premise that unchecked power in any hands whatsoever is intolerable."[22] "Unchecked power" emphatically was not confided to the judiciary; as Hamilton wrote in Federalist No. 81, the Justices may be impeached for usurpation of legislative power.[23] President Taft, no wild-eyed radical, acknowledged in 1911 that the judicial system was not working as it should, and stated, "Make your judges responsible. Impeach them. Impeachment of a judge would be a very healthful thing in these times."[24] Cumbersome as impeachment is, it is yet not so difficult as amendment, which requires approval by three-fourths of the States. At one time Brandeis and Frankfurter, it needs to be remembered, favored an amendment that would remove the due process clause from the Constitution altogether.[25] But such heroic measures would be unnecessary in the face of an aroused public opinion, a

20a. See supra Chapter 21 at note 41.

21. United States v. Butler, 297 U.S. 1, 79 (1936), dissenting opinion.

22. "Myth and Reality in Supreme Court Drama," 48 Va. L. Rev. 1385, 1405 (1962).

23. Quoted supra Chapter 15 at note 50.

24. Quoted in Joseph P. Lash, *From the Diaries of Felix Frankfurter* 113 note 3 (1975). See also Lusky 80. The Supreme Court, by Justice Frankfurter, stated, "Restraints on our jurisdiction are self-imposed only in the sense that there is from our decisions no immediate appeal short of impeachment or constitutional amendment." Rochin v. California, 342 U.S. 165, 172 (1952).

25. Louis Jaffe, "Was Brandeis an Activist? The Search for Intermediate Premises," 80 Harv. L. Rev. 986, 989 (1967). In 1924 Frankfurter stated that "The due process clause ought to go." "The Red Terror of Judicial Reform," 40 *New Republic* 110, 113, reprinted in Frankfurter, *Law and Politics* 10, 16 (Macleish and Pritchard eds. 1939).

The requirements for amendment or impeachment, it may be suggested, are so onerous as to render the Court's decisions all but irrevocable. "[I]f the policy of the govern-

mighty engine, as President Nixon learned after the "Saturday Night Massacre."[26] "The Court," wrote Charles L. Black, "could never have had the strength to prevail in the face of resolute public repudiation of its legitimacy."[27]

A prime task of scholarship, therefore, is to heighten public awareness that the Court has been overleaping its bounds. "[S]cholarly exposure of the Court's abuse of its powers," Frankfurter considered, would "bring about a shift in the Court's viewpoint."[28] Such awareness is a necessary preliminary for, as Mason observed, "only that power which is recognized can be effectively limited."[29] Calls for disclosure of the Court's real role have been made by both proponents and opponents of judicial "adaptation" of the Constitution. Justice Jackson, it will be recalled, called on the Justices in the desegregation case to disclose that they were "making new law for a new day"; and Judge Learned Hand declared that "If we do need a third [legislative] chamber it should appear for what it is, and not as the interpreter of inscrutable principles."[30]

Forty years ago the philosopher Morris R. Cohen wrote to Professor Frankfurter, "the whole system is fundamentally dishonest in its pretensions (pretending to say what the Constitution lays down when they

ment is to be irrevocably fixed by the decisions of the Supreme Court," said Lincoln in his First Inaugural Address, "the people will have ceased to be their own rulers." Quoted in Morton Keller, *Affairs of State* 17–18 (1977).

26. Attorney General Elliot Richardson resigned rather than discharge Special Prosecutor Archibald Cox at the insistence of President Nixon. Deputy Attorney General William Ruckelshaus was discharged for refusal to discharge Cox.

27. *The People and the Court* 209 (1960).

28. Quoted in Lash, supra note 24 at 59. Rodell referred to "the reverential awe-bred-of-ignorance, with which most Americans regarded the Court" in 1937. *Nine Men* 247 (1955). Professor Charles Black urges that lawyers "never cease to call the Court to account, and to urge reason upon it. Inadequate reason, lack of responsiveness to counter-argument [as in Reynolds v. Sims]—these are self-wounding sins in any court." Address, "The Judicial Power as Guardian of Liberties," before a symposium on "The Supreme Court and Constitutional Liberties in Modern America," Wayne State University, Detroit, Mich., Oct. 16, 1976, at 9. Arrogation of power withheld is far worse.

29. Mason, supra note 22 at 1405. Mason states, "once the public recognizes the personal nature of the judicial power, it would become difficult for the judiciary to function at all." Id. 1399.

30. *The Bill of Rights* 70 (1962); see also A. S. Miller and R. F. Howell, "The Myth of Neutrality in Constitutional Adjudication," 27 U. Chi. L. Rev. 661, 695 (1960).

[the Justices] are in fact deciding what [they think] is good for the country.)"[31] But Martin Shapiro argued: "Suicide is no more moral in political than in personal life. It would be fantastic indeed if the Supreme Court, in the name of sound scholarship, were to disavow publicly the myth on which its power rests . . . If the myth . . . is destroyed . . . the Court loses power."[32] Power in the service of moral imperatives must not rest on a sham.[33] It is not "scholarship," but obedience to constitutional limitations that calls for a halt. "The foundation of morality," said Thomas Huxley, "is to have done, once and for all, with lying."[34] On a practical level, as Presidents Lyndon Johnson and Richard Nixon learned, nondisclosure to the people creates a credibility gap.[35]

The nation cannot afford to countenance a gap between word and deed on the part of its highest tribunal, a tribunal regarded by some as the "national conscience." It should not tolerate the spectacle of a Court that pretends to apply constitutional mandates while in fact revising them in accord with the preference of a majority of the Justices who seek to impose *their* will on the nation. Richard Nixon learned at last that even a President cannot set himself above the law, that he is obliged " 'to take Care that the Laws be faithfully executed.' It is necessary and right that the nine Justices be held to a like standard."[36] "The people," in the words of five early State Constitutions, "have a right to require of their . . . magistrates an exact and constant observance" of the "fundamental principles of the Constitution."[37] Among the most fundamental is the exclusion of the judiciary from policymaking.

31. Letter to Felix Frankfurter, January 27, 1936, L. C. Rosenfield, *Portrait of a Philosopher: Morris Raphael Cohen in Life and Letters* 270 (1962), quoted in Lash, supra note 24 at 55. There is a "credibility gap between the Court's pretensions and its actions." P. B. Kurland, *Politics, the Constitution and the Warren Court* xxiii (1970).

32. Supra note 18 at 27; see also supra Chapter 7 at notes 56–57.

33. Cf. Paul Brest, *Processes of Constitutional Decisionmaking: Cases and Materials* 1146 (1975).

34. Quoted in H. T. Mencken, *Treatise of Right and Wrong* 197 (1934).

35. "The contrast between morality professed by society and immorality practiced on its behalf makes for contempt of law." On Lee v. United States, 343 U.S. 747, 758–759 (1952), Justice Frankfurter, dissenting opinion.

36. Lusky 20.

37. Supra Chapter 15 at note 18.

Let it not be said of us as Gibbon said of Rome: "The *image* of a free constitution was preserved with decent reverence. The Roman senate *appeared* to possess the sovereign authority, and devolved on the emperors all the executive powers of government."[38] Here no Senate devolved the policymaking powers on the Court; they are self-conferred and survive only because the American people are unaware that there is a yawning gulf between judicial professions and practice. An end, I would urge, to pretence. If government by judiciary is necessary to preserve the spirit of our democracy, let it be submitted in plainspoken fashion to the people—the ultimate sovereign—for their approval.

## Supplementary Note on the Conclusion

The foregoing pages furnish proof positive, in my judgment, that both the Founding Fathers and the framers of the Fourteenth Amendment held a narrow view of the judicial role—that of nay-sayer policing the constitutional boundaries, which were to be settled largely by resort to the original intent. And, to borrow from Raymond Aron, these conclusions justify themselves "by the falseness of the [opposing] beliefs."[1] If instead a judge resorts to his "individual sense of justice," Benjamin N. Cardozo commented, "That might result in a benevolent despotism if the judges were benevolent men. It would put an end to the reign of

---

38. 1 Gibbon, *The History of the Decline and Fall of the Roman Empire* 215 (Nottingham Soc. undated) (emphasis added). He said of the Roman emperors that "they surrounded their throne with darkness, concealed their irresistible strength, and humbly professed themselves the accountable ministers of the senate, whose supreme decrees they dictated and obeyed." Id. 303.

1. Raymond Aron, "Pensées," N.Y. Times, Oct. 23, 1983, E19. Justice Thomas McKean told the Pennsylvania Ratification Convention that "refutation of an argument begets a proof." 2 *Debates in the Several State Conventions on Adoption of the Federal Constitution* 541 (Jonathan Elliot ed. 1836).

law."[2] Today the "very notion of the rule of law is at issue."[3] Activists forget that the struggle for a written Constitution, as Justice Black noted, "was to make certain that men in power would be governed by *law*, not the arbitrary fiat of the man or men in power."[4] Put differently, we are "to be governed by the same pre-established rules and not by the whims of those charged with executing those rules."[5] Preestablished rules serve the requirements of certainty and predictability so that people may conduct themselves accordingly.[6] Additionally, such rules deserve respect because they represent wisdom accumulated over the centuries. Activists would brashly toss that wisdom on the scrap heap. Wisdom, wrote Learned Hand, "is to be gained only as we stand upon the shoulders of those who have gone before"; it can be achieved "only by accumulation."[7] A wise judge draws upon "the distilled knowledge of many generations of men, each decision based on the experience of those who came before and tested by the experience of those after, and it is wiser than any individual can possibly be."[8]

2. Benjamin N. Cardozo, *The Nature of the Judicial Process* 136 (1921).

3. Mark Tushnet, "Legal Realism, Structural Review, and Prophecy," 8 U. Dayton L. Rev. 809, 811 (1983).

4. In re Winship, 397 U.S. 358, 384 (1970), dissenting opinion.

5. Philip Kurland, "Curia Regis: Some Comments on the Divine Rights of Kings and Judges 'To Say What the Law Is,' " 23 Ariz. L. Rev. 581, 582–583 (1981). Solicitor General Robert Jackson, soon to be a Justice, believed that "the rule of law is in unsafe hands when the courts cease to function as courts and become organs for control of policy." Robert H. Jackson, *The Struggle for Judicial Supremacy* 322 (1941).

6. "Certainty is so essential to law, that law cannot even be just without it." Catherine D. Bowen, *Francis Bacon: The Temper of a Man* 146 (1963).

7. Learned Hand, "The Spirit of Liberty," in *Papers and Addresses of Learned Hand* 283 (Irving Dilliard ed. 1977).

8. J. G. A. Pocock, *The Ancient Constitution and Feudal Law: A Study of English Historical Thought in the Seventeenth Century* 35 (1987). Pocock expatiates: "Institutions which have survived . . . for a long time must be presumed to have solved innumerably more problems than the men of the present age can imagine, and experience indeed shows that the efforts of the living, even mustering their best wisdom for the purpose to alter such institutions in the way that seems best to their own intelligence have usually done more harm than good. The wisdom which they embody has accumulated to such a degree that no reflecting individual can in his lifetime come to the end of it, no matter how he calls philosophy and theoretical reason to his aid." Id. 36. Long before, Hamilton said, "Experience is the oracle of truth; and where its responses are unequivocal, they ought to be conclusive and sacred." Federalist No. 20 at 124 (Mod. Lib. ed.).

One of the virtues of the common law is that it sought to resolve problems in the light of common sense. Common sense is especially relevant to constitutional construction, for which we have the authority of Justice Story:

> Upon subjects of government, it has always appeared to me that metaphysical refinements are out of place. A Constitution of government is addressed to the common sense of the people; and never was designed for trials of logical skill or visionary speculation.[9]

A striking example of "visionary speculation" is furnished by Professor J. M. Balkin, who relies on the "principle of iterability," that is, different readers may read texts differently. He explains that "texts cannot be understood unless they can be misunderstood—cannot be read unless they can be misread."[10] It does not follow, however, that misreadings acquire

9. Robert Bork, "Styles in Constitutional Theory," 26 S. Tex. L.J. 383, 385 (1985). Story was anticipated by Jefferson. In a letter to Justice William Johnson, June 12, 1823, Jefferson wrote, "Laws are made for men of ordinary understanding, and should, therefore, be construed by the ordinary rules of common sense. Their meaning is not to be sought for in metaphysical subtleties, which may make anything, mean everything or nothing, at pleasure." Thomas Jefferson, 15 *The Writings of Thomas Jefferson* 450 (1903) (Andrew A. Lipscomb ed. 1903). See Raoul Berger, "Some Reflections on Interpretivism," 55 Geo. Wash. L. Rev. 1, 7 (1986).

Francis Bacon perceived the inadequacy of philosophers to deal with mundane matters: "As for the philosophers, they make imaginary laws for imaginary commonwealths; and their discourses are as the stars, which give little light because they are so high. For the lawyers, they write according to the states where they live, what is received law and not what ought to be the law." *The World of the Law: The Law as Literature* xvi (Ephraim London ed. 1960). Budding "legal philosophers" apparently are unaware of the observation by the highly regarded English philosopher G. E. Moore: "Philosophical questions are so difficult, the problems they raise are so complex, that no one can fairly expect, now, any more than in the past, to win more than a very limited assent." Robert Skidelsky, *John Maynard Keynes: Hopes Betrayed, 1883–1920* 138 (1986). Charles Fried, professor of jurisprudence at Harvard Law School, deplores "the uncontrolled eruption into law" of philosophy and "the poor quality of the philosophy." Charles Fried, "Jurisprudential Responses to Legal Realism," 73 Cornell L. Rev. 331 (1988).

10. J. M. Balkin, "Constitutional Interpretation and the Problem of History," 63 N.Y.U. L. Rev. 911, 932 (1988). Balkin adverts to "the possibility that a text will mean something different to a given reader in a given context than it meant to earlier readers in other contexts." Id. This is a chameleon theory—the text changes color according to who looks at it; it torpedoes the precept that the Constitution is binding, for a document that can mean anything to anybody has no binding force. See Raoul Berger, "History,

canonical status. To the contrary, Western tradition seeks to rectify, not to build upon, mistakes, as the course of science abundantly demonstrates. Then too, Balkin assumes, to borrow from Judge Frank Easterbrook, that "Readers, not writers, are sovereign,"[11] despite the centuries-old rule that the intention of the writer prevails. Finally, I would commend to activists the caution of Gerhard Casper, President of Stanford University: "The American concept of the legitimacy of government is closely tied to the Constitution ["the secular equivalent of the Bible"]. Its limitless manipulation may endanger the very legitimacy that has been the greatest accomplishment of American constitutionalism."[12]

---

Judicial Revisionism, and J. M. Balkin," 1989 B.Y.U. L. Rev. 759, 772–778.

Maitland observed that "the Chancellors were tempted to forget how plain and rough good law should be." 2 *Historians at Work* 320 (Peter Gay et al. eds. 1975). Albert Einstein was "opposed to all metaphysical undertakings" and had as his "first principle the strictest and most comprehensive ascertainment of fact. All theories and requirements are to rest exclusively on this ground of facts and find here their ultimate criterion." Ronald W. Clark, *Einstein: The Life and Times* 154 (1971).

11. Frank H. Easterbrook, "The Influence of Judicial Review on Constitutional Theory," in *A Workable Government? The Constitution After 200 Years* 170, 173 (Burke Marshall ed. 1987).

12. Gerhard Casper, "Constitutionalism," in 2 *Encyclopedia of the American Constitution* 480 (Leonard W. Levy et al. eds. 1986). In 1934, Edward S. Corwin urged the Court "to give over attempting to supervise national legislative policies on the basis of a super-constitution which, in the name of the Constitution, repeals and destroys that historic document." Edward S. Corwin, *The Twilight of the Supreme Court* 182 (1934).

# APPENDIX A

# *Van Alstyne's Critique of Justice Harlan's Dissent*

Professor Van Alstyne's article[1] constitutes the most extended attempt to refute Justice Harlan's dissent in *Reynolds v. Sims*.[2] In the course of my discussion of suffrage, reapportionment, and the "open-ended" theory I sought to take account of his views. That portion of his article which dealt with the "remedy" aspect of Harlan's analysis has in part been discussed in connection with Justice Brennan's adoption of the Van Alstyne argument.[3] Van Alstyne also attributes to Harlan the view that "§2 equally precludes the application of any earlier provisions of the Constitution to state voting rights."[4] He considers that "there was probably no reliable understanding whatever that §2 would preclude Congress (or the courts) from employing sources of constitutional authority other than §2 to affect state suffrage"[5] and spends many pages demonstrating that there was no such consensus.

Now Harlan was not at all concerned with "other" constitutional provisions; save for a footnote reference to Bingham's explanation of a "republican form of government."[6] Harlan concentrated on the Fourteenth Amendment. Here is his thesis in his own words: "The history of the adoption of the Fourteenth Amendment provides conclusive evidence that neither those who proposed nor those who ratified the amendment

1. "The Fourteenth Amendment, The 'Right' to Vote, and the Understanding of the Thirty-Ninth Congress," 1965 S. Ct Rev. 33.
2. 377 U.S. 533, 589 (1964).
3. Supra Chapter 5 at notes 102–106.
4. Van Alstyne 39.
5. Id. 45.
6. Quoted, id. 41.

believed that the Equal Protection clause limited the power of the States to apportion their legislatures as they saw fit."[7] Apparently Van Alstyne bases his inference of preemption of "other" provisions on Harlan's statement that "§2 expressly *recognizes* the States' power to deny or, in any way, abridge the right" to vote.[8] To recognize a State power falls short of holding that the Amendment "precludes the application of any earlier provisions of the Constitution." So to hold would imply that "earlier provisions," if any, had been repealed by implication. It cannot be presumed that Harlan was unaware of the elementary proposition that repeals by implication are not favored and require evidence that a repeal was intended.

Apart from a few radical dissentients,[9] there was a wide consensus that control over suffrage had from the beginning been left with the States, as was categorically stated by Stevens, Fessenden, Conkling, Bingham, and many others.[10] To placate the dissentients there were assurances that the "representation" provision left other provisions, if any, untouched; in other words, they were not repealed by implication. A typical colloquy between Higby and Stevens is cited by Van Alstyne. Higby objected that the "representation" proposal "gives a power to the States to make governments that are not republican in form," and asked Stevens

> if it does not acknowledge a power in a State to do such a thing.
> Mr. Stevens. Yes, sir, it does acknowledge it, and it has always existed under the Constitution.
> Mr. Higby. I do not acknowledge that it is in the Constitution as it now is.
> Mr. Stevens. Then we do not give it to them.

Van Alstyne finds Stevens' response "confusing."[11] To "acknowledge" that States *have* a power is not to *give* it to them. At another point Stevens

7. 377 U.S. at 595.
8. Van Alstyne 39.
9. Cited, id. 49–51.
10. Supra Chapter 4.

11. Van Alstyne 50–51; *Globe* 428. This exchange occurred early in the session. Higby profited from the debates and later stated, "The Government of the United States does not propose or attempt to go into every one of the States now in close fellowship with

stated, "the States have the right . . . to fix the elective franchise," and the representation provision "does not take it from them."[12]

Rejection of the dissentient appeal to "other" constitutional sources for federal power over suffrage[13] is demonstrated by the fact that a subcommittee of the Joint Committee reported an Amendment "Congress shall have power . . . to secure . . . the same political rights,"[14] thereby expressing its view that Congress did not enjoy that power. And it is confirmed by the passage of the Fifteenth Amendment.[15] If there were "other" constitutional powers for the purpose the Fifteenth Amendment was superfluous. From 1789 to 1866 it was generally accepted that suffrage had been left to regulation by the States,[16] a view reiterated in 1875 by Chief Justice Waite:

> The Fifteenth Amendment does not confer the right of suffrage upon any one. It prevents the State from giving preference, in this particular, to one citizen of the United States over another on account of race. Before its adoption this could be done. It was as much within the power of a State to exclude citizens from voting on account of race . . . as it was on account of age, property, or education. Now it is not.[17]

---

the Government and represented here, and say to them that all classes of citizens without distinction of race or color shall vote. It is true that the general principle has been to leave the question to each of the States." *Globe* 2252.

12. *Globe* 536.

13. Chief of these was the guarantee of "a republican form of government"; Van Alstyne 50.

14. Quoted, id. 48 note 46.

15. Auerbach states, "Students of the history of the Fourteenth Amendment agree that the 'congressional understanding of the immediate effect of [the Fourteenth Amendment] enactment on conditions then present' was that it would not deal with the right of suffrage. Otherwise the Fifteenth Amendment would not have been necessary, as Mr. Justice Harlan pointed out." "The Reapportionment Cases: One Person, One Vote— One Vote, One Value," 1964 S. Ct. Rev. 1, 75. The point was made by the Court in Minor v. Happersett, 88 U.S. (21 Wall.) 162, 175 (1874).

16. Supra Chapter 4 at notes 42, 43, 45–48, 57, 64; Chapter 5 at note 49.

17. United States v. Reese, 92 U.S. 214, 217–218 (1875). Looking at "equal protection" in 1964, Auerbach considers it an "astonishing result" that would read "equal protection" to allow a State to deny "the right to vote in a state or local election . . . for reasons which have nothing to do with race, color . . . but which nevertheless result in an arbitrary classification." Auerbach, supra note 15 at 77–78. But that view is a product of

Of course, this does not dispose of the question: were there such other powers? Van Alstyne, however, makes no attempt to demonstrate that there were. My study of the guarantee of a republican form of government, upon which the dissentients cited by Van Alstyne heavily rely, led me to doubt their existence.[18] Those doubts were strongly reinforced by the historical materials Justice Stewart collected in his opinion in *Oregon v. Mitchell*.[19] In any event, Van Alstyne's elaborate argument that the Fourteenth Amendment does not preclude the application of "other" provisions of the Constitution does not shake Harlan's demonstration that suffrage was excluded from the Amendment itself.

Van Alstyne's attempt to downgrade Stevens' testimony stands no better. Stevens did not consider Negroes prepared for suffrage, nor the North ready to accept it; he had stated that the right of a State to disfranchise "has always existed," that the proposed "representation" provision "does not take it from" the States.[20] One could hardly ask for greater clarity. Against this, Van Alstyne quotes Stevens, "If any State shall exclude any of her adult citizens from the elective franchise . . . she shall forfeit her right to representation in the same proportion," and asks whether this evidences Stevens' understanding "that an exception was to be read into the unqualified language of § 1 and that the Equal Protection Clause could not be applied against partial and oppressive laws denying the freedmen their voice in the government."[21] This quotation did not address that issue; but the above quotations plainly indicate Stevens' view that suffrage was to remain the province of the States; that is an "exception" built into "equal protection" by the

---

our times, not at all responsive to the intention of the framers, either in 1787 or in 1866. See supra Chapter 5 after note 77. In New York v. Miln, 36 U.S. (11 Pet.) 102, 139 (1837), the Court declared, "a State has the same undeniable and unlimited jurisdiction over all persons and things, within its territorial limits, as any foreign nation, where that jurisdiction is not surrendered or restrained by the Constitution of the United States." For the standard of proof required to establish such "surrender" see supra Chapter 1 note 57.

18. Fessenden commented on Article I, § 2(3), re qualifications of electors in each State, "it has always been considered that the clause . . . acknowledged the rights of the States to regulate the question of suffrage. I do not think it has ever been disputed." *Globe* 1278.

19. 400 U.S. 112, 288–291 (1970), concurring and dissenting in part.

20. Supra Chapter 4 at notes 25, 64, 46.

21. Van Alstyne 56. But see Bickel, supra Chapter 6 at note 27.

entire Republican leadership. Bingham stated: "The amendment does not give . . . the power to Congress of regulating suffrage in the several States."[22] Senator Howard explained that "the first section of the proposed amendment does not give . . . the right of voting."[23] Toward the close of the session Senator Sherman said, "we have refused" to require the rebel "States to allow colored persons to vote."[24] And after passage of the "equal protection" clause, Bingham lent his aid to Tennessee's exclusion of black suffrage, notwithstanding "we are all for equal and exact justice, but justice for all is not to be secured in a day"[25] —eloquent testimony that "equal protection" was not viewed as a bar to denial of suffrage.

Van Alstyne's statement that Stevens "greatly favored Negro suffrage and constantly supported all efforts to that end, to the extent he thought them politically feasible"[26] is not very revealing. In fact, as C. Vann Woodward wrote, "Stevens was not yet prepared to enfranchise the Negro freedmen . . . apart from political reasons he had other doubts about the wisdom of the measure . . . he doubted that the freedmen were prepared for intelligent voting."[27] Eric McKitrick stated, "beyond doubt" Stevens "tipped the balance . . . Being none too keen on direct enactment of Negro suffrage."[28] It was on Stevens' motion that the Joint Committee on Reconstruction preferred a reduction of representation proposal to one prohibiting discrimination, by a vote of 11 to 3.[29] He was taunted during the final debate by Charles A. Eldredge, a Democrat from Wisconsin: "Why is it that the gentleman from Pennsylvania gives up universal suffrage . . . It is . . . for the purpose of saving their party in the next fall election."[30] Another Democrat, Andrew Rogers, asserted, "The committee does not dare submit

22. *Globe* 2542.
23. Id. 2766.
24. Id. 3989.
25. Id. 3979.
26. Van Alstyne 46.
27. *The Burden of Southern History* 92 (1960); supra Chapter 4 at note 25.
28. *Andrew Johnson and Reconstruction* 348 (1960).
29. Kendrick 51.
30. *Globe* 2506.

the broad proposition to the people . . . of negro suffrage."[31] In September 1866, when the Amendment was a campaign issue, Stevens assured the Pennsylvania voters that the "Amendment does not touch social or political rights."[32]

It is Van Alstyne who would "read into" the words "equal protection" the very suffrage so unmistakably excluded by the framers. For centuries the canon of interpretation has been that a thing may be within the language and yet not within the intention of the framers and therefore not "within the statute."[33] "Equal protection" had limited scope for the framers; it barred discriminatory laws with respect to specified "fundamental rights"—no more.[34]

The difficulties that confront Van Alstyne's attack on Harlan's analysis may be gathered from his own statement. He makes

> several observations generally in agreement with Mr. Justice Harlan's view of what was implied by §2. First, the fact that the Joint Committee considered an amendment to prohibit voting discrimination on racial grounds [and let it wither on the vine] does seem to imply that it otherwise regarded state laws providing for such discrimination as constitutional. Second, the fact that a more limited reduction-of-representation-basis alternative was simultaneously considered and adopted, that the proposal to prohibit discrimination on the basis of race was not adopted [such proposals were voted down by the Senate by very heavy majorities] appears to imply that §2 itself recognizes the exclusive power of states over suffrage qualifications. Beyond this, the speeches by Stevens and Conkling in support

31. Id. 2538. See Van Alstyne's Summary, supra Chapter 4 at note 16.

32. James 201. Van Alstyne cites a Stevens statement of two years later: "Since the adoption of the fourteenth amendment . . . I have no doubt of our power to regulate the elective franchise." Van Alstyne recognizes that such a "retrospective view . . . must, of course, be discounted to that extent"; Van Alstyne 64–65; it was in flat contradiction of representations made to secure adoption. Such retrospective statements are to be totally discounted. See supra Chapter 3 at notes 51–52; see also Raoul Berger, "Judicial Review: Counter Criticism in Tranquillity," 69 Nw. U. L. Rev. 390, 399–401 (1974). In any event, Stevens' later views did not carry the day because Congress passed the Fifteenth Amendment to fill the gap.

33. See supra Chapter 1 note 24; Chapter 10 at note 94. See also Pierson v. Ray, discussed supra Chapter 1 note 57.

34. See supra Chapter 10.

of H. R. No. 51 [a predecessor provision cast in terms of racial discrimination] initially appear to the same effect.[35]

To the "speeches by Stevens and Conkling" should be added those of other prominent leaders, Fessenden, Bingham, Howard and still other Republicans, copiously quoted in Chapters 3 and 4 supra, and unmistakably confirmed by the Joint Committee Report. How Van Alstyne can extract from these statements the conclusion that "its [§ 2] principal proponents emphasized that it did not acknowledge the constitutionality of state disenfranchisement laws"[36] escapes my grasp.

Among the facts Van Alstyne musters to counteract an "initial favorable" impression is his "package" argument. In demonstrating that § 2 illuminated the exclusion of suffrage from § 1 of the Amendment, Justice Harlan stated: "the Amendment is a single text. It was introduced and discussed as such in the Reconstruction Committee, which reported it to Congress. It was discussed as a unit in Congress and proposed as a unit to the States, which ratified it as a unit."[37] This is one of the "serious exaggerations" Van Alstyne lays at Harlan's door: "Far from being a single text . . . the Fourteenth Amendment was a package of proposals, the more significant of which were pieced together from independent bills by different men at different times and originally debated as wholly separate amendments."[38]

Let it be admitted that the different bills were " *'originally'* debated as wholly separate amendments"; but down the line they were "discussed as a unit" in the form of an amendment combining five sections, and "ratified . . . as a unit" by the States. And though the several sections were introduced "by different men at different times," they were debated in the very same Congress and same short space of time.[39] Mem-

35. Van Alstyne 48–49.
36. Id. 44.
37. 377 U.S. at 594.
38. Van Alstyne 42–43.

39. For example, § 2 "was debated in the Senate in February and March of 1866," id. 43. In February Bingham reported the Joint Committee resolution, H. R. No. 63, a progenitor of the § 1 "privileges or immunities" and "equal protection" provisions and explained them, Bickel 33; *Globe* 1033–1034, "while Trumbull's bills on the same subject of civil rights were prominently before Congress and the country." James 83. TenBroek,

bers turned from one subject to the other and then back again, time after time. Throughout the debates discussion of "representation," which became the subject of §2, alternated with discussions of the Civil Rights Bill and the Bingham amendment, the antecedents of §1. Explicit recognition that Negro suffrage was beyond the achievable was the leitmotiv of all the discussions. Are we to assume that the members of Congress erased from their minds all reference made to suffrage because made in the context of the Bill or alternately in that of "representation"? Men do not thus insulate important discussions in airtight mental compartments. For example, Stevens referred in the course of the debate on the Amendment to the Black Codes and stated, "I need not enumerate these partial and oppressive laws," patently because they had been frequently mentioned, and to underscore the obvious said that the "civil rights bill secures the same thing."[40] With respect to Howard's proposal that citizenship be defined in §1, Fessenden said, "I should like to hear the opinion of the Chairman of the Committee on the Judiciary [Senator Trumbull], who has investigated the civil rights bill so thoroughly, on the subject."[41] Certainly Bingham regarded the Amendment as a "unit," for he said, "The second section excludes the conclusion that by the first section suffrage is subjected to congressional law."[42] Howard said that "the theory of this *whole* amendment is to leave" suffrage with the States.[43] Van Alstyne himself states that "the brevity of the three-day House debate on . . . the packaged Fourteenth Amendment bill, is probably attributable to the fact that its most significant components had previously been considered at length."[44] That no recapitulation of these

---

226, states that the "speeches in the May and June debates which deal with the meaning of §1 (whether for or against) other than by specific allusion to the Civil Rights Act do so precisely in the terms employed in the February debate."

40. *Globe* 2459.

41. Id. 2893.

42. Id. 2542.

43. Id. 3039 (emphasis added).

44. Van Alstyne 43. He considers that §2 "became a part of the Fourteenth Amendment largely through the accident of political exigency rather than the relation which it bore to the other sections of the amendment"; id. 43–44. The central "relation" was that Negro suffrage was unacceptable, both in §1 and §2, and those sections could be "packaged" in a unit that was understood by all. As the Joint Committee report stated, the §2

"components" was deemed necessary is underscored by the frequent statements that the Amendment was designed to constitutionalize the Civil Rights Act. In short, Congress was thoroughly aware of a common purpose to exclude Negro suffrage that animated discussion of the Civil Rights Bill, and of §§ 1 and 2. On Van Alstyne's own reading of Justice Harlan, § 1 was "understood at the time of its promulgation not to apply to suffrage qualifications as determined by the states";[45] it is therefore *in pari materia* with § 2 which exhibits a similar understanding. Because "they relate to the same thing, they ought all"—Civil Rights Bill, §§ 1 and 2—"to be taken into consideration in construing any one of them."[46] Plainly Van Alstyne's "package" analysis does not vitiate Harlan's documentation.

Finally, Justice Harlan correctly stated that the Joint Committee on Reconstruction, which fashioned the § 2 "representation" provision, "regularly rejected explicitly enfranchising proposals in favor of plans which would postpone enfranchisement, leave it to congressional discretion, or abandon it altogether." And, as he pointed out, "the abandonment of negro suffrage as a goal exactly corresponded with the adoption of provisions to reduce representation for discriminatory restrictions on the ballot."[47]

---

"representation" provision was adopted because an outright grant of suffrage proved unacceptable. Supra Chapter 5 at note 49.

45. Van Alstyne 38.

46. United States v. Freeman, 44 U.S. (3 How.) 556, 564 (1845). The rule is centuries old: "If any part of a statute be obscure it is proper to consider the other parts; for the words and meaning of one part of a statute frequently lead to the sense of another." Matthew Bacon, *A New Abridgment of the Laws of England*, "Statute" I (2) (3d ed. 1768).

47. Oregon v. Mitchell, 400 U.S. 112, 170–171 (1970), dissenting opinion.

# *Judicial Administration of Local Matters*

In a recent evaluation of the Court's assumption of the policymaking role, Archibald Cox wrote:

> [W]here the older activist decisions merely blocked legislative initiatives, the decisions of the 1950's and 1960's forced changes in the established legal order. The school desegregation cases overturned not only the constitutional precedents built up over three quarters of a century but the social structure of an entire region . . . The one man, one vote rule asserted that the composition of the legislatures of all but one or two of the 50 states was unconstitutional and had been unconstitutional for fifty or a hundred years [or more] . . . *New York Times Co. v. Sullivan* overturned the law of libel as it had prevailed from the beginning.

Cox comments:

> Decisions mandating reforms in the on-going activities of other branches of government often require affirmative action. The affirmative action can be secured [lacking voluntary cooperation, only] by the courts themselves embarking upon programs having typically administrative, executive and even legislative characteristics heretofore thought to make such programs unsuited to judicial undertaking [and arguably therefore never comprehended in the original grant of judicial power].
>
> The most prominent examples are the school desegregation cases. The court determines which students will be assigned to each school, how teachers shall be selected, what security measures shall be adopted, and even where new schools shall be built. When trans-

portation is required, the court directs the expenditure of hundreds of thousands of dollars.

. . . In Boston, for example, the city was induced by fear of fiscal disaster to plan the elimination of 191 teachers. The federal court went down the list, school by school, even hearing the personal pleas of individual teachers, and decided to allow 60 layoffs and disallow 131.

Desegregation decrees have all the qualities of social legislation . . . I can think of no earlier decrees with these characteristics in all constitutional history.[1]

All this on the theory that "the Constitution requires busing"!

A summary of judicial takeovers of legislative and executive prerogatives is furnished in the following article by Wayne King:

A Federal court ruling ordering Mobile to scrap its city government and replace it with a new one more favorable to blacks has generated a storm of protest in this city, including a petition drive to impeach the judge.

"This is the first time," said Mayor Lambert C. Mims in an interview, "that the Federal Government has told a free people what kind of government they must have."

"If they can do that, they can tell you what time to go to bed, what time to get up, and whether to have pork and beans for lunch."

Yesterday, a newly formed group called the Constitutional Crisis Committee began distributing petitions calling for the impeachment of Federal Judge Virgil Pittman of the Southern District of Alabama.

Judge Pittman two weeks ago ruled in a class-action suit brought by city blacks that the Mobile system of government, a three-member city commission, with each member elected by citywide vote, "precludes a black voter from an effective participation in the election system."

1. Archibald Cox, "The New Dimensions of Constitutional Adjudication," 51 Washington L. Rev. 791, 802, 814–815 (1976). [The "dominating characteristic of judicial review . . . is that it is ordinarily a *negative* power only—a power of *refusal*. The Court can forbid somebody else to act but cannot usually act itself; in the words of Professor (Thomas Reed) Powell, it 'can unmake the laws of congress, but cannot fill the gap.' " Edward S. Corwin, *The Twilight of the Supreme Court*, 122 (1934) (emphasis in the original).]

He ordered that in the municipal election next year the commission was to be replaced by a mayor elected by citywide vote and
nine council members elected from single-member districts.

Given the city's racially polarized voting pattern, this would likely
result in the election of at least three and possibly four blacks.

The court found that the vote of Mobile's blacks, 35 percent of
the population, was "diluted" by the white majority, making it unlikely to elect a black in a citywide vote.

The ruling is believed to be the most extensive intrusion by the
courts so far into legislative and executive affairs. The Mobile City
Commission was established under legislative power of the State of
Alabama in 1911 and has twice been retained by popular vote of the
city's voters.

There have been a number of recent examples of state and Federal judicial action taking over prerogatives normally reserved to the
executive or legislative branches of Government.

In Alabama, Mississippi and Louisiana, Federal courts have ordered state prisons to be brought up to standards set by the courts,
in most cases involving large expenditures of state funds.

In New York City, a Federal court ordered the aging Tombs
Prison closed and a new facility built.

In New Jersey, a state court in effect ordered the Legislature to
enact an income tax by declaring the closing of public schools until
adequate financial support was made available—possible only
through enactment of the income tax.

In Chicago, a Federal court ordered affirmative action in the hir-
ing of policemen, a step that has also been taken in numerous other
places.

In Boston, parts of the operation of public schools have been directed by Federal Judge Arthur Garrity in an effort to correct racial
imbalances.

These are part of the growing trend toward "activist" court decisions forcing the requirements of the judiciary onto other branches
of Government.

Besides the question of separation of powers among the legislative, executive and judicial branches, these and similar court actions
have raised the question of "accountability" of judges—most of

whom, particularly those on the Federal bench, are not elected but appointed for terms up to life without review.

In a speech to the new Constitutional Crisis Committee, Mr. Mims, the current Mayor under a rotation system among the commissioners, said: "This decision, if not reversed, could be the beginning of the end for local government and the open door for complete Federal takeover of community affairs."

The city has set aside $500,000, including $200,000 in Federal revenue-sharing money, to fight the decision.

Eugene McKenzie, a furniture store owner who is head of the crisis committee, said in an interview that the petitions for impeachment of Judge Pittman were based on "usurpation of the voters' right to choose their form of local government as guaranteed by the Alabama Constitution."

The petition also maintains that the 10th Amendment of the United States Constitution delegating certain powers to the Federal Government and reserving others to the states had been breached by the ruling.

Mayor Mims said in an interview that the issue was not racial. "If we'd been bad to blacks, been mean old honkies, then maybe we'd deserve this," he said. "I just hope that blacks will realize that the issue is if a judge can order this, he can order Ku Klux Klansmen into city government."

In his ruling, Judge Pittman observed that "there is no formal prohibition against blacks seeking office in Mobile" and that "since the Voting Rights Act of 1965, blacks register and vote without hindrance."

However, the judge found that "one indication that local political processes are not equally open is the fact that no black person has ever been elected to the at-large city commission."

Although the judge found no current examples of "overt gross discrimination" in city services, he said in his ruling that there were "significant differences and the sluggishness" in responding to needs in black areas as compared to white areas.

Moreover, he found significant racial imbalances in city administrative agencies appointed by the city commissioners.

Mayor Mims said that while such imbalances appear to exist,

blacks did have minority representation on all such boards and said
that appointments were made according to qualifications and not
according to race.

Judge Pittman's ruling is being appealed to the Court of Appeals
for the Fifth Circuit in New Orleans. No hearing date has been set,
and no ruling is expected before the date of the municipal elections
next August. The city will ask for a stay of the order, if necessary, to
continue to elect the commissioners as its form of Government. The
Mayor also said that the city would continue its appeals to the
United States Supreme Court if necessary.[2]

2. Wayne King, "Mobile in Uproar Over U.S. Judge Who Told It to Revise Government," N.Y. Times, Nov. 13, 1976, 1 at 38.

# The Writings of Raoul Berger

## BOOKS

*Congress v. The Supreme Court* (Cambridge, Harvard University Press, 1969).

*Impeachment: Some Constitutional Problems* (Cambridge, Harvard University Press, 1973).

*Executive Privilege: A Constitutional Myth* (Cambridge, Harvard University Press, 1974).

*Government by Judiciary: The Transformation of the Fourteenth Amendment* (Cambridge, Harvard University Press, 1977).

*Death Penalties: The Supreme Court's Obstacle Course* (Cambridge, Harvard University Press, 1982).

*Federalism: The Founders' Design* (Norman, University of Oklahoma Press, 1987).

*Selected Writings on the Constitution.* Foreword by Philip B. Kurland (Cumberland, Va., James River Press, 1987).

*The Fourteenth Amendment and the Bill of Rights* (Norman, University of Oklahoma Press, 1988).

## ARTICLES

"Usury in Instalment Sales," 2 *Law & Contemporary Problems* 148 (1935).

"Exhaustion of Administrative Remedies," 48 Yale Law Journal 981 (1939).

"From Hostage to Contract," 35 Illinois Law Review 154, 281 (1940).

"Intervention by Public Agencies in Private Litigation in the Federal Courts," 50 Yale Law Journal 65 (1940).

"Constructive Contempt: A Post-Mortem," 9 University of Chicago Law Review 602 (1942).

"Freezing Controls: The Effects of an Unlicensed Transaction" (with Boris Bittker), 47 Columbia Law Review 398 (1947).

"Meeting Competition Under the Robinson-Patman Act" (with Abraham S. Goldstein), 44 Illinois Law Review 315 (1949).

"Government Immunity From Discovery" (with Abe Krash), 50 Yale Law Journal 1451 (1950).

"The Status of Independent Producers Under the Natural Gas Act" (with Abe Krash), 30 Texas Law Review 29 (1951).

"Estoppel Against the Government," 21 University of Chicago Law Review 680 (1954).

" 'Disregarding the Corporate Entity' for Stockholders' Benefit," 55 Columbia Law Review 808 (1955).

"Removal of Judicial Functions From Federal Trade Commission to a Trade Court: A Reply to Mr. Kintner," 59 Michigan Law Review 199 (1960).

"Administrative Arbitrariness and Judicial Review," 65 Columbia Law Review 55 (1965).

"Executive Privilege v. Congressional Inquiry" (Parts 1 & 2), 12 UCLA Law Review 1044, 1288 (1965).

"Administrative Arbitrariness: A Rejoinder to Professor Davis' 'Final Word,' " 114 University of Pennsylvania Law Review 816 (1966).

"Administrative Arbitrariness: A Reply to Professor Davis," 114 University of Pennsylvania Law Review 783 (1966).

"Administrative Arbitrariness: A Sequel," 51 Minnesota Law Review 601 (1967).

"Do Regulations Really Bind Regulators?" 62 Northwestern University Law Review 137 (1967).

"Retroactive Administrative Decisions," 115 University of Pennsylvania Law Review 371 (1967).

"Administrative Arbitrariness: A Synthesis," 78 Yale Law Journal 965 (1969).

"Dr. Bonham's Case: Statutory Construction of Constitutional Theory," 117 University of Pennsylvania Law Review 521 (1969).

"Standing to Sue in Public Actions: Is It a Constitutional Requirement?" 78 Yale Law Journal 816 (1969).

"Impeachment of Judges and 'Good Behavior' Tenure," 79 Yale Law Journal 1475 (1970).

"Impeachment for 'High Crimes and Misdemeanors,' " 44 Southern California Law Review 395 (1971).

"The Presidential Monopoly of Foreign Relations," 71 Michigan Law Review 1 (1972).

"War-Making by the President," 121 University of Pennsylvania Law Review 29 (1972).

"Impeachment: A Counter Critique," 49 Washington Law Review 845 (1974).

"The Incarnation of Executive Privilege," 22 UCLA Law Review 4 (1974).

"Judicial Review: Countercriticism in Tranquility," 69 Northwestern University Law Review 390 (1974).

"The President, Congress, and the Courts," 83 Yale Law Journal 1111 (1974).

"Congressional Subpoenas to Executive Officials," 75 Columbia Law Review 865 (1975).

"Executive Privilege: A Reply to Professor Sofaer," 75 Columbia Law Review 603 (1975).

"Executive Privilege: Some Counter Criticism," 44 University of Cincinnati Law Review 166 (1975).

"Executive Privilege, Professor Rosenblum, and Higher Criticism," 1975 Duke Law Journal 921.

"Protection of Americans Abroad," 44 University of Cincinnati Law Review 741 (1975).

"Bills of Attainder: A Study of Amendment by the Court," 63 Cornell Law Review 355 (1978).

"The Constitution and the Rule of Law," 1 Western New England Law Review 261 (1978).

"Dean Green: Some Personal Recollections," 56 Texas Law Review 475 (1978).

"The Fourteenth Amendment: Facts v. Generalities," 32 Arkansas Law Review 280 (1978).

"Government by Judiciary: Some Countercriticism," 56 Texas Law Review 1125 (1978).

"War, Foreign Affairs, and Executive Secrecy," 72 Northwestern University Law Review 309 (1978).

" 'Chilling Judicial Independence': A Scarecrow," 64 Cornell Law Review 822 (1979).

"The Fourteenth Amendment: The Framers' Design," 30 South Carolina Law Review 495 (1979).

"The Fourteenth Amendment: Light From the Fifteenth," 74 Northwestern University Law Review 311 (1979).

"Government by Judiciary: John Hart Ely's Invitation," 54 Indiana Law Journal 277 (1979).

" 'Government by Judiciary': Judge Gibbons' Argument Ad Hominem," 59 Boston University Law Review 783 (1979).

" 'Law of the Land' Reconsidered," 74 Northwestern University Law Review 1 (1979).

"Must the House Consent to Cession of the Panama Canal?" 64 Cornell Law Review 275 (1979).

"The Scope of Judicial Review: An Ongoing Debate," 6 Hastings Constitutional Law Quarterly 527 (1979).

"The Scope of Judicial Review and Walter Murphy," 1979 Wisconsin Law Review 341.

" 'The Supreme Court as a Legislature': A Dissent," 64 Cornell Law Review 988 (1979).

"A Comment on 'Due Process of Law,' " 31 South Carolina Law Review 661 (1980).

"Congressional Contraction of Federal Jurisdiction," 1980 Wisconsin Law Review 801.

"The Ninth Amendment," 66 Cornell Law Review 1 (1980).

"A Political Scientist as Constitutional Lawyer: A Reply to Louis Fisher," 41 Ohio State Law Journal 147 (1980).

"The President's Unilateral Termination of the Taiwan Treaty," 75 Northwestern University Law Review 577 (1980).

"The Scope of Judicial Review: A Continuing Dialogue," 31 South Carolina Law Review 171 (1980).

"Ely's 'Theory of Judicial Review,' " 42 Ohio State Law Journal 87 (1981).

"Incorporation of the Bill of Rights in the Fourteenth Amendment: A Nine-Lived Cat," 42 Ohio State Law Journal 435 (1981).

"Paul Brest's Brief for an Imperial Judiciary," 40 Maryland Law Review 1 (1981).

"Residence Requirements for Welfare and Voting: A Post-Mortem," 42 Ohio State Law Journal 853 (1981).

"Soifer to the Rescue of History," 32 South Carolina Law Review 427 (1981).

"Paul Dimond Fails to 'Meet Raoul Berger on Interpretivist Grounds,' " 43 Ohio State Law Journal 285 (1982).

"Incorporation of the Bill of Rights: A Reply to Michael Curtis' Response," 44 Ohio State Law Journal 1 (1983).

"Insulation of Judicial Usurpation: A Comment on Lawrence Sager's Court-Stripping Polemic," 44 Ohio State Law Journal 611 (1983).

"Mark Tushnet's Critique of Interpretivism," 51 George Washington Law Review 532 (1983).

"Michael Perry's Functional Justification for Judicial Activism," 8 University of Dayton Law Review 465 (1983).

"A Study of Youthful Omniscience: Gerald Lynch on Judicial Review," 36 Arkansas Law Review 215 (1983).

"The Activist Legacy of the New Deal Court," 59 Washington Law Review 751 (1984).

"Death Penalties and Hugo Bedau: A Crusading Philosopher Goes Overboard," 45 Ohio State Law Journal 863 (1984).

"G. Edward White's Apology for Judicial Activism," 63 Texas Law Review 367 (1984).

"Lawyering v. Philosophizing: Facts or Fancies," 9 University of Dayton Law Review 171 (1984).

"A Response to D. A. J. Richards' Defense of Freewheeling Constitutional Adjudication," 59 Indiana Law Journal 339 (1984).

"Constitutional Law and the Constitution," 19 Suffolk University Law Review 1 (1985).

"Benno Schmidt v. Rehnquist and Scalia," 47 Ohio State Law Journal 709 (1986).

"Cottrol's Failed Rescue Mission," 37 Boston College Law Review 481 (1986).

"McAffee v. Berger: A Youthful Debunker's Rampage," 22 Willamette Law Review 1 (1986).

"New Theories of 'Interpretation': The Activist Flight From the Constitution," 47 Ohio State Law Journal 1 (1986).

" 'Original Intention' in Historical Perspective," 54 George Washington Law Review 296 (1986).

"Some Reflections on Interpretivism," 55 George Washington Law Review 1 (1986).

"Death Penalties: A Response to Stephen Gillers," 24 Willamette Law Review 1 (1988).

"Federalism: The Founders' Design: A Response to Michael McConnell," 57 George Washington Law Review 51 (1988).

"Justice Brennan v. The Constitution," 29 Boston College Law Review 787 (1988).

"Originalist Theories of Constitutional Interpretation," 73 Cornell Law Review 350 (1988).

"The Founders' Views—According to Jefferson Powell," 67 Texas Law Review 1033 (1989).

"History, Judicial Revisionism, and J. M. Balkin," 1989 Brigham Young University Law Review 759.

"Original Intent and Leonard Levy," 42 Rutgers Law Review 255 (1989).

"Fantasizing About the Fourteenth Amendment," 1990 Wisconsin Law Review 1043.

"The Jury's Role in Capital Cases Is Immune From Judicial Interference," 1990 Brigham Young University Law Review 639.

"Justice Samuel Chase v. Thomas Jefferson: A Response to Stephen Presser," 1990 Brigham Young University Law Review 873.

"The Ninth Amendment: The Beckoning Mirage," 42 Rutgers Law Review 951 (1990).

"Robert Bork's Contribution to Original Intention," 84 Northwestern University Law Review 1167 (1990).

"Activist Censures of Robert Bork," 85 Northwestern University Law Review 993 (1991).

"Incorporation of the Bill of Rights: A Response to Michael Zuckert," 26 Georgia Law Review 1 (1991).

"Lawrence Church on the Scope of Judicial Review and Original Intention," 70 North Carolina Law Review 113 (1991).

"Original Intent: Bittker v. Berger," 1991 Brigham Young University Law Review 1201.

"Original Intent and Boris Bittker," 66 Indiana Law Journal 723 (1991).

"Bruce Ackerman on Interpretation: A Critique," 1992 Brigham Young University Law Review 1035.

"Natural Law and Judicial Review: Reflections of an Earthbound Lawyer," 61 University of Cincinnati Law Review 5 (1992).

" 'Original Intent': A Response to Hans Baade," 70 Texas Law Review 1535 (1992).

"The Transfiguration of Samuel Chase: A Rebuttal," 1992 Brigham Young University Law Review 559.

"Activist Indifference to Facts," 61 Tennessee Law Review 9 (1993).

"Constitutional Interpretation and Activist Fantasies," 82 Kentucky Law Journal 1 (1993).

"Incorporation of the Bill of Rights: Ahkil Amar's Wishing Well," 62 University of Cincinnati Law Review 1 (1993).

"Original Intent: The Rage of Hans Baade," 71 North Carolina Law Review 1151 (1993).

"An Anatomy of False Analysis: Original Intent," 1994 Brigham Young University Law Review 715.

"The Ninth Amendment, as Perceived by Randy Barnett," 88 Northwestern University Law Review 1508 (1994).

"Suzannah and—The Ninth Amendment," 1994 Brigham Young University Law Review 51.

"A Lawyer Lectures a Judge," 18 Harvard Journal of Law and Public Policy 851 (1995).

"Liberty and the Constitution," 29 Georgia Law Review 585 (1995).

"Judicial Manipulation of the Commerce Clause," 17 Texas Law Review 695 (1996).

"The 'Original Intent'—As Perceived by Michael McConnell," 91 Northwestern University Law Review 242 (1996).

"Jack Rakove's Rendition of Original Meaning," 72 Indiana Law Journal 619 (1997).

"Ronald Dworkin's 'Moral Reading of the Constitution,' " 72 Indiana Law Journal [no. 4] (1997).

# Bibliography

### I. FEDERAL DOCUMENTS

Act of April 9, 1866, Ch. 21, 14 Statutes 27.

*Annals of the Congress of the United States*, 1789–1824, 42 vols. (Washington, Gales & Seaton, 1834).

Avins, Alfred, ed. *The Reconstruction Amendments' Debates* (Richmond, Va., Virginia Commission on Constitutional Government, 1967).

*The Congressional Globe*, 1833–1873, 46 vols. (Blair & Rives, 1834–1873).

*Hearings on Executive Privilege Before the Subcommittee on the Separation of Powers of the Senate Committee on the Judiciary*, 92d Congress, 1st Session (July 1971).

*Hearings on the Supreme Court Before the Subcommittee on the Separation of Powers of the Senate Committee on the Judiciary*, 90th Congress, 2d Session (June 1968).

Richardson, James D., comp. *The Messages and Papers of the Presidents* (Washington, Government Printing Office, 1889–1905).

### II. BOOKS

Acheson, Dean. *Morning and Noon* (Boston, Houghton Mifflin, 1965).

Ackerman, Bruce. *We the People: Foundations* (Cambridge, Harvard University Press, 1991).

Adams, Henry. *John Randolph* (Boston and New York, Houghton Mifflin, 1882).

Adams, John Quincy. *Life in a New England Town: 1787, 1788. Diary of John Quincy Adams* (Boston, Little, Brown, 1903).

Adams, Samuel. *The Writings of Samuel Adams*, Harry A. Cushing, ed. 4 vols. (New York, G. P. Putnam's Sons, 1904–1908).

Allen, Sir C. K. *Law in the Making*, 6th ed. (Oxford, Clarendon Press, 1958).

Bacon, Francis. *Selected Writings of Francis Bacon* (New York, Mod. Lib. ed., 1937).

Bacon, Matthew. *A New Abridgment of the Laws of England*, 8 vols., 3d ed. (London, 1768).

Bailyn, Bernard. *The Ideological Origins of the American Constitution* (Cambridge, Harvard University Press, 1967).

493

Baldwin, Henry. *A General View of the Origin and Nature of the Constitution and Government of the United States* (Philadelphia, J. C. Clark, 1837).

Barnett, Randy E., ed. *The Rights Retained by the People*, 2 vols. (Fairfax, Va., George Mason University Press, 1993).

Bemis, Samuel F. *John Quincy Adams and the Foundation of American Foreign Policy* (New York, Knopf, 1949).

———— . *John Quincy Adams and the Union* (New York, Knopf, 1956).

Benedict, Michael Les. *A Compromise of Principle: Conservative Republicans and Reconstruction, 1863–1869* (New York, Norton, 1974).

Berenson, Bernard. *Conversations With Berenson* [by] Umberto Morra. Translated from the Italian by Florence Hammond (Boston, Houghton Mifflin, 1965).

Berger, Raoul. *Congress v. The Supreme Court* (Cambridge, Harvard University Press, 1969).

————. *Executive Privilege: A Constitutional Myth* (Cambridge, Harvard University Press, 1974).

————. *The Fourteenth Amendment and the Bill of Rights* (Norman, University of Oklahoma Press, 1989).

————. *Government by Judiciary: The Transformation of the Fourteenth Amendment* (Cambridge, Harvard University Press, 1977).

————. *Impeachment: The Constitutional Problems* (Cambridge, Harvard University Press, 1973).

————. *Selected Writings on the Constitution* (Cumberland, Va., James River Press, 1987).

Biancolli, Louis. *The Book of Great Conversations* (New York, Simon and Schuster, 1948).

Bickel, Alexander M. *The Least Dangerous Branch: The Supreme Court at the Bar of Politics* (Indianapolis, Bobbs-Merrill, 1962).

————. *The Supreme Court and the Idea of Progress* (New York, Harper & Row, 1978).

Black, Charles L., Jr. *The People and the Court: Judicial Review in a Democracy* (New York, Macmillan, 1960).

Blackstone, William. *Commentaries on the Laws of England*, 4 vols. (London, 1765–1769).

Boorstin, Daniel J. *The Discoverers* (New York, Random House, 1983).

————, ed. *American Primer* (New York, Dutton, 1968).

Bork, Robert H. *The Tempting of America: The Political Seduction of the Law* (New York, Free Press, 1990).

Boswell, James. *The Life of Samuel Johnson*, Everyman ed. (New York, Knopf, 1992).

Bowen, Catherine D. *Francis Bacon: The Temper of a Man* (Boston, Little, Brown, 1963).

Bracton, Henry de. *Treatise on the Laws and Customs of England*, Samuel Thorne, ed. (Cambridge, Harvard University Press, 1968).

Brest, Paul. *Processes of Constitutional Decisionmaking: Cases and Materials* (Boston, Little, Brown, 1975).

Brinton, Crane, John B. Christopher, and Robert L. Wolff. *A History of Civilization* (Englewood Cliffs, N.J., Prentice-Hall, 1960).

Brock, W. R. *An American Crisis: Congress and Reconstruction, 1865–1867* (London, Macmillan, 1963).

Brodie, Fawn M. *Thaddeus Stevens: Scourge of the South* (New York, Norton, 1959).

Brooks, Van Wyck. *Days of the Phoenix* (New York, Dutton, 1957).

Butterfield, Sir Herbert. *George III and the Historians* (New York, Macmillan, 1969).

Cahn, Edmond N., ed. *Supreme Court and Supreme Law* (Bloomington, Indiana University Press, 1954).

Cardozo, Benjamin N. *The Growth of the Law* (New Haven, Yale University Press, 1924).

———. *The Nature of the Judicial Process* (New Haven, Yale University Press, 1921).

———. *The Paradoxes of Legal Science* (New York, Columbia University Press, 1928).

———. *Selected Writings of Benjamin Cardozo*, Margaret Hall, ed. (New York, Fallon, 1947).

Choper, Jesse H. *Judicial Review and the National Political Process* (Chicago, University of Chicago Press, 1980).

Chrimes, S. B. *English Constitutional Ideas in the Fifteenth Century* (Cambridge, Cambridge University Press, 1936).

Clark, Ronald W. *Einstein: The Life and Times* (New York, Thomas Y. Crowell, 1971).

Coke, Edward. *Institutes of the Laws of England*, 4 vols. (London, 1628–1644).

Commager, Henry Steele, ed. *Documents of American History*, 7th ed. (New York, Appleton-Century, 1963).

Cooley, Thomas. *A Treatise on the Constitutional Limitations*, 8th ed. (Boston, Little, Brown, 1927).

Corwin, Edward S. *American Constitutional History*, A. T. Mason and G. Garvey, eds. (New York, Harper & Row, 1964).

———. *The Doctrine of Judicial Review: Its Legal and Historical Basis and Other Essays* (Princeton, Princeton University Press, 1914).

———. *The Twilight of the Supreme Court* (New Haven, Yale University Press, 1934).

Cover, Robert. *Justice Accused: Antislavery and the Judicial Process* (New Haven, Yale University Press, 1975).

Cox, Archibald. *The Role of the Supreme Court in American Government* (New York, Oxford University Press, 1976).

Curtis, Michael B. *No State Shall Abridge: The Fourteenth Amendment and the Bill of Rights* (Durham, Duke University Press, 1986).

Donald, David. *Charles Sumner and the Coming of the Civil War* (New York, Knopf, 1960).

———. *Charles Sumner and the Rights of Man* (New York, Knopf, 1970).

———. *The Politics of Reconstruction* (Baton Rouge, Louisiana State University Press, 1965).

Durant, Will. *The Age of Faith* (New York, Simon and Schuster, 1950).

Dwarris, Fortunatus. *A General Treatise on Statutes* (London, W. Benning, 1848).

Elkins, Stanley, and Eric L. McKitrick. *The Age of Federalism: The Early American Republic, 1788–1800* (Oxford, Oxford University Press, 1993).

Elliot, Jonathan, ed. *Debates in the Several State Conventions on the Adoption of the Federal Constitution*, 4 vols., 2d ed. (Washington, D.C., J. Elliot, 1836).

Elliott, Ward E. Y. *The Rise of a Guardian Democracy* (Cambridge, Harvard University Press, 1974).

Ely, John H. *Democracy and Distrust: A Theory of Judicial Review* (Cambridge, Harvard University Press, 1980).

Fairman, Charles. *Mr. Justice Miller and the Supreme Court* (Cambridge, Harvard University Press, 1939).

———. *Reconstruction and Reunion, 1864–1888*, vol. 6, pt. 1, of *History of the Supreme Court of the United States* (New York, Macmillan, 1971).

Farrand, Max, ed. *The Records of the Federal Convention of 1787*, 4 vols. (New Haven, Yale University Press, 1911).

*The Federalist* (New York, Modern Library ed., 1937).

*The Federalist Papers.* Introduction and commentary by Garry Wills (New York, Bantam, 1982).

Flack, Horace. *The Adoption of the Fourteenth Amendment* (Baltimore, Johns Hopkins University Press, 1908).

Frankfort, Henri A., et al. *The Intellectual Adventure of Ancient Man: An Essay on Speculative Thought in the Ancient Near East* (Chicago, University of Chicago Press, 1977).

Frankfurter, Felix. *The Commerce Clause Under Marshall, Taney, and Waite* (Chapel Hill, University of North Carolina Press, 1937).

———. *Law and Politics*, A. Macleish and E. F. Prichard, eds. (New York, Harcourt Brace, 1938).

———. *Mr. Justice Holmes and the Supreme Court* (Cambridge, Harvard University Press, 1938).

———. *Of Law and Men*, Philip Elman, ed. (New York, Harcourt Brace, 1956).

Freedman, M., ed. *Roosevelt and Frankfurter: Their Correspondence, 1928–1945* (Boston, Little, Brown, 1967).

Gay, Peter, et al., eds. *Historians at Work*, 4 vols. (New York, Irvington Publishers, 1975).

Gibbon, Edward. *The History of the Decline and Fall of the Roman Empire* (New York, Nottingham Society, undated).

Gillette, William. *The Right to Vote: Politics and the Passage of the Fifteenth Amendment* (Baltimore, Johns Hopkins University Press, 1965).

Goebel, Julius. *Antecedents and Beginnings to 1801*, vol. 1 of *History of the Supreme Court of the United States* (New York, Macmillan, 1971).

Goebel, Julius, and T. R. Naughton. *Law Enforcement in Colonial New York, 1664–1776* (Montclair, N.J., Patterson Smith, 1970).

Gough, John W. *Fundamental Law in English Constitutional History* (Oxford, Clarendon Press, 1955).

Graglia, Lino A. *Disaster by Decree* (Ithaca, Cornell University Press, 1976).

Graham, Howard Jay. *Everyman's Constitution* (New York, Norton, 1968).

*The Great Debate: Interpreting Our Constitution* (Washington, D.C., Federalist Society, 1986).

Griffith, Kathryn. *Judge Learned Hand and the Role of the Federal Judiciary* (Norman, University of Oklahoma Press, 1973).

Gunther, Gerald, ed. *John Marshall's Defense of McCulloch v. Maryland* (Stanford, Stanford University Press, 1969).

Haines, Charles G. *The Revival of Natural Law Concepts* (Cambridge, Harvard University Press, 1930).

Hale, Sir Matthew. *History of the Pleas of the Crown* (London, 1736).

Hamilton, Alexander. *The Papers of Alexander Hamilton*, H. C. Syrett and J. E. Cooke, eds., 27 vols. (New York, Columbia University Press, 1961–1981).

———. *Works of Alexander Hamilton*, H. C. Lodge, ed., 12 vols. (New York, Knickerbocker Press, 1904).

Hand, Learned. *The Bill of Rights* (Cambridge, Harvard University Press, 1962).

———. *The Spirit of Liberty: Papers and Addresses of Learned Hand*, Irving Dilliard, ed. (New York, Knopf, 1952).

Harris, Robert J. *The Quest for Equality* (Baton Rouge, Louisiana State University Press, 1960).

Hart, Henry M., and Albert Sacks. "The Legal Process: Basic Problems in the Making and Application of Law" (unpublished manuscript, 1958).

Hatton, Christopher. *A Treatise Concerning Statutes and Acts of Parliament and the Exposition Thereof* (London, 1677).

Hauser, Arnold. *The Social History of Art*, 4 vols. (New York, Vintage Books, undated).

Heller, Francis H. *The Sixth Amendment to the Constitution of the United States* (Lawrence, University of Kansas Press, 1951).

Hickok, Eugene W., ed. *The Bill of Rights: Original Meaning and Current Understanding* (Charlottesville, University Press of Virginia, 1991).

Himmelfarb, Gertrude. *Victorian Minds* (New York, Knopf, 1968).

Hobbes, Thomas. *Leviathan* (Cambridge, Cambridge University Press, 1991).

Hockett, H. C. *The Constitutional History of the United States, 1826–1876* (New York, Macmillan, 1939).

Hofstadter, Richard. *Anti-Intellectualism in American Life* (New York, Knopf, 1963).

Holmes, Oliver Wendell, Jr. *Collected Legal Papers* (New York, Harcourt Brace, 1920).

———. *The Common Law* (Boston, Little, Brown, 1881).

Hook, Sidney. *Philosophy and Public Policy* (Carbondale, Southern Illinois University Press, 1980).

Horwitz, Morton J. *The Transformation of American Law* (Cambridge, Harvard University Press, 1977).

Howe, Mark de W., ed. *Holmes-Laski Letters: The Correspondence of Mr. Justice Holmes and Harold J. Laski* (Cambridge, Harvard University Press, 1953).

Hughes, Charles Evans. *The Autobiographical Notes of Charles Evans Hughes*, D. J. Danielski and J. S. Tulchin, eds. (Cambridge, Harvard University Press, 1973).

———. *The Supreme Court of the United States: Its Foundation, Methods, and Achievements, an Interpretation* (New York, Columbia University Press, 1928).

Hurst, James Willard. *The Legitimacy of the Business Corporation in the Law of the United States* (Charlottesville, University Press of Virginia, 1970).

Hyman, Harold M. *A More Perfect Union* (New York, Knopf, 1973).

————, ed. *New Frontiers of the American Reconstruction* (Urbana, University of Illinois Press, 1966).

Jackson, Robert H. *The Struggle for Judicial Supremacy: A Study of a Crisis in American Political Power* (New York, Knopf, 1941).

James, Joseph B. *The Framing of the Fourteenth Amendment* (Urbana, University of Illinois Press, 1965).

Jefferson, Thomas. *Writings*, Paul Leicester Ford, ed., 10 vols. (New York, G. P. Putnam's Sons, 1892–1899).

————. *The Writings of Thomas Jefferson*, Andrew A. Lipscomb, ed., 20 vols. (Washington, D. C., 1903).

Keller, Morton. *Affairs of State* (Cambridge, Harvard University Press, 1977).

Kendrick, Benjamin. *The Journal of the Joint Committee of Fifteen on Reconstruction* (New York, Columbia University Press, 1914).

Kent, James. *Commentaries on American Law*, 9th ed., 4 vols. (Boston, Little, Brown, 1858).

Kluger, Richard. *Simple Justice* (New York, Knopf, 1976).

Kurland, Philip B. *Politics, the Constitution, and the Warren Court* (Chicago, University of Chicago Press, 1970).

Lacy, Dan. *The White Use of Black in America* (New York, Atheneum, 1972).

Lash, Joseph P. *From the Diaries of Felix Frankfurter* (New York, Norton, 1975).

Lerner, M., ed. *The Mind and Faith of Justice Holmes* (Garden City, N.Y., Halcyon House, 1943).

Levy, Leonard. *Against the Law: The Nixon Court and Criminal Justice* (New York, Harper & Row, 1974).

————, et al., eds. *Encyclopedia of the American Constitution*, 4 vols. (New York, Macmillan, 1986).

————. *Judgments: Essays in American Constitutional History* (Chicago, Quadrangle Books, 1972).

————, ed. *Judicial Review and the Supreme Court* (New York, Harper & Row, 1967).

————. *Original Intent and the Framers' Constitution* (New York, Macmillan, 1988).

————, ed. *The Supreme Court Under Earl Warren* (New York, Quadrangle Books, 1972).

Locke, John. *An Essay Concerning Human Understanding*, Raymond Wilburn, ed. (New York, Dutton, 1947).

————. *Two Treatises of Government*, Peter Laslett, ed. (Cambridge, Cambridge University Press, 1960).

London, Ephraim, ed. *The World of Law: The Law as Literature* (New York, Simon and Schuster, 1960).

Lusky, Louis. *By What Right?* (Charlottesville, Michie, 1975).

McClellan, James. *Joseph Story and the American Constitution: A Study in Political and Legal Thought With Selected Writings* (Norman, University of Oklahoma Press, 1971).

McCloskey, Robert G. *The American Supreme Court* (Chicago, University of Chicago Press, 1960).

McDonald, Forrest. *The American Presidency: An Intellectual History* (Lawrence, University Press of Kansas, 1994).

———. *Novus Ordo Seclorum: The Intellectual Origins of the Constitution* (Lawrence, University Press of Kansas, 1985).

McDowell, Gary L. *The Constitution and Contemporary Constitutional Theory* (Cumberland, Va., Center for Judicial Studies, 1985).

McIlwain, Charles H. *Constitutionalism: Ancient and Modern*, rev. ed. (Ithaca, Cornell University Press, 1947).

———. *The High Court of Parliament and Its Supremacy* (New Haven, Yale University Press, 1910).

McKitrick, Eric L. *Andrew Johnson and Reconstruction* (Chicago, University of Chicago Press, 1960).

McRee, G. J. *Life and Correspondence of James Iredell*, 2 vols. (New York, Appleton, 1857–1858).

Madison, James. *Letters and Other Writings of James Madison*, congressional edition, 4 vols. (Philadelphia, J. B. Lippincott, 1865).

———. *Writings*, Gaillard Hunt, ed., 9 vols. (New York, Putnam, 1900–1910).

Marshall, Burke, ed. *A Workable Government? The Constitution After 200 Years* (New York, W. W. Norton, 1987).

Mason, Alpheus T. *Brandeis: A Free Man's Life* (New York, Viking Press, 1946).

———. *Harlan Fiske Stone: Pillar of the Law* (New York, Viking Press, 1956).

———. *Security Through Freedom: American Political Thought and Practice* (Ithaca, Cornell University Press, 1955).

———. *The States Rights Debate: Antifederalism and the Constitution* (Englewood Cliffs, N.J., Prentice-Hall, 1964).

———. *The Supreme Court: Palladium of Freedom* (Ann Arbor, University of Michigan Press, 1962).

Mason, Alpheus T., and W. M. Beaney. *American Constitutional Law* (Englewood Cliffs, N.J., Prentice-Hall, 1954).

Mencken, Henry T. *Treatise of Right and Wrong* (New York, Knopf, 1934).

Mendelson, Wallace. *Justices Black and Frankfurter: Conflict in the Court* (Chicago, University of Chicago Press, 1961).

———. *The Supreme Court: Law and Discretion* (Indianapolis, Bobbs-Merrill, 1967).

Meyer, Michael J., and William A. Parent, eds. *The Constitution of Rights: Human Dignity and American Values* (Ithaca, Cornell University Press, 1992).

Meyers, Marvin, ed. *The Mind of the Founders: Sources of Political Thought of James Madison* (Indianapolis, Bobbs-Merrill, 1973).

Miller, Charles A. *The Supreme Court and the Uses of History* (Cambridge, Harvard University Press, 1969).

Morgan, J. H. *John, Viscount Morley; An Appreciation and Some Reminiscences* (Boston, Houghton Mifflin, 1924).

Morison, Samuel Eliot. *The Oxford History of the American People* (New York, Oxford University Press, 1965).

Muller, Herbert. *Uses of the Past* (New York, Oxford University Press, 1952).

Murphy, Paul. *The Constitution in Crisis Times, 1918–1969* (New York, Harper & Row, 1972).

Nelson, William E. *The Fourteenth Amendment: From Political Principle to Judicial Doctrine* (Cambridge, Harvard University Press, 1988).

Nevins, Allan. *The Emergence of Lincoln* (New York, Charles Scribner's Sons, 1950).

Nock, Albert J. *Jefferson* (New York, Harcourt, Brace and Company, 1926).

Oakeshott, Michael. *Rationalism in Politics and Other Essays* (London, Methuen and Co., 1962).

Onuf, Peter, ed. *Jeffersonian Legacies* (Charlottesville, University Press of Virginia, 1993).

*Oxford Dictionary of Quotations*, 3d ed. (New York, Oxford University Press, 1979).

Padover, Saul K. *Jefferson*, abridged ed. (New York, Penguin, 1970).

Paludan, Phillip S. *A Covenant With Death* (Urbana, University of Illinois Press, 1975).

Patterson, Caleb P. *The Constitutional Principles of Thomas Jefferson* (Austin, University of Texas Press, 1953).

Pendleton, Edmund. *Letters and Papers*, D. J. Mays, ed., 2 vols. (Charlottesville, University Press of Virginia, 1967).

Perry, Michael J. *The Constitution, the Courts, and Human Rights* (New Haven, Yale University Press, 1982).

Pocock, J. G. A. *The Ancient Constitution and Feudal Law: A Study of English Historical Thought in the Seventeenth Century* (Cambridge, Cambridge University Press, 1987).

Poore, Benjamin Perley, ed. *Federal and State Constitutions, Colonial Charters,* 2 vols. (Washington, D.C., Government Printing Office, 1877).

Posner, Richard. *The Federal Courts: Crisis and Reform* (Cambridge, Harvard University Press, 1985).

Powell, J. *Essay Upon the Law of Contracts and Agreements,* 2 vols. (London, 1790).

Powell, Thomas Reed. *Vagaries and Varieties in Constitutional Interpretation* (New York, Columbia University Press, 1956).

Randall, J. R. *The Making of the Modern Mind* (Boston, Houghton Mifflin, 1940).

Ray, Gordon N. *Thackeray: The Age of Wisdom, 1847–1863* (New York, McGraw Hill, 1958).

Roberts, C., ed. *Has the Court Too Much Power* (1974).

Roberts, Owen. *The Court and the Constitution* (Cambridge, Harvard University Press, 1951).

Rodell, Fred. *Nine Men* (New York, Random House, 1955).

Rossiter, Clinton. *Alexander Hamilton and the Constitution* (New York, Harcourt, Brace & World, 1964).

Rowse, A. L. *A Cornishman at Oxford* (London, J. Cape, 1965).

Rutherforth, Thomas. *Institutes of Natural Law,* 2 vols. (Cambridge, J. Bentham, 1754–1756).

Samuels, Ernest. *Henry Adams: The Major Phase* (Cambridge, Harvard University Press, 1964).

Schlesinger, Arthur M., Jr. *The Disuniting of America* (New York, Norton, 1992).

Schwartz, Bernard, ed. *The Fourteenth Amendment: Centennial Volume* (New York, New York University Press, 1970).

Selden, John. *Table Talk: Being the Discourses of John Selden, Esq.* (London, 1696).

Shapiro, Martin. *Law and Politics in the Supreme Court* (New York, Free Press of Glencoe, 1964).

Skidelsky, Robert. *John Maynard Keynes: Hopes Betrayed, 1883–1920* (New York, Viking Press, 1986).

Smith, Homer W. *Man and His Gods* (Boston, Little, Brown, 1953).

Smith, Page. *John Adams,* 2 vols. (Garden City, N.Y., Doubleday, 1962).

Speaight, Robert. *The Life of Hilaire Belloc* (London, Hollis & Carter, 1957).

Stampp, Kenneth M. *The Peculiar Institution* (New York, Vintage Books, 1956).

Storing, Herbert J., ed. *The Complete Antifederalist,* 7 vols. (Chicago, University of Chicago Press, 1981).

Story, Joseph. *Commentaries on the Constitution of the United States,* 2 vols., 5th ed. (Boston, Little, Brown, 1905).

Strickland, S. P., ed. *Hugo Black and the Supreme Court: A Symposium.* Foreword by C. L. Black (Indianapolis, Bobbs-Merrill, 1967).

Swift, Zephaniah. *A System of the Laws of the State of Connecticut*, 2 vols. (Windham, Conn., 1795–1796).

Swiggett, Howard. *The Extraordinary Mr. Morris* (Garden City, N.Y., Doubleday, 1952).

TenBroek, Jacobus. *Equal Under Law* (London, Collier Books, 1965).

Thorne, Samuel, ed. *A Discourse Upon the Exposicion & Understandinge of Statutes* (San Marino, Calif., Huntington Library, 1942).

Tocqueville, Alexis de. *Democracy in America*, 2 vols. (New York, Colonial Press, 1900).

Trevelyan, G. M. *An Autobiography and Other Essays* (Salem, N.H., Ayer Company Publishers, 1949).

———. *Illustrated History of England* (London, Longmans, Green, 1956).

Twiss, Benjamin R. *Lawyers and the Constitution* (Princeton, Princeton University Press, 1942).

Van Doren, Carl. *Benjamin Franklin* (New York, Viking Press, 1968).

Washington, George. *Writings*, J. Fitzpatrick, ed., 39 vols. (Washington, D.C., Government Printing Office, 1940).

White, G. Edward. *The American Judicial Tradition* (New York, Oxford University Press, 1976).

———. *Earl Warren: A Public Life* (New York, Oxford University Press, 1982).

Wilson, Edmund. *Europe Without a Baedeker* (New York, Farrar Strauss, 1966).

———. *Patriotic Gore* (New York, Oxford University Press, 1962).

Wilson, James. *The Works of James Wilson*, R. G. McCloskey, ed., 2 vols. (Cambridge, Harvard University Press, 1967).

Wood, Gordon S. *The Creation of the American Republic, 1776–1789* (Chapel Hill, University of North Carolina Press, 1969).

———. *The Radicalism of the American Revolution* (New York, Knopf, 1991).

Woodward, C. Vann. *The Burden of Southern History* (Baton Rouge, Louisiana State University Press, 1960).

Wright, Benjamin F. *American Interpretations of Natural Law: A Study in the History of Political Thought* (Cambridge, Harvard University Press, 1931).

———. *The Growth of American Constitutional Law* (New York, Henry Holt, 1942).

### III. ARTICLES

Abraham, Henry J. " 'Equal Justice Under Law' or 'Justice at Any Cost' "? The Judicial Role Revisited: Reflections on *Government by Judiciary*," 6 Hastings Constitutional Law Quarterly 467 (1979).

Adler, Mortimer. "Robert Bork: The Lessons to Be Learned," 84 Northwestern University Law Review 1121 (1990).

Alexander, Larry A. "Modern Equal Protection Theories: A Metatheoretical Taxonomy and Critique," 42 Ohio State Law Journal 3 (1981).

Alfange, Dean, Jr. "On Judicial Policymaking and Constitutional Change: Another Look at the 'Original Intent' Theory of Constitutional Interpretation," 5 Hastings Constitutional Law Quarterly 603 (1978).

Allen, Francis. "The Constitution: The Civil War Amendments: XIII–XV," in Daniel J. Boorstin ed., *American Primer* 165 (1968).

Amar, Akhil R. "The Bill of Rights and the Fourteenth Amendment," 101 Yale Law Journal 1193 (1992).

Annan, Noel. "Introduction," in Isaiah Berlin, *Personal Impressions* (1981).

Arnold, Thurman. "Professor Hart's Theology," 73 Harvard Law Review 1298 (1960).

Aron, Raymond. "Pensées," New York Times, October 23, 1981, at E19.

Auden, W. H. "Introduction," in Sydney Smith, *Selected Writings of Sydney Smith* (W. H. Auden ed. 1956).

Auerbach, Carl. "The Reapportionment Cases: One Person, One Vote—One Vote, One Value," 1964 Supreme Court Review 1.

Baade, Hans W. " 'Original Intention': Raoul Berger's Fake Antique," 70 North Carolina Law Review 1523 (1992).

Balkin, J. M. "Constitutional Interpretation and the Problem of History," 63 New York University Law Review 911 (1988).

Bell, Derrick. "Book Review," 76 Columbia Law Review 350 (1976).

———. "The Burden of Brown on Blacks: History Based on Observations of a Landmark Decision," 7 North Carolina Central Law Journal 25 (1975).

Beloff, Max. "Arbiters of America's Destiny," The Times Higher Education Supplement (London), April 7, 1978, at 11.

Berger, Raoul. "Bruce Ackerman on Interpretation: A Critique," 1992 Brigham Young University Law Review 1035.

———. "Constitutional Interpretation and Activist Fantasies," 82 Kentucky Law Journal 1 (1993).

———. "Constructive Contempt: A Post-Mortem," 9 University of Chicago Law Review 602 (1942).

———. "Cottrol's Failed Rescue Mission," 37 Boston College Law Review 787 (1988).

———. "The Founders' Views—According to Jefferson Powell," 67 Texas Law Review 1033 (1989).

———. "The Fourteenth Amendment: Light from the Fifteenth," 74 Northwestern University Law Review 311 (1979).

———. " 'Government by Judiciary': Judge Gibbons' Argument Ad Hominem," 59 Boston University Law Review 783 (1979).

———. "History, Judicial Revisionism, and J. M. Balkin," 1989 Brigham Young University Law Review 759.

———. "Incorporation of the Bill of Rights: A Nine-Lived Cat," 42 Ohio State Law Journal 435 (1981).

———. "Incorporation of the Bill of Rights: A Reply to Michael Curtis' Response," 44 Ohio State Law Journal 1 (1983).

———. "Incorporation of the Bill of Rights: A Response to Michael Zuckert," 26 Georgia Law Review 1 (1991).

———. "Judicial Review: Counter Criticism in Tranquillity," 69 Northwestern University Law Review 390 (1974).

———. "Justice Brennan's 'Human Dignity' and Constitutional Interpretation," in Michael J. Meyer and William A. Parent, eds., *The Constitution of Rights: Human Dignity and American Values* (1992).

———. "Justice Brennan vs. the Constitution," 29 Boston College Law Review 787 (1988).

———. "Natural Law and Judicial Review: Reflections of an Earthbound Lawyer," 61 University of Cincinnati Law Review 5 (1992).

———. "Original Intent: The Rage of Hans Baade," 71 North Carolina Law Review 1523 (1993).

———. " 'Original Intent': A Response to Hans Baade," 70 Texas Law Review 1535 (1992).

———. "Original Intention in Historical Perspective," 54 George Washington Law Review 296 (1986).

———. "Paul Brest's Brief for an Imperial Judiciary," 40 Maryland Law Review 1 (1981).

———. "Soifer to the Rescue of History," 32 South Carolina Law Review 427 (1981).

———. "Some Reflections on Interpretivism," 55 George Washington Law Review 1 (1986).

———. "War-Making by the President," 121 University of Pennsylvania Law Review 29 (1972).

Bickel, Alexander M. "Is the Warren Court Too 'Political'?" *The New York Times Magazine*, September 25, 1966, in Leonard Levy, ed., *The Supreme Court Under Earl Warren* 216 (1972).

————. "The Original Understanding and the Segregation Decision," 69 Harvard Law Review 1 (1955).

Bickel, Alexander M., and Harry Wellington. "Legislative Purpose and the Judicial Process: The Lincoln Mills Case," 71 Harvard Law Review 1 (1957).

Bishop, Joseph W., Jr. "The Warren Court Is Not Likely to Be Overruled," *The New York Times Magazine*, September 7, 1969, in L. Levy, ed., *The Supreme Court Under Earl Warren* 93 (1972).

————. "What Is a Liberal—Who Is a Conservative?" 62 *Commentary* 47 (September 1976).

Black, Charles L., Jr. Address, "The Judicial Power as Guardian of Liberties, Before a Symposium on 'The Supreme Court and Constitutional Liberties in Modern America,' " Wayne State University, Detroit, Mich., October 16, 1976.

Bork, Robert H. "Address," in *The Great Debate: Interpreting Our Written Constitution* (1986).

————. "Foreword," in Gary L. McDowell, *The Constitution and Contemporary Constitutional Theory* (Cumberland, Va., Center for Judicial Studies, 1985).

————. "Neutral Principles and Some First Amendment Problems," 47 Indiana Law Journal 1 (1971).

————. "Styles in Constitutional Theory," 26 South Texas Law Journal 383 (1985).

Braden, George D. "The Search for Objectivity in Constitutional Law," 57 Yale Law Journal 571 (1948).

Brest, Paul. "Book Review," New York Times, December 11, 1977, sec. 11 at 10.

————. "The Fundamental Rights Controversy: The Essential Contradictions of Normative Constitutional Scholarship," 90 Yale Law Journal 1063 (1981).

————. "The Misconceived Quest for the Original Understanding," 60 Boston University Law Review 204 (1980).

————. "Who Decides?" 58 Southern California Law Review 661 (1985).

Bridwell, Randall. "Book Review," 1978 Duke Law Journal 907.

————. "The Scope of Judicial Review: A Dirge for the Theorists of Majority Rule?" 31 South Carolina Law Review 617 (1980).

Bronner, Ethan. "S-t-r-e-t-c-h-i-n-g the Constitution," Boston Sunday Globe, May 8, 1988, at A27.

Burleigh, John. "The Supreme Court vs. The Constitution," 50 *Public Interest* 151 (1978).

Burns, James McGregor. "Dictatorship—Could It Happen Here?" in C. Roberts, ed., *Has the Court Too Much Power* 234 (1974).

Cahn, Edmond. "Brief for the Supreme Court," *The New York Times Magazine*, October 7, 1956, in Leonard Levy, ed., *The Supreme Court Under Earl Warren* 28 (1972).

———. "Jurisprudence," 30 New York University Law Review 150 (1955).

Calabresi, Guido. "What Clarence Thomas Knows," New York Times, July 28, 1991, sec. 4, at 15.

Casper, Gerhard. "Constitutionalism," in 2 Leonard W. Levy et al., eds., *Encyclopedia of the American Constitution* (1986).

Chayes, Abram. "The New Judiciary," 28 Harvard Law School Bulletin 23 (1976).

Church, W. Lawrence. "History and the Constitutional Role of Courts," 1990 Wisconsin Law Review 1071.

Claggett, Bruce M. "Book Review," 27 Harvard Law School Bulletin 3 (1976).

Coles, William. "A Passionate Commitment to Experience," New York Times, May 29, 1983 (Book Review Section).

Commager, Henry Steele. "Constitutional History and the Higher Law," in Conyers Read, ed., *The Constitution Reconsidered* 225 (1938).

———. "Judicial Review and Democracy," 19 *Virginia Quarterly Review* 417 (1943).

Cooper, Tim. "Freund: 40 Years of Supreme Court History Recalled," 64 Harvard Law School Record 1 (1977).

Corwin, Edward S. "The Decline of Due Process Before the Civil War," 24 Harvard Law Review 460 (1911).

———. "The 'Higher Law' Background of American Constitutional Law," 42 Harvard Law Review 149 (1928).

Cover, Robert. "Book Review," *New Republic*, January 14, 1978, at 26.

Cox, Archibald. "The New Dimensions of Constitutional Adjudication," 51 Washington Law Review 791 (1976).

Curtis, Charles P. "A Better Theory of Legal Interpretation," 3 Vanderbilt Law Review 407 (1950).

———. "Judicial Review and Majority Rule," in Edmond N. Cahn, ed., *Supreme Court and Supreme Law* 170 (1954).

———. "The Role of the Constitutional Text," id. 64.

Curtis, Michael K. "The Bill of Rights as a Limitation on State Authority: A Reply to Professor Berger," 16 Wake Forest Law Review 45 (1980).

Dahl, Robert. "Decision-Making in a Democracy: The Supreme Court as a National Policy-Maker," 6 Journal of Public Law 279 (1957).

Dershowitz, Alan M. "Book Review," *New York Times Book Review*, September 21, 1975, at 1.

———. "Inside the Sanctum Sanctorum," New York Times, November 2, 1980.

Dimond, Paul. "Strict Construction and Judicial Review of Racial Discrimination Under the Equal Protection Clause: Meeting Raoul Berger on Interpretivist Grounds," 80 Michigan Law Review 462 (1982).

Dixon, Robert. "Reapportionment in the Supreme Court and Congress: Constitutional Struggle for Fair Representation," 63 Michigan Law Review 209 (1964).

Douglas, William O. "Stare Decisis," 49 Columbia Law Review 735 (1949).

Downing, Rondel G. "Judicial Ethics and the Political Role of the Courts," 35 *Law and Contemporary Problems* 94 (1970).

Dworkin, Ronald. "The Forum of Principle," 56 New York University Law Review 469 (1981).

Easterbrook, Frank H. "The Influence of Judicial Review on Constitutional Theory," in Burke Marshall, ed., *A Workable Government? The Constitution After 200 Years* (1987).

Ely, John Hart. "Constitutional Interpretivism: Its Allure and Impossibility," 53 Indiana Law Journal 399 (1978).

———. "Foreword: On Discovering Fundamental Values," 92 Harvard Law Review 5 (1978).

———. "The Wages of Crying Wolf: A Comment on Roe v. Wade," 82 Yale Law Journal 920 (1973).

Erler, Edward J. "The Ninth Amendment and Contemporary Jurisprudence," in Eugene W. Hickok, ed., *The Bill of Rights: Original Meaning and Current Understanding* 432 (1991).

Fairman, Charles. "Does the Fourteenth Amendment Incorporate the Bill of Rights?" 2 Stanford Law Review 5 (1949).

Farber, Daniel. "Book Review," 6 *Constitutional Commentary* 564 (1989).

Finn, Chester E. "Book Review," *Commentary* 78, April 1, 1976.

Fiss, Owen M. "The Supreme Court, 1978 Term—Foreword: The Forms of Justice," 93 Harvard Law Review 1 (1979).

Foner, Eric. "The Supreme Court's Legal History," 23 Rutgers Law Journal 243 (1992).

Frank, John. "Review and Basic Liberties," in Edmond Cahn, ed., *Supreme Court and Supreme Law* 109 (1954).

Frankfurter, Felix. "John Marshall and the Judicial Function," 69 Harvard Law Review 217 (1955).

———. "Memorandum on 'Incorporation' of the Bill of Rights Into the Due Process Clause of the Fourteenth Amendment," 78 Harvard Law Review 764 (1965).

———. "The Supreme Court and the Public," 83 *Forum* 329 (1930).

Frantz, Laurent B. "Congressional Power to Enforce the Fourteenth Amendment Against Private Acts," 73 Yale Law Journal 1353 (1964).

———. "Is the First Amendment Law?—A Reply to Professor Mendelson," 51 California Law Review 729 (1963).

Fried, Charles. "Jurisprudential Responses to Legal Realism," 73 Cornell Law Review 331 (1988).

Friendly, Henry J. "The Bill of Rights as a Code of Criminal Procedure," 53 California Law Review 929 (1965).

Gangi, William. "Judicial Expansionism: An Evaluation of the Ongoing Debate," 8 Ohio Northern University Law Review 1 (1981).

Garrison, William Lloyd. "The Liberator," in Henry Steele Commager, ed., *Documents of American History*, 7th ed. (1963).

Gibbons, John. "Book Review," 31 Rutgers Law Review 839 (1978).

Graglia, Lino A. " 'Interpreting' the Constitution: Posner on Bork," 44 Stanford Law Review 1019 (1992).

Grant, J. A. C. "The Natural Law Background of Due Process," 31 Columbia Law Review 56 (1931).

Grey, Thomas C. "Do We Have an Unwritten Constitution?" 27 Stanford Law Review 703 (1975).

———. "Origins of the Unwritten Constitution: Fundamental Law in American Revolutionary Thought," 30 Stanford Law Review 843 (1978).

Griswold, Erwin N. "Due Process Problems Today in the United States," in Bernard Schwartz, ed., *The Fourteenth Amendment* (1970).

Gunther, Gerald. "Some Reflections on the Judicial Role: Distinctions, Roots, and Prospects," 1979 Washington University Law Quarterly 817.

———. "Too Much a Battle with Strawmen," Wall Street Journal, November 25, 1977, at 4.

Haines, Charles G. "The Law of Nature in State and Federal Judicial Decision," 25 Yale Law Journal 617 (1916).

Hamilton, Walton H. "The Path of Due Process of Law," in Conyers Read, ed., *The Constitution Reconsidered* 167 (1938).

Hand, Learned. "Chief Justice Stone's Conception of the Judicial Function," 46 Columbia Law Review 696 (1946).

Hawkins, Vaughan. "On the Principles of Legal Interpretation, With Reference Especially to the Interpretation of Wills," 2 Juridical Society Papers 298 (1860).

Henkin, Louis. "Human Dignity and Constitutional Rights," in Michael J. Meyer and William A. Parent, eds., *The Constitution of Rights* 210 (1992).

———. " 'Selective Incorporation' in the Fourteenth Amendment," 73 Yale Law Journal 74 (1963).

———. "Some Reflections on Current Constitutional Controversies," 109 University of Pennsylvania Law Review 637 (1961).

Hooker, Roger W. "A 'Quiet, Undramatic' Leader," New York Times, August 19, 1976.

Horn, Robert H. "Book Review," 88 Harvard Law Review 1924 (1975).

Horwitz, Morton J. "The Conservative Tradition in the Writing of American Legal History," 17 *American Journal of Legal History* 275 (1973).

———. "The Emergence of an Instrumental Conception of American Law, 1780–1820," in 5 *Perspectives in American Legal History* 287 (1971).

Hurst, James Willard. "The Process of Constitutional Construction," in Edmond N. Cahn, ed., *Supreme Court and Supreme Law* 55 (1954).

———. "The Role of History," in Edmond N. Cahn, ed., *Supreme Court and Supreme Law* 60 (1954).

Hutcheson, Joseph C. "The Judgment Intuitive: The Function of the 'Hunch' in Judicial Decision," 14 Cornell Law Quarterly 274 (1929).

Hutchinson, Allan C. "Alien Thoughts: A Comment on Constitutional Scholarship," 58 Southern California Law Review 701 (1985).

Hutson, James. "The Creation of the Constitution: The Integrity of the Documentary Record," 65 Texas Law Review 1 (1986).

Hyman, Harold. "Federalism: Legal Fiction or Historical Artifact?" 1987 Brigham Young University Law Review 905.

Jaffe, Louis. "The Supreme Court Debated—Another View," *The New York Times Magazine*, June 5, 1960, in Leonard Levy, ed., *The Supreme Court Under Earl Warren* 199 (1972).

———. "Was Brandeis an Activist? The Search for Intermediate Premises," 80 Harvard Law Review 986 (1967).

Jurow, Keith. "Untimely Thoughts: A Reconsideration of the Origins of Due Process," 19 *American Journal of Legal History* 265 (1975).

Kauper, Paul. "Penumbras, Peripheries, Emanations, Things Fundamental, and Things Forgotten: The Griswold Case," 64 Michigan Law Review 235 (1965).

———. "Some Comments on the Reapportionment Cases," 63 Michigan Law Review 243 (1964).

Kay, Richard S. "Book Review," 10 Connecticut Law Review 800 (1978).

Kelly, Alfred H. "Clio and the Court: An Illicit Love Affair," 1965 Supreme Court Review 119.

———. "Comment on Harold M. Hyman's Paper," in Harold M. Hyman, ed., *New Frontiers of the American Reconstruction* 41 (1966).

———. "The Fourteenth Amendment Reconsidered: The Segregation Question," 54 Michigan Law Review 1049 (1956).

Kommers, Donald. Book Review, "Role of the Supreme Court," 40 *Review of Politics* 409 (1978).

Korman, Edward R. "Book Review," 4 Hofstra Law Review 549 (1976).

Kurland, Philip. "Curia Regis: Some Comments on the Divine Right of Kings and Courts 'To Say What the Law Is,' " 23 Arizona Law Review 581 (1981).

Kutler, Stanley I. "Raoul Berger's Fourteenth Amendment: A History or Ahistorical," 6 Hastings Constitutional Law Quarterly 511 (1979).

Levinson, Sanford. " 'The Constitution' in American Civil Religion," 1979 Supreme Court Review 123.

———. "Fidelity to Law and the Assessment of Political Activity," 27 Stanford Law Review 1185 (1975).

———. "The Turn Toward Functionalism in Constitutional Theory," 8 University of Dayton Law Review 567 (1983).

Levitan, David. "The Foreign Relations Power: An Analysis of Mr. Justice Sutherland's Theory," 55 Yale Law Journal 467 (1946).

Lewin, Nathan. "Avoiding the Supreme Court," *The New York Times Magazine*, October 17, 1976, at 31.

Lewis, Anthony. "Historical Change in the Supreme Court," *The New York Times Magazine*, June 2, 1962, in Leonard Levy, ed., *The Supreme Court Under Earl Warren* 77 (1972).

———. "A Man Born to Act, Not to Muse," *The New York Times Magazine*, June 30, 1968, in Leonard Levy, ed., *The Supreme Court Under Earl Warren* 151 (1972).

———. "A Time to Celebrate," New York Times, May 13, 1974, at 29.

———. "What Qualities for the Court?" *The New York Times Magazine*, October 6, 1957, in Leonard Levy, ed., *The Supreme Court Under Earl Warren* 114 (1972).

———. "Winners and Losers," New York Times, October 18, 1989, at A17.

Linde, Hans. "Judges, Critics, and the Realist Tradition," 82 Yale Law Journal 227 (1972).

Lofgren, Charles A. "United States v. Curtiss-Wright Export Corporation: An Historical Reassessment," 83 Yale Law Review 51 (1973).

Lusky, Louis. "Government by Judiciary: What Price Legitimacy?" 6 Hastings Constitutional Law Quarterly 403 (1979).

Lynch, Gerald. "Book Review," 63 Cornell Law Review 1091 (1978).

McArthur, John B. "Abandoning the Constitution: The New Wave in Constitutional Theory," 59 Tulane Law Review 280 (1984).

McCloskey, Robert G. "Due Process and the Supreme Court: An Exhumation and Reburial," 1962 Supreme Court Review 33.

McConnell, Michael W. "Review of *Federalism: The Founders' Design*, by Raoul Berger," 54 University of Chicago Law Review 1484 (1987).

McDonald, Forrest. "How the Fourteenth Amendment Repealed the Constitution," *Chronicles* 29 (October 1989).

McDougal, Myres, and Asher Lans. "Treaties and Congressional-Executive or Presidential Agreements: Interchangeable Instruments of National Policy," 54 Yale Law Journal 184 (1945).

McGovney, D. O. "Privileges and Immunities Clause, Fourteenth Amendment," 4 Iowa Law Bulletin 219 (1918).

Macedo, Stephen. "Originalism and the Inescapability of Politics," 84 Northwestern University Law Review 1203 (1990).

———. "Reason, Rhetoric, and the Ninth Amendment: A Comment on Sanford Levinson," 64 Chicago-Kent Law Review 163 (1988).

Maitland, Frederic W. "The History of English Law Before the Time of Edward I," in Peter Gay et al., eds., 3 *Historians at Work* 320 (1975).

Maltz, Earl M. "Federalism and the Fourteenth Amendment: A Comment on *Democracy and Distrust*," 42 Ohio State Law Journal 209 (1981).

———. "Murder in the Cathedral: The Supreme Court as Moral Prophet," 8 University of Dayton Law Review 623 (1983).

Martin, Douglas. "Yale Chief Opens Constitution Talks by Faulting Meese," New York Times, February 22, 1987, sec. 1 at 46.

Mason, Alpheus T. "The Burger Court in Historical Perspective," 47 New York State Bar Journal 87 (1975).

———. "Myth and Reality in Supreme Court Drama," 48 Virginia Law Review 1385 (1962).

Mendelson, Wallace. "Mr. Justice Black's Fourteenth Amendment," 53 Minnesota Law Review 711 (1969).

———. "Mr. Justice Frankfurter: Law and Choice," 10 Vanderbilt Law Review 333 (1957).

———. "Raoul Berger's Fourteenth Amendment: Abuse by Contraction vs. Abuse by Expansion," 6 Hastings Constitutional Law Quarterly 437 (1979).

Miller, Arthur S. "The Elusive Search for Values in Constitutional Interpretation," 6 Hastings Constitutional Law Quarterly 487 (1979).

———. "An Inquiry Into the Relevance of the Intention of the Founding Fathers, With Special Emphasis Upon the Doctrine of Separation of Powers," 27 Arkansas Law Review 584 (1973).

Miller, Arthur S., and Ronald F. Howell. "The Myth of Neutrality in Constitutional Adjudication," 27 University of Chicago Law Review 661 (1960).

Mommsen, Theodor. "History of Rome," in Peter Gay et al., eds., 3 *Historians at Work* 288 (1975).

Monaghan, Henry P. "The Constitution Goes to Harvard," 13 Harvard Civil Rights–Civil Liberties Law Review 117 (1978).

———. "Our Perfect Constitution," 56 New York University Law Review 353 (1981).

Morrison, Stanley. "Does the Fourteenth Amendment Incorporate the Bill of Rights?" 2 Stanford Law Review 140 (1949).

Murphy, Walter. "Book Review," 87 Yale Law Journal 1752 (1978).

Nathanson, Nathaniel. "Book Review," 56 Texas Law Review 579 (1978).

Neal, Phil C. "Baker v. Carr: Politics in Search of Law," 1962 *Supreme Court Review* 252.

Nelson, William E. "History and Neutrality in Constitutional Adjudication," 72 Virginia Law Review 1237 (1986).

Newmeyer, Kent. "Book Review," 19 *American Journal of Legal History* 66 (1975).

Nye, R. B. "Comment on C. V. Woodward's Paper," in Harold M. Hyman, ed., *New Frontiers of the American Reconstruction* 148 (1966).

"Opinions Considered: A Talk With Tom Wicker," New York Times, January 5, 1992, sec. 4 at 4.

Packer, Herbert. "The Aim of Criminal Law Revisited: A Plea for a New Look at 'Substantive Due Process,' " 44 Southern California Law Review 490 (1971).

Perry, Michael J. "The Authority of Text, Tradition, and Reason: A Theory of Constitutional Interpretation," 58 Southern California Law Review 551 (1985).

———. "Interpretivism, Freedom of Expression, and Equal Protection," 42 Ohio State Law Journal 261 (1981).

———. "Review of *Government by Judiciary: The Transformation of the Fourteenth Amendment*, by Raoul Berger," 78 Columbia Law Review 685 (1978).

Pollak, Louis. "The Supreme Court Under Fire," 6 Journal of Public Law 428 (1957).

Pollock, Frederick. "Judicial Caution and Valour," in *Jurisprudence in Action* (The New York Bar Association, 1953).

Posner, Richard. "Address," 35 Harvard Law Bulletin 34 (1987).

———. "Bork and Beethoven," 42 Stanford Law Review 1365 (1990).

Pound, Roscoe. "Common Law and Legislation," 21 Harvard Law Review 383 (1908).

Powell, H. Jefferson. "How Does the Constitution Structure Government? The Founders' Views," in Burke Marshall, ed., *A Workable Government? The Constitution After 200 Years* (1987).

———. "The Modern Misunderstanding of Original Intent," 54 University of Chicago Law Review 1513 (1987).

———. "The Original Understanding of Original Intent," 98 Harvard Law Review 885 (1985).

Rapaczynski, Andrzej. "The Ninth Amendment and the Unwritten Constitution: The Problems of Constitutional Interpretation," 64 Chicago-Kent Law Review 177 (1988).

Richards, David A. J. "Abolitionist Political and Constitutional Theory and the Reconstruction Amendments," 25 Loyola of Los Angeles Law Review 1187 (1992).

Richardson, H. G., and G. O. Sayles. "Parliament and Great Councils in Medieval England," 77 Law Quarterly Review 213 (1961).

Rodell, Fred. "The Crux of the Court Hullabaloo," *The New York Times Magazine*, May 29, 1960, in Leonard Levy, ed., *The Supreme Court Under Earl Warren* 192 (1972).

———. "It Is the Warren Court," *The New York Times Magazine*, March 13, 1966, in Leonard Levy, ed., *The Supreme Court Under Earl Warren* 136 (1972).

———. "The 'Warren Court' Stands Its Ground," *The New York Times Magazine*, September 27, 1964, in Leonard Levy, ed., *The Supreme Court Under Earl Warren* 209 (1972).

Rostow, Eugene V. "The Democratic Character of Judicial Review," 66 Harvard Law Review 193 (1952).

———. "The Japanese-American Cases—A Disaster," 54 Yale Law Journal 489 (1945).

Sandalow, Terrance. "Constitutional Interpretation," 79 Michigan Law Review 1033 (1981).

———. "The Distrust of Politics," 56 New York University Law Review 446 (1981).

———. "Judicial Protection of Minorities," 75 Michigan Law Review 1162 (1977).

Saphire, Richard B. "Judicial Review in the Name of the Constitution," 8 University of Dayton Law Review 45 (1983).

Scalia, Antonin, "Originalism: The Lesser Evil," 57 University of Cincinnati Law Review 849 (1989).

Schauer, Frederick. "Easy Cases," 58 Southern California Law Review 399 (1985).

Shattuck, Charles E. "The True Meaning of the Term 'Liberty' in Those Clauses in the Federal and State Constitutions Which Protect 'Life, Liberty and Property,' " 4 Harvard Law Review 365 (1891).

Sherry, Suzanna. "The Ninth Amendment: Righting an Unwritten Constitution," 64 Chicago-Kent Law Review 1010 (1989), reprinted in 2 Randy E. Barnett, ed., *The Rights Retained by the People* 283 (1993).

Simon, Larry. "The Authority of the Constitution and Its Meaning: A Preface to a Theory of Constitutional Interpretation," 56 Southern California Law Review 603 (1985).

Sloan, Herbert. "The Earth Belongs in Usufruct to the Living," in Peter Onuf, ed., *Jeffersonian Legacies* 281 (1993).

Soifer, Aviam. "Protecting Civil Rights: A Critique of Raoul Berger's History," 54 New York University Law Review 651 (1979).

Sowell, Thomas. "A Black 'Conservative' Dissents," *The New York Times Magazine*, August 8, 1976, at 14.

Steel, Lewis M. "Nine Men in Black Who Think White," *The New York Times Magazine*, October 13, 1968, in Leonard Levy, ed., *The Supreme Court Under Earl Warren* 82 (1972).

Stephenson, D. G. "Book Review," 61 Virginia Law Review 1338 (1975).

Sutherland, Arthur E. "Privacy in Connecticut," 64 Michigan Law Review 283 (1965).

TenBroek, Jacobus. "Use by the United States Supreme Court of Extrinsic Aids in Constitutional Construction," 27 California Law Review 399 (1939).

Thayer, James Bradley. "The Origin and Scope of the American Doctrine of Constitutional Law," 7 Harvard Law Review 129 (1893).

Tushnet, Mark. "Civil Rights and Social Rights: The Future of the Reconstruction Amendments," 25 Loyola of Los Angeles Law Review 1207 (1992).

———. "Following the Rules Laid Down: A Critique of Interpretivism and Neutral Principles," 96 Harvard Law Review 781 (1983).

———. "Legal Realism, Structural Review, and Prophecy," 8 University of Dayton Law Review 809 (1983).

———. "A Note on the Revival of Textualism in Constitutional Theory," 58 Southern California Law Review 683 (1985).

———. "Truth, Justice, and the American Way: An Interpretation of the Public Law Scholarship in the Seventies," 57 Texas Law Review 1307 (1979).

Van Alstyne, William W. "The Fourteenth Amendment, The 'Right' to Vote, and the Understanding of the Thirty-Ninth Congress," 1965 Supreme Court Review 33.

Warren, Charles. "The New 'Liberty' Under the Fourteenth Amendment," 39 Harvard Law Review 431 (1926).

White, G. Edward. "Judicial Activism and the Identity of the Legal Profession," 67 *Judicature* 246 (1983).

———. "Reflections on the Role of the Supreme Court: The Contemporary Debate and the 'Lessons' of History," 63 *Judicature* 162 (1979).

Wiecek, William M. "The Constitutional Snipe Hunt," 23 Rutgers Law Journal 253 (1992).

Wilkins, Roger. "Racial Outlook: Lack of Change Disturbs Blacks," New York Times, March 3, 1978, sec. A at 26.

Wills, Garry. "Introduction," in Garry Wills, ed., *The Federalist Papers of Alexander Hamilton, James Madison, and John Jay* (1982).

Wofford, John. "The Blinding Light: The Uses of History in Constitutional Interpretation," 31 University of Chicago Law Review 502 (1964).

Woodward, C. Vann. "Seeds of Failure in Radical Race Policy," in Harold M. Hyman, ed., *New Frontiers of the American Reconstruction* 12 (1966).

Wright, J. Skelly. "Professor Bickel, the Scholarly Tradition, and the Supreme Court," 84 Harvard Law Review 769 (1971).

Zuckert, Michael. "Book Review," 8 *Constitutional Commentary* 149 (1991).

# Index of Cases

Abbott v. Bayley, 6 Pick. 89 (Mass. 1827), 41, 42, 46, 59, 181, 213

Ableman v. Booth, 62 U.S. (21 How.) 506 (1858), 246, 249

Adamson v. California, 332 U.S. 46 (1947), 48, 51, 67, 136, 157, 158, 159, 167, 168, 169, 171, 175, 178, 179, 182, 231, 232–33, 234, 273, 284, 406

Adkins v. Children's Hospital, 261 U.S. 525 (1923), 146, 190, 292, 346

Allgeyer v. Louisiana, 165 U.S. 578 (1897), 290

A.F. of L. v. American Sash Co., 335 U.S. 538 (1949), 283, 286

American Security Co. v. District of Columbia, 224 U.S. 491 (1912), 199

The Antelope, 23 U.S. (10 Wheat.) 66 (1825), 304, 334

Anti-Fascist Refugee Committee v. McGrath, 341 U.S. 123 (1951), 438

Aptheker v. Secretary of State, 378 U.S. 500 (1964), 442

Aumeye's Case (1305), 414

Baker v. Carr, 369 U.S. 186 (1962), 90, 100, 198–99, 286, 367

Baldwin v. Missouri, 281 U.S. 586 (1930), 17, 282, 287, 436–37, 462–63

Barron v. Baltimore, 32 U.S. (7 Pet.) 243 (1833), 155, 163, 165, 180, 181, 182, 211

Bartkus v. Illinois, 359 U.S. 121 (1959), 178

Beauharnais v. Illinois, 343 U.S. 250 (1952), 171, 174

Bell v. Maryland, 378 U.S. 226 (1964), 145, 192, 406, 429

Belmont Bridge v. Wheeling Bridge, 138 U.S. 287 (1891), 90

Bennecke v. Insurance Co., 105 U.S. 355 (1881), 173

Bertonneau v. Bd. of Directors of City Schools, 3 F. Cas. 294 (C.C.D. La. 1878) (No. 1,361), 150

Blake v. McClung, 172 U.S. 239 (1898), 58

Blask v. Sowl, 309 F. Supp. 909 (W.D. Wis. 1967), 369

Board of Education v. Barnette, 319 U.S. 624 (1943), 287, 316, 322

Bolling v. Sharpe, 347 U.S. 497 (1954), 236, 390, 396, 442

Boyd v. United States, 116 U.S. 616 (1886), 288

Boys Market v. Clerks' Union, 398 U.S. 235 (1970), 346

Bradwell v. State, 38 U.S. (16 Wall.) 130 (1872), 40

Brown v. Allen, 344 U.S. 443 (1953), 347

Brown v. Board of Education, 347 U.S. 483 (1954), 25, 117, 132, 141, 144,

Brown v. Board of Education (*continued*) 146, 151, 254, 264–66, 287, 309, 311, 333, 349, 361, 366, 389, 392–93, 396, 444

Buchanan v. Warley, 245 U.S. 60 (1917), 66

Buckley v. Valeo, 424 U.S. 1 (1976), 390

Burnet v. Coronada Oil & Gas Co., 285 U.S. 393 (1932), 344

Butchers' Union Co. v. Crescent City Co., 111 U.S. 746 (1884), 211

Calder v. Bull, 3 U.S. (3 Dall.) 386 (1798), 274, 302, 330

Campbell v. Morris, 3 H. & McH. 535 (Md. 1797), 41,42, 46, 181, 201

Cantwell v. Connecticut, 310 U.S. 296 (1940), 442

Carpenter v. Pennsylvania, 58 U.S. (17 How.) 456 (1854), 412

Carr v. Corning, 182 F.2d 14 (D.C. Cir. 1950), 137

Chambers v. Baltimore & Ohio R.R., 207 U.S. 142 (1907), 58

Chambers v. Florida, 309 U.S. 227 (1940), 239

Champion v. Ames, 188 U.S. 321 (1902), 20

Chapman v. Alabama, 386 U.S. 18 (1967), 358–59

Chicago, M. & St. P.R. Co. v. Minnesota, 134 U.S. 418 (1890), 159, 232–33

The Chinese Exclusion Case, 130 U.S. 581 (1889), 379

Church of the Holy Trinity v. United States, 143 U.S. 457 (1891), 219

Civil Rights Cases, 109 U.S. 3 (1883), 55, 96, 148, 219, 246

Cohens v. Virginia, 19 U.S. (6 Wheat.) 264 (1821), 434

Coleman v. Alabama, 399 U.S. 1 (1970), 319, 363, 448

Colgate v. Harvey, 296 U.S. 404 (1935), 57

Collins v. City of Harker Heights, 112 S. Ct. 1061 (1992), 188

Commonwealth v. Caton, in 2 *Letters and Papers of Edmund Pendleton* 416 (D. J. Mays ed. 1967), 330

Connecticut General Ins. Co. v. Johnson, 303 U.S. 77 (1938), 92, 123, 174, 179

Corfield v. Coryell, 6 F. Cas. (No. 3230) 546 (C.C.E.D. Pa. 1823), 31, 38, 39–40, 41, 42, 44, 46, 48, 59, 60–61, 62, 66, 68, 112, 120, 167

Cory v. Carter, 48 Ind. 327 (1874), 150

Dandridge v. Williams, 397 U.S. 471 (1970), 287

Davidson v. New Orleans, 96 U.S. 97 (1877), 230

Decatur v. Paulding, 39 U.S. (14 Pet.) 497 (1840), 327

Dennis v. United States, 341 U.S. 494 (1951), 145

Detroit Bank v. United States, 317 U.S. 329 (1943), 236

Dred Scott v. Sandford, 60 U.S. (19 How.) 393 (1857), 63, 180, 230, 246, 279, 397

Duncan v. Louisiana, 391 U.S. 145 (1968), 156, 158, 175, 239, 281, 293, 311, 450, 456

Duplex Co. v. Deering, 254 U.S. 443 (1921), 190

Eakin v. Raub, 12 S. & R. 330 (Pa. 1825), 318–19

Eckenrode v. Pennsylvania R. Co., 16 F.2d 996 (3d Cir. 1947), 94

Eisner v. Macomber, 252 U.S. 189
(1920), 409, 436

Entick v. Carrington, 19 How. St. Tr.
1029 (1765), 277, 288

Erie R.R. Co. v. Tompkins, 304 U.S.
64 (1938), 152, 318, 370, 393, 459

Ernst & Ernst v. Hochfelder, 425 U.S.
185 (1976), 192–93, 424

Ex parte Bain, 121 U.S. 1 (1887), 9

Ex parte Bollman, 8 U.S. (4 Cranch)
75 (1807), 222

Ex parte Grossman, 267 U.S. 87 (1925),
409

Ex parte McCardle, 74 U.S. (7 Wall.)
506 (1868), 398

Ex parte Virginia, 100 U.S. 339 (1879),
92, 245, 398

Federal Power Comm'n v. Natural Gas
Pipeline Co., 315 U.S. 575 (1942),
414

Ferguson v. Skrupa, 372 U.S. 726
(1963), 280–81, 287

Flast v. Cohen, 392 U.S. 83 (1968), 322,
324

Fletcher v. Peck, 10 U.S. (6 Cranch)
87 (1810), 276

Florida v. Williams, 399 U.S. 78 (1970),
448

Flournoy v. Hewgley, 234 F.2d 213
(10th Cir. 1956), 173

Foucha v. Louisiana, 112 S. Ct. 1780
(1992), 187

Furman v. Georgia, 408 U.S. 238
(1972), 283, 348, 462

Gardner v. Newburgh, 2 Johns. Ch.
162 (N.Y. 1816), 276

Gassies v. Ballon, 31 U.S. (6 Pet.) 761
(1832), 64

Georgia v. Rachel, 384 U.S. 780 (1966),
47, 48, 153, 400

Gibbons v. Ogden, 22 U.S. (9 Wheat.)
1 (1824), 20, 45, 384, 397, 405,
432–33

Gideon v. Wainright, 372 U.S. 335
(1963), 442

Gitlow v. New York, 268 U.S. 652
(1925), 158, 291–92

Gompers v. United States, 233 U.S. 604
(1914), 435, 437

Graves v. O'Keefe, 306 U.S. 466 (1939),
319

Gray v. Sanders, 372 U.S. 368 (1963),
104

Gregg v. Georgia, 96 S. Ct. 2909 (1976),
283, 359

Griswold v. Connecticut, 381 U.S. 479
(1965), 19, 56, 86, 118, 281, 284, 286,
288, 316, 322, 324–25, 350, 371, 442

Haley v. Ohio, 332 U.S. 596 (1948), 283

Hammer v. Dagenhardt, 247 U.S. 251
(1918), 383

Harper v. Va. Bd. of Elections, 383 U.S.
663 (1966), 159, 219, 228, 285, 315

Hawaii v. Mankichi, 190 U.S. 197
(1903), 8, 194

Hawke v. Smith, 253 U.S. 221 (1920),
19, 403, 409

Helvering v. Davis, 301 U.S. 619 (1937),
386

Hepburn v. Griswold, 75 U.S. (8 Wall.)
603 (1869), 280

Hewitt v. Painter, 1 Bulstrode 174, 80
Eng. Rep. 864 (1611), 417–18

Heydon's Case, 3 Co. Rep. 7a, 76 Eng.
Rep. 637 (1584), 419

Home Building & Loan Assn. v.
Blaisdell, 290 U.S. 398 (1934), 429

Houston v. Moore, 18 U.S. (5 Wheat.)
1 (1820), 25, 312

Hurtado v. California, 110 U.S. 516
(1884), 4, 223, 225, 231, 237–38, 395

Immigration & Naturalization Serv. v.
  Chadha, 462 U.S. 919 (1983), 380
In re Winship, 397 U.S. 358 (1970),
  274, 295, 302, 312, 467

Johnson v. Louisiana, 406 U.S. 356
  (1972), 307, 343–44
Johnson v. United States, 163 F. 30 (1st
  Cir. 1908), 50, 407, 436

Kamper v. Hawkins, 3 Va. (1 Va. Cas.)
  20 (1793), 332
Katz v. United States, 389 U.S. 347
  (1967), 315
Katzenbach v. Morgan, 384 U.S. 641
  (1966), 198, 249, 251
Keifer & Keifer v. R.F.C., 306 U.S. 381
  (1939), 407
Kent v. Dulles, 357 U.S. 116 (1958),
  442
Kentucky v. Dennison, 65 U.S. (24
  How.) 66 (1858), 250
Kirby v. Illinois, 406 U.S. 682 (1972),
  364

Livestock Dealers & Butchers' Ass'n
  v. Crescent City Live-stock &
  Slaughter-House Co., 15 F. Cas. 649
  (Cir. Ct. D. La. 1870), (No. 8408),
  51, 153, 401
Livingston's Executor v. Story, 36 U.S.
  (11 Pet.) 351 (1837), 364
Loan Association v. Topeka, 87 U.S. (20
  Wall.) 655 (1874), 4, 279
Lochner v. New York, 198 U.S. 45
  (1905), 287, 298, 348, 436
Louisiana ex rel. Francis V. Resweber,
  329 U.S. 459 (1947), 282
Lucas v. Colorado Gen. Assembly, 377
  U.S. 713 (1964), 108, 285
Luther v. Borden, 48 U.S. (7 How.) 1
  (1849), 100

Lynch v. Household Finance Corp.,
  405 U.S. 538 (1972), 288

M'Culloch v. Maryland, 17 U.S. (4
  Wheat.) 316 (1819), 3, 21, 58, 126,
  277, 330–31, 370, 381–82, 430–32,
  433, 439, 446
McGautha v. California, 402 U.S. 183
  (1971), 348
McPherson v. Blacker, 146 U.S. 1
  (1892), 384
Magdalen College Case, 11 Co. Rep.
  66b, 77 Eng. Rep. 1235 (1615), 415
Magg v. Miller, 296 F. 923 (D.C. Cir.
  1924), 94
Marbury v. Madison, 5 U.S. (1 Cranch)
  137 (1803), 21, 23, 305, 313, 314,
  327, 381, 388, 394, 434
Martin v. Hunter's Lessee, 14 U.S. (1
  Wheat.) 304 (1816), 26
Mastro Plastics Corp. v. Labor Board,
  350 U.S. 270 (1956), 193, 424
Maxwell v. Dow, 176 U.S. 581 (1900),
  48, 240
Messon v. Liberty Fast Freight Co., 124
  F.2d 448 (2d Cir. 1942), 94
Metropolitan Board of Excise v. Barrie,
  34 N.Y. 657 (1866), 279
Meyer v. Nebraska, 262 U.S. 390
  (1923), 290
Michael H. v. Gerald D., 491 U.S. 110
  (1989), 188
Millar v. Taylor, 4 Burr 2303 (1769),
  418
Miller v. Herzfeld, 4 F.2d 355 (3d Cir.
  1925), 94
Miller v. McQuerry, 17 F. Cas. (No.
  9853) 332 (C.C.D. Ohio, 1853), 277,
  304
Minersville School District v. Gobitis,
  310 U.S. 586 (1940), 283

Minor v. Happersett, 88 U.S. (21 Wall.) 162 (1874), 28, 40, 52, 86, 96, 102–3, 105, 175, 181, 312, 379, 473

Miranda v. Arizona, 384 U.S. 436 (1966), 459

Missouri v. Holland, 252 U.S. 416 (1920), 433–36, 437

Missouri v. Jenkins, 495 U.S. 33 (1990), 380

Missouri v. Lewis, 101 U.S. 22 (1879), 213

Mitchell v. W. T. Grant Co., 416 U.S. 600 (1974), 347

Mobile & Ohio Railroad v. Tennessee, 153 U.S. 486 (1894), 239

Morehead v. Tipaldo, 298 U.S. 587 (1936), 290

Murray's Lessee v. Hoboken Land & Improvement Co., 59 U.S. (18 How.) 272 (1856), 224, 278–79

Myers v. United States, 272 U.S. 52 (1926), 380, 384

N.A.A.C.P. v. Alabama, 357 U.S. 449 (1958), 442

National Ins. Co. v. Tidewater Co., 337 U.S. 582 (1949), 221, 276, 332, 438

National Labor Relations Board v. Thompson Products, 141 F.2d 794 (9th Cir. 1944), 190

Nebbia v. New York, 291 U.S. 502 (1934), 333

Nevada v. Hall, 440 U.S. 410 (1979), 304

New York v. Miln, 36 U.S. (11 Pet.) 102 (1837), 473–74

New York Times Co. v. Sullivan, 376 U.S. 254 (1964), 442, 480

New York Trust Co. v. Eisner, 256 U.S. 345 (1921), 108

Nixon v. Herndon, 273 U.S. 536 (1927), 198

Ogden v. Saunders, 25 U.S. (12 Wheat.) 213 (1827), 212, 219, 309, 370, 394, 432

Olmstead v. United States, 277 U.S. 438 (1928), 459

On Lee v. United States, 343 U.S. 747 (1952), 465

Oregon v. Mitchell, 400 U.S. 112 (1970), 8, 72, 75, 84, 86, 87, 97, 105, 108–15, 116, 117, 235, 245, 251, 286, 352, 376, 418, 468, 474

Osborn v. Bank of the United States, 22 U.S. (9 Wheat.) 738 (1824), 331, 385, 433

Owings v. Hull, 34 U.S. (9 Pet.) 606 (1835), 173

Palko v. Connecticut, 302 U.S. 319 (1937), 181, 293, 294, 296

Parker v. Munday, (N.J. 1791), 1 Coxe's L. Rep. 70 (1816), 454

Patton v. United States, 281 U.S. 276 (1930), 448

People ex rel. King v. Gallagher, 93 N.Y. 438 (1883), 150

Pepper v. Hart [1993] A.C. 593, H.L. (E.), 418–19

Phillips v. Gookin, 231 Mass. 250, 120 N.E. 691 (1918), 94

Pierson v. Ray, 386 U.S. 547 (1967), 17, 28, 151, 180, 249, 454, 476

Planned Parenthood of Southeastern Pennsylvania v. Casey, 112 S. Ct. 2791 (1992), 394

Plessy v. Ferguson, 163 U.S. 537 (1896), 142, 149, 150, 347

Poe v. Ullman, 367 U.S. 497 (1961), 280–81, 295, 300

Pollock v. Farmers Loan & Trust Co., 157 U.S. 429 (1895), 5, 344

Pollock v. Farmers Loan & Trust Co., 158 U.S. 601 (1895), 5

Powell v. McCormack, 395 U.S. 486 (1969), 370, 393, 447

Prigg v. Pennsylvania, 41 U.S. (16 Pet.) 539 (1842), 78, 246, 249

Providence Bank v. Billings, 29 U.S. (4 Pet.) 514 (1830), 433

Prudential Ins. Co. v. Cheek, 259 U.S. 530 (1922), 291

Rainwater v. United States, 356 U.S. 590 (1958), 68

Ramsay v. Allegre, 25 U.S. (12 Wheat.) 611 (1827), 274

Reid v. Covert, 354 U.S. 1 (1957), 414

Reno v. Flores, 113 S. Ct. 1439 (1993), 188

Reynolds v. Sims, 377 U.S. 533 (1964), 3, 4, 8, 71, 81, 87, 90, 94, 97, 104, 108, 114–15, 309, 366, 464, 471–72

Rhode Island v. Massachusetts, 37 U.S. (12 Pet.) 657 (1838), 412

Roberts v. City of Boston, 59 Mass. (5 Cush.) 198 (1849), 150

Roberts v. Louisiana, 96 S. Ct. 3001 (1976), 360

Robinson v. California, 370 U.S. 660 (1962), 295

Rochin v. California, 342 U.S. 165 (1952), 5, 226, 281, 284, 315, 463

Runyon v. McCrary, 96 S. Ct. 3586 (1976), 461

Satterlee v. Mathewson, 27 U.S. (2 Pet.) 380 (1829), 304

Schwegmann Bros. v. Calvert Distillers Corp., 341 U.S. 384 (1951), 8

Sheldon v. Sill, 49 U.S. (8 How.) 441 (1850), 247

Slaughter-House Cases, 83 U.S. (16 Wall.) 36 (1872), 7, 17, 41, 45, 48, 51, 57–58, 60, 61, 63–68, 69, 80, 96, 159, 176, 178, 182, 211, 237

Smith v. Allwright, 321 U.S. 619 (1944), 319

Sniadach v. Family Finance Corp., 395 U.S. 337 (1969), 284

Snyder v. Massachusetts, 291 U.S. 97 (1934), 294

South Carolina v. United States, 199 U.S. 437 (1905), 409

South Carolina State Highway Department v. Barnwell Bros., 303 U.S. 177 (1983), 20

Southern Pacific Co. v. Jensen, 244 U.S. 205 (1917), 344

Sparf v. United States, 156 U.S. 51 (1895), 405

State ex rel. Garnes v. McCann, 20 Ohio St. 198 (1871), 150

State ex rel. Stoutmeyer v. Duffy, 7 Nev. 342 (1872), 150

State v. Cincinnati, 19 Ohio 178 (1850), 150

State v. Kieran, 5 R.I. 497 (1858), 279

Stockdale v. Hansard, 112 E.R. 1112 (Q.B. 1839), 429

Stone v. Powell, 96 S. Ct. 3037 (1976), 358

Strauder v. Virginia, 100 U.S. 303 (1879), 198, 461

Stuart v. Laird, 5 U.S. (1 Cranch) 299 (1803), 212

Sugarman v. Dougall, 413 U.S. 634 (1973), 240

Swift v. Tyson, 40 U.S. (16 Pet.) 1 (1842), 319, 370, 393

Terminiello v. Chicago, 337 U.S. 1 (1948), 390

T.I.M.E. v. United States, 359 U.S. 464 (1959), 247

Townsend v. Sain, 372 U.S. 293 (1963), 449

Trop v. Dulles, 356 U.S. 86 (1958), 274–75, 315, 343, 348

Truax v. Corrigan, 257 U.S. 312 (1921), 229

Twichell v. Pennsylvania, 74 U.S. (7 Wall.) 321 (1868), 171

Twining v. New Jersey, 211 U.S. 106 (1908), 385

Tyson v. Banton, 273 U.S. 418 (1927), 334

Ullmann v. United States, 350 U.S. 422 (1956), 289, 384

Union Starch & Refining Co. v. National Labor Rel. Board, 186 F.2d 1008 (7th Cir. 1951), 190

United States v. Arredondo, 31 U.S. (6 Pet.) 691 (1832), 181, 247

United States v. Ash, 413 U.S. 300 (1973), 364

United States v. Babbitt, 66 U.S. 55 (1861), 8–9

United States v. Barnes, 222 U.S. 513 (1912), 64

United States v. Burr, 25 F. Cas. (No. 14,693) 55 (C.C. Va. 1807), 16–17, 28, 409, 454

United States v. Butler, 297 U.S. 1 (1936), 463

United States v. Carolene Products Co., 304 U.S. 144 (1938), 234, 296–97, 444

United States v. Cruikshank, 92 U.S. 542 (1875), 105, 163, 212

United States v. Cruikshank, 25 F. Cas. (No. 14,897) 707 (C.C.D. La. 1874), 213, 219, 249

United States v. Curtiss-Wright Export Corp., 299 U.S. 304 (1936), 447

United States v. Darby, 312 U.S. 100 (1941), 173

United States v. Federal Power Commission, 191 F.2d 796 (4th Cir. 1951), 157

United States v. Freeman, 44 U.S. (3 How.) 556 (1845), 8–9, 138, 479

United States v. Gilliland, 312 U.S. 86 (1941), 64

United States v. Lovett, 328 U.S. 303 (1946), 334, 438

United States v. Morton Salt Co., 338 U.S. 632 (1950), 390

United States v. Oglesby, 163 F. Supp. 203 (W.D. Ark. 1958), 369

United States v. 1,629.6 Acres of Land, County of Sussex, Del., 503 F.2d 764 (3d Cir. 1974), 369

United States v. Pan-American Petroleum Co., 55 F.2d 753 (9th Cir. 1932), 173

United States v. Rabinowitz, 339 U.S. 56 (1950), 347

United States v. Reese, 92 U.S. 214 (1875), 24, 86, 473

United States v. Smith, 18 U.S. (5 Wheat.) 153 (1820), 45, 222

United States v. Wade, 388 U.S. 218 (1967), 364

United States v. Wheeler, 354 U.S. 281 (1920), 45

United States v. Wong Kim Ark, 169 U.S. 649 (1898), 409

United States v. Worrall, 2 U.S. (2 Dall.) 384 (C.C.D. Pa. 1798) (17,766), 303

Van Camp v. Board of Education, 9 Ohio 407 (1859), 14

Van Horne's Lessee v. Dorrance, 2 U.S. (2 Dall.) 304 (1795), 288

Veazie Bank v. Fenno, 75 U.S. (8 Wall.) 533 (1869), 232, 274

Walker v. Sauvinet, 92 U.S. 90 (1875), 237–38

Walz v. Tax Comm'n, 379 U.S. 664 (1970), 319, 393

Ward v. Flood, 48 Cal. 36 (1874), 150

Ware v. Hylton, 3 U.S. (3 Dall.) 199 (1796), 9, 19, 20, 333

Wayman v. Southard, 23 U.S. (10 Wheat.) 1 (1825), 18, 335, 379

Weems v. United States, 217 U.S. 349 (1910), 436

Wesberry v. Sanders, 376 U.S. 1 (1964), 92

West Chester & Philadelphia Railroad Co. v. Niles, 55 Pa. 209 (1867), 194

West Virginia State Bd. of Ed. v. Barnette, 319 U.S. 624 (1943), 390

Wheeler v. Montgomery, 397 U.S. 280 (1970), 340

Whitney v. California, 274 U.S. 357 (1927), 282, 292

Williams v. Florida, 399 U.S. 78 (1970), 343, 448–56

Windham v. Felbridge, Y.B. 33 Hen. 4, f.38, 212

Wisconsin R.R. Comm. v. C.B. & Q.R.R. Co., 257 U.S. 563 (1922), 157

Wright v. Vinton Branch, 300 U.S. 440 (1937), 157

Wynehamer v. The People, 13 N.Y. 378 (1856), 159–60, 277–79, 443

Yates v. United States, 354 U.S. 298 (1957), 47

Yick Wo v. Hopkins, 118 U.S. 356 (1886), 198

Youngstown Sheet & Tube Co. v. Sawyer, 343 U.S. 579 (1952), 428, 437, 447

Zorach v. Clauson, 343 U.S. 306 (1952), 385

Zweifon v. Mitchell, 516 F.2d 594 (D.C. Cir. 1975), 319

# General Index

Abolitionists (antislavery movement)
and abolitionist theory: and belief
in racial equality, 13, 199; and Bill of
Rights incorporation, 166; Bingham
as conduit of, 134, 254–57; and
*Brown v. Board* briefs, 254; and courts,
246; Cover on, 253; division among,
267; and *Dred Scott* decision, 230;
and due process, 229, 231, 233;
enmity in North, 11–12, 268; and
equality, 199; and Fourteenth
Amendment, 10; influence of,
253–70; and intermarriage, 193; Kelly
on, 258; and Negrophobia, 255, 257;
and racism, 269; Richards on, 267.
*See also* Neoabolitionists
Abortion cases: and Burger Court, 365;
and moral consensus, 335–36
Abraham, Henry J.: legitimacy of
judicial review, 391
Absolute rights, 67, 207–12. *See also*
Fundamental rights
Acheson, Dean: on equal protection,
265; on personal predilections, 312
Ackerman, Bruce: on *Brown v. Board*,
25; on *Corfield*, 48; criticizes Berger,
24
Activists, 22, 389–401; and discrepant
evidence, 24; Dworkin, 27–28;
libertarian (Jackson), 320; low state

of scholarship, 185. *See also* Judicial
revision; Supreme Court revisionism
Act of March 3, 1875, 247–48
Acton, Lord: on states' rights, 26
Adams, Henry: on states' rights, 26
Adams, John: on exact observance, 310;
and judicial power, 370; on laws'
importance, 311; and Massachusetts
Constitution, 310; and natural law,
275, 303; on property, 288
Adams, John Quincy: on
malapportionment, 92–93; on the
Justices, 356
Adams, Samuel: on absolute rights, 54;
on vague laws, 116
Adler, Mortimer: on unjust and
unconstitutional, 334, 387
African-Americans. *See* Blacks; School
segregation; Suffrage
Alexander, Larry: on desegregation,147
Alfange, Dean, Jr.: on Bill of Rights,
178
Aliens: and Civil Rights Bill, 242
Alighieri, Dante: on usurpation, 393
Allen, Francis: on "open-ended"
Fourteenth Amendment, 116
Amar, Akhil: on Bill of Rights, 175; on
Fourteenth Amendment, 176
Ambiguity: and judicial interpretation,
300

Ambiguous language. *See* "Open-ended" theory

Amendment process, 19, 145, 402; and abolition of "separate but equal," 310; and common law, 344; vs. "general acceptance," 356; and Graham on school desegregation, 301; vs. judicial revision, 19, 145, 301, 339–42, 371, 429, 447

Ames, Chief Justice (R.I.): on due process, 278–79

Annan, Lord Noel: on judges as diviners, 382

Antioriginalism propaganda: not acknowledging personal preferences, 385; Levy on, 22; offers no alternative, 389, 420

Antislavery societies: impact of, 256, 257

Antislavery theorists. *See* Abolitionists and abolitionist theory

Arnold, Thurman: on power, 314; on rule of law, 320

Aron, Raymond: on refutation, 421, 466

Articles of Confederation: Article IV of, 66; privileges and immunities in, 45

Articles of U.S. Constitution. *See under* Constitution, U.S.

Ashley, Representative James (Ohio): on suffrage, 72, 103

Auden, W. H.: on "guardians," 333

Auerbach, Carl: on Court's failure, 71; on republican form of government, 100; on "open-ended" terms, 117, on suffrage, 473

Baade, Hans W.: critique of Berger, 24

Bacon, Francis: judges do not make law, 18–19, 379; on natural law, 30; on philosophers, 468

Bacon, Matthew: intention governs, 8–9; on jury, 451; on original intention, 404; statutes and common law, 17; on statutory construction, 479; words common law meaning, 8–9, 230, 407

Bagehot, Walter: on history, 10

Bailyn, Bernard: on law binding, 23

Baker, Representative Jehu (Ill.): on due process, 231; on §5, 249

Baldwin, Abraham: on minute regulation, 58; on federal corporations, 422

Baldwin, Justice Henry: on Marshall, 433; on precedents, 364

Balkin, J. M., 420, 468–69

Bancroft, George: on *Dred Scott*, 246

Banks, Representative Nathaniel P. (Mass.): on suffrage, 76, 83

Barnett, Randy: on Ninth Amendment, 56

Beck, James M.: on judicial revision, 3–4

Bedford, Gunning: on judicial review, 374

Bell, Derrick A., Jr.: on desegregation, 349–50; on equality, 199

Beloff, Lord Max: on judicial revision, 28

Benedict, Michael L.: on centrist control, 270; on House radicals, 256, 259, 260; on states' rights, 218; on suffrage, 71

Benson, Egbert: on *expressio unius*, 247; on free speech, 155

Bereford, Chief Justice: on maker interprets, 414

Berger, Raoul: criticism of, 23–24; on history of the Fourteenth Amendment, 7–8; Kommers on, 388; legitimacy of judicial review differs from scope, 317; on Nelson, 87; on predilections, 6; on resurrecting Four Horsemen, 354; Soiter on, 23–24, 146

Bickel, Alexander: on Bill of Rights incorporation, 178; on binding intent, 340; on Bingham, 135, 137, 162, 164; on Black Codes, 35; on black unpreparedness for unsegregated schools, 149; on *Brown v. Board*, 254; on Civil Rights Act, 49, 196; on compression of Constitution, 58; on Constitution as symbol, 317; on court as moralist, 333; courts not for policy, 379; on Court reasoning, 366; and desegregation, 118, 133; on due process clause, 228; on Fairman 157; on Frankfurter, 142; Holmes on rule of law, 344; on judicial review, 332; Kelly on, 136; on limited objectives, 120; on Moderates' views, 196–97; Nelson on, 87; and "open-ended" theory, 111, 116–26; on original understanding, 405–6; recants, 119; on segregation, 143; on subjective judgments, 392; and suffrage, 75, 87; on Vinson's death, 347; on Watergate and Warren Court, 460

Bill of Rights: absorption of, 294; and antislavery theory, 254; Bingham on, 165; enforcement by courts, 441–42; extends to states, 155–56; inapplicable to states, 155–56, 212; incorporation of, 50, 155–89, 284, 294, 359, 392; Levy on due process as catchall for, 226; Madison on, 55, 375; and "privileges and immunities," 159; rejection of incorporation, 392; as response to specific excesses, 186; as restrictions of power, 55, 213; tenBroek on application of, 211–12; and Warren Court, 363, 396–97

Bingham, Representative John A. (Ohio): as abolitionist conduit, 134, 254; and abolitionist theory, 254, 255–57, 258, 261; on admission of Tennessee, 99, 113; and apportionment, 92, 93, 101, 102; and Bill of Rights incorporation, 157, 160–66, 172, 177, 182–84, 185; and "citizen" vs. "person," 241–44; and Civil Rights Act, 32, 42, 46–47, 62, 130, 134–37, 149, 161, 173, 196, 238; and court intrusion, 398; and due process, 127–28, 160, 161, 229–31, 230, 232, 253, 262, 395; on 1866 elections, 260; and enforcement, 250; and equal protection, 202–3, 204, 205–6, 206–7, 208, 210–11; —, expansive effort of, 214–16, 229, 230, 240; inapplicable to North, 189; inflated rhetoric of, 128, 164; justice takes time, 206; Kelly on goal of, 258, 262; and language of Fourteenth Amendment, 262; on meaning of "due process," 127; and "open-ended" theory, 119, 127–28; and privileges or immunities, 58, 62–63, 181; protection of corporations, 122; and record of Stevens' remark, 421–22; and Report of Joint Committee, 103; and republican form of government, 101–2, and states' rights, 399; Stevens on, 128; and suffrage, 81, 85, 99, 112–13, 165; on Supreme Court, 27, 246

Bishop, Joseph W., Jr.: distrust of people, 338; on judicial review, 369

Black, Charles L., Jr.: on *Brown v. Board*, 141, 366; colonial judges interpreters, 379–80; on constitutional legality, 460; on judicial review, 370–71; meandering approval of judicial activism, 364–68

Black, Justice Hugo L.: on Amendment, 118, 145, 227–28, 371, 429; and apportionment, 92; on Bingham, 136; —, compared to Madison, 164, 182; on canons of decency, 284; on capital punishment, 348; on "conscience of people," 350; and Council of Revision proposal, 322; on Court's economic program, 5; and death penalty, 359; on discard of precedent, 346; due process clause, 159, 227–28, 233, 234, 239, 273, 281, 287–88; —, not blank check, 285, 361; on elections as state controlled, 286; on Fourteenth Amendment and corporations, 179; Fourteenth Amendment embodied Civil Rights Bill, 51; incorporation theory of, 155–59, 166; and judicial amendment, 19, 315, 406; Levy on, 284, 350; on "natural law due process notion," 274; on Ninth Amendment, 55–56, 442; and "open-ended" theory, 117; and "ordered liberty", 295; and rule of law, 311–12, 467; and substantive due process, 289, 302

Black Codes: and Civil Rights Act, 34–35, 51, 65, 66, 172, 203; and equal protection, 263; and "liberty," 54; Stevens' reference to, 478

Blacks: pre-1937 Court's failure to protect, 353–54; and Sumner's impression of slaves, 11, 267; whites' hostility toward, 11–16, 75, 109, 255–56, 257, 268, 400. *See also* Racism; School segregation; Suffrage

Blackstone, William: on court role, 381; and due process, 225; on fundamental or natural rights, 30–31; on generality, 200; on judges' role, 19, 385; on jury, 449, 451; on law and equity, 328; and liberty, 31, 54; parliament omnipotent, 325; and triad of rights, 30–31, 386

Blaine, Representative James G. (Me.): black representation, 82, 92, 93; Fourteenth Amendment hard fought, 197

Bloodworth, Timothy: contra latitudinarian, 446

Bolingbroke, Viscount: fixed constitution, 313

Bologna bloodletting case, 194

Boorstin, Daniel J.: on changing convictions, 23

Bork, Robert H.: Adler on, 334; on *Brown v. Board*, 151; on Constitutional interpretation, 239, 410; construct new rights, 314; on contemporary academicians, 20; on equal protection, 151, 152, 154; on limited government, 343; and privileges or immunities, 44–45; on Warren's opinions, 108

Boston, school desegregation in, 481, 482

Boudinot, Elias: on fixed Constitution, 340

Boutwell, Representative George S. (Mass.): on black representation, 70; no discrimination, 256; on republican form of government, 113; on suffrage, 84, 101

Bowen, Catherine D.: on certainty, 467

Bracton, Henry de: judicial predilections, 379

Braden, George: on consensus, 282; on policymaking, 285, 297

Bradley, Justice Joseph P.: on Civil Rights Act identical with Fourteenth Amendment, 51, 153, 401; on Congressional power, 96; on enforcement, 213, 218, 249; on Fourteenth Amendment limitations, 148–49, 175; on pursuit of happiness, 41; on § 5, 175; and *Slaughter-House* decision, 41, 67

Brandeis, Justice Louis D.: on amendments that nullified decisions, 344; and due process, 282, 463; on free speech and press, 291–92; on government extension, 176–77; on judicial usurpation, 370, 393, 459; on precedents vs. Constitution, 318–19; protection by legislature, 584; on separation of powers, 380; on states' rights, 152

Brennan, Justice William J.: and apportionment, 108–15; on Constitutional revision, 364, 384; and Constitutional rights, 53; on death penalties, 25–26, 382; and enforcement, 245; and "open-ended" theory, 116; rejects Harlan, 109; on § 5, 249, 251; and subjective standards, 285; and suffrage, 75, 81, 86, 87; and Supreme Court as Platonic Guardians, 384

Brest, Paul: on advocacy scholarship, 22, 420; on Berger, 146; competence confers jurisdiction, 391; Constitution at core of civil religion, 29; Constitution not binding, 394; on fixed meanings, 408–9; on fundamental rights, 54, 186–87, 386, 389; original intention, 411

Brewer, Justice David J.: anarchism, 5, 355

Bridwell, Randall: assesses debate, 421; on minority rule, 387

Bright, John: on black vote, 71

Brinton, Crane: on Robespierre, 333

Brock, W. R.: on equality, 13, 400

Broomall, Representative John M. (Pa.): on Civil Rights Bill, 62; on due process, 228–29; Fourteenth Amendment and citizens, 243; on representation, 84

Brown, Justice Henry B.: moneyed influence, 5

Browne-Wilkinson, Lord: intention governs, 419

Bryant, William Cullen: original intention, 21

Burckhardt, Jacob: power as evil, 315

Burger, Chief Justice: on amendment process, 340; on Court as "continuing constitutional convention," 319; on death penalty, 348; on right to counsel, 448; prefers Constitution to precedents, 319, 363

Burger Court, 358–60; Black on, 365; and jury trials, 456; and Levy critique, 362, 364

Burke, Edmund: continued consent, 394

Burns, James McGregor: on Court, 353

Butterfield, Sir Herbert: on audience, 14; on discrepant evidence, 10

Cahn, Edmond N.: judges' moral sense, 355; too late to reopen, 369; on separate but equal, 25, 310

Calabresi, Guido: despises Court, 20, 333, 382

Camden, Lord: on discretion, 328; innovation requires clarity, 277; on property, 288

Canons of construction. *See* Rules of construction

Capital punishment. *See* Death penalty
Cardozo, Justice Benjamin N.: on free
    speech, 293; on fundamental
    principles, 181; on individual sense
    of justice, 23, 314, 385, 466; on
    justice, 334; Marshall on judicial
    power, 331; on ordered liberty, 294;
    on statute controls, 312
Casper, Gerhard: constitutional
    manipulation, 469
Chase, Chief Justice Salmon: states'
    rights, 78
Chase, Justice Samuel: clear case for
    overturn, 330; on natural law, 274–75;
    on privileges and immunities, 41,
    45–46, 201; rejects common law
    crimes, 303; on separation of powers,
    18–19
Chayes, Abram: judicial revolution, 298,
    380, 397
Chemerinsky, Erwin: on *Corfield*, 48
Choate, Joseph H.: on communism, 5;
    on laundresses' hours, 290
Choper, Jesse H.: minority rights, 187,
    387
Chrimes, S. B.: on original intention,
    415
Church, W. Lawrence: judicial
    administration of schools, 380; on
    original intention, 21, 419
Churchill, Winston: on democracy, 339
Citizenship: both U.S. and state, 57,
    60, 64–65, 69; in Civil Rights Bill,
    61, 241; national privileges and
    immunities, 57–69; and "persons" vs.
    "citizens," 240–44; suffrage not
    attribute of, 105; not voting, 41, 48
Civil rights, 186–87; Bingham on Civil
    Rights Bill, 46–47, 127, 134; and
    Burger Court, 358; in Civil Rights
    Act, 401; and Civil Rights Act veto,

235; "no discrimination," 34, 133–37,
    149; liberty vs. property, 287–89;
    limited category of, 153; political
    privileges absent from, 202–3; Wilson
    on no desegregation, 36, 133
Civil Rights Act (1866), 32–44; "all
    discrimination" defeated, 195–96; not
    applicable to North, 172–73, 208,
    237; and due process clause, 228, 243;
    and enumerated rights, 34, 39, 42,
    44, 120, 135, 136, 153–54; and
    equal-protection clause, 124, 201–2,
    203, 204, 238; Flack on, 170; as
    "formal expression," 295; Fourteenth
    Amendment as embodying, 27,
    32–33, 262; and fundamental rights,
    64, 243; identical with Fourteenth
    Amendment, 48–52, 62, 92, 120–21,
    136, 168, 170, 203; Kelly on, 134,
    136–37, 172–73, 191–92, 263; and
    liberty, 54; limited aims of, 36, 48,
    195–97, 400–401; opponents' reading
    of, 191–92, 196; and "persons" vs.
    "citizens," 240–43; and private school
    discrimination, 461–62; privileges or
    immunities clause and Article IV,
    32, 58–60, 66; Raymond on, 61, 236;
    and school segregation, 26–27,
    133–39, 148; scope of, 66; §5
    enforcement, 248–52; Shellabarger
    on discrimination within race, 91; and
    suffrage, 37–39, 71–73, 112; and
    Trumbull, Fourteenth Amendment
    and Civil Rights Act identical, 92; —,
    not suffrage, 130; Van Alstyne on,
    130; veto of, 194–195, 201–2, 235;
    and whites, 66
Civil Rights Act (1871), 247
Civil Rights Act (1875): and
    congressional role, 122; and school
    segregation, 148

Claggett, Bruce M.: change by amendment, 341; on original intention, 309

Clark, Senator Daniel (N.H.): on black codes, 228; goal to check, 235; postwar South, 16, separate schools, 139

Clark, Kenneth, 287

Clark, Justice Tom: on *Brown v. Board*, 347; on segregation, 143

Clifford, Justice Nathan: judicial review limited, 279

Cohen, Morris R.: judicial predilections, 464–65; quality of Justices, 356

Coke, Edward: Bonham's case, 222; on due process, 225, 226; Jefferson on, 224; on law of land, 222, 223, 226–27; and original intention, 415; rules of construction, 404; 12-man jury, 449; on usage as law, 448

Comity clause (Article IV), 40, 42, 165

Commager, Henry Steele: condemned Court, 6, 308, 353–54; on natural law, 276; segregation untouched, 135

Commerce clause, 308

Committee on Reconstruction. *See* Joint Committee on Reconstruction

Common law: common sense in, 468; and Constitution, 453, 468; and Constitutional adaptation, 344–45; and Continental Congress, 225; immunity of judges in, 28, 180; and instrumentalism, 328–29, 344; Madison on, 304; and natural rights (Kelly), 43; and original intention, 414–21; and trial by jury, 450

Common law meaning of words, 45, 282, 409

Common law of crimes, federal, 303

Common understanding at adoption, 169

Comstock, Justice: on natural law, 278

Congressional power: corrective only, 211, 213–20

Conkling, Representative Roscoe (N.Y.): and apportionment, 82–83, 98–99, 103, 172; on representation, 70; emancipation not political rights, 129; on slaves, 59; and states' rights, 78–79; and suffrage, 76, 78–79, 82–83

Consent of governed: and authority of Constitution or law, 23, 317–18, 394

Conservative majority, 259, 270

Constitution(s): not subtle interpretation, 416, 468

Constitution, U.S.: activist view, 351; amendment of, 19, 145 (*see also* Amendment process); and American civil religion, 29, 394; and commerce clause, 308; common law words in, 451, 282, 409; continued consent, 394; and Declaration, 106; as fixed, 313–14, 331, 381, 409; Jefferson on, inalterable by construction, 314, 357, 360, 403, 460; —, original intention, 423–24; judges sworn to support, 393–94; on judicial expansion, 309; limits on powers, 276; and modern rights, 186–87; reverence for, 321; and rights, 53; weight of precedents, 318, 319

Constitutional construction: Frankfurter on history, 143; Senate Committee on, 412–13. *See also* Judicial revision; Original intention

Constitutionalism, elements of: and rule of law, 22, 311, 459–60. *See also* Rule of law

Construction, manipulation of, 469. *See also* Rules of construction

Continental Congress, First, 225, 450

Contract: Civil Rights Act on right of, 33, 37, 38, 138; liberty of, 290–91; and miscegenation, 193–94

Cook, Representative Burton C. (Ill.): peonage, 60

Cooley, Chief Justice Thomas: acquiescence in usurpation, 319, 393; fixed constitution, 381; Fourteenth Amendment limited, 399; limited goals, 293–94

Corbin, Francis: limited powers, 276

Corporations: Fourteenth Amendment, 92, 123, 179; Justice Black on, 92

Corwin, Edward S.: activism proponent, 402; on construction, 404; on democracy, 325; on due process, 226, 395; on *Federalist*, 427; on judicial review, 374, 375, 481; on liberty, 291; on natural law, 30, 278

Council of Revision, proposal for, 322–25

Counsel, right to, 363–64

Court-packing, 346, 359

Courts: and abolitionist influence, 266–67; activist decisions, 480–84; and Founders' distrust of, 306; Hamilton on, 316; legitimacy of judicial review, 369–401; limited role of, 315–16, 325–27, 329–32, 379, 381; and moral choices, 334–36; as nay-sayer, 326; and § 5, 245–46. *See also* Judges; Precedent

Cover, Robert: Constitution not binding, 22, 25, 387; on natural law, 275, 305; on neoabolitionists, 253, 268, 443

Cowan, Senator Edgar (Penn.): on blacks, 75; no desegregation, 139, 140; on due process, 229; exclude

North, 172; on racism, 257, 268; on Thirteenth Amendment, 129

Cox, Archibald: was activism, 4, 90; on *Brown v. Board* as revolutionary, 132, 458, 459; Burger Court predilections, 360; Court negatived, 327; on desegregation decisions, 480–81; on due process, 232–33; on judicial activism, 298, 480; on legitimacy of judicial review, 372; libertarian turnabout, 337, 338; and natural law, 280, 441; on obscenity, 349; and personal liberties vs. property rights, 289; reapportionment, 4, 97; on Warren Court, 298

Cranch, Judge William: limit discretion, 329

Criminal proceedings: and Court vs. public opinion, 348; and "due process," 227; and Fourteenth Amendment, 156, 170; and original understanding, 460–61; and Supreme Court (1937–1961), 358. *See also* Jury

Curtis, Justice Benjamin: and due process 224, 227, 279, 381, 395, 438

Curtis, Charles P.: on adaptation, 339; construction, 407; on intent, 7–8

Curtis, George Ticknor: on Thirteenth Amendment, 176, 180

Curtis, Michael Kent: incorporation of Bill of Rights, 176, 180; radicals and antislavery, 269

Dante. *See* Alighieri, Dante

Davis, Representative Thomas T. (N.Y.): not perfect equality, 202, 215, 242

Death penalty: and Brennan, 25–26, 382; public backlash, 283

Declaration of Independence: and antislavery theory, 254; and consent of governed, 317; and Fourteenth-Amendment framers, 443; and suffrage, 104, 105–7; Sumner appeals to, 140

Delano, Representative Columbus (Ohio): not jurors, 195, 256; protect whites in South, 131, 188–89

Denman, Lord Chief Justice: doubts ruling power, 429

Dershowitz, Alan: mediocre justices, 391

Desegregation: Bickel on, 117; *Brown v. Board* no popular mandate, 25–27; 132–54, 480–84; Cox on, 458; Learned Hand on, 247; and public opinion, 349–50; shift after Vinson, 141–42, 347. *See also* School segregation

Dickinson, John: against licentious, 106; on ex post facto, 409; on judiciary, 324

Disclosure, 131

Discrimination: not all forms, 114, 199, 209, 214–15; only enumerated rights, 153–54; and equal protection, 201–2, and equal protection clause, 201, 204–7

District of Columbia: segregated schools in, 26, 137–38, 141, 147–48

Donald, David: on Bingham's political realism, 256; on Democrats, 265; on equality, 152–53, 267; on Moderates' control, 259; not North, 91; on racism, 13, 267; Republicans horrified, 188; on Sumner, 98, 113, 140, 200, 246, 258, 397

Donnelly, Representative Ignatius (Minn.): on representation, 70; on separate schools, 139

Doolittle, Senator James R. (Wisc.): on Civil Rights Act and Fourteenth Amendment, 120–21, 168;

Republicans frightened, 15; on suffrage, 13, 76, 79, 82, 264

Douglas, Justice William O.: on canons of decency, 284; on Constitution vs. personal preference, 385; and Council of Revision, 324; on full disclosure, 131; and judicial revision, 219; and jury trial, 343–44; Levy on, 350, 363; and ordered liberty, 295; and privacy, 286–87, 325; on rule of law, 315, 319; on §5, 251; on social legislation, 280; on substantive due process, 324–25; and Warren Court, 307

Downing, Rondel G.: on Court revision, 403

*Dred Scott* decision, 246

Dual (U.S. and state) citizenship, 57, 64–65, 69

Due process, 221–27; Bingham on, 127, 230; and Justice Black, not blank check, 227–28, 273, 281, 285–87; —, impartial trial, 234; Continental Congress, 225, 450; of "convenient vagueness," 221, 281–82; and Council of Revision, 324; economic vs. libertarian, 287–89; and equal protection, 206–7; and Frankfurter, 282–83, 299, 438–39; and free speech or press, 291–93; Hamilton on, 395; Hand on, 222–23; Holmes on, 17, 437; and Howard, 205; indeterminate (Schmidt), 394–95; and laissez faire, 5; law of the land, 223–24; not legislative, 222; and natural law theories, 280; and "open-ended" phraseology, 117; and original understanding, 460–61; reapportionment (Cox), 90; removal of, recommended, 463; Scalia on, 187–88; solely procedural, 222–26, 235, 239; vs. social legislation,

Due process (*continued*)
280–81, 282; Supreme Court
expanded, 282; Wilson on, 243–44.
*See also* Economic-substantive due
process; Libertarian due process;
Substantive due process
Dworkin, Ronald: no original intention,
411; on segregation, 27–28

Easterbrook, Judge Frank H.:
interpretation policies, 420; writer's
intention, 469
Eckley, Representative Ephraim R.
(Ohio): provide security, 62, 243; on
representation, 81
Economic-substantive due process, 5;
Court abandons, 287, 289
Einstein, Albert: emphasizes facts, 469
"*Ejusdem generis*," 64
Eliot, Charles W.: cherishes democracy,
339
Eliot, Representative Thomas D.
(Mass.): on suffrage, 196
Elkins, Stanley: collective interest, 52
Elliott, Ward: black vote political,
70–71; not blank check, 116; on
reapportionment, 90; on suffrage, 84,
108
Ellsworth, Oliver: overleap limits, 313,
325
Ely, John Hart: on *Bolling v. Sharpe*,
396; on Civil Rights Act/Fourteenth
Amendment, 49; on due process, 395;
on equal protection, 152; on
Fifteenth Amendment, 88; on
invitation to revise, 27; on judges as
moral arbiters, 335; on judicial
predilections, 384–85; on neutral
principles, 309; on privileges or
immunities clause, 44
Enforcement of Fourteenth
Amendment: §5, 245–52

Equality: and abolitionists, 199; in Civil
Rights Bill, 33, 153; and Declaration
vs. Constitution, 106; Douglas
changes, 219; of enumerated
privileges and immunities, 42; equal
protection of laws narrower, 206;
feared, 267; incomplete for blacks,
36–38, 89; limited, 201, 202, 206; as
one person-one vote, 87 opposition
to, 14–15, 400; vagueness of, 267
Equal protection, 199–220, 235;
Acheson on, 265; and apportionment,
91; and Bingham, 127, 160–61; and
*Brown v. Board*, 144; corrective vs.
general Congressional power,
213–20; Frankfurter on, 144–45, 199;
freedom from discrimination vs.
absolute rights, 207–12; Graham not
desegregation but imperfect
understanding of, 140–41, 301;
Holmes on, 198; limited scope of,
201, 263; and "one person, one vote,"
108; and "open-ended" phraseology,
118–19; and reapportionment, 90;
and republican form of government,
100, 101; what rights protected,
201–7; substantive, 219–20; and
suffrage, 203, 473–75, 476; and
Warren, 236, 265
Erler, Edward J.: Civil Rights Act and
Fourteenth Amendment, 49
Executive discretion and judicial review,
327
*Expressio unius* rule, 64, 181

Fairman, Charles: activist obscurantism,
281; and Bill of Rights incorporation,
171, 174, 175–76, 178; on Bingham
and due process, 161, 164; and Civil
Rights Act/Fourteenth Amendment,
32; historical study by, 185; on
Howard and Bill of Rights, 167, 168;

Kelly's dismissal of, 10; on neoabolitionists, 264; and privileges or immunities, 37; and §5, 249, 250; on state sovereignty, 163; and suffrage, 40–41

Farnsworth, Representative John F. (Ill.): on apportionment, 94; equality frightening, 13; on equal protection, 235, 244; on intermarriage, 194; on original intention, 412; on suffrage, 83, 139

Federal Farmer: on original intention, 411

Federalism: Brandeis on, 152; and Founders, 377; limited reform, 263, 398–99; as obstacle, 173; *Slaughter-House* on, 178

*Federalist:* as opinion at Convention, 427; cited, 316, 317

Fessenden, Senator William P. (Me.), 24; on abolitionist theory, 257; on Civil Rights Act scope, 196; on dual citizenship, 65; Joint Committee, 116, 259; Kelly on goal of, 258; on limited program, 116, 202, 261, 264; on need for compromise, 167; and radicals, 257, 260, 268; on representation provision, 24, 85, 103, 139; on republican form of government, 98; and state power, 208; and suffrage, 38, 76, 79, 81, 85, 104, 474; on Sumner, 258; on trick, 123–24

Field, Justice Stephen: assault upon capital, 5; on Civil Rights Bill, 61; courts save democracy, 326, 355; some discriminations, 211; on judicial process, 379; and Negro jurors, 92; on privileges and immunities, 51, 57–58, 66; and *Slaughter-House* decision, 67

Fifteenth Amendment: filled gap, 24; Frankfurter on, 198–99; Justice Miller on, 80; as political response to, 71, 88; is preventative, 473; suffrage not conferred by Fourteenth Amendment, 86

Fifth Amendment: absence of equal protection, 236; Bingham on due process clause, 232; Charles Curtis on due process clause, 395; death penalty, 25; —, Brennan on, 382; and equal protection, 236; and free speech, 292; and liberty vs. property, 288

First Amendment: assembly, 212; Cox on vulgarity, 349; Learned Hand on, 298; speech not fundamental, 292

Fiss, Owen M.: competence confers power, 391; on predilections, 385

Flack, Horace: on Bill of Rights and states, 175; Civil Rights Act/Fourteenth Amendment identical, 33, 51, 92, 170; on Civil Rights Act scope, 190–91; on Fourteenth Amendment scope, 171; general power, 216; on incorporation, 168; on Radicals' nondisclosure, 121; on silence, 167; and states' rights, 79

Foner, Eric: Reconstruction revolution, 398

Fortescue, Chief Justice: on maxims, 404

Founders: community vs. individual, 52–53; and natural law, 303; and original intention, 405; positivist viewpoint of, 275; property over liberty, 288; and rule of law, 314–15, 320; sought limited government, 276; and state autonomy, 308; and "unjust" not "unconstitutional," 334. *See also* Framers of Constitution

Four Horsemen, 220, 354

Fourteenth Amendment, 3; and *Brown v. Board*, 132 (*see also* Desegregation; School segregation); and corporations, 92; and Court's jurisdiction, 397–98; enforcement of, 245–52; and fears of Southern dominance, 15–16; general language vs. specific intentions of, 396; Learned Hand on terms of, 222–23; Justice Miller on, 80; and "one man-one vote" doctrine, 24–25; and original intention, 8–9; as political tactic, 109; purpose, 238. *See also* Framers of Fourteenth Amendment

Framers of Constitution: and charters of incorporation, 417, 432; Council of Revision rejected by, 322–23, 324, 325; and "due process," 226; and judicial review, 332, 378; and Marshall on intention, 219; and natural law, 275–77, 305; original intention of, 4; and rule of law, 313; state enclave, 53

Framers of Fourteenth Amendment: and abolitionists, 14; changes explicitly provided by, 180; Court's intrusion resented by, 397–398; and equal protection, 153, 208; and federalism, 399; and northern states, 188–89; and original intention, 412; and "property" over "pursuit of happiness," 41

France, Anatole, 288

Frankfurter, Justice Felix: and Bickel, 117, 132–33; and *Brown v. Board*, 137, 141–45; and commerce clause, 308; on constitutionality, 292; Constitution what Justices say, 300; on distinguishing among powers, 287; distrust of courts, 316; due process conveniently vague, 221, 226,

234, 281, 282, 299, 438–39; on equal protection, 100, 101; and guarantee of republican government, 101; impact of scholarship, 464; on incorporation, 169, 178; and judicial change, 437; —, common law meaning, 438; on judicial divination, 282–86; on judicial legislation, 322; on judicial power, 274, 315; judiciary encroaches, 274; on legal history, 414; legislative history, 8, 334; McCloskey on, 356; on Marshall and Constitution, 428; and natural law, 276; original intent, 414, 438; on predilections, 283, 390, 459; and preferred freedom, 298; on privileges or immunities clause, 67; on remarks of proponents, 157; remove due process by amendment, 463; and rule of law, Constitution above decisions, 319; on segregation, 143; on shifts in personnel, 347; on suffrage, 198–99

Frantz, Laurent B.: on representations, 376–77

Freedmen: and citizenship, 63–64; protection of, 65–66

Freedom of speech, 291–93; applicability to states proposed (Madison), 181–82, 212; and *Gitlow v. New York*, 158; not in state constitutions, 292

Fried, Charles: on legal philosophers, 468

Frowycke, Chief Justice, 415

Fugitive Slave Act, 249, 277, 304; and decisions, 246, 443

Fundamental rights, 52–68, 186; Blackstone on, 30–31; Brest on, 186–87; and citizenship, 59, 61–62, 63, 66; and Civil Rights Bill, 43, 44, 64, 243, 443; and compelling government interest test, 298; enumerated rights, 34; existing law identified, 186; free speech not fundamental, 292; protection of, 238; voting as, 198

Gangi, William: on opposing views, 421

Garfield, Representative James A. (Ohio), 395; on due process, 234; federal guarantees, 59; Fourteenth Amendment and Civil Rights Act, 51; on original intent, 421–22; on state jurisdiction, 218; on suffrage, 83

Garrison, William Lloyd: bitter racism in North, 268; conservative antislavery, 253, 256; on suffrage, 75

Gay, Peter: historian impartial, 149

Gerry, Elbridge: amendment exclusive, 341; Bill of Rights against federal government, 155; judges not share in policymaking, 323; on original intention, 446; trusts legislature, 325, 384

Gibbon, Edward: on judge's discretion, 328; power disguised, 466

Gibbons, John G.: on Berger, 24

Gibson, Justice: on precedent vs. principle, 318, 319

Gillette, William: on Negro swing vote, 88; on suffrage, 92

Goebel, Julius: on due process, 224; on fixed Constitution, 313; on jury trial, 451

Goldberg, Justice Arthur J.: cites opponents, 192; on Ninth Amendment, 442

Gorham, Nathaniel: on apportionment, 91; judges on policy, 323

Government by consent, 317–18

Graglia, Lino A.: on *Brown v. Board*, 146; on Bork, 154; on equality, 151;

on "horribles," 392; on incorporation, 176; on originalism, 393

Graham, Howard Jay: and abolitionist theory, 37, 253–54, 257, 259–60; on Bill of Rights, 165; and *Brown v. Board*, 133–34, 144; on Civil Rights Act/Fourteenth Amendment, 33; on *Corfield*, 41; on discrimination, 43; and due process, 230–31, 232; and federalism, 80, 399; forgot antislavery usage, 257; mistrust of courts, 246; on racism, 140–41; on Reconstruction racism, 263; and school segregation, 26, 301, 311; on Trumbull, 67

Grant, J. A. C.: on due process, 274

Grant, Ulysses, S.: on Legal Tender Acts, 346; on suppression of Negro rights, 68

Gray, Justice Horace: on original intent, 405

Grayson, William: on jury, 451, 452

Grey, Thomas C.: and due process, 226; on effectuation of original understanding, 460–61; and incorporation of Bill of Rights, 158; on judicial attitude, 342; on judicial review, 369; and judicial revision, 378, 428, 440–44; natural law, 445; on natural rights, 305–6; on originalism, 410; on originalist view, 389, 440; and Warren Court, 307; cited, 116, 179, 253, 264

Grimes, Senator James W. (Iowa): states' rights, 77

Grinnell, Representative Josiah B. (Iowa): on natural rights, 36; separate schools, 139

Gunther, Gerald: on judges and injustice, 390; on judicial candor, 432

Haines, Charles G.: due process and natural law, 280; on natural law, 303

Hale, Sir Matthew, 30, 451

Hale, Judge Robert S., 172, 249

Hale, Representative Robert (N.Y.): on Bill of Rights, 213; on Bingham, 165; on blacks, 11; and equal protection, 204; no general grant, 215; on state protection, 163, 208;

Hamilton, Alexander: agent cannot remodel power, 314; on amendment, 371; binding until amended, 340, 446; on breach of law as precedent, 351; on consent, 22; counts bulwark, 315–16; on due process, 222, 395; on impeachment, 316–17; on judicial usurpation, 370; on judiciary, 19; 397; on minority veto, 386; not spirit of law, 316; on original intention, 417; respect for experience, 467; respect for legislative intention, 316; on reverence for Constitution, 321; on rules and precedents, 329, 404; on rules of interpretation, 414; on state authority, 55, 178; on treaty power, 426, 434

Hamilton, Walton H., 221

Hand, Learned: on *Brown v. Board*, 27, 247; on Constitutional amendment, 371; on Constitutional interpretation, 360; on Court's role, 326–27, 360, 464; on cumulative wisdom, 467; on First Amendment vs. other interests, 298; on historical interpretation, 198; on judges' divining public opinion, 283; on judges' points of view, 354–55; on judicial legislation, 464; on judicial review, 273, 310; on "last formal expression," 295; and legislative prerogatives, 247; on personal preferences, 299, 354; and Platonic Guardians, 384; and

property vs. liberty, 288; on substantive due process, 282; on sweeping terms of Fifth and Fourteenth Amendments, 222

Harlan, Senator James (Iowa): on desegregation, 147–48

Harlan, Justice John Marshall: on Civil Rights Act, 134; on criminal administration, 358; on due process clause, 239, 281; on historical arguments, 299–300; on incorporation of Bill of Rights, 175; judicial amendment, 3; and jury trial, 456; on original intention, 352, 418; on privileges and immunities clause, 235; and reapportionment, 114, 445, 471–79; states exempt from Bill of Rights, 156; and suffrage, 8, 71, 81, 86, 105

Harris, Robert J.: distrust courts, 246; on equal protection, 236; on §5, 250

Hart, H. M.: on legislative intention, 8

Hartley, Thomas: on apportionment, 93

Hatton, Lord Chancellor: on original intention, 415, 416–17

Hawkins, Vaughan: on original intention, 409

Henderson, Senator John B. (Mo.): on Civil Rights Act, 38, 39; on equality, 206; on racism, 43; on suffrage, 76, 79, 82; on Thirteenth Amendment, 33

Hendricks, Senator Thomas A. (Ind.): on Civil rights, 201; impact of Democrats, 256; North feared black invasion, 12

Henkin, Louis: judicial predilections, 350; on rights, 303; selective incorporation, 158; state enclave, 53

Henry, Judge (Va.): not legislators, 332

Henry, Patrick: on amendments, 341; on jury, 455

Hierarchy of authorities, 186–86
Higby, Representative William (Calif.):
on Chinese, 209; on Fifteenth
Amendment, 86; on representation,
472; republican in form, 99
Hill, Representative Ralph (Ind.), 99
Himmelfarb, Gertrude, 315
Historicist fallacy, 9
History: Cooley on individual rights,
294; Court's use of, 342; Kelly
manipulated, 95; and meaning of
words, 282
Hobbes, Thomas: on good and evil,
385; on original intent, 21
Holdsworth, Sir William: on existing
rights, 53–54
Holmes, Oliver Wendell, Jr.: on
abolitionists, 257, 268; on arrogation
of power, 393; and common law, 344;
on constitutionality, 146; on court
role, 287; on Court's economic
theory, 348; and due process, 282;
on equal protection clause, 198; on
fear of socialism, 5; on Fourteenth
Amendment, 287; on free speech,
291; on intimation of legislative will,
50; and judicial revision, 433–37; on
justice vs. law, 312; on legislative
intention, 407; on liberty of contract,
290; on literal meaning, 199; on
meaning of words, 408, 416; omit
emotion, 11; on original intention,
414; on original understanding, 169,
405; and policymaking by Court,
383; on precedents vs. Constitution,
318–19; on role of courts, 334, 381;
on state power limitation, 17, 462; on
value of history, 108; on words as
conduct, 7
Hook, Sidney: on ends and means, 23;
Justices vs. people, 382; on majority
rule, 387

Hooker, Roger W., Jr.: on rule of law,
312
Horn, Robert H.: young precedents,
364, 379
Horwitz, Morton J.: on discrimination
and judicial will, 327–28; on natural
law, 275, 277; on ongoing debate,
389
Hotchkiss, Representative Giles W.
(N.Y.): and equal protection, 215;
on §5, 251
Howard, Senator Jacob M. (Mich.): and
Bill of Rights incorporation, 166–69;
and Civil Rights Act, 33, 36; on *Dred
Scott* decision, 397; and enforcement,
214, 251; and equal protection,
204–5, 210, 235; Kelly on goal of,
258; ordinary rights, 168; and
privileges or immunities, 62, 63, 64,
120; and purposes of Fourteenth
Amendment, 214, 243; and suffrage,
24, 38, 74, 77, 81–82, 85, 107, 112,
121, 124–25, 172, 413, 475, 477; on
Thirteenth Amendment, 129
Howe, Senator Timothy (Wisc.): on
Black Codes, 52; Civil Rights
Act/Fourteenth Amendment,
184–85; equal justice, 249
Hubbard, Justice (N.Y.): on natural law,
278
Hughes, Chief Justice Charles Evans:
Constitution what judges say, 318;
on impairment of contract, 428–29;
on perception, 377
Humpty-Dumpty, meaning of, 414–15
Hurst, Willard: on Article V, 371; on
corporate charter, 439; distrusts
power, 311; on policy choices, 339;
power and meaning, 467; rulemaking
to Congress, 251; states' rights, 17
Hutcheson, Judge Joseph: "hunch" first,
461

Hutchinson, Allan C.: activist desperation, 389
Hutchinson, Chief Justice Thomas (Mass.): judge not legislator, 328
Hutson, James: records unreliable, 421–25
Huxley, Thomas H.: stop lying, 465; submit to facts, 3
Hyman, Harold M.: due process, 211; on Fairman, 185; on Negrophobia, 398; states preeminent, 79, 400; on Thirteenth Amendment, 129

Impeachment: Hamilton on, 316–17; Taft on, 463
Implied power(s): and Fugitive Slave Act case, 249, 250; Lusky's theory, 445–46; over state officers, 250
Indiana: Congress may not supervise education, 150; Negros excluded from, 14
Instrumentalism, 328–29, 345, 351, 352
Iredell, Justice James: on amendment, 341; on consent, 23; delegates are agents, 317; and judicial review, not within boundaries, 19; —, only if clearly invalid, 330; —, delegation of power of attorney, 380–81; —, no despotic power, 325; —, of legislative power, 275; on jury, 450; and natural law, 275, 302; on original understanding, 9; on usurpation, 317, 457

Jackson, Andrew: usurpation impeachable, 317
Jackson, James: stay within bounds, 176; trust Congress, 155–56
Jackson, Justice Robert H.: on *Brown v. Board*, 372; on Court counter to public, 353; on incorporation, 174; on infallibility, 347; McCloskey on, 356;

on pre-1937 Court, 4; on role of court, 300; on rule of law, 319–20; and school segregation, 141, 143, 146; on §5, 245
Jaffe, Louis: on conscience of people, 283, 284–85, 349; on judicial insensitivity, 358
James, Joseph B.: on Civil Rights Bill/Fourteenth Amendment, 50–51, 131; on due process, 229, 230; Fourteenth Amendment applied to South, 189; on radicals, 260
James, William: on facts, 28
Japanese relocation case, 353
Jarvis, Charles: on amendment, 341
Jefferson, Thomas: chains of Constitution, 276; on charters of incorporation, 432; on Coke, 224; on *Federalist*, 427; on free press, 293; on interpretation, 21, 190; judges as moral arbiters, 335; on judicial powers, 328; on laws for ordinary understanding, 468; on limited judiciary, 404; majority rule, 387; on natural right, 52; on original intention, 21, on race relations, 106
Johnson, Andrew: on Civil Rights Act veto, 194–95, 201–2, 235; on schools for Negroes, 139–40
Johnson, Justice A. S (N.Y.): on substantive due process, 278
Johnson, Dr. Samuel: on critics, 23; on facts, 29; on novice, 185
Johnson, Justice William: on discretion, 329; expansiveness of power, 274
Joint Committee on Reconstruction: on all distinctions, 114; Report of, 103; on representation, 475; on §2, 85; on suffrage, 74, 85, 103
Judges: accumulated wisdom, 385; class values of, 354–55; common-law role

of, 328; current role of, 380; discretion feared, 20; distrusted, 306, 411; Founders' dislike of, 306; individual sense of justice and rule of law, 23, 385; as moral arbiters, 335; not legislators, 379; and public opinion, 283, 385; special competence, 391–92; sworn to support Constitution, 393–94. *See also* Courts

Judicial administration of local matters, 480–84

Judicial discretion, 327–32; fear of, 344

Judicial review: Bickel on personal preference, 143; bounds of, 273; Commager on, 308; Constitution itself the ultimate, 319; in Convention, 374–78; Hamilton on, 329; Iredell on, 275; as negative only, 481; Pendleton on, 330; Ratification approval, 426–27; Wilson on, 378

Judicial revision, 3, 4, 18–19, 297, 299, 457–58; and accidents of Court membership, 338, 346–47, 354; activist arguments for, 389–401; vs. amendment process, 145, 301, 339–42, 371; awareness needed, 464–66; backwards reasoning, 110, 344–45, 361, 461; common law distinguished, 344; constitutional government harmed by, 459–60; and Court as continuing constitutional convention, 319, 361, 458; and Frankfurter, 437–39; and Grey, 440–44; and Holmes, 433–37; and instrumentalism, 327–29, 345, 351–52; and Lusky, 444–47; vs. majoritarianism, 337–39; and Marshall, 19, 428–33, 439, 446; and public sentiment, 348–50; rollback of, 461–62; as threat to security

(Madison), 403. *See also* Policymaking

Julian, Representative George W. (Ind.): on intermarriage, 194; on racism, 13; on representation, 70

Jurow, Keith, 224–25

Jury: and Bill of Rights incorporation, 171; and black jurors, 133, 195; and equal protection, 461; and historical content of "jury," 282; includes attributes, 453; not natural right, 43; number of jurors, 343, 350, 448–56

Just compensation, 162

Justice: Cardozo's search for, 334; and government of laws, 312; indefinite standard, 284; and rule of law, 311; unjust not unconstitutional, 323

Kauper, Paul: on reapportionment, 90; on republican form of government, 100

Kay, Richard: on cherished assumptions, 23; on original intention, 20–21

Keller, Morton: on Black Codes, 34–35; on suffrage, 73, 122

Kelley, Representative William (Pa.): on suffrage, 84; whites, visitors to South, 188

Kelly, Alfred H.: on abolitionist impact, 253, 258, 262, 266; on apportionment, 91; on argument from silence, 167; on Bingham and Bill of Rights, 165, 177; on Black Codes, 172; on Civil Rights Act, 134, 136; and Constitution as racist, 106; on *Corfield*, 40, 42; and equal protection, 203, 204, 205; and Fairman, 10; Fourteenth Amendment revolutionary, 191–92; and incorporation of Bill of Rights, 168; on judicial manipulation, 342; on

Kelly, Alfred H. (*continued*)
manipulation of history, 95; on
narrow civil rights, 36; and natural
rights, 43; on Negro reform program,
80; and "open-ended" theory,
126–27; and privileges or immunities,
42; on radical influence, 233; on
Radical Republicans, 196, 259–60;
on rights of Englishmen, 186; and
school segregation, 133, 135–36, 138,
254–55
Kendrick, Benjamin: on Bingham
amendment, 160, 162; on Howard,
166, 184
Kent, James: and Blackstone, 31;cited
by Civil Rights Act sponsors, 32, 36;
law reasoning to goal, 344–45; on
rights, 61; on state sovereignty, 163
Kerr, Representative Michael C. (Ind.):
on Bill of Rights, 213
King, Rufus: on Bank, 432; on judicial
role, 324; on treatymaking, 426
Kluger, Richard: on *Brown v. Board*,
132, 136, 141; on judicial candor,
143–44; revised Fourteenth
Amendment, 146; and school
segregation, 25
Kommers, Daniel: on Berger, 388–89
Korman, Edward R.: on reaction to
convictions, 358
Kurland, Philip: on Court, 327; on
judicial usurpation, 378–79; on
Justices, 356; on reapportionment,
90, 285; on rule of law, 420; on
segregation cases, 350; on Warren
Court, 363
Kutler, Stanley: on judicial shift, 20; on
political vacuum, 390

Lane, Senator Henry S. (Ind.): access
to courts, 228; on racism, 13; on
suffrage, 79

Lash, Joseph P.: on Frankfurter, 142
Laski, Harold: hierarchy of authority,
185
Latham, Representative George R.
(W. Va.): Civil Rights Act and
Fourteenth Amendment identical,
32; on internal policies of states, 172
Law of the land, 237–38
Lawrence, Representative William
(Ohio): and Hamilton's due process,
395; on jurors, 195; on natural rights,
211; and privileges or immunities,
47; on representation, 84 on rights,
34, 37, 38
Lawyer's history, 95, 342
Lee, Francis Lightfoot, 132
Legal Tender cases, 346
Levinson, Sanford: on original
intention, 460
Levy, Leonard W.: on abolitionist
theory, 253, 266; on activist judges,
350; antiquarian historicism, 310;
on Justice Black, 284, 350; on Burger
Court, 358, 360–64; and Court-made
policy, 289; on Court's activism, 298;
on Court's civil rights record, 353; on
due process, 226; on Fairman,
157–58; on incorporation of Bill of
Rights, 177; on judicial review, 365,
372, 373; judicial review and the
people, 371; and judicial usurpation,
370; on Madison's notes, 423; on
means and ends, 459; on
Nonoriginalists, 385; on original
meaning, 408; on political
appointments, 351; on
result-oriented jurisprudence, 320;
on Rostow, 308; on Supreme Court
appointments, 356; and vagueness
of "due process" and "equal
protection," 221; on Warren
approach, 309

Lewis, Anthony: continuing Convention, 4; on personnel, 356; revisory Court, 20; poverty and race intractable, 349; vacuum theory, 390; on Warren Court, as instrument of social change, 22, 307; —, as "keeper of national conscience," 3; —, as legal revolution, 22, 156, 307; —, revisory Court, 20; Warren's Platonic Guardians, 350

*Liberator, The*, closing of, 256

Libertarian due process, 160, 234, 287, 289

Libertarian judicial activists, 320

Libertarians: turnabout of, 337–57

Liberty: Blackstone on, 31, 187; of contract, 290–91; and freedom of speech or press, 291

Lieber, Francis: on rights, 54

Lincoln, Abraham: abolition amendment submitted by, 268; on judicial policymaking, 463–64; personnel choice, 346; and racial equality, 12, 193–94; and states' rights, 77

Linde, Hans: Constitution preferred, 343; on instrumentalism, 345

Litwack, Leon: on segregation, 12

Livingston, Chancellor: on treatymaking, 426

Local government, federal court administration of, 480–84

Locke, John: on delegation, 390; on natural law, 30; on original understanding, 21; on property, 288

Logan, Representative John A. (Ill.): on Fourteenth Amendment, 131

Lusky, Louis: on Justice Black, 284; on *Carolene* footnote, 296–98; on Court role, 21–22, 307, 312, 316, 343, 371, 380, 444–47, 458; and equal protection, 220; on ordered liberty, 294–95; on unpopular decisions, 283

Lynch, Gerald: on revision, 392

McArthur, John B.: on moral issues, 335–36; on nonoriginalism, 389

McClellan, James, 420; on the "living Constitution," 428

McCloskey, Robert G.: Court as savior, 355; on Court's personnel, 356; on judicial activism, 187, 273, 281

McConnell, Michael W.: state governments as guardians, 53

McDonald, Forrest: on M. Curtis, 186; liberty of community, 53

McDougal, Myres: anti-amendment, 340; antioriginalism, 311; on philosopher kings, 338

McDougall, Senator James A. (Calif.): on Civil Rights Act, 120

Macedo, Stephen: on antioriginalism, 335–36

McGovney, D. O.: on privileges and immunities, 7, 57

McIlwain, Charles H.: on criticism, 29; on goals, 22; on natural law, 302

McKean, Chief Justice Thomas: refutation is proof, 421

McKee, Representative Samuel (Ky.): on Court access, 228; on racism, 71; on suffrage, 84

Mackintosh, Sir James: on precedents, 385

McKitrick, Eric L.: on public good, 52; on racism, 192; on suffrage, 475

Maclaine, Archibald: on delegation, 317

McLean, Justice John: on natural law, 277

McReynolds, Justice James Clark: Freund on, 356; on liberty, 290

Madison, James: on altering Constitution, 314; on Bill of Rights,

Madison, James (*continued*)
441–42; —, aimed at federal
government, 55; —, invalidation, 375;
—, sought to apply to states, 155–56;
on chartering corporations, 314; on
common law, 222, 304; on
constitutional boundaries, 313; on
Constitutional change, 384, 434, 460;
on Constitutional Convention
records, 422; on enumeration of
powers, 37; on free-speech extension
to states, 292–93; on judicial
policymaking, 383; and judicial
review, 273–74, 375–76, 377; on
judicial role, 326; on jury trial, 195,
452, 455; on *M'Culloch* decision,
430–31; and "open-ended" terms,
121; and original intention, 4, 21; on
power, 315; on property, 288; and
republican government, 97; on
treatymaking, 425

Magna Charta, 222, 223, 224

Maitland, Frederic William: on legal
simplicity, 469

Majority rule: academics'
disillusionment with, 337–39; on
minority protection, 386–87

Maltz, Earl M.: on alternatives to
originalism, 389; on original intent,
419

"Mandate from heaven," 275, 283, 294,
302, 445–46

Marriage, interracial, 193–94

Marshall, Chief Justice John: on Bill
of Rights, 211; on citizenship, 64;
on commerce clause, 308; on
common-law meanings, 45, 222;
congressional power, 376; on
Constitution, fixed, 292, 381, 394;
—, judicial revision, 219, 428–33; —,
not narrow construction, 429; —,
on prolixity, 126; on incomplete
records, 423; intention sacred, 21;
interpret not make, 18; judicial
review, on invalidation, 19, 325–26;
—, not judicial will, 385, 433; —,
limits not transcended, 231, 305, 314,
388; —, plain usurpation required,
330–31; —, Ratification records,
426–27; —, no squatter sovereignty,
369–70; and judicial revision, 433;
on judicial role, 18–19, 331; on limited
powers, 3–4; on morality vs. law, 334;
and natural law, 276, 277; on original
intention, 414; on plain expression,
16; on plain words to control states,
180; rely on representatives, 438; on
role of judges, 393–94; on rule of law,
313; on slavery, 304; and "treason,"
409; on unwise vs. unconstitutional,
386

Marshall, Representative Samuel S.
(Ill.): internal sovereignty, 78

Mason, Alpheus T.: Court as legislature,
286–87; on judicial predilections,
464; on "penumbra," 316; on states'
rights, 52–53; on unchecked power,
463

Mason, George: on jury, 450

Massachusetts Constitution (1780): on
equal protection, 200; exact
observance of, 370; on fundamental
principles, 310; on separation of
powers, 383

Matthews, Justice Stanley: due process,
231, 237–38; on limited powers, 4;
on suffrage, 198

Mendelson, Wallace: on chameleon due
process, 117, 221; on Court as
national conscience, 352; on
Frankfurter, 286; on law and justice,
312; on rule of law, 320

Meyers, Marvin: on limited powers,
304

Mill, John Stuart: on imposing preferences, 462

Miller, Arthur S., and Howell, Ronald F.: no consensus on judicial role, 353; on Frankfurter, 286; on historicist fallacy, 9; on imposing preferences, 462; on incorporation of Bill of Rights, 170; on original intention, 300, 406; on Justices' inadequacy, 388; result-oriented judicial decisions, 310; on school segregation, 264; on subjectivity, 309

Miller, Representative George F. (Pa.): on §5, 249; on suffrage, 83–84

Miller, Justice Samuel: on abolitionists, 257; clear language for federal incursion, 96; on due process, 230, 237; on federalism, 80; Fourteenth Amendment confined to Negroes, 211; on judges' class interests, 355; natural law, 279; privileges or immunities, 57, 58, 63, 64, 65–67; on unlimited power, 4

Miscegenation laws, 193–94

Missouri Constitution: anticipated Fourteenth Amendment, 33

Moderates' influence, 259; Bickel on, 124; Donald on, 259; and equal protection, 124; narrow objectives, 120; and radical leadership, 257

Modern rights, 186–89; Perry on, 55, 187

Mommsen, Theodor: on self-determination, 387

Monaghan, Henry P.: on modern rights, 187; on original intent, 421; on racial equality, 269

Montesquieu: on judiciary, 446

Moody, Justice William H.: on predilections, 385

Moore, G. E.: philosophic difficulties, 468

Morality: and full disclosure, 131; judges not arbiters of, 334–35; moral disarray, 335

Morley, John: on individual rights, 53

Morrill, Representative Justin S. (Vt.): on specificity, 34

Morrill, Senator Lot M. (Me.): opposing Sumner, 140

Morris, Gouverneur: on judicial review, 326, 383

Morrison, Stanley: on Bingham, 164; on Black's incorporation, 289; on privileges and immunities, 57

Morton, Senator Oliver (Ind.): on Fifteenth Amendment, 88

Moulton, Representative Samuel W. (Ill.): on Black Codes, 35; on equal protection, 201; on jurors, 195; on miscegenation, 194

Muller, Herbert: mandate from heaven, 275

Murphy, Paul: on lynching, 6; on new doctrine, 296; on policing, 326; on Warren, 144, 265–66, 310

Murphy, Walter: on privileges and immunities, 47

Myers, Leonard: on equal protection, 153–54

NAACP: and desegregation, 133, 134, 135

Nagel, Robert: on individual rights, 53

National Advisory Commission on Civil Disorders, Report of: on racism, 349

Natural law, 274–80, 302–6; as arbitrary, 275; and Bill of Rights absorption (Black), 158; and Black on ordered liberty, 295; and Coke, 222; and due process, 233; and Founders, 275–77; Grey on, 440–41, 442–43; and intermarriage, 194; Iredell on, 280; not for judges, 277, 304; late

Natural law (*continued*)
appearance of, 302; preindependence appeal to, 305–6; and substantive due process, 274–75, 277–83, 302
Natural rights, 120; civil rights as (Wilson), 36, 119; and Civil Rights Act, 238; and Framers, 305–6; Grinnell on, 36; Jefferson on, 52; not jury trial, 195; limited meaning of, 236; received meaning for, 43; not suffrage, 129
Neal, Phil C.: on apportionment, 97; equality statewide, 213
Nebraska, admission of: on suffrage, 101
Nelson, William: on abolitionist influence, 266–67; on Fairman, 185; Fourteenth Amendment and Civil Rights Act linked, 48; on incorporation, 174; limited goals, 400; on suffrage, 87
Neoabolitionists: Bingham as conduit, 134; and Bingham on suffrage, 81; and control of 39th Congress, 233; and desegregation case, 254–55; and due process clause, 233; Fairman on, 264; Graham on, 257; Senator Howard on suffrage, 107; legislative history as read by, 42, 366–67
Newmeyer, Kent: on racist Constitution, 106
Ninth Amendment, 55–56, 440, 441–42
Nixon, Richard: appointees of, 356; and instrumentalism of Santarelli, 351
Nock, Albert J.: hierarchy of authority, 185
Northern states: Civil Rights Act not applicable to North, 172; effect of incorporation, 172–74, 189; miscegenation in, 193; racism (Negrophobia) in, 11–15, 108–9, 192,

257, 267; and reapportionment, 91–92; segregated schools in, 26, 137, 147–48, 152
Nye, Senator James W.: on *Dred Scott*, 397; on equal protection, 200
Nye, Russell R.: political problem, 256; racism during Reconstruction, 261, 267; racist policy, 16

Oakeshott, Michael: on property, 288
Obscenity: and popular opinion, 349; subjective decisions, 392
"One person one vote," 24–25, 71, 87, 104
"Open-ended" theory: Justice Black on, 123; Cooley on fixed Constitution, 381; Radical strategy, 262; Van Alstyne on, 128
Ordered liberty, 294–95
Oregon, Negroes excluded from, 14
Original intention, 402–11; and American scene, evidence of opposition, 190–97, 425–27; Bickel on, 340; Bork on, 239; Brest on, 22, 393–94; and *Brown v. Board* briefs, 254; challenge to Brown, 388; consequences of honoring, 392; effectuates limits, 20–21; and English common law sources, 414–21; and Harlan, 86, 352; Marshall on, 414, 433; as rule of construction 194, 405; rule of law, 21; scope of application of, 460; —, Bork's version of, 154; Supreme Court on, 410
Otis, James: on rights of Englishmen, 54
Owen, Robert Dale: on suffrage, 111; —, modified, 125

Packer, Herbert: on due process, 5, 219–20; fundamental rights, 289
Paludan, Phillip S.: Court anti-Negro, 280; on federalism, 398–99; on

racism, 13, 267; on state sovereignty, 156, 173

Parker, Chief Justice Isaac (Mass.): on privileges and immunities, 42, 46; on suffrage, 41

Parliament, omnipotent, 325

Parsons, Theophilus: on natural rights, 387

Paternalism, 391

Paterson, Justice William: on property, 288

Patterson, Caleb B.: on interpretation, 460

Patterson, Senator James (N.H.): on limited goal, 269

Peckham, Justice Rufus Wheeler: on privileges or immunities, 240

Pendleton, Edmund: on amendment, 341; on judicial review, 330

*Pepper v. Hart* (H.L.): applies original intent, 418–19

Perry, Michael J.: on activists, 386; no antioriginalist alternative, 389; on Court as moral arbiter, 335; incorporation of Bill of Rights, 178; on judicial policymaking, 379, 383; and modern "rights," 55, 386; and "open-ended" phraseology, 118; on segregation, 147

Phelps, Representative William (N.J.): on racism, 148

Phillips, Wendell: on party trick, 112

Philosophy: and law, 468

Pike, Representative Frederick A. (Me.): on suffrage, 196

Pinckney, Charles: on judicial legislators, 324

Platonic Guardian(s), 338, 355–56, 357; Warren as, 350

Pocock, J. G. A.: on accumulated wisdom, 467

Poland, Senator Luke (Me.): compromises, 167; Declaration of Independence, 107; enforcement, 249, 250; Fourteenth Amendment and Article IV, 184; and privileges or immunities, 45; and suffrage, 82

Policymaking: judicial takeover, 390, 339–40; judiciary excluded from, 316, 383, 397

Political rights or privileges, 202; Brennan on, 110; equal protection clause, 461

Pollak, Louis: on Bank, 432; original intent, 405

Pomeroy, John Norton: on Fourteenth Amendment, 401; on state autonomy, 399

Pomeroy, Senator Samuel C. (Kans.): on suffrage, 72, 74

Positivism: and the Founders, 275, 277

Posner, Judge Richard: on activism, 397; on appointments, 392; on *Brown v. Board*, 146; on predilections, 385

Postenactment remarks, 68

Pound, Roscoe: on mandate from heaven, 275; on natural law, 302

Poverty: and judicial cure, 349

Powell, H. Jefferson: on original intent, 412, 416–18; on predilections, 20

Powell, Justice Lewis F.: on the Court, 358–59

Powell, Thomas R.: on judicial lawmaking, 481; on split Court, 346

Power: abdication of, 390; and clarity of grant, 277; congressional usurpation of, 317, 376; Constitution limits, 314; Court to police limits, 326; distrust of, 311; evil encroaching, 315; judicial usurpation of, 274, 284, 317, 369–70, 378–79, 393; and justice, 312; limited, 305; vs. means, 430; obtain from people, 357; not unchecked, 463; warnings against, 274, 276, 314, 315

Precedent: Burger on, 363; and
  Constitution, 318, 319; as curb on
  judicial discretion, 344; Hamilton on,
  329
"Preferred position" theory (*Carolene*),
  296–98
Prettyman, Judge E. Barrett: on
  segregated schools, 137
Price, Representative Hiram (Iowa): on
  Article IV, 161
Prisot, Chief Justice: on
  contemporaneous constructions, 212
Privacy: Douglas on, 286–87; Lusky on,
  444
Privileges or immunities, 243; Article
  IV of Constitution, 31, 38, 45–46,
  58–60, 181; —, construed narrowly,
  47; Bingham on, 134; Chase on,
  201; "citizens" as reference of,
  240–41; *Corfield v. Coryell*, 39–40, 42,
  167; derivation of terms, 44–48;
  derived from Articles of
  Confederation (Article IV), 45;
  Howard on, 120, 167; "open-ended"
  interpretation, 116–31;
  *Slaughter-House* narrowed, 57–69;
  substantive rights, 235; and suffrage,
  103
Property: and Declaration vs.
  Constitution, 106; as Founders' value,
  288; vs. liberty, 288–89
Puritans: on judges, 411

Racism: in Constitution, 106; and
  Fourteenth Amendment, 11–13, 398;
  Negroes excluded from Indiana, 13;
  in North, 11–16, 108–9, 267, 269,
  349, 350; during Reconstruction, 261
Radicals: Bickel on, 121; and black vote,
  70–71; defeat of program of, 259–61;
  factional, 233; outnumbered, 127,
  259; and suffrage, 100

Randolph, Edmund: on arrogation of
  power, 311; on Council of
  Revision, 322; judiciary plan of, 376;
  and jury trial, 451, 452; on natural
  rights, 303; on republican
  government, 97
Rapaczynski, Andrzej: on morals, 335
Ratification: and undisclosed objectives,
  131, 171, 173
Raymond, Representative Henry J.
  (N.Y.): on absolute equality, 216;
  court access, 228; legislative
  inequality, 60, 236; on residents, 61
Realist canon, 345
Reapportionment, 90–98; and Black,
  285; and Brennan, 108–15; and equal
  protection, 90; and Frankfurter, 198,
  286; and Harlan, 281, 445; northern
  states, 91–92, 100; and republican
  form of government, 94, 97–103; and
  standards, 315; Van Alstyne's critique
  of Harlan, 471–79; Warren on,
  104–8, 366
Reconstruction: and abolitionist theory,
  257; and Negrophobia, 255, 398;
  racism during, 267
Rehnquist, Justice William H.: on
  "persons," 240
Report of the Joint Committee on
  Reconstruction, 103
Representation: of states (§2), 80–82,
  114–15, 479; and suffrage, 82
Republican form of government,
  97–103; and apportionment, 94;
  Bingham on, 101–2; and
  representation, 472; and suffrage, 99,
  113; and Sumner, 233–34
Republicans: and black equality, 14–16;
  desired ascendancy, 70, 90; Fifteenth
  Amendment and ascendancy, 88;
  necessarily conservative, 259; and
  Negro suffrage, 109; racism of, 11–13

Result-oriented jurisprudence, 310, 320; advocacy scholarship, 22; Charles Black on, 365; Levy on, 360

Rhett, Edmund: perpetuate peonage, 35

Richards, David A. J.: three abolitionist schools, 267

Richardson, H. G.: on our views and past, 9

Rights: and activist constructs, 187; of assembly, 212; Blackstone's triad of life, liberty, and property, 30–31; Civil Rights Bill, 33, 51, 54; of community vs. individual, 52–53; of Englishmen, 31, 186; given by existing laws, 53–54; of national citizenship, 57–69

Roberts, Justice Owen: on ordered liberty, 295; as swing man, 345–46

Robespierre: on mandated virtue, 333

Rodell, Fred: on *Brown v. Board*, 347; on the Court, 464; on Justice Roberts, 346; result oriented, 289, 309, 324, 337; on Truman appointees, 356

Roosevelt, Franklin: and Frankfurter, 300

Rossiter, Clinton: on *Federalist*, 427

Rostow, Eugene V.: on Japanese relocation, 353; on judicial review, 308, 340

Rowse, A. L.: revere facts, 389

Rule of law, 23, 311–21, 466–67; Kurland on, 420; limits discretion, 329; Nixon's denial of, 351

Rules of construction: common-law meaning, 45; consider whole for obscure part, 478; not to defeat intention, 64; *expressio unius*, 247; holds boundaries, 420; opposition discounted, 190, 192–93; original intentions supra intention vs. text, 8; pari materia, 138; "plain language" required, 28, 180; principal includes attributes, 453

Rutherforth, Thomas: on original intention, 404–5

Sacks, A.: evidence of intention, 8

Sandalow, Terrance: change by legislature, 392; on original intention, 414

Sankey, Lord Chancellor: ends and means, 459

Santarelli, Donald E., 460; on activist credo, 351

Sargent, Senator Aaron (Cal.): on racism, 148

"Saturday Night Massacre," 464

Sayles, G. O. *See* Richardson

Scalia, Justice Antonin: on liberty, 187–88; on nonoriginalism, 420

Schauer, Frederick: current disdain for originalism, 410–11

Schenck, Representative Robert C. (Ohio): on elevating Negro, 124; on suffrage, 131

Schlesinger, Arthur, Jr.: on racism, 149

Schmidt, Benno: on intermediate due process, 394–95; on race relations, 396

School segregation: Bickel on, 117–18; Bork on, 151–54; and *Brown v. Board*, 132–33, 141–46; and Civil Rights Act, 26–27, 133–37; in District of Columbia, 137–38, 147–48; in northern states, 26, 147–48; and *Plessy v. Ferguson*, 149–50; and present-day America, 149; untouched by Fourteenth Amendment, 27

Schurz, Carl: on "colored schools," 139

Selden, John: on original intention, 415

Selden, Justice: on natural law, 278

Senate: and treatymaking, 425–26

"Separate but equal" doctrine, 139, 149–50

Separation of powers: Massachusetts Constitution, 383; and judicial review, 371; Marshall on, 335; Washington on, 380

Shapiro, Martin: on Court's neutrality, 343, 351–52; on judicial candor, 465; on judicial review, 310

Shattuck, Charles E.: Blackstone's "liberty," 290–91; on due process, 227

Shaw, Chief Justice Lemuel: on natural rights, 277; on school segregation, 101, 150

Shellabarger, Representative Samuel (Ohio): on citizenship rights, 60; on Civil Rights Bill, 34, 47, 91, 242; on discrimination, 213–14; and equal protection, 153, 206; and republican form of government, 99

Sherman, Senator John (Ohio): and Civil Rights Bill, Fourteenth Amendment embodies, 92; —, specifies, 34, 39; on defeat of radicals, 260; Negroes disliked, 255; Northern ascendancy, 16; states' rights, 80; and suffrage, 256–57

Sherman, Roger: on policymaking, 324

Sherry, Suzanna: on moral choices, 334–35; on natural rights, 305

Silence, argument from, 167

Simon, Larry: moral disarray, 335

Smith, Page: on property, 288

Smith, Zephaniah: on judicial lawmaking, 328

Socialism, fear of, 5

Social legislation: due process used against, 280–81, 282; Supreme Court as frustrating, 20

Soifer, Aviam: ad hominem criticism, 23–24

Sources (historical), 7–8, 421–27

Spencer, Samuel: on treatymaking, 426

Spooner, Lysander: abolitionist theorist, 32; on due process, 233; result oriented, 269

Stampp, Kenneth M.: on slavery, 33, 228

States: Bill of Rights in state constitutions, 156; commerce clause, 308; corrective vs. general Congressional power, 213–20; Founders' view on, 373; and framers' design, 17; and free speech, 181–82, 291–93; and equal protection, 214; framers' attachment to, 54, 77–80, 308; migratory birds, 434; Negro suffrage, 73–77, 138; and school segregation, 147–48

States' rights, 77–80; Acton on, 26; Henry Adams on, 26; Bingham on, 134; Founders' concern, 52–53; and Fourteenth Amendment framers, 216, 398, 400

Stevens, Representative Thaddeus (Pa.): on Bingham, 128; on citizenship, 64; and "citizens" vs. "persons," 242; on Civil Rights Bill, 49; on Civil Rights Bill proposals, 196; compromised, 169; disliked, 257; and due process, 231; and enforcement, 249, 250; on equality, 113–14; and equal protection, 203, 204, 215–16, 217; on Fifteenth Amendment, 88; Fourteenth Amendment and Civil Rights Act, 136; Joint Committee differences, 166; Negro mistress of, 193; on race and Constitution, 106; and Report of Joint Committee, 103; on representation, 472–73; and Republican ascendancy, 15–16; on school segregation, 140; on social equality, 15; and suffrage, 75, 79, 83, 111, 125, 203, 474–76; on Sumner, 258

Stewart, Justice Potter: on Bill of
Rights, 175; on capital punishment,
283; on predilections, 108; on
reapportionment cases, 285; on
suffrage, 97
Stewart, Senator William M. (Nev.):
on amendment, 123; Civil Rights
Act applies to South, 189; on Civil
Rights Bill, 48; and racism, 13, 14; on
representation, 115; on rights, 62;
on Stevens, 258; and suffrage, 99, 114
Stone, Chief Justice Harlan F.: on
*Carolene*, 234, 296–98; on liberty and
property, 5; on liberty of contract,
290; on need for self-restraint, 463;
on predilections, 298–99; on Tenth
Amendment, 173
Storm, Representative John B. (Pa.; 42d
Congress): broad construction
rejected, 171
Story, Justice Joseph: ability of Justices,
392; and apportionment, 91; common
law controls discretion, 326; on
common-law definitions, 222; on
common-sense construction, 468; on
Constitutional amendment, 390;
Constitutions not for subtleties, 416;
Court cannot add to grants, 312; due
process, 226–27; on exceeding grants,
388; on fixed construction, 381, 394;
on fundamental rights, 54; limited
grants, 402–3; on Ninth Amendment,
55; on original intention, 405; on
repudiation of representation, 425; on
state sovereignty, 26; on strict
standard for interpretation, 404; on
unbounded jurisdiction, 304
Substantive due process, 159–60,
273–74; abolitionists' conceptions of,
10, 233, 253–54; and Bingham, 255;
and *Dred Scott*, 230, 279; economic

vs. libertarian, 287, 289; and
Frankfurter, 438; and fundamental
rights, 188; Learned Hand on, 282;
natural law as, 274–75, 279; and
privacy cases, 444
Substantive equal protection, 219–20
Suffrage: admission of Tennessee,
76–77, 100–102, 113; and Article IV,
38; Bingham on, 112–13; Brennan
on, 112–13; and Civil Rights Act, 38,
71, 72–73, 136; Declaration of
Independence, 107; Dixon on, 84;
Doolittle on, 76, 79, 82, 264; Elliot
on, 84; and equal protection, 205–6,
476; and Fifteenth Amendment, 24,
86, 88; Finck on, 256; Holmes on,
198–99; hostility to, 122; Howard on,
81–82, 85; Negro suffrage political
dynamite, 72; Ohio rejection of, 256;
Pike on, 196; and privileges or
immunities clause, 103; and
republican form of government, 97,
101–2; and §2 of Amendment, 80–84,
86, 115, 479; Sherman on, 475; state
control of, 41, 413, 473; and Stevens,
75, 79, 83, 111, 114, 125; and
Sumner, 72, 75, 76, 259; Van Alstyne
on, 72–73, 128–31, 203, 471–79; and
white attitudes, 87; —, on exclusion
of suffrage, 86–87; —, on express
amendments for, 104–5
Sumner, Senator Charles, 11, 18, 26;
and apportionment, 91, 93–94; Civil
Rights Act proposal, 196; dislike felt
toward, 113, 258; and equality, 200,
228, 233; and Fourteenth
Amendment, 258, 260; Massachusetts
unsympathetic to, 98; and northern
states, 188; on original intention,
409–10; and republican form of
government, 97; and segregated

Sumner, Senator Charles (*continued*)
schools, 137, 140, 148; and suffrage, 72, 75, 76, 259

Supreme Court, 3–6; ability of members, 356, 391–92; accidents of membership on, 345–47; on Bill of Rights and states, 156; and civil over economic liberties, 289–90; and civil liberties jurisprudence, 187; as "conscience of people," 281, 333, 350, 352–55, 382; and Constitution, 108, 300–301, 318, 319, 372, 465; as continuing constitutional convention, 3–4, 361, 393; Cox on, 327; disclosure of role, 464; and feelings of society, 283; as Founders' surrogate (Lusky), 445; and Founders' views of judges, 383; on Fourteenth Amendment, 52, 198; Frankfurter on, 282; and liberty of contract, 290–91; Lusky on role of, 327; on opposition statements, 192–93; and original intention, 405–6; and postenactment remarks, 68; on preferred position theory, 296–300; and public opinion, 464; unconstitutional conduct of, 459–60

Supreme Court revisionism: Black on, 118; Frankfurter shifts, 221; theorizing, 22–24, 27–28, 320, 389–401

Sutherland, Arthur: on due process, 226; on Frankfurter, 284; on shift of theory, 337

Sutherland, Justice George, 356

Taft, Chief Justice William Howard: on equality, 229; on judges, 463; on judicial "Bolsheviki," 355

Taney, Chief Justice Roger Brooke: on fugitive slaves, 250

TenBroek, Jacobus: and abolitionist theory, 10, 253, 254, 257, 258, 261, 266, 268; on Bill of Rights, 165–66, 177; on Bingham, 236; "citizen" vs. "person," 244; and Civil Rights Act, 238; on Declaration of Independence, 105, 106; on due process, 229; on equal protection, 207–9, 214, 215, 216–17, 218; on Fourteenth Amendment debates, 477–78; on original intention, 410; on privileges and immunities, 37, 43

Tennessee, readmission of (sans suffrage): Bingham on, 99, 101–2, 113, 475; and republican form of government, 99, 101–2, 113

Tenth Amendment, 16–17, 96, 173, 177, 286

Thackeray, W. M.: on Negroes, 267

Thayer, James Bradley: on policing boundaries, 19, 326–27

Thayer, Representative Martin Russell (Pa.): enumerated rights, 36–37; on identity of Civil Rights Act and Fourteenth Amendment, 50

Thirteenth Amendment, 200, 241; suffrage not conferred, 129

Thomas, Representative John L. (Md.): limited equality, 138–39

Thorne, Samuel: on actual intent, 415

Thucydides: use available records, 423

Tiffany, Joel: Blackstone's triad, 32; slavery unconstitutional, 268

Tilton, Theodore: Stevens on, 15

Tocqueville, Alexis de: on imprudent appointments, 357; on miscegenation, 193; on racial prejudices 11–12

Treason: accepted meaning, 409, 454; and republican form of government, 102

Treaties: Holmes on migratory birds, 434–35; treatymaking by Senate, 425–26

Trevelyan, G. M.: on British appointees, 383; on free controversy, 390

Truman, David: on Court's neutrality, 343

Truman, Harry: on appointees, 356

Trumbull, Senator Lyman (Ill.): and Bill of Rights and states, 189; on citizenship, 63, 478; civil, not political, rights, 38; on Civil Rights Act, 32, 35, 38–39, 41, 48–49, 52, 54, 168, 172–73, 192, 208, 234–35, 237, 400; —, applies to whites, 66; —, and Fourteenth Amendment identical, 50, 92; —, not to suffrage, 130; on equality, 200; and "equal protection," 124; on Freedmen's Bureau Bill, 172, 192; and fundamental rights, 61; and Judiciary Committee, 270; on opposition assertions, 191; postenactment statement, 67–68; and privileges or immunities clause, 42–43, 45, 46, 47, 58, 60, 61, 68–69, 262; and states as depositories of rights, 399 and suffrage, 38, 112; on Sumner, 258

Tucker, Thomas: Bill of Rights not to states, 155, 156

Tushnet, Mark: on academic activism, 336, 396–97; on jurors, 195; on rule of law, 466–67

Twenty-sixth Amendment and "self-governance," 87

Twiss, Benjamin R.: on due process, 227

Van Aernam, Representative Henry (N.Y.): Civil Rights Act and Fourteenth Amendment, 169

Van Alstyne, William W.: and "open-ended" phraseology theory, 128–31; and reapportionment, 8, 72–73, 90–99, 100–102, 114, 471–79; on suffrage, 203

Vinson, Chief Justice Fred M.: on segregation, 141, 346–47

Virginia Ratification Convention (1788): on amending, 341; on judicial review, 330, 388, 427; on jury, 450, 451, 452; "is power enumerated?" 132; rights protection, 54

Wade, Senator Benjamin F. (Ohio): on citizen, 63

Waite, Chief Justice Morrison R.: on Fifteenth Amendment, 473; not lawmaking, 312; state protects, 163; on suffrage, 105

Wallace, J. Clifford: on judicial wisdom, 392

Warner, Representative Samuel L. (Conn.): distrusted Court, 246

Warren, Charles: on free speech, 292–93, 294

Warren, Chief Justice Earl: apportionment, 91, 104–8; on *Bolling v. Sharpe*, 396; on Constitution, 315, 343; on death penalty, 348, 359; on disregard of evidence, 264–66; and equal protection clause, 396; and intention of framers, 458; Levy on, 350; on means and ends, 459; neoabolitionist history inconclusive, 367; result oriented, 309–10; and suffrage, 71, 87

Warren Court, 307–10; Bill of Rights, 363; and *Brown v. Board*, 141–46, 311; Cox on, 298, 459; discarded precedents, 363; Lewis on (*see under* Lewis, Anthony); and negative role, 326; and public opinion, 359

Washington, Representative Elihu B. (Ill.): suffrage holdout, 166

Washington, George: on separation of powers, 380; on usurpation, 320–21, 393

Webster, Daniel: on Article IV, 181

Wechsler, Herbert: on burden of persuasion, 152; on judicial review, 373; on segregation, 367

Wellington, Harry: on result orientation, 366

White, Alexander: change by amendment, 318

White, Justice Byron R.: on due process, 293; on jury trial, 451, 452, 453, 454, 455; on predilections, 295; on 12–man jury, 448–49, 455

White, Chief Justice Edward D.: on Article IV, 45; on English practice, 436

White, G. Edward: on Berger, 413; common law adjudication, 344; on court-packing, 359; on judicial revision, 187, 391; on Warren, 396

Wicker, Tom: on racism, 149

Wiecek, William H.: on Berger, 24, 146–47

Wilkins, Roger: on racism, 149

Williams, Senator George H. (Ore.): on representation, 70

Wills, Garry: federal not local jurisdiction, 178

Wilson, Edmund: "bed-fellow" argument, 429; criticism of slavery in South, 293–94

Wilson, Senator Henry (Mass.): on Black Codes, 34; on freedom to come and go, 50, 56; on racism, 89, 261; on separate schools, 12, 137; on state blockage, 138; and suffrage, 76, 82; on Thirteenth Amendment and suffrage, 129

Wilson, James: aversion toward judges, 306; on constitutionality of unjust laws, 323; on continuous consent, 22–23; on corporate charters, 422; distrust of judges, 382–83; on

impeachment, 317; on judge-assisted veto power, 381; judicial review, 427, on judicial role, 19, 379; on jury trial, 452–53; on majority rule, 386; and natural law, 275; on original meaning, 405; on policing boundaries, 325, 378; and Senate treatymaking, 426

Wilson, Representative James F. (Iowa): apportionment, 107–8; on Bill of Rights, 161; on Black Codes, 35; Civil Rights Act, 31, 36, 39, 46, 47, 130, 136, 152, 156–57, 192, 195, 238, 241; distrust of judiciary, 246; on due process clause, 160, 229, 243–44; and equal protection, 201, 206, 209, 216; and freemen's exclusion, 110; and northern states, 189; and "open-ended" theory, 123; on racism, 13; on rights, 37, 54, 60; on school segregation, 26–27, 133–34; and suffrage, 15

Wilson, Woodrow: rejects government by experts, 391

Windom, Representative William (Minn.): Civil Rights Bill limited, 51–52, 185, 202; on Fourteenth Amendment, 235; not voting 139

Wofford, John: on incomplete records, 406; meaning changes, 408

Wood, Gordon S.: community, not individual, rights, 52, 187; fear of discretion, 20, 328; Founding, a revolution in thinking, 377; protect common law liberties of people against rulers, 53; punishment as disgrace, 382

Woodbridge, Representative Frederick E. (Vt.): Blackstonian triad, 62, 161 against discrimination, 209, 210; on Fourteenth Amendment, 250

Woods, Judge William: on separate schools, 150

Woodward, C. Vann: on abolitionist unpopularity, 257; on condition of Negroes, 12; on equality, 14, 206; historian must respect records, 11; on Northern ascendancy, 71, 85; Stevens on suffrage, 475

Wright, Benjamin F.: on Council of Revision, 322; on judicial policymaking, 323, 332; on natural law, 303; state, not individual, rights, 53

Wright, Judge J. Skelly: framers made choices, 345; government by experts, 391

Wythe Committee: on jury, 450

Yates, Senator Richard (Ill.): accepted moderate program, 265; proposes no discrimination, 195–96; speech in South, 188; on state sovereignty, 77–78; on suffrage, 72, 82

Yates, Robert: on judicial review, 376

Zuckert, Michael: Bill of Rights history ambiguous, 177; on free speech in North, 189; rejects tie between Civil Rights Act and Fourteenth Amendment, 50

This book is set in Janson Text, which for many years was incorrectly ascribed to the Dutch punch-cutter Anton Janson. The typeface was actually based on the work of Miklós Kis, a Hungarian punch-cutter, typefounder, and printer who worked in Amsterdam. His types are some of the greatest in the Dutch old face style. Linotype Janson was created by C. H. Griffith in 1937 and derives from an original face cut by Kis between 1670 and 1690.

Printed on paper that is acid-free and meets the requirements of the American National Standard for Permanence of Paper for Printed Library Materials, z39.84-1984. ∞

Book design by Louise OFarrell, Gainesville, Florida
Typography by Alexander Graphics, Ltd., Indianapolis, Indiana

Printed and bound by Worzalla Publishing Company, Stevens Point, Wisconsin